GW00686135

To
Chief Justice Yvonne Kauger
and

Joseph Cohen
whose support made this book possible

CONTENTS

I. INTERNATIONAL FRAMEWORK

II. NATIONAL CONTEXT

A. Scandinavia and Asia

PREFACE

Growing up in Muskogee, Oklahoma—the ''Capitol of the Five Civilized Tribes''—I have always been fascinated by Indian culture. My mother, Rachael Wiley Price, was born in Tamaha, Indian Territory, before Oklahoma was a state. My grandfather, James Marshall Wiley, with whom I lived as a child, was a Baptist minister who was active in local politics and Indian affairs. He served as solicitor for Bacone College, a school for Indians in Muskogee. He was instrumental in preventing the closing of the Nuyaka Mission Indian School in Okmulgee in the 1920s and he fought for special admissions criteria for Indian students at Oklahoma Baptist University in Shawnee. ''Dandy,'' as I called him, spoke both the Choctaw and Creek languages, however, he would not teach them to me. He told me that I didn't ''need'' to learn them. Mother said that we were part Cherokee, but I have never been able to find any records to support her claim. All I know is that Indians were respected and admired by my family and that we practiced many Indian customs.

It is only natural then, that when my interest in the international legal rights of the child coincided with my interest in Indian culture, I should try to put them both together. On a visit to see my mother in 1991, I learned of the Sovereignty Symposium, an annual conference on Indian law sponsored by the Oklahoma State Supreme Court. At the suggestion of Supreme Court Justice Hardy Summers, I contacted the coordinator of the Symposium, Justice Yvonne Kauger, to see if I could be a participant. My first presentation had to do with the Convention on the Rights of the Child and its possible future application in tribal venues.

After studying the Sovereignty Symposium program, I realized that while it was comprehensive, it did not have an international component. Justice Kauger agreed to let me organize a panel on international indigenous issues for the following year. It was sufficiently successful for me to be able to persuade Justice Kauger that in 1993, in honor of the International Year for the World's Indigenous People, I should have more than one panel. Happily, I was given an entire day—four panels—to fill with international presentations under the title, ''International Law and the Rights of Indigenous Peoples.'' By 1994, the international section of the Sovereignty Symposium had become an annual event. Participants came from many countries, at their own expense, to present papers and to experience Indian culture ''Oklahoma style.'' This meant that they were able to interact with Indians who did not live on reservations and whose tribal affiliations had independent legal systems that were respected by the Oklahoma Supreme Court.

Unfortunately, the excellent papers presented on these panels were published only as Sovereignty Symposium documents, and usually did not reach the general public. One year, at a preliminary dinner for my panelists, one of them said, "Why don't you publish these papers in a book?" I immediately got up from the table and called Heike Fenton of Transnational Publishers to see if she would be interested. Her answer was affirmative.

When I returned to New York, we signed a contract and assumed that the book would be ready in less than a year. After all, I had more than enough authors. Nothing could have been further from reality. While most of the authors agreed to write and submitted their chapters on time, others took many months to produce their promised contributions. By the time that all of the chapters were ready, some of the earlier ones were out of date and required revisions—all of which added months to the publication process. Assuring that footnote style was uniform presented a particular challenge, since only five of the fifteen authors were familiar with American legal footnoting style. Fortunately, for this task I had the assistance of Susan Kilbourne, a colleague who had footnoting experience from working on the *Georgetown University Journal on Fighting Poverty*. Susan carefully studied the footnotes, made stylistic corrections and noted incomplete citations. Of course, this meant that some authors then had not only to update their manuscripts, but they also had to track down the missing information, some of which had been misplaced. To their credit, none of the authors complained. Thanks to the wonders of E-mail, everyone responded to these requests in record time.

Putting the final touches on this manuscript has reminded me of the many people involved in the publication process to whom I owe a debt of gratitude. First, I want to express my very great appreciation to Chief Justice Yvonne Kauger, who gave me total freedom to organize the international panels at the Sovereignty Symposium, which gave me the opportunity to become more fully acquainted with the growing field of indigenous rights. I would also like to thank my wonderful cooperative authors, who helped to make this important project a reality—as well as Susan Kilbourne, whose footnote diligence helped to speed up the editing process. A special thanks goes to Professor Keith Nunes (Orlando School of Law) and Professor Siegfried Wiessner (St.Thomas University School of Law) for encouraging me to undertake this project. Finally, I am especially grateful to Heike Fenton of Transnational Publishers, who never abandoned the book, even though she may have had serious doubts about whether the project would ever be completed.

Cynthia Price Cohen
December 1997

CONTRIBUTORS

Hugh Beach: (B.A., Harvard College; Ph. D., Uppsala University). Professor Beach is a Swedish-American associate professor of cultural anthropology at Uppsala University, Sweden. He has specialized in the study of the Saami and other circumpolar peoples and has many years of field experience in Swedish Lapland with Saami reindeer pastoralists. He has also herded reindeer in Alaska.

Professor Beach has also written for a general audience, for example, ''A Year in Lapland,'' Smithsonian Institute Press, 1993. For many years he was a Board member of the Swedish Minority Rights Group, and he serves as expert advisor in Saami affairs to the Swedish Ombudsman Against Ethnic Discrimination.

Deepak Kumar Behera: (M.A., *Gold Medalist,* and Ph.D., Anthropology, Sambalpur University) Dr. Behera is the editor of the international *Journal of Social Sciences.* He has written extensively and has edited books concerning such areas as childhood studies, gender issues and indigenous and tribal matters. Dr. Behera is Reader and Head, Department of Anthropology, Sambalpur University Jyoti-Vihar Burla, Orissa, India.

Julian Burger: (Ph.D.) Dr. Burger is Secretary of both the Working Group on Indigenous Populations and the Commission on Human Rights working group on the draft United Nations Declaration on the Rights of Indigenous People. He is also responsible for the indigenous peoples programme in the Office of the High Commissioner for Human Rights at the United Nations.

Dr. Burger is the author of many articles and several books on indigenous peoples including *Report from the Frontier: The State of the World's Indigenous Peoples* (1987), *Aborigines Today: Land and Justice* (1988), and *Atlas of First Peoples: A Future for the Indigenous World* (1990). He is also the author/editor of the Independent Commission on International Humanitarian Issues Report, *Indigenous Peoples: A Global Quest for Justice* (1989). His books have been translated into several languages including Danish, German, Japanese, Russian, and Spanish.

Cynthia Price Cohen: (B.A., *summa cum laude,* The City College of New York; M.A., Political Science, The City University of New York Graduate Center; J.D., New York Law School, Human Rights Award, J.S.D., Law Studies Institute of the Polish Academy of Sciences). Executive Director of ChildRights International Research Institute, which she founded in 1992. As the representative of a nongovernmental organization, Dr. Price Cohen participated in the drafting of the United Nations Convention on the Rights of the Child from 1983 until it was adopted by the General Assembly in 1989. She systematically follows the deliberations of the Committee on the Rights of the Child (the Convention's monitoring body) and other international activities relating to the rights of the child.

Dr. Price Cohen takes a scholarly interest in the rights of indigenous people. She is a regular participant in the annual Sovereignty Symposium (Tulsa, Oklahoma)—an Oklahoma Supreme Court sponsored conference on Indian law where she organizes and chairs a series of panels on international law and the rights of indigenous peoples. She lectures on the rights of the indigenous child at conferences and symposia and has published numerous essays on this topic, including "United Nations Convention on the Rights of the Child: Relevance for Indigenous Children" in *Children and Childhood in Our Contemporary Societies,* (Deepak Kumar Behara, ed.). Dr. Price Cohen is a member of the Oklahoma Indian Bar Association and the Indian Law section of the Oklahoma Bar Association.

Alice de Jonge: Lecturer in law within the Department of Business Law and Taxation at Monash University, Australia's largest university. She lectures in International Trade Law and Asian Business Law. Her main interest is in Asia-Pacific legal systems and comparative constitutional law, and she has published on women's rights in China and on constitutional issues in the Marshall Islands.

In 1995, Professor de Jonge spent six weeks working as an investigating lawyer for the Ombudsman Commission of Papua New Guinea. She is currently living as a resident tutor in law at Queen's College (University of Melbourne) and is completing an S.J.D. thesis at the University of Melbourne.

Bob Freedman: (B.A., New College, University of South Florida; M.P.A. and L.L B., Queen's University, Kingston, Ontario; L.L.M., University of Virginia, *international human rights law*.) Associate lawyer at Ratcliff & Company in North Vancouver, British Columbia. Mr. Freedman practices in the area of Native law, concentrating his work in the areas of land claims litigation, Aboriginal rights and title litigation, and social development issues.

Mr. Freedman is also an Adjunct Professor in the Faculty of Law at the University of British Columbia, where he teaches courses in self-government and treaty negotiations. He has published widely in the area of Native law. He was a law clerk to the Hon. Mr. Justice Lambert at the British Columbia Court of Appeal in 1992-1993.

Lynda Frost: (B.A., *honors* Amherst College; J.D. *high honors* University of Iowa; M.A. international education; Ph. D. educational administration.)Assistant Professor, General Faculty, University of Virginia School of Law She has clerked for judges on the European and Inter-American Courts of Human Rights, as well as the U.S. Court of Appeals for the Eighth Circuit.

For over a decade, she has worked with educators in Latin America, both as a teacher in international schools and as a consultant for nongovernmental organizations. In the early 1990s, Professor Frost assisted in the restructuring of the educational system of the North Atlantic Autonomous Region of Nicaragua pursuant to the 1987 Autonomy Statute. In 1992, with the support of the Inter-American Institute of Human Rights, she organized and directed a three-day seminar on human rights and bilingual/intercultural education for educators and politicians in the North Atlantic Autonomous Region. In 1995, she helped the Colombian National Indigenous Organization develop a human rights education curriculum to teach tribal leaders in Colombia about international protections for indigenous rights.

Professor Frost would like to express her appreciation for the generosity of many people in the North Atlantic Autonomous Region of Nicaragua, who made her research possible and who devoted many hours to introduce her to various aspects of the coastal educational system. She would also like to acknowledge the helpful comments and suggestions of my colleagues Enrique Carrasco, Greg Sergienko, and Jonathan Stubbs, and my research assistants Lily Garcia, H. Christine Kim, and Timothy Lyden. Professor Frost thanks S. James Anaya for encouraging her to study the educational ramifications of the political and administrative change in the Atlantic Coast of Nicaragua.

Gail Goodwin Gomez: (Ph.D. in Linguistics, Columbia University) Professor of Anthropology, Rhode Island University. Dr. Goodwin Gomez has been working among the Yanomami Indians of northern Brazil since 1984 under the auspices of the Pro-Yanomami Commission (CCPY), a Sao Paulo-based NGO, which is internationally known for its human rights work on behalf of the Yanomami Indians.

Kirke Kickingbird: (J. D. University of Oklahoma) Director of the Native American Legal Resource Center, Oklahoma City University School of Law, a member of the faculty and Chair in Native American Law. Professor Kickingbird was elected to a one year term on the American Bar Association Board of Governors in August 1996 and to full three year term in August of 1997. Professor Kickingbird has served as the Oklahoma Governor's Special Counsel on Indian Affairs, chairman of the Oklahoma Indian Affairs Commission, and president of Oklahoma Indian Legal Services. He was also a member of three U.S. delegations to the United Nations dealing with rights of indigenous people. He was President of the Native American Bar Association during 1996-1997. Professor Kickingbird is a member of the Kiowa Tribe.

Osvaldo Kreimer: (J. D., Universidad de Buenos Aires; Ph.D., Communication Research, Stanford University) Lawyer with the Executive Secretariat of the Inter-American Commission on Human Rights of the Organization of American States, in Washington D.C. Since 1989 Dr. Kreimer has worked as Senior Specialist Lawyer at the Inter-American Commission on Human Rights, and been in charge of the preparation of and consultation on the future Inter-American Declaration on the Rights of Indigenous Peoples. After completing his advanced education, Dr. Kreimer taught at Boston University and Rutgers University.

From 1977 until 1989 he was Unit Chief, and then Director of the Educational Development Program of the Organization of American States (OAS-PREDE).

Bradford Morse: (B.A., Rutgers University, History and Sociology; L.L.B., University of British Columbia; L.L.M., Osgoode Hall Law School, York University) Professor of Law at the University of Ottawa, Faculty of Law where he has been teaching since 1976. He has written extensively on a variety of Aboriginal legal issues in Canada and several other countries. Professor Morse has served as legal advisor to many First Nations and other Aboriginal groups in Canada, as well as in New Zealand and Australia for over 20 years. Morse also has advised royal commissions and government departments in several countries.

Professor Morse was awarded a Fulbright Senior Scholar Fellowship in 1997 that was spent at the Native American Legal Resource Centre of Oklahoma City University, which is under the superb direction of Professor Kirke Kickingbird, and where much of the work for his contribution to this book was conducted.

Professor Morse would particularly like to thank the Canada—U.S. Fulbright Program for providing the opportunity along with the Oklahoma City University School of Law with its Native American Legal Resource Center under the direction of Dean Rennard Strickland and Professor Kirke Kickingbird respectively for kindly providing the environment and collegiality in which to complete this contribution.

Frank Orton: Swedish Ombudsman against Ethnic Discrimination (DO). The office of the DO was established by the Parliament on 1 July 1986, through the Law against Ethnic Discrimination. The DO shall counteract ethnic discrimination in society by helping individuals subjected to discrimination, by recommending legislation, and by shaping opinion. Frank Orton, the second DO, took office on 1 January 1992.

Douglas Sanders: Professor, Faculty of Law University of British Columbia. Professor Sanders has worked on indigenous legal issues in Canada and other countries since the 1960s. He teaches courses on international human rights law and on indigenous peoples at the University of British Columbia. He reported on international law developments for the Canadian Royal Commission on Aboriginal Peoples.

Lee Swepston: (B.A., University of North Carolina at Chapel Hill; J.D., Columbia University Law School) Chief of the Equality and Human Rights coordination Branch in the International Labour Office. He joined the ILO after working with the International Commission of Jurists. Mr. Swepston is the author of numerous books and article on human rights, labour rights, indigenous and tribal peoples and children's rights.

Richard Wilson: Professor of Law and Director of the International Human Rights Law Clinic at the Washington College of Law, American University, in Washington, D.C. He has written and spoken extensively in the US, Latin

America and Europe about legal education and teaching methods, as well as human rights and the criminal trial process, with particular emphasis on access to justice for disadvantaged persons. He has lived or worked in several Latin American countries, including Mexico, Guatemala, El Salvador, Nicaragua, Costa Rica, Panama, Colombia and Chile. Professor Wilson was a Peace Corps volunteer in Panama from 1966-1968, a Fulbright Scholar in Colombia in 1986, director of the law school's summer study program in Chile in 1995 and 1996, and a Visiting Lecturer at Daito Bunka University in Tokyo, Japan in the fall of 1995.

Kevin J. Worthen: (A.S., College of Eastern Utah; B.A. and J.D., Brigham Young University). Professor of Law at the J. Reuben Clark Law School at Brigham Young University in Provo, Utah. Prior to joining the faculty at B.Y.U., Professor Worthen clerked for Judge Malcolm R. Wilkey of the D.C. Circuit and Justice Byron R. White of the U.S. Supreme Court, and practiced with the firm of Jennings, Strouss & Salmon in Phoenix, Arizona. In 1994 he was a Fulbright Scholar at the University of Chile Law School in Santiago, Chile.

Professor Worthen would like to express his appreciation to the Fulbright Commission for the grant that enabled him to teach and research at the University of Chile Law School in 1994. This article reflects a portion of the research conducted during that time. Earlier versions of the ideas presented in this article were presented at The Sovereignty Symposium in Tulsa, Oklahoma, in June 1995, and at the Constitutional Law Section of the Inter-American Bar Association Conference in Quito, Ecuador, in November 1995.

INTRODUCTION

The *Human Rights of Indigenous Peoples* was inspired by the need to create a greater public awareness of indigenous peoples' human rights and to fill the void caused by lack of relevant materials. Eleven of the fifteen chapters were written by participants in the Oklahoma Supreme Court's Sovereignty Symposium. While some of the chapters are based on papers presented at the Symposium, many are the result of entirely new research. All of the authors are personally familiar with their subject-matter.

The chapters are arranged to give the reader a well-rounded understanding of this emerging field of international law. The book is divided into two sections. The first section lays out the evolving international standards and identifies the players in the standard-making process: the United Nations Commission on Human Rights, the International Labour Organisation and the Inter-American Commission on Human Rights. The second section gives the reader a close-up view of the real life concerns of indigenous people in a variety of geographic settings and highlights the necessity of strengthening international standards. Together, the fifteen chapters provide an excellent overview of the current situation of indigenous peoples.

Part I: International Framework covers the sources of international standards: the United Nations Commission on Human Rights (Julian Burger and Cynthia Price Cohen); the International Labour Organisation (Lee Swepston) and the Organization of American States (Osvaldo Kreimer). All authors are thoroughly familiar with their topics, having personally been involved in the drafting of the relevant treaties and declarations. To give some idea of the interplay between international organizations and indigenous groups, Part I includes a chapter on the participation of indigenous peoples in these standard-setting processes as ''quasi-nongovernmental organizations'' (Douglas Sanders).

Part II: National Context is divided into two sections, one covering indigenous peoples in Scandinavia and Asia and the other discussing indigenous peoples in South and North America. Together they present a fascinating, kaleidoscopic of the worldwide indigenous rights picture. The countries surveyed range from highly developed to somewhat primitive. Problems of the various tribal groups vary, as do government responses to their needs. Some indigenous people are very sophisticated while others are relatively uncivilized. Some are reasonably well-off financially, while others live in the direst poverty.

Notwithstanding these differences, certain similarities emerge from the authors' descriptions. In every situation, whether poor or affluent, the general standard of living of indigenous peoples in any given geographic area is lower than that of the majority or dominant group. Two basic themes are repeated throughout this section: problems relating to the environment, land claims and land-usage; and tensions between modernity and tradition.

The first chapter in *Section A (Scandinavia and Asia), A New Era for the Saami People of Sweden* by Frank Orton (Swedish Ombudsman Against Ethnic Discrimination) and Hugh Beach (Professor of Anthropology, Uppsala University) gives an enlightening overview of the Saami people who inhabit the northern regions of several Scandinavian countries. A light-haired, fair-skinned, semi-nomadic group, they nevertheless have much in common with their darker-skinned indigenous brothers to the South when it comes to dealing with the dominant culture.

The two Asian chapters expose indigenous problems in two vastly different countries: India and Papua New Guinea. It is like comparing an elephant to a mouse. *"So-Called Development" and Its Impact on the Rights of Indigenous People in India* by sociology professor Deepak Kumar Behera overwhelms the reader with the sheer size of India and makes it clear how easy it is for indigenous matters to get lost in day to day political concerns. On the other hand, Professor Alice de Jonge's *Human Rights of Indigenous People in Papua New Guinea* gives the reader an understanding of the clashes between tradition and modernity as the government and tribal groups attempt to reconcile the two differing sets of practices.

Section B (The Americas) covers both South and North America. This section gives a dramatic example of the variety of indigenous experience. The South American chapters cover four distinctly different situations—each describing an aspect of the current status of indigenous peoples in these various countries, some more difficult than others, but all in a continuing state of flux. While all of the authors are professors from the United States, each of them has spent considerable time in the particular country, studying the indigenous people whose lives they describe.

In *Of Robots and Indians: Human Rights and Educational Change in Nicaragua* by Professor Lynda Frost writes about the confusion and waste in well-meaning efforts by the government to educate indigenous children in their native language. Professor Gail Goodman Gomez's contribution, *Indigenous Rights and the Case of the Yanomami Indians in Brazil* depicts the hope and frustration of efforts to establish the Yanomami Park in the Amazon region of Brazil. It too highlights the clashes between tradition and modern society. In *Environmental, Economic, Social and Cultural Rights of the Indigenous Peoples of Chiapas, Mexico*, Professor Richard Wilson looks at the explosively intense political situation in the Chiapas region of Mexico, while Professor Kevin Worthen explores the situation of Chilean indigenous peoples in relation to the state in *The Role of Indigenous Groups in Constitutional Democracies: A Lesson from Chile and the United States*.

The three North American chapters are about indigenous peoples closer to home, in countries (Canada and the United States) that, while having had a less than honorable early association with Indians, are now seeking to correct these mistakes through court cases, legislation and administrative decisions that ameliorate conditions caused by policies of the past and to establish necessary assistance for various tribal groups.

Professor Bob Freedman sets the stage with a critical analysis of an important Canadian Supreme Court case: *Does Section 35 of the Constitution Act, 1982 Have Any Real Meaning? An Analysis of the "Reasonable Limits" Test in* Sparrow v. The Queen. This is put into a broader context by Professor Bradford Morse's political-historical overview of the Canadian relationship with its aboriginal people, *Two Steps Forward and One Step Back: The Frustrating Pace of Building a New Aboriginal-Crown Relationship in Canada.* In it Professor Morse makes a point of comparing the Canadian and United States experiences.

The final chapter, *American Indians in the International Arena: A Brief History from a United States Perspective,* is unique for three reasons. First, it sheds new light on the Indian as an actor in international affairs. Second, Professor Kirke Kickingbird knows his subject from the inside out. As a member of the Kiowa nation, he was part of the American delegation that worked on ILO Convention (No. 169). Moreover, he is regularly called upon to consult in other countries on matters relating to indigenous peoples. Finally, Professor Kickingbird is the only indigenous author in this collection. We are honored to have him among our contributors.

Indigenous peoples exist throughout the world. While these essays cover only a small segment of the population of indigenous peoples, it is hoped that they will heighten the reader's interest in indigenous issues.

I. INTERNATIONAL FRAMEWORK

CHAPTER 1

INDIGENOUS PEOPLES AND THE UNITED NATIONS

*Julian Burger**

In April 1996, the United Nations Commission on Human Rights took an unprecedented step and, for the first time in its fifty-year history recognized that the issues of indigenous people required special attention and merited a separate item on the Commission's busy agenda. For most of the last half-century, indigenous peoples have been absent from the deliberations of the world organization. Only in 1982, with the establishment of the Working Group on Indigenous Populations (a working group of independent human rights experts), were indigenous peoples given an opportunity to make their concerns known to the United Nations. Since then, indigenous peoples have been pressing member States to recognize their rights and provide opportunities for full participation in matters of concern to them. This article describes some of the main activities undertaken by the United Nations as a result of the growing presence and persistence of indigenous organizations.

I. WORKING GROUP ON INDIGENOUS POPULATIONS

It is useful, although not entirely accurate, to state that indigenous people were given their first formal acknowledgment by the United Nations when the Working Group on Indigenous Populations (Working Group) was established in 1982.[1] Initially, the Working Group was given the dual mandates of: 1) reviewing

---

*Note: The views expressed in this article are those of this author and not necessarily those of the United Nations.

[1] The pioneer among indigenous activists at the international level is generally acknowledged to be the Iroquois Chief Deskaheh who spent several months lobbying the League of Nations (forerunner of the United Nations) at its headquarters in Geneva in 1923. *See* Chapter 5, Douglas Sanders, *The Legacy of Deskaheh: Indigenous Peoples as International Actors* in this collection of essays.

In 1970, the Sub-Commission on Prevention of Discrimination and Protection of Minorities recommended that a complete and thorough study of the problem of discrimination against indigenous populations be undertaken. The study, prepared by the Special Rapporteur José Martinez Cobo, was published in a series of documents between 1973 and 1984. *See* CONSOLIDATED REPORT OF THE SPECIAL RAPPORTEUR ON DISCRIMINATION AGAINST INDIGENOUS POPULATIONS, U.N. Sub-Commission Prevention of Discrimination and Protection of Minorities. (1987).

developments pertaining to the promotion and protection of the human rights of indigenous peoples; and 2) giving special attention to the evolution of standards.[2] Since its first session, the Working Group has expanded its interests and, in recent years, has also considered a wide range of other topics including: treaties between indigenous peoples and States; indigenous intellectual and cultural property rights; the possibility of a permanent forum for indigenous peoples; the activities of the International Year and International Decade of the World's Indigenous People; and proposals for expert seminars on key themes. At its 1996 session, under its review of recent developments, the Working Group focused its attention on indigenous health and, in 1997, on environment, land, and sustainable development.

Participation in the Working Group has grown rapidly over the last several years. Thirty people participated in 1982; the Working Group now has an attendance of over 700 delegates representing governments, intergovernmental organizations, indigenous peoples, and nongovernmental organizations. The flourishing state of the forum is largely attributable to the flexible and open working methods adopted early in its life. Unlike other United Nations bodies, where participation is restricted to nongovernmental organizations holding consultative status with the Economic and Social Council, the Working Group decided to allow all indigenous representatives the possibility of addressing the meeting, even if they had not obtained any official recognition by the United Nations.

The decision to open the Working Group to indigenous people led to the broadening of its work agenda and the strengthening of its authority as a temperature gauge on indigenous issues worldwide. In reality, it would be highly undemocratic for participation to be restricted to the fifteen officially recognized indigenous nongovernmental organizations, most of which are based in the North.[3] Furthermore, indigenous peoples do not fit comfortably among nongovernmental activists, as they have nearly always had their own governments and institutions for managing their affairs—which may range from village-based councils to elected parliaments such as that of the Home Rule Government of Greenland. In some cases national governments recognize these institutions and in others they do not. But, whether States formally acknowledge indigenous

---

[2] The Working Group on Indigenous Populations was established by Economic and Social Council resolution 1982/34 of 7 May 1982 (ESCOR Res. 1982/34 (1982)), and mandated to meet annually for up to five days.

[3] The fifteen indigenous organizations with consultative status with the Economic and Social Council are: Aboriginal and Torres Strait Islander Commission; Four Directions Council; Grand Council of the Crees (Quebec); Indian Council of South America; Indian Law Resource Center; Indigenous World Association; International Indian Treaty Council; International Organization of Indigenous Resources Development; Inuit Circumpolar Conference; National Aboriginal and Islander Legal Services Secretariat; National Indian Youth Council; Saami Council; Asociación Kunas Unidos por Nabguana; Asociación Cultural Sejekto de Costa Rica; and World Council of Indigenous Peoples.

governments or not, indigenous peoples consider that they have a historic and continuing interest in running their own affairs and have thus avoided presenting themselves at the United Nations as nongovernmental entities.

At the first session of the Working Group in 1982, a recommendation was made to establish a fund to assist indigenous people with travel and expenses so that representation from all communities could be assured. However, it was not until 1988 that the Voluntary Fund for Indigenous Populations[4] became operational and was able to fund the first delegations. Since then, more than 200 indigenous representatives from many different communities around the world, including the African, Asian, and Pacific regions, have been given assistance that enables them to attend the Working Group. The United Nations Voluntary Fund, together with the travel funds created by nongovernmental support groups, have helped to ensure that financial considerations do not prevent indigenous organizations from participating in the Working Group. The United Nations Voluntary Fund is administered by a Board of Trustees that meets for five days each April to recommend grants. All members of the board are indigenous persons.[5]

The Working Group, despite its success in attracting indigenous participation, is nonetheless low down in the hierarchy of the United Nations system. It is composed of the independent human rights experts of the Sub-Commission on Prevention of Discrimination and Protection of Minorities.[6] Its activities are thus approved by the Sub-Commission which, in turn, reports to the Commission on Human Rights, an intergovernmental organ. The Commission itself must pass its decisions through the Economic and Social Council to the General Assembly. The Working Group cannot undertake human rights investigations, make financial commitments, or pass judgments on specific violations. It may only determine its own working agenda within the broad framework of its mandate and make recommendations to its parent bodies.

However, and probably because of these limitations, the Working Group has served within the United Nations system as a think tank on indigenous questions. It has generated proposals for studies and expert seminars, and launched the idea of an International Year (1993) which led to the International Decade of the World's Indigenous People (1995–2004). Additionally, it is in the

---

[4] The Voluntary Fund for Indigenous Populations was established by General Assembly Resolution 40/131 of 13 December 1985, and is financed through voluntary contributions from governments and nongovernmental organizations.

[5] The present membership of the Board of Trustees is: Vicky Tauli-Corpuz (Philippines), Ole Ntimama (Kenya), Nina Pacari Vega (Equador), Tove Sovendahl Petersen (Denmark/Greenland), and Michael Dodson (Australia).

[6] The present members of the Working Group are: Mrs. Erica-Irene Daes (Greece), Mr. Miguel Alfonso Martinez (Cuba), Mr. Vladimir Boutkevich (Ukraine), Ribot Hatana (Japan), and Mr. El-haj Guissé (Senegal). Mrs. Daes has been its Chairperson-Rapporteur since 1984.

forefront of the push for a new type of forum in the United Nations in which indigenous people can be decision makers rather than observers. Possibly most important of all, the Working Group devoted some five years to drafting a Declaration on the Rights of Indigenous Peoples that reflects by and large a consensus of what indigenous people consider their fundamental human rights. Since 1996, each year the Working Group has focused on a key issue affecting indigenous people. At its 1998 session, the Working Group will highlight the issue of education.

II. DRAFT DECLARATION ON THE RIGHTS OF INDIGENOUS PEOPLES

The draft United Nations Declaration on the Rights of Indigenous Peoples was completed by the Working Group on Indigenous Populations in 1993, the International Year for the Worlds Indigenous People.[7] In 1994, it was adopted by the Sub-Commission on Prevention of Discrimination and Protection of Minorities, an international forum of independent human rights experts, and received by governments in February 1995 at the Fiftieth Session of the Commission on Human Rights.

The Commission on Human Rights has now established a working group of its own to review the draft Declaration. This group met for the first time during two weeks in November 1995 and examined the text section by section in order to identify areas of potential difficulty and possible consensus. Before commenting on the Commission's November meeting, it may be useful to see how the draft Declaration developed and what it says.

The draft Declaration is a unique instrument of the United Nations system because it has been drafted with participation from victims of the human rights violations and the future beneficiaries of its provisions. While the draft Declaration is not an indigenous document, it reflects a broad consensus of an extraordinarily wide range of indigenous experiences. Contributors to the final text have included: traditional leaders; indigenous lawyers and activists; women's and youth organizations; survivors of genocidal State-sponsored policies against indigenous people; and community workers. Indigenous people have spoken about their vulnerability in times of armed conflict; their loss of lands and resources; the impact of dams, deforestation, and other national development; racial discrimination; over-imprisonment; social and economic deprivation; environmental concerns; loss of language and culture, and many other issues. The draft Declaration, with its forty-five articles—an exceptional length for such an instrument—goes a considerable way toward capturing these diverse concerns and providing the necessary protection.

---

[7] *Draft Declaration on the Rights of Indigenous Peoples*, U.N. Working Group on Indigenous Populations, U.N. Doc. E/CN.4/Sub.2/1994/2/Add.1 (1993) [hereinafter *Draft Declaration*].

The draft Declaration is composed of a preambular introduction of nineteen paragraphs and an operational part of forty-five articles, divided into nine sections. The first section proposes some general principles and assures indigenous people their equal status with other groups;[8] their right to full participation;[9] their right to maintain their distinctive characteristics;[10] and their right to self-determination.[11] Article 3 of the draft Declaration, which is considered by indigenous organizations as fundamental to the entire text, reads:

> Indigenous peoples have the right of self-determination. By virtue of that right they freely determine their political status and freely pursue their economic, social and cultural development.

The second section affirms the right of indigenous peoples to life and existence[12] and, in particular, condemns policies of ethnocide.[13] It may be noted that the concept of ethnocide does not exist in other United Nations human rights instruments, although it may be understood as being closely associated with genocide, which is outlawed by the Convention on the Prevention and Punishment of the Crime of Genocide[14] that came into force in 1951. Ethnocide and cultural genocide of indigenous peoples is described in article 7 as:

a) Any action which has the aim or effect of depriving them of their integrity as distinct peoples, or of their cultural values or ethnic identities;

b) Any action which has the aim or effect of dispossessing them of their lands, territories or resources;

c) Any form of population transfer which has the aim or effect of violating or undermining any of their rights;

d) Any form of assimilation or integration by other cultures or ways of life imposed upon them by legislative, administrative or other measures;

---

[8] *Draft Declaration, supra* note 7, art. 2.

[9] *Draft Declaration, supra* note 7, art. 4.

[10] *Draft Declaration, supra* note 7, art. 4.

[11] *Draft Declaration, supra* note 7, art. 3.

[12] *Draft Declaration, supra* note 7, art. 6.

[13] *Draft Declaration, supra* note 7, art. 7.

[14] Convention on the Prevention and Punishment of the Crime of Genocide. GA Res. 260 A (III) 9 Dec. 1948.

e)   Any form of propaganda directed against them.[15]

The third section focuses on the rights of indigenous peoples to their cultures and tradition, including the protection of sacred sites.[16] This section also requests that states take effective measures so that indigenous people may be understood in political, legal, and administrative proceedings through the provision of interpretation or other means.[17]

The fourth section deals with rights related to education and language. Article 15 of the draft Declaration provides for a right of access to all levels of education of the State[18] as well as the right of indigenous peoples to establish and control their own educational systems and institutions in their own languages.[19] Article 16 recognizes the right of indigenous peoples to have their cultures and histories appropriately reflected in education and the media.

The fifth section enumerates provisions protecting the economic and social rights of indigenous peoples, such as their rights to improvements in health, employment, and other conditions.[20] It also re-affirms their right to participate in the decision-making processes of the State.[21] Article 21 may be considered of special interest to indigenous peoples living in relatively self-sufficient ways. It reads:

> Indigenous peoples have the right to maintain and develop their political, economic and social systems, be secure in the enjoyment of their own means of subsistence and development, and to engage freely in all their traditional and other economic activities. Indigenous peoples who have been deprived of their means of subsistence and development are entitled to just and fair compensation.[22]

The sixth section covers rights to the land and resources, recognizing collective ownership over land,[23] restitution of lost territory,[24] preservation of the environment,[25] and control over development on their lands.[26] The six articles in this

---

[15] *Draft Declaration, supra* note 7, art. 7

[16] *Draft Declaration, supra* note 7, art. 13.

[17] *Draft Declaration, supra* note 7, art. 14.

[18] *Draft Declaration, supra* note 7, art. 15.

[19] *Draft Declaration, supra* note 7, art. 15.

[20] *Draft Declaration, supra* note 7, art. 22.

[21] *Draft Declaration, supra* note 7, arts.19 and 20.

[22] *Draft Declaration, supra* note 7, art. 21.

[23] *Draft Declaration, supra* note 7, art. 26.

[24] *Draft Declaration, supra* note 7, art. 27.

[25] *Draft Declaration, supra* note 7, art. 28.

[26] *Draft Declaration, supra* note 7, art. 30.

section constitute the basis for the land and resource rights indigenous peoples seek, while article 25 underscores the spiritual and material relationship indigenous peoples have to their lands. Article 26 reads:

> Indigenous peoples have the right to own, develop, control and use the lands and territories, including the total environment of the lands, air, waters, coastal seas, sea-ice, flora and fauna and other resources which they have traditionally owned or otherwise occupied or used. This includes the right to full recognition of their laws, traditions and customs, land tenure systems and institutions for the development and management of resources, and the right to effective measures by States to prevent any interference with, alienation of or encroachment upon these rights.[27]

Equally important for indigenous peoples who have been the victims of rapacious national development is article 30, which recognizes indigenous peoples' right to determine and develop priorities and strategies for the development or use of their lands, territories, and resources, including the right to require that States obtain their free and informed consent prior to the approval of any project affecting their lands.

The seventh section establishes indigenous peoples' rights to autonomy and their own political institutions.[28] It also speaks of the right of recognition and observance of treaties.[29] Article 31, considered by certain indigenous organizations as a limitation of their right to self-determination and by some governments as extending too many competencies to indigenous institutions, states:

> Indigenous peoples, as a specific form of exercising their right to self-determination, have the right to autonomy or self-government in matters relating to their internal and local affairs, including culture, religion, education, information, media, health, housing, employment, social welfare, economic activities, land and resources management, environment and entry by non-members, as well as ways and means for financing these autonomous functions. [30]

The eighth section identifies a number of measures to be undertaken by States and the United Nations. This particular section has been criticized by certain governmental delegations that claim that the draft Declaration puts obligations upon States that are not in keeping with the non-binding character of

---

[27] *Draft Declaration, supra* note 7, art. 26.

[28] *Draft Declaration, supra* note 7, art. 31.

[29] *Draft Declaration, supra* note 7, art. 36.

[30] *Draft Declaration, supra* note 7, art. 31.

the instrument.[31] The final section provides some concluding general principles, in particular the notion that the rights of the draft Declaration constitute the minimum standards for the survival, dignity, and well-being of indigenous peoples of the world.[32]

Some further points about the uniqueness of the draft Declaration may also be made. The draft speaks of indigenous peoples as collectivities, making it similar in character to the African Charter on Human and Peoples Rights,[33] and different from the major international human rights instruments which to date protect only individual rights. The draft Declaration strikes a balance between the right of indigenous peoples to be different and to control their own affairs, and their right to participate fully in the wider society. Probably one of the most important features of the draft Declaration is its insistence on the concept of consent as a basis for the relationship between States and indigenous peoples.

The Commission on Human Rights' working group considered this draft in its session in November 1995.[34] Already there were signs of profound disagreement about the text between indigenous peoples and governments, as well as among the governments themselves. Indeed, for certain Asian governments, consideration of the draft Declaration should be held off until a satisfactory definition of the term ''indigenous peoples'' has been determined by the United Nations. Although such a view is a minority one, it may be observed that according to the working definition of indigenous peoples used by the Working Group on Indigenous Populations and its own practice, the vast majority of the world's indigenous people live in the Asian region.[35]

---

[31] A United Nations Declaration creates no legal obligations for states, but exerts a moral pressure and may be referred to in practice by courts. Covenants or conventions are forms of treaties between states and the United Nations by which the state agrees to comply with the treaty's obligations.

[32] *Draft Declaration, supra* note 7, art. 42.

[33] *See* African Charter on Human and People's Rights, *done at* Banjul, June 26, 1981, *entered into force,* Oct. 21, 1986, O.A.U. Doc. CAB/LEG/67/3 Rev. 5, *reproduced in* 21 I.L.M. 59 (1982). The African Charter includes several articles protecting people's rights, *see e.g.,* article 21(1): All peoples shall freely dispose of their wealth and natural resources. This right shall be exercised in the exclusive interest of the people. In no case shall the people be deprived of it.

[34] The Working Group was established by Commission on Human Rights resolution 1995/32 of 3 March 1995 (*See Report of the Working Group on Indigenous Populations* established in accordance with Commission on Human Rights Res. 1995/23, U.N. Commission on Human Rights, 51st Sess., U.N. Doc. E/1995/32 (1995)). The report this session of the Working Group is contained in document E/CN.4/1996/84 (*Report of the Working Group on Indigenous Populations,* U.N. Commission on Human Rights, 52nd Sess., U.N. Doc. E/CN.4/1996/84 (1996)). *See also Report of the Working Group on Indigenous Populations,* U.N. Commission on Human Rights, 53rd Sess., U.N. Doc. E/CN.4/1997/102 (1997).

[35] This article has avoided discussion of the definition of the term ''indigenous peoples'' mainly for reasons of space. The United Nations does not have an official definition of the term, although the Working Group on Indigenous Populations has usually referred

Another source of potential difficulty is the use of the term "peoples" in the plural, which for some States may be understood to denote a right of self-determination. In the same vein, the majority of States—although by no means all—are presently unwilling to endorse article 3, because it recognizes the right of indigenous peoples to self-determination in line with article 1 of both the International Covenant on Civil and Political Rights and the International Covenant on Economic, Social and Cultural Rights.[36] In addition, the sections dealing with land and resource rights and autonomy arrangements may also prove to be major sources of disagreement.[37]

An area of initial concern to indigenous peoples has been the procedure established to give their organizations a right to participate in the Working Group on Indigenous Populations. The Commission invited all interested indigenous organizations to make their requests to participate, through the Centre for Human Rights, to the so-called NGO Committee, the intergovernmental body which reviews and recommends nongovernmental status. The States concerned are similarly invited to make their own comments on the indigenous applications. In practice, and despite some fears that governments would restrict indigenous participation, more than 100 indigenous organizations have been approved; no indigenous organization has yet been rejected by the NGO Committee. Furthermore, the General Assembly decided to expand the mandate of the Voluntary Fund for Indigenous Populations, allowing it to provide travel and living allowance grants to indigenous people seeking to attend both the Working Group on Indigenous Populations of the Sub-Commission and Human Rights Commission's working group.

There is no clear time-frame for the completion of the draft Declaration. At a recent session of the Commission on Human Rights, several governmental delegations called for adoption early in the International Decade. Indigenous peoples, optimistically, have urged the Commission to adopt the text as elaborated by the Working Group on Indigenous Populations without change. Notwithstanding the difficulties that lie ahead, indigenous peoples may take comfort in the fact that, after more than a decade of persistence and dedication, they convinced the members of the Working Group on Indigenous Populations to

---

to a working definition prepared by Martinez Cobo in his study. *See* José Martinez Cobo, Study of the Problem of Discrimination against Indigenous Populations, U.N. Sub-Commission on Prevention of Discrimination and Protection of Minorities, at §§ 378–82, U.N. Doc. E/CN.4/Sub.2/1986/7/Add.4 (1986). Also of interest may be the note prepared by the Chairperson-Rapporteur, Mrs. Daes, on this question (Erica-Irene Daes, *Note on the Concept of Indigenous People*, U.N. Doc. E/CN.4/Sub.2/AC.4/1995/3 (1995).

[36] International Covenant on Civil and Political Rights, *adopted* Dec. 16, 1966, 999 U.N.T.S. 171 (*entered into force* Mar. 23, 1976); International Covenant on Economic, Social and Cultural Rights, *adopted* Dec. 16, 1966, 993 U.N.T.S. 3 (*entered into force* Jan. 3, 1976).

[37] *See* Section VI of the draft United Nations Declaration on the Rights of Indigenous Peoples.

agree upon a text that they found acceptable. A similar patient conviction could bring similar results with regard to the final adoption of the text by the General Assembly.

III. STUDIES AND SEMINARS

A number of research activities related to indigenous peoples have been undertaken by the United Nations in recent years. In 1989, Mr. Miguel Alfonso Martinez was appointed Special Rapporteur of the Sub-Commission on the Study of Treaties, Agreements and Other Constructive Arrangements Between States and Indigenous Populations. This study, due to be completed in August 1998, comprises a preliminary report and two progress reports, and provides a partial review—mainly in the form of case studies—of historical treaties.[38] In 1990, Ms. Erica-Irene Daes was appointed Special Rapporteur of the Sub-Commission on the Study on the Protection of the Cultural and Intellectual Property of Indigenous Peoples. Her study was completed in 1993 and, in 1994, the Special Rapporteur prepared some draft principles and guidelines for the protection of the heritage—a term she prefers to "cultural and intellectual property"—of indigenous peoples.[39] Mrs. Daes' supplementary report on the draft principles and guidelines was presented to the Sub-Commission in 1996.

It may be expected that the treaty study will result in a series of recommendations, perhaps in relation to monitoring of existing and future treaties, particularly because the study shows how many of the provisions of the historic treaties States have violated. The study on indigenous heritage has already resulted in some proposals for guidelines that might serve as a basis for a future international instrument for the protection of indigenous rights. In 1997, the Commission on Human Rights authorized a third study on the relationship of indigenous peoples to their land; it is being undertaken by Erica-Irene Daes. A first working paper was presented to the Sub-Commission in August 1997.[40]

One slightly unusual study should also be mentioned: the series of reports conducted by the former United Nations Centre on Transnational Corporations. This study, which looks at the impact of transnational corporations on the lands, environments, and human rights of indigenous peoples in the Americas, Africa,

---

[38] *Second Progress Report of the Special Rapporteur on Treaties*, U.N. Sub-Commission on the Study of Treaties, U.N. Doc. E/CN.4/Sub.2/1995/27 (1995).

[39] *Final Report of the Special Rapporteur on the Protection of the Heritage of Indigenous People*, U.N. Sub-Commission on the Study of the Protection of the Cultural and Intellectual Property of Indigenous Peoples, U.N. Doc. E/CN.4/Sub.2/1995/26 (1995).

[40] *Indigenous People and Their Relationship to Land*, preliminary working paper prepared by Mrs. Erica-Irene Daes, Special Rapporteur. U.N. Doc. E/CN.4/Sub.2/1997/17 (1997).

and Asia was made at the request of the Working Group on Indigenous Populations.[41]

In addition to the studies mentioned above, the United Nations has initiated a series of expert seminars on often sensitive themes related to indigenous peoples. Expert seminars have been held on racism (Geneva 1989),[42] self-government (Nuuk 1991),[43] and sustainable development (Santiago 1992).[44] More recently, the United Nations organized an expert seminar on practical experiences regarding indigenous land rights and claims (Whitehorse 1996).[45] The expert seminars are organized to allow frank discussions, unfettered by national political considerations, about issues on which widely differing opinions are held. The conclusions and recommendations are advisory only and commit only the individuals who attend in their personal capacity as experts.

In practice, an unusual balance has been struck between governments and indigenous peoples in these seminars. The United Nations invites equal numbers of indigenous and governmental experts, and the two officeholders—Chairperson and Rapporteur—are designated from both groups. Another feature of the expert seminars is the use of the local indigenous language as an official language of the meeting. Thus, in the meeting on self-government held in Nuuk, Greenland, simultaneous interpretation and documentation was available in Greenlandic Mapudungum. The language used by the largest number of indigenous people in Chile, the Mapuche, was one of the official languages of the Santiago conference on sustainable development.

The expert seminar in Greenland considered the scope of internal autonomy, fiscal and administrative arrangements, and the legislative steps leading to self-government. The experts concluded that indigenous peoples have the right of self-determination as provided for in the International Covenants on Human Rights.[46] They also considered that indigenous self-government was not merely

---

[41] *Final Report on Transnational Investments and Operations on the Lands of Indigenous Peoples*, U.N. Centre on Transnational Corporations, U.N. Doc. E/CN.4/Sub.2/1994/40 (1994)

[42] *Report of the United Nations Seminar on the Effects of Racism and Racial Discrimination on the Social and Economic Relations Between Indigenous Peoples and States*, U.N. Doc. E/CN.4/1989/22 and Add.1. (1989).

[43] *Report of the United Nations Meeting of Experts on Practical Experience in the Realization of Internal Self-Government of Indigenous Peoples* (Nuuk, Greenland, 24–27 September 1991). U.N. Doc. E/CN.4/1992/42 and Add. 1 (1992).

[44] *Report on the United Nations technical conference on practical experience in the realization of sustainable and environmentally sound self development of indigenous people* (Santiago, Chile, 18–22 May 1992), U.N. Doc. E/CN.4/Sub.2/1992/31

[45] *Report of the Expert Seminar on Practical Experiences Regarding Indigenous Land Rights and Claims* (Whitehorse, Canada, March 24–28, 1996.) U.N. Doc. E/CN.4/Sub.2/AC.4/1996/6 (1996).

[46] *See supra* note 38.

a right of indigenous peoples, but also could be beneficial to the state and the natural environment.[47] The expert conference in Santiago was held one month prior to the June 1992 United Nations conference on Environment and Development. There the experts looked specifically at the traditional practices of indigenous resource management and at ways to strengthen sustainable and environmentally sound self-development of indigenous peoples. They urged United Nations agencies responsible for development to ensure indigenous participation in the planning, implementation, and evaluation of projects.

The United Nations expert seminar on Practical Experiences Regarding Indigenous Land Rights and Claims was held in Whitehorse, Canada, from March 24–28, 1996. The experts recognized the distinctive spiritual and material relationship that indigenous peoples have with their lands; it also noted the important link between self-determination and indigenous rights to the land. One recommendation made by the experts concerned the request to governments to denounce discriminatory legal policies which included doctrines of *terra nullius*—the notion that indigenous communities do not have the capacity to own land collectively—and the doctrine of imposing extinguishment of indigenous land rights, titles, or ownership.[48]

IV. THE YEAR, THE DECADE, AND THE UNITED NATIONS SYSTEM

During the 1990s, indigenous peoples began to have an influence on other parts of the United Nations in addition to the human rights area. With the notable exception of the International Labour Organisation, which adopted a convention on indigenous and tribal populations in 1957[49] and revised it in 1989 as Convention No. 169 on Indigenous and Tribal Peoples.[50] Prior to the latter 1980s the United Nations system had taken little action in favor of indigenous peoples. The first formal recognition by the United Nations of indigenous peoples' human rights can be found in articles 17, 29, and 30 of the Convention on the Rights of the Child, adopted by the General Assembly in 1989.[51] The Convention on

---

[47] *See* Greenland, *supra* note 43.

[48] *See Report on U.N. Expert Seminar on Practical Experiences Regarding Indigenous Land Rights and Claims*, *supra* note 45.

[49] ILO Convention Concerning Indigenous and Tribal Populations in Independent Countries (No. 107) 1957.

[50] ILO Convention Concerning Indigenous and Tribal Peoples in Independent Countries (No. 169) 1983. For details, *see* Chapter 2, Lee Swepston, *The ILO Indigenous and Tribal Peoples Convention (No. 169): Eight Years After Adoption*.

[51] Convention on the Rights of the Child, G.A. Res. 44/25, 44 U.N. GAOR Supp. (No. 49) at 165, U.N. Doc. A/44 736 (1989). Although article 30 specifically speaks in a generalized way about the rights of indigenous children, their rights are also protected by articles 17 and 29. *See* Chapter 3, Cynthia Price Cohen, *International Protection of the Rights of Indigenous Children*.

Biological Diversity, adopted in 1992, also includes in article 8(j) a provision relating to indigenous people.[52]

Historically, indigenous people have been largely absent from high-level international conferences. This changed in 1992, when, for the first time, indigenous people gathered in Rio de Janeiro in June at the time of the Conference on Environment and Development. One indigenous representative was invited to address the plenary of the conference. A year later, at the World Conference on Human Rights in Vienna, some dozen indigenous speakers were given an opportunity, in common with foreign ministers and heads of State, to address the plenary of the meeting from the podium. A similar situation occurred at the inauguration of the 1993 International Year for the World's Indigenous People, when indigenous leaders were invited to address the General Assembly.

These opportunities, though largely symbolic, are nonetheless a mark of how far the indigenous issue has traveled in the United Nations system over the last ten years. The General Assembly proclaimed 1993 as the International Year for the World's Indigenous People in part as a response to this newfound recognition. The year was launched under the theme "Indigenous Peoples: A New Partnership" with the goal of strengthening international cooperation for the solution of problems faced by indigenous people in the areas of human rights, the environment, development, education, and health. One year was hardly enough time to reorient the United Nations in new directions or to mobilize governmental policymakers, and this frustration was felt by certain indigenous people and governments alike. Nevertheless, there was unanimity on the need to create a framework for continuing, long-term action by the world organization.

The General Assembly's launch of the International Decade of the World's Indigenous People (1995 to 2004) is aimed at establishing such a framework. The theme of the Decade is "Indigenous People: Partnership in Action" and emphasis is placed on the development of projects and programs by the operational arms of the United Nations. Additionally, the Office of the High Commissioner for Human Rights (OHCHR) is authorized to open a special fund to support indigenous projects administered with the participation of indigenous people. Priorities for the OHCHR include human rights training of indigenous representatives—a priority which is being realized through an indigenous fellowship program open to human rights activists proposed by their community or organization.

V. THE FUTURE: A PERMANENT FORUM IN THE UNITED NATIONS

While the next few years should provide opportunities for practical progress in the socioeconomic field, there is also a movement to establish a permanent

---

[52] United Nations Convention on Biological Diversity, Na. 92 7807, 5 June 1992, 31 I.L.M. 818 (1992).

indigenous presence within the United Nations itself. Consideration of a possible permanent forum within the United Nations was a recommendation made by the Vienna Conference on Human Rights. The proposal is strongly supported by the government of Denmark which, in June 1995, hosted a workshop in Copenhagen on this question. A number of elements were identified by indigenous people as being integral to any new forum. First, the mandate of the proposed forum should include issues such as environment, development, and other concerns, as well as human rights matters. Second, the forum should "have teeth" and be able to take action on serious human rights violations. Finally, but most important, indigenous people must participate in the decision making of the new body.

The Secretary-General submitted a review of existing mechanisms for indigenous people within the United Nations system at its Fifty-First Session in 1996. Subsequently, in June 1997, a second workshop on a permanent forum for indigenous people in the United Nations was held in Santiago de Chile, at which it was recommended that the Economic and Social Council take up the issue.[53] The fate of the permanent forum is probably linked to the progress on the draft Declaration on the Rights of Indigenous Peoples. Both initiatives depend on a fundamental change of governmental positions on indigenous issues in the United Nations. At present, there is still a long way to go before consensus is reached on either of these two critical matters.

There have certainly been achievements at the United Nations, but no one could claim that day-to-day living conditions of the vast majority of indigenous people have improved significantly. Many of the world's estimated 300 million indigenous people live in extreme poverty and are deprived of access to basic necessities, such as educational and health services or shelter. One has to attend only a single session of the Working Group on Indigenous Populations to be made aware of a catalog of human rights violations of which indigenous people can claim to have been victims: forced dispossession of their lands and natural resources; extrajudicial killings; torture and arbitrary imprisonment of their leaders; discrimination; destruction of religious and spiritual sites; and much more. It is hard not to ask the question—as many do—what exactly is the United Nations doing about these alleged injustices? What is needed is a giant leap in understanding and action, but the United Nations seems to move forward only with slow and cautious steps.

---

[53] *See* Review of Existing Mechanisms, Procedures and Programmes within the United Nations Concerning Indigenous People. Report of the Secretary-General to the 51st Session of the General Assembly.

U.N. Doc. A/51/493 (1996). *Also see* Report of the Second Workshop on a Permanent Forum for Indigenous People, Santiago, Chile, June 30 June-July 1, 1997. U.N. Doc. E/CN.4/1998/11 (1997).

CHAPTER 2

THE ILO INDIGENOUS AND TRIBAL PEOPLES CONVENTION (NO. 169): EIGHT YEARS AFTER ADOPTION

Lee Swepston*

I. INTRODUCTION

The International Labor Conference of the International Labor Organization (ILO) adopted the Indigenous and Tribal Peoples Convention (No. 169)[1] in 1989, initiating a major advance in international protection of these peoples. Four years after the Convention came into force,[2] it can be safely said that the Convention has moved the indigenous peoples debate forward significantly, that it has had a very positive effect—but that it has not yet had the full effect desired.

This essay will analyze Convention No. 169 itself, and the ILO's work surrounding the Convention, and will make a first attempt to assess its impact. It will also examine, at this critical juncture, the direction in which international law on this subject is moving, and what the ILO Convention's role in this will be. It can be said already that the kind of influence Convention No. 169 has exerted is sometimes surprising and not always what the drafters of the Convention thought it was designed to do, but that this influence appears to be uniformly beneficial. Convention No. 169 has definitely exercised an upward pressure on both national law and practice, and on international standard-setting such as the United Nations' Draft Declaration on the Rights of Indigenous Peoples,[3] and

---

*Note: The views expressed in this article are those of the author and not necessarily those of the International Labor Organization.

[1] Convention on Indigenous and Tribal Peoples in Independent Countries (No. 169), *adopted by* the International Labor Conference at its 76th Session on June 27, 1989 [hereinafter Convention].

[2] Convention No. 169 entered into force on September 5, 1991, one year after the second ratification was registered. Most ILO Conventions require two ratifications to enter into force.

[3] For more information, *see* Chapter 1, Julian Burger, *Indigenous Peoples and the United Nations,* in this volume.

on the draft Inter-American Declaration on the Rights of Indigenous Peoples.[4] Convention No. 169 has had a similar effect on the operational guidelines of various development agencies that assist indigenous and tribal peoples. It remains to be seen whether the Convention will continue to exert the influence it has had in the past.

II. THE ILO AND INDIGENOUS AND TRIBAL PEOPLES

A first question that has to be answered whenever this subject is discussed is, why have the only international conventions on indigenous and tribal peoples been adopted by the International Labor Organization, rather than by the United Nations. What, in fact, is the interest of the ILO in this subject?

The ILO was established in 1919 as part of the settlement of World War I. Its first Constitution was part of the Treaty of Versailles, and it was one of the two international organizations created as a result of that conflict. The League of Nations was responsible for the political and military peace, and the ILO for the social peace. As the Constitution of the ILO states, "there can be no lasting peace without social justice." For this reason, the ILO began to address the situation of "native workers" as early as 1921. One of the outcomes of that effort was the adoption in 1930 of the ILO's Forced Labor Convention (No. 29), conceived originally to protect the "native workers" in overseas colonies of the European powers.

The principal method employed by the ILO in its fight for social justice was, and continues to be, the adoption and supervision of international conventions. This has resulted, in the adoption, to date, of 181 conventions on different subjects—mostly concerned with the world of work, but some with wider application. In addition to those conventions dealing directly with indigenous and tribal peoples, others establishing work-related protection are of equally direct reference to these poorest of working people.

When the United Nations was created in 1945 to replace the defunct League of Nations, it found that the ILO had survived World War II with its experience of adopting conventions intact. The ILO then began to broaden its pre-war examination of the situation of indigenous *workers* to cover the problems of indigenous *peoples* as a whole.[5] It undertook leadership of the Andean Indian Programme—a system-wide, multidisciplinary program to assist Indians in the Andean countries—which lasted from 1952 to 1972. One of the earliest outcomes

---

[4] For more detail, *see* Chapter 4, Osvaldo Kreimer, *The Future Inter-American Declaration on the Rights of Indigenous Peoples: A Challenge for the Americas,* in this volume.

[5] The words "peoples" and "populations" had not at that point acquired the emotional resonance they took on later. The ILO used the two interchangeably for years. *See* Chapter 1, Julian Burger, *Indigenous Peoples and the United Nations. Also see* Part IV, this chapter.

of this programme was a request from the U.N. system for the ILO to use its standard-setting experience to adopt a convention on the subject.

In 1953 the ILO published a book entitled *Indigenous Peoples*,[6] a worldwide survey of the living and working conditions of these peoples, that remains a valid reference in some countries. Nothing like it has been published since. Shortly after this survey, the ILO began working on the adoption of what would become the Indigenous and Tribal Populations Convention (No. 107), adopted in 1957.[7]

Convention No. 107 was the only international treaty that had ever been adopted on this subject. It would remain unique until the ILO revised it in 1989.[8] Deliberations for Convention No. 107 were undertaken under the ILO's responsibility, with the active participation of the rest of the United Nations system: the U.N. itself, and specialized agencies including the United Nations Educational, Scientific and Cultural Organization (UNESCO), the Food and Agriculture Organization (FAO), and the World Health Organization (WHO). In effect, the ILO thus adopted Convention No. 107 on behalf of the entire United Nations system, and enlisted the help of the other organizations in supervising its implementation, as well as in carrying out the Andean Indian Programme.[9] Convention No. 107 was eventually ratified by 27 countries, 14 of which were in the Americas, but that also included Bangladesh, India, and Pakistan, as well as several African and Arabic-speaking countries.

Convention No. 107 had the same basic structure as does the later Convention No. 169, and covered most of the same subjects: administration, land, health and social security, labor, and education. Its provisions were at once protective and patronizing, as will be explained below. The Convention's major fault was that it reflected the values of the time in which it was adopted, ignoring the indigenous perspective in favor of integration and assimilation.

III. THE ADOPTION OF CONVENTION NO. 169

In time, the United Nations itself began to examine the question of indigenous populations.[10] This coincided with the beginning efforts of indigenous peoples to organize themselves on the international level. As a consequence of these

---

[6] INTERNATIONAL LABOR ORGANIZATION, INDIGENOUS PEOPLES (1953).

[7] Convention on Indigenous and Tribal Populations (No. 107), ILO (1957).

[8] Though of course all international human rights standards apply to these peoples.

[9] *See* discussion *infra* Part V (describing the ILO's supervisory procedures for ratified conventions).

[10] The terminology used here is that adopted by the United Nations at the time. *See* text *infra* Part IV (discussing terminology and meaning).

activities, Convention No. 107 was called into question as being "integrationist." In 1972, the United Nations began working on a *Study of the Problem of Discrimination against Indigenous Populations*[11] (Study) and, in 1981, it set up a Working Group on Indigenous Populations within the Sub-Commission on Prevention of Discrimination and Protection of Minorities of the Commission on Human Rights. The Study called for the revision of Convention No. 107, and asked the United Nations to begin examining the question of standards. The U.N.'s review of possible standards has taken the form of a draft Declaration on the Rights of Indigenous Peoples which, as of late 1997, was before a working group of the Commission on Human Rights.

Responding to calls for the revision of Convention No. 107—which came from indigenous and tribal peoples as well as from the United Nations—the ILO began an examination of this question in 1985. Again with the cooperation of the rest of the U.N. system, and this time with the participation of a number of indigenous representatives as well as of the Inter-American Indian Institute, it completed the revision in 1989.[12]

The ILO is a tripartite organization. This means that governments—which are the members of the ILO—are not the only ones to have votes. Every country is represented at the Conference by four delegates: two government representatives, and one each from its employers' and the workers' organizations. Twenty-five percent of the votes in the ILO Conference are thus allotted to the workers' representatives, and twenty-five percent to the employers' representatives. Thus, the ILO is at once far more open than the U.N. to participation in its deliberations by nongovernmental organizations (NGOs) because half the votes are allotted to workers' and employers' representatives; and yet much less open, because these groups are presumed to represent all NGO interests relevant to the ILO's work.

In the discussions leading to the adoption of Convention No. 169, special arrangements were made for indigenous representation in order to overcome this exclusivity in the ILO's concept of NGOs. Indigenous peoples participated in their capacity as NGOs (in the sense in which this is known in the United Nations.)[13] As such, they were able to intervene directly at defined times in the discussion, to lobby for their point of view, and to express their opinions throughout the deliberations. Governments had been asked to consult them in drawing

---

[11] *See* J. Martinez-Cobo, *Study of the Problem of Discrimination against Indigenous Populations*, U.N. Sub-Commission on Prevention of Discrimination and Protection of Minorities, U.N. Doc. E/CN.4/Sub.2/1986/7/Add. 4 (1986).

[12] For a detailed account of the adoption of Convention No. 169, *see* Lee Swepston, *A New Step in International Law on Indigenous and Tribal Peoples: ILO Convention No. 169 of 1989*, 15 OKLA. CITY U. L. REV. 699 (1990).

[13] For information regarding NGOs, indigenous peoples, and the United Nations, *see* Chapter 5, Douglas Sanders, *The Legacy of Deskaheh: Indigenous Peoples as International Actors,* in this volume.

up their replies to the written phase of consultations preceding the Conference discussions.[14] The ILO and some indigenous organizations, particularly the World Council of Indigenous Peoples, held a series of regional consultations in Latin America to inform indigenous people of the issues at stake and help them lobby their own countries' representatives. In addition, indigenous representatives were part of a large number of delegations on government, employer, and worker benches, because some delegations had taken special pains to provide for this representation.

The most important factor in indigenous representation was a working arrangement by which the Workers' Group of the Conference Committee, considering the adoption of the Convention, opened its caucuses to indigenous representatives and submitted to the Committee the amendments to the text which were given to them by the indigenous forum at the Conference. All in all, for the first time at the international level, indigenous representatives had a significant part in the discussions leading to the adoption of a treaty (Convention No. 169) that will have an impact on their lives. The lessons learned in this process have been put to excellent use in later discussions at the United Nations.

IV. WHAT DOES CONVENTION NO. 169 PROVIDE?

The Convention consists of thirty-four substantive articles, divided into sections on general principles, land rights, labor, vocational training, handicrafts and rural industries, social security and health, education and means of communication, contacts and cooperation across borders, and other provisions.

Terminology is a major factor in understanding Convention No. 169. This is important in two ways: the Convention refers to "indigenous" *and* "tribal" peoples, and it refers to "peoples" instead of "populations."

It is simplest to refer only to "indigenous" peoples or populations, omitting reference to "tribal" peoples—and this is the current usage in the United Nations. However, this is not sufficient from a legal and sociological point of view to cover all the situations that should be covered. "Indigenous" implies historical precedence in a particular area, and this is sufficiently true in the Americas and in parts of Oceania to be a useful term. However, only some ten percent of the indigenous and tribal peoples in the world live in North and South America. In much of the rest of the world, those who are covered by the two ILO Conventions were probably not in the region before other groups that now form the dominant population. In India alone, there are over sixty million tribal people—more than twice as many as there are in North and South America combined—who are no more indigenous than anyone else.[15] The same situation

---

[14] Though only one government—Canada's—did so in a way which allowed the secretariat to take opinions expressed by the indigenous representatives in that country directly into consideration in drafting the Convention.

[15] For a discussion of the "indigenous" peoples of India, designated "tribal" by the Indian Constitution, *see* Chapter 7, Deepak Kumar Behara, *"So-Called Development" and Its Impact on the Rights of the Indigenous People in India,* in this volume.

applies to nomadic peoples in the North African deserts, to Pygmy and Masai in sub-Saharan Africa, and to the tribal peoples in South-East Asia. The ILO Conventions therefore have a wider frame of reference than "indigenous" in the strict sense.[16] To put it simply, the historical presence, which is a determining factor in U.N. discussions, is only one of the factors taken into account in the ILO. When this was put to the membership during consultations leading to the adoption of Convention No. 107, and later for Convention No. 169, the point was accepted.

The second, and more controversial, point of terminology is that Convention No. 169 refers to indigenous and tribal "peoples," a point that required much discussion before it was accepted by the Conference. Convention No. 107 had referred to "populations," and many States did not want to make any change because to adopt the word "peoples" would be a recognition of the right to self-determination in international law. Even those countries that use the term "peoples" in their internal law sometimes took this position. The problem remains that no one knows what the right to self-determination implies. Many fear, however, that using the term "peoples" would open the door to self-determination in the sense of *authorizing secession* from existing States. This is an ongoing debate, but the ILO is not the competent body to resolve the question. The ILO Conference therefore was forced to insert the following provision as paragraph 3 of Article 1:

> The use of the term "peoples" in this Convention shall not be construed as having any implications as regards the rights which may attach to the term under international law.

What does this mean for self-determination? In itself, it means nothing in the context of deciding what "self-determination" actually implies. If self-determination means—in part at least—autonomy within state boundaries, then Convention No. 169 is consistent with all degrees of autonomy and other expressions of self-determination within the boundaries of existing States. The Convention takes no position whatsoever on the question of political autonomy outside the boundaries of existing States; this is a question for the United Nations in a larger political context.

Some have said that the solution found in the ILO Convention will destroy any chance that the term "peoples" might be used in United Nations instruments. This is yet to be seen, but this author regards that as improbable. The U.N. Draft Declaration uses the term "peoples," but some governments have

---

[16] Indeed, the ILO has raised this problem in the context of the U.N. Draft Declaration on the Rights of Indigenous Peoples (*Draft Declaration on the Rights of Indigenous Peoples*, U.N. Working Group on Indigenous Populations, U.N. Doc. E/CN.4/Sub.2/1994/2/Add.1 (1993)) now before the U.N. Commission on Human Rights, cautioning the United Nations not to adopt terminology that could turn the Declaration into a regional human rights instrument.

already announced that they will try to remove it as the draft U.N. declaration is discussed in the Commission on Human Rights. The name of the U.N. Working Group remains "on Indigenous *Populations*," and the International Year[17] and the International Decade[18] have been designated by the United Nations as being for indigenous "people," rather than "peoples."[19] If the use of the term "peoples" in the ILO Convention has any impact on discussions in the United Nations, it will be to lower resistance to its use, not to raise it. The ILO believes that it will contribute to a broader understanding of the rights of peoples within states.

Another criticism is that Article 1(3) somehow limits the rights of indigenous peoples to self-determination. Again, this patently is not so. Convention No. 169 simply refers the decision on the content of this right to the United Nations, where it rightly belongs.

A. Basic Philosophy

The basic philosophy of Convention No. 169 is the major thing that distinguishes it from Convention No. 107. Whereas the earlier Convention presumed the eventual disappearance of indigenous and tribal populations as they were gradually integrated into the countries in which they live, the 1989 instrument adopted an attitude of respect for the cultures and ways of life of these peoples. Convention No. 169 presumes their right to continued existence and to development along the lines they themselves wish.[20] It also provides, in a number of articles, for the right of these peoples to be involved in the decision-making process as it affects them.[21] There was a debate during the Conference discussions about whether the right to take part in decisions that affect them meant, on the one hand, a right of veto by indigenous peoples over development projects, or, on the other hand, a meaningless and *pro forma* consultation. The response to this discussion is found in article 6(2) of the Convention: "The consultations carried out in application of this Convention shall be undertaken, in good faith and in a form appropriate to the circumstances, with the objective of achieving agreement or consent to the proposed measures." Thus, there is neither a right of veto, nor the possibility of carrying out empty consultations, if the Convention is correctly applied. The Convention requires a true dialogue.

---

[17] The year 1993 was designated The International Year for the World's Indigenous People.

[18] The United Nations has designated the years 1995–2004 as the International Decade of the World's Indigenous People. *See* Burger, *supra* note 3.

[19] In French and Spanish, the term used is "populations" and "poblaciones" respectively, a setback for those promoting the term "peoples."

[20] Convention, *supra* note 1, art. 7.

[21] Convention, *supra* note 1, arts. 6, 7, 12, 15, 17, 20, 22, 23, 25, 27, 28, and 33.

There are two other areas in which the Convention expresses respect for the cultures and ways of life of indigenous and tribal peoples. The first is that a number of articles[22] require that consultations and other activities take place through traditional institutions. This obviously will support the continuance of indigenous cultures, as well as put a certain pressure on indigenous communities to revive their political structures where they may have lapsed.

The second way in which traditional cultures are supported is that the Convention requires a transfer of responsibility in some respects to indigenous communities and other indigenous entities, to the degree that they want it and are capable of exercising it. This will be explored below under sections dealing with *education* and with *health* in particular. It is not restricted to these two subjects, however—indigenous responsibility is an attitude that permeates the Convention.

B. General Provisions

Some of the articles in the "General Provisions" section of the Convention (articles 1 through 12) have already been described; the most important is article 6, which lays down the requirement of consultation. There are also other important provisions in this section.

Article 2 of the Convention provides that governments "have the responsibility for developing, with the participation of the peoples concerned, coordinated and systematic action to protect the rights of these peoples and to guarantee respect for their integrity." This implies that governments must focus their "indigenous policy" and integrate it into wider decision-making policies, and that indigenous and tribal peoples must be involved in setting policy and carrying out that process.

A series of articles embodies respect for customary indigenous law, while at the same time limits the credit given to it. Essentially, these provisions require that customary law be given credit where it does not conflict with fundamental provisions of national and international law. An example might be that indigenous family and social control rules should apply within their communities, and that national courts should respect their rules for such matters as when a marriage has been accomplished, how possessions are transferred from one person to another, or the age at which a young person becomes an adult for tribal purposes. However, where there is a major conflict, national law would probably prevail.

One important limitation is that individuals have the right to all rights granted to other citizens, and that international human rights law must be respected. Two illustrations will indicate what this means. First, women often suffer discrimination under traditional law that is not tolerated under international law, and this would not be permitted under the Convention. Second, some

---

[22] *See, e.g.*, Convention, *supra* note 1, arts. 6(1)(a), 8(2), 9(1), and 12.

groups might have rituals or practices—such as those involving a high degree of physical pain—that would be unacceptable to the international community. As a consequence, it is likely that such practices could be restricted under Convention No. 169.

Article 7 allows indigenous and tribal peoples to exercise control over their own fates by providing for indigenous peoples to ''have the right to decide their own priorities for the process of development as it affects their lives, beliefs, institutions and spiritual well-being and the lands they occupy or otherwise use.'' This article also provides for their participation in the formulation, implementation, and evaluation of plans and programs for national and regional development. A very important aspect of article 7 is that it requires the governments of ratifying countries to ''. . . ensure that, whenever appropriate, studies are carried out, in co-operation with the peoples concerned, to assess the social, spiritual, cultural and environmental impact on them of planned development activities.'' All these aspects together contribute to the sense that indigenous and tribal peoples are not—or should not be—passive victims of development, but that they have the right to take part in and control the development process as it affects them

C. Land Rights

The special importance of land rights for indigenous and tribal peoples, and the place this concept occupies in national constitutions, guaranteed a difficult discussion in the ILO Conference when it adopted Convention No. 169. The result is a complex set of provisions, and an advance over Convention No. 107.

The basic land rights provision is article 14, the first sentence of which reads: ''The rights of ownership and possession of the peoples concerned over the lands which they traditionally occupy shall be recognized.'' The obligation is for the State to ''recognize,'' and not to ''grant,'' the lands of traditional occupation—in other words, the Convention makes it clear that rights do exist whenever lands have been traditionally occupied. The form of those rights may vary, whether they constitute ownership or possession, or both, and the ILO Committee of Experts has confirmed that the Convention does not necessarily require full title, as long as possession is secure. This article also provides for cases in which there is shared use of lands, such as when nomadic peoples or herders have long used lands to which they do not have title. There is an important obligation on governments to take steps to identify the lands of traditional occupation, to guarantee effective protection of the rights, and to resolve land claims.

''Resource'' rights are covered in article 15. This provision was hotly contested by governments who noted that many national constitutions provided that all resources, or all mineral or subsurface resources depending on the country, belonged to the State, and they saw no reason to make an exception for indigenous and tribal peoples. The indigenous representatives made the obvious rejoinder that surface land rights alone were not what interested them. If oil or gold was mined without their consent in their traditional lands, this destroyed the quality of life, and damaged their cultures and livelihoods. The resulting compromise recognizes that governments will seldom modify their constitutional principles, but that rights can be established which are consistent with them.

The article therefore provides that "The rights of the peoples concerned to the natural resources pertaining to their lands shall be specially safeguarded." If the government does retain ownership of mineral or subsurface rights, it must consult these peoples to determine whether their interests would be damaged before permitting either "exploration" or "exploitation" of resources on their lands. Indigenous and tribal peoples then have to be compensated for any damages resulting, and shall wherever possible participate in the benefits. It is important to read this requirement in light of article 6 (see above), which requires effective consultations, and with the last sentence of article 15(1): "These rights include the right of these peoples to participate in the use, management and conservation of these resources."

The difficult issue of "removal from traditional lands" is covered in article 16. Indigenous and tribal peoples have been subject to being simply expelled from the lands they occupy, for as long as human history has been recorded. This is usually done on the pretext that, when too few people occupy good land that the dominant population wants for itself, "progress" is impaired. This article of Convention No. 169 begins with the assertion that indigenous and tribal peoples "shall not be removed from the lands which they occupy." Nevertheless, removals may take place, some for reasons that can be accepted in the general framework of national development or for other reasons. The article goes on to provide that where their relocation (note the word used is "relocation," and not merely "removal") is considered necessary *as an exceptional measure*, it shall take place only with their "free and informed" consent and, where this cannot be obtained, after procedures including public inquiries where appropriate.

When might such relocations be necessary? The Conference decided in 1989 that to spell out cases would be to grant license for them, one of the weaknesses in Convention No. 107. The easiest to accept are such things as war, physical emergency such as disease or flood, and ecological disaster. The more difficult to justify are "national development" reasons. A recent study by the World Bank illustrates what everyone active in this field has known for years: almost no major hydroelectric project anywhere in the world has been built without removing indigenous peoples from the land to be flooded. Yet these removals will take place, and all citizens of the country are subject to them. The Convention therefore sets up a series of hurdles to be passed, with public hearings as insurance against abuse. This will not always prevent abuse but, if observed, it will diminish the risk.

Article 16 goes on to provide that these peoples shall have the *right to return* to their traditional lands when the reason for removal ceases, and the right to compensation and replacement lands. This author knows of no other instance in international law where such provisions are made.

D. Labor, Health, and Education

Articles 20 to 32 lay down guarantees on a variety of subjects, no less important but which require less explanation than the earlier articles. As concerns *labor,* article 20 provides for equal treatment with other citizens, in a degree of detail which indicates the labor abuses to which indigenous and tribal peoples are subjected. This is a case in which equal treatment requires "special measures to ensure the effective protection . . . of workers belonging to these peoples." The reader will recall that the revolt of the Indian populations in southern Mexico at the beginning of 1994 was very largely a revolt against labor abuses aggravated by a perception of exploitation of indigenous peoples.

Article 20 covers admission to employment, and equal pay for work of equal value. Indigenous and tribal peoples, like other workers, must be allowed to form and join trade unions for their protection. Seasonal and casual indigenous workers need special protection from abuses by labor contractors, and need to be informed of their rights and how to protect them. Indigenous women have to be protected from sexual harassment (again the only case in an international treaty where this appears, for any population group). Particular attention is to be given to labor inspection in areas where they live.

Articles 21 to 23 cover the "economic life" of indigenous communities, providing first for their admission to general measures of vocational training and guidance, and then for promotion of their traditional economies "as important factors in the maintenance of their cultures and in their economic self-reliance and development."[23] Under articles 24 and 25, special attention should be given to the health needs of these peoples, from the training of community-based health care workers, to incorporation of traditional health care practices. Article 25 calls for these services to be provided with the resources "to allow them to design and deliver such services under their own responsibility and control."

Education is covered in articles 26 through 31. These articles provide, *inter alia*, for the history and values of indigenous peoples to be taken into account in the national educational system as well as in the education provided to these peoples. They also provide, in a very important innovation, for these peoples to assume control over their educational systems, if they wish to do so, while preserving minimum standards of education available to others in the national population.

---

[23] Convention, *supra* note 1, art. 23(1).

Other provisions of the Convention protect the right to contacts across borders (article 32), and require ratifying States to take the measures necessary to implement the Convention. Article 34 calls for the Convention to be implemented in a flexible manner, taking account of the conditions in each country—a very important provision for a convention as detailed as this one is, and that applies to so many different situations.

V. THE ILO'S SUPERVISORY SYSTEM

It is not productive to adopt an international instrument without ensuring that its application will be supervised. The ILO has the most sophisticated supervisory system in international law. It is not well known to many in the human rights field, because most ILO conventions focus on labor matters, an aspect of international human rights law that has been badly neglected by many. The system was radical when it was developed between 1919 and 1927; in some ways, it is even more so now.

The supervisory system is based on article 22 of the ILO Constitution. Ratifying States are required to send reports on treaty compliance to the ILO at regular intervals—between one and five years, depending on various factors. The ILO receives and examines some 2,000 government reports each year. At the same time, governments are required to send copies of these reports to workers' and employers' organizations inside their country, who then have their own right to comment: for example, they might state that the government is misrepresenting the situation, or has not provided full information.

These reports are examined by the Committee of Experts on the Application of Conventions and Recommendations, which meets once a year. The Committee of Experts makes any comments it feels are necessary—asking questions about application, or indicating that the national law and practice are not in conformity and requesting changes. This is done in two forms: ''direct requests'' and ''observations.'' ''Direct requests'' are unpublished[24] and consist of less serious or more preliminary points. They request further information or ask for minor adjustments. ''Observations'' are published comments that appear in the annual reports of the Committee of Experts[25] and are submitted to the International Labor Conference for possible discussion.

The Report of the Committee of Experts—known as ''the green book'' for its cover—is already a powerful tool for those who want to compare their country's performance with its international obligations, and with the situation in

---

[24] Direct requests are not published in book form, and are not submitted to the Conference as are observations. However, they are not confidential, and are published in the ILOLEX database which appears on CD-ROM annually. All Committee of Experts comments have recently been made available on the Internet at http://www.ilo.org. The separate arrangements for direct requests are purely a practical matter to deal with enormous volumes of information.

[25] Report I(4A) to each session of the Conference.

other countries. The process does not stop there, however. The International Labor Conference meets every June, and has a Committee on the Application of Standards which is composed of representatives of governments and of employers and workers. This Committee will usually decide to discuss in public session about fifty cases of the several hundred published in the Committee of Experts' report. The Committee of Experts invites the representative of the government concerned to appear before the Committee and explain the reasons for the problem noted by the Committee. This representative then takes part in a dialogue with the Committee, usually led by the employers' and workers' spokespersons. The representative is asked to clarify statements, to indicate a timetable for the implementation of measures the Committee of Experts has requested, or to commit the government to inviting the International Labor Office to carry out "direct contacts" to resolve the problems. These sessions can be very difficult for government representatives, and often result in promises of improved performance.

Convention No. 169 has not yet been in force long enough for many observations on its application to come before the Conference, but there have been frequent discussions on the application of Convention No. 107—most recently for Brazil and India, though these are not the only ones that have been discussed. The issues that come up before the Conference under Convention No. 107 are no different than they would be if the same countries had ratified Convention No. 169. For instance, in Brazil, the Conference has followed the Committee of Experts in being particularly concerned about the invasion of Yanomami lands by the *garimpeiros* (independent gold miners);[26] in India, the principal preoccupation has been the displacement of tribal populations by the massive hydroelectric Sardar Sarovar Dam and Power Project.[27]

However, in 1995 the first instance of a discussion of the application of Convention No. 169 arose when the Conference asked Mexico to explain the relationship between protection of indigenous peoples under the Convention and the events in Chiapas.[28] The Conference Committee asked the government to accept the ILO's technical assistance, and discussions continue on how the ILO can most effectively help the government improve the situation of the Indians in the country.

In addition to the regular supervisory procedure, there are two main "complaints procedures" in the ILO. Under article 26 of the Constitution, any government, any delegate to the International Labor Conference, or the governing body

---

[26] For greater detail about the situation in Brazil, *see* Chapter 10, Gail Goodwin Gomez, *Indigenous Rights and the Case of the Yanomami in Brazil,* in this volume.

[27] *See* Behara, *supra* note 15.

[28] For a discussion of the situation in Chiapas, *see* Chapter 11, Richard Wilson, *Environmental, Economic, Social and Cultural Rights of the Indigenous Peoples of Chiapas, Mexico*, in this volume.

of the ILO may file a "complaint" alleging the violation of a Convention by a country that has ratified it. This results in the establishment of a Commission of Inquiry, which holds hearings in Geneva, visits the country concerned, and makes findings as to whether the Convention is being violated. Under article 24 of the Constitution, a "representation" may be filed by any workers' or employers' organization alleging violation of a ratified Convention. This results in the appointment of a tripartite Governing Body Committee, which decides the case, usually on the basis of an exchange of correspondence. This procedure is especially effective in cases where the facts are not in doubt. While neither procedure has ever been used in relation to Convention No. 107, the representation procedure has recently been invoked for the first time regarding Convention No. 169. The availability of these procedures probably has a dissuasive effect if governments believe they might be invoked.

A. Indigenous and Tribal Peoples and ILO Supervision

How may the supervisory procedures of the ILO be used for the advantage of indigenous and tribal peoples? The first thing to recognize is that the ILO has no procedure for individual submissions of information or complaints—in fact, organizations other than trade unions or employers' organizations have no "formal" access to the system at all. This does not mean that the ILO does not receive and use information generated by other organizations, however. There are several ways in which this can come about.

First, of course, the country must have ratified the ILO Convention concerned to get the full benefit of the ILO's supervisory system. As indicated in more detail below, this does not necessarily mean Convention No. 107 or 169, because other ILO conventions also apply to indigenous and tribal peoples. Ratification is a voluntary act by a government, and if it does not ratify a convention soon after it is adopted, it may take a great effort by interest groups inside the country to achieve ratification. The efforts being made to achieve ratification of Convention No. 169 in several countries are examined below. However, even if the country has not ratified a particular convention, it can still be useful as a reference. No government likes to have it pointed out that it is acting contrary to international human rights law, even where the Convention has not been ratified.

How can ILO standards best be used if the Convention *has* been ratified? It helps, of course, if an indigenous organization is a workers' or employers' organization, and there are trade unions in various countries that were formed to represent indigenous occupational interests. Such a body would have automatic standing with the ILO. What does this give it the right to do? First—and this is often neglected in favor of a formal complaints procedure—this workers' organization would have the right under article 23 of the ILO Constitution to submit information directly to the ILO on the government's performance of the country's obligations. These "comments" by employers' and workers' organizations represent a unique possibility for nongovernmental bodies to play a formal part in the international supervisory process. They are frequently used. For example, in recent years, more than 300 such comments have been received annually on some 2,000 government reports. The comments are sent to the government concerned for its observations, and are given considerable attention by the Committee of Experts in the examination of the government's report. This can have as great an effect as does a formal complaint, and is usually much faster than following a formal procedure. A workers' organization of indigenous and tribal peoples would also have the right to file a representation of the type mentioned above.

If an indigenous organization is not a trade union or employers' organization, it may be able to form an alliance with one. There are several cases in which national or international trade union organizations have submitted information to the ILO on behalf of an NGO, when it believed this information was credible. For instance, Survival International has, on several occasions, persuaded the International Confederation of Free Trade Unions or the International Federation of Plantation, Agricultural and Allied Workers to submit very substantial material on violations of Convention No. 107 in Brazil and India. A national-based trade union could do the same, and occasionally has.

A new way of taking advantage of ILO's supervisory power has emerged in Norway. A Saami Parliament was created in this country some time ago, and it has gradually assumed a greater role in managing the internal autonomy of the Sami people. Based on a suggestion made in the "Report Form" on Convention No. 169,[29] the government of Norway has begun to send its reports on Convention No. 169 to the Saami Parliament for comment, and transmits the parliament's comments to the ILO as part of its own report. The government has also asked the ILO to open a parallel dialogue with the parliament, giving the representatives of the Saami people a formal part to play in the supervisory process. While no exactly similar arrangement has emerged in any other country, the ILO Committee of Experts has been urging governments for some years to consult their indigenous peoples in drawing up their reports, and to state what these consultations have yielded.

What if a government has not ratified Convention No. 107 or No. 169? As already said, most governments have not yet ratified the new Convention, and therefore no supervision can be carried out by the ILO on how it is being applied. However, No. 169 is only one of the ILO's 181 Conventions adopted to date. There are many others that can be used, in all the ways described above, to defend the interests of indigenous and tribal peoples as workers. In many countries, these peoples suffer from forced labor and debt bondage—a situation recently examined in a representation against Brazil under article 24 of the ILO

---

[29] For each convention, the ILO Governing Body adopts a Report Form, which is designed to help governments make their periodic reports. These forms contain questions to illustrate the kind of information desired under various articles, as well as more general guidelines on reporting on each individual instrument.

Constitution in relation to the ILO forced labor conventions. Indigenous peoples are discriminated against in access to employment and after they enter employment. They cannot gain access to vocational training programs and institutions, and are frequently relegated to the lowest-paid forms of migrant agricultural labor. Often they are not allowed to join or to form trade unions. These are classic ILO matters, and conventions exist on all of these questions. Even if a government has not ratified Convention No. 169, almost all ILO Member States have ratified Convention No. 29 on forced labor, Convention No. 87 on freedom of association and protection of the right to organize, Convention No. 111 on discrimination in employment, and ILO conventions on the protection of wages (No. 95), minimum wages (Nos. 26, 99, and 131), and others. It may take more research, but these conventions can offer a great deal of protection.

B. Ratification of Convention No. 169

The earlier Convention, No. 107 of 1957, was eventually ratified by only twenty-seven countries, of which fourteen were in the Americas. Part of the reason for revising Convention No. 107 was the awareness that many countries, which had more progressive approaches to the indigenous and tribal peoples within their borders, did not want to ratify it because of that convention's integrationist approach.

Convention No. 169 has, as of the fall of 1997, ten ratifications. The first two countries to ratify were Norway and Mexico (1990), which was sufficient to bring the Convention into force on September 5, 1991. It has subsequently been ratified by Bolivia, Colombia, Costa Rica, Denmark, Guatemala, Honduras, Panama, and Peru. All of these except Denmark, Guatemala, Honduras and Norway had previously ratified Convention No. 107.[30] Several countries are expected to file their formal ratifications in the near future. The Netherlands, for instance, is expected to ratify very soon, in order to guide its foreign development assistance.

The ratification of Convention No. 169 by Guatemala in 1996 is worth noting. The ratification process ran into significant opposition from military and business leaders, whose objections were based on two concepts: the idea that the Convention would create "a State within a State" (see below), and the land rights provisions. However, the Convention's ratification was a vital element in the peace negotiations being carried out under U.N. auspices, both sides apparently agreed that ratification was necessary to provide a framework for bringing the seventy percent or more of the population who are Indians within the rule of law in the country. After the Indian negotiators made it clear that signing the peace agreement depended on a government commitment to ratify, the agreement was signed and the Convention ratified.

---

[30] Under ILO procedures, the fact that these countries have ratified a convention revising an earlier convention means that they have automatically denounced Convention No. 107.

At the time of this writing, there were two rather strange situations in which the Convention has caught the imagination of a segment of the public and has even been approved by the national legislatures, but the ratification has not been submitted to the ILO. Argentina's parliament approved ratification more than two years ago, but the Foreign Ministry refuses to communicate the instrument that would give Convention No. 169 international force. In the meantime, while Convention No. 169 has been adopted as national law, Argentina remains bound by Convention No. 107, which it had earlier ratified. Fiji is in something of the same situation: the approval of the Convention's ratification by Parliament has not been followed up by a communication of the instrument of ratification.

There were at least two major countries where the Convention was providing a framework for discussion in a process that would probably lead to ratification. In the Russian Federation, the government asked the ILO on two occasions to provide technical assistance in considering proposed new indigenous legislation to begin to fill the complete legal vacuum in many subjects. The ILO was invited to testify to the Duma in November 1994, and did so. Those meetings brought about a proposal for an international agencies and donors conference. This took place in September 1995 under the sponsorship of the Ministry of National Minorities and the Ministry of Labor. Its purpose was to help provide Russia with the legal and logistical framework which would allow it to ratify the Convention.

Another situation existed in the Philippines, where there was a long tribal insurgency against the government. The ILO is carrying out a series of development projects in that country that focus on indigenous peoples. In 1994 it convened a series of meetings which led to the two tribal factions joining forces for the first time—in the conference room at least—to discuss their situation with the government. Further development projects have now been put into place, and the Government has requested the ILO to provide a complete training package for government officials who work with indigenous peoples, so that they may understand the Convention and help to move the country toward ratification. This supplements the training of indigenous leaders, which was the opening phase of this project. Ratification went before the Senate, after more ILO assistance and further discussions.

Other countries are being more cautious about ratification, and in some cases are even flatly opposed to it. In several Latin America countries, the requirements of article 6, outlined above, have given rise to a fear that the Convention would create ''a State within a State'' by giving indigenous peoples the right to veto any national development project that may affect them, and by recognizing that they have an identity separate from the dominant sector of the population. The explanations provided above will, it is hoped, serve to indicate that this is an exaggeration of the Convention's statement of the need for full participation by all national citizens in the process of development, and their empowerment as an essential element of democracy. Nevertheless, these fears have proven difficult to contradict for those not given to careful analysis.

The obstacles to ratification in Sweden and Finland—and quite probably in others—hinge on the land rights provisions. In both countries, as in Norway, there is a long-standing examination of the question of land rights between the Saami populations and others that occupy the same areas.[31] There appears to be an interpretation of the Convention's article 14 that ratification would necessarily result in full title being granted to all indigenous peoples who had any claim of rights to any lands. This would mark a fundamental change to a traditional shared-rights position and complicate a difficult and ongoing negotiation over land use. There is some suggestion that this interpretation may result, in part, from an inaccurate translation of the Convention. In any case, it will be evident from the first part of this essay that Convention No. 169 does not require recognition of full title wherever there is a claim to land rights, but instead supports a wide range of solutions as long as a kind of rights appropriate to the situation and needs of those involved is recognized.

VI. THE EFFECT OF CONVENTION NO. 169 THUS FAR

Convention No. 169 appears to have had an effect on three different levels, and not always in those areas in which its influence was expected when it was drafted. First, in those countries which have ratified it, the Convention has contributed to and accelerated a reexamination of indigenous policy, which is, of course, exactly what it was meant to do. In Bolivia, Mexico, and Peru, ratification was accompanied by revision of the national constitutions to recognize the multi-ethnic nature of the national population, and the preexistence of the indigenous populations, as well as other legislative changes. In Colombia, ratification was followed by a decision to cede large portions of the Amazon forest to the indigenous populations that inhabited them. Norway has used the Convention's ratification as an impetus to move toward the resolution of land-rights discussions that have been going on for years.[32]

The second effect has been on countries that have not yet ratified the Convention, but are using it as a basis for examining the situation of their indigenous and tribal peoples. The situations in the Russian Federation and the Philippines have been described above. The Convention is also a large factor in Brazil, where the constitution's provisions on indigenous populations and the current Indian Act are under examination. As indicated above, Finland and Sweden are using the Convention as a basis for reflection on their own land laws concerning the Saami. Much more recently, several countries in Southeast Asia, including Cambodia, Laos, Thailand, and Viet Nam, have asked the ILO for policy assistance based on the Convention. There are other situations as well, including some of which the ILO is itself unaware.

---

[31] The situation of Saamis in Sweden is described in Chapter 6, Frank Orton & Hugh Beach, *A New Era For the Saami People of Sweden,* in this volume.

[32] A Norwegian Saami Rights Committee has now finished a long study of various points, including land rights, but no decision has yet been taken on whether and how to implement its recommendations.

Finally, the Convention's adoption has had a major effect on international reflection on the subject of indigenous peoples. The one that has the most current visibility is the discussion in a working group of the U.N. Commission on Human Rights of the draft Declaration on the Rights of Indigenous Peoples, described in Chapter 1. A reading of the draft, and of the analytical commentary prepared by the U.N. secretariat, will indicate the influence the ILO Convention has had on its text. There remain areas about which the ILO is concerned—notably the draft Declaration's use of the term "indigenous" without the additional term "tribal" or some other qualification of the meaning of "indigenous"—but this is a battle yet to be resolved.

An equally great ILO influence may be found in the draft Inter-American Declaration on the Rights of Indigenous Peoples, now circulating for comments. The influence of Convention No. 169 is apparent there, and the text adopted will, it may be hoped, continue the upward movement of international human rights law.

A less obvious influence is in international technical assistance for indigenous and tribal peoples around the world. This has taken two shapes. The first is that the World Bank and the Asian Development Bank (ADB) have adopted operational directives for their technical assistance which affects indigenous and tribal peoples, and in both cases these guidelines reflect closely the influence of Convention No. 169. In December 1995, the ADB called a conference to examine its future work in this regard; though inconclusive, it confirmed the importance of these international standards to its efforts.

Another mechanism remains too little known. The Regional Fund for Indigenous Development—established in the Andean countries on the initiative of Bolivia, and partially funded by the government of Spain, the World Bank, and the Inter-American Development Bank—is closely based on Convention No. 169. Its aims are to fund development projects put forward by indigenous communities and governments, and both are represented on the fund's governing body. The fund is not, however, receiving adequate contributions.

The Convention has also had a marked effect on the technical cooperation work of the ILO itself, and of international donors. The Danish International Development Agency (DANIDA) has been the most active solicitor of the ILO's technical assistance, and has funded major assistance programs in the Philippines, India, Bolivia, Guatemala, and others. It has been the major source of funding for the ILO's Inter-Regional Programme to Support Self-Reliance of Indigenous and Tribal Communities through Co-operatives and other Self-Help Organizations (INDISCO). The Netherlands has joined in this funding effort in various capacities. Most recently, DANIDA is funding a project to promote the aims of Convention No. 169 and its ratification, and to provide technical assistance directly to indigenous and tribal peoples.

In the end, the influence of the Convention on the technical assistance provided by the international community may prove to be as important as the direct influence of the Convention on the laws and practice of the countries that ratify it. Which is the more important of the two kinds of impact is unimportant, as long as the principles contained in the Convention continue to influence States' practice, and as long as the representatives of indigenous and tribal peoples themselves continue to defend their cause at the national, regional, and international levels.

A final word concerns the two drafting efforts now going on in the United Nations and in the OAS. Since the establishment of the League of Nations, and the even more rapid development of international human rights law after the United Nations was established, there has been an almost unbroken progression in the principles in conventions, declarations, resolutions, and other statements adopted by the international community. It is vitally important that this progression not be broken by the desire of some States to roll back what has already been achieved in Convention No. 169.

This is not to say the U.N. draft Declaration and the draft OAS instrument must conform to the ILO Convention. This would be senseless; the three instruments have different purposes, different audiences, and different people involved in their drafting. But in no case must the latter instruments sink below the level of Convention No. 169, either in scope or in protection. This would be a betrayal of indigenous and tribal peoples around the world, and a failure of the principles of the United Nations system itself.

CHAPTER 3

INTERNATIONAL PROTECTION OF THE RIGHTS OF INDIGENOUS CHILDREN

Cynthia Price Cohen

I. INTRODUCTION

The world is currently in the midst of celebrating the International Decade of the World's Indigenous People (1995–2004). Undoubtedly, this will assure that the international indigenous rights movement—which began in 1982 with the establishment of the Working Group on Indigenous Populations in the Sub-Commission on the Prevention of Discrimination and the Protection of Minorities of the United Nations Commission on Human Rights—will continue to flourish. However, for those who are concerned about the rights of the child, a word of caution is advised. At the present time, both the United Nations and the Organization of American States are in the process of finalizing draft declarations on indigenous peoples' rights,[1] while two international treaties dealing with specific aspects of indigenous rights—labor and children[2]—have already gone into force. The two declarations and the labor treaty do not recognize established international rights of indigenous children.[3] Moreover, they are especially attuned to the needs of the "group," a concept that is strongly supported

---

[1] *See* Draft Declaration on the Rights of Indigenous Peoples, U.N. Doc. E/CN.4/1995/2 (1995) [hereinafter Draft U.N. Declaration]. *See infra* notes 84–89 and accompanying text. *Also see* Draft Inter-American Declaration on the Rights of Indigenous Peoples, OAS Inter-Am. Comm. on Hum. Rts., 1333rd Sess., Doc. OEA/Ser/LV/II.90, Doc. 9, rev. 2 (1997) [hereinafter Draft Inter-American Declaration]. *See infra* notes 90–94 and accompanying text.

[2] *See* Convention on Indigenous and Tribal Peoples in Independent Countries (No. 169), *adopted by* the International Labor Conference at its 76th Session on June 27, 1989 [hereinafter ILO Convention]. *See infra* notes 77–83 and accompanying text. The childrens treaty was drafted by the U.N. Commission on Human Rights (the Convention on the Rights of the Child). *See infra* notes 4–76 and accompanying text. Both were adopted in 1989.

The author would like to draw attention to the fact that treaties (Conventions, Covenants, etc.) are legally binding on nations that ratify them, while declarations are merely a set of agreed-upon principles, with no implementation mechanism.

[3] Although both declarations have preambular paragraphs referring to other human rights treaties, neither one mentions the Convention on the Rights of the Child.

by those who seek to preserve indigenous culture. In contrast, the Convention on the Rights of the Child,[4] which contains specific articles protecting the rights of the indigenous child, is essentially a general human rights treaty for children and therefore emphasizes the rights of the individual child. The two draft declarations, which have yet to be adopted, will not be binding and will have no implementation mechanisms. The labor treaty is in force, and has been ratified by a number of countries. However, the individual rights of the indigenous child, protected by the Convention on the Rights of the Child, are now legally enforceable in 191 countries.[5]

There is a danger that in the rush to protect the rights of the indigenous group, the declarations will inadvertently treat indigenous children as tribal property. The text of the labor treaty is open to similar interpretation. Considering that the "child as property" concept is completely antithetical to the principles of the Convention on the Rights of the Child, if existing child rights principles are not appropriately recognized by those in the indigenous rights movement, there is the possibility that this could create serious tensions at some time in the future. It would be wise for the Commission on Human Rights and the Inter-American Human Rights Commission to give close attention to the standards of the Convention on the Rights of the Child before adopting the final drafts of their declarations.

It is the purpose of this chapter to explain the international law of indigenous child's rights by surveying the relevant standards of the Convention on the Rights of the Child, and to consider the significance to children of the tensions between the international protection of group rights and the individual rights standards of the Convention.

II. UNITED NATIONS CONVENTION ON THE RIGHTS OF THE CHILD: RELEVANCE FOR INDIGENOUS CHILDREN

When the Polish government proposed the drafting of a treaty protecting the child's human rights to celebrate the 1979 International Year of the Child,[6] there was no indication that it might one day include protection of the rights of the indigenous child. Yet the final draft not only has specific provisions to meet the indigenous child's needs, but the entire Convention is relevant for indigenous children.[7]

---

[4] Convention on the Rights of the Child, G.A. Res. 44/25, 44 U.N. GAOR, Supp. No. 49 at 165, U.N. Doc. A/44/736 (1989).

[5] As of 1997, the United States and Somalia were the only countries that had not ratified the Convention on the Rights of the Child.

[6] See U.N. Doc. E/CN.4/L.1366/Rev.1 (1978).

[7] See infra notes 14–76 and accompanying text.

In the process of making its proposal for the Convention on the Rights of the Child, the Polish government submitted two separate draft models of the treaty to the Commission on Human Rights, neither of which made any mention of indigenous child rights. The first draft model of the Convention that Poland presented to the Commission in 1978[8] was essentially a replication of the 1959 Declaration of the Rights of the Child, with the addition of an implementation mechanism. This model was rejected by the Commission on Human Rights as being too vague. It then established the Open-Ended Working Group on a Draft Convention on the Rights of the Child (Working Group) to begin the elaboration of a new international human rights instrument that would adequately protect the rights of the child.

Using a second, newly revised, Polish draft model Convention[9] as its guide, the Working Group set out to create a human rights treaty that would satisfy the demands of vastly differing cultural, political, and economic systems. In bits and pieces the Working Group added on and took apart the Polish model, until it was approximately double in length. The result was that many of the additional articles were actually augmentations of the original Polish proposal. As the drafting progressed, these "augmenting" articles were given numerical designations that linked the new article to the original by adding "bis" or "ter" to the old number. For example, the Polish article protecting the child's right to express an opinion (article 7) gave rise to articles on: freedom of information and expression (article 7 *a*); freedom of religion (article 7 *bis*); freedom of association and assembly (article 7 *ter*); and the right to privacy (article 7 *quarter*). These articles were later renumbered as 12, 13, 14, 15, and 16. [10]

The Working Group was chaired by Professor Adam Lopatka of Poland, who skillfully directed the drafting so as to keep tensions at a minimum. Whenever there was considerable disagreement on a text, he would assign it to a small drafting party made up of the disputing delegations. Usually, they would return to the Working Group with a text that would be acceptable to almost everyone and adopted with minimal changes.[11] All drafting was done on the basis of consensus.

It should be noted that drafting of the Convention on the Rights of the Child took place in two stages: the "first reading" (1979–1988), [12] during which the

---

[8] U.N. Doc. E/1978/34 (1978).

[9] U.N. Doc. E/CN.4/1349 (1979).

[10] The legislative history of the Convention, including the renumbering, can be found in UNITED NATIONS CONVENTION ON THE RIGHTS OF THE CHILD, A GUIDE TO THE *Travaux Préparatoires*, Sharon Detrick, ed. 1992 [hereinafter Detrick].

[11] For an example of how the Chairman used the "small drafting party" mechanism during the "second reading" of the Convention, *see Report of the Working Group on a Draft Convention on the Rights of the Child in* THE RIGHTS OF THE CHILD, 31 (Maria Rita Saulle, ed. 1995).

[12] The first reading was completed at the Working Group's January 1988 session. For the first reading text, *see* U.N. Doc. E/CN.4/1988/WG.1/WP.1/Rev.1.

basic text of the Convention was developed, and the "second reading" (1989),[13] in which the text was finalized. As the Convention on the Rights of the Child evolved from a simple model that held little interest for the international community to a full-fledged human rights treaty with broad international support, the drafters saw fit to include special protections for the indigenous child. In its final form, the Convention on the Rights of the Child is a human rights treaty whose forty-two substantive articles cover the entire range of human rights (civil-political, economic-social-cultural, and humanitarian), modified to meet the needs of *all* children.

Implementation provisions of the Convention on the Rights of the Child are found in articles 43–45. They follow the basic implementation format of most United Nations human rights treaties in that they require ratifying countries (States Parties) to submit reports to a committee of experts who evaluate the progress that has been made in implementing the Convention. The Convention's ten experts are known as the Committee on the Rights of the Child.

A State Party is required to submit its initial report to the Committee two years after the Convention goes into force for that country. Once the report is received, it is studied by members of the Committee, along with any additional material that may have been submitted by U.N. bodies and NGOs. The Committee then submits a list of questions to the State Party, which must answer them in writing. After that, the Committee holds a public hearing on the report. At the end of the hearing, the Committee drafts its Concluding Observations, which are then published in the Committee's report to the General Assembly.

A. Protection of the Rights of the Indigenous Child

The Convention on the Rights of the Child protects the indigenous child's rights in three ways: 1) through general principles; 2) through articles protecting specific rights of the indigenous child; and 3) through rights applicable to all children. "General principles" are those articles of the Convention that the Committee on the Rights of the Child has deemed applicable to the entire Convention. The articles "protecting specific rights of the indigenous child" are those articles in which the word "indigenous" appears. Finally, the rights "applicable to all children" include the remainder of the Convention's articles.

Because the task of reporting on the Convention's forty-two substantive articles threatened to be overwhelming, both for States Parties and for Committee members, the Committee drafted *General Guidelines Regarding the Form and Content of Initial Reports (Guidelines)*[14] to assist States Parties in preparing their

---

[13] Although the second reading actually took place in November-December 1988, all documentation is dated 1989, when the report was adopted by the Commission on Human Rights.

[14] *See Committee on the Rights of the Child: General Guidelines Regarding the Form and Content of Initial Reports to be Submitted by States Parties Under Article 44, Paragraph (a) of the Convention*, U.N. Doc. CRC/C.5 (Oct. 30. 1991) [hereinafter *Guidelines*]; U.N. Doc. A/47/41 (1992) at Annex III. It should be noted that article 44

reports. Under the *Guidelines*, the Convention's articles are separated into eight clusters according to topic, rather than being listed in sequence. Each of the clusters includes a specific set of articles. Sections I and II of the *Guidelines* ask comprehensive questions about the country (demographics, etc.), the measures that have been taken to implement the Convention (article 4), and how the State Party defines the word "child" (article 1). The remaining articles are clustered into sections: III. General Principles; IV. Civil Rights and Freedoms; V. Family Environment and Alternative Care; VI. Basic Health and Welfare; VII. Education; Leisure and Cultural Activities; and VIII. Special Protection Measures. The "specific rights of the indigenous child" fall within sections: IV. (article 17, access to appropriate information); VII. (article 29, aims of education); and VIII. (article 30, minority and indigenous children).

B. General Principles

The Committee on the Rights of the Child has designated four articles as applicable to the entire Convention. These articles—article 2 (protection from discrimination), article 4 (best interests of the child), article 6 (survival and development), and article 12 (respect for the views of the child)—interact with one another and with the Convention's other articles, thus strengthening the child rights structure. For example, the article 3 "best interests" of the child standard would of necessity demand that the child should not be subjected to discrimination—a requirement of article 2. Similarly, the "best interests" standard would also be consistent with ensuring the child's survival (article 6) and the child's right to be heard (article 12).

Each of these articles is applicable to the indigenous child. Arguably, the group versus individual rights issue would not be a factor in applying the Convention's article 6 protections, because "survival" is central to the group as well as to the individual. The same can be said of the article 2 proscription against "discrimination." However, when it comes to article 3 ("best interests of the child") and article 12 ("respect for the views of the child"), the situation is not so clear. Who should decide the "best interests" of the child? The tribe or the state? What criteria should be applied? More important, what role will the child have in the decision-making process? Who should protect the individual child's interests? None of these issues are adequately addressed by current indigenous rights declaration drafting exercises. Because virtually the entire world has pledged itself to uphold the individual rights of the Convention on the Rights of the Child, violation of these rights by a tribal council could put it in conflict with the State and therefore might destabilize international measures aimed at ensuring the indigenous group's autonomy.

---

requires states parties to submit their initial reports two years after the Convention goes into effect for that country, with periodic reports every five years thereafter. The Committee has also issued a comprehensive set of Guidelines for the upcoming periodic reports.

C. Articles That Protect the Specific Rights of the Indigenous Child

One unique characteristic of the Convention on the Rights of the Child is that it contains three articles that apply specifically to the indigenous child. To understand why and how the Convention on the Rights of the Child relates to indigenous children, it is useful to track the origins of these articles and to discover how they came to be a part of the Convention's text.

In reviewing each article's legislative history, the reader should be cognizant of the successful efforts of indigenous groups to ensure that any reference to "indigenous *populations*" was replaced by other linguistic formulations. The preferred term is "peoples;" the term "populations" has been looked on with disapproval by indigenous groups, even though the drafting of the Declaration on the Rights of Indigenous Peoples took place under the auspices of the Working Group on Indigenous Populations.[15] On the other hand, governments have been hesitant to use the word "peoples," because, under international law, it implies a right to self-determination that might lead indigenous groups to try to secede from the dominant State and set up independent States of their own. Because the Convention's drafters were sensitive to possible international ramifications of the word "peoples," it does not appear in the Convention on the Rights of the Child. Neither does the word "populations."[16]

1. Article 17—Access to Appropriate Information

Article 17 was originally put forward as article 9 of the second Polish model Convention. The initial text focused on the negative aspects of the media and called for governments to "protect the child against any harmful influence that mass media . . . may exert on his mental and moral development." From 1979, when the second Polish model convention was submitted to the Commission on Human Rights, until 1989, when the Convention's text was finalized, this one-paragraph article was subjected to many modifications.

The first Working Group discussions of article 17 took place in 1981, with a new submission from Poland (based on its 1979 revised text), and one from Australia, which proposed a text that linked lack of control of the child's exposure to inappropriate materials to child abuse. A steady stream of recommendations for modifications of article 17 can be found in reports of the Working Group sessions for 1981, 1982, 1983, 1984, 1987, and 1989. Not surprisingly, each time that the article was debated, it became longer and more detailed.

---

[15] For a discussion of the activities of the Working Group on Indigenous Populations, *see* Chapter 1, Julian Burger, *Indigenous Peoples and the United Nations.*

[16] A full discussion of the significance of the word "people" can be found in Chapter 2, Lee Swepston, *The ILO Indigenous Peoples' Convention (No. 169): Eight Years After Adoption.*

The indigenous child was first introduced into article 17 in 1983, when the Baha'i International Community submitted a five-sub-paragraph text to the Working Group. Sub-paragraph (c) of the Baha'i draft called for States Parties to:

> encourage mass media agencies to disseminate their child-oriented programmes not only in the official language(s) of the State but also in the language(s) of the State's minority and *indigenous groups*;[17]

However, that Working Group session concluded without taking action, on article 17.

It was not until 1984 that the drafting of article 17 became more than a repeated submission of proposals. At that session, Poland retabled a two-paragraph Soviet-initiated article from the 1982 Working Group session that dealt with types of information and parental responsibility. Also submitted were a slightly modified draft of the 1983 Baha'i proposal, sponsored by a coalition of nongovernmental organizations (NGOs) known as the Informal NGO Ad Hoc Group on the Drafting of the Convention on the Rights of the Child (NGO Group;[18] and a United States proposal on free flow of information across borders. In addition, Finland offered what amounted to a new introduction to the original Baha'i draft, while the Ukrainian SSR proposed a new, three-paragraph variation of the 1982 Soviet-initiated proposal. Interestingly, the second sentence of the first paragraph of the Ukrainian text reads:

> Information shall be produced and disseminated in both the official language(s) of the State and the State's minority groups and *indigenous peoples.*[19]

In other words, of the many different texts that were proposed for article 17, two recognized the special needs of the indigenous child. Curiously, neither of these were submitted by an indigenous organization.

Because the multiplicity of proposals posed a threat to the efficiency of the drafting process, the Chairman of the Working Group assigned article 17 to a small drafting party made up of Canada, France, the Netherlands, Poland, the Ukrainian SSR, the United Kingdom, the United States, and the Baha'i International Community. The result of their deliberations was an article with an introduction and four subparagraphs. It called on governments to encourage mass

---

[17] U.N. Doc. E/CN.4/1983/WG.1/WP.2 (1983) (emphasis added).

[18] *See* Cynthia Price Cohen, *Role of Nongovernmental Organizations in the Drafting of the Convention on the Rights of the Child*, 12 Hum. Rts. Q. 137 (1990).

[19] U.N. Doc. E/CN.4/1984/71 (1984) (emphasis added).

media to institute certain programmatic policies beneficial to children. It contained no mention of the indigenous child.

The Ukrainian SSR once again introduced its alternative proposal and pressed for inclusion of the phrase "indigenous *peoples*."[20] However, it was ultimately decided that the text by the small drafting party should be used as a basis for further deliberations. Sub-paragraph (c) of that text had called on States Parties to "encourage the mass media to have particular regard to the linguistic needs of minority groups."

The Canadian delegation then urged that if there was to be a reference to "minority groups," a similar reference should be made regarding "indigenous *peoples*."[21] Objections were made to the use of the term "indigenous *peoples*," with the Working Group finally agreeing to use the term "indigenous *populations*." After a great deal of debate, at its 1984 session, the Working Group finally adopted a modified four-sub-paragraph text of article 17 that included the following sub-paragraph:

(c)   Encourage the mass media agencies to have particular regard to the linguistic needs of the child who belongs to a minority group or an *indigenous population*. . . .[22]

The 1984 session of the Working Group did not mark the end of debates over article 17. The article was again revisited by the Working Group in 1987, resulting in the addition of another sub-paragraph between existing sub-paragraphs (b) and (c). The text of the remainder of the article was left unchanged at the end of the first reading.

The first reading consensus was broken as soon as debates over the content of article 17 were reopened during the second reading. At that time, new proposals were made by Turkey, Venezuela, and a coalition of Latin American NGOs. As a consequence, a new small drafting party was established to deal with these proposed revisions. This time, the party was made up of Venezuela, Turkey, the United States, and Yugoslavia. The proposals that they had before them included everything from elimination of all of the sub-paragraphs to adoption of the text as it stood at the end of the first reading. One proposal urged a change in the language of what was now sub-paragraph (d) to eliminate the disagreeable phrase "indigenous *populations*." Recommended substitutions were "indigenous *people*," "indigenous *child*," and "*the child who is* indigenous." This latter modi-

---

[20] U.N. Doc. E/CN.4/1984/71 (1984).

[21] U.N. Doc. E/CN.4/1984/71 (1984).

[22] U.N. Doc. E/CN.4/1984/71 Annex I (1984) (emphasis added).

fication is the one that was adopted. The final text of article 17 was revised so that sub-paragraph (d) now binds States Parties to:

> Encourage the mass media to have particular regard to the linguistic needs of the child who belongs to a minority group or who is *indigenous.*[23]

2. Article 29—Aims of Education

In the 1979 second Polish model Convention, the article 29 (then designated article 16), aims of education, appeared in a two-paragraph version:

1. The States Parties to the present Convention recognize that the bringing up and education of the child should promote the full development of his personality, his respect for human rights and fundamental freedoms.

2. The child shall be prepared for an individual life in a free society, in the spirit of understanding, tolerance and friendship among all peoples, ethnic and religious groups and educated in harmony with the principles of peace proclaimed by the United Nations.[24]

The text for article 29 was not actually discussed by the Working Group until 1985. But every year, beginning in 1982 with a Polish modification of its original text,[25] more proposals were tabled.[26] In 1983, the Baha'i International Community introduced a very long three-paragraph, multiple sub-paragraph article. The first paragraph had to do with education and training, the second with various aspects of the purpose of that education, the third paragraph was similar in scope, but also spoke of parental responsibility.[27] The following year saw submissions by China,[28] the NGO Group,[29] World Association for the School as an Instrument of Peace (an NGO), and the Canadian delegation.[30] Drafting of

---

[23] U.N. Doc. E/CN.4/1989/48 (1989) (emphasis added).

[24] *See* U.N. Doc E/CN.4/1349 (1979).

[25] *See* U.N. Doc. A/C.3/36/6. Part II (1982).

[26] A joint NGO comment was also submitted that urged revisions of the Polish text to bring it into line with article 13(2) of the *International Covenant on Economic, Social and Cultural Rights.* Obviously, this 1982 proposal pre-dates the 1983 establishment of the NGO Ad Hoc Group on the Drafting of the Convention on the Rights of the Child. *See* U.N. Doc. E/CN.4/1982/WG.1/WP. 1 (1982) at p. 5.

[27] *See* U.N. Doc E/CN.4/1983/WG.1/WP.2 (1983).

[28] *See* U.N. Doc. E/CN.4/1984/71 Annex II (1984).

[29] *See* U.N. Doc E/CN.4/1985/WG.1/WP.1 (1985). *See* Cohen, *supra* note 18.

[30] *See* U.N. Doc. E/CN.4/1985/WG.1/WP.1 (1985).

the text of article 29 was an exceptionally contentious process. It sparked lengthy debates in 1985, 1987, 1988, and during the second reading.

When it began its consideration of article 29, the 1985 Working Group had before it for consideration all of the previously submitted drafts of article 29, plus five new ones that were tabled at that session. These new proposals came from: Algeria,[31] the United States,[32] the Netherlands,[33] the Baha'i International Community,[34] and Canada.[35] Canada's proposal became the basis of the Working Group discussions. The ensuing lengthy dialogue had the following participants: the Netherlands, Finland, the USSR, the United States, China, Algeria, Australia, Canada, the German Democratic Republic, the Ukrainian SSR, the Federal Republic of Germany, France, the United Kingdom, and the NGO Group.[36] Although no final text was adopted at the 1985 Working Group session, there was support for the Netherlands' proposal.

At the end of the first reading in 1988, the text of article 29 was made up of two paragraphs. The first paragraph, which was substantially based on the 1985 Canadian text, had four subsections. The second was roughly the same as the Netherlands' proposal.[37] There was still no reference to the indigenous child.[38]

Between the first and second readings, the Working Group requested that the Secretary-General undertake a "technical review" of the Convention. As a part of this process, the various branches of the U.N. were asked to examine the text of the Convention and their comments were ultimately published in a U.N. document.[39] The most influential comments on article 29 came from the United Nations Educational, Scientific and Cultural Organization (UNESCO), the United Nations Children's Fund (UNICEF), the World Health Organization (WHO), and the International Labor Organization (ILO). All of these recommendations were given consideration at the second reading. To more efficiently address this complex article, the Working Group Chairman appointed a small drafting party to sort out the options. Participants in the drafting party were

---

[31] See U.N. Doc. E/CN.4/1985/64 Annex II (1985).

[32] See U.N. Doc. E/CN.4/1985/WG.1/WP.13 (1985).

[33] See U.N. Doc. E/CN.4/1985/64 para. 90 (1985).

[34] See U.N. Doc. E/CN.4/1985/64 para. 89 (1985).

[35] See U.N. Doc. E/CN.4/1985/64 para. 88 (1985). The 1984 Canadian draft had included protection of the child from conscription and armed combat. This was deleted in the 1985 version. It was subsequently retabled as a separate article.

[36] See U.N. Doc. E/CN.4/1985/64 paras. 88–103 (1985).

[37] See U.N. Doc. E/CN.4/1988/WG.1/WP.1 (1988).

[38] Id.

[39] U.N. Doc. E/CN.4/1989/WG.1/CRP.1 (1989).

Canada, Colombia, Italy, Norway, Yugoslavia, UNESCO, and the ILO. Paragraph 1(d) of their resulting joint proposal called on States Parties to direct the education of the child to:

> The preparation of the child for a responsible life in a free society, in the spirit of understanding, peace, tolerance, equality of sexes, and friendship among all peoples, ethnic, religious and *indigenous groups.*[40]

This joint text was used for creating the final version of article 29.

Among the countries taking part in the final debates over article 29 were Ireland, the United States, India, the United Kingdom, the Holy See, Venezuela, Argentina, the Federal Republic of Germany, and Italy. Discussions about subparagraph (d) focused on the part of the sentence that followed the words "equality of sexes." The United States urged that the wording be changed to ". . . and friendship among all members of the human race, without discrimination."[41] The Australian delegation preferred ". . . and friendship among all peoples without discrimination on the basis of ethnicity, religion or *indigenous origin.*"[42] Neither of these proposals met with a consensus, and there was some discussion of completely omitting the reference to "indigenous *origin.*" However, the Canadian delegate explained that, in Canada and other countries, indigenous people were not considered to be members of ethnic groups, so that a specific reference was necessary. The Canadian delegation suggested the wording: ". . . and friendship among all peoples, ethnic, national and religious groups and persons of *indigenous origin.*"[43] Because there were no objections to this proposal, the Canadian text was adopted.[44]

The final version of article 29(d) says that the State Parties agree that the education of the child shall be directed to

> the preparation of the child for responsible life in a free society, in the spirit of understanding peace and tolerance, equality of sexes and friendship among all peoples, ethnic, national and religious groups and persons of *indigenous origin.*[45]

3. Article 30—Children of a Minority or an Indigenous Group

Unlike articles 17 and 29, article 30 did not have its roots in a Polish model convention. It was an entirely new article, for which proposals were introduced

---

[40] U.N. Doc. E/CN.4/1989/WG.1/WP.60 (1989) (emphasis added).

[41] *See* U.N. Doc. E/CN.4/1989/48 (1989) at para. 484.

[42] *See* U.N. Doc. E/CN.4/1989/48 (1989) at para. 486 (emphasis added).

[43] *See* U.N. Doc. E/CN.4/1989/48 (1989) at para. 487 (emphasis added).

[44] *See* U.N. Doc. E/CN.4/1989/48 (1989) at para. 488.

[45] U.N. Doc. E/CN.4/1989/48 (1989) (emphasis added.)

in 1983, 1985, and 1986. Despite general interest in the inclusion of an article protecting the rights of minorities, consideration of this article did not take place until the 1987 session of the Working Group.

In 1986, the Four Directions Council, an indigenous rights group, submitted a text that made direct reference to indigenous persons and the goal of the article's four sub-paragraphs was to protect indigenous children's education, culture, language, and customs.[46] Comments on this draft were entered by both Mexico and Australia in 1986, but detailed discussions were postponed until the following year.[47]

At the 1987 session of the Working Group, Norway tabled a new, shorter alternative text for article 30 that would be applicable to both minority and indigenous children. Australia urged consideration of the Four Directions Council's text, although Australia, along with Austria, the German Democratic Republic, the Netherlands, Poland, and Sweden, expressed a preference for the Norwegian proposal. Additionally, India, Japan, Mexico, and the United States entered their concern about what they saw as a requirement in both texts that States Parties expend extra money to ensure that indigenous children would be educated in their native languages. The competing positions regarding article 30 once again caused Chairman Lopatka to set up a small drafting party to decide on alternative language. This drafting party was made up of Norway, the Four Directions Council, Australia, and Finland. The drafting party proposed the following text:

1. The States Parties to the present Convention shall take all appropriate measures to preserve and enhance the linguistic, cultural and religious heritage of children belonging to *indigenous populations* or ethnic, linguistic or religious minorities.

2. In particular States Parties shall, where the best interests of the child render foster care or adoption necessary, avoid where possible the removal of the child from their own group or community.[48]

Joining in the ensuing discourse were the delegations from: the United Kingdom, the Netherlands, the United States, Austria, Venezuela, Brazil, Australia, the German Democratic Republic, Mexico, India, and Canada. The Canadian and several other delegations gave various opinions as to why it would be better to eliminate the second paragraph from this article and to incorporate these principles in the article that dealt with adoption. This led the Working Group to adopt the text originally proposed by Norway:

---

[46] *See* U.N. Doc. E/CN.4/1986/391 (1986) at paras. 65–67.

[47] *See* U.N. Doc. E/CN.4/1985/WG.1/NGO.1 (1985).

[48] U.N. Doc. E/CN.4/1987/25 (1987) (emphasis added).

In those States in which ethnic, religious or linguistic minorities or *indigenous populations* exist, a child belonging to such minorities or populations shall not be denied the right, in community with other members of its group, to enjoy its own culture, to profess and practice its own religion, or to use its own language.[49]

The second reading revisions of article 30 primarily involved linguistic changes that would be responsive to the concerns of indigenous people. Although a small drafting party made up of Brazil, France, Italy, Norway, Senegal, and Yugoslavia considered a number of new proposals, they were unable to arrive at a consensus. The end result was that the text was maintained more or less as it had been adopted at the first reading. Changes were confined to matters of gender neutrality and the elimination of the word ''populations'' to refer to indigenous peoples. The final text of article 30 resolved both of these problems:

In those States in which ethnic, religious or linguistic minorities or persons of *indigenous origin* exist, a child belonging to such a minority or *who is indigenous* shall not be denied the right, in community with other members of his or her group, to enjoy his or her own culture, to profess and practice his or her own religion, or to use his or her own language.[50]

D. Articles Applicable to All Children

Based on the nondiscrimination requirements of article 2, all of the articles of the Convention on the Rights of the Child apply to indigenous children. Therefore, using the Committee's *Guidelines* as a model, the following is a brief survey of the internationally recognized rights of the indigenous child. To enable the reader to understand just how comprehensive these rights are, the articles in sections IV–VIII will be listed, followed by a designation for the rights protected and a brief commentary. The three articles protecting indigenous children will also be listed in their appropriate section, but will not be covered by the commentary, since they were discussed in detail above.

1. Section IV: Civil Rights and Freedoms

Article 7 (name and nationality), article 8 (preservation of identity), article 13 (freedom of expression), article 14 (freedom of religion), article 15 (freedom of association and peaceful assembly), article 16 (protection of privacy), article 17 (access to appropriate information), and article 37(a) (protection from torture, and deprivation of liberty).

The article 7 right of the child to a name and nationality has long been recognized in international law. It can be found in the Declaration of the Rights

---

[49] U.N. Doc. E/CN.4/1989/48 (1989) (emphasis added).

[50] U.N. Doc. ECN.4/1989/48 (1989) (emphasis added).

of the Child, as well as in both the first and second Polish model Conventions. In addition, this right is supported by article 24 of the International Covenant on Civil and Political Rights.[51] Article 8, on the other hand, is an entirely new international concept. This article, ensuring preservation of the child's identity, was proposed by the Argentine government as a method of preventing the "disappearances" of children that had taken place in a prior political regime.[52] Articles 13 (freedom of expression), 14 (freedom of religion), 15 (freedom of association), and 16 (right to privacy) were all submitted by the United States.[53] These articles make the rights, such as those in the International Covenant on Civil and Political Rights and the American "Bill of Rights," applicable to children. The article 37(a) protection against torture and deprivation of liberty were based on a proposal by the government of Canada and strongly supported by Amnesty International and other NGOs.[54]

2. Section V: Family Environment and Alternative Care

Article 5 (parental guidance), article 9 (separation from parents), article 10 (family reunification), article 11 (illicit transfer and non-return), article 18(1) (2) (parental responsibilities), article 19 (abuse and neglect, including article 39—rehabilitative care), article 20 (child without a family), article 21 (adoption), article 25 (periodic review of placement), article 27(4) (recovery of maintenance).

Article 5, recognizing the child's right to parental guidance—tempered by acceptance of the child's evolving capacities—is based on proposals submitted by the United States and Australia. It was not adopted until the end of the second reading.[55] The article 9 protection against separation from parents was part of the second Polish model Convention. It was adopted in 1983, relatively early in the drafting process.[56] Article 11 (illicit transfer and non-return), which is based on the Hague Convention on the Civil Aspects of International Child Abduction, was submitted by the Untied States delegation in 1981; it was not adopted until 1983.[57] Article 18, on parental responsibilities, was one of the original articles in the second Polish model Convention. It was put before the Working Group

---

[51] *See* International Covenant on Civil and Political Rights, *adopted* Dec. 16, 1966, 999 U.N.T.S. 171 (*entered into force* Mar. 23, 1976) at art. 24.

[52] *See* Detrick, *supra* note 10, art. 8, 291 96.

[53] *See* Detrick, *supra* note 10, arts. 13, 14, 15, 16, at 229–37; 238–48; 249–55; 255–62.

[54] *See* Detrick, *supra* note 10, art. 37, at 458–78.

[55] *See* Detrick, *supra* note 10, art. 5, 157–61.

[56] *See* Detrick, *supra* note 10, art. 9, at 162 82.

[57] *See* Detrick, *supra* note 10, art. 11, at 208–23.

in 1981 and was adopted at that same session.[58] On the other hand, article 19 (protection from abuse and neglect) was first proposed by the United States in 1982. The proposal was amended, but not discussed, in 1983, and was addressed and adopted during the Working Group deliberations of 1984.[59] Articles 20 (child without a family) and 21(adoption) proved to be quite controversial, owing to the fact that adoption is not a recognized practice in Islamic countries. Only by careful wording, and the addition to article 20 of the *"Kefala* of Islamic law'' as a form of alternative care, was it possible to find an acceptable text by the end of the second reading.[60] Article 25 (periodic review of placement) has its roots in an early United States proposal that was never discussed. A year later a similar article was proposed by Canada. The article was adopted in 1986, after lengthy debate.[61] Article 27 (standard of living) is another of those articles that was part of the second Polish model Convention. It was discussed by the Working Group in 1983, but was not adopted until 1985.[62] Finally, article 39 on rehabilitative care was officially tabled by the Norwegian government in 1988. However, the text was based on an NGO Group proposal from the previous year. After a modest amount of debate, it was adopted at the end of the first reading.[63]

3. Section VI: Basic Health and Welfare

Article 6(2) (survival and development), article 18 (parental responsibilities), article 23 (disabled children), article 24 (health and health services), article 26 (social security), and article 27 (standard of living).

The child's right to survival and development (article 6) was first raised by the Indian delegation at the last session of the first reading. Although strongly supported by UNICEF, it nevertheless raised an intense debate as those who supported a right to life, and those who preferred not to include anything that might disturb the delicately drafted definition of the child as ''any human being,'' opposed the article on the grounds that it might imply that the Convention should apply to the unborn child. It was ultimately adopted with the addition of a first paragraph stating that ''every child has the inherent right to life,'' implying that this does not necessarily include the right ''to be born.''[64] Article 18, defining parental responsibilities for the child's upbringing, was part of the original Polish model Convention and was adopted in 1981 with a modest amount of debate.[65]

---

[58] *See* Detrick, *supra* note 10, art. 18, at 263–71.

[59] *See* Detrick, *supra* note 10, art. 19, at 271 78.

[60] *See* Detrick, *supra* note 10, arts. 20, 21, at 296–318.

[61] *See* Detrick, *supra* note 10, art. 25, at 360–63.

[62] *See* Detrick, *supra* note 10, art. 27, at 371 81.

[63] *See* Detrick, *supra* note 10, art. 39, at 454–58.

[64] *See* Detrick, *supra* note 10, art. 6, 120–23.

[65] *See supra* note 58 and accompanying text.

The article 23 protections of the disabled child were also part of the Polish model, but were much more controversial. It was first discussed in 1982 and again in 1983, before drafting of the text, which was spearheaded by Canadian proposals, was finally adopted.[66] The article on health and health services (article 24) was another of the Polish model Convention articles that was introduced in one year (1983), was not discussed by the Working Group, and languished for two years with additional proposals being tabled before it was finally debated in 1985. Although a basic text had already been adopted, an additional proposal was introduced in 1986. The article was then reopened for discussion in 1987 and again in 1988, when the first reading text was adopted.[67] Articles 26 (social security) and 27 (standard of living) were also part of the Polish model Convention, but were adopted with considerably less debate than article 24. They, too, were strongly influenced by Canadian proposals. Article 26 was adopted with minimal debate in 1984, the first year that it was before the Working Group.[68] The basic text of article 27 was also adopted in its first year of discussion (1985), but it was reopened in 1987 to consider a submission from Bangladesh that had been drafted by the NGO Group. This resulted in the addition of a fourth paragraph relating to parental responsibility for child support when living separately from the child.[69]

4. Section VII: Education, Leisure, and Cultural Activities

Article 28 (education), article 29 (aims of education), and article 31 (leisure, recreation, and cultural activities).

The three articles in this section are somewhat interlinked. All three were proposed by Poland in its second model Convention. All three were adopted by the Working Group in 1985. However, unlike article 31, which sparked little debate, both articles 28 and 29 were the source of much controversy during the second reading. To a large extent, these difficult negotiations were the result of pressures arising from the fact that the second reading would be the last time that governments would have an opportunity to introduce new concepts or ideas into the Convention's text and because these three articles were the most likely places that some of their concerns might be addressed.[70]

5. Section VIII: Special Protection Measures—Children in Situations of Emergency, in Conflict with the Law, and in Situations of Exploitation

Article 22 (refugee child), article 30 (minority or indigenous child), article 32 (economic exploitation), article 33 (drug abuse), article 34

---

[66] See Detrick, *supra* note 10, art. 23, at 329–43.

[67] See Detrick, *supra* note 10, art. 24, at 343–59.

[68] See Detrick, *supra* note 10, art. 26, at 360–63.

[69] See Detrick, *supra* note 10, art. 27, at 371 81.

[70] See Detrick, *supra* note 10, arts. 28–29, at 383–408.

(sexual exploitation and abuse), article 35 (sale, trafficking, and abduction), article 36 (other forms of exploitation), article 37 (capital punishment and deprivation of liberty), article 38 (armed conflicts, including article 39—rehabilitative care), and article 40 (juvenile justice).

The article protecting the rights of the refugee child (article 22) was first tabled in 1981 as an additional paragraph for the article on adoption. However, after a fair amount of discussion in 1982, the text was adopted as a separate article.[71] Article 32, prohibiting child labor, was another of the articles that was included in the second Polish model Convention. Canada submitted revised texts in 1983 and 1984, and the Polish delegation revised its proposal in 1985. The article was finally addressed by the Working Group in 1986, and the first reading text was adopted at that session.[72]

Protection from drugs had been mentioned as a sub-paragraph in the Polish second model Convention. However, in 1985, a new proposal was put forward by the Chinese delegation. Oddly, its two paragraphs addressed totally different concerns. Paragraph 1 dealt with drug use, while paragraph 2 protected the interests of children born out of wedlock. However, in 1986, two proposals, one from the Chinese delegation omitting its second paragraph and one from the NGO Group ended the stalemate and led to a speedy consensus. Article 33 was adopted at that session.[73] Articles 34 (sexual exploitation), 35 (sale, trafficking, and abduction), and 36 (other forms of exploitation) were simultaneously before the Working Group in 1987.

Article 34 was a joint proposal by France and the Netherlands, which were joined by Venezuela when they simultaneously tabled a text for article 36. Article 35 was a submission from the NGO Group. The debates were lengthy, as it was necessary to agree upon details as to what constituted sexual exploitation, and whether it was necessary to have an article on ''other forms of exploitation.''[74] Article 38 (armed conflicts) and article 40 (juvenile justice) were among the most hotly debated articles in the second reading. Both required the establishment of small drafting parties, which labored for more than a week before reaching agreement on a compromise text. In the case of article 30, the drafting party was unable to decide whether the minimum age for participation in armed combat should be 18 or 15. The ultimate choice was age 15, because the United States delegation refused to support the higher age limit.[75] The juvenile justice article was contentious for reasons that were technical as much as political. For example, in the first reading draft, torture and deprivation of liberty were linked

---

[71] *See* Detrick, *supra* note 10, art. 22, at 319–29.

[72] *See* Detrick, *supra* note 10, art. 37, at 438–58.

[73] *See* Detrick, *supra* note 10, art. 33, at 426–29.

[74] *See* Detrick, *supra* note 10, art. 34, 429–54.

[75] *See* Detrick, *supra* note 10, art. 38, at 502 17.

solely with juvenile justice, which ignored the fact that children are often the objects of politically based actions. This was resolved by separating the juvenile justice protections from the prohibition of torture through the creation of a new article (article 37). The basic approach to juvenile justice did provoke a difference of opinion that was somewhat philosophical in nature. This had to do with whether article 40 should follow the model of the ''Beijing Rules'' on the Prevention of Juvenile Delinquency which minimized punishment and took a more preventative approach, or a ''due process'' model. The compromise text, which speaks of the child's ''dignity and worth,'' also provides such due process guarantees as: a prohibition on ex post facto laws; the presumption of innocence; the right to a speedy trial and an interpreter; protection from self-incrimination; and the right to appeal.[76]

It should be noted that articles 30, 37, and 39, which are included in section VIII of the *Guidelines*, were omitted from the overview of this section because they were examined above, in connection with other sections.

III. OTHER INTERNATIONAL LEGAL INSTRUMENTS IMPACTING ON THE RIGHTS OF INDIGENOUS CHILDREN

As mentioned above, there are three other international legal instruments—one treaty and two draft declarations—that aim to protect the rights of indigenous peoples, and therefore have an impact on the rights of the indigenous child. All three of these instruments have a group focus and, as a result, have given no special attention to the indigenous child. This seems odd, considering that, in many tribal societies, children are believed to be the repository of the tribe's future.

A. International Labor Organization Convention No. 169 Concerning Indigenous and Tribal Peoples in Independent Countries[77]

The International Labor Organizaation Convention No. 169 Concerning Indigenous and Tribal Peoples in Independent Coauntries[78] (ILO Convention) is made up of eight sections containing thirty-two substantive articles and an implementation mechanism. The rights of indigenous children are touched on in only two articles of the ILO Convention: articles 28 and 29. These are found within section VI, Education and Means of Communication. Note that both

---

[76] *See* Detrick, *supra* note 10, art. 37, at 458–79.

[77] For a detailed account of the drafting and application of ILO Convention (No. 169), *see* Chapter 2, Lee Swepston, *The ILO Indigenous and Tribal Peoples Convention (No. 169): Eight Years After Adoption* in this volume.

[78] *See* ILO Convention, *supra* note 2.

articles speak of the indigenous child as a possession or property. Article 28(1) states:

> . . . children *belonging to the peoples concerned* shall, wherever practicable, be taught to read and write in their own indigenous language or in the language most commonly used by the group to which they belong.[79]

The remainder of article 28 elaborates on the measures that the State must take in order to achieve this goal. Article 29 has a somewhat contradictory rule that requires States Parties to undertake a dual task because:

> . . . the imparting of general knowledge and skills that will help *children belonging to the peoples* concerned to participate fully and on equal footing in their own community and in the national community shall be the aim of the education of these peoples.[80]

In other words, as exhibited in the language of these two articles, the aim of the ILO Convention is to protect indigenous peoples' traditional ways, while also assuring their children's future access to modern life. However, describing children as "belonging to the peoples concerned" raises the question of whether, under these circumstances, children would be given a voice in the decisions that affect them—a requirement of the Convention on the Rights of the Child.[81]

Considering the ILO's long history of treaties to end various types of child labor, one might have expected more references to children in the ILO Convention. This historical background makes the absence of a minimum age for employment of indigenous children a striking omission. Such standards could have been incorporated into the sections dealing with Recruitment and Conditions of Employment[82] and with Vocational Training, Handicrafts and Rural Industries.[83]

B. U.N. Draft Declaration on the Rights of Indigenous Peoples[84]

Children are similarly overlooked by the United Nations draft Declaration on the Rights of Indigenous Peoples.[85] They are mentioned in only four of the

---

[79] *Id.* at art. 28 para.1 (emphasis added).

[80] *Id.* at art. 29 (emphasis added).

[81] *See supra* note 4 at art. 12.

[82] *See* ILO Convention, *supra* note 2, at section III.

[83] *Id.* at section IV.

[84] For more detailed information regarding the status of the U.N. Draft Declaration *see* Chapter 1, Julian Burger, *Indigenous Peoples and the United Nations* in this volume.

[85] *See* draft U.N. Declaration, *supra* note 1.

draft Declaration's forty-five articles: articles 6 (right to life); 11 (protection from armed combat); 15 (education); and 22 (special measures).

The purpose of article 6 is to protect the indigenous person's right to life and liberty and to eliminate genocide. One of its two paragraphs refers to children and gives indigenous people the

> ... collective right to live in freedom, peace and security as distinct peoples and to full guarantees against genocide or any other act of violence, including the removal of indigenous *children* from their families and communities under any pretext.[86]

Article 11 addresses the rights of indigenous people in times of armed conflict and is aimed at protecting civilians and prohibiting recruitment of indigenous peoples into the armed forces. It is paragraph (b) that applies to children. It unequivocally affirms that "States Parties shall not:"

> (b)   Recruit indigenous *children* into the armed forces under any circumstances;[87]

Article 15 sets out the right to education. It gives indigenous peoples the right "to establish and control their own educational systems and institutions ..." and also guarantees to children two different but interlocking rights:

> Indigenous *children* have the right to all levels and all forms of education of the State ... and Indigenous *children* living outside their own communities have the right to be provided access to education in their own culture and language.[88]

> Note the similarity between article 15 and the children's rights articles in ILO Convention (No. 169). Again, this illustrates the difficulties indigenous communities face in maintaining their cultural traditions, while also trying to function in a modern society.

Article 22 recognizes the right of indigenous peoples to "special measures for the ... continuing improvement of their economic and social conditions." Areas specified include "sanitation, health and social security," among others. In regard to these requirements the article notes that:

---

[86] *Id.* at arts. 6, 107 (Emphasis added). This article appears to have been drafted in response to situations similar to those in the United States and Canada, in which Indian children were taken from their families and sent away to distant boarding schools, or adopted by non-Indian families.

[87] *Id.* at art. 11, at 108 (emphasis added).

[88] *Id.* at art. 15, at 109 (emphasis added).

Particular attention shall be paid to the rights and special needs of indigenous elders, women, youth, *children* and disabled persons.[89]

Genocide, armed combat, education, and special care are the only topics in the draft U.N. Declaration in which children are singled out as rights holders. Such important issues as child labor, juvenile justice, disabilities, survival and refugee/internal displacement—areas that would seem to be appropriate for specific indigenous rights standard-setting, and for which there are existing international norms—are, oddly, omitted.

C. Draft Inter-American Declaration on the Rights of Indigenous Peoples[90]

The draft Inter-American Declaration on the Rights of Indigenous Peoples[91] is made up of twenty-four articles. It has a preamble and six sections, two of which are devoted to definitions and general caveats. The other four sections cover: Human Rights (articles II–IV); Cultural Development (articles VII–XIII); Organizational and Political Rights (articles XIV–XVII); and Social Economic and Property Rights (articles XVIII–XX). The original draft was modified based on criticisms from various indigenous groups after the draft Declaration was distributed for review. Children were originally mentioned in only one article; there are now two articles that touch on the rights of the indigenous child: article VI (special guarantees against discrimination) and article XI (family relations and family ties).

Article VI contains two paragraphs that lay out the parameters of the non-discrimination standards which governments should ensure to indigenous peoples. Children are specifically mentioned in paragraph 1:

Indigenous peoples have the right to special guarantees against discrimination that may have to be instituted to fully enjoy internationally and nationally-recognized human rights; as well as measures necessary to enable indigenous women, men and *children* to exercise, without any discrimination, civil, political, economic, social, cultural and spiritual rights. The states recognize that violence exerted against persons because of their gender and *age* prevents and nullifies the exercise of those rights.[92]

Note also the reference to ''age.''

---

[89] *Id.* at art. 22, at 111 (emphasis added).

[90] For more detailed information about the Inter-American Declaration of Human Rights, *see* Chapter 3, Osvaldo Kreimer, *The Future Inter-American Declaration on the Rights of Indigenous Peoples: A Challenge for the Americas* in this volume.

[91] *See* Draft Inter-American Declaration, *supra* note 1.

[92] *Id.* at art. IV (emphasis added).

Article IV is particularly significant, because the most recent draft guarantees "internationally and nationally-recognized human rights" and includes children among the group that can exercise these rights. This was not true of earlier drafts, which mentioned only "men and women" and made no mention of "age." These changes were made as a result of the drafter's policy of actively seeking suggestions from indigenous and human rights groups. The words "children" and "age" are there largely because of correspondence between ChildRights International Research Institute and the Inter-American Commission on Human Rights. ChildRights pointed out that the rights of the child were not adequately recognized by the draft Declaration and made a number of recommendations. The Inter-American Commission's response to ChildRights' extensive suggestions for additions to the text was to incorporate the words "children" and "age" to the existing text of article VI, but to ignore the other suggestions.[93] While it is gratifying that the Inter-American Commission at least

---

[93] ChildRights International Research Institute recommended the following modifications and additions to the text of the Inter-American Draft Declaration on the Rights of Indigenous Peoples (amendments to existing text are in italics):

PREAMBLE

8. *Human rights instruments and other advances in international law.*

Paragraph 2:

[M]indful of the progress achieved by the States and indigenous organizations in codifying indigenous rights, especially in the sphere of the United Nations and the International Labor Organization, and in this regard recalling the *ILO Convention 169, the Convention on the Rights of the Child* and the Draft UN Declaration on the subject.

Article V. No forced assimilation

2. The States shall not take any action which forces indigenous peoples to assimilate and shall not endorse any theory or engage in any practice, that imports discrimination, destruction of a culture or the possibility of the extermination of an ethnic group, *including the removal of indigenous children from their homes for purposes of education or the adoption of indigenous children by non-indigenous families, without the indigenous community's prior approval.*

Article VI. Special guarantees against discrimination

2. The States shall also take the measures necessary to enable [*delete* both] indigenous women, men *and children* to exercise, without any discrimination, civil, political, economic, social and cultural rights. The States recognize that violence asserted against persons because of their gender *or age* prevents and nullifies the exercise of those rights.

Article XII. Health and well-being (additional paragraph)

6. States shall provide indigenous peoples with the information and technology to enable the application of modern techniques to assist the mentally or physically disabled child to lead a full and productive life and to diminish infant mortality. States shall encourage the elimination of traditional practices that are prejudicial to the health of the child.

made some of the recommended changes, it is unfortunate that the drafters did not go on to indicate how the word "children" is to be defined, and whether there are any limitations on indigenous children's exercise of these rights.

Article XI is also a two-paragraph article. Here, it is the second paragraph that is relevant. The first paragraph, after affirming that, "The family is the natural and basic unit of societies and must be respected and protected by the state," goes on to declare that "... the state shall recognize and respect the various forms of indigenous family, marriage, family name and filiation." It continues in paragraph 2:

> In determining the *child's* best interest in matters relating to the protection and adoption of *children* of members of indigenous peoples, and in matters of breaking of ties and other similar circumstances, consideration shall be given by courts and other relevant institutions to the views of the peoples, including individual, family and community views.[94]

This article is interesting for the reason that its approach to adoption would seem to be at odds with the standards of the U.N. draft Declaration. Note the difference between this paragraph, which makes provisions for "breaking of ties" and article 6 of the U.N. draft Declaration, which prohibits "the removal of indigenous children from their families and communities under any pretext."[95] This anomaly cannot be resolved by turning to the Convention on the Rights of the Child, because it has no article on the adoption of indigenous children. It does, however, have a general adoption article, which addresses some of the same ideas, including the requirement of consent. Article 21(a) of the Convention requires States Parties to:

> Ensure that the adoption of a child is authorized only by competent authorities who determine, in accordance with applicable law and procedures and on the basis of all pertinent and reliable information, that the adoption is permissible in view of the child's status concerning parents, relatives and legal guardians and that, if required, the persons

---

NEW ARTICLE. Rights of the indigenous child

The indigenous child shall be entitled to all of the rights of the child recognized under international law including the right: to freedom of expression, religion, association; to be heard in judicial and administrative proceedings; to health care, education, social security, a standard of living; and to juvenile justice procedural protections; as well as protection from discrimination and exploitation.

[94] *See* Draft Inter-American Declaration, *supra* note 1 at art. XI (emphasis added.)

[95] *See supra* note 86 and accompanying text.

concerned have given their informed consent to the adoption on the basis of such counselling as may be necessary. . . .[96]

IV. CONCLUSIONS

The fact that the rights of indigenous children were not part of some great original plan for the Convention on the Rights of the Child, and that they were actually included in a rather ad hoc manner, does not diminish their importance. These rights were debated by a diverse group of government delegations and were accepted by the Working Group as sound principles worthy of protection under international law. More important, they have now been legally recognized by 191 nations, which have implicitly agreed to implement the enumerated rights of indigenous children as part of their national law.

During the years that it has been examining States Parties' reports, the Committee on the Rights of the Child has reviewed the reports of more than 80 countries. Many of these were countries with large numbers of indigenous children. In its Concluding Observations, the Committee has systematically raised questions about the status of the indigenous child.[97] To date, the Committee's observations and recommendations have centered on issues relating to poverty, health, general education, and native language education. It has not yet touched on the child's individual rights. However, if the indigenous rights movement continues its current emphasis on the rights of the group—ignoring the individual rights of the child—and if indigenous peoples are granted sovereignty over their people in such matters as juvenile justice, child abuse, and child custody, it is possible that there could be a clash between a State's obligation to implement the Convention on the Rights of the Child and its obligation to recognize the rights of indigenous peoples.

The Convention has had an enormous impact on the world's attitude toward children. Not only has it made a change in the way that subsequent child-related treaties were drafted, it has also inspired changes in child policy at both the national and international levels. For example, when drafting was begun on the Hague Convention on the Protection of Children and Cooperation in Respect of Intercountry Adoption,[98] the first draft was essentially a treaty aimed at enabling governments to assist their nationals in obtaining children from other countries.

---

[96] *See* Convention, *supra* note 4 at art. 27.

[97] *See, e. g,. Concluding Observations* for: Paraguay, U.N. Doc. CRC/C/15/Add. 75 (1997); Colombia, U.N. Doc. CRC/C/15/Add.15 (1994), Bolivia, U.N. Doc. CRC/C/15/Add.1 (1993); Nicaragua, U.N. Doc. CRC/C/Add.36 (1995); and Guatemala, CRC/C/15/Add.58 (1996). Both the Committee's *Concluding Observations* and the States Parties' reports are available on the internet at: <www.unhchr.ch>.

[98] *See* Hague Conference on Private International Law: Final Act of the 17th Session, Including the Convention on Protection of Children and Co-operation in respect of Intercountry Adoption, *opened for signature* May 29, 1993, 31 I.L.M. 1134 (1993) [hereinafter *Convention on Intercountry Adoption*].

However, in a complete reversal, the final text of the Intercountry Adoption treaty is a child-centered instrument that emphasizes the importance of helping the child to find a family. Also reflecting the influence of the Convention on the Rights of the Child are: the treaty's "best interests" of the child standard;[99] its reference to children as "him and *her*,"[100] and its requirement that the child must have a chance to express his or her views with regard to the adoption.[101] A similar response to the Convention can be seen in the behavior of ratifying nations that are carefully revising their child-related policies and legislation and are setting up children's ombudsman offices.[102] Reaction to the impact of the Convention can also be found in the revised policies of such international bodies as the United Nations High Commissioner for Refugees and the United Nations Children's Fund, both of which have been inspired to make major changes in their programs and the way that they work with children.[103] Naturally, the International Labor Organization Convention (No. 169) Concerning Indigenous and Tribal Peoples in Independent Countries does not replicate the child rights Convention's standards because it was adopted the same year as the Convention and the Convention had not yet gone into force. However, because all other subsequent international human rights instruments that impinge on the rights of children have taken the Convention's standards into account, it is surprising that neither of the draft declarations has seen fit to recognize the importance of the Convention on the Rights of the Child.

Because of the Convention on the Rights of the Child, States can no longer allow children to be treated as objects or as "pre-human" beings. Each child has been guaranteed the right to respect as an individual under international law. It might be said that the resulting tensions between concepts of group rights and the individual are an echo of the tensions between tradition and modernity that

---

[99] *See supra* note 4 at art. 3.

[100] Prior to the Convention on the Rights of the Child, human rights treaties were always written with the singular possessive pronouns in the masculine gender. The Convention on the Rights of the Child changed this by using both the masculine and feminine pronouns: "him and her" or "his and her."

[101] *See supra* note 98 at art. 12, which protects the child's right to express his or her views.

[102] Sweden, in particular, established its Office of Ombudsman as an effort to fulfill its obligations under the Convention on the Rights of the Child. Although other national Children's Ombudsman Offices were established earlier (Austria, Norway, New Zealand, etc.), many of these were inspired by the drafting of the Convention.

[103] *See Note on Refugee Children*, U.N. HCR, UN Doc. EC/SCP/46 (1987). *See* also Refugee Children, U.N. HCR Executive Comm., 38th Sess., No. 47 (1987), *in* U.N. HCR EXECUTIVE COMM., CONCLUSIONS ON THE INTERNATIONAL PROTECTION OF REFUGEES 105 (1988); *Guidelines on Refugee Children*, UNHCR U.N. Doc. E/CN 4/28 (1988) and REFUGEE CHILDREN, GUIDELINES ON PROTECTION AND CARE. (1994). *See* Rebeca Rios-Kohn, *The Impact of the Convention on the Rights of the Child on UNICEFs Mission*, 6 TRANSNT'L L.& CONTEMP. PROB. 287 (1996).

can be seen in the ILO Convention and U.N. draft Declaration's education articles.

The traditional view of children as property is now totally out of date. As the world moves through the International Decade of the World's Indigenous People, one of the tasks facing indigenous peoples will be to decide how to deal with the tradition vs. modernity dilemma—how to keep the "old ways" while benefiting from modern technology. It is true that not all that is modern is good, and that modern society is beginning to appreciate traditional practices (i.e., the use of herbal remedies and respect for the environment), but indigenous children are being caught in the crossfire. It behooves those charged with responsibility for international indigenous rights norm-setting to be certain that the rights of the indigenous child are adequately protected.

CHAPTER 4

THE FUTURE INTER-AMERICAN DECLARATION ON THE RIGHTS OF INDIGENOUS PEOPLES: A CHALLENGE FOR THE AMERICAS

Osvaldo Kreimer*

I. THE ORGANIZATION OF AMERICAN STATES AND THE INTER-AMERICAN COMMISSION ON HUMAN RIGHTS (IACHR): BACKGROUND IN PROMOTING AND PROTECTING THE HUMAN RIGHTS OF INDIGENOUS PEOPLES

As early as 1933, the VIIth American International Conference, held in Montevideo, Uruguay, called for organizing a hemispheric congress to study the problems of indigenous populations.[1] The first of these "Indianist congresses" was held in Patzcuaro, Michoacán, México, in 1940,[2] and led to the creation

---

*Note: The views expressed in this article are those of the author and not necessarily those of the Organization of American States.

[1] This resolution by the American governments coincided with a general concern about social issues by these Inter-American Conferences, as shown by other resolutions on social guarantees (IX Conference, Res. XXIX, 1948), workers' and unions' development and free expression (VIII Conference, Res. VIII, 1938), and against racism and religious persecution (VIII Conference, Res. XXXVII, 1938). (Carnegie Endowment for International Peace "Conferencias Internacionales Americanas" Primer Suplemento 1938–1942. Washington, 1943, and "Segundo Suplemento" Departamento Juridico, Union Panamericana, Washington, 1956).

[2] All American countries, except for Haiti and Paraguay, assented to the congress, which issued 72 agreements, including several on land distribution; soil degradation; irrigation works; alphabets for indigenous languages; linguistics; Indian crafts protection; creation of schools and free school food services; medical services; indigenous education; social and political situation of the Indians in the Americas; and established the 19th of April as an "Indian Day" to be celebrated in the Americas (Union Panamericana "Serie sobre Congresos y Conferencias," No. 30 Acta Final del Primer Congreso Indigenista Interamericano, Washington, 1940).

of the Inter-American Indian Institute in 1942. In 1948, the IXth American International Conference created the Organization of American States in its present structure. The conference also proclaimed the Inter-American Declaration on the Rights and Duties of Man, as well as the Inter-American Charter on Social Guarantees. The Social Guarantees Charter, in its article 39, approached the subject of indigenous rights with an attitude that, albeit protectionist, was progressive for a time that was dominated by the goals of integration of indigenous culture into the dominant national culture. Its last paragraph on indigenous land is still relevant.[3]

More recently, the Inter-American Commission on Human Rights (IACHR) has analyzed human rights situations of indigenous populations in several of its country reports on Colombia,[4] Guatemala,[5] Chile,[6] Bolivia,[7] Surinam,[8] Brazil;[9]

---

[3] Article 39 of the Inter-American Charter of Social Guarantees (IX Conference, Res. XXIX, 1948), awkwardly included within the Section on "Rural Labour," reads:

> In countries where the problem of an indigenous population exists, the necessary measures shall be adopted to give protection and assistance to the Indians, safeguarding their life, liberty and property, preventing their extermination, shielding them from oppression and exploitation, protecting them from want and furnishing them an adequate education.

> The state shall exercise its guardianship in order to preserve, maintain, and develop the patrimony of the Indians or their tribes, and it shall foster the exploitation of the natural, industrial or extractive resources or any other sources of income proceeding from or related to the aforesaid patrimony, in order to ensure in due time the economic emancipation of the indigenous groups.

> Institutions or agencies shall be created for the protection of Indians, particularly in order to ensure respect for their lands, to legalize their possession thereof, and to prevent encroachment upon such lands by outsiders.

[4] Inter-American Commission on Human Rights—Organization of American States, Report on the Situation of Human Rights in Colombia, OEA/Ser.L/V/II.84, doc. 39, rev. 1 (1993).

[5] Inter-American Commission on Human Rights—Organization of American States, Report on the Situation of Human Rights in Guatemala, OEA/Ser.L/V/II.83, doc. 16, rev. 1 (1993).

[6] Inter-American Commission on Human Rights—Organization of American States, Report on the Situation of Human Rights in Chile, OEA/Ser.L/V/II.66, doc. 17 (1985).

[7] Inter-American Commission on Human Rights—Organization of American States, Report on the Situation of Human Rights in Bolivia, OEA/Ser.L./V/II.53, doc. 6, rev. 2 (1981).

[8] Inter-American Commission on Human Rights—Organization of American States, Report on the Situation of Human Rights in Suriname, OAS/Ser.L./V/II.61, doc. 6 rev. 1 (1983); and "Second Report," OAS/Ser.L./V/II.66, doc. 21, rev. (1985)

[9] Inter-American Commission on Human Rights—Organization of American States, Report on the Situation of Human Rights in Brazil (released Nov. 1997).

in the special reports on the Miskito Indians in Nicaragua (1987);[10] and in the report about the "Communities of Peoples in Resistance" in Guatemala (1994).[11]

In the area of litigation, the IACHR also has addressed specific issues of indigenous communities in cases such as *Aloeboetoe et al. v. Suriname*,[12] which was taken to the Inter-American Court on Human Rights, headquartered in San Jose de Costa Rica. The Inter-American Court in its decisions on that case accepted the IACHR argument and endorsed the importance of ethnic differences, and explicitly took into account indigenous "customary law" in its family law decisions.

With certain regularity, the IACHR receives and processes individual cases presented about alleged violations against indigenous peoples, both as individuals and as communities. The cases are administered and analyzed mainly under the provisions of the American Convention on Human Rights or, for countries like the United States and Canada that have not ratified the Convention, under the American Declaration on the Rights and Duties of Man. However, at present there is no Inter-American legal instrument for application and expansion of those rights in relation to the special situations and issues pertinent to the indigenous peoples.[13]

II. THE PROCESS OF PREPARATION TO DATE

In 1989, the IACHR presented a proposal to the OAS General Assembly on the need to develop an Inter-American instrument on the rights of indigenous

---

[10] Inter-American Commission on Human Rights—Organization of American States, Report on the Situation of Human Rights of a Segment of the Nicaraguan Population of Miskito Origin, OEA/Ser.L/V/II.62, doc. 10, rev. 3 (1983).

[11] Inter-American Commission on Human Rights—Organization of American States, Report on the Situation of Human Rights of the "Communities of Population in Resistance" in Guatemala, OEA/Ser.L/V/II.86, doc. 5, rev. 1 (1994).

[12] Additionally, the Commission adressed specific issues of indigenous communities in the cases of *Gangaram Panday* and *Aloeboetoe*. INTER-AMERICAN COMMISSION ON HUMAN RIGHTS, ANNUAL REPORT OF THE COMMISSION 1992–93, OEA/Ser.L./V/II.83, doc. 14, corr. 1, Mar. 12, 1993 at 23 [hereinafter 1992–93 ANNUAL REPORT]. In the *Gangaram Panday* case, Mr. Panday was illegally detained by Suriname and he died while in the government's custody. Dinah Shelton, *The Jurisprudence of the Inter-American Court of Human Rights*, 10 AM. U. J. INT'L L. & POL'Y 333, 352 (1994). The *Aloeboetoe* case involved Surinamese soldiers who had attacked a group of twenty males of the Sarama tribe of maroons, seven of whom died. *Id.* at 364 n.185. Both of these cases were brought before the Inter-American Court on Human Rights, which is headquartered in San Jose, Costa Rica. INTER-AMERICAN COURT OF HUMAN RIGHTS, ANNUAL REPORT OF THE COURT (1995) OAS/Ser.L./V/III.33, doc. 4, Jan. 22, 1996, at 1. The court found violations of the American Convention on Human Rights in these cases and awarded compensation to the victims.

[13] While other international instruments about human rights can be applied by the IACHR by virtue of, among others, article 29(d) of the American Convention on Human

peoples,[14] and the General Assembly issued a resolution recommending that IACHR prepare an "Inter-American legal instrument on the rights of indigenous populations."[15] Then, in 1990, the IACHR held a consultative meeting of Indian leaders from North, Central, and South America and other experts at the Inter-American Indian Institute in Mexico City. The objective of the consultation was to obtain guidance on the establishment of priorities, as well as on demands and approaches and methodologies to be employed for preparation.

In 1991, the IACHR approved a participatory methodology for the preparation of the instrument and began a first round of consultations about issues and approaches to be taken into account in the future document. The consultation was based on a lengthy questionnaire about individual rights (mostly reflecting those contained in the American Convention on Human Rights) and about collective rights. The responses from twenty-one indigenous organizations, eleven governments, and two intergovernmental organizations were published in summarized form in 1993.[16]

In 1994, the Executive Secretariat of the Commission prepared a "Draft for Discussion" to be taken up by the IACHR at its meetings in April and September 1995.[17] The responses to the first round of consultation provided

---

Rights, its application is always indirect. An inter-American instrument—like this Declaration—will give a more forceful mandate for the Commission and the Court, besides addressing problems and approaches more peculiar and pertinent to the OAS member states.

[14] INTER-AMERICAN COMMISSION ON HUMAN RIGHTS, IACHR ANNUAL REPORT 1988–89, OEA/Ser.L/V/II.76, doc. 10 (1989).

[15] AG/RES 1022 (XIX–0/89) at O.A.S. General Assembly Proceedings, 19th Regular Session, Vol.1 OEA/Ser.P/XIX.0.2, Washington, 1989.

[16] See OAS INTER-AMERICAN COMMISSION ON HUMAN RIGHTS, IACHR ANNUAL REPORT 1992–93, at 281, 330, Doc. OEA/Ser.L/V/II.83, doc. 14 (1993). Answers were received from the governments of Canada, Chile, Colombia, Costa Rica, Guatemala, Mexico, Panama, Peru, Saint Lucia, the United States, and Venezuela, and from the following intergovernmental organizations: A.E.K. Consultorio Jurídico Pueblos Indígenas de Panamá, Colonizadores del Trópico Boliviano, the Andean Commission of Jurists (Peru), the Consejo Regional Indígena del Cauca (Colombia), the Comisión Interamericana de Juristas Indígenas (Steering Office in Argentina), the Centro de Estudios Aymaras Quechuas (Bolivia), Fundación Comunidades Colombianas, the Assembly of First Nations (Canada), the Council of Crees (Canada), the Indigenous Bar Association of Canada, the World Council of Indigenous Peoples (International), the Center for Indigenous Culture (Brazil), the MARKA Center (Peru), the Comisión Jurídica de los Pueblos de Integración Tawantinsuyana (Peru), the Fundación del Aborigen Argentino (Argentina), the CINAMI A.C. Central Nacional de Ayuda a las Misiones Indígenas (Mexico), SER A.C. Servicios del Puelo Mixe (Mexico), the Vicaría de Solidaridad de la Prelatura de Ayaviri (Peru), Inuit Tapirisat of Canada, and the Indian Law Resource Center (U.S.).

[17] OAS Inter-Am. Comm. on Hum. Rts., *Inter-American Declaration on the Rights of Indigenous Peoples, Draft for Discussion*, at OAS IACHR ANNUAL REPORT (1995) OEA /Ser.L/V/II.91, Feb. 1996 217–230.

the main guidelines for the document.[18] Other sources included the U.N. draft Declaration[19] and ILO Convention No. 169,[20] as well as national constitutional and legislative texts, decisions by the IACHR and other OAS bodies, and suggestions by experts.[21]

On September 18, 1995, during its 90th Regular Meeting, the IACHR approved a ''Draft of the Inter-American Declaration on the Rights of Indigenous Peoples,''[22] to be used for final broad consultation with governments, indigenous organizations, and experts.

From October 1995 to December 1996, the Commission embarked on a broad round of consultations concerning the text of that draft. A number of different mechanisms were used for the purpose of this consultation: a) direct consultation by correspondence to about three hundred indigenous organizations and experts, as well as to governments; b) presentation and discussion of the draft at specialized technical meetings; c) consultation of indigenous organizations at a national and multinational level; and d) regional meetings.

The draft was presented and examined at various technical meetings: in Arequipa, Peru, at the ''First World Meeting of Indigenous Peoples,'' which was organized by the World Council of Indigenous Peoples in October of 1995; on February 27, 1996, in Ottawa at ''Widening the Circle,'' a meeting organized by FOCAL, the University of Ottawa and the World Council of Indigenous Peoples, and attended by more than 100 delegates from the entire hemisphere; in Guatemala City, at a special meeting organized by the Inter-American Institute of Human Rights in March of 1996; at the General Kuna Congress in Ogubscun, Panama, in 1996; and at the 1996 Sovereignty Symposium, held in Tulsa, Oklahoma.

For the national and regional consultations, the IACHR acted as coordinator, with assistance from the Inter-American Indian Institute; the Unit for the Promotion of Democracy; the Inter-American Institute of Human Rights; and the Inter-American Fund for the Development of Indigenous Peoples (headquartered in Bolivia); and with cooperation from the Inter-American Development Bank.

---

[18] Report on the 1st Round of Consultations on the Inter-American Legal Instrument on the Rights of Indigenous Populations. *See* ANNUAL REPORT OF THE INTER-AMERICAN COMMISSION ON HUMAN RIGHTS (1993) OEA/Ser.L/V/II.83, Doc. 14, Mar. 1993.

[19] *See* United Nations Draft Declaration on the Rights of Indigenous Peoples, U.N. Doc. E/CN.4/Sub.2/1994/2/Add.1 (April 20, 1994).

[20] *See* Lee Swepston, *International Labour Organization and Convention 169* in INDIGENOUS PEOPLES AND INTERNATIONAL ORGANIZATIONS (M.T. van de Fliert, ed., 1994).

[21] For a review of national constitutional law in the Americas, *see* Raidza Torres, *The Rights of Indigenous Populations: The Emerging International Norm,* 16 YALE J. INT'L. L. 127–75.

[22] *See* OAS Draft Inter-American Declaration on the Rights of Indigenous Peoples, OAS Inter-Am. Comm. on Hum. Rts., 1278th Sess., Doc. OEA/Ser/L/V/II.90, doc. 9, rev. 1 (1995) [hereinafter *Draft Inter-American Declaration*].

National consultations and special meetings with indigenous organizations and leaders were held in Argentina, Bolivia, Brazil, Canada, Chile, Colombia, Costa Rica, Ecuador, El Salvador, Honduras, Mexico, Panama, Paraguay, Peru, and the United States. Both the Indian Council of Central America and the Coordinating Committee of Indigenous Peoples of the Amazon Basin held consultation meetings with their individual organization members. In an effort to go from the local to the subregional level, two major meetings were held: one in Guatemala City, for representatives of Central America and the Caribbean, and the second in Quito, Ecuador, for the South American national Indian leaders.

The IACHR received many detailed and specific comments from these meetings, as well as from governments,[23] experts[24] and organizations.[25] While most of the comments from indigenous organizations and their fifteen national meetings were very specific technical suggestions about the texts, in the regional meetings many participants requested more time for additional consultations. The IACHR considered that while new consultations could be useful in the next steps, it had sufficiently elaborated indications and input from indigenous peoples in order to revise the draft, and that additional consultations could be more productive at the national level.

The revised draft was prepared by a technical meeting of experts[26] and Commissioners, held in Washington in January 1997, and was presented to the plenary of the IACHR for consideration at its 96th Meeting in February 1997. The IACHR approved the text as its Proposal[27] and sent it to the General Assembly for consideration in June 1997. The IACHR also proposed that the General

---

[23] Comments were received from the governments of Argentina, Brazil, Canada, the United States, Honduras, El Salvador, Mexico, and Venezuela. The government of Bolivia endorsed the observations of the national consultation.

[24] Responses and comments were also received from the International Labor Organization (ILO) and from the United Nations Mission in Guatemala (Minugua); also from the Indian Law Resource Center (U.S.), the Inter-American Dialogue, ChildRights International Research Institute, the International Indian Treaty Council (U.S.), and Hutchins, Soroka Dionne (Ottawa, Canada).

[25] From experts: August Willemsen Diaz, (Guatemala), Aureliano Turpo Choquehuanca (World Council on Indigenous Peoples), Professor Fernand de Varennes (Murdoch University, Australia), Prof. Joe Palacio (UWI, Belize), and Hugo Mondragon (Colombia).

[26] The participants at the meeting included IACHR rapporteur members Dr. Carlos Ayala Corao and Ambassador John Donaldson, and experts Dr. Magdalena Gomez Rivera (Director of Legal Prosecution at the National Indigenous Institute of Mexico), Dr. Patrick Robinson (a former member of the Commission and initial rapporteur on the topic); Wilton Littlechild, Q.C. (Indian lawyer and member of the Canadian Parliament), and IACHR principal specialist lawyer, Dr. Osvaldo Kreimer.

[27] See 1996 Annual Report of the Inter-American Commission on Human Rights, OEA/Ser. L/V/II.95, doc. 7, rev. Mar. 1997. It can be seen at Internet: www.oas.org.

Assembly, when it considers the Declaration, request the member countries to take appropiate measures to approve the Declaration at its annual session in 1998, in commemoration of the 50th Anniversary of the Organization of American States and of the American Declaration on the Rights and Duties of Man.

The General Assembly issued a resolution instructing the Permanent Council of the OAS to study the proposal, and expressed the view that the text "of the Proposed Declaration should reflect the concerns of indigenous populations as well as the work of the United Nations in this area."[28] In successive steps, it outlined the methodology to follow: first, it asked the governments to transmit their observations by December 31, 1997, to the Permanent Council. Then, with those comments as well as those from the Inter-American Indian Institute and the Inter-American Juridical Committee, the Permanent Council "shall convene a meeting of government experts in this field. . . ." with a view to possible adoption of the "Proposed American Declaration on the Rights of Indigenous Peoples" by the General Assembly of the OAS in 1998.[29]

III. SEVEN MAIN PRINCIPLES BEHIND THE PROPOSED AMERICAN DECLARATION ON THE RIGHTS OF INDIGENOUS PEOPLES

A careful reading of the Proposed American Declaration on the Rights of Indigenous Peoples prepared by the IACHR reveals seven basic assumptions that are at its foundation and synthesize its philosophy:

1) The explicit acknowledgment by the OAS's Inter-American community of States about the importance of their indigenous peoples, their *cultures, dignity, and contributions* to national and universal cultures.

2) The *pluricultural* nature of these societies: That is, that indigenous peoples are not viewed as diverse or different from the general population, but rather that each State is internally diverse, and shall be united by a common framework for all segments of society.

3) The *integrity* of States: Recognition by the State of indigenous peoples' ethical integrity, without duplicities or discrimination; and at the same time ensuring that each State shall be a unity, integrating its different segments in an internal dynamics that enriches that unity.

4) The *inherent nature* of indigenous rights: Indigenous peoples, because of their preexistence to contemporary States, and because of

---

[28] AG Res. doc. 3573/97 on June 5, 1997.

[29] OAS General Assembly, 27th Regular Session, June 1, 1997. *See* OEA/Ser./P/AG/ Doc. 3573/97.

their cultural and historical continuity, have a special situation, an inherent condition that is juridically a source of rights.

5) The right of indigenous peoples to *self-government* and internal autonomy: This principle articulates acknowledgment of their culture, because self-government is an application and implementation of those cultures, traditions, and systems of authority.

6) The preeminence and *primacy of human rights:* The Declaration explicitly states collective rights as necessary conditions for the full enjoyment of individual human rights.

7) The need for compensatory and special measures: To repair historical discrimination and dispossession, without trying to deny history, but accepting the real situations and sufferings of indigenous peoples today, and trying to create conditions for the realization of their full potential.

A. Overriding Principles

References to these seven principles are found throughout the Declaration's Preamble and 26 articles. For example, the Preamble states that "they have a *special role* to play," and further recalls "that some of the democratic institutions and concepts embodied in the constitutions of American States originate from institutions of indigenous peoples" (preamble, paragraphs 1 and 2) (emphasis added).

Preambular paragraph 3 refers to the respect and special relation of indigenous peoples with the environment and the ecology. Preambular paragraph 5 discusses their specific forms of control and ownership of land, territories, and resources. The whole third section, on cultural developments, emphasizes the importance of indigenous peoples' historic and archaeological heritage, languages, outlook and philosophy, family organization, tradition of medicine and health practice. Section four acknowledges the value of their traditional ways of association, meeting, and expression. In one of the most progressive articles of the Declaration (article XVI), indigenous law is presented as part of the State's legal system. Section five recognizes indigenous forms of ownership and dominion, as well as their intellectual property rights in relation to scientific, genetic, and technological developments, and original designs. Article XXI affirms their right and capacity to decide on the values, goals, and strategies that will govern and steer their development.

The principle of *pluriculturality* is explicitly stated at the beginning of the preamble, and in the rejection of forced assimilation (article V). Section three, on cultural development, recognizes such *pluralism* when it acknowledges and requires respect for the different expressions of indigenous cultures, ownership rights, and the particular communal ways of these ownerships, even if different from those protected by ordinary law.

Article IX declares that the States shall include in their general educational system "content reflecting the *pluricultural* nature of their societies (emphasis added)," and article XVII includes provisions to facilitate the inclusion in the States' organizational structures of the institutions and traditional practices of indigenous peoples.

B. Specific Rights

Integrity of the States is of special importance, and the Declaration is very clear in this respect, with numerous references to the states and their institutions. For example, the Preamble begins by reminding States "that the indigenous peoples are a segment of their population," then affirms that "they [the indigenous peoples] have a *special role* to play in strengthening the institutions of the State and in establishing national unity based on democratic principles (emphasis added)."

Article I borrows the following statement from International Labor Organization Convention No. 169: "the use of the term peoples in this instrument shall not be construed as having any implication with respect to any other rights that might be attached to that term in international law."

Article IV, while stating that indigenous peoples have the right to have their legal personality fully recognized, qualifies it by saying that it shall be within the State's legal system.

Article IX, on indigenous educational systems, states that they shall be complementary to national educational systems and shall guarantee equal education and teaching opportunities for the entire population, either indigenous or nonindigenous.

In article XVI, indigenous law is recognized as part of the State's legal system. In reference to the ownership of minerals and resources of the subsoil, and for those cases in which they belong to the State (article XVIII), special compensation is foreseen for indigenous peoples who inhabit those territories.

In article XXI, "Right to Development," the Declaration states that indigenous peoples are part of the national State, as are other segments of society.

Article XXV indicates that "nothing in this instrument shall be construed as granting any rights to ignore boundaries between states."

And Article XXVI concludes by stating that "nothing in this Declaration may be construed as permitting any activity contrary to the purposes and principles of the OAS, including sovereign equality, territorial integrity, and political independence of the state."

The inherent nature of certain rights of indigenous peoples is at the origin of many of the provisions of the Declaration in section four, in particular, "self government and internal autonomy," as well as those in section five, in reference to ownership rights and particular styles of developments.

As to self-government and internal authority, the Declaration underlines both that the indigenous institutions and their systems are building blocks of the States, and that their functioning shall be exercised within the framework of the national States.

The Declaration affirms a strong right of indigenous peoples to master their own affairs, a right that they may or may not implement in regard to education, health, cultural issues, internal judicial system, plans and projects that deal with the environment, and habitat (section three). Section four speaks specifically to self-government and indigenous laws; article XXI covers the right of indigenous peoples to decision-making and implementing their own development.

Preeminence of human rights is clearly established in paragraph 7 of the preamble and in article II. Both in relation to reparation and compensation for past dispossessions, as well as to the establishment of special guarantees to ensure the present and future enjoyment of human rights by indigenous peoples, the Declaration includes the important provision that indigenous peoples shall intervene in the determination of those guarantees. These special measures appear in article VI, on discrimination; in article VII, about restitution of cultural property; in article XII, about the elimination of health conditions that fall below standards; and in article XVIII, regarding restitution of land, territories, and resources.

Finally, the proposed Declaration demands special guarantees to prevent and punish intruders and unauthorized use of indigenous peoples' properties (article XVIII).

IV. FUTURE STEPS

The draft Inter-American Declaration on the Rights of Indigenous Peoples, as approved by the IACHR, is a strong document proposing advances in international law in this area, but well-grounded in existing domestic constitutional law in the Americas and in the work of the U.N., ILO, and indigenous conferences.

The OAS political bodies are now in charge of making it a juridical reality. The meeting of governmental experts to be held in 1998 may introduce changes before its final approval by the General Assembly. Some indigenous organizations, while supporting the proposed Declaration, have expressed concern about attempts to weaken it.[30] Undoubtedly, the final outcome will much depend upon the interest and actions of the indigenous organizations and the political systems in each OAS member country.

---

[30] *See,* for instance, the editorial from The Indian Law Resource Center newsletter "Indian Rights Human Rights" Spring 1997, Vol 4. No. 1. Similarly, a pronouncement by 24 Mexican Indigenous Organizations, issued in Mexico D.F. on May 28, 1997 (In file with the Inter-American Commission on Human Rights. OAS)

CHAPTER 5

THE LEGACY OF DESKAHEH: INDIGENOUS PEOPLES AS INTERNATIONAL ACTORS

Douglas Sanders

The success of colonialism in Africa, Asia, and the Americas meant that indigenous peoples became subjects, regulated by colonial authorities or new States. In the Americas, traditional rights only survived in hinterland areas or in the pockets of reserve lands. Treaties were broken with impunity. Indigenous peoples were denied any international legal personality or access to international tribunals.

Some indigenous leaders actively resisted this imposition of "domestic law" status. Protests took place within imperial structures, with Indian leaders from British Columbia traveling to London in 1906 and 1909 to seek redress. Other protests were at the international level. Indigenous leaders tried to petition the League of Nations after its formation in 1919. The doors were not open. No minority rights provisions had been written into the Covenant of the League of Nations, apparently because Australia and New Zealand wanted to avoid any international scrutiny of their treatment of Aboriginals and Maori.[1]

In 1923 and 1924, the Iroquois patriot Deskaheh was in Geneva, representing the traditional Confederacy government of Six Nations in Ontario.[2] Deskaheh claimed that Canada was planning to invade the lands of the Six Nations. He sought recognition of the Confederacy as a State in international law. The governments of the United Kingdom and Canada went to some lengths to prevent debate on the question. The Netherlands tried to get Deskaheh's petition on the agenda of the League's Council. Ireland, Panama, Persia and Estonia attempted to bring it before the League's Assembly and sought an advisory opinion from the Permanent Court of International Justice. The Canadian government's reply to the Iroquois petition was published in the Official Journal of the League. While Deskaheh was still in Europe, the Canadian government dissolved the traditional council at Six Nations, imposing an elected system under the rules

---

[1] WARWICK A. MCKEAN, EQUALITY AND DISCRIMINATION UNDER INTERNATIONAL LAW 14–15 (1983). The League was a potential forum, and a support organization existed in Geneva, the Bureau International pour la Defense des Indigenes.

[2] *See* RICHARD VEATCH, CANADA AND THE LEAGUE OF NATIONS, Chapter 7, *The Appeal of the Six Nations* 1975.

found in the federal Indian Act. No Indian consent to this change was obtained. The new system was rejected by Confederacy supporters, who formed a majority of band members. Six Nations had been invaded and an illegitimate government installed by the settler state of Canada.[3]

Ratana, the Maori leader, visited Geneva in 1924 to petition the League of Nations and visited Japan on his return trip to New Zealand to see an example of a colored race running its own country. In 1945, Iroquois representatives went to San Francisco for the conference that established the United Nations. Their petition to the new world body was reprinted in an Ontario High Court judgment dealing with the question of whether Six Nations was subject to the Canadian Indian Act.[4]

There were no provisions on minority rights or decolonization in the United Nations Charter or the Universal Declaration of Human Rights. While Indians annually petitioned the United Nations after its formation, the petitions were never publicly acknowledged.[5] Three British Columbia Indians took a petition to the United Nations in New York in 1953. John Humphrey, the Canadian who headed the Human Rights Division, advised them to go to Ottawa.

The International Labor Organization has been involved with labor issues concerning indigenous peoples since the 1920s. In the 1950s, the ILO coordinated the Andean Indian Program. This work led to the drafting of a convention on indigenous and tribal populations in 1957. While the roots of the concern were in Latin America, the convention was signed by States in Africa and Asia as well. It was not signed by Canada, the United States, Australia, or New Zealand. The convention had dual themes of protection and assimilation, and was rejected by indigenous political leaders. In 1989, the ILO completed a revision of the convention to bring it more into line with current attitudes.[6]

I. FINDING A PLACE IN MODERN INTERNATIONAL LAW

Indigenous issues could have been considered at the United Nations under one or more of the following headings: a) racial discrimination, b) decolonization

---

[3] When Canada accepted the jurisdiction of the World Court in 1931, it made a reservation concerning domestic issues. Prime Minister Bennett, speaking in the House of Commons, stated that the reservation would prevent any discussion of Indian treaties or the treatment of Indians, obviously reflecting Canada's embarrassment over Deskaheh's work at the League: 1931, Vol. II, Debates, House of Commons, 1628 (May 15, 1931).

[4] The Six Nations petition to the founding meeting of the United Nations is reprinted in the judgment of the Ontario High Court in Logan v. Styres, (1959) 20 Dominion Law Reports (2d) 416 at 422 24. The court ruled that the Indian Act did apply to Six Nations.

[5] The special collection of the papers of John Humphrey in the library of the Faculty of Law, McGill University, Montreal, contains unpublished listings of communications received by the United Nations.

[6] *See* Lee Swepston, *A New Step in International Law on Indigenous and Tribal Peoples: ILO Convention No. 169 of 1989,* 15 OKLA. CITY U. L. Rev. 677–714 (1990).

or self-determination, c) the rights of cultural minorities, or d) individual human rights. Other themes, such as labor, economic development, the activities of transnational corporations, the environment, health, or the status of treaties with indigenous peoples, could also have been invoked, though they were limited bases for international concern. The most logical themes were minority rights or decolonization/self-determination. But both areas were politically sensitive and both were restrictively handled at the United Nations.

A strategic decision was taken in the mid-1960s by Augusto Willemsen Diaz, a lawyer from Guatemala on the staff of the United Nations Centre for Human Rights in Geneva, to route a concern with indigenous peoples through the work underway on racial discrimination. As a result of his work, a 1970 interim report of a study on racial discrimination recommended a separate study on indigenous populations. While Willemsen Diaz saw "discrimination" as an incomplete description of the issues involved, it was possible for indigenous peoples to get on the agenda of the United Nations through this door.[7] A study on discrimination against indigenous populations was authorized by the Economic and Social Council in 1971. Indigenous issues finally moved outside the context of racial discrimination with the establishment of the Working Group on Indigenous Populations in 1982. A U.N. seminar in January 1989 still reflected the earlier approach: "The United Nations Seminar on the Effects of Racism and Racial Discrimination on the Social and Economic Relations between Indigenous Peoples and States."[8]

The study authorized by the Economic and Social Council in 1971, on discrimination against indigenous populations, was the responsibility of José R. Martinez Cobo, a diplomat from Ecuador and a member of the Sub-Commission on Prevention of Discrimination and Protection of Minorities. Inadequate staffing and funding at the United Nations Centre for Human Rights meant that the work fell almost exclusively to Augusto Willemsen Diaz. He was constantly called on to do other work as well. Mr. Martinez Cobo took a couple of trips as part of the work, but wrote nothing. The study was completed by Willemsen Diaz in 1983.[9]

In this period a new international concern with indigenous peoples was developing. The pioneer support organizations, the International Work Group

---

Also see Chapter 2, Lee Swepston, *The ILO Indigenous and Tribal Peoples Convention 1989 (No. 169): Eight Years After Adoption,* in this volume.

[7] Personal discussions with Augusto Willemsen Diaz.

[8] Douglas Sanders, *Another Step: The UN Seminar on Relations between Indigenous Peoples and States,* 4 CAN. NATIVE L. REP. 37–47 (1989).

[9] E/CN.4/Sub.2/1986/7 and Add. 1–4. The Working Group on Indigenous Populations was established before the completion of the report. As a result, the report did not play a significant role in the establishment of a forum on indigenous issues at the United Nations. The report is long and not easily available.

for Indigenous Affairs (IWGIA), based in Copenhagen, and Survival International, based in London, were both formed at the end of the 1960s around concerns with ethnocide and genocide in South America. The Programme to Combat Racism of the World Council of Churches sponsored a symposium on South America in 1971. The meeting produced a groundbreaking decolonizing statement by a group of prominent South American anthropologists; the Declaration of Barbados.[10]

The first modern international indigenous organizations, the World Council of Indigenous Peoples (WCIP) and the International Indian Treaty Council (IITC), were both formed in 1975.[11] The World Council held conferences in Sweden in 1977 and Australia in 1981, both times with financial support from the host country. The conference in Australia discussed a draft treaty on indigenous rights. The International Indian Treaty Council began an active lobbying presence at the United Nations. It was the primary indigenous organization involved in the two conferences on indigenous peoples which were held under NGO auspices in United Nations facilities in Geneva in 1977 and 1981.[12] The 1977 conference produced a Declaration of Principles for the Defence of the Indigenous Nations and Peoples of the Western Hemisphere.

Significantly, Norway included a Sami leader in its delegation to the United Nations World Conference on Racism, held in Geneva in 1978. The final conference statement devoted a section to indigenous rights. A 1981 United Nations regional seminar in Nicaragua, held as part of the Decade to Combat Racism and Racial Discrimination, included a specific concern with indigenous peoples, and the Fourth Russell Tribunal, held in Rotterdam in 1980, heard a series of cases of the denial of rights of Indian peoples in the Americas.[13] Finally, the Federation of Saskatchewan Indians organized the World Assembly of First Nations in Regina in 1982, drawing indigenous representatives from most parts of the Americas.

Certain States promoted the concern with indigenous peoples at the United Nations. Through links between Helge Kleivan of the International Work Group

---

[10] Symposium on Inter-Ethnic Conflict in South America, Barbados, January 1971, co-sponsored by the Programme to Combat Racism and the Churches' Commission on International Affairs of the World Council of Churches, together with the Ethnology Department, University of Berne. *See* Declaration of Barbados, INTERNATIONAL WORK GROUP FOR INDIGENOUS AFFAIRS, DOCUMENT #1, Copenhagen, 1971; W. DOSTAL, THE SITUATION OF THE INDIAN IN SOUTH AMERICA, World Council of Churches, 1972.

[11] *See* Douglas Sanders, *The Re-Emergence of Indigenous Questions in International Law,* CAN. HUM. RTS. Y.B., 3–30 (1983); Douglas Sanders, *The Formation of the World Council of Indigenous Peoples,* INTERNATIONAL WORK GROUP FOR INDIGENOUS AFFAIRS, DOCUMENT No. 29, Copenhagen (1977).

[12] *Basic Call to Consciousness, Akwesasne Notes,* New York (1978), (no author named), deals with the 1977 Conference.

[13] Ismaelillo, Robin Wright, *Native Peoples in Struggle* in CASES FROM THE FOURTH RUSSELL TRIBUNAL AND OTHER INTERNATIONAL FORUMS (1982).

for Indigenous Affairs and Thorvald Stoltenberg, then foreign minister of Norway, Norway began identifying indigenous peoples in its foreign aid policies, including annual grants to both IWGIA and WCIP. Norway urged the other Nordic States to support indigenous issues internationally. The Netherlands became a strong supporter, and the Dutch Parliament passed a resolution on indigenous rights after the 1980 Russell Tribunal hearings in Rotterdam.

With leadership from Theo Van Boven, the Dutch head of the United Nations Centre for Human Rights, and support from certain northern European States, the decision was taken by the United Nations in 1982 to establish a Working Group on Indigenous Populations as a pre-sessional Working Group of the Sub-Commission on Prevention of Discrimination and Protection of Minorities.[14] As a Working Group of the Sub-Commission, it would draw its five members from the Sub-Commission. As a pre-sessional group, it would meet immediately before the annual four-week August meetings of the Sub-Commission. The Working Group has a mandate to review developments of concern to indigenous peoples and to draft international law standards on indigenous peoples. In 1993, the Working Group completed a draft Declaration on the Rights of Indigenous Peoples. It continues to meet every summer, and has been involved with specific studies on treaties and on cultural heritage. In 1995, the United Nations Commission on Human Rights, a superior body to the Sub-Commission, began its consideration of the draft Declaration, a process being handled by a working group of the Commission.[15]

II. INDIGENOUS PARTICIPATION

In 1982, at the first session of the Sub-Commission's Working Group, it was decided that any indigenous person or representative of an indigenous group could participate in the annual sessions. In almost all other United Nations fora, participation is limited to States, intergovernmental organizations, accredited nongovernmental organizations, or special observers such as the Holy See or recognized liberation movements. The Working Group on Indigenous Populations is the most open body in the entire system of the United Nations and the specialized agencies.[16]

---

[14] The creation of the Working Group was proposed by the Sub-Commission on Prevention of Discrimination and Protection of Minorities in its resolution 2 (XXXIV) of September 8, 1981, endorsed by the Commission on Human Rights in its resolution 1982/19 of March 10, 1982, and authorized by the Economic and Social Council in its resolution 1982/34 of May 7, 1982. The initiative did not come at the level of the Economic and Social Council, but that is the body that formally established the Working Group in 1982.

[15] *See* Russel Barsh, *Indigenous Peoples and the UN Commission on Human Rights,* 18 HUM. RTS. Q. 782 (1996).

[16] Since the innovation in the Working Group, two other bodies have adopted a similar approach: the Working Group on Contemporary Forms of Slavery and the new Commission on Sustainable Development, which grew out of the Earth Summit in Rio

Another innovation facilitating indigenous participation was the creation of the United Nations Voluntary Fund for Indigenous Populations, which each year funds a number of indigenous representatives to attend the Working Group sessions. Three nonindigenous support organizations also have a "human rights fund" for indigenous participation. These two funding sources have been important, in particular, in increasing indigenous or tribal representation from Asia and Africa.

A third innovation that facilitated indigenous participation was a relaxed approach to the rules of the Economic and Social Council (ECOSOC) for the formal accreditation of indigenous organizations as "nongovernmental organizations" (NGOS) in "consultative status" with the Council. Formal NGO status allows organizations to attend and speak in many of the human rights bodies of the United Nations. Most of the thirteen indigenous organizations that have gained NGO status did not meet ECOSOC criteria for accreditation at the time they were considered. An organization like the Grand Council of the Cree (Quebec), while it has played a constructive role in the Working Group sessions, did not meet normal criteria because it is not an international organization. In contrast, groups like the Inuit Circumpolar Conference, the Sami Council, and the World Council of Indigenous Peoples are organizations that obviously met the criteria. The general criteria for accreditation have now been changed for all nongovernmental organizations, permitting the accreditation of appropriate national or local organizations.

There is almost no secondary literature describing any of the indigenous organizations with NGO status. As of 1995, there were thirteen such organizations:

(1) *World Council of Indigenous Peoples* (WCIP). This organization was a project of the National Indian Brotherhood of Canada (now the Assembly of First Nations). It was the most international of all indigenous organizations. In recent years, its activity has largely been confined to Central America and parts of South America. It is not now particularly active at the Working Group.

(2) *International Indian Treaty Council* (IITC). The Treaty Council was established by the U.S. American Indian movement around the goal of international law recognition for treaties between Indian tribes and states. Representatives of IITC did the basic early lobbying at the United Nations in the 1970s, as documented in the film "Indian Summer in Geneva."[17] The organization has ceased to be very active.

---

de Janeiro which itself, like other recent U.N. conferences, allowed otherwise unaccredited NGOs to participate in its work.

[17] The film was produced by Volkmar Ziegler in 1985 and is available from Broadcast Studio, 28 Montbrillant, 1201, Geneva, Switzerland. It has footage from the first or second session of the Working Group and an interesting interview with the major IITC individual who lobbied at the United Nations in the 1970s.

(3) *Indian Law Resource Centre* (ILRC). ILRC is a public interest law firm acting for traditional indigenous governments in the United States, with involvement, as well, in indigenous issues in Nicaragua. Its director, Tim Coulter, played a major role in the early years of the Working Group. It remains active, but in a limited way.

(4) *Four Directions Council.* This group originally represented four indigenous peoples, but now is a voice for the Mikmaq. Russel Barsh, a nonindigenous lawyer and academic, represented the Council for many years and was the single most active person at the United Nations on indigenous issues. He no longer represents the Council.

(5) *National Indian Youth Council.* This is a United States organization which got accredited fairly early, but is no longer active.

(6) *National Aboriginal and Islander Legal Services Secretariat.* This Australian organization was the personal vehicle of Paul Coe, a long-time Aboriginal activist. He regularly attended the Working Group after it was established in 1982, but was not present in 1994 or 1995.

(7) *Inuit Circumpolar Conference* (ICC). ICC represents Inuit in the United States, Canada, Greenland/Denmark, and Russia. ICC is normally active in the Working Group. It was very active at the Vienna U.N. World Conference on Human Rights in June 1993.

(8) *The Indian Council of South America* (CISA). CISA began as a regional body within the structure of the World Council of Indigenous Peoples.

(9) *Saami Council.* The Council represents Saami in Norway, Sweden, Finland, and the Russian Federation. It remains a regional member of the World Council of Indigenous Peoples. It applied for separate NGO status after it became frustrated by the decline in activity of the World Council.

(10) *Grand Council of the Crees (Quebec).* This organization is regularly represented at the Working Group by Ambassador Ted Moses, former Grand Chief of the Cree, and Robert Epstein, a long-time non-indigenous adviser. The Grand Council was also active at the U.N. World Conference on Human Rights in Vienna in June 1993.

(11) *Indigenous World Association.* This organization was originally the personal vehicle of Professor Roxanne Dunbar Ortiz, a controversial figure who had been very active in the International Indian

Treaty Council. After being ousted from the Treaty Council a few times, Ms. Ortiz formed her own organization. She was an important figure in early lobbying at the United Nations, both before and after the formation of the Working Group. The organization frequently accredits nonmembers, as it did in 1995.

(12) *International Organization of Indigenous Resource Development* (IOIRD). This organization was formed jointly by the Council of Energy Resource Tribes in the United States, and the Hobbema Four Nations in Alberta, Canada, who have substantial energy revenues. In 1992, IOIRD made detailed presentations on specific wording for the draft Declaration, based on discussions at a special tribal gathering in the United States.

(13) *Aboriginal and Torres Strait Islander Commission.* This organization is established by the government of Australia. Its members are elected by aboriginal people in elections conducted by Australia. It is essentially a government advisory body, with some program management capacity. It has been very active at the United Nations, but it does not fit into a traditional understanding of the category "nongovernmental organization," though as an advisory body, it has some independence in practice.

This brief overview of the accredited indigenous NGOs gives no sense of the patterns of indigenous involvement in the Working Group. Far more indigenous people speak for nonaccredited groupings than on behalf of the thirteen accredited indigenous NGOs. With some exceptions, the thirteen do not play a role in coordinating indigenous participation. The Aboriginal and Torres Strait Islander Commission of Australia plays that kind of role for Australian Aboriginals. Regional organizations like CISA, Asia Indigenous Peoples Pact, and Pacific/Asia Council of Indigenous Peoples play no apparent role in coordinating or organizing indigenous participation for their regions. National, tribal, or local organizations—as opposed to regional or international bodies—predominate. The open rules of the Working Group have meant that there is no pressure on indigenous representatives to participate under the auspices of the existing accredited organizations or even of the nonaccredited regional organizations.

Indigenous delegates to the Working Group regularly caucus during its sessions. For a number of years, they held evening meetings, with translation services provided on a volunteer basis by United Nations translators. In recent years, when the Working Group has met on its own for a morning or afternoon, it has turned over the meeting room and the simultaneous translation services to the indigenous representatives. These caucus sessions have produced common positions on both the text of the draft Declaration and on the drafting process. In 1992, a common position that demanded the recognition of an unqualified right of self-determination in the draft Declaration was adopted. In 1993, the delegates adopted a common position asking that the draft not be completed that year.

In 1995, the United Nations Human Rights Commission established a new open-ended intersessional working group to consider the draft declaration (after the completion of drafting work at the level of the Sub-Commission on Prevention of Discrimination and Protection of Minorities). The Commission established a new process for accrediting "organizations of indigenous people" (not already in consultative status) for participation in the sessions of the Commission's working group. Accreditation involves the Coordinator of the International Decade of the World's Indigenous People and the NGO Committee of the Economic and Social Council. The working group of the Commission, according to Resolution 1995/32, has the "sole purpose" of considering the draft Declaration. It will not assume the other work of the Working Group of the Sub-Commission.

When the International Labor Organization undertook the revision of Convention (No. 107) on Indigenous and Tribal Peoples, it opened the process to some indigenous participation. The ILO encouraged its regular delegations (representing states, employer organizations, and employee organizations) to include indigenous individuals. It also permitted representatives of Survival International and the World Council of Indigenous Peoples to participate in the sessions.

III. DISCUSSIONS ON A "PERMANENT FORUM"

The idea of formalizing a role for indigenous peoples within the United Nations system developed in the decade of the 1990s, but there is not yet any agreement on an appropriate body.

The idea of a "permanent forum" originated in the United Nations seminar on self-government held in Greenland in 1991. The 1992 United Nations Conference on the Environment and Development called upon United Nations organs, programs, and specialized agencies to adopt mechanisms that would ensure the coherent and coordinated incorporation of the views of indigenous people in the design and implementation of all policies and programs. The 1993 United Nations World Conference on Human Rights recommended that the General Assembly establish a permanent forum for indigenous people within the United Nations system. General Assembly resolution 48/163 in 1993, proclaiming the International Decade of the World's Indigenous People, requested the Human Rights Commission to give "priority consideration" to the establishment of a permanent forum for indigenous people. The Commission asked the Working Group to consider the issue at its session in 1994. The Working Group discussed the issue, but came to no conclusion.[18] A workshop on the issue was held in Copenhagen, Denmark, in June 1995.

---

[18] The Working Group had a note by Madam Daes, E/CN.4/Sub.2/AC.4/1994/13, a note by the Secretary General E/Cn.4/Sub.2/AC.4/1994/11, and a paper by Denmark E/CN.4/Sub.2/AC.4/1994.CRP.3. Denmark's paper is reprinted in The Indigenous World

There were two expert background papers at the Copenhagen workshop. They were authored by Madam Daes, chair of the Working Group, and Professor Rodolfo Stavenhagen of Mexico.[19] Madam Daes proposed a body along the lines of the United Nations Development Fund for Women (UNIFEM). UNIFEM has a developmental focus and is located at United Nations Headquarters in New York. In addition, it has 10 subregional offices in Asia and the Pacific, Latin America, and Africa. In countries without an office, the fund works through the offices of the United Nations Development Program. Madam Daes suggested the new body should promote international cooperation activities and coordinate all United Nations activities that directly affect indigenous people. It would report to the Economic and Social Council. She felt the body should convene workshops and discussions with the staff of specialized agencies, United Nations operational bodies, and indigenous peoples at all levels. She suggested a body with ten members, five representing governments and five representing indigenous peoples. The governmental members would be selected by the Economic and Social Council from the five U.N. regions. The indigenous representatives would be appointed by the Secretary-General from a list of nominations made every four years by organizations of indigenous peoples; the five indigenous representatives would not have to be from the five U.N. regions. Participation in meetings would be open, as it has been in the Working Group, though a special system of accreditation might be established. She felt the existing Working Group at the sub-Commission level could continue as "an advisory body on matters that deal with the rights of indigenous people." The permanent forum would be able to "concentrate its efforts more on other, lesser known matters, knowing that it has a reliable advisory body when it comes to indigenous rights."

Professor Rodolfo Stavenhagen saw a parallel in the "Indigenous Fund," the Fund for the Development of the Indigenous Peoples of Latin America and the Caribbean established by the Ibero-American heads of State in 1992. The Fund has no money of its own, but has been given some resources by the Inter-American Development Bank, the World Bank, the European Union, and a number of other donors. The governing general meeting is composed of delegations from the eighteen States participating in the Fund. Each delegation is

---

1994–95, a yearbook published by the International Work Group for Indigenous Affairs in Copenhagen in 1995 at page 211. Other documentation has also been generated on the issue, including a report of the secretariat, a note by Madame Daes, a discussion paper by Denmark/Greenland, analysis by the Aboriginal and Torres Strait Islander Commission and written comments by Canada. The ATSIC analysis can be found in E/CN.4/Sub.2/AC.4/1994/11/Add.2. The Canadian statement can be found in E/CN.4/Sub.2/AC.4/1994/11/Add.1. The report of the secretariat notes some of the suggestions that have been made:

> . . . the proposal to establish a Commission on Indigenous Peoples within the United Nations, an advisory body, a permanent seat for indigenous people, an office for indigenous affairs, a High Commissioner for Indigenous Peoples, and a suggestion that observer status be granted to one or more indigenous organization at the General Assembly.

[19] Both are reprinted in E/CN.4/Sub.2/AC.4/1995/7/Add.2.

to be composed of one governmental and one indigenous representative. The indigenous representative is to be named by the government after consultations with indigenous organizations. The board of directors is composed of nine members elected by the general meeting and representing the governments of the States of the Latin American and Caribbean region, the indigenous peoples of those States, and the governments of the other member States outside the region.[20] Professor Stavenhagen commented:

> To my knowledge, the Indigenous Fund is the first intergovernmental institution in which indigenous peoples as such participate in the governing bodies. However, there is no doubt that States maintain control of the Fund, since under the Constituent Agreement, decisions are taken by unanimous affirmative vote of the delegates of member States of the region, together with a majority of affirmative votes of representatives of other member States (currently two) and a majority of affirmative votes of delegates of indigenous peoples. As is the case with meetings of the United Nations Working Group on Indigenous Populations, indigenous participation in the Fund's first General Meeting was free and unrestricted.

The Copenhagen workshop did not reach a conclusion on the structure for a permanent forum.[21] Some suggested entrusting the work to a reformed Trusteeship Council. Others proposed a new body reporting to the Economic and Social Council. Still others spoke of expanding the mandate of the existing Working Group at the Sub-Commission level. A second workshop on the permanent forum was hosted by Chile in July 1997.[22]

In the meantime, the Working Group on Indigenous Populations of the Sub-Commission is continuing to meet. The 1994 report of the Working Group commented:

> 153. The members of the Working Group believed that the Working Group would continue to serve important and necessary functions. Those included its present functions, in particular additional standard setting in fields in which members of the Working Group were engaged in technical studies, and ensuring continuity in the unique dialogue

---

[20] The board is currently composed of representatives from Bolivia, El Salvador, and Mexico, plus the representatives of the two states outside the region, Spain and Portugal, and indigenous representatives from Colombia, Honduras, and Paraguay. The elected indigenous members of the board of directors were nominated by the indigenous participants.

[21] *Report of the United Nations Workshop on a Permanent Forum for Indigenous People,* E/CN.4/Sub.2/AC.4/1995/7.

[22] For details on these working groups, *see* Chapter 1, Julian Burger, *Indigenous Peoples and the United Nations,* in this volume.

between indigenous peoples, Governments and the United Nations system which had evolved into a major and routine part of the Working Group's annual sessions. Both indigenous peoples and Governments had stated that they greatly valued the opportunity they had had since 1982 to meet annually at Geneva and to engage in a frank exchange of views, on a basis of equality, which had developed into a constructive dialogue.[23]

The Commission on Human Rights, in its annual resolution authorizing the Working Group to continue, sets out a description of its ongoing role. Resolution 40 of 1996:

(5) invites the Working Group to take into account in its deliberations on developments pertaining to the promotion and protection of the human rights of indigenous people the work, within the framework of their respective mandates, of all thematic special rapporteurs, special representatives, independent experts and working groups as it pertains to the situation of indigenous people;

(6) urges the Working Group to continue its comprehensive review of developments and of the situation and aspirations of the world's indigenous people . . . ;

(8) invites the Working Group to consider whether there are ways in which the contribution of expertise from indigenous people to the work of the Working Group might be enhanced.

Working Group member Miguel Alfonso Martinez reiterated his view in the 1996 session that the Working Group of the Sub-Commission is a permanent forum, and any new body should not deal with the issues dealt with by the Working Group.[24]

IV. THE DRAFT DECLARATION ON THE RIGHTS OF INDIGENOUS PEOPLES

The most controversial part of the draft Declaration on the Rights of Indigenous Peoples, as approved by the Working Group and the Sub-Commission in 1993, is the article stating that indigenous peoples have the right of self-determination. This article was a substantial victory for indigenous representatives, but will be the most difficult issue in consideration of the draft at the Commission level. There are other important parts to the draft Declaration.

---

[23] E/CN.4/Sub.2/1994/30, par. 153. The self-congratulatory style of the paragraph is common to U.N. statements.

[24] E/CN.4/Sub.2/1996/21, par. 120.

A. Individual and Collective Rights

There has always been concern about the balance between "individual rights" and "collective rights" in the draft; indigenous people argue strongly for an almost exclusive focus on "collective rights."

The first two preambular paragraphs begin the document with a positive invoking of collective differences:

Affirming that indigenous peoples are equal in dignity and rights to all other peoples, while recognizing the right of all peoples to be different, to consider themselves different, and to be respected as such;

Affirming also that all peoples contribute to the diversity and richness of civilizations and cultures, which constitute the common heritage of humankind.

These first two paragraphs affirm that general human rights apply equally to indigenous peoples and indigenous individuals. Articles 19 and 20 grant rights of full participation in the institutions of the state within which the indigenous people finds itself. This is, in effect, the anti-apartheid provision. Apartheid provided for "group rights," but denied the residents of the homelands equal rights with other South Africans outside the homelands.

The issue of collective and individual rights has been contentious over the last decade.[25] Perhaps now the idea of the coexistence of both categories of rights is accepted.

There is a concern with what limits may be placed on indigenous self-government to protect the human rights of individual members of the self-governing units. Paragraph 33 of the draft reads as follows:

Indigenous peoples have the right to promote, develop and maintain their institutional structures and their distinctive juridical customs, traditions, procedures and practises, in accordance with internationally recognized human rights standards.

At the specific suggestion of the Canadian government delegation in 1993, another article stating a human rights norm was introduced, one taken from the Constitution Act of 1983. Article 43 of the draft reads: "All the rights and freedoms recognized herein are equally guaranteed to male and female indigenous individuals; . . ." Articles 33 and 43 were not opposed by indigenous representatives.

---

[25] *See* Douglas Sanders, *Collective Rights,* 13 Hum. Rts. Q. 368 (1991).

B. Lands and Territories

The provisions on lands are very strong:

Article 25. Indigenous peoples have the right to maintain and strengthen their distinctive spiritual and material relationship with the lands, territories, waters and coastal seas and other resources which they have traditionally owned or otherwise occupied or used, and to uphold their responsibilities to future generations in this regard.

Article 26 gives indigenous peoples ownership and control over the lands and resources "they have traditionally owned or otherwise occupied or used. . . ." Article 27 provides for the restitution of lands taken without the free and informed consent of the indigenous peoples (while recognizing that compensation, preferably in the form of land, is a possible alternative to restitution). Development projects on indigenous lands require "free and informed consent" under article 30.

C. Cultural and Intellectual Property

Two articles deal with indigenous cultural and intellectual property. The first focuses primarily on material culture and the second on intellectual property, though content tends to overlap:

Article 12. Indigenous peoples have the right to practice and revitalize their cultural traditions and customs. This includes the right to maintain, protect and develop the past, present and future manifestations of their cultures, such as archaeological and historical sites, artefacts, designs, ceremonies, technologies and visual and performing arts and literature, as well as the right to the restitution of cultural, intellectual, religious and spiritual property taken without their free and informed consent or in violation of their laws, traditions and customs.

Article 29. Indigenous peoples are entitled to the recognition of the full ownership, control and protection of their cultural and intellectual property. They have the right to special measures to control, develop and protect their sciences, technologies and cultural manifestations, including human and other genetic resources, seeds, medicines, knowledge of the properties of fauna and flora, oral traditions, literatures, designs and visual and performing arts.

D. Powers of Self-Government

There was debate whether there should be a list of powers of indigenous self-government or a more general description of the purposes of self-government. The result was article 31:

Indigenous peoples, as a specific form of exercising their rights to self-determination, have the right to autonomy or self-government in matters relating to their internal and local affairs, including culture, religion, education, information, media, health, housing, employment, social welfare, economic activities, land and resources management, environment and entry by non-members, as well as ways and means for financing these autonomous functions.

This basic provision is supplemented by provisions on membership/citizenship in the indigenous collectivity (article 32), indigenous law (article 33), education (article 15), media (article 17), child welfare (article 6), health and housing (article 23).

E. Treaties

The draft has two references to treaties. The thirteenth preambular paragraph reads:

> ... treaties, agreements and other constructive arrangements between States and indigenous peoples are properly matters of international concern and responsibility.

The substantive provision is article 36:

> Indigenous peoples have the right to the recognition, observance and enforcement of treaties, agreements and other constructive arrangements concluded with States or their successors, according to their original spirit and intent, and to have States honour and respect such treaties, agreements and other constructive arrangements. Conflicts and disputes which cannot otherwise be settled should be submitted to competent international bodies agreed to by all parties concerned.

Perhaps by giving the right only to indigenous peoples, the article leaves open the possibility of indigenous peoples regarding particular treaties as unequal, imposed, or unfair.

F. The Concept of "Indigenous Peoples"

The draft Declaration has no definition of the term "indigenous." The International Labor Organization suggested that the draft Declaration should follow the ILO usage and refer to both "indigenous" and "tribal" peoples. This would have made it clear, for example, that the Declaration was to apply to groups in India and Bangladesh where domestic law uses the term "tribe" and the government rejects the idea that the tribes are "indigenous peoples."[26] The decision against adding "tribe" or "tribal," and the lack of a definition of

---

[26] India, Bangladesh, and Nigeria insisted at the 1996 session of the Working Group of the Sub-Commission that a definition was necessary: E/CN.4/Sub.2/1996/21, par. 34.

"indigenous," means that the question of the applicability of the Declaration to some peoples is left unresolved, for the moment. There is broad agreement on a large core group of peoples who are "indigenous": those in the Americas, Australia, and the Nordic states. The draft Declaration leaves the scope of the category open to an evolution in understanding and usage.

The working group of the Commission has been concerned with this issue, prompting continuing attention to "the concept" of indigenous peoples by the Working Group of the Sub-Commission. In their 1996 Report, the Working Group of the Sub-Commission noted:

> . . . that representatives of indigenous peoples and many governmental delegations expressed the view that it was neither desirable nor necessary to elaborate a universal definition of "indigenous peoples."[27]

Madam Daes expressed her view that it was neither possible nor useful to define "indigenous peoples" because of their diversity.[28] It is equally true that international human rights law does not define the terms "minority" or "peoples."

V. WHERE ARE WE?

Indigenous rights became an important part of the human rights work of the United Nations in the final quarter of the twentieth century. The rather staid meetings of the world body have been transformed by the presence of a colorful array of indigenous peoples from all regions of the world. Discussion on indigenous peoples occurs in the full range of U.N. human rights fora. As well, international financial institutions are concerned with the impact of their decisions on indigenous peoples.

Is the change substantial? The first recognition of indigenous peoples in United Nations human rights standard setting came in the references to indigenous children in the Convention on the Rights of the Child. There has been no real progress, as of this writing, on the draft Declaration on the Rights of Indigenous Peoples at the level of the Commission on Human Rights. But it was clear that the process would be slow at that level, as it had been at the level of the Sub-Commission. U.N. bodies have not been able to come to any conclusion on the proposal for a "permanent forum" for indigenous peoples, but the debate goes on. The International Year of the World's Indigenous People and the International Decade are symbolic gestures. They are underfunded (or unfunded), but in the same way that other symbolic designations are unfunded in this era of financial troubles at the United Nations. Nevertheless, the progress on indigenous rights at the United Nations is substantial, though we are still at an early stage in standard setting and participation.

---

[27] E/CN.4/Sub.2/1996/21, par. 153.

[28] *Id.* par. 19. Madam Daes' paper on the question is found in E/CN.4/Sub.2/AC.4/1996/2.

II. NATIONAL CONTEXT
A. Scandinavia and Asia

CHAPTER 6
A NEW ERA FOR THE SAAMI PEOPLE OF SWEDEN

Frank Orton* and Hugh Beach

I. INTRODUCTION

The Saami, or Lapps, are the native people of the area in northernmost Europe known as Lapland. Because of the national borders forced upon them, the Saami have been divided into four separate countries: Norway, Sweden, Finland, and Russia. There were social, economic, and linguistic differences within the general Saami population before the lands were divided into separate states, but these were, and largely still are, subordinated to the overall unity of Saami ethnic identity. Unlike many other ethnic minorities, the Saami maintain access to much of *their* land, despite ongoing debates concerning questions of their legal rights to the land.

Estimates vary, but common figures given for the population of the Saami are: 60,000 Saami, of whom 40,000 are in Norway, 15,000 in Sweden, 4,000 in Finland, and 1,500 to 2,000 in Russia.[1] There is a growing tendency for those Saami who earlier sought to avoid public admission of their ethnic roots for fear of stigmatization to take new pride in their ethnic membership.

The Saami call themselves "saemie," "sápmi," "saa'm" or similar dialectical variations. For many years, Saami spokesmen have campaigned to substitute "Saami" for "Lapp" (considered by many Saami to be a derogatory term). During the 1960s and 1970s, "Saami" (in Swedish and Norwegian, "Same") has come to replace "Lapp" in all official texts. Similar replacement has gained momentum internationally. For a small minority people, threatened with assimilation, the destruction of their resource base, and deterioration of their language, gaining authentication for their own name for themselves by others is a symbolically significant step toward international recognition of their cultural needs and rights to self-determination.

---

*Note: The views expressed in this article are those of the author and not necessarily those of the Swedish Ombudsman Against Ethnic Discrimination.

[1] Hugh Beach, *The Saami of Lapland*, in POLAR PEOPLES: SELF-DETERMINATION AND DEVELOPMENT (1994). *See also* SAMERNA: I HISTORIEN OCH NUTIDEN, (I. Ruong ed., 1982).

Despite a broad range of traditional subsistence lifestyles and adopted modern livelihoods, the Saami are best known to the world for their reindeer herding. Yet the reindeer-herding Saami are a small minority of the entire Saami population; in Sweden, for example, only about ten to fifteen percent of Saami practice this profession.[2] Characteristic of Saami, however, whether herders or nonherders, is that they regard the reindeer as a basic guardian of their culture, their language, and identity.

In practice, the policies of their encompassing Nation States have commonly shrunk Saami resource rights to privileges and conferred these exclusively upon the reindeer-herding Saami. Still, the Saami preoccupation with reindeer stretches far beyond the resource rights practiced by the herders alone. The herding livelihood is something all Saami will fight to protect to the fullest. It is regarded as the source of their culture and the flame that keeps their identity as Saami alive.

II. BACKGROUND

The history of the Saami can be discussed according to three phases or major forms of influence: 1) an early colonial tax period; 2) a policing period to regulate Saami-settler relations; and 3) a rationalization period with increasing focus on meat productivity and welfare norms at the expense of ethnic land rights and cultural elements. Of course, the characterizations of these periods are to some extent arbitrary, and aspects of one period can be found to persist in later periods. Nonetheless, we believe they will be helpful in organizing this historical sketch and will elucidate the essential facets of Saami relations with Nation States. This sketch cannot strive for completeness. It is designed rather as background for an appreciation of current affairs.

A. Early Colonization

When the growing Fennoscandian kingdoms first turned their attentions to Lapland, the national borders in the north were far from fixed. Reindeer-herding Saami migrated through different spheres of influence. Some Saami paid tax to three courts at the same time (including, in the 14th century, the Republic of Novgorod), even if they were registered under the protection of one authority. Should this authority prove too demanding, a nomad might well shift his allegiance to another. The kings who laid claim to regions in Lapland often followed a rather Saami-friendly course, for they could ill afford to estrange "their" Saami. Not only did the Saami supply valuable goods in the form of taxes, but their allegiance to a particular king helped him to register a claim on the territory used by them.[3]

---

[2] *See* Beach, *supra* note 1. *Also see* SOU 1975:99 and 100; *Samerna i Sverige*; and *Bilagor* (1975).

[3] *See* T. CRAMÉR, SAMERNAS VITA BOK-STOCKHOLM (1968–81). *Also see* F. HULTBLAD ÖVERGA'NG FRA'N NOMADISM TILL AGRAR BOSÄTTNING I JOKKMOKKS SOCKEN. NORDISKA, Museet ACTA LAPPONICA XIV, Lund. (1968).

The 1751 Codicil[4] exemplifies early far-sighted, pro-Saami legislation, which in practice, however, has since been watered down. The Norwegian-Swedish border in the northern districts was not specified until 1751, when a boundary agreement was made. Saami had migrated in traditional paths without hindrance between the Baltic Sea and the North Sea in these northern districts and were guaranteed the right to continue to do so in a codicil to the boundary agreement. Immemorial territories of the different Saami groups (such a group was previously called a *Lappby* in Swedish and later renamed a *sameby*) were crosscut by the national border, but, with the Codicil, Swedish Saami traditional grazing rights were respected in Norway, and the traditional grazing rights of Norwegian Saami were respected in Sweden. This 1751 Codicil has been termed the "Saami Magna Charta," as it grants the old *Lappby* a central position.[5] It has never been canceled, but its implementation has been regulated by bilateral commissions, the last and now operative one from 1972.[6] Swedish Saami access to Norwegian grazing is now tightly constrained. While some penetration across the border is allowed for some *sameby*s, the time of stay in Norway and the distance of penetration permitted are highly controlled. Renewed implementation of the agreement regulating this reindeer traffic must, however, be in place by 2002.

B. Conflicts with Settlers

In time, the administration of Saami dedicated to the levying of taxes was transformed, largely as a result of the spread of farming and of the inevitable conflicts between farmers and herders. The old system of administration had been devised basically to ensure the even distribution and efficiency of tax-producing operations. Later legislation, however, became increasingly devoted to the strict regulation and inspection of herding in order to smooth herder-settler relations.[7]

---

[4] The full text of this codicil appears in: T. CRAMÉR AND G. PRAWITZ, STUDIER I RENBETESLAGSTIFTNING, (1970)

[5] *See* T. CRAMÉR, *supra* note 3, and T. CRAMÉR AND G. PRAWITZ, *supra* note 4.

[6] SOU 1986:36, *Samernas Folkrättsliga Ställning* (Statens Offentliga Utredningar, The Swedish Government Official Reports). Delbetänkande av samerätts-utredningen, Justitiedepartementet, Stockholm. Information on the commission and resulting convention: pp. 89–91 (1986). *See also* PER GUTTORM KVENANGEN, SAMERNAS HISTORIA,. (1996) at 97–99.

[7] The first Reindeer Grazing Act was passed by the Swedish Parliament in 1886. Others followed in 1898 and 1928. The full texts of these acts can be found in T. CRAMÉR AND G. PRAWITZ, STUDIER I RENBETESLAGSTIFTNING. (1970). A Reindeer Herding Act came in 1971 (SFS 1971:437. *Rennäringslagen,* Sofiero, June 18, 1971) and is still current, although it has been modified somewhat through the years. For a discussion concerning the details of this legislation and its effects, *see* BEACH, HUGH, REINDEER-HERD MANAGEMENT IN TRANSITION: THE CASE OF TUORPON SAAMEBY IN NORTHERN SWEDEN. ACTA UNIV. UPS, UPPSALA STUDIES IN CULTURAL ANTHROPOLOGY 3. (1981).

It was generally believed that conflicts (such as reindeer trampling a farmer's fields or consuming his hay) could be avoided by separating geographically the herding and farming systems as much as possible. In Sweden, the *Lappby* members were made collectively responsible for the damages caused farmers by the reindeer.[8] Anything such as a farming commitment and a permanent house which might cause the herder to leave the nomadic life or neglect his reindeer—allowing them to spread unattended and cause damages—was frowned upon by the authorities. For example, were a herding family to own more than four goats, this would be construed as farming, and the family would be expelled from the *Lappby*.

Social Darwinism became a common ideology by the late nineteenth century, and the Saami were often considered beings of a lower order who should not be given the same legal status as the non-Saami Nordic peoples nor stand in the way of higher civilization. As mining, hydroelectric, and logging interests spread throughout Lapland, the rights of the Saami became construed as privileges that must bow to progress, commonly without due process or just compensation.

The basic tenet of Swedish Saami policy, formulated during this period (the early 1900s) and still in effect today, is that the Swedish State will grant certain special resource privileges to the Saami in order to preserve their unique culture. Saami culture is then narrowly recognized by the government to mean only reindeer herding.[9] A Saami who strays from this livelihood must give up his special rights. Moreover, the collective herding unit, the *sameby,* may engage in no economic activity other than herding. In this manner, Saami self-determination has been severely limited.

It should be emphasized that, in the first two Reindeer Grazing Acts,[10] there is nothing that says that only herders have Saami hunting and fishing rights. The Reindeer Grazing Act of 1886 says simply that all herders should belong to a *Lappby*; it does not say that hunters and fishermen did not or could not belong

---

[8] Beach, Hugh, with Myrdene Anderson and Pekka Aikio, *Dynamics of Saami Territoriality within the Nation-States of Norway, Sweden and Finland*, in MOBILITY AND TERRITORIALITY: SOCIAL AND SPATIAL BOUNDARIES AMONG FORAGERS, FISHERS, PASTORALISTS AND PERIPATETICS, (Michael Casimir and Aparna Rao, eds. 1991).

If reindeer destroyed crops, it was no longer necessary for the injured party to identify whose reindeer had perpetrated the act. Any reindeer-inflicted damage within a specific *Lappby's* range was compensated in payment from that *Lappby* with all of its herders sharing the expense.

[9] This is relevant because it is the basis of Swedish Saami policy. In effect, that Saami culture which the state sees fit to protect and favor is only reindeer herding, a form of livelihood which is practiced by only a small minority of Saami and which has *never* been the major Saami livelihood. The only Saami rights remaining were linked solely to reindeer herding. *See* Beach, *supra* note 1.

[10] I mean here the Reindeer Grazing Act of 1886 and the Reindeer Grazing Act of 1898. *See supra* note 7.

to *Lappbys*, or that these had no "immemorial rights" in their *Lappbys*.[11] As noted, the goal was to get the herders registered to a *Lappby* so that they would be *collectively* responsible for reindeer damages to farmers within the area when one could not specify the exact owner of those reindeer which had caused the damages. However, it is one thing to say that only *Lappby* members can herd, and quite another to say that only herders are *Lappby* members. The Herding Act of 1928,[12] however, brought together for the first time both of these regulations.

According to the Act of 1928, maintained in the Act of 1971,[13] all herders and only herders can be *Lappby/sameby* members.[14] While the State grandly decreed all Saami to possess "immemorial" herding rights (which include hunting and fishing rights), it deftly subverted the true implication of this admission with the further decree that only the *Lappby/sameby* members have the right to *exercise* these rights.

To this day, a major conflict within the Saami population concerns the ability of the Saami outside of the *samebys* to exercise their "immemorial" rights (hunting and fishing as well as herding). Still today, membership in the "closed shop" *sameby* is regulated by the vote of the current *sameby* members.

C. The Rationalization Period and Welfare Ideology

As the twentieth century progressed, farming declined drastically in the north. Small-scale farmers had little choice but to move south or find some other employment. Job opportunities became scarce, and large rural areas were gradually depopulated. The conflicts between herders and farmers, which had once preoccupied the authorities, subsided, and the emerging welfare States turned their attention to maximizing profits for the sake of higher living standards. This was the period marked by the policy of "rationalization."

---

[11] This is of vital importance because it explains the conflict over rights between the registered herders (*Lappby/Sameby* members) and those who cannot herd but who have *immemorial* rights on the land as Saami. This was also important to the authorities who wanted to know whom they should collectively bill for any reindeer-inflicted damage to farmers' crops within the *Lappby* range. For an explanation of the term "immemorial," *see* notes 22–24, *infra,* and accompanying text.

[12] The Reindeer Grazing Act of 1928, Lag om de svenska Lapparnas rätt till renbete i Sverige, Stockholm Palace, July 18, 1928. While all Saami who have a parent or grandparent who has practiced herding as a steady livelihood are said to possess herding rights, paragraph 1 of the Act of 1928 delimits which of these Saami have the right to *practice* their herding rights, i.e., only those who are *Lappby* members.

[13] Reindeer Herding Act of 1971 (SFS 1971:437. *Renñaringslagen,* Sofiero, June 18, 1971). This Act has 102 paragraphs and is 19 pages in length. Paragraph 1 of the Act of 1971 maintains the same principles of Paragraph 1 of the Act of 1928 in regulating which of the Saami have herding rights and which of these can practice them.

[14] *See* para. 8 of the Act of 1928, and the similar paragraph, para. 11, in the Act of 1971.

Some of the motivations that prompted the program of rationalization were based on humane values of caring and compassion. Medical surveys showed the "vital statistics" of the Saami to be comparable with those of people in underdeveloped countries,[15] despite the fact that, in principle, the Saami shared with their non-Saami neighbors the benefits of the national health programs. Shocked by the poor living standards (usually calculated only in monetary terms) and high infant mortality rates among its herding population, the Nordic States sought to raise the living standard of the Saami and considered that in doing so one would automatically help preserve Saami culture. These two goals, however, do not necessarily integrate without difficulty. In Sweden, a two-pronged plan was adopted: structure rationalization and production rationalization. The ideals of the former advocated a thirty percent reduction of the herding labor force on the grounds that there were currently more herders than necessary to do the job. Moreover, the fewer the herders, the more reindeer each might own. The ideals of the latter, production rationalization, advocated modern ranching methods, with calf slaughter, etc., to maximize the amount of meat produced per grazing unit—methods quite counter to Saami traditions and not always rational by the State's own definition.[16]

III. THE NEW ERA

The rationalization period lingers on despite its often misdirected goals and serious obstacles, like the effects of the Chernobyl nuclear disaster and the faltering reindeer-meat market.[17] However, the last ten years have been momentous for the Saami, and we feel it fair to say that, despite many difficulties, they have embarked upon yet a new era, featuring both a new sense of transnational ethnic solidarity and a set of new relations with regard to their encompassing Nation States. Today's growing pan-Saami international unity is directed toward greatly increased political and juridical presence in the international arena through forums such as the U.N. Human Rights Committee and the European Court of Human Rights. Norway and Sweden have finally established democratically elected Saami Parliaments ("Sametings") and, especially in Norway, altered significant aspects of governmental Saami policy following upon the extensive work of special Saami Rights Commissions. Although Finland had a Saami Parliament well in advance of both Norway and Sweden, here too significant policy changes have been enacted, largely in light of important new findings from research into Saami resource rights and because of efforts to harmonize Saami policies within the Nordic countries. The establishment of a Nordic Saami

---

[15] See S. Haraldson, *Levnads-och dödlighetsförha'llanden i de nordligaste svenska lappbyarna*, 59 SVENSKA LÄKARTIDNINGEN 2829 (1962).

[16] See Hugh Beach, *Reindeer-Herd Management in Transition: The Case of Tuorpon Saameby in Northern Sweden*, 3 UPPSALA STUD. IN CULTURAL ANTHROPOLOGY 454 (1981).

[17] See Hugh Beach, *Perceptions of Risk, Dilemmas of Policy: Nuclear Fallout in Swedish Lapland*, 30 SOC. SCI. & MED. 729–38 (1990).

Parliament with representatives from each of the national Saami Parliaments is firmly on the agenda.

The dissolution of the Soviet Union has had a profound effect on the Saami of the Kola Peninsula. With the economy in shambles, the Russian government terminated the old State-owned farms (''sovkhozes'') including the reindeer sovkhozes in which many of Russia's Saami were employed. Farm capital (reindeer stock) has been thrown onto the open market for purchase by the highest bidder. Yet this economic turmoil is accompanied by new freedoms, and the Kola Saami have in record time organized themselves politically, made firm connections with their Saami neighbors to the west (cultural and educational exchange programs, for example) and even joined the Nordic Saami Council, first as observers, but by 1992, as full voting members.

With this as background, this chapter will now turn to the main course of change for the Saami over the last ten years or so and indicate why this is characterized as a ''new era.'' At the same time the essay will be touching upon many unresolved issues, and will attempt to point in the direction of future developments.

A. Saami Rights Litigation

Flushed with victory in the *Altevatn* case in Norway whereby the ''immemorial'' grazing rights of Swedish Saami to certain Norwegian grazing areas were upheld by the Norwegian Supreme Court,[18] the Swedish Saami embarked, in 1966, upon a similar course of action in the Swedish courts. This case, the *Skattefjäll* or *Taxed Mountain* case, in which the Saami sought clarification of their resource rights, came to be the longest case ever in the Swedish courts and did not come to a close until 1981 with a verdict from the Swedish Supreme Court.[19] The verdict was long, complex, and frequently misunderstood. Briefly stated, it can be said to contain two main aspects: one a ruling on the conditions necessary for the Saami to have established true ownership rights over lands utilized by them traditionally, and the other a ruling as to whether or not the particular region in question fulfilled these conditions.[20] While the Saami did not win their particular claim to the contested Taxed Mountain land areas, they did win important points of principle with regard to the conditions recognized to establish land ownership. The Supreme Court was well aware that these conditions might be met by the Saami with respect to other regions. Thus, the

---

[18] *See* Altevatn Case, L. nr. 42, nr. 8/1966. (1966).

[19] *See* Taxed Mountain Case (''Skattefja llsma'l''), NJA 1981 s. 1, (1981)

[20] *See* B. Bengtsson, *Skattefjällsma'let och dess efterverkningar, in* SAMESYMPOSIUM 15 (Marjut Aikio & Kaisa Korpijaakko, eds. 1991).

verdict established new and liberal standards by which to test Saami land ownership claims, and it did not constitute a precedent denying Saami land ownership
throughout Lapland.[21]

Moreover, aside from the ownership issue, the Supreme Court did confirm
exclusive Saami "immemorial" rights to herd, hunt, and fish on lands traditionally (and continuously) used by them.[22] A description of "immemorial" rights
is given in the 15th chapter of Jordabalken, the old Swedish Code of Land Laws
from 1734,[23] now retained in point 6 in the promulgation to the new Jordabalken:

> It is *immemorial* right, when one has had some real estate or right for
> such a long time in undisputed possession and drawn benefit and utilized
> it that no one remembers or can in truth know how his forefathers or
> he from whom the rights were acquired first came to get them.[24]

Nonetheless, bowed by what many Saami conceived of as a total defeat, the
Saami involved decided not to pursue the case further in the international arena—despite a dissenting opinion by a prominent member of the court in favor
of Saami hunting and fishing rights, and the elaborated and detailed advice of
their counsel.[25] The politics of litigation seemed bankrupt, and the Swedish
Saami turned instead toward the politics of negotiation.

Meanwhile in Norway, events took a more dramatic turn. In protest against
the damming of the Kautokeino-Alta river, which would destroy valuable reindeer herding zones, Saami from many regions, together with supporters from
various environmental protectionist groups, banded together at the dam site to
stop the construction. Finally, a large police force had to be called in to remove

---

[21] Bertil Bengtsson, one of the judges of the Supreme Court in the *Taxed Mountain
Case* and also the court's main referent during this case, has clarified the court's complex
verdict in a number of articles. *See* Bertil Bengtsson, *Statsmakten och äganderätten.* SNS
Förlag. 10 ff. (1987). *See also* Bertil Bengtsson, *Ny lagstiftning ma'ste ga' till samernas
fördel, in* SAMEFOLKET Nr. 6–7, (1988); and Bertil Bengtsson, *Samernas rätt i ny belysn-
ing. in* SVENSK JURISTTIDNINGEN. A'RG. 75, HÄFTE 2 (1990).

[22] *Id. Also see* T. CRAMÉR, *supra* note 3, and Hugh Beach, *Den Svenska Samepoliti-
ken,* IVANDRARE OCH MINORITETER (D. SCHWARZ ed., Nr. 2, April, 1992).

[23] In addition to chapter 15 of the 1734 Jordabalken, the reference to "immemorial"
rights can be found in the 1971, or earlier editions, of the semi-official Swedish Law
Book, SVERIGES RIKES LAG.

[24] Jordabalken: 15; Promulgation of the new Jordabalken, SFS 1970:995; cf. Undén,
1969:142 (1969) (emphasis added).

[25] *See* Taxed Mountain Case ("Skattefjällsma'l"), *supra* note 19. The judge with the
dissenting opinion was the Supreme Court judge Bertil Bengtsson (also the court's main
referent during the *Taxed Mountain Case*) who, in a special statement (NJA 1981:1 page
249 ff., published together with the text of the Supreme Court's verdict), has made it
clear that he takes exception to the government's Saami policy with regard to Saami
hunting and fishing rights, a policy which puts the regulation of these rights under
State patronage.

the protesters by force. The sight of indigenous people being manhandled while trying to protect their land, or of Saami hunger strikers in front of the Norwegian Parliament in Oslo, made international headlines, alerted the world to the moral argument of the Saami, and moved much of the majority population to sympathize with them.

B. Saami Rights Commissions

Largely as a result of this confrontation, the Norwegian government commissioned a royal investigation into Saami rights in 1980. This Norwegian Saami Rights Commission was to deal with issues of a general political character, with the issue of a Norwegian Saami Parliament, and with economic issues. It was to investigate questions about Saami rights to natural resources and make recommendations toward new legislation. In 1983, Sweden also established a Saami Rights Commission directed to revise legislation concerning Saami in keeping both with the international covenants Sweden had ratified[26] and also with the verdict of the Swedish Supreme Court in the *Taxed Mountain* case. By a directive of the government[27] the Swedish Saami Rights Commission was instructed to consider: 1) the advisability of strengthening the Saami legal position with regard to reindeer herding; 2) the question of whether a democratically elected Saami organization should be established; and 3) the need for measures to strengthen the position of the Saami language. Later the Commission's directives were broadened to encompass the situation of the Saami as an indigenous people.[28]

In 1984, the Norwegian Saami Rights Commission, led by Professor (now Chief Justice) Carsten Smith presented its first partial report, *On the Legal Position of the Saami*,[29] a work of enormous breadth and solid scholarship. It was as a result of the recommendation of this Norwegian Commission that the

---

[26] It is only through application of the U.N. Human Rights Committee (which monitors the International Covenant on Civil and Political Rights) and the European Court at Strasbourg (European Convention on Fundamental Rights and Freedoms of 1950) that purported transgressions of international law ratified by Sweden can be addressed with judgments that are binding for Sweden, and it is here Saami efforts are concentrated.

[27] *See* Dir. 1982:71, *Vissa fra'gor om samernas ställning i Sverige.* Kommittedirektiv, Beslut vid regeringssammanträde 1982 09–02. Chefen for justitiedepartementet, statsra'det Petri, anför. Sweden.

[28] Dir. 1983:10, Kommittédirektiv. Tilläggsdirektiv till kommitten med uppgift att utreda vissa fra'gor om samernas ställning i Sverige.

Had the directive been followed, it would have permitted the Commission to carry out a broad historical investigation of Swedish Saami policy, thereby casting light on injustices that should be addressed. It could also have led to a discussion about Saami rights as a people and not simply about Saami needs as perceived by the state.

[29] *See* NOU 1984:18, *Om samenes rettsstilling,* Norges Offentlige Utredninger, Avgitt til Justisdepartementet (15 juni 1984) Universitetsforlaget, Oslo.

Norwegian Parliament voted to establish a Norwegian Saami Parliament.[30] Still, despite the gains made, there are many points on which Saami demands were not met by the commission. Many Saami demanded that this Saami Parliament be empowered with a veto on land encroachments injurious to Saami land usage. In the realm of international law, the Norwegian Saami Rights Commission (echoed by the Swedish Saami Rights Commission) has stated that the Saami cannot be considered a "people" according to the meaning of the term in the United Nations 1966 International Covenant on Civil and Political Rights and its 1966 International Covenant on Economic, Social and Cultural Rights.[31] Without this recognition, the Saami are not considered to possess the right of self-determination. Instead, the commission argued that the Saami come under the safeguards of article 27 of the Covenant on Civil and Political Rights, and interpreted this article to require positive discrimination for minorities and indigenous populations.[32]

Unlike the Norwegian Commission, and despite the fact that the Swedish Commission was to recommend adjustments of Swedish Saami policy in light of the *Taxed Mountain* verdict, the Swedish Commission left aside the important questions of the historical rights of the Saami and, instead. concerned itself solely with comparing the situation of the Saami in Sweden to the minimal requirements of international conventions on human rights.[33] Yet, essential to any Swedish commission on Saami involving resource rights, culture, and political organization is a thorough analysis of "immemorial" rights. The Commission was set up to investigate whether contemporary pressures from extractive industries had threatened herding to the point that protective measures should be taken to maintain Saami culture. If so, the Commission was to make concrete proposals for such protective measures. This manner of framing the issues constituted an implicit acceptance of the premise that herding is something to be supported (or perhaps not) as a kind of sympathy action for the Saami. In short,

---

[30] *See* Ot prp nr 33 (1986–87), *Om lov om Sametinget og andre samiske rettsforhold (sameloven),* Justis-og politidepartementet, Norway.

[31] *See* International Covenant on Civil and Political Rights, GA Res. 2200A (XXI) 21 U.N. GAOR Supp. (No. 16) at 52, U.N. Doc. A/6361 (1966), 999 U.N.T.S. 171 (March 23, 1966) and International Covenant on Economic, Social and Cultural Rights, GA Res. 2200A (XXI) 21 UN GAOR Supp. (No. 16) at 49; U.N. Doc. A/6316 (1996) Jan. 3, 1976. *Also see supra* note 26 and acompanying text. For an explanation of the international ramifications of the word "peoples," *see* Chapter 2, Lee Swepston, *The ILO Indigenous and Tribal Peoples Convention (No. 169): Eight Years After Adoption,* in this volume.

[32] SOU 1986:36, Samernas Folkrättsliga Ställning (1986). Delbetänkande av samerättsutredningen. Justitiedepartementet, Stockholm. The investigation's judgment about positive discrimination for the Saami appears on pp. 160–61. The investigation's judgment that the Saami do not constitute a "people" according to international law is discussed in the above source on pp. 117–21. *Also see* Covenant on Civil and Political Rights, *id.* at art. 27.

[33] *See, e.g., supra* note 26.

the legal rights of the Saami to herd, and their rights to shield their herding from extractive industries, were here treated merely as a special privilege which the State could give or withhold depending upon its own perception of Saami needs. The legal issues of land ownership and resource rights remain ignored in favor of a new slight adjustment of welfare.[34]

C. The Swedish Saami Parliament

Following the example of the Norwegian Saami Rights Commission, in 1989 the Swedish Commission suggested the creation of a democratically elected Saami Parliament, a "Sameting," as part of a general effort to "harmonize" Saami policy of the Nordic nations.[35] The Commission also suggested revisions in the Reindeer Herding Act of 1971 in an effort to strengthen herding interests in relation to exploitive industries (mostly government owned).[36] Among other things, the Commission recommended that the Saami language be given increased status and financial support.[37]

---

[34] *See* H. Beach, *A Summary of MRG's Second Discussion Day Concerning the Saami,* about the Saami Rights Commission's work on Saami rights and a "Sameting," (SOU 1989:41) (1990).

[35] SOU 1989:41, *Samerätt och Sameting.* Huvudbetänkande av samerättsutredningen. Justitiedepartementet, Stockholm.

As the historical presence of the Saami has been similar in Norway, Sweden, and Finland, and, as these countries have in various unions shared kings and governments, it is natural for them to entertain the idea that Saami rights should be quite similar in each of these modern nations. The Saami too prefer pan-Saami solutions, so that, for example, a person recognized as a Saami in one country will also fit into the definition of Saami in one of the other countries.

[36] SOU 1989:41, *Samerätt och Sameting.* Huvudbetänkande av samerättsutredningen. Justitiedepartementet, Stockholm.

Saami reindeer herding is seriously threatened by the ever-increasing encroachments of extractive industries, notably the timber, mining, hydroelectric power, and even tourist industries. Each industry has its own history, and yet none can be grasped in isolation of the others. Much of the labor force brought north by the hydro-electric power industry, for instance, has shifted to the timber industry. The road cut through the wilderness to transport a huge generator and other building materials to a dam site can later open the nearby forests to logging by the timber industry (*see* BEACH, *supra* note 7). The mines have often established large cities around them with a wide transportation system and populations which demand recreation opportunities. The various extractive industries have together created populations in the North which dwarf the local Saami into a minority position (with proportionately reduced political power) in most of the municipalities of their core area.

Section 30 of the Reindeer Act of 1971 calls for a ban on specific land exploitation only if the encroacher causes changes of "appreciable discomfort" for herding—known among herders as one of the "rubber clauses," for how does one judge this discomfort?

[37] SOU 1989:41, *Samerätt och Sameting.* Huvudbetänkande av samerättsutredningen. Justitiedepartementet, Stockholm.

The suggestion (not implemented) was to make the Saami language an official lan-

In 1992, the Swedish government (now ruled by a conservative coalition instead of the Social Democrats) presented a bill to the national Parliament concerning the creation of a Swedish Saami Parliament, a Sameting.[38] However, this same bill contained much more than a suggestion to establish a Sameting. While it claimed to recognize Saami "immemorial" rights in its revision of the Herding Act of 1971, no meaningful changes were made in support of this claim. Were Saami "immemorial" rights to be recognized in practice, Saami resource rights would extend far beyond the Herding Act and pertain to more than the members of the herding collectives.

The appropriate application of "immemorial" rights guarantees the right of present and future generations to continue with the traditional resource utilization of their forefathers, assuming this was undisputed and well-grounded. However, there is much that needs clarification. Is "immemorial" right only an individual right or a collective right of each specific herding organization? If it is a civil right, not merely a privilege, how is it that the State regulates its practice so as to deny the non-herding Saami access to their "immemorial" resources without due process or just compensation? Why have Saami "immemorial" rights to hunting and fishing been ignored, and if they were to be recognized in practice, what would this entail? The questions are many, and one would have thought that they were items for the strict scrutiny of the Swedish Saami Rights Commission. Unfortunately, despite the fact that the Commission could have given its directives an interpretation broad enough to grapple with these issues, the Commission chose not to, thereby allowing the problems to fester and pushing the matter over to the courts, both national and international.

The bill presented in 1992 took a tack very different from the recommendations of the former Swedish Saami Rights Commission. The significant changes the bill prescribed for the Reindeer Herding Act were basically a tightening of restrictions and regulations on the herders rather than adjustments to strengthen herding interests.[39] The most hurtful and unexpected blow to the Saami was the removal of Saami hunting and fishing exclusivity on lands heretofore reserved for their use alone.[40]

---

guage in two northern municipalities. Saami would thus be able to receive and to answer government administrative communications in Saami. Funding would also be provided for increased Saami language schooling.

[38] *See* Proposition 1992/93:32, *Samerna och samisk kultur m.m.*, 1 Riksdagen 1992/93, 1 samling, Nr. 32, Sweden.

[39] *See id.* The Reindeer Herding Act was given an environmentalist orientation with the goal to maintain "sustainable development." In practice, this has meant regulations permitting authorities to demand herd-size limitations for individual herders along with the imposition of fines if these limitations are not met. To the Saami, who had campaigned for veto powers against proposed logging in areas harmful to herding, and who had hoped for real improvement in the negotiating powers of the herding industry, the changes to the Reindeer Herding Act were quite disappointing.

[40] *See* Proposition 1992/93:32, Samerna och samisk kultur m.m., 1 Riksdagen 1992/93, 1 samling, Nr. 32, Sweden, (1992). The section which has to do with the confiscation of Saami small game hunting rights is contained in section 2.14 of this bill, pp. 131 52.

At an extra meeting called by a Swedish Saami Association and occasioned by this bill, a copy of the bill was publicly burned in front of national news TV cameras. The major Swedish Saami organizations passed resolutions calling for the acceptance of the Sameting, but rejected all other portions of the bill, at least until the newly formed Sameting had the opportunity to convene and to discuss these vital matters.[41] Obviously, they argued, this is the stated goal of such a Sameting, and it would defeat its own purpose if the State institutionalized a Sameting without its having the chance to express itself on the most significant legislative changes for the Saami presented during the last 20 years, and on the implementation of the 1981 *Taxed Mountain* judgment.

Be this as it may, and despite references by those knowledgeable about northern affairs to the expropriation of Saami hunting and fishing exclusivity as ''pork'' for the northern non-Saami voters (in no voting community in Sweden do the Saami hold a majority position), the bill was passed by Parliament on December 15, 1992, with an overwhelming majority.[42]

Each of the three Fennoscandian countries hosting Saami populations now has a Sameting, but the cost to the Saami has been high, at least in Sweden. Besides the points already mentioned, the Swedish bill rejected an addendum to the constitution proclaiming special responsibility for the indigenous Saami minority similar to that accepted by Norway,[43] it did not grant official status to the Saami language when used in regard to Saami livelihoods (as the Saami Rights Commission had advocated[44]), and it made plain Sweden's intent not to

---

See also Hugh Beach, *Shots Heard Round the World, in* BESLUTET OMSMA'VILTJAKTEN-EN STUDIE I MYNDIGHETSUTÖVNING (Agneta Arnesson-Westerdahl, ed. 1994), utgiven av Sametinget.

Although government authorities had long ago taken the responsibility to issue hunting licenses (with the justification that the Saami were incapable of dealing with such decisions), the rights they were administering were still Saami exclusive hunting and fishing rights to the area above, or west of, the Agriculture Line. In Proposition 1992/93:32, the government declared the parallel right of the Crown to hunt in this area, claiming it to be Crown land (although the Supreme Court made it plain in its verdict in the *Taxed Mountain Case* that the ownership of this land was still not resolved).

[41] *See Regeringens Samepropositon,* in SAMEFOLKET, 12 28 Nr. 11 (1992).

[42] *See Samerna i Riksdagen, in* SAMEFOLKET. Nr. 1, (1993) (pp. 8–26 contain the full text of the Parliamentary debate on Dec. 15, 1992, concerning Proposition 1992/93:32).

[43] *See* Proposition 1992/93:32, Samerna och samisk kultur m.m., 1 Riksdagen 1992/93, 1 samling, Nr. 32, Sweden (pp. 30–33) (1992). The Saami Rights Commission's suggested addendum to the constitution, *Förslag till ändring I regeringsformen,* is also reprinted as Appendix 1.2.2 in Proposition 1992/93:32 (1992).

[44] *See* SOU 1990:91, *Samerätt och Samiskt Spra'k,* final report of the Saami Rights Commission (1990). The portions of this report which specify the Commission's recommendations concerning the Saami language are reprinted in Proposition 1992/93:32 as Appendix 1.3.1, 1.3.2, and 1.3.3.

The government's rejection of the legal right to utilize the Saami language in official

ratify ILO Convention (No. 169) on Indigenous and Tribal Peoples in Independent Countries.[45]

Even with regard to the content of the new Sametings structures in Norway and Sweden, the Saami have cause for disappointment. As is the case in Finland, the new Sametings have only advisory status to the government. In addition, they have no veto over land exploitation in delicate herding areas. Moreover, the Saami parliaments are departments of government, theoretically subject to government directives and, therefore, unable to represent the Saami in national or international courts against the State.

Yet, despite these weaknesses, the creation of Sametings in Norway and Sweden has been a much-desired goal. Their hope is that these Sametings will in time mature into administrative bodies of increasing autonomy and respect. Saami interest groups and organizations are not politically organized or activated to the same extent, and it may take a good deal of time before the new Saami parliaments actually do represent the full spectrum of Saami. In the meantime, there is always the risk that the small or unorganized group within the general Saami category will lose its voice with respect to the State.

The Saami parliaments hold a promise of improved Saami-state relations, but, at least initially, this may be achieved only with internal Saami strife. Of course, this is an unavoidable consequence of the democratic process, and such strife is certainly not something new. However, the bureaucratic parliamentary

---

contexts can be found in Proposition 1992/93:32, Samerna och samisk kultur m.m., 1 Riksdagen 1992/93, 1 samling, Nr. 32, Sweden (1992) (pp. 53–56).

[45] *See* Beach, *supra* note 40.

The main obstacle to ratification by Sweden is §14 of this convention which states among other things that: ''The rights of ownership and possession of the peoples concerned over the lands which they traditionally occupy shall be recognized.'' When the text of this convention was still in draft form, Sweden and a number of other nations sought to have this article changed so as to recognize the peoples' right of use rather than right of ownership. Failing this, Sweden has declined ratification, despite the fact that the text was adopted by the International Labor Conference before being opened up for ratification by member states. Norway, however, has taken another tack and ratified the convention, thus accepting its many safeguards for and positive attitude toward indigenous peoples, while at the same time presenting a special interpretation of §14. According to Norway's special interpretation, strongly protected rights of usage must be viewed as satisfactorily fulfilling ILO's demand for admission of indigenous land ownership, as the Norwegian state cannot grant ownership rights to the Saami for vast land areas occupied by other people, often in the possession of what would then become conflicting private ownership claims. Norway has thereby taken the risk of being declared in violation of the convention, and the Swedish Saami minister, Per Unckel, has made it plain in his presentation of the new Swedish Saami policy to the Swedish national Parliament on December 15, 1992, that Sweden intends to let Norway be the ''guinea pig'' on this issue.

For a detailed discussion of ILO Convention (No. 169) *see* Chapter 2, Lee Swepston, *The ILO Indigenous and Tribal Peoples Convention (No. 169): Eight Years After Adoption,* in this volume.

process itself is not Saami. The gains from this new model will be brought from within a context of increased cultural encapsulation. The Saami must try to mold their parliaments to themselves rather than merely to the demands of State processes, and to maintain general Saami concerns despite shortsighted gains to be made by any one faction temporarily in a position of power.

As previously mentioned, the Saami in Norway and Finland have not experienced the same kind of political tradeoff as have the Swedish Saami in obtaining a democratically elected representative body at the expense of practical content to their "immemorial" rights. Publication of a doctoral dissertation by Kaisa Korpijaakko in 1989 on the legal rights of the Saami in Finland[46] has had a major effect on Finnish Saami policy formulations, which will probably be echoed to some degree in Sweden and Norway as well. Because her research deals with the period when Sweden and Finland were one country, it is plain that her results bear upon the legal rights of the Swedish Saami, too. Her research proves that the Swedish/Finnish government recognized that Saami people owned their lands, as witnessed by taxation records. Thus, at that time the Saami were not simply considered landless nomads, but rather their land titles were incorporated into the state's land tenure system. While the *Taxed Mountain* verdict in Sweden ruled that such ownership was not the case for the Saami with regard to the *Taxed Mountain* lands in Jämtland, it stated clearly the possibility that ownership title could be substantiated for the Saami elsewhere.[47] This has now come to pass, although not yet in the courts. Korpijaakko's work in Finland, following upon the trail blazed in Sweden by Tomas Cramér, the attorney for the Saami in the *Taxed Mountain* case, has documented Saami land claims to an extent which can no longer be ignored. It is hard to imagine that herding rights based on privilege can long stand against "immemorial" rights and outright "ownership" rights.

Korpijaakko serves as a legal counsel on Finland's Advisory Committee on Saami Affairs and, in June 1990, this Committee presented its proposal for a Saami Act to the Finnish government.[48] This act advocates the restoration of

---

[46] *See* Kaisa Korpijaakko-Labba, Om Samernas Rättsliga Ställning I Sverige-Finland, (1994), Kakimiesliiton Kustannus. Helsingfors, Juristförbundets Förlag, at 499– (a Swedish translation of her Finnish doctoral dissertation presented in 1989).

[47] *See* Taxed Mountain Case, *supra* note 19.

See also B. Bengtsson, *Skattefjällsma'let och dess efterverkningar*, in Samesymposium 15 (Marjut Aikio & Kaisa Korpijaakko, eds. 1991).

[48]Saamelaisasiain neuvottelukannan mietintö I. Ehdotus saamelaislaiksi ja erinäisten lakien muuttaniseksi (Proposal for a Saami Act and Other Legal Reforms), Helsinki, Komiteanmietintö 1990:32 (1990).

See also Lennard Sillanpää, *Political and Administrative Responses to Sami Self-Determination* (a comparative study of public administrations in Fennoscandia on the issue of Sami land title as an aboriginal right), *in* Societas Scientiarum Fennica, Commentationes Scientiarum Socialium 48 (1994).

land and water rights in the Saami homeland regions to the Saami. Norway, too, through the continued work of its Saami Rights Commission, seeks to address the vital issue of Saami land title. The Norwegian Saami Rights Commission is currently engaged in studying the land rights of the Saami in the Finnmark region of Norway. Sweden, however, terminated its Saami Rights Commission and refuses to confront the issue of Saami "immemorial" rights or land ownership rights squarely. Instead, by legislative procedure, it has to date ignored the ruling of its own Supreme Court upholding Saami hunting and fishing exclusivity.[49]

Given this situation, the Saami have little choice but to revert to litigation. This time, however, we shall see the Saami approaching international as well as national forums with a new spirit of unity stretching across Saamiland. The Swedish Saami will most surely seek to appeal the confiscation of their hunting and fishing rights to international courts, but they will also be aided by pan-Saami organizations such as the Saami Council, which enjoys NGO status[50] with the United Nations, and in time by the future Nordic Saami Parliament. To what extent the national Saami parliaments will be able to participate in such a confrontation with their governments is, of course, unclear, but they will undoubtedly press their advantage to the fullest. A government that muzzles its Saami parliament would suffer mightily in international stature.

IV. CONCLUSION

To understand the situation of the Saami, it is important to consider what it is that the Saami are hoping to achieve. Few if any Saami would advocate the building of an independent Saami State as a viable and serious alternative. What they do want, however, is the ability to protect their lands of traditional use against heavy exploitation. This is not to say that they will automatically oppose all development, only that they insist on being a decisive part of all negotiations. Similarly, the Saami are not necessarily opposed to allowing a broader use of their hunting and fishing rights. But these must be recognized as *their* rights, the revenues from which should accrue to them. Their main desire is to protect

---

[49] The Swedish "obviousness requirement" (*uppenbarhetsrekvisitan*) in the Constitution (RF 11:14) allows the courts to condone violations of the Swedish Constitution so long as they are not overly glaring. Obviously, legislation passed by Parliamentary majority will not be considered to be in obvious violation of the Constitution. It is argued that the "obviousness requirement" ensures government by democratically elected representatives rather than by politically appointed judges.

[50] The term NGO refers to "nongovernmental organizaton." The role of NGOs at the United Nations is the result of a resolution of the Economic and Social Council which, under the Untied Nations Charter, has the power to made arrangements for their participation in U.N. deliberations. For an overview of indigenous peoples and NGOs in the United Nations, *see* Chapter 5, Douglas Sanders, *The Legacy of Deskaheh: Indigenous Peoples as International Actors*, in this volume.

their wildlife resources within a program of sustainable use. Within that ecological framework, and after their own needs have been met, they have indicated that they would not be averse to allocating a share of the harvestable resource to others. A kind of comanagement program for renewable resources involving government scientists and administrators as well as Saami expertise, similar to that comanagement enjoyed by the aboriginals of the Canadian Northwest, would probably be welcomed by the Saami. It is high time for concepts such as ''subsistence use'' and ''preferential quotas'' for the local population to be given content in Saamiland.

Even though they are encapsulated by government and minimally empowered, the Saami parliaments, now in all three of the Nordic Saami countries, open to the Saami new avenues of action, both within each Nation State, but also as a unified transnational entity. With these democratically elected representative parliaments the Saami will be in a position to clarify their own position and to mount a unified front. These bodies and their future combined manifestation, armed with the recent and emerging body of international jurisprudence regarding indigenous rights, place the Saami in a better position than ever before of forcing the practical recognition of the rights they already have in each of their separate Nation States and of partaking in the new rights being developed by the international community. Fundamentally new is the possibility for the Saami now to speak with *one* representative voice. The Fennoscandian governments might no longer find it possible to follow the old Roman dictum *divide et impera*, split and rule, divide and conquer.

The greatest threat to the Saami today is the widespread ignorance about their situation, their history, and their rights in the countries in which they reside. Most Swedes know a little about the American Indians, but seem to know even less about Sweden's indigenous people. Ignorance means inaction in addressing the wrongs done them. Knowledge, understanding, and, not least, uncomfortable questions from the international community are among the most effective means of bringing pressure to bear on the Fennoscandian States to implement changes benefiting the Saami and aiding their ability to survive as a people with a distinct culture and language.

CHAPTER 7

"SO-CALLED DEVELOPMENT" AND ITS IMPACT ON THE HUMAN RIGHTS OF INDIGENOUS PEOPLE IN INDIA

Deepak Kumar Behera

I. INTRODUCTION

The post-independent India witnessed the race of developmental activities through the execution of large development projects to alleviate poverty, remove economic stagnation, increase employment potential, provide basic amenities, etc. Although this ''so-called development'' was successful in increasing the GNP and harnessing the natural resources, it has given rise to certain adverse effects and unintended consequences. Its negative impacts on the environment, disturbing the delicate ecological balance, are well known to all of us. The ''so-called development'' has also brought about the uprooting and dismemberment of social, moral, and economic webs of indigenous life that were built over generations. Morever, it has caused irreparable damage to the indigenous people. These people have been marginalized and pushed to the periphery of society to pay the cost of rich and powerful people's urge for industrialization and development. The irony is that the cost is being paid by the people who are least able to afford it and who will benefit the least from the fruits of development.

Development cannot be conceived in general terms for the Indian nation as a homogeneous and indivisible whole. Indian society is multiracial, multicultural, multireligious, and multilinguistic. It comprises not a single social reality but multiple realities of various groups and communities.

The recently concluded ''People of India Project'' by the Anthropological Survey of India recorded 4,835 indigenous communities distributed over thirty-two states and Union Territories.[1] Of these 4,835 communities, a vast majority directly depend on natural capital. In other words, they are hunter-gatherers, shifting cultivators, fisher folk, small peasants, etc. For our purposes, such groups have been referred to as tribal peoples or indigenous communities. These are the defenseless people who always get just enough to fill their bellies. In such

---

[1] People of India Project, ANTHROPOLOGICAL SURVEY OF INDIA.

communities, the skills for earning a living are transferred from mother to daughter and from father to son. A common feature of the indigenous people is their remoteness and the marginal quality of their territorial resources. These indigenous people are socially oppressed and economically exploited.

Dispossession of indigenous people to make way for mammoth capital-intensive development projects has become a distressingly routine phenomenon. It is thus reasonable to hold that, although the dispossession of indigenous people in India began during the colonial era, the question of their survival did not become critical until post-colonial times.

Thus, the present day ''so-called development'' sacrifices the legitimate rights and interests of indigenous people just because they are not organized, articulate, or violent, or because they are not politically equipped to fight back and obstruct the process of development or sue the government in a court of law for due compensation for losses that are both material and intangible.[2] Obviously then, concern about indigenous people is neither romantic nor adhoc. It is of very great contemporary significance.

Against this background, this essay endeavors to analyze the concept of ''development'' from an indigenous people's perspective. Data regarding the subject of this paper have been culled exclusively from second-hand sources. Admittedly, the data are sparse, but this chapter seeks to raise important basic issues concerning the human rights of indigenous people in the context of the ''so-called developmental'' projects. The first section highlights some of the major issues of the indigenous people of India in relation to dam, mining, industrial, commercial, and shrimp farming projects; cases included in the analysis are purposefully selective and therefore may be seen as a major limitation of the study. The second part of the paper critically examines the concept of ''development'' from an indigenous perspective. Finally, the chapter presents a summary of its findings.

II. "SO-CALLED DEVELOPMENT"

It can be argued that environmental degradation in India arises primarily because of a ruthless exploitation of the biosphere by a small clique of greedy people who are unmindful of the suffering of the vast majority of indigenous people and unconcerned about the future. This is possible because that group controls a disproportionately large part of the biosphere, especially the land: the agricultural, forest, and urban space. The ''so-called development'' has made India's living resources most vulnerable and left its biodiversity exposed to various ecological threats. India remains, perhaps, the only major country that does not require a mandatory environmental impact assessment prior to the initiation of development projects.

---

[2] *See* L.K. MOHAPATRA, TRIBAL DEVELOPMENT IN INDIA: MYTH AND REALITY 13 (1993).

The "so-called development" has displaced a large number of people by acquiring their land. Recent estimates indicate that in India between 1951 and 1990 nearly 18.5 million persons were displaced as the result of various development projects. The vast majority of them are indigenous people. The magnitude of displacement of people in relation to various projects is illustrated in the table below.

A Comparative Estimate of Persons Displaced by
Various Categories of Project (1951–1990)

Types of Projects	Number Displaced
Dams	14,000,000
Mines	2,100,000
Industries	1,300,000
Sanctuaries	600,000
Others	500,000

Sources: Fernandes et al., 1992: 6.

As one can see from the statistics, displacement due to irrigation and power projects (dams) is highest, followed by that attributable to mines and industries.

The adverse impact of such projects on the ecosystem and the consequent deprivation and disturbance suffered by certain indigenous people is often lightly dismissed as the "price for development."[3] It is unfortunate that compensation of displaced people is viewed exclusively from an economic point of view. Human beings cannot be reduced to mere economics. Their cultural, social, and psychological links and needs are shattered when they are displaced. No amount of economic assistance can diminish the pain caused in the process of displacement. At best, the government can only try to make the displacement less painful by providing all the facilities—such as health care, education, safe drinking water, shelter, employment, and land—that are conducive to their holistic development. Reducing compensation to pure economics is a degradation of human beings. In practice, however, not even the economic rehabilitation of indigenous people is taken seriously.

During the process of development planning by the central/state governments, there has been no clear policy formulated to handle involuntary displacement. The absence of a national policy can be attributed to the government's apathy toward the cause of the displaced indigenous people and the stubborn

---

[3] S.N. Ratha and D.K. Behera, *Displacement and Rehabilitation: Data from the Resettled Colonies Around the Steel Plant at Rourkela, Orissa*, III MAN IN ASIA 10 (1990).

technical bias displayed by the development agencies that undermines the social and human implications.[4] Indigenous people's increased awareness of their rights has resulted in the development of a protest movement. Its goal is to protect the livelihood of indigenous people from distorted development.

A. Dam Projects

Various dam projects have helped to irrigate large tracts of land belonging mostly to medium and big farmers. But for tribal and marginal farmers this has only resulted in the pain of being uprooted from their homeland with little prospect for their rehabilitation. One example is the Narmada Project, the most controversial dam project in the history of India. This project will eventually include 30 major, 135 medium, and 3,000 minor dams on the Narmada river, which flows through Madhya Pradesh, Maharashtra, and Gujarat. Of the 30 major dams, five will be hydro, six will be multipurpose and 19 will be irrigation projects. While 10 of these dams will be on the Narmada itself, 20 will be on its tributaries.[5]

The two issues at the center of the dispute from the project's inception have been the resettlement and rehabilitation of oustees and the environmental impact of the project. The main controversy centers on the Sardar Sarovar Project (SSP) in Gujarat. It is estimated to cost Rs.13,000 crores, although the final figure is likely to be considerably higher. The SSP envisages an irrigation component for 187 thousand hectares and 1,450 MW power. To achieve this it will submerge 39,134 hectares—13,744 hectares of which are forests and 11,318 hectares of which are agricultural land. It will also displace 66,675 indigenous people, the majority of whom are tribal.[6]

The issue of the social and environmental costs of this project has been raised by environmental groups as far back as the early 1980s. At that time, it was naively assumed that the states concerned would be able to satisfy the criteria laid down by the 1979 Narmada Dispute Tribunal Award for all oustees—that they be given two hectares of these states—or that the project authorities had a clear estimate at that time of the extent of displacement likely to be caused by the project. Ironically, while the figure originally projected stood at 6,605 families, today it is an incredible 40,000 indigenous families.

It has been evident for some time that there is just not enough land to settle all the oustees. The Gujarat Government alone has stuck to the Narmada Dispute Tribunal Award and formulated a resettlement policy that gives every oustee

---

[4] *See* W. Fernandes et al., DEVELOPMENT, DISPLACEMENT AND REHABILITATION IN THE TRIBAL AREAS OF ORISSA (1992).

[5] *See* K. Sharma, *Narmada Project—Built* on Broken Promises, in THE HINDU SURVEY OF THE ENVIRONMENT 107 (Shri N. Ravis, ed., 1993).

[6] *See id.*

(landed or landless) and his/her major sons a minimum of two hectares of irrigable land. Partly in response to this, the state government was able to defuse the opposition from one of the main opponents, the Arch-Vahini, which is now supporting the project.

However, Maharashtra and Madhya Pradesh, where a majority of those affected is located, recognize only landed oustees for entitlement. The resettlement policy in both of these states is based on the principle of "land for land." The indigenous tribal people cannot claim title to the land they have tilled for generations, because it is not listed as revenue land (it is usually forest land, either reserved or protected). Therefore, they may not get land at all. Little or no thought has been given as to how these landless oustees will be rehabilitated. The nongovernmental organizations, like Narmada Bachao Andolon, that have been fighting for the rights of these tribal oustees conclude that the majority will be forced to migrate to the nearest town or city to seek daily wage labor. Such environmental refugees are already a phenomenon among the urban poor in many cities. The project has floundered on this basic issue.

Even the 1985 Credit and Loan agreement with the World Bank laid down that the project should ensure adequate resettlement and rehabilitation for the oustees. However, in 1985, the exact number of potential oustees was not known. It is possible that, if the World Bank had sought an independent assessment on the extent of displacement and whether reasonable resettlement was possible, it would have reconsidered its involvement in the project, or at least it would have suggested that the project be modified. The World Bank did no such thing, despite the fact that as early as 1984—before it finalized the agreement with the Indian government—the World Bank's appraisal team had informed it that crucial information on resettlement was lacking. However, the World Bank continued its financing of the project until March 1992.

The turning point in the relationship between the World Bank and the SSP came in 1990 when the World Bank, then under Barber Conable, was forced to accede to the requests of Indian and international environmental and human rights groups to review the project. Mr. Conable initiated the process just before he relinquished charge of the World Bank to Lewis Preston. The inquiry led to the appointment of the former Under Secretary-General of the United Nations Development Programme as administrator and Bradford Morse as chairperson of an independent review of the SSP.

Mr. Morse and his team[7] came to India in 1991. They traveled extensively for six months in the area affected, met with those for and against the project, as well as with the officials in all three states, and with representatives of the Central Government. In June 1992, they handed over their final report to the World Bank president.

---

[7] The investigatory team was made up of Bradford Morse and three other notable persons.

The Morse report was extremely critical of the project. It stated: ''We think the Sardar Sarovar projects as they stand are flawed, that resettlement and rehabilitation of all those displaced by the projects have not been properly considered or adequately addressed. Moreover, we believe that the Bank shares responsibility with the borrower for the situation that has developed.'' The team also found that the project was inadequate in meeting environmental considerations. ''The history of the environmental aspects of Sardar Sarovar is the history of non-compliance,'' stated the report. ''There is no comprehensive statement. The nature and magnitude of environmental problems and solutions remain elusive. This feeds the controversy surrounding the projects.''

Apart from the submergence of forests, another environmental problem raised was that of losing forest land for rehabilitation. As there is not enough revenue land to resettle the oustees, both Maharashtra and Madhya Pradesh are trying to persuade the Union Ministry of Environment and Forest to give them permission to release forest land for resettlement. Under the 1986 Environment Protection Act,[8] the states are expressly forbidden to ''dereserve'' reserved forests in the light of information on India's greatly depleted forest cover. Under pressure, the Ministry had to agree to the Maharashtra government's request to release 2,700 hectares of forest in Taloda for the oustees. Recently, another such request for an additional 1,500 hectares has been cleared, although it runs contrary to India's conservation policy.

What is extraordinary about the Narmada Project is that, despite the controversy, the pressure from the World Bank, and agitations by environmental groups like the Narmada Bachao Andolan, the environmental amelioration remains grossly inadequate. A measure like compensatory afforestation, for instance, which was supposed to keep pace with the construction, is so far behind that it has become a purely academic exercise.

Unfortunately, cancellation of the final installment of the World Bank loan has diminished the pressure on the project-implementing agency to adhere to these social and environmental requirements. Completing the dam at all costs has become the prime concern. Even the financial shortfall has been made up with those in charge declaring the SSP as a ''national project'' and promising the equivalent amount from the Eighth Plan funds.

While the Narmada controversy is by no means a closed chapter, the events of 1992–93 hold lessons for future development projects. The first lesson is that foresight is cheaper that hindsight. Nothing illustrates this better than the Sardar Sarovar project. If a complete and accurate assessment of the social and environmental costs had been made in the initial stages, the cost-benefit ratio of the project would have been altered. This might have led to rethinking on the size of the project or its design. Instead, as the extent of displacement and environmental

---

[8] Environment Protection Act, (1986).

requirements became known, financial adjustments were made without any regard to the ultimate cost-benefit ratio.

The costs were far in excess of what was projected, even after adjusting for inflation. Additionally, the size of the displacement ought to have been calculated well ahead of time so that the governments concerned would have been able to assess whether land for the oustees was available. Today, it is evident that there is insufficient land to settle all the SSP oustees. Yet no estimate has been made of the displacement that the other major dam projects will cause or how rehabilitation and resettlement will take place there.

The Morse report makes some significant points in its conclusion that are valid for all such major development and infrastructure projects, especially in a poor country like India. "Failure to consider the human rights of the displaced and failure to consider environmental impacts occur in the development of mega projects in both developed and developing countries."

B. Mining Projects

A second major source of environmental degradation is intensive mining. A critical look at the state of some of the mines in India portrays a none-too-encouraging picture as far as precautionary and remedial measures for environmental degradation are concerned. The indiscriminate quarrying and mining by both leaseholders and public sector miners in different hill regions of the country is nothing less than the "rape of Mother Earth." India's mining industry has witnessed a phenomenal growth since independence. Most mineral reserves are within about 40 contiguous districts of central and eastern India. These districts also happen to be the country's tribal belt and its major forest area. Minerals are, by their nature, a nonrenewable resource. Thus, the damage done to these resources has to be viewed in the context of indigenous people depending upon natural capital.

The khazan lands of Goa (about 18,000 hectares), east of the alignment, must not be dismissed as a peripheral issue. The irreversible damage through surface iron ore mining cannot be overestimated. In Goa, under the Portuguese, 70 percent of mining concessions were given in the forest areas. Slopes and hillsides have been cut for mining as well as for new settlements, resulting in landslides, gullying, and soil erosion. The mining process produces about twenty-six million tons of mining rejects per annum. These rejects damage forests and, during monsoons, the leakage affects agriculture fields, khazan lands, rivers and streams. Barges transporting iron ore pollute khazan lands with sulphuric acid that damages both agriculture and pisciculture.

According to the 1981 Indian Bureau of Mines study of the 37 mines that contribute 80 percent of the total mineral production of Goa, it was found that 252 hectares of agricultural land close to the reject dumps had been damaged;

forests had been damaged; pollution of rivers, streams, and natural springs was taking place; groundwater was being depleted, depriving villagers of well water; silting of waterways was rampant; and flooding of adjacent fields while pumping out water for mining was visible. The committee therefore recommended strongly that mining concessions in forest areas be reconsidered and that a Mining Monitoring Board be set up to monitor the ecological damage from mining and disposal of mining rejects, so that the environment and the indigenous people of Goa would not be affected adversely.

Another example of environmental disregard can be found in the Doon valley, which is lavishly endowed by nature and surrounded by the Himalayan Shivalik ranges and the Ganga and Yamuna rivers. This valley in Uttar Pradesh has been ruthlessly exploited for its mineral wealth, particularly the large deposits of national limestone. Because it has high purity and low silica content, the limestone of this area is considered unique, which is also why its exploitation is proportionately greater. Thousands and thousands of hectares of the valley have been given on lease.

It is recommended that hilly areas have 60 percent tree cover; today this region has a tree cover of only 12 percent. As a result, numerous streams have dried up and the soil's water retention has been lowered considerably. The lives of thousands of indigenous people from the surrounding villages have been threatened because of debris that turns the rich agricultural land into wasteland. Exact figures on this are, unfortunately, not available, but the plight of the thousands of villagers in and around the mining areas is even stronger evidence than mere statistics. For instance, the villagers of Khairi Man Singh in the Doon valley have had to abandon their village because of the large-scale loss of agricultural land. Canals have been totally clogged, which affects irrigation and even causes drinking water shortage. In addition, floods create great havoc in the area every year.[9]

The khazan land of Goa and the Doon valley of Uttar Pradesh are but the tip of the iceberg in which pure private interest masquerading as national development is destroying natural resources and those who depend on them.

C. Industrial and Commercial Projects

Most of the big industries in India have located in the tribal predominated belts. That is why tribal people constitute an important segment of the workforce of those industrial settings. As a consequence, those industries—by introducing a variety of new technologies into different tribal regions—have brought about many far-reaching changes in the socioeconomic life of Indian tribal peoples.

---

[9] *See* P. Viegas and G. Menon, The Impact of Environmental Degradation on People (1989).

A typical example is the Rourkela Steel Plant (RSP) in the state of Orissa. The installation of RSP was a very remarkable event in the history of the tribal people of Northern Orissa. The construction of RSP was started in 1956 with the collaboration of a private German firm, Krupp Demag, and partial financial aid provided by the West German government.

During construction, tribal people of 32 villages were displaced and resettled in a few colonies within the vicinity occupied by the plant. Sometime toward the middle of 1955, the Ganjus, or headmen, of those affected villages convened a meeting at Mohania Began, where it was resolved that the natives did not want the steel plant in their neighborhood. It was further resolved that if the government felt that there was no alternative to the establishment of the plant on the site already selected, the displaced cultivators should be given an equal amount of agricultural land as compensation at a suitable place of their liking. A small committee was also set up to press the government to accept these demands. With the passage of time, an organization called ''Steel Plant Site People's Federation'' came into existence.

Gradually, opposition to the plant was no longer confined to holding meetings and sending deputations. In several villages, it took the form of ''noncooperation.'' The RSP found it difficult to recruit local labor, especially in those villages where agricultural lands were under notice of acquisition. The movement continued, demanding adequate compensation for the victims.

After a protracted negotiation, in 1955 the government of Orissa issued a press notice, accepting the full responsibility for rehabilitation of the displaced persons. Under this scheme, the government laid down three settlement colonies,[10] and leased out housing plots, 18.29 x 12.29 meters (60 x 40 ft.), to each displaced family on a long-term basis. The term of payment was Rs.5 per year, and the allottee was constrained from selling or mortgaging the plot or the building construction on it. Besides those settlements, fifteen reclamation areas were opened within a radius of 100 kms. from Rourkela. In those reclamation areas, the displaced tribal people were to reclaim land for which a subsidy of Rs.100/per acre was proposed. The compensation that the tribal people received from the government was very nominal and far from satisfactory.

Such an alternative arrangement of resettlement led to family disorganization. As expected, the older generation tended to settle in the reclamation centers, whereas the younger generation, in large number, stayed in resettled colonies. This did not lead to harmonious interpersonal relationships. Thus, the process of rehabilitation brought a division within the tribal family.

At the time of rehabilitation, an assurance was given to the displaced tribal people that they would receive preference for all jobs for which they were

---

[10] These settlements were known as Jalda (5 kms. south of steel plant site), Jhirpani (7 kms. north of steel plant), and Bondamunda (6 kms. east of steel plant).

qualified. It was obvious that, among the displaced persons, there was hardly anyone who would be able to qualify for the higher supervisory and administrative posts. But there were some opportunities for those who were semiskilled, and considerable employment available for unskilled laborers.

Under this policy, about 800 displaced persons were employed as unskilled and semiskilled laborers by the RSP. Many displaced persons, however, preferred to work under private contractors, as the latter paid them better wages. The employment picture began to deteriorate with the completion of many construction projects in 1960–61. The situation further deteriorated with the adoption of a new policy by the RSP on February 25, 1961.

The new policy discontinued the preferential treatment extended to displaced persons. While highest priority was given to displaced persons who were already in the RSP, the next priority was given to other persons who had put in at least one year of approved services under the RSP. The other displaced persons were given a lower priority. The RSP rationalized that they had already accommodated the bulk of the displaced persons of working age at the time of displacement and could not undertake the obligation to future generations. In other words, those who were minors at the time of displacement were denied the preference to accommodate nondisplaced persons who had already put in at least one year's work in RSP.

This logic did not satisfy the displaced tribal population. In April 1961, a large number of tribal people squatted in front of the office of the Sub-Divisional Officer and the residence of the Deputy General Manager of the RSP and demanded to be immediately employed in the plant. As these squatters refused to leave, and there was apprehension of trouble, the police arrested a number of them, including their leaders. The agitation went on for quite some time but, because of lack of coordination, it did not make much of an impact.

In fact, in September 1961, 450 displaced workers, the bulk of whom were females, were declared "surplus" by the RSP and retrenched. The explanation given by the RSP for such retrenchment was that the scope of employment for females is extremely limited. However, the situation improved slightly in 1962 with the expansion work of the RSP. Consequently, some displaced persons were reemployed and the tension ceased to a great degree. Indigenous people entered into the factory in order to get jobs and to raise their standard of living. In achieving these two goals, they are undergoing accelerated but painful changes. These changes promise to be exceedingly complex, requiring difficult internal adjustments and institutional adaptations.

The large-scale industrialization at Rourkela has been geared to the general economic development of the country, without much conscious effort to benefit the local indigenous communities. This has led to social disruption among these communities. The advent of an exotic external system has weakened and destabilized the indigenous social fabric. The processes of industrialization have mutilated the tribal worker of the RSP into a fragment of a man, degraded him to the level of an appendage of a machine. It has distorted the conditions under which he works, and subjected him during the labor-process to a despotism the more hateful for its meanness. It has further converted his life into working time.[11]

D. Shrimp-Farming Project

Big businesses have the resources and the technical managerial skills for executing large-scale projects that can create an increase in the export of fish and fish products. But what will be the impact on traditional fisherfolk who have depended on inland fisheries for several generations? The export-oriented growth of the marine fishery has already led to significant erosion of their livelihood, provoking several protest movements of traditional fisherfolk in the coastal areas. Undoubtedly, there will be a repetition of this disturbing trend in the inland fishery.

This is where the issues raised in the Chilka Lake controversy became relevant. Chilka is India's largest brackish (mixture of fresh and seawater) lake, covering 900 to 1,100 sq. kms. in the Puri and Ganjam districts of Orissa. Apart from being a spot of scenic beauty on the Orissa tourist map, this lake is home to many species of fish (estimated at well over 100) and birds (around 153, including the migratory ones that are a major attraction of this lake and its environs). Among the factors that created the lake was the formation of sandy ridges, which tend to close its access to the sea. The 35 km. long Magarmukh channel, the lake's main link to the sea, is heavily silted and a mere 100 meters wide in some sections.

At the center of the present controversy is the fact that the lake has long been the source of livelihood for an estimated 1,000 fishermen. Initially, as prawn exporting became lucrative, several rural families, who were not traditional fisherfolk, decided to take up fishing. In addition, there were some anti-social elements who also stepped in to try to earn quick money. Thus, even before the advent of big business, the rights of indigenous fisherfolk had been threatened, although on a much smaller scale.

The bigger threat came in 1992 in the form of an Integrated Shrimp Farming Project (ISFP), which acquired 400 hectares of land that included 300 hectares of pond area. A public limited company called Chilka Aquatic Farms Limited (CAF) was formed; the state government held 49 per cent shares, Tata Iron & Steel Co. Ltd. held 20 percent, Tata Oil Mills Co. Ltd. held 18 per cent, and Oil India Private Ltd., held three per cent.[12]

---

[11] *See* S.N. Ratha and D.K. Behera, *supra* note 3.

[12] *See* B. Dogra, *Chilka Lake Under Relentless Attack, in* THE HINDU SURVEY OF THE ENVIRONMENT 103 (Shri N. Ravis, ed., 1993).

Although the project promised nothing but benefits to the indigenous fisherfolk in this area (by way of seedlings, etc.), a different picture emerged after a visit to the villages around the lake. Discussions with the fisherfolk, the villagers, the village representative, and the social activists revealed their apprehensions about the project. As a result, the ''save Chilka movement'' continues to oppose the project despite the several repressive measures taken by the police. The villagers feared that the project would erode their livelihood and ruin their resource base by causing pollution. The indigenous fishing communities have been paying the state government for fishing rights, particularly for prawn, but their land rights have not been recorded properly. Consequently, those with money have been able to exploit the situation by getting the rights transferred in their favor. So far, such questionable transfers have been on a relatively small scale.

The arbitrary leasing of hundreds of acres to the ISFP, without consulting those affected, raised more concerns, especially because this involved a new capital-intensive method of fishing. Moreover, it is widely believed—and news reports were also published to this effect—that other such large-scale leases to big business interests will follow.

The embankment constructed for the ISFP keeps some fishermen away from their fishing areas. To the detriment of others, the land that earlier received seawater is now cut off from the sea, leading to the destruction of fishing grounds. Yet another group faces the prospect of having their grazing land submerged. Altogether, this creates the impression that the livelihood of many indigenous people will be affected adversely. Modernization and the consequent takeover of the fish industry by capitalists have served to increase the exploitation of indigenous people by outsiders to such an extent that the fishermen have become ''virtually slaves of usurious money lenders and greedy middlemen.''[13]

Indigenous people also fear that the high-protein feed and chemicals used in the new technology will soon pollute the lake. Once big businesses recover their investment and make substantial profits, they can conveniently move to greener pastures and the indigenous fisherfolk will be left with a polluted lake and a much lower fish yield.

In addition, purse-seining and trawling (particularly bottom trawling) cause irreversible damage to the spawning ground, leading to a sizable reduction in the annual fish catch. More important, the violation of fishing limits by trawlers and purse-seiners makes it not only uneconomical, but also impossible, for indigenous fisherfolk to carry on their traditional occupation.

Finally, the issue that united fisherfolk and nonfisherfolk was the threat of floods and waterlogging. The project involved construction of a 13 km. long

---

[13] *A Well Rehearsed Clergy Revolt*, The HINDU, June 10, 1984.

embankment, which can disrupt the existing drainage and direct floodwater toward the villages, in addition to inundating the fields.

The experience of Chilka Lake exposes the falsehood of the long-cherished myth that, once big money comes into an area, some benefits are also bound to reach the weaker sections: the trickle-down effect. The grim reality is that the indigenous people may not even remain to absorb the trickle as the entry of big business and other outsiders displaces them from the traditional occupation.

The objections to this project have to be seen in the context of the experience of other countries that have tried to implement large-scale aquaculture projects of this kind. From neighbouring Bangladesh, there are reports of fields being ruined by water-logging and salinity. Peasants have been forced to migrate after big business interests finished exploiting their area. Similarly, reports from Thailand tell of the damage done by pollution caused by the new technology; the experience of some African countries speaks of some big budget projects ending up as financial disasters because they were designed without taking into account the ecology and people of the area. By improving the resource base and helping the indigenous people dependent on it, the shrimp yield can be increased significantly, avoiding the pitfalls of ISFP-type projects. Use of the considerable variety of indigenous skills and traditional Indian techniques can be ecologically sustainable. Their use needs to be encouraged and revived rather than displaced by modern ones.

III. OUTCOMES OF "SO-CALLED DEVELOPMENT"

The contemporary development process and the consequent dispossession problem are of a qualitatively different order, generated by the unequal social-political structure, both at the national and global levels, and the unilateral imposition of the supposedly universal model of development. Present-day development practices have not only wrecked the physical survival of the defenseless indigenous people, but also their very cultural and cognitive survival and social reproduction as collective categories. The nexus between development projects and physical and occupational displacement of individuals conveys a partial truth in order to conceal the unpalatable whole truth of capitalist exploitation and imperialist control.

It may be asserted that although people other than those who are indigenous have also been ousted in the name of development in the ''national interest,'' the acuteness of the gloom that is suffered is disproportionately high among indigenous people. As mentioned earlier, common features shared by most indigenous people are their remoteness and the marginal quality of their territorial resources. In the past, exploitation of such poor regions was found difficult or uneconomical. But the recent rapid technological advancement and unrivaled economic and political strength of world capitalism, and the rising power of neocolonialism, have created favorable conditions for the invasion and extraction of natural resources from the ecologically fragile territories of the indigenous people.

The outrageous technological model of development and the notion of national interest have progressively depleted the survival bases of the indigenous people and their already limited political autonomy. It has also irretrievably mutilated the indigenous people's distinguishing sociocultural-cognitive framework.[14]

A study showed that around 56 percent of the slum dwellers in India's major cities belong to castes and tribal peoples who were forced to leave their villages because of developmental schemes such as the Green Revolution, dams, mines, and industrial infrastructure. These projects have displaced the local inhabitants without proper compensation and rehabilitation.[15]

In the cities, they seek to solve problem of indigenous peoples' accommodation and other facilities by erecting settlements that are disdainfully referred to by the upper classes as "slums," and regarded as an eyesore.[16] There, displaced tribal people lead a life of perpetual discomfort, characterized by almost subhuman living conditions. Hardly any public civil services are available in these squatter settlements. Sanitary and hygienic conditions are extremely unsatisfactory.

By and large, the response of the city planners to slums has been either apathetic or authoritarian. The apathy is evidenced by the fact that although the slum problem has coexisted with rapid industrialization for the last three decades or more, not much has been done in terms of its solution. Still today, the majority of slum dwellers remain uncovered by slum improvement schemes. The authoritarian response is expressed through legislation such as the much-debated Delhi "Anti-Encroachment Bills" passed by the communities of Lok Sabha and Rajya Sabha in May 1984.

Given the fact that the slum dwellers are the city's poorest residents, these bills seem to be a direct attack on them. Without the bargaining power or the capacity to withstand such affronts—which their richer counterparts may possess—these slum dwellers seem to bear the consequences of these laws. In other words, the indigenous poor are pushed out of the rural areas by the "so-called developmental" pattern. But the urban decision makers try to protect the cities from the displaced poor, rather than deal with the causes that have led to their migration.

---

[14] *See* J. Pathy, *Development Syndrome and Dispossession of the Defenseless* 4, paper presented in the National Seminar on Displacement and Rehabilitation of Project Affected People (1993).

[15] *See* A. De Souza, *Slums and Squatter Settlements in Metropolitan Cities, in* URBAN PROBLEMS AND POLICY PERSPECTIVES 183 (G. Bhargava ed., 1981).

[16] *See id.*

In the past few decades, the overwhelming desire of industry and commerce to squeeze out profits from the natural resources, and their consequent commercialization, has led to the loss of all interest in preserving the ecological equilibrium. In addition to the increasing demand for raw materials for industrial and commercial purposes, there is also pressure to use the forest to meet the revenue requirements of the country. The state perceives forests almost exclusively as a source of revenue, without concern for regeneration. Thus, there has been massive deforestation by the reckless extraction of forest resources by national and international industrial and commercial concerns in collusion with the obliging techno-bureaucratic apparatus of the state.[17] This deprives indigenous people from the forest regions of the life system on which they have depended for centuries. When regeneration of forests is attempted, it is more often than not in the shape of the monoculture of commercial species from which the indigenous people get little or no benefit. Therefore, deforestation resulting from the combination of industrial, commercial, and revenue interests has had adverse consequences on the ecology and, more important, on the forest dwellers. It has destroyed the source of their fuel, food, fodder, and their cultural religious identity. As a result, they have been trapped in the vicious circle of impoverishment, indebtedness, land alienation, and bondage.

The transfer of protected forests to the reserve category implies a reduction in the availability of forest products for the forest dwellers, particularly tribal people, whose dependence on forests is considerable. Each tribe inhabiting a particular geographical area observed a cultural practice—known to ethnography as totemism—to safeguard the flora and fauna of its immediate environment.[18] Now the traditional totemism is in a skeletal form; it is no longer a device to protect the environment. The symbiotic relationship (constructive dependence) between the forest and forest dwellers has now been transformed into a destructive dependence on the forest.[19] Compared to the traditional culture that protected forests from overexploitation, the new culture is one that views forests solely as a source of income. Tribal people are slowly losing interest in preserving forests for the future. This has happened over the last four decades because of the ''so-called development'' in which forests have been treated purely as raw material or as a source of revenue. This industry-revenue orientation has resulted in the clear-cutting of vast forest areas and in deforestation. The forest dwellers have thus been forced into indebtedness and have no choice but to destroy forests for survival as headloaders or wage earners under forest contractors.

In their desperate attempt to survive today, indigenous people are required to forsake their tomorrow and overuse their environment. A classic example of

---

[17] *See* D.K. Behera, *Impact of Deforestation on the Life of the Plain-Bhuiyans (A Case Study of Two Villages of North Orissa)*, 4 J. HUM. ECOLOGY 256 (1993).

[18] *See* S.N. Ratha and D.K. Bekera, *Rethinking Totemism: Understanding Man-Nature Relationship*, 70 MAN IN INDIA 245 (1990).

[19] *See* W. Fernandes et al., *supra* note 4, at 149.

this phenomenon can be found in impoverished tribal areas where millions of households are forced to cut forest every day and sell wood to get, at best, half-a-meal a day. All this does not come cheaply in terms of personal costs. Tribal women wake up before dawn, walk miles to the ever-dwindling forests to cut and bundle wood, and then carry their heavy load tens of kilometers to nearby towns. After all that effort, what they get is a mere pittance. Thus, the forest dwellers are forced to overstrain the meager resources that are left in their control, and are then portrayed as ecological culprits.

A major point that needs to be highlighted in the context of development is the inequitable sharing of developed resources, amenities, services, infrastructure, and employment potential, which came into being because of implementation of the projects. The indigenous people who are being displaced are not necessarily those who have been targeted to benefit under the new project. Invariably, their part of the bargain is only to lose, to become victims in the process of development of, for, and by others. They lose two ways: once, when they are displaced from their original land and environment and, again, when they are denied the benefits flowing from their sacrifice.

The capital-intensive development projects fail to recruit indigenous people for pretextual reasons such as lack of skill, alleged irregularity, lethargy, and the like. Meanwhile, the indigenous people are forced to live in juxtaposition with alien capitalist relations and cultures with traumatic results. They are pushed into the ever-expanding low-paid, insecure, transient, and destitute labor market. That poverty, malnutrition, mortality, morbidity, illiteracy, unemployment, debt bondage, and serfdom are markedly higher among them is thus not surprising. This is nothing short of ethnocide. At stake is their economic and cultural survival.

Although publicized as serving the common interest of the Indian people, these monstrosities (the "so-called development" projects) benefit only a small affluent elite, and multinational funding agencies and other obsequious stooges of world capitalism. Despite crucial differences, indigenous peoples across the country face more or less similar problems: the recent recolonization of their territories, general economic subjugation, and sociocultural stigmatization. Their customary holistic and anticipatory conception of nature, generic and corporate character of land, community-oriented values and collective identities, self-management systems, linguistic framework, and consensual decision making process are unrecognized and castigated, thereby resulting in silent and subtle forms of ethnocide. The cultural hegemony of the dominant global and national society prevents the perpetuation of their collective existence—an indication of irreversible ethnocide.[20]

---

[20] *See* Pathy, *supra* note 41, at 14.

IV. OBSERVATIONS

Why do the indigenous people protest against the ''so-called development''? Why are such social protests gaining ground? The interplay between ideologies of domination and subordination are crucial to the understanding of such social protests. This struggle is not just an effort to stop a few dams, industries, or mines, or to prevent deforestation. It is fundamentally a struggle for recovering the access and control over productive natural resources by the indigenous people. Thus, the indigenous people's fight to reclaim their rights will be a long one.

This brings us back to the central issue of our discussion. What is sustainable development? It is argued that development can have meaning only within the framework of the people. To the extent that this is lacking, ''development'' is regressive and even dehumanizing. It is because of the lack of this dimension in its truest form that most Indian development schemes have turned out to be fragmentary and, at times, even cross-purposive. In contrast, true development believes in a moral economy, which provides for the needs of the indigenous people and ecologically sound programs. Second, true development is for the people, of the people, and by the people. In this case, ''people'' does not mean the microscopic minority who are rich and powerful, who own or control or manipulate the means of production, those members of the ''upper class'' who indulge in conspicuous consumption and vulgar displays of possessions. Rather, ''people'' must mean that vast majority of indigenous people who are socially oppressed, economically exploited, and culturally suppressed. Third, any genuine developmental program should address itself to the specifics of the situation: to the needs of the indigenous people and their communities. The local communities should have a fundamental and inalienable right of access to their environment and natural resources. Therefore, a developmental program cannot succeed unless it enlarges its ambit and becomes a ''people's program.'' The participation of indigenous people at all levels can be the only realistic approach to any substantial development in India. Finally, genuine development should mean the removal of the dehumanizing processes that are the consequences of the ''so-called development.''

The survival and sustainable development of the indigenous people depend on a system of self-development that is based upon their own creative force, corporate productive resources, and cognitive structures where the dynamics are defined by the concerned people themselves. Of course, such a holistic ecologically sustainable and culturally specific model of development will be against the current top-down technocratic and neocolonial model of development. The attempts of the representatives of the ''so-called development'' to silence the voice of dissent and to evict the indigenous people from their ancestral homes and habitat should be condemned. Honest adherence to democratic norms and full regard for the human rights of the indigenous people is essential. So far as the issue of use of natural resources is concerned, no indigenous community, as a rule, should be deprived of its right over the resources on which it may depend for its living without: 1) prior willing consent of the community; and 2) advance provision to the community of an acceptable, hounorable alternative means of livelihood.

Our analysis reveals that there are linkages between the "so-called development" activities leading to the exploitation of natural resources, and the dominant social, economic, and political forces that are operative within the larger framework of inequality and social injustice. Those human beings who have the power and the means to exploit nature are often motivated by greed. They deprive others of benefits and inflict on them the consequences of exploitation, which causes inequality and injustice in society. It is in this context that one can truly understand the human rights of indigenous people.

CHAPTER 8

THE HUMAN RIGHTS OF INDIGENOUS PEOPLES IN PAPUA NEW GUINEA

Alice de Jonge

I.   INTRODUCTION

A.   The Problem of Human Rights in a Pacific Context

Until very recently, international human rights thinking has largely been dominated by Western and First World values and traditions. In human rights discourse, the "world community has tended to ignore the Pacific region with its small nations spread across a vast ocean."[1] Because they struggle with more important and immediate concerns and find much in international rights discourse that lacks relevance, if not meaning, in a non-Western cultural and economic context, Pacific States have not become parties to international rights covenants. With some notable exceptions, Pacific States did not even have any profile in the extended deliberations on the draft United Nations Declaration on the Rights of Indigenous Peoples,[2] or in the preparation of the Draft Pacific Charter.[3] Only three nongovernmental organizations (NGOs) from the Pacific states were represented during the formulation of the recent Bangkok NGO Declaration on Human Rights.[4] It seems hard to deny the potential relevance

---

[1] A.H. Angelo, *Lo Bilong Yumi Yet*, 22 VICTORIA U. OF WELLINGTON L. REV./ MONOGRAPH 433, 441 (1992) (*citing* explanatory memoranda to the recently drafted Pacific Charter of Human Rights).

[2] U.N. Doc. E/cN.4/1995/2 Annex (1995). For an overview of U.N. action regarding the rights of indigenous peoples, *see* Chapter 1, J. Burger, *Indigenous Peoples and the United Nations*, in this volume.

[3] *Supra* note 1. Angelo does not indicate which Pacific States provide the exceptions to this general trend of nonparticipation.

[4] Represented at the Asia-Pacific NGO Conference on Human Rights were the Bougainville Independence (represented by Mr. Moses Havini); the Bougainville Support Group (represented by Ms. Rosemarie Gillespie) and the National Coucil of Maubere Resistance (represented by Mr. Jose Ramos Horta): *See List of Participants* 263 at 280 in OUR VOICE: BANGKOK NGO DECLARATION ON HUMAN RIGHTS; REPORTS OF THE ASIA PACIFIC NGO CONFERENCE ON HUMAN RIGHTS AND NGOS STATEMENTS TO THE ASIA RE-GIONAL MEETING, Asia Cultural Forum on Development (ACFOD) on behalf of the Organizing Committee and Coordinating Committee for Follow-Up Asia Pacific Conference on Human Rights (1993), List of Participants.

and importance of these endeavors to the Pacific area, but it is quite clear that they are not regarded as matters of high priority by the Pacific States, or by major Pacific NGOs themselves.

Human rights thinking raises a number of problems for Pacific nations. It is not part of the local landscape and is, like much else of the current political environment, seen as imposed from outside. In the post-independence era, any treaty obligation, as an undertaking to the international community, may simply be seen as a new form of external tie, when States would rather be left alone. Particularly so when they perceive that attitudes to human rights are very often dictated by political self-interest. Many Pacific States also feel substantial pressure from external economic dominance or dependence and may wish at least to retain control in the rights area. The substantial cost burdens associated with human rights undertakings are an added disincentive.

B. The Concept of Indigenous Rights in Papua New Guinea

The concept of rights for indigenous peoples poses a particular problem in the context of Papua New Guinea (PNG). Most references to indigenous rights in international and regional conventions have been drafted with the needs of indigenous *minority groups* in mind. In PNG, however, no such groups can readily be identified. Rather, what has now emerged in post-colonial PNG is a population of approximately 4.3 million (as of late 1995) people, mainly of Melanesian descent whose earliest ancestors came to the island nation more than 50,000 years ago.[5] Small expatriate communities, mostly from Australia and New Zealand but also including Chinese, Filipinos, and Indians, tend to be concentrated in the urban centers (Port Moresby, Lae, etc.). Otherwise most of the population (around 85%) is scattered throughout the rural areas with the highest concentrations (outside the National Capital District) in the Highlands regions.[6] Indigenous Melanesian and other ethnic groups making up the bulk of the population speak a total of over 750 different languages, found within over 800 identifiable community groupings.[7] English, *Hiri Motu*, and *Tok Pisin* (New Guinea Pidgin) are the three official languages.

---

[5] TONY WHEELER AND JON MURRAY, PAPUA NEW GUINEA: A TRAVEL SURVIVAL KIT (5th ed. 1993), 11 and 14. It is believed that humans reached PNG more than 50,000 years ago by island-hopping across the Indonesian archipelago from Asia. The earliest settlers were hunters and gatherers, with agriculture and animal husbandry only being gradually introduced to northern coastal areas as recently as 4,500 years ago. Early societies were everywhere small, kin-based and locally autonomous, sharing broad cultural and linguistic similarities. At the same time, however, there were, and always have been, numerous local variations, and rarely were the many (nearly 1,000) different local languages mutually intelligible. *Ibid.* and *see* Ron Crocombe and Robin Hide, *New Guinea: Unity in Diversity* in LAND TENURE IN THE PACIFIC 324 (Ron Crocombe ed.(3rd ed., 1987).

[6] *Id.*

[7] *Id.*

The recognition of indigenous rights in PNG thus requires that the country itself, at both the national and the local level, should be run according to the customary principles recognized by the various indigenous groupings. Indeed, the nation's 1975 Constitution expressly recognizes this fact.[8] At the national level, the National Goals and Directive Principles (NGDPs) provide that the future development of the country should be achieved "primarily through the use of Papua New Guinean forms of social and political organization" (Fifth National Goal).[9] The Fifth National Goal further recognizes that to achieve this will require:

> a fundamental re-orientation of our attitudes and the institutions of government, commerce, education and religion towards Papua New Guinea forms of participation, consultation, and consensus, and a continuous renewal of the responsiveness of these institutions to the need and attitudes of the People; and

> recognition that the cultural, commercial and ethnic diversity of our people is a positive strength, . . . for . . . respect for, and appreciation of, traditional ways of life . . . as well as for a willingness to apply these ways dynamically and creatively for the tasks of development; and

> traditional villages and communities to remain as viable units of Papua New Guinean society and for active steps to be taken to improve their cultural, social, economic and ethical quality.

C. Recognition of Customary Laws and Practices

One of the most important ways in which these three Directives are carried out in PNG is through the incorporation of customary laws and practices as part of the national legal system. This is done in section 9 of the PNG Constitution, which provides that:

> The laws of Papua New Guinea consist of—this Constitution; and the Organic Laws; and the Acts of the Parliament, and Emergency Regulations; and laws made under or adopted by or under this Constitution or any of those laws, including subordinate legislative enactments made under this Constitution or any of those laws; and the underlying law, and none other.[10]

---

[8] See *Preamble,* CONSTITUTION OF THE INDEPENDENT STATE OF PAPUA NEW GUINEA, Revised Laws of Papua New Guinea Ch. No. 1. The Papua New Guinea Statute Law is now contained in a Revised Edition. This revision was made in 1975. "Ch. No." indicates the legislation chapter number in the Revised Edition.

[9] Fifth National Goal, *National Goals and Directive Principles,* CONSTITUTION OF THE INDEPENDENT STATE OF PAPUA NEW GUINEA, Revised Laws of Papua New Guinea Ch. No. 1.

[10] *Id.*

Schedule 2 of the Constitution provides that the underlying law consists of (a) custom and (b) the principles and rules of English common law and equity as they existed immediately before independence. In the case of inconsistency between these two sources of underlying law, custom is to prevail. However, Schedule 2.1(1) also provides that "custom is adopted and shall be applied and enforced, as part of the underlying law" only to the extent that it is not inconsistent with a Constitutional law or a statute, "or repugnant to the general principles of humanity." Schedule 2.1 also gives the national Parliament power to determine the procedural and substantive mechanisms by which customary law can be pleaded, proved, recognized, applied, and enforced, as well as power to provide for the resolution of conflicts of custom. In the case of conflict between statutory rules and customary rules of procedure, statutory law would, of course, prevail.

The Constitution thus establishes a hierarchy of laws, with the underlying law, and custom as part of it, at the very lowest level. In doing so, the Constitution sets up a tension between introduced Western notions of "justice" and "rights," with its liberal beliefs in individual freedom and autonomy on the one hand, and customary laws, beliefs, and practices—largely based on a belief in *social* (as opposed to individual) justice and the importance of the group—on the other. The rest of this essay explores the way in which the conflicts between these two culturally different approaches to the concept of "rights" has so far become apparent in two important areas: in the creation of a Western-style registration system for customary land ownership, and in the criminal law jurisdiction of the village courts, which are responsible for the resolution of local disputes in accordance with customary laws and practices.

II. RESOLVING CONFLICTS BETWEEN WESTERN LAW AND CUSTOM IN LAND REFORM

A. Introduction

At the national level, possibly the most important result of the legal system's recognition of indigenous rights and customary laws has been the fact that approximately 97 percent of the land in the country remains under customary land ownership.[11] As Professor R.W. James has noted, this is at least partly the result of a historical colonial legacy:

> The land policy adopted by the Colonial powers was one of paternalism. This policy was reflected in a variety of legislation which prohibited direct dealings between traditional landowners and expatriates, and protected the former from expropriation of their lands by the state so that they would have no land shortage . . . that policy remained the

---

[11] *National Goals and Directive Principles*, Constitution of the Independent State of Papua New Guinea, Revised Laws of Papua New Guinea Ch. No. 1; Schedule 2.3.

single most important dominant one and its success is reflected in the fact that alienated land still represents less than 3 percent of the total land area of the country.[12]

Both before and even more so after independence, however, this situation has been complicated by the other major determinant of land law policy formation in PNG—the government's acute awareness of the need to make customary land holdings compatible with the demands of foreign investment and economic development in a modern era of free-flowing capital. A number of factors make this particularly important in the case of PNG, most notably the economy's almost total dependence upon revenues from mining and agriculture,[13] but also the country's acute lack of skilled labor and reliable infrastructure, which only serves to increase the nation's dependence upon foreign capital and know-how.

Proposals for land law reform in PNG have been dominated by the tension that has always existed between these two sides of the policy debate, and an element of dualism has always been present. By the 1970s, proposals for land reform were being expressed by the options of "Westernization" and "indigenization."[14] The latter option emphasized collectivist processes, and inspired the Land Groups Incorporation Act 1974.[15] In the case of freehold land, the Land (Ownership of Freehold) Act[16] now provides that no foreign investor or noncitizen is allowed to own freehold land.

The Land Groups Incorporation Act facilitates the incorporation of traditional groups for purposes of registering their group titles. So far, however, few landowning groups have applied for such incorporation. Moreover, the national legislation required to implement registration of corporate landholdings has so

---

[12] Professor R.W. James, *Land Mobilisation Programme in Papua New Guinea*, 18 MELANESIAN L.J. 38, 39 (1990).

[13] The minerals and petroleum sector dominates the economy in terms of contribution to GDP, exports, and government revenue. In 1994, mineral exports comprised sixty-seven percent of total merchandise exports; by 1996, this figure had risen to 71.5% of total merchandise exports. Agriculture, the other important sector in the economy, supports—directly or indirectly—about eighty-five percent of the population. The agriculture, forestry, and fisheries sector represented an estimated thirty percent of the GDP in 1996, and is projected to contribute the same in 1997. Department of Foreign Affairs and Trade, Commonwealth of Australia, COUNTRY ECONOMIC BRIEF: PNG: August 1995, at 16 and COUNTRY ECONOMIC BRIEF: PNG: March 1997, at 18, 21.

[14] *See* James, *supra* note 12, at 39–40.

[15] Land Groups Incorporation Act (Revised Laws of Papua New Guinea Ch. No. 147 (1974). The Business Groups Incorporation Act of 1974 was also passed at this time, and enables customary groups to incorporate as business entities for the purpose of undertaking business activities. Business Groups Incorporation Act (Revised laws of Papua New Guinea Ch. No. 144) (1974).

[16] Land (Ownership of Freehold) Act (Revised Laws of Papua New Guinea Ch. No. 359).

far taken the government over twenty years to draft,[17] and is unlikely to be put into effect soon, having proven too controversial to implement without nation-wide protest.[18]

Increasing pressure for improved access to land and finance for develop-ment, however, has resulted in a proliferation of piecemeal legislation and the recognition of fictitious arrangements to achieve land mobilization. The most important legal mechanisms relied upon in the absence of any provision for general registration of customary land are Land Tenure Conversion,[19] Lease-Lease-back,[20] and State Leases.

In 1983, the Task Force on Customary Land Issues recommended a system of "sporadic" registration,[21] and since then both national and provincial govern-ments have taken steps to encourage this. The East Sepik Province has passed two acts to facilitate voluntary registration and encourage landowning groups to collaborate with foreign investors in the development of their land.[22]

Under the current Land Act, interests in customary land cannot be trans-ferred otherwise than in accordance with custom.[23] The only exception relates to transactions with the State.[24] Hence, before a foreign investor can obtain any

---

[17] See James, *supra* note 12, at 39–40.

[18] See Part D, below.

[19] The Land (Ownership of Freeholds) Act (Revised Laws Ch. No. 359) creates a machinery for the voluntary surrender of freehold and the substitution of a government lease for 99 years in its place. See Land (Ownership of Freeholds) Act. Because leasehold interests can be transferred to foreigners, this enables the State to grant the land to a foreign company for development, or to utilize the land as security for raising foreign capital.

[20] Section 15A of the Land Act (Revised Laws of Papua New Guinea, Ch. No. 185) provides that where the owners of customary land wish to develop their land for special agricultural or other business projects, and to use the land as security for any loan or credit obtained for the purpose, the Minister may lease the land from the owners and hold it for such period as is considered sufficient for the purpose of the business, and he may sublease it to the customary owners. *See* Land Act (Revised Laws of Papua New Guinea C. No. 185). § 15A.

[21] *See* James, *supra* note 12, at 40.

[22] The East Sepik Acts, drafted by Dr. Fingleton, are the Land Law (1987) and the Customary Land Registration Act (1987). Discussed in James, supra note 12, at 40–41 and in ROBERT D. COOTER, ISSUES IN CUSTOMARY LAND LAW (Institute of National Affairs Discussion Paper No. 39; Port Moresby 1989), 8 and 54.

[23] *See* Land Act (Revised Laws of Papua New Guinea, Ch. No. 185). Under section 73 of this Act, indigenous owners have no power to sell, lease, or dispose of customary land otherwise than to other indigenous persons in accordance with custom.

[24] This exception is found in chapter 185, section 15 of the Land Act, which provides that if customary owners are willing to dispose of their land otherwise than in accordance with custom, the Minister may purchase or lease it on such terms as are agreed. Before

interest in such land, the State must first lease or purchase the land from customary landowners. The urgent need for foreign capital to finance infrastructure, mining and other projects provides an obvious incentive for the State to make use of its right to acquire customary land. In the mining, and petroleum sector particularly, the practice in the past has been for the government to purchase customary land which is then leased to developers. Leasehold land is usually leased to the developer company for a ninety-nine-year term, under a specific-purpose lease agreement. Unlike freehold land which cannot be transferred to noncitizens, leasehold interests in land may be freely dealt with. Both leasehold and freehold land must be registered with the Registrar of Titles.

B. The World Bank and the Government's Land Mobilization Program

The World Bank and other donors have insisted that economic development, if not economic survival, requires major reforms in land administration.[25] Within PNG, as the commodity notion of land has increased during the 1980s and 1990s, restrictions and prohibitions on land alienation have been attacked as "transactional costs" that are inefficient, unnecessary, and expensive, and simply serve to hinder development. With little choice but to agree, and on the basis of World Bank and Australian government involvement, the government introduced the Land Mobilization Program (LMP) in the late 1980s.[26] Supported by a tripartite funding arrangement, the LMP has so far focused on the strengthening of the Department of Lands and Physical Planning (DLPP),[27] the installation of a new computerized Papua New Guinea Land and Geographical Information System (PNGLAGIS),[28] and the development of controversial draft legislation aimed at streamlining administrative procedures for customary and alienated land.[29]

According to the World Bank, which supports the LMP, the program is necessary "to ensure continued control of traditional land by traditional landowners while improving their ability to generate income."[30] The Bank also

---

doing so, however, the Minister must be satisfied that the land is not required or likely to be required by the owners or by persons who will or may inherit the land under custom.

[25] Rowan Callick, *World Bank backs $466m plan*, AUSTRALIAN FINANCIAL REVIEW, September 12, 1995; Ludger Mond, *Papua New Guinea: The Joke of World Bank/IMF—PNG: questioning "development,"* 10:3 PACIFIC NEWS BULL. 8, 9–10 (March 1995) and Anon., *Papua New Guinea: "the hot issue of land"— what do we mean by "development"?* 10:7 PAC. NEWS BULL. 8–9 (May 19, 1995).

[26] *See* James, *supra* note 12, at 42ff (summarizing and reviewing the Land Mobilization Programme); citing DEPARTMENT OF LANDS AND PHYSICAL PLANNING, LAND MOBILISATION PROGRAMME: PROGRAMME DESCRIPTION (1988).

[27] *Id.* at 42, 44.

[28] *Id.*

[29] *Id.*

[30] *See* Callick, *supra* note 25.

argues that ''land disputes are a major cause of tribal warfare,''[31] and that land reform is needed to address the country's law and order problem.[32] It points to the fact that disputes over land are everywhere rife, and on a number of occasions have led to outbreaks of violence resulting in destruction of crops and houses, injuries, and even death.[33] Local landowners seeking land compensation payouts have occupied and blockaded disputed areas, causing development projects worth millions of kina to be halted or abandoned, and disrupting local schooling, water supply, and transport services.[34] In some cases, magistrates traveling out to disputed land after an adjudication (to oversee the marking out of disputed territory) have been greeted by literally hundreds of warriors from the losing side in full traditional war dress and armed with traditional weapons![35] Crime and civil unrest remain a severe, and expensive, threat to foreign investment interests—as Australian mining giant CRA found when rivalries among local landowners forced it to pull out of the otherwise highly lucrative Mt. Kare Gold Mine.

The World Bank's position has received vigorous support from a number of sources, including senior government politicians and officials, major donors, and *The National* daily newspaper, one of PNG's two major dailies. A recent *National* editorial, for example, claimed that PNG's biggest crisis was ''the lack of control of land and resources by the government of Papua New Guinea.'' All economic ills and political instability in the country,'' said the paper, were caused by landowner dissatisfaction. Landowner compensation claims were described as ''the shackles that are restraining national progress and even strangling the life out of the country.'' The editorial added that the government must soon ''begin a nationwide registration of traditional land, buy out whole chunks of land from those willing to sell or even contemplate compulsory acquisition. It will never have total control otherwise. The nation can never be fully developed until then.''[36]

---

[31] *Id.*

[32] *See* Mond, *supra* note 25.

[33] *See* Michael John Trebilcock, *Customary Land Law Reform in Papua New Guinea: Law Economics and Property Rights in a Traditional Culture,* 9 ADELAIDE L. REV. 191, 192 93 (1983); citing World Bank, PAPUA NEW GUINEA, DEVELOPMENT POLICIES AND PROSPECTS FOR THE 1980s (1981)

[34] A 1982 daily newspaper in PNG reported that outstanding land compensation claims against the government amounted to close to one million kina, and stated that promoting land compensation claims is the ''biggest growth industry in the country.'' Nor has the situation improved since that time, as cited and discussed in Trebilcock, *id.* at 93.

[35] See the incidents cited by Michael Trebilcock in Trebilcock, *id.* at 192–93.

[36] THE PORT MORESBY NATIONAL, April 18, 1995, as cited and discussed in Anon., *supra* note 25.

Groups like the PNG Trade Union Congress and Melanesian Solidarity (*Melsol*) point, however, to the close business and financial links between *The National* and Malaysian timber giant Rimbunan Hijau, a company whose logging operations in PNG have repeatedly been criticized.[37] Such companies benefit directly from government ownership of PNG land—the necessary prerequisite to the grant of a logging or mining lease. The Trade Union Congress and *Melsol* also point to the disastrous effects of land mobilization/registration schemes in other Third World countries, suggesting that such programs "throw indigenous people into poverty and despair once they give away land rights to the State or big corporation."[38]

The poverty and despair referred to here is that which arises from a loss of identity, and of a whole way of life. For no matter how much compensation may be received by landowners who agree to give up their land, what is lost in return for such payment is something that cannot be valued in Western (monetary) terms. Land in PNG, and indeed throughout Melanesia, is something "valued," if at all, in spiritual, social, and cultural terms. Being priceless in economic terms, land has never traditionally been something that could be traded or exchanged. Yet the immense significance and importance of land pervades all aspects of traditional lifestyles. As Burton-Bradley, a long-time resident and researcher in PNG, notes:

> . . . the indigenous person has a psychological attachment to his land transcending the purely economic and legal arrangements of the superimposed alien culture, . . . he may go along with the formal arrangements . . . but in his thinking and at a deeper level his basic attitude to what is his land remains substantially unchanged throughout life, independent of any transactions and exchanges which have taken place. His land is the place where he was born, where he was subjected to primary enculturation, where he has lived the most important aspects of his life, where the values of his cultural-linguistic group have been constantly reinforced, and where, in most instances, he may die. As he grows up he learns that it is the place where his ancestors preceded him, and to which they may return, thus giving the attachment a magico-religious sanction. It is the place where his children and his children's children will follow. At the psychological level it is clearly an extension of the concept of self.[39]

---

[37] *See* Anon., *supra* note 25.

[38] *Supra* note 36.

[39] Burton-Bradley, *The Psychological Dimension, in* Problems of Choice: Land in Papua New Guinea's Future 32 (Peter G. Sack, ed., 1974). *See also* Trebilcock, *supra* note 33, at 201.

The ILO Convention (No. 169) *Concerning Indigenous and Tribal Peoples in Independent Countries*[40] expressly recognizes, in Part II, "the special importance for the cultures and spiritual values of the peoples concerned of their relationship with the lands . . . which they occupy or otherwise use, and in particular the collective aspects of this relationship." Article 15 further recognizes the "right of the peoples concerned . . . to participate in the use, management and conservation of . . . the natural resources pertaining to their lands." Article 16 recognizes the right of indigenous persons not to be removed or relocated away from their traditional lands unless warranted by "exceptional circumstances."

C. Mining, Miners, and Landowners

In the case of PNG, however, the rights embodied in articles 15 and 16 of the ILO Convention have only recently begun to be recognized. It was not until 1988 that the government finally made a number of significant policy changes to involve landowners in decision making and facilitate participation in major development projects. The "development forum" process that was established now has statutory backing under the Mining Act 1992 (No. 195).[41] Essentially, this is a consultation forum where all parties interested in a project (the national government, local government bodies, project developers, and landowners) convene to discuss and to agree on proposed projects. The procedure, as used in the Porgera, Misima, and Kutuba projects, usually results in three sets of agreements. The first are the agreements between the State and the project developers. The second are subsidiary agreements between the State and provincial governments, and the third agreements are made between the State and landowners to outline their mutual rights and obligations to each other. Landowners are usually, for example, required to "cooperate" and "consult," and "not to disrupt the operations of the Project. . . ," while the government in return might undertake to provide certain services to the local community.[42] Such provisions represent a key feature of the government's attempt to use the consultative process to alleviate landowner discontent, and to prevent the kind of (often violent) forms of "self-help" actions that have occurred in the past.

In practice, however, the consultative agreements have not always had the desired effect. Without any mechanism for enforcement, landowners have not

---

[40] International Labor Organization Convention (No. 169) Concerning Indigenous and Tribal Peoples in Independent Countries, adopted during the 76th session of the ILO, 1989, article 13, as extracted *in* BASIC DOCUMENTS ON HUMAN RIGHTS 303–16 (Ian Brownlie, ed., 3rd ed. 1992).

[41] Mining Act (Revised Laws of Papua New Guinea No. 195), replaced by a new Mining Act (1992).

[42] *See* John Nonggorr, *Resolving Conflicts in Customary Law and Western Law in Natural Resource Developments in Papua New Guinea*, 16 UNSW L.J. 433 (1993) at 446–56.

hesitated in resorting to self-help. As Dr. John Nonggorr points out, it is also unrealistic to expect landowners to pay damages for breach of contract where, for example, a blockade stops the operation of a mine causing millions of kina to be lost.[43] Nor do such agreements solve the essential problem and the primary cause of landowner discontent—the often devastating social, economic, and environmental effects of large mining and development operations.

The socially destructive and disruptive nature of mining operations soon becomes obvious upon a visit to any of the country's major mining sites. At Porgera, for example, a modern mining operation in a remote mountainous area in Enga Province, local communities were dislocated, and residents were relocated away from the area to make way for the plant. Seventy-five to 80 percent of the current mine workforce are PNG nationals who have migrated to the mine site, many of whom have wives and children still back in the village. Most, however, are young, single males who find themselves with money and nothing to spend it on. Away from traditional social constraints that operate back home in the village, these men turn to gambling, drinking, fighting, and prostitutes. Social discord, tribal fighting, and general instability have disrupted mining operations, damaged mining equipment and buildings, and generally cost the mining companies involved a considerable amount of time and money.[44] Nor are the Porgera investors the only foreign companies to have suffered such losses.

Slowly it seems, the lessons are being learned. In the agreements establishing the most recent major gold-mining project on Lihir Island, for example, an effort has been made to maintain the viability and stability of local village communities. Thus, in the case of the Putput Community, villages are to be relocated to sites as close as possible to their original positions, and payments will be made to families required to relocate.[45] Lihir Management Company (LMC), the company responsible for managing mining operations on Lihir, has also promised "to assist the development of community infrastructure" including water supply, waste disposal, and electricity services for the relocated villages.[46] Under clause 5 of the Community Agreement, LMC is to establish a Putput Plantsite Community Trust Fund.

Under the Compensation Agreement, LMC must use its best endeavors to avoid disturbing any graves or burial grounds located within areas affected by the establishment of the plant site. Where recent grave sites (less than 20 years old) are to be disturbed, LMC will relocate the grave to a new site, and pay

---

[43] *See id.* at 450.

[44] J. Connell, *"Logic is a capitalist cover-up"*: *Compensation and Crisis in Bougainville, Papua New Guinea, in* RESOURCES, DEVELOPMENT AND POLITICS IN THE PACIFIC ISLANDS 30 (S. Henningham & R.J. May, eds., 1992).

[45] *See* Draft Putput Community Agreement, Lihir Mining Area Landowners Assn (Inc.) and Lihir Management Co. Pty Ltd., cl. 4 (Apr. 13, 1995).

[46] *Id.*, cl. 3.

compensation to relatives of the deceased.[47] The company has undertaken to "assist landowners from the Putput Plant area establish business opportunities which will allow them to participate in the business spin-offs from the Project's construction and operation"[48] and has also been noted for its policy of preferring to employ suitably qualified local Lihirians in mining and related operations where this is feasible.

Compensation for environmental destruction and social disruption has always been a controversial issue, and a flood of compensation claims have been launched by landowners over recent years. Frustrated by this growing flood, the government has recently taken steps to prevent landowners from having access to the courts. Its most recent, and most controversial, move in this direction is the introduction of the Mining (Ok Tedi Restated Eighth Supplemental Agreement) Bill 1995,[49] proposed legislation that effectively renders invalid and illegal any compensation claim or compensation proceedings in any court against Ok Tedi Mining Ltd. or any of its shareholders.[50] This bill has been attacked as a blatant breach of constitutional rights, and the Australian company involved, Broken Hill Proprietary Limited, was found guilty of contempt by a Victorian Supreme Court for its role in drafting the contentious legislation.

D. The Registration of Customary Land

The other highly controversial, and much criticized, move by the government under the auspices of its land mobilization program is the introduction of the Land Registration (Customary Land) (Amendment) Bill 1995.[51] This legislation provides for the determination of rights and interests in customary land, and for registration of ownership of, and dealings in, such lands. The primary aim of the law is to "free up" customary landholdings, and to facilitate leases

---

[47] *See* Compensation Agreement for Land, Crops, Water and Air for the Lihir Gold Project, Lihir Island, Lihir Management Co. Pty Ltd., Lihir Mining Area Landowners Assn (Inc.), Block Executives (For and on Behalf of the Landowners), Catholic Mission, Kavieng Property Trust, and The United Church in PNG and the Solomon Islands, cl. 9 (undated, but Recitals indicate sometime in 1995).

[48] Putput Community Agreement, *supra* note 45, cl. 6.

[49] Mining (Ok Tedi Restated Eighth Supplemental Agreement) Act (1995), introduced into Parliament as a Bill in September-October 1995 amid great controversy and legal action in the Victorian Supreme Court against BHP for its role in preparing the draft legislation. *See* Matthew Stevens, *BHP contempt finding aggravates Ok Tedi woes*, THE AUSTRALIAN, 20 Sept. 1995, 1; Rachel Hawes and Mary Louise O'Callaghan, *BHP in contempt over PNG mine role*, THE AUSTRALIAN, Sept. 10, 1995, 1 and Mary Louise O'Callaghan, Matthew Stevens and Rachel Hawes, *PNG snubs Ok Tedi ruling*, THE AUSTRALIAN, Sept. 20, 1995, 41.

[50] The current shareholders are the Independent state of PNG, BHP Minerals Holdings Limited, and Inmet Mining Corporation, who hold respectively 30, 52, and 18 percent of shareholdings.

[51] Land Registration (Customary Land) (Amendment) Bill (1995).

and joint-ventures between landownders and foreign investors. Under the proposed law, banks will be able to lend money to landowning groups on the security of a lease of the land, and land will also be able to be used as equity for landowner participation in joint ventures. The act effectively eliminates the current prohibition on any form of direct alienation of interests in land by landowners other than to the State, and thus avoids the current need for all leasing and other transactions to go through the State. The hope is that this will provide landowners with a greater degree of direct control over decisions concerning their land, facilitate economic activity among landowners, reduce the number of cases in which land is acquired outright by the State, and reduce the number of compensation claims.

The proposed implemention of land registration has been so controversial—leading to widespread rioting and demonstrations throughout the country—that the government has now been forced to postpone indefinitely any further consideration of the reforms. The fact is that, despite the arguments in favor of land registration reform, serious problems remain. First, given the current lack of experience or training in business and fund management among most villagers, to assume that funds obtained directly or indirectly through the use of registered land will be used for the benefit of the community involved, or even used wisely, is at best overly optimistic and, at worst, dangerously misleading. This becomes even more of a problem when the project financed by the land is one which has only a fixed lifetime, so that benefits cease once the viable life of the project, or the agreeement under which it was established, expires. Unless early steps are taken to provide for the future (such as the setting up of a trust fund), a community may find itself at the end of a project with no money and little more than an empty area of polluted land, or land from which all fertility has been drained.

A second, more fundamental, problem is that the proposed reforms do not affect mining projects—still the most important source of non-aid income for the country. In other words, there is still no *direct* avenue for landowners to participate in the most important area of the nation's economic development. Under the common law system, which PNG has inherited from colonial times, all gold and silver resources are vested in the Crown by prerogative right. State ownership of all other minerals under the surface of the land is also given statutory force by the Mining Act 1992[52] and the Petroleum Act.[53] Thus, only the State has power to grant or alienate the right to extract such resources. The problem here for Papua New Guineans is that:

> . . . the existence of different interests in land such as licences, easements or leases, and the separation of minerals from the surface soil

---

[52] Mining Act (Revised Laws of Papua New Guinea Ch. No. 195), *replaced* by a new Mining Act (1992) in 1992. *See* sec. 2 of the old Mining Act and sec. 5 of the new.

[53] Petroleum Act (Revised Laws of Papua New Guinea Ch. No. 198.); *See* sec. 5.

contradict their ideas of land ownership. They cannot comprehend, let alone accept, why land which has always been theirs and upon which their livelihood and existence depend, can be divided into such fictions. . . .

Very few, if any Papua New Guineans will accept the idea that while they own the surface soil, somebody else owns resources found on, under or above it. Even educated Papua New Guineans including lawyers find this difficult to grasp. For example a Papua New Guinean Attorney-General, a former judge of the National Court, when referring to the question of mineral ownership in Papua New Guinea, after stating the government position that minerals on customary land in the country are owned by the state, said: "As a Minister of State and the Attorney-General, the law is correct, but as a "native" or as a villager, that is not correct, I will never agree with it."[54]

As Nonggorr points out, such differences in understandings about land and ownership only serve to exacerbate distrust between landowners on the one hand, and the State and investors on the other.[55] Nonggoor then suggests, as a solution to this conflict, that all mineral ownership should be vested in landowners—a suggestion with much to recommend it.[56] Not only would such a move be in accordance with the Draft Pacific Charter,[57] which provides, in article 21, that "All peoples shall have the right to dispose of their wealth and natural resources freely," it would also be in line with the terms and the spirit of PNG's national Constitution.[58]

A final, and potentially the most serious, problem with the proposed new land registration law, has to do with its effect on usufructuary and other more

---

[54] Nonggorr, *supra* note 42, at 445–46.

[55] *See id.* at 446.

[56] *See id.* at 446 and 457.

[57] Draft Pacific Charter of Human Rights, as extracted *in Essays and Documents on Human Rights in the Pacific*, 22 VICTORIA U. OF WELLINGTON L. REV./MONOGRAPH 4, Appendix 1: V, at 145–59.

[58] For example, the Fourth NGDP, dealing with "Natural resources and environment" states:

We declare our fourth goal to be for Papua New Guinea's natural resources and environment to be conserved and used for the collective benefit of us all, and be replenished for the benefit of future generations.

WE ACCORDINGLY CALL FOR—
wise use to be made of our natural resources and the environment in and on the land or seabed, under the land, and in the air, in the interests of our development and in trust for future generations;

Constitution of the Independent State of Papua New Guinea (Revised Laws of Papua New Guinea Ch. No. 1), National Goals and Directive Principles, 4th National Goal.

indirect rights in land under the customary system. Under this system, group land rights are generally focused at the level of the subclan or lineage, although common rights to hunting territories, etc., are often shared among a larger group constituting the wider clan or community. The subclan will be either patrilineal or matrilineal, and this in turn determines such things as how decisions on the allocation of land other than by inheritance are made. Usufructuary rights, such as the right to intensive use (e.g., gardening), are usually enjoyed by the household or by individuals.

What is important to note here is the complex nature of the relationship between individual and group rights and obligations in relation to land. For example, a household might customarily recognize an obligation to allow a neighbor or relative in need to share in the cultivation of household land and/or in the produce from such cultivation. A number of neighboring families might customarily share the cultivation of several pieces of land, and recognize an obligation to share, lend, and borrow garden produce among each other as required.

Such rights are not, however, recognized or provided for in the proposed land registration legislation. Rather, the bill provides for a list of names of all those said to belong to the group that ''owns'' the land according to custom to be recorded in the Register.[59] Thus, for example, all adult descendants of the patrilineal line in a traditionally patrilineal subclan would have the right to have their names included on such a list. Their spouses, and those from the community not within the patrilineal line, would not. Nor would they enjoy any right to have a say in the making of decisions concerning the land. Moreover, if a man's name was on the register, but he was not the eldest male descendant of the line, for example, neither his wife's name nor those of their children could be registered. Potentially, his wife and children could be left landless in the event of his death. Even though traditionally his relatives would have recognized an obligation to look after his widow and children, the new law imposes no obligation upon them to do so if in fact they decide not to.[60]

E. Finding a Solution—Is It possible?

Here again the essential problem—different understandings and conceptions of what land ''rights'' really means—can be found. Land, under custom, was never, and can never be, equated with Western conceptions of ''property'' and ''ownership.'' Rather, as the Chief-of-Staff of Uni Tavur pointed out during the height of the demonstrations against the registration law in May 1995, land in

---

[59] Land Registration (Customary Land) (Amendment) Bill 1995.

[60] With many thanks to Freda Bagai, law student at the University of PNG, Port Moresby, for explaining these difficulties.

PNG is an extension of the person, and a part of individual and group identity. He continued:

> People in Papua New Guinea hold land close to their hearts. It sustains them, it means life itself and it has a spiritual meaning to them. They will do anything to protect and safeguard their land if they feel that their right to the land is threatened. In fact, many regard it as foolhardy for anyone—even for the state—to consider trying to register land and wrest ownership from the people of this country.[61]

Herein lies the essence of the dilemma. For, looked at closely, there is no conflict between what is being said on both sides of the land reform debate. Indeed, there cannot be, because the arguments being made are about different priorities, different objectives, and different realities. The argument put forward by the World Bank, the government, and foreign donors and investors that land mobilization will achieve objective "A" (economic growth, increased incomes, and employment opportunities), whatever its merits, is one that becomes totally irrelevant for local villagers whose main concern is that objective "B" (the preservation of a way of life and the viability of the local community) will not be met.

And so the tension remains and continues to grow. As any observer of local current affairs in PNG will note, land has been, and remains, the hottest and most contentious issue of the 1990s. When and how some sort of resolution will be reached, only time can tell. What remains certain, however, is the essential irreconcilability between the interests and issues currently at stake, and that it is likely to take a very long time before anything more than an uneasy truce can be realized.

III. RESOLVING CONFLICTS BETWEEN WESTERN LAW AND CUSTOM IN THE CRIMINAL LAW SPHERE

A. Introduction

Historically, criminal law in colonial PNG was governed by the provisions of the Queensland Criminal Code as adopted.[62] In 1974, the two adopting enactments (as amended) in the Teritories of New Guinea and Papua were repealed

---

[61] See Anon., supra note 25.

[62] The Criminal Code Ordinance of 1902, section 1, adopted Queensland's Criminal Code Act of 1899 in the Territory of Papua. The Act was adopted in the Territory of New Guinea in 1921, by the Laws Repeal and Adopting Act Schedule 2, and later repealed and re-adopted, with some amendments, by the Law Repeal and Adopting Ordinance of 1924. While section 13 of the Laws Repeal and Adopting Act of 1921 provided that the Queensland Code provisions should be applied only "so far as the same are applicable to the circumstances of the Territory," the adoption in the Territory of Papua contained no such qualification. But see R. v. Ebulya, PNGLR 200, 221 22 (1964), where, although the court expressly "observed that the Criminal Code of Queensland was adopted as and to be the law of [Papua] without the qualification of circumstantial applicability or of repugnancy to existing laws," the court also went on to say that parts of the Code were

and replaced by the Criminal Code Act.[63] The Act, which has application throughout PNG, is virtually identical to the Queensland Code, and pays little regard to the unique economic, political, and social circumstances of the country.

Customary law and perceptions in PNG have played quite a significant role in civil law areas such as marriage, family laws, and inheritance.[64] In criminal matters, however, recognition of custom has always been extremely limited in scope. This has remained the case, even after the promulgation of the Native Customs (Recognition) Act 1963[65] (now the Customs Recognition Act).[66] That Act provided, for the first time, a systematic scheme for dealing with customary law throughout PNG.[67]

The current legal position under section 4 of the Customs Recognition Act is that, in criminal matters, the courts may take custom into account only for the purposes of (1) ascertaining the state of mind of a person; (2) deciding the reasonableness of an act, default, or omission of a person; (3) deciding the reasonableness of an excuse; (4) deciding whether to proceed to the conviction of a guilty party; or (5) determining the penalty to be imposed on a guilty party. This limited applicability of custom in criminal cases is further subject to an

---

clearly inapplicable and unenforceable, such as those calling for trial by jury, or granting rights of appeal to a "Full Court," which did not exist at the time of the adoption.

[63] Criminal Code Act (Revised Laws of Papua New Guinea, Ch. No. 262), (1974).

[64] In Papua, for example, the Courts and Laws Adopting Ordinance of 1888 adopted generally the law of Queensland as the basic law of Papua, subject to local legislation, "so far as the laws are applicable to the circumstances of the Possession" (section 10). No legislative enactment specifically recognized customary law in the Territory. In practice, however, the colonial courts did receive and consider evidence as to custom.

In New Guinea, for example, the section 10 of the Laws Repeal and Adopting Ordinance of 1921 provided, in keeping with the terms of the League of Nations Mandate Agreement, that:

> The tribal institutions, customs and usages of the aboriginal natives of the Territory shall, subject to the provisions of the Ordinances of the Territory from time to time in force, be permitted to continue in existence in so far as the same are not repugnant to the general principles of humanity.

In both Territories, Native Regulations enacted between 1939 and 1962 also provided for the recognition and application of customary law relating, *inter alia*, to marriage and intestate inheritance of property.

[65] Native Customs (Recognition) Act, Act No. 28 of 1963. Omitted from the Revised Laws of Papua New Guinea under s. 5 of the Revision of the Laws Act 1973.

[66] Customs Recognition Act (Revised Laws of Papua New Guinea Ch. No. 19). The Native Customs (Recognition) Act on which the current version of the Customs Recognition Act is based was originally promulgated by the Legislative Council of the (then) Territory of Papua and New Guinea as Act No. 28 of 1963.

[67] *See also* Local Courts Act, Act No. 65 of 1963, §§ 31 33 (1963). Local Courts Act 1963 was omitted from the Revised Laws under s. 5 of the Revision of the Laws Act 1973.

overriding limitation in section 3 that customs cannot be recognized insofar as: (1) enforcement would result in injustice or would not be in the public interest; or (2) enforcement would not be in the best interests of a child under 16.[68]

Taken together, sections 3 and 4 of the Customs Recognition Act have operated, in conjunction with a judiciary trained in common law precedent rather than customary traditions, to ensure that custom continues to play a severely limited and often ignored role in the criminal process. In practice, custom has been utilized in cases involving provocation as a defense,[69] and is often used at the sentencing stage in deciding upon a punishment to suit the accused,[70] but is rarely relied upon in the determination of substantive questions of criminal law or issues of criminal responsibility. Moreover, even at the sentencing stage, sometimes wide variations can appear in the extent of recognition granted to custom in cases decided by individual judicial officers who may differ enormously in their knowledge of, and attitude toward, customary practices.

The hierarchy of laws established by the the PNG Constitution, which places custom at the very lowest level of this hierarchy, was detailed above. Together with the limitations contained in section 3 of the Customs Recognition Act, the establishment of such a hierarchy sets up a tension between introduced Western liberal notions of "justice" and "the public interest" on the one hand, and traditional customary notions of "justice" and "social harmony" on the other. And just as is currently the case in the area of land law, the working out of this tension between values and norms drawn from two very different societies has had a significant influence upon the administration of criminal law, most noticeably at the village court level.

B. Law, Order, Politics, and the Village Courts

The administration and enforcement of criminal justice in any jurisdiction inevitably involves relationships of authority and power. In PNG, the general consensus among modern historians recognizes that

> Ultimately, the early colonizer was concerned with control of the new dependencies. . . . Control of the country was the aim . . . and in many

---

[68] "Custom" is defined in section 1 of the Act as "the customs and usages of indigenous inhabitants of the country existing in relation to the matter in question at the time when and the place in relation to which the matter arises, regardless of whether or not the custom or usage has existed from time immemorial."

[69] *See, e.g.,* R. v. Hamo-Time, PNGLR 9 (1963), R. v. Iawe-Mama, PNGLR 96 (1965–1966), R. v. Robert, PNGLR 180 (1965–1966), and R. v. Yanda-Piaua, PNGLR 482 (1967–1968) (willful murder reduced to manslaughter because of provocation in the form of sorcery).

[70] *See, e.g.,* Acting Public Prosecutor v. Nitak Mangilonde Taganis of Tampitanis, PNGLR 299 (1982), Acting Public Prosecutor v. Uname Aumane, PNGLR 510 (1980), and R. (The Queen) v. Iu Ketapi & Anor., PNGLR 44 (1971 1972). *See also* D.R.C. CHALMERS ET AL., CRIMINAL LAW AND PRACTICE OF PAPUA NEW GUINEA 635–40 (1985).

areas this was carried out peremptorily and callously. . . . The courts held by the *kiaps* (administrative field officers) were in no way intended to adapt law, they were intended to rapidly dispense justice as one of the duties of general administration.[71]

Imported British and Australian law formed the basic law. Insofar as it was to be tolerated and permitted, custom would only ever enter into the official legal system as ''an adjunct to maintaining harmony within the community.''[72]

In light of this history, Mr. John Kaputin, then Minister for Justice, described the significance of the passing of the Village Courts Act 1973[73] in the following terms:

> The major piece of legislation which attempts to place the law back in the hands of the people is the *Village Courts Act*. This piece of legislation is . . . important because village communities will be able to continue to mediate and to decide disputes within those communities with the full approval of the written law of the land. . . .
>
> I see two great benefits as likely to follow the establishment of the Village Courts. . . . Firstly, customary law will from now on be a real part of the national law, and will stand up beside the imposed law. In the past, lip service has been paid to our law by means of the *Native Customs (Recognition) Ordinance* 1963, but, since it operated in a court structure designed for the operation of the foreign law and conceptually only capable of employing the foreign law, it could never be effective.
>
> The second benefit, though more indirect, will be that the Village Courts will be a great source of information as to the content of customary law, and will be of great assistance as the imposed law is reformed.
>
> . . . Village Court magistrates who will be appointed because of their knowledge of customary law will be a vital source of information and, indeed, a catalyst for reform.[74]

Several writers have recognized, however, that the consideration which had a much greater impact upon the renewal of official interest in the (previously

---

[71] D.R.C. Chalmers, *A History of Traditional Dispute Settlement Procedures in the Courts of Papua New Guinea, in* LAW AND SOCIAL CHANGE IN PAPUA NEW GUINEA 169 at 170 (D. Weisbrot et al., eds., 1982).

[72] *Id.* at 175.

[73] Village Courts Act (Revised Laws of Papua New Guinea, Ch. No. 44) (1974).

[74] B.M. Narokobi, *Adaptation of Western Law in Papua New Guinea*, 5 MELANESIAN L.J. 52 (1977) (quoting John Kaputin).

rejected)[75] idea of locally based village courts than any desire "to place law back in the hands of the people," was the desire, and perceived need, to strengthen the government's control over law and order maintenance.[76] A 1971 Law Department inquiry into the "system of lower courts and the operation of the police with particular reference to the rural areas" indicates that the official view at the outset of the 1970s was directed toward keeping the worsening law and order situation under control.[77]

1. The Breakdown of Law and Order

The breakdown of law and order, and the failure of the courts to control the situation during the 1960s and 1970s, has been attributed to several factors. The first of these was the official system's failure to recognize substantive customary laws in all but a few criminal matters. Offenses considered serious in customary law, such as breaking tabus on places or crops, or unorthodox behavior by women, were completely ignored by officialdom. District officers often failed to take seriously certain matters, such as sorcery and disputes over land, which in fact were major causes of disputes and disorder, but which rarely appeared before the official government courts. In this respect, Andrew Strathern cites the example of the bitterness felt by Hageners in the Highlands when the administration refused their request to order people off their land after an assault on the president of a neighboring council.[78] This was interpreted by the Hageners as demonstrating the ineffectiveness of the alien court system.

The administration of justice in the official courts was also characterized by a failure to recognize or appreciate Melanesian ideas of reciprocity, with little imagination used by the courts in sentencing or making orders. The usual common law penalties of fine or imprisonment were all too often automatically

---

[75] Although the proposal for native courts was revived in 1955 when a Native Courts Bill was drafted by a leading advocate in favor of native courts, the Australian Minister for External Territories Paul Hasluck refused to consider the proposal, and stuck resolutely to a policy of a single integrated court system. The idea was also opposed by the Chief Justice Sir Alan Mann.

Professor David Derham outlines the background and debate over native courts in his report: D. DERHAM, REPORT ON THE SYSTEM OF ADMINISTRATION OF JUSTICE IN THE TERRITORY OF PAPUA AND NEW GUINEA (1960) 129–31. He also pointed to the lack of training of local magistrates, and the growth of unofficial courts. However, the arguments that were made by Derham in 1960 against the establishment of native courts were essentially those made by Hasluck—it was more desirable to have a single, integrated court system. See Chalmers, *supra* note 71, at 180–81.

[76] See, e.g., A. Paliwala, LAW AND ORDER IN THE VILLAGE: THE VILLAGE COURTS, in LAW AND SOCIAL CHANGE IN PAPUA NEW GUINEA 191 at 196 (D. Weisbrot et al., eds., 1982). See also Chalmers, *supra* note 71, at 181 82.

[77] See Chalmers, *supra* note 71, at 182.

[78] See A.J. Strathern, *The Supreme Court, A Matter of Prestige and Power*, 1 MELANESIAN L.J. 23 (1972).

imposed, and novel punishments more in accordance with local perceptions of justice and fairness ignored. Marilyn Strathern's research also reveals what is perhaps the major incongruence between the imported and traditional legal systems: Papua New Guineans see matters in the context of intergroup relations, whereas the Western-styled courts see individual guilt and responsibility as the crucial issue.[79] A related "conceptual defect" from which the courts suffered was to view criminal and civil law as separate divisions. Customary law does not see such distinctions.[80]

A second factor was the overly formal nature of courtroom procedures. Evidentiary procedures, in particular, remain bewildering and intricate, despite the relatively recent introduction of less formal oral proceedings. The alienating effect of bewildering rules and procedures was in many instances (even after attempts were made, in the 1960s, to localize the magistracy) compounded by the arrogance, youth, and/or inexperience of individual *kiaps,* magistrates, and other government officials. It was attitudes like these that helped to generate a local lack of confidence in the official system.[81]

Language difficulties also added to the problems. Interpreters were not readily available, and even when they were, lengthy tracts of interpreted evidence often represented a barrier to the efficient administration of justice.[82] The conduct and attitudes of officialdom, as well as the narrow legalism of professional ethics and courtroom conflict, were particularly alienating and misunderstood in a society where traditional dispute settlement mechanisms promoted harmony, group justice, compromise, concern for succeeding generations, and popular participation.[83]

A third factor blamed for the breakdown in law and order during the 1960s and 1970s was limited to the changes wrought in rural society by the impact of colonialism. The introduction of Western religion, Western education, and Western consumerism was accompanied by a growth of discontent and consequent unruliness, particularly among the young. Economically, the development of peasant cash cropping and ancillary service and process activities transformed village relationships. Instead of the whole community being involved, only a small group were able to take substantial advantage of the economic opportunies available. Many of this group were traditional "big men," but others were people whose economic strength was derived primarily through their links with

---

[79] *See* Marilyn Strathern, *Legality and Legitimacy: Hageners' Perception of the Judicial System*, 1 MELANESIAN L.J. 5 (1972).

[80] *See* Chalmers, *supra* note 72 at 180, *citing* T.E. Barnett, *Law and Justice Melanesian Style* in ALTERNATIVE STRATEGIES FOR PAPUA NEW GUINEA 73 (A. Clunies Ross and I. Langmore, eds., 1973).

[81] *See* Chalmers, *supra* note 71, at 169–77.

[82] *See id.* at 178 and 180.

[83] *See* Narakobi, *supra* note 73, at 54.

the outside world. The result was an increase in disputes, particularly land disputes and tribal fighting, as economic and political power relationships were gradually rearranged.

The development of unofficial dispute resolution mechanisms by local communities was a final important factor in the failure of the official court system. Fenbury, for example, sums up indigenous attitudes toward the official courts by saying that there were two expressions in Highlands pidgin for courts: *"Kot bilong Gavment"* (government courts) and *"Kot bilong mipela* ("our courts"). In other words, the people in rural areas, if not in the urban centers, never perceived the official courts as their own. The very existence of "our courts," unofficial courts, was to become one of the forceful reasons offered for establishing local courts in the early 1960s. The same argument was to be resurrected in the 1970s when the debate arose over village courts.

Paliwala describes the way in which unofficial forms of dispute settlement, based on traditional methods, continued to flourish. He begins by noting essential differences between the introduced adversarial techniques of dispute settlement on the one hand, and traditional forms of dispute resolution—based primarily on negotiation, mediation, community involvement, and "getting to the root of the problem as opposed to dealing with symptomatic causes"—on the other.[84] His main point, however, is that traditional dispute resolution forms survived primarily through a process of transformation to accommodate new forms of leadership introduced into village society during the colonial period.

2. New Forms of Leadership

The most important new forms of leadership were the district and patrol officers known as *kiaps*. Traditional leadership became subordinate to the authority of the *kiap* who had magisterial powers. Even after local and district courts were introduced in the 1960s, *kiaps* continued to exercise judicial authority in many areas. Other important new forms of authority were the "village constables" in Papua, and the *luluai* and *tultul* in New Guinea. These were normally selected from among the existing village leadership ("big men" or, in some areas, hereditary leaders). In the 1960s, local government councils were established with elected councilors. Again, the "big men" could, and often did, become councilors. While the new leadership remained subordinate to the colonial administration, it wielded significant power and influence at the local level.

Right from the beginning there was a tacit acceptance of unofficial dispute settlement by the colonial authorities, because the *kiap*, and later the local court magistrates, could not deal with all the disputes in the village. Many disputes, particularly those arising within the community, continued to be settled by traditional leaders—the difference was a shift in power favoring those "big men" who had the perceived authority and support of the state behind them, for now

---

[84] *See* Paliwala, *supra* note 76, at 193–94.

they were *luluai*, *tultul*, or *bosbois*[85] as well. Gradually, these officials developed dispute settlement functions as a natural extension of their colonial authority. The villagers accepted their decisions, and their right to preside over village tribunals, because of their apparent role as part of the government dispute settlement machinery. Later, the unofficial dispute settlement functions of the *luluai* and *tultul* were taken over by local government councillors and their representatives in each council ward known as the *komiti*. These officials tended to employ traditional techniques, and to adopt a role similar to that of "big men" in their settlement of disputes. The difference was, however, that in adopting that role, they had the apparent backing of the colonial authorities. According to Paliwala, this brought about "subtle changes in the power balance between the intervener, the parties and the community in favour of the former."[86]

The tacit acceptance by the colonial administration of unofficial dispute settlement by *luluai*, *tultul*, councilors, and "big men" indicates that there is no great contradiction between some aspects of customary dispute settlement and colonial interests. Paliwala concludes that growing concerns about law and order transformed this acceptance into a perception by the State of a need to both control and strengthen the unofficial dispute settlement machinery by giving it State backing. According to Paliwala, "it was this double need which led to the establishment of the village courts."[87]

Finally, Paliwala also notes that the introduction of village courts in different parts of the country was ultimately a matter of convincing the village leadership that the courts were a good thing.[88] In the early 1970s, this leadership consisted of an amalgam of the customary leadership and new forms of leadership such as the local government councils introduced by or linked to the State. State-backed leadership increased the power of the leaders in relation to the people, who were never given a role in the introduction or operation of the village court system, which remains in the hands of local government functionaries.[89]

The successful introduction and operation of village courts has thus depended upon a coalition of interests between national officialdom and holders

---

[85] In highland areas such as Simbu, the *bosbois* (group leaders) appointed by the *kiap* had as their main official function bringing offenders to government stations and reporting on trouble, and, in addition, took on an informal dispute settlement role as an extension of their official duties.

[86] Paliwala, *supra* note 76, at 195.

[87] *Id.*

[88] *Id.* at 201. *Also see* Law and Social Change in Papua New Guinea 191, 201 (A. Paliwala and A. Sawyerr, eds., 1982).

[89] These include the Village Courts Secretariat, responsible for overall planning and the training of magistrates, and the district supervising magistrate, responsible for appointing new magistrates. More recently, Provincial governments have also become important in planning the introduction of the courts.

of power under traditionally based and informal systems operating at the local level. The courts have operated most effectively in places where the official desire to increase social control at the rural level has coincided with the interests of a new village elite. This group is interested in law and order, the protection of their new property (such as trucks and trade stores), and in an efficient dispute settlement system. The control of the village courts by members of this group has supported their needs. More important, the practical operation of criminal law enforcement at the local level has reflected their political and economic concerns and preoccupations.

C. The Village Court Act 1973[90]

The Village Court Act provides that the primary duty and function of the court is "to ensure peace and harmony in the area for which it is established by mediating in and endeavouring to obtain just and amicable settlements of disputes."[91] The court (constituted at this stage by a single magistrate) has an obligation to attempt to reach a settlement by mediation before resort is made to the compulsive jurisdiction of the court. When the parties do invoke the compulsive jurisdiction of the court, section 27 ensures that "a Village Court is not bound by any law other than this Act that is not expressly applied to it, but shall, subject to Subsection (2)[92] and to Section 26, decide all matters before it in accordance with substantial justice." Section 26 provides that "in all matters before it a Village Court shall apply any relevant custom as determined in accordance with Sections 2, 3 and 7 of the *Customs Recognition Act*.)"[93]

Under section 2 of the Customs Recognition Act, the court is instructed to ascertain questions of custom "as though they were matters of fact," and in doing so, the court is given full discretion to "inform itself as it thinks proper." Section 7 of the act gives the court additional discretion in cases where it is not satisfied as to which of two or more systems of custom should prevail. These discretionary powers are very wide indeed, and include the power to:

(1) consider all the circumstances and adopt the system the court is satisfied the justice of the case requires;

(2) apply, with the necessary modifications and as nearly as may be, the ordinary rules of the underlying law;

---

[90] Village Court Act (Revised Laws of Papua New Guinea, Ch. No. 44) (1973).

[91] Village Court Act § 16 (Revised Laws of Papua New Guinea, Ch. No. 44) (1973).

[92] Subsection 27(2) states that "A person charged with a criminal offence before a Village Court shall be presumed innocent until proved guilty."

[93] Customs Recognition Act (Revised Laws of Papua New Guinea, Ch. No. 19). Bayne goes on to note, however, that since most magistrates cannot read, "it is unlikely that they bother to attempt to apply these complex provisions." Peter Bayne, *Village Courts in Papua New Guinea* in JUSTICE PROGRAMS FOR ABORIGINAL AND OTHER INDIGENOUS COMMUNITIES 75, 79 (K.M. Hazelhurst, ed., 1985).

(3) vary the principles set out in section 7 in any case to the extent required by the justice of the case.

Section 26 of the Village Courts Act and section 3 of the Customs Recognition Act together allow the court to deviate from custom whenever it considers that deviation is required either "in the public interest" or by the "justice" of the case before it. Thus, as Peter Bayne has noted, while it is

> commonly said that the village courts are a means of bringing customary ways into the judicial system, and that they were intended to apply customary law according to customary procedures . . . [e]ven as a matter of what they are obliged by law to do, this is only partly true. . . . while the Act does at points suggest this, the courts may if they wish ignore custom.[94]

Bayne goes on to note that allowing village courts to ignore custom if they so wish was in full conformity "with the views of the politicians who introduced and supported the Act."

> Their major concern was to restore order in the rural and urban villages. To them, it was a question of giving the power of control to village leaders; whether the power would be exercised according to custom was secondary. . . . The *restoration* or *preservation* of a fixed body of customary law was certainly far from the minds of the advocates of the courts. It would be foolish to think in these terms.[95]

The government's aim of restoring law and order in rural areas by controlling and strengthening traditional social control mechanisms was also furthered by section 27(3) of the Village Courts Act. That subsection bestows upon local government councils the power to make rules "declaring what is to be taken as the custom relating to any matter, and such a declaration is binding on village courts." That little use has been made of this power is perhaps a reflection of the fact that decisions of village courts have largely coincided with the interests of the local elite, including powerful council members, without the need for the council's rule-making power to be exercised. Nor is this coincidence of interests left to chance, but is practically ensured by the fact that a councilor, a ward committee member, or an employee of a council can be, and often will be, a village court magistrate. As a matter of form, the local government councils make the rules, while the village court merely enforces them. In local eyes, and as a matter of practical reality, however, councilor-magistrates may simply be exercising their traditional powers as "big men" to both make and enforce the rules.

---

[94] *Id.* at 81.

[95] *Id.*

D. The Village Courts in Operation

As Peter Bayne has noted, it becomes virtually impossible in this kind of environment to insist that local courts and council bodies should operate "in accordance with some separation of powers notion by which you separate rule making from rule enforcement. It is not going to be a distinction which is appreciated. If you have courts constituted by people who are local leaders, then obviously their introduction will have an effect upon local power relationships." [96]

In a situation where power relations are fluid, becoming a village court official is a means of access to power. To be a magistrate, in particular, will enhance political as well as social and economic power. This becomes especially important in communities where traditionally there is an acceptance of the principle that persons of public prominence and wealth will take care of close relatives and neighbors. Thus, a magistrate might use his or her (it is rarely her) influence to obtain extra land, or a government loan, either personally or for a favored clan or family member. It was on this basis that one of the major arguments put forward against the introduction of village courts was the likelihood that corruption and nepotism would result. In practice, there have been occasions where the courts have operated in ways which run counter to Western conceptions of objectivity, justice, and due process.

Some courts, for example, have used the power to fine excessively, even where compensation might be a more appropriate remedy. This may partly be to impress the parties with the court's authority, but it can also be due to a desire to impress the local government council which receives the fine. There is also an emphasis on enforcement and collection of council tax liabilites. Fines and taxes collected by village courts boost council revenue. Another council rule being enforced more rigorously is the rule under which the village people have to do communal work one day a week to keep the village clean. However, where the court officials are dissatisfied with their council, or where there is some degree of political competition between the council and court officials, the courts tend to reduce the amount of fines, and/or become less industrious in enforcing council rules:

> Thus Kiburu village court in Mendi in the Southern Highlands imposed about K2000 worth of fines in its first year of operation. Subsequently, the amount of fines levied was reduced greatly, and council officials attributed this to laziness on the part of court officials. The court officials, however, said that they did not get enough support from the council; therefore they did not see why they should support it with the peoples' money.[97]

---

[96] *Id.* at 82.

[97] Paliwala, *supra* note 76, at 205.

In some instances, the court has shown a marked subservience to and a considerable attempt to settle disputes by mediation in cases involving village leaders.[98] In other cases, young people or the disadvantaged *rabismen* (rubbish men) have been given short shrift. This is particularly likely where fighting, bad language, or drunkenness is involved. Courts near urban centers like Port Moresby have used their powers to control young men who come home to the village during the weekend and get drunk. Young people are often considered to be a real problem in the village, and local magistrates have dealt with them accordingly.

A concern to preserve traditional conceptions of law and order is also evident in magisterial attempts to control women who, in their view, "had become too flighty."[99] In one early episode, cited by Bayne, a village court decided that it was contrary to custom for women to smoke in the town market, and women were prosecuted for smoking, despite the fact that women had for years smoked in the market.[100] In another, more recent case, a woman was sentenced to six months in jail by a village court for shouting at her husband. On appeal to the National Court, she was later released from jail. In releasing the woman, Judge Tracey Doherty noted that she had also recently released a 35–year-old widow with six children who had been jailed after she had been seen in the company of another man! Her Honor then went on to state that, although the National Court system recognised traditional laws "as the basis of PNG law, many customs are not legal under the Constitution."[101]

Procedurally, the courts have often had difficulty in escaping Western-style formalism, despite various efforts in the act to relieve them of procedural constraints.[102] Paliwala, for example, describes the Western trappings found in many

---

[98] *See id.* Paliwala cites the example of an animal trespass case in Kerowagi involving two prominent Simbu leaders. Tempers in the dispute had run high, and guns were involved. Yet the court was far more concerned to settle the dispute amicably than with establishing the rights and wrongs of the case.

[99] *Id.* at 208.

[100] *See* Bayne, *supra* note 93, at 82.

[101] *PNG Court Frees "Cross" Woman*, as digested by John A. MacDougall *in* RNZ News, PACNEWS ED-1, based on television broadcast Dec. 15, 1993.

[102] *See generally,* Chalmers, *supra* note 71. *See also* Bayne, *supra* note 93, at 79.

Scaglion is one anthropologist, however, who reaches the conclusion that village courts have been generally successful in enabling disputants to avoid formal court procedures. He summarizes his study of one court by stating that:

> On the basis of 1975 data and village court caseloads, nearly seventy per cent of all conflict cases arising in the villages do not enter the formal introduced system in any way. Yet magistrates often mediate [informally] in their role as big men, and their status as village court magistrates gives more weight to their opinions. . . . . Other than the fact that such mediation is not formally recorded, hearings of this sort fulfill the expectations of the *Village Courts Act* 1973. They are heard traditionally and are based on customary law and compromise.

courts, and the way in which the courts have "developed an efficient, crisp interrogatory style which does not permit much deviation from parties or wit-nessses. . . . [and in which] audience participation is discouraged."[103] In criminal cases, this emphasis on following formal procedures has tended to shift the initiative away from the parties, and to give court officials control over a case. Paliwala cites the example of a Rigo case where the parties had patched up their quarrel by the time the dispute came to court. Despite the complainant's state-ment that he wanted to withdraw his case and did not want any compensation, the court imposed a criminal fine on the defendant, against the express wishes of both parties.[104]

A tendency to adopt the procedural style and methods of Western courts can also result in a Western-oriented attitude toward the dispute in question. For example, some courts have developed an almost Western approach to limitations. Debts are traditionally not subject to limitations and may even be levied against successors of the debtor. Yet, in one case in the Southern Highlands, involving the debt of a valuable "kina" shell given eleven years before, the court had this to say:

> You must settle it yourselves. If it was 4 or 5 years ago it would be alright. But if we let your case proceed now it is not only setting a bad precedent, but may revive tensions and exacerbate the problem.[105]

Western-style court procedures and Western judicial attitudes have also meant a tendency for village courts to deal only with the conflicting rights of the immediate parties to the dispute in question, rather than examining wider con-cerns in order to get to the "root" of the problem (as occurs in traditional mechanisms). This approach is taken sometimes in cases where counterclaims are raised. Traditionally, a debt owed to one member of a family could often be offset by a debt owed to another member. Yet village courts may not allow pooling of claims in this fashion:

> In one case in Kainantu, U gave a pig to K, and K agreed to pay 50 kina. When K failed to pay, U claimed the money. During the proceed-ings, K's cousin claimed that he had given U a pig and that U had

---

Only when such mediation is unsuccessful are cases brought before the full court.

R. Scaglion, *Formal and Informal Operations of a Village Court in Maprik*, 7 Melane-sian L. J. 116, at 128–29 (1979). *See also* G. Westermark, *Village Courts in Question: The Nature of Court Procedure*, 6 Melanesian L. J. 79 (1978) (reaching similar conclusions in relation to courts from another part of the country).

[103] Paliwala, *supra* note 76, at 203.

[104] *See id.* at 203. Paliwala's comments and observations are based on fieldwork done during three years (1975–1978) carried out in various parts of the country but based mainly in the Kerowagi area of the Simbu Province in the New Guinea Highlands. *Id.* at 191.

[105] See Paliwala, *supra* note 76, at 204.

promised to pay him some money. The court was very upset with K's cousin for raising this matter. The magistrate said, ''We are not going to hear this case because, to us, this is a 'revenge' case. You should have brought your [the cousin's] case in the proper way a few days ago. So leave this court.''[106]

E. The Village Courts and the Constitution

A dilemma faced the drafters of the PNG *Constitution* in the early 1970s. Section 37 of the Basic Rights Division in the Constitution was being drafted to provide for a comprehensive set of protections for those caught up in the criminal justice system—rights relating to arrest, bail, information of a charge, burden of proof, etc. It was quickly realized, however, that it would be nearly impossible for village courts to operate according to that model. Indeed, it is a model rarely achieved in many Western countries. The solution adopted, in section 37(21) and (22) of the Constitution, was to say that section 37 just does not apply to village courts. All that they are obliged to do is to accord natural justice, a concept which allows for great flexibility in procedure in the village court system. It also avoided the difficulties inherent in asking village court magistrates, who by and large lacked English language skills and/or legal training, to adjudicate legal disputes in accordance with complex procedural requirements often couched in archaic English language.

''Revenge'' cases have been a major cause of concern in the criminal law area. The traditional view that revenge is allowed, even obligatory, in some cases is one that conflicts with modern Western notions of justice. Where such cases do come before the courts, the conflict between Western legal and traditional customary principles becomes strikingly obvious, and creates moral, as well as legal, difficulties that the courts have struggled to deal with. In one case, for example, it was submitted on sentence that the prosecutrix was raped by the prisoner as dictated by custom (as payback—here the prosecutrix's brother had allegedly raped the prisoner's sister). The court, however, was unable to accept this, and held that even if this was a custom, it was repugnant to the dictates of the Constitution.[107]

In another case, the two accused, each aged about fifty years, were villagers from the Goilala area of Central Province.[108] When the first accused's daughter began to live with the son of the second accused, her father objected to the lack of brideprice payment and other symbols of marriage, and took his daughter back. He also stated that he took objection to the couple living together because

---

[106] Paliwala, *supra* note 76, at 204.

[107] *See* State v. Wasale Nerius & Ramilang Tingas, N. No. 397, (National Court, 1982), *cited in* Criminal Law and Practice of Papua New Guinea 30 (Donald R.C. Chalmers, David Weisbrot, and Warwick John Andrew, eds., 1985).

[108] *See* Public Prosecutor v. Apava Keru and Aia Moroi, PNGLR 78 (1985) (Supreme Court).

the son "and his father previously killed my four sons by sorcery."[109] When the second accused's son came to reclaim his "wife" and took her away, the first accused followed them and, while they were resting, killed the young man. Shortly afterwards, upon hearing the news of the murder, the second accused left his own village to avenge his son's death. Finding the first accused's own son, he killed him while he was "unarmed and unsuspecting," ignorant of the first murder by his father.[110]

At first instance, the trial judge sentenced both accused to six years' imprisonment.[111] On appeal by the Public Prosecutor against the inadequacy of the sentence, the Supreme Court, noting that the second murder, by the second accused, was a payback killing for the first murder, held that the trial judge had committed an error by regarding this fact as a mitigating factor:

> We consider that there should never be a reduction in any case for the custom of payback. The reason is that under the *Customs Recognition Act* (Ch No 19), s. 4(e), custom, formerly called in the legislation "native custom," is to be taken into account in determining the penalty (if any) to be imposed on a guilty party. But that provision is subject to s. 3 of that Act which provides that custom should not be recognised or enforced if the court considers that enforcement of it "would not be in the public interest," and to Sch. 2.1 of the *Constitution* which provides that custom is not to be applied if it is repugnant to "the general principles of humanity."
>
> ... Whatever the exact ambit of the custom [of payback], we consider it not in the public interest to recognise that custom by giving a reduced sentence for a murder committed pursuant to that custom. We also consider that custom ... repugnant to the "general principles of humanity" ... [as well as] contrary to the "Right to Life" contained in the *Constitution*, s 35.[112]

In the result, the sentence of the second accused was increased to one of life imprisonment.[113]

In the case of the first accused, however, the court held that considerations of custom could give rise to the application of "a well known principle of mitigation in Papua New Guinea and elsewhere ... sometimes called 'de facto

---

[109] *Id.* at 79.

[110] *Id.* at 80.

[111] *Id.* at 78.

[112] Public Prosecutor v. Apava Keru and Aia Moroi, PNGLR 78 (1985), 82.

[113] *Id.* at 84.

provocation.' ''[114] Applying this to the first accused, the court concluded that the first accused was "entitled to some reduction in sentence for de facto provocation. The man he killed took his daughter away against his wishes and without having paid brideprice.''[115] The first accused's sentence was increased to fifteen years imprisonment with hard labor.[116]

In *Public Prosecutor v. Kerua*, the Supreme Court again held that the trial judge had erred in regarding custom as a mitigating factor, and further held "that, in any event, his sentences were inordinately low.''[117] The relevant custom in that case was the alleged local custom "from 'time before' . . .—to kill the adulteress, mutilate her and throw her in the river and to kill the man too.''[118] Stating that "it is not in the public interest that a man should torture and murder his wife for adultery and kill her lover,''[119] the court affirmed that "the custom of payback is . . . contrary to . . . the general principles of humanity.''[120] In addition, the court also refused to accept the trial judge's decision that the defendant was "enraged or provoked on seeing his wife and [her lover] together.''[121] Rather, the accused had formed the intention to assault them during the month or more in which the couple had been living together. Finally, the Supreme Court took strong objection to the trial judge's statement that the accused's wife and her lover "must be held responsible for part of this trouble. They brought about this trouble by their adulterous relationship.''[122] Holding that the victim's conduct could not be used to reduce sentence in such cases, the court increased the sentence imposed on the accused for the murder of his wife from four years, three months to eleven years.[123]

In contrast to the courts' treatment of payback cases, however, is the judiciary's willingness to take customary compensation payments into account when sentencing a guilty party. In *State v. Robert Kupara*,[124] the accused was upset

---

[114] *Id.* at 83.

[115] *Id.* at 83.

[116] *Id.* at 84.

[117] Public Prosecutor v. Sidney Kerua and Billy Kerua, PNGLR 85 (1985) at 91.

[118] *Id.* at 89.

[119] *Id.*

[120] *Id.*

[121] *Id.*

[122] *Id.* at 90.

[123] *Id.* at 91. In addition to the 11-year sentence for murder, the accused was sentenced by the appeal court to concurrent sentences of four years and three years respectively for wounding and false imprisonment of the wife's lover, making a total cumulative sentence of 15 years. *Id.*

[124] State v. Kupara, PNGLR 312 (1985).

over his wife's playing cards with other people, and asked her to leave. When she refused, the argument developed into a struggle, and the accused used a billum (woven bag made of fiber) to hit the side of his wife's body. This ruptured an enlarged spleen, which eventually caused her death. Upon sentence, the accused sought to rely upon payment of customary compensation by himself and his family to the relatives of the deceased as a mitigating factor.[125] Upholding the trial judge's decision to take the compensation payment into account, Kapi DCJ expressed the view that:

> the effect of . . . the *Customs Recognition Act* (Ch No 19), s 4(e), . . . is that . . . a court may take into account custom insofar as it may give full explanation of the circumstances of the accused . . . relevant on sentence. . . . [and that this was] . . . altogether a different matter from recognising, enforcing or adopting custom as part of the underlying law under the *Constitution*. Custom may be taken into account without enforcing it as part of the underlying law. . . . It follows from this reasoning that the *Customs Recognition Act*, s 3, and the *Constitution*, Sch 2.1 cannot be applicable. They are applicable where custom as such is adopted as part of the underlying law.[126]

Noting that this conclusion was contrary to the reasoning of the Supreme Court in *Public Prosecutor v. Apava Keru and Aia Moroi*,[127] his Honor was careful to distinguish that case on the basis that:

> The court there was considering the influence on an accused person to act in accordance with the custom of payback. . . . I would be bound by that decision on the custom of payback. However, I am here concerned with customary compensation.[128]

A further concern in the human rights area has been the tendency for lower-level courts in particular to adopt an attitude of extreme "traditionalism" in cases concerning women. In some cases, the equality provisions of the Constitution, which specifically provide for equality within as well as outside of the marriage relationship, appear to have been violated. In one case in Mendi in the Southern Highlands, for example:

> . . . a woman had run away from her husband a second time, in spite of a preventive order from the village courts which enjoined both parties

---

[125] *See id.* at 313.

[126] *Id.* at 14–315.

[127] *See* Public Prosecutor v. Apava Keru and Aia Moroi, PNGLR 78 (1985).

[128] State v. Kupara, PNGLR 312 (1985), 315.

to stay together in peace. The husband had beaten the wife very badly and the wife refused, before the court, to go back to the husband. She said that if the court insisted on her going back, she would commit suicide. The court insisted that she should give the marriage another try and ordered the husband to give one cassowary as compensation for the injury. The wife rushed to the river. She did not commit suicide but smashed the fingers of her hand with a stone, saying to the court, "You may force me to go back, but I will be no use to him as I can't dig his garden and can't cook his food."[129]

Many village courts are also enforcing the "sik mun" or menstruation taboo customs quite strictly. In Tari, also in the Southern Highlands, courtship customs under which a girl is not allowed to be alone with a boy are being enforced. In another case in Mendi,

> The wife claimed that the husband had not given her any money to buy clothes, etc., when she had her baby. . . . The court said, "This thing of money is a new thing. We never had money and a man was never supposed to give money to a woman. We have our gardens. You should not bring to us questions about money."[130]

Sorcery has also been a problem that both government officials and the courts have struggled to deal with. In the leading 1980 case of *State v. Uname & Ors*, four men were found guilty of the wilful murder of an old woman, who was alleged to be a sorceress responsible for the deaths of at least twenty people.[131] Each of the defendants was sentenced by the trial judge to three months' imprisonment with hard labor and ordered to pay compensation of five pigs to the deceased's son upon release.[132] In reaching this sentence, the trial judge took into account "the genuine belief by the accused that the victim was a sorceress and responsible for numerous deaths,"[133] the background of the accused, including the fact that they "came from a remote part of the country with minimal contact with the outside world,"[134] and the cultural setting of the accused, including "the effect of sorcery or belief in it in the minds of believers."[135]

---

[129] Described in Cyndi Banks, Women in Transition: Social Control in Papua New Guinea 36 (1993), *citing* A. Paliwala, *Law and order in the village: Papua New Guinea's Village Courts, in* Crime, Justice and Underdevelopment 193, 222. (C. Sumner, ed., 1982).

[130] *Id.*

[131] *See* Acting Public Prosecutor v. Uname Aumane and Ors, PNGLR 510 (1980).

[132] *See id.* at 510–11.

[133] *Id.* at 528, per Andrew J.

[134] *Id.* at 513, per Kidu C.J.

[135] *Id.*

An appeal by the Prosecutor was heard by five judges of the Supreme Court.[136] The five judges unanimously upheld the appeal, quashing the order for compensation and imposing a six-year sentence on the four accused. All agreed that the penalty imposed by the trial court was "grossly inadequate for the crime of wilful murder,"[137] and that the trial judge had "over-emphasized the belief in sorcery" in reaching his sentencing decision.[138]

Later cases have followed this Supreme Court decision. In the 1988 case of *State v. Osborn Kwayawako & Ors,*[139] for example, six accused pleaded guilty to a charge of wilful murder of an elderly man, again alleged to be a sorcerer responsible for the death of an unspecified number of people.[140] In the National Court of Justice, Kapi DCJ noted that section 4(e) of the Customs Recognition Act, which allows the court to take custom into account for determining the sentence to be imposed upon a defendant,[141] had to be read subject to the Sorcery Act (No. 274).[142] He then went on to hold that, even though under Section 20 of the Sorcery Act 1971 an act of sorcery may be a wrongful act or insult for the purposes of the defense of provocation in limited circumstances, it did not allow the court "to take the customary belief of the power of sorcery into account in sentencing" the accused.[143] The accused were sentenced to 15 years each with hard labor.[144]

F. The Village Courts in an International Context

The establishment of a Village Court system in PNG can be seen as a recognition of the rights outlined in article 9 of the ILO's 1989 Convention Concerning Indigenous and Tribal Peoples in Independent Countries. This article provides that:

---

[136] Acting Public Prosecutor v. Uname Aumane & Ors, PNGLR 510 (1980).

[137] *Id.* at 513–14.

[138] *Id.* at 513, per Kidu C. J. Both Kidu C. J. and Andrew J. also noted that the trial judge had even gone so far as to find "that the victim did in fact kill twenty people" (per Andrew J. at 528), and felt that this, in turn, had led the trial judge to treat the case as one of diminished responsibility (at 529).

[139] State v. Osborn Kwayawako & Ors, PNGLR 174 (1988).

[140] *See id.* at 174.

[141] *See* Customs Recognition Act § 4(e), (Revised Laws of Papua New Guinea, Ch. No. 19). The Native Customs (Recognition) Act on which the current version of the Customs Recognition Act is based was originally promulgated by the Legislative Council of the (then) Territory of Papua and New Guinea as Act No. 28 of 1963.

[142] *See* Sorcery Act (Revised Laws of Papua New Guinea, Ch. No. 274) § 20, (1971).

[143] Kwayawako, PNGLR 174, at 176.

[144] *Id.* at 174–75. Only one of the six accused men in *Kwayawako*, who did not particpate in the actual killing, was given a lighter sentence of 12 years with hard labor: *Id.*

(6) To the extent compatible with the national legal system and internationally recognised human rights, the methods customarily practised by the peoples concerned for dealing with offences committed
by their members shall be respected.

(7) The customs of these peoples in regard to penal matters shall be
taken into consideration by the authorities and courts dealing with
such cases.

In many other ways, however, the village courts have not acted in ways
at all compatible with the Western conceptions of human rights contained in
international human rights conventions. Areas of Western-influenced international human rights thinking, which can and do often conflict with the operation
of custom in the Village Courts, include those related to communal work, freedom of religion, the due process provisions of article 14 of the International
Covenant on Civil and Political Rights,[145] and the requirements for equality
between men and women as elaborated in the Convention on the Elimination
of all Forms of Discrimination against Women.[146]

VI. CONCLUSION

Pacific nations such as PNG continue to wrestle with international, Western-
influenced concepts of human rights. The current emphasis in international human rights thinking on the rights of indigenous peoples' is particularly problematic. While international conventions appear to require the recognition of custom
as a fundamental right of indigenous peoples, this requirement is almost always
made subject to "the national legal system and . . . internationally recognized
human rights."[147] Given that the recognition of custom so often conflicts with
Western-derived national and international beliefs about rights, it is perhaps
small wonder that "the experience of local communities of the interpretation in
domestic courts of human rights in the customary context has . . . led to a degree
of reserve about human rights."[148]

If human rights thinking is to be made more acceptable to Pacific communities, there appears to be a need to address more seriously what Professor Angelo

---

[145] *See* International Covenant on Civil and Political Rights, 1966, *reproduced* in
BASIC DOCUMENTS ON HUMAN RIGHTS 125 (art. 14) (Ian Brownlie, ed., 3rd ed., 1992).

[146] *See* U.N. Convention on the Elimination of All Forms of Discrimination Against
Women, 1979; *reproduced* in BASIC DOCUMENTS ON HUMAN RIGHTS 169 (Ian Brownlie,
ed., 3rd ed. 1992).

[147] *See*, for example, Article 8 of the International Labor Organization Convention
Concerning Indigenous and Tribal Peoples in Independent Countries (No. 169) (1989)
supra note 40.

[148] Angelo, *supra* note 1, at 37.

has described as the question of "how to accommodate customary rights and emerging international norms expressed in multilateral treaties."[149] As this chapter has sought to demonstrate, such a need has always been evident in the criminal law area. And, as the twenty-first century approaches, an even more important area where the need for greater accommodation exists is the area of land law. In this area (as in the area of criminal law), serious questions remain about the capacity of a legal system modeled on Western lines to adequately accommodate traditional social values which emphasize the importance of the community. The fear is that a Western-style legal system, by purportedly attempting to place control over land in the hands of the people, is simply not equipped to accommodate customary notions, such as those of reciprocity and group responsibility. These concepts are noticeably absent from Western views of property rights, and may simply disappear when Melanesian situations are seen through "Anglo-Australian cognitive lenses," and governed by an Anglo-Australian-style legal system.

In this respect, the criminal justice experience of the village courts provides a warning. At the very least, it demonstrates that difficult value judgments must be made, and a variety of individual and social interests taken into account, in any attempt to amalgamate and accommodate legal forms and methods from two such different cutures. The danger is that, in the absence of such carefully considered judgments, raw political and economic power will instead be allowed to determine some of the most important issues at stake in the future of this young and vulnerable nation.

---

[149] *Id.* at 33.

B. The Americas

CHAPTER 9

OF ROBOTS AND INDIANS: HUMAN RIGHTS AND EDUCATIONAL CHANGE IN NICARAGUA

Lynda E. Frost

I. INTRODUCTION

When indigenous peoples strengthen recognition of their human rights through a struggle for self-determination, the resulting legal changes frequently encompass increased control over the regional educational system. Nonetheless, political realities often minimize the nature and extent of subsequent educational reform. The complex role of outsiders who provide technical assistance and financial support to an impoverished educational system can dramatically affect the realization of regional autonomy in the administration of that system.

The northern region of the Atlantic Coast of Nicaragua provides an ideal context in which to explore issues of human rights, indigenous peoples, external assistance, and educational change. The northern coastal region is ethnically diverse,[1] and a decade ago the area gained political and administrative autonomy

---

[1] The Atlantic Coast is ethnically, culturally, religiously, and linguistically distinct from the western part of the nation. A mix of indigenous populations, blacks from the Caribbean, and U.S. missionaries comprises a region very dissimilar to the western part of the country. The beliefs and customs of the people differ from those of the West, which is predominantly Catholic, mestizo (mixed European and Native American ancestry), and urbanized. *See* Roxanne Dunbar Ortiz, *Indigenous Rights and Regional Autonomy in Revolutionary Nicaragua*, 14(1) LATIN AM. PERSP. 43–66 (1987). Estimates of the population size for the various ethnic groups in the coastal region vary dramatically depending upon the source. The Nicaraguan government provided the following estimates of coastal population groups in 1986: Miskitos—80,000; Sumos—10,000; Garifunos—1500; Ramas—800. *See* Government of Nicaragua, Art. 9 CERD Report, U.N. Doc. CERD/C/128/Add.1, at 4 (1986). *See also* F.J. Docherty, *Educational Provision for Ethnic Minority Groups in Nicaragua*, 24 COMP. EDUC. 193, 201 (1988) (*citing* 1987 General Assembly order papers to support the following estimates: Mestizos—182,000; Miskitos—75,000; Creoles—26,000; Sumos—9000; Garifunos—1750; Ramas—850). The London-based Minority Rights Group makes the following estimates: Mestizos—80,000 to 180,000; Miskitos—70,000 to 150,000; Creoles—30,000; Sumos—5,000 to 10,000. *See* ROXANNE DUNBAR ORTIZ, THE MISKITO INDIANS OF NICARAGUA 4 (Minority Rights Group Report No. 79, 1988) [hereinafter ORTIZ, THE MISKITO INDIANS].

Historically, the Atlantic Coast has been separate from the rest of the country. The geography is rough; during the rainy season, transportation is almost impossible. A road connecting the Atlantic and Pacific coasts was not completed until 1982. Communication

from the central Nicaraguan government in Managua.[2] Prior to the political changes, the coastal educational system was developed and controlled by the educational ministry in Managua with assistance from private and foreign organizations. A new Autonomy Statute gave the regional government responsibility for administering educational programs on the Atlantic Coast,[3] and the Miskito Indians became heavily involved in managing most important aspects of coastal life. Nevertheless, outside actors still had a major impact on the local educational system. Perhaps because of the nature of this outside assistance, the regional educators were only moderately successful in implementing new educational policies more respectful of local needs and values.

One incident dramatically illustrates the complicated influence of outsiders on educational rights and autonomy in the region.[4] Prior to 1980, nearly all the educators on the Atlantic Coast were mestizos[5] from Managua and the western portion of the state or Moravian missionaries, and classes were taught in Spanish with Spanish textbooks. The system was under the control of the Ministry of Education in Managua, and functions, such as textbook selection and teacher training, were centralized.[6] But, during the years of struggle for autonomy, the

---

between the Coast and the West is also difficult, and a telecommunications system was not installed in Puerto Cabezas, the capital of the NAAR, until 1992. The territory is sparsely populated and, although the Atlantic Coast departments contain almost sixty percent of the Nicaraguan territory, less than ten percent of the population lives in that region. *See* AMNESTY INTERNATIONAL, NICARAGUA: THE HUMAN RIGHTS RECORD (1986); Ortiz, The Miskito Indians, *supra,* at 4.

[2] In 1987, the departments of Zelaya Norte and Zelaya Sur on the Atlantic Coast of Nicaragua received autonomous status through the Estatuto de Autonoía de las Regiones de la Costa Atlántica de Nicaragua, Autonomy Statute for the Regions of the Atlantic Coast of Nicaragua, Law No. 28, Sept. 7, 1987, *reprinted in* DOCUMENTS ON AUTONOMY AND MINORITY RIGHTS 386 (Hurst Hannum ed., 1993) [hereinafter Autonomy Statute], and became the North and South Atlantic Autonomous Regions (NAAR and SAAR, respectively). For a description of the process leading to autonomy, *see* Theodore Macdonald, *The Moral Economy of the Miskito Indians: Local Roots of a Geopolitical Conflict, in* ETHNICITIES AND NATIONS: PROCESSES OF INTERETHNIC RELATIONS IN LATIN AMERICA, SOUTHEAST ASIA, AND THE PACIFIC 107–53 (Remo Guidieri et al., eds., 1988).

The two regions of the Atlantic Coast have very different characteristics. The north is predominantly indigenous, with Miskito the most common language, followed by Spanish, English, and Sumo. In the south, English is the dominant language, with some Spanish and indigenous languages spoken. Both regions are less developed than the western part of the country, and the NAAR lags significantly behind the SAAR in providing for the material needs of the population. The educational system in the NAAR traditionally has been more basic and sparse than the system in the SAAR.

[3] *See* Autonomy Statute, *supra* note 2, at art. 8.2.

[4] Much of the background information in this chapter comes from a series of interviews with educators in Puerto Cabezas, the capital of the NAAR, in July of 1990 and May of 1992.

[5] *See supra* note 1 for a definition of mestizos.

[6] The Nicaraguan public educational system, like many systems in Latin America, uses a national curriculum with standard textbooks for all public school students. *See*

coastal public educational system changed. Residents of the Coast fought for greater sensitivity to local conditions and increased regional control over the educational system.[7] During the 1980s, the central government responded by initiating a program of long-distance education for teacher training on the Atlantic Coast through which more Miskitos were trained and hired in the public educational system.[8] These new educators became increasingly dissatisfied with this system. They echoed the residents' concerns that the central government neglected the needs of the Coast and that the pedagogical materials provided by the Ministry of Education ignored or distorted the realities of many of their students. With the aid of the Center for Investigation and Documentation of the Atlantic Coast (CIDCA) and linguists from universities in the United States and Europe,[9] these new teachers labored long, unpaid hours to develop a series of textbooks that not only translated Spanish text into Miskito, but also included examples and illustrations more familiar to the indigenous coastal communities of the north.[10] They developed a program of bilingual/intercultural education designed to meet the needs of the local population, which is predominantly

---

ROBERT F. ARNOVE, EDUCATION AS CONTESTED TERRAIN: NICARAGUA, 1979–1993 34–35, 80–93 (1994) (describing various standard Nicaraguan textbooks) [hereinafter ARNOVE, CONTESTED TERRAIN].

[7] The 1980 passage and gradual implementation of the Law on Education in Indigenous Languages on the Atlantic Coast (Bilingual Education Decree 571) is an outgrowth of that struggle. *See* Michael Shapiro, *Bilingual-Bicultural Education in Nicaragua's Atlantic Coast Region,* 14(1) BICULTURAL EDUC. 67–86 (1987). The law "obliges the Minister of Education to plan, organize, coordinate, and evaluate the teaching of pre-primary and the first four grades of primary school in Miskito and English in the areas where native and Creole communities are found on the Atlantic Coast of Nicaragua." *Id.* at 72.

[8] *See* Robert F. Arnove & Anthony Dewees, *Teacher Education in Revolutionary Nicaragua, in* FIT TO TEACH: TEACHER EDUCATION IN INTERNATIONAL PERSPECTIVE 105–25, 114–15 (Edgar B. Gumbert ed., 1990). Distance education is a means of providing education to populations in areas remote from the university campuses. Rather than attend frequent class sessions, students in distance education programs prepare lessons independently and gather infrequently for intensive sessions that include discussion of the material and evaluation of students' mastery. *See id.*

[9] *See id.* at 117. For a statement of issues involving language on the Coast, *see* Linguists for Nicaragua, *Language Rights on the Nicaraguan Atlantic Coast,* 13(3) CULTURAL SURVIVAL Q. 7–10 (1989).

[10] Standard, government-issued textbooks frequently ignore or mischaracterize the history and traditions of minority groups. *See* ROY PREISWERK & DOMINIQUE PERROT, ETHNOCENTRISM AND HISTORY: AFRICA, ASIAN AND INDIAN AMERICA IN WESTERN TEXTBOOKS (1978); Stephen Gottlieb, *In the Name of Patriotism: The Constitutionality of "Bending" History in Public Secondary Schools,* 62 N.Y.U. L. REV. 497–578 (1987). Joseph Farrell and Stephen Heyneman have compiled a list of issues to be addressed in textbook development. *See* Joseph Farrell & Stephen Heyneman, *Textbooks in Developing Countries: Economic and Pedagogical Choices, in* TEXTBOOKS IN THE THIRD WORLD: POLICY, CONTENT, AND CONTEXT (Philip G. Altbach & Gail P. Kelly, eds. 1988).

Miskito,[11] and a first set of textbooks, entitled *Tuba Lupia* (Little Child), was published in 1987.

While educators were pleased to have materials in their students' native language, the black-and-white textbooks illustrated with line drawings and reproduced on low-grade paper certainly left room for improvement. When the United States Agency for International Development (USAID) expressed interest in supporting education on the Coast, the Ministry of Education in Managua suggested it fund a translation into Miskito of a national primary school textbook series entitled *Azul y Blanco.* [12] USAID decided to fund the new series, which was called *Siakni Bara Pihni (Azul y Blanco)*. Coastal educators, however, became concerned when they were not consulted during the development of the series. To assist in adapting the texts to suit regional realities, they felt they needed to be involved in the development process. However, USAID was unresponsive to these concerns. In the end, the new texts were translated verbatim by Miskitos in Honduras and published in Colombia.

When 40,000 copies of the colorful, attractive new books were delivered, the teachers realized their fears had been well founded. They identified numerous problems with the series, including dialectical differences with the Miskito spoken in Honduras, pedagogical errors in the order in which concepts were presented, inappropriate instructions and illustrations based on materials unknown to Miskito communities, and even racist illustrations and stories. For example, *Siakni Bara Pihni* used a respected pedagogical technique of introducing letters in the order of their frequency of usage, but it used the frequency of the letters in Spanish, not in Miskito. Exercises in the Spanish version designed to help students distinguish between "b" and "v" or "c" and "z" became fill-in-the-blank exercises in the Miskito translation because "v," "c," and "z" do not exist in Miskito, a language with a seventeen-letter alphabet in contrast to the twenty-nine-letter Spanish alphabet. Further, some exercises required the use of crayons,[13] which were not available in the region, or a dictionary,[14] which did not exist for the Miskito language. Many illustrations in the texts had characters with European features, and artifacts such as sewing machines and traffic lights, which were almost unheard of in the region.[15]

---

[11] *See supra* note 1 (population estimates for coastal region).

[12] *Azul y Blanco* is Spanish for "blue and white," the colors of the Nicaraguan flag. USAID had earlier funded the wholesale replacement of Nicaraguan textbooks in Spanish published during the Sandinista regime, in the end providing over seven million textbooks. The *Azul y Blanco* series was one of the textbook series funded by USAID. *See* ARNOVE, CONTESTED TERRAIN, *supra* note 6, at 68.

[13] Many lessons in the first-grade SIAKNI BARA PIHNI book are based on the use of crayons. *See, e.g.*, Rocio C. Rojas & Samuel D. Rivero, 1 SIAKNI BARA PIHNI 17, 77.

[14] *See* Rocio C. Rojas & Samuel D. Rivero, 3 SIAKNI BARA PIHNI 15.

[15] *See* Rojas & Rivero, 1 SIAKNI BARA PIHNI, *supra* note 13, at 47, 81, 112. At the time *Siakni Bara Pihni* was published, the North Atlantic Autonomous Region, an area

The texts also contained short stories and fairy tales from various countries. Many of these stories depicted settings that were unfamiliar, and arguably inaccessible, to Miskito students. Even more surprisingly, the stories occasionally depicted indigenous peoples in stereotyped and racist ways. One story in a second-grade text told of a family that relied on a robot to care for the children when their parents were away. One day, the robot malfunctioned and began to talk nonsense. The children in the story complained that the robot was "speaking like an Indian" because its speech was unintelligible.[16] In the Miskito version, this story was illustrated with a robot in complete feather headdress.[17]

When the new textbooks were delivered to teachers in the North Atlantic Autonomous Region (NAAR), they refused to use them. The textbooks were placed in a warehouse and several administrators in the region lost their jobs during the course of the conflict with the Ministry of Education in Managua. In the end, the teachers agreed to use the new textbooks as a reference source, but continued to teach from the older *Tuba Lupia* series. Meanwhile, the central educational administration in Managua failed to understand why the attractive textbooks were not used. The whole incident amounted to a discouraging waste of energy and funding.

What caused this frustrating situation? Four years after the 1987 Autonomy Statute granted the NAAR control over the administration of the regional educational system, why were educators expected to teach children from a text unsuited to the needs of their pupils? What led to the invention of the racist and stereotypical Indian robot image?

This chapter examines the educational rights of the indigenous peoples, in the NAAR and elsewhere. It explores the impact of the Miskitos' struggle for self-determination on the regional educational system and examines outside influences on educational reforms in the region. It concludes that, to truly realize educational rights and self determination, indigenous peoples must gain not only increased local control through formal legal and policy statements, but also true influence through the successful implementation of educational reform.

II. INDIGENOUS PEOPLES AND EDUCATIONAL RIGHTS

The 1987 Autonomy Statute formalized a consensus in Nicaragua that the Atlantic Coast should enjoy some independence as to matters of considerable local impact. In recognition of cultural distinctions between the northern and southern regions, the Autonomy Statute divided the Coast into two autonomous

---

encompassing over twenty-five percent of the Nicaraguan national territory, had one traffic light.

[16] Rojas & Rivero, 3 SIAKNI BARA PIHNI, *supra* note 14, at 118.

[17] A Norwegian anthropologist working in the region, Hans Buvollen, describes these and other complaints about the series in *Ideas Para Mejorar Educación a Costeños y Defender Autonomia*, BARRICADA, June 5, 1991, at 3 (on file with author).

regions. Regional council elections were held in 1990, and the NAAR and the SAAR regional governments were officially installed.

The process of political and administrative structural change in the NAAR was followed, and at times influenced, by many outside organizations and states. International law and practice regarding self-determination provided a legal framework for the struggle for autonomy.[18] The international system for the protection and promotion of human rights affected developments in the region a number of times.[19] The following review of legal provisions and policy statements on the educational human rights of indigenous peoples provides a framework for comprehending the implementation of political and administrative legal changes in the educational system of the NAAR.

Numerous international legal instruments have firmly established a child's right to education.[20] From its inception, the United Nations (U.N.) has recognized the importance of education in achieving its goals of international cooperation, peace, and mutual respect. An early U.N. General Assembly resolution, the Universal Declaration of Human Rights (Universal Declaration) proclaimed that "everyone has the right to education."[21] While it specified some of the aims of education, the Universal Declaration also gave parents the right to determine the kind of education their children receive.[22] A later instrument, the International Covenant on Economic, Social and Cultural Rights elaborated on the "right of everyone to education" articulated in the Universal Declaration.[23] The Covenant did not address issues of cultural diversity and education, but it guaranteed "the liberty of parents . . . to choose for their children schools . . . to ensure the

---

[18] A thorough review of this framework is beyond the scope of this chapter. For insightful analyses of international self-determination and indigenous peoples, *see* S. JAMES ANAYA, INDIGENOUS PEOPLES IN INTERNATIONAL LAW (1996); Catherine Iorns, *Indigenous Peoples and Self-Determination: Challenging State Sovereignty*, 24 CASE W. RES. J. INT'L L. 199 (1992).

[19] On-site investigations and reports by nongovernmental and intergovernmental human rights organizations drew international attention to events in Nicaragua and influenced the negotiating postures of the government and the indigenous representatives. *See* America's Watch, *The Miskitos in Nicaragua 1981–84* (1984); Amnesty International, *Nicaragua: The Human Rights Record* (1986); Amnesty International, *The Americas: Human Rights Violations Against Indigenous Peoples* (1992); Inter-American Commission on Human Rights, *Report on the Situation of Human Rights of a Segment of the Nicaraguan Population of Miskito Origin*, O.A.S., OEA/Ser.L/V/II.62, Doc. 10, Rev. 3 (1983).

[20] For a general analysis of the right to education, *see* UNESCO, THE CHILD'S RIGHT TO EDUCATION (Gaston Mialaret, ed., 1979).

[21] Universal Declaration of Human Rights, G.A. Res. 217 (III 1948) at art. 26(1). It further states that elementary education shall be free and compulsory.

[22] *See id.* at art. 26(3).

[23] International Covenant on Economic, Social and Cultural Rights, 993 U.N.T.S. 3, 6 I.L.M. 360 (1967) at art. 13.

religious and moral education of their children in conformity with their own convictions.''[24]

The United Nations Organization for Education, Science and Culture (UN-ESCO) was created in 1945 with a partial mandate to coordinate and promote United Nations activities in the field of education.[25] UNESCO has been especially instrumental in furthering the recognition of education as a right, rather than a privilege. In 1960, the General Conference of UNESCO adopted the Convention Against Discrimination in Education (Nondiscrimination Convention).[26] The Nondiscrimination Convention echoed the education provision in the Universal Declaration and, as a convention, gave that provision binding force.[27]

Finally, the recent Convention on the Rights of the Child elaborated upon the educational rights mentioned in the Covenant, recognizing the right of the child to education and specifying that education shall be directed to ''the development of respect for . . . his or her own cultural identity, language and values.''[28] The Convention on the Rights of the Child has received nearly unprecedented support in the international community and was ratified by most states within a few years of its adoption by the General Assembly.[29]

The educational rights established by the international instruments discussed above apply to children and individuals regardless of their ethnicity. In addition, there are other international instruments that specifically address the rights of indigenous peoples and give detailed attention to their education. Over the years, these instruments have changed significantly in their approach to educational issues. The two International Labor Organization (ILO) conventions on the rights of indigenous peoples differ dramatically in their approaches to indigenous education. The tenor of the 1957 Convention is reflected in the pedagogical goal

---

[24] *Id.* at art. 13(3).

[25] *See* PETER I. HAJNAL, GUIDE TO UNESCO 1–19 (1983).

[26] Convention Against Discrimination in Education, 429 U.N.T.S. 93 (1960). For a description of the Convention, *see* NATAN LERNER, GROUP RIGHTS AND DISCRIMINATION IN INTERNATIONAL LAW 147–50 (1990); PATRICK THORNBERRY, INTERNATIONAL LAW AND THE RIGHTS OF MINORITIES 287–90 (1991).

[27] As a declaration rather than a convention, the Universal Declaration would not be legally binding upon the states that adopted it unless the rights it mentions had become customary international law. *See* OSCAR SCHACHTER, INTERNATIONAL LAW IN THEORY AND PRACTICE 84–90, 335–42 (1991).

[28] U.N. Convention on the Rights of the Child, U.N.G.A. Res. 44/25 (XLIV), 44 U.N. GAOR, Supp. (No. 49), U.N. Doc. A/RES/44/25 (1989), *reprinted in* 28 I.L.M. 1448 (1989), arts. 28, 29(1)(c). *Also see* Chapter 3, Cynthia Price Cohen, *International Protection of the Rights of Indigenous Children.*

[29] As of mid-1997, 191 countries had ratified the Convention on the Rights of the Child with only the United States and Somalia remaining as non-ratifying States.

of "help[ing] children become integrated into the national community."[30] By contrast, the 1989 Convention viewed education as "help[ing] children . . . participate fully and on an equal footing in their own community and in the national community."[31] The language of the ILO conventions moved from the 1957 emphasis on integrating indigenous children into a larger society to the 1989 focus on respect for the integrity of the indigenous community reflected in a goal of enabling children to participate in both their indigenous communities and larger societal groups.[32]

In 1982, under the auspices of the Commission on Human Rights, a Working Group on Indigenous Populations was formed within the Sub-Commission on the Prevention of Discrimination and the Protection of Minorities. Among the tasks it assumed was the drafting of a Declaration on the Rights of Indigenous Peoples.[33] The Working Group met annually and, in 1994, it adopted a final text of the draft Declaration.[34] The draft was referred to the Sub-Commission on the Prevention of Discrimination and the Protection of Minorities, which approved it in 1995 and referred it to the Commission on Human Rights.[35]

---

[30] International Labor Organization Convention (No. 107) Concerning the Protection and Integration of Indigenous and Other Tribal and Semi-Tribal Populations in Independent Countries, 328 U.N.T.S. 247, art. 24.

[31] International Labor Organization Convention (No. 169) Concerning Indigenous and Tribal Peoples in Independent Countries, International Labor Conference, Draft Report of the Committee on Convention No. 107, Appendix I, C.C. 107/D. 303, Art. 29. For a detailed dicussion of this treaty, *see* Chapter 2, Lee Swepston, *The ILO Indigenous and Tribal Peoples Convention (No. 169): Eighty Years After Adoption.*

[32] The shift from an integrationist approach to an approach based on the integrity of the indigenous community is paralleled by the attitudes of educators toward diverse school populations. In the 1960s, educators generally followed remedial and compensatory models of education, seeking to compensate for perceived cognitive deficiencies or substandard social environments of culturally different students. In the next decade, educators began a move toward a bridge model in which the goal was to narrow the gap between the white, middle-class culture of the public schools and the different cultures of many public school students. For a description of various models of education for culturally diverse populations in the United States, *see* Lynda E. Frost, *"At-Risk" Statutes: Defining Deviance and Suppressing Difference in the Public Schools*, 23 J. L. & EDUC. 123, 127–29 (1994).

[33] *See* Erica-Irene A. Daes, *Equality of Indigenous Peoples Under the Auspices of the United Nations—Draft Declaration on the Rights of Indigenous Peoples*, 7 ST. THOMAS L. REV. 493 (1995). Dr. Daes is the Chairperson/Rapporteur of the United Nations Working Group on Indigenous Populations. The Draft Declaration has particular importance because of the significant participation of indigenous tribes and organizations in the drafting process. *See* Douglas Sanders, *The UN Working Group on Indigenous Populations*, 11 HUM. RTS. Q. 406,407 (1989).

[34] United Nations Draft Declaration on the Rights of Indigenous Peoples, U.N. ESCOR, Comm. on Hum. Rts., 11th Sess., Annex I, U.N. Doc. E/CN.4/Sub.2 (1993) [hereinafter Draft Declaration].

[35] The Working Group was established by Commission on Human Rights resolution 1995/32 of 3 March 1995 (*See Report of the Working Group established in accordance*

This draft Declaration on the Rights of Indigenous Peoples contains some provisions addressing the education of indigenous children. Article 13 provides, in relevant part, that "[i]ndigenous peoples have the right to manifest, practise, develop and teach their spiritual and religious traditions, customs and ceremonies. . . ."[36] Article 14 continues, "[i]ndigenous peoples have the right to revitalize, use, develop and transmit to future generations their histories, languages, oral traditions, philosophies, writing systems and literatures. . . ."[37] Article 16 provides that "[i]ndigenous peoples have the right to have the dignity and diversity of their cultures, traditions, histories and aspirations appropriately reflected in all forms of education and public information. . . ."[38] These articles emphasize the rights of indigenous peoples to preserve and strengthen their indigenous traditions, in part through education.

Article 15 of the draft Declaration elaborates on the nature of these educational rights:

> Indigenous children have the right to all levels and forms of education of the State. All indigenous peoples also have this right and the right to establish and control their educational systems and institutions providing education in their own languages, in a manner appropriate to their cultural methods of teaching and learning.

> Indigenous children living outside their communities have the right to be provided access to education in their own culture and language.

> States shall take effective measures to provide appropriate resources for these purposes.[39]

Significantly, article 15 not only permits local control over education, but also mandates the allocation of resources to realize that control.

---

with Commission on Human Rights Res. 1995/23, U.N. Commission on Human Rights, 51st Sess., U.N. Doc. E/1995/32 (1995)). The report this session of the Working Group is contained in document E/CN.4/1996/84 (*Report of the Working Group on established in accordance with Commission on Human Rights resolution 1995/32, U.N. Commission on Human Rights, 52nd Se*ss., U.N. Doc. E/CN.4/1996/84 (1996)). *See also Report of the Working Group on established in accordance with Commission on Human Rights resolution 1995/32, U.N. Commission on Human Rights, 53nd Sess.,* U.N. Doc. E/CN.4/1997/ 102 (1997). For details about the draft Declaration and the Commission on Human Rights working group, *see* Chapter 1, Julian Burger, *Indigenous Peoples and the United Nations* in this volume.

[36] *See* Draft Declaration *supra* note 34, at art. 13.

[37] *Id.* at art. 14.

[38] *Id.* at art. 16.

[39] *Id.* at art. 15.

Most recently, the Organization of American States (OAS), through the Inter-American Commission on Human Rights, began work on an Inter-American Declaration on the Rights of Indigenous Peoples. In 1989, the OAS General Assembly passed a resolution directing the Inter-American Commission to draft a legal instrument clarifying indigenous rights.[40] To collect information necessary for the drafting process, in 1992 the Commission sent a questionnaire to OAS Member States and organizations representing indigenous peoples. In their responses, several countries mentioned their concerns about educational issues, such as "the child's inalienable rights to education in his/her native language, history and culture, as part of the academic curriculum" and the contention that "the history of the indigenous populations and their present circumstance should be taught, without the distortions and misrepresentation that bring about prejudice; the content and methods should be tailored to the regions inhabited by the indigenous populations and their customs."[41] The Commission approved a draft Declaration in 1995 for use in consultation with governments and other interested groups.[42] In 1997, the Commission approved a revised draft in response to views received from governments, indigenous organizations, and other experts.[43] The revised draft contains a number of educational provisions.[44]

---

[40] OEA/Res. 1022 (XIX-)/89).

[41] Annual Report of the Inter-American Commission on Human Rights 1992–1993, OEA/Ser.L/V/II.83, doc. 14, corr. 1, at 279–80, 287 (1993).

[42] Draft of the Inter-American Declaration on the Rights of Indigenous Peoples, approved by the IACHR at the 1278th session held on Sept. 18, 1995, *Annual Report of the Commission 1995*, OEA/Ser.L/V/II.91, doc. 7 rev. (Feb. 28, 1996) at 207.

[43] Proposed American Declaration on the Rights of Indigenous Peoples, approved by the IACHR at the 1333rd session held on Feb. 26, 1997, *Annual Report of the Commission 1996*, OEA/Ser.L/V/II.95, doc. 7 rev. (Mar. 14, 1997), at 633. The Commission hopes the OAS General Assembly will give the commission final approval in 1998. *Id.* at 632.

[44] Draft Article IX reads:

1. Indigenous peoples shall be entitled a) to establish and set in motion their own educational programs, institutions and facilities; b) to prepare and implement their own educational plans, programs, curricula and materials; c) to train, educate and accredit their teachers and administrators. The states shall endeavor to ensure that such systems guarantee equal educational and teaching opportunities for the entire population and complementarity with national educational systems.

2. When indigenous peoples so decide, educational systems shall be conducted in the indigenous languages and incorporate indigenous content, and they shall also be provided with the necessary training and means for complete mastery of the official language or languages.

3. The states shall ensure that those educational systems are equal in quality, efficiency, accessibility and in all other ways to that provided to the general population.

4. The states shall take measures to guarantee to the members of indigenous

The evolutionary trend in the approach of international instruments to indigenous education is encouraging. From the 1957 ILO Convention to the U.N. draft Declaration on the Rights of Indigenous Peoples and the draft American Declaration, the framers of international instruments have systematically moved away from the goal of assimilation toward that of harmonious coexistence. While the most recent instruments still reflect remnants of the older perspectives, they have nonetheless progressed far beyond the initial instruments in their respect for the autonomy of indigenous peoples.

Although Nicaragua has not ratified either of the ILO conventions, and did not respond to the OAS questionnaire used to draft the Inter-American Declaration on the Rights of Indigenous Peoples,[45] it has become a state party to other conventions that establish educational rights. Specifically, Nicaragua has ratified the International Covenant on Economic, Social and Cultural Rights, the Convention Against Discrimination in Education, and the Convention on the Rights of the Child. As a result, Nicaragua is legally bound to recognize and implement the educational rights established in those conventions.

III. EDUCATIONAL IMPERIALISM

International instruments affecting indigenous peoples have indeed abandoned the assimilationist perspective. Yet the educational systems of indigenous peoples do not necessarily evidence the scope of these changes.[46] Many educational systems remain highly politicized and reflect goals that are distant from

---

peoples the possibility to obtain education at all levels, at least of equal quality with the general population.

5. The states shall include in their general educational systems, content reflecting the pluricultural nature of their societies.

6. The states shall provide financial and any other type of assistance needed for the implementation of the provisions of this article.

Id. at 637–38.

[45] For a detailed discussion of the American Declaration on the Rights of Indigenous Peoples, *see* Chapter 4, Osvaldo Kreimer, *The Future Inter-American Declaration on the Rights of Indigenous Peoples: A Challenge for the Americas,* in this volume.

[46] Although a comprehensive examination of educational systems other than the Nicaraguan system is beyond the scope of this chapter, developments in the U.S. Bureau of Indian Affairs-administered schools present an interesting case study. The Indian Self-Determination and Education Assistance Act of 1975, particularly as amended, aimed to maximize tribal participation and reduce federal bureaucracy. 25 U.S.C. § 450 (1988 & Supp. 1995). Nonetheless, the implementation of the Act was repeatedly delayed and the educational autonomy promoted by the Act was diluted through measures such as the Goals 2000: Educate America Act that imposed national priorities on the schools. 20 U.S.C. § 5801 (Supp. 1995). *See* John Tippeconnic, *The Education of American Indians: Policy, Practice and Future Direction,* in AMERICAN INDIANS: SOCIAL JUSTICE AND PUBLIC POLICY (Donald Green & Thomas Tonnesen, eds. 1991); Joy Snyder & K. Zoann, *Self-Determination in American Indian Education: Educators' Perspectives on Grant, Contract, and BIA-Administered Schools,* 34 J. AM. INDIAN EDUC. 20 (1994).

the aspirations of the indigenous populations they serve and perhaps even goals that conflict with the legal and policy framework of the countries in which they are located.

Educators and anthropologists have explored the complicated uses of education in a political context. Most educators speak of education as central to both individual and societal development. This view of education has been propounded by authors at all points on the political spectrum, from Fidel Castro to the Reagan administration's National Commission on Excellence in Education.[47] The political context of education can have an extraordinary impact on a child's development.

Education also plays an important role in building the cohesion of a nation and the identity of a social group. Researchers have long recognized the profound effect of education on the political development of children.[48] From the earliest classes, schools teach children about the role of national heroes in the nation's history. Patriotic songs and stories are an important part of most formal curricula. Many schools are named after national political figures. Thus, through repeated and varied techniques, public school students are socialized into the national culture.[49]

Many scholars, however, condemn the nation-building and identity-shaping character of education. Some criticize the imperialistic ends of Latin American educational systems that are strongly influenced by North American pedagogical and conceptual frameworks.[50] Other scholars argue that the process of socialization through education acquires an imperialist flavor through the manner in which it coopts the vulnerable into a preconceived system. For example, Vine Deloria, Jr., one of the critics of the imperialistic function of education, argued that for decades, Indian educational programs in the United States sought to integrate students into mainstream society, thereby obliterating native traditions and values.[51] Similarly, anthropologist Claude Levi-Strauss argued that literacy was of prime importance to the State because it enabled the State to control its subjects.[52]

---

[47] See FIDEL CASTRO, EDUCACIÓN Y REVOLUCIÓN (1974); NATIONAL COMMISSION ON EXCELLENCE IN EDUCATION, A NATION AT RISK (1983).

[48] See ROBERT COLES, THE POLITICAL LIFE OF CHILDREN (1986); POLITICAL SOCIALIZATION, CITIZENSHIP EDUCATION, AND DEMOCRACY (Orit Ichilov, ed., 1990).

[49] For a description of the socialization process in Nicaragua under the Ortega and Chamorro governments, see ARNOVE, CONTESTED TERRAIN, supra note 6.

[50] See ADRIANA PUIGGRÓS, IMPERIALISMO Y EDUCACIÓN EN AMÉRICA LATINA (1980).

[51] See Vine Deloria, Jr., Education and Imperialism, 19 INTEGRATED EDUCATION 58 (1982).

[52] See CLAUDE LEVI-STRAUSS, TRISTES TROPIQUES 1298 (1973).

The cooptation process is far from obvious. Educators refer to the mechanisms through which students are socialized as the "hidden curriculum."[53] This hidden curriculum often contradicts the explicit curriculum. Thus, a teacher may teach democracy in an autocratic classroom. A teacher may teach about freedom of speech and expression in a classroom that prohibits all communication without the express permission of the teacher. Students receive mixed messages from the interplay between the hidden and the explicit curriculum in such a classroom. In a newly autonomous region, a teacher hired and paid by the central government may teach a curriculum designed by the central government, using textbooks designed and provided by that government. While this teacher may speak of autonomy, the hidden curriculum belies that message, conveying instead a message of external dependency and control.

The educational system of the NAAR has had numerous outside influences. Over a century ago, Moravian missionaries arrived in the region and established schools for the children. In fact, the private Moravian schools still serve many local children today. National development agencies have donated funds and personnel to strengthen the educational system in the NAAR. For example, USAID sponsored the ill-fated project to fund elementary school textbooks. A Norwegian development agency for a number of years supported an employee who assisted the bilingual/intercultural education program of the regional school system.[54] Various nongovernmental organizations have also participated in diverse ways.[55]

These outside forces are not necessarily threatening to the autonomy of the regional educational system. During a decade of struggle in the Sandinista period, the NAAR had experienced large-scale population movements and infrastructure erosion.[56] These years of conflict led the local population to depend on

---

[53] One scholar identifies four primary meanings of the term "hidden curriculum": unofficial expectations, unintended learning outcomes, implicit messages, and the curriculum created by students. *See* John Portelli, *Exposing the Hidden Curriculum*, 25 J. CURRICULUM STUD. 343, 345–46 (1993). For an intelligent, historically grounded view of the changing meanings of the "hidden curriculum," *see* Peter Hlebowitsh, *The Forgotten Hidden Curriculum*, 9 J. CURRICULUM & SUPERVISION 339 (1994).

[54] For a description of the bilingual/intercultural education project, *see* Lynda Frost, *The Bilingual Education of Indigenous Children in Nicaragua under the 1987 Autonomy Statute: The Effective Limits of Legal Change*, 3 INT'L J. CHILDREN'S RTS. 51, 60–64 (1995).

[55] For example, the Inter-American Institute of Human Rights, located in San Jose, Costa Rica, held a three-day symposium on "Human Rights and Bilingual/Intercultural Education in the North Atlantic Autonomous Region" in Puerto Cabezas in 1992. *See* Lynda Frost, *Human Rights Education Programs for Indigenous Peoples: Teaching Whose Human Rights?*, 7 ST. THOMAS L. REV. 699, 717 (1995). For a more general description of roles of human rights organizations in relation to indigenous peoples, *see* *id.* at 709–12.

[56] In 1982, the Sandinista government relocated approximately 8,500 Miskitos from northern villages to a resettlement camp called Tasba Pri and destroyed the villages. Many more Miskitos fled across the border to Honduras. When the Miskitos were released

outside agencies to provide needed resources and services.[57] However, after the victory of Chamorro in 1990, many politically oriented assistance organizations departed, leaving the regional government alone in its struggle to meet the needs of a population that had been uprooted from its traditional sources of sustenance. Ironically, the shift of international attention away from the region jeopardized the ability of the regional government to strengthen its governance and realize autonomy in a powerful way.

Now, even if the newly autonomous region occasionally has a temporary need for outside assistance, the need does not preclude the NAAR from considering whether the philosophy of outside supporters is consistent with the values of the region. An instructive precedent is the law and development movement that, along with the Alliance for Progress, strongly influenced U.S. relations with Latin America during the 1960s. Under the Kennedy administration, U.S. foreign policy focused increasingly on issues of development, especially in Latin America. The law and development movement, a coalition of governmental and nongovernmental actors, sent hundreds of U.S. lawyers to Latin America intent on sharing U.S. solutions to the problems of legal education and practice. Justice Douglas enthusiastically called for lawyers "to serve as architects of free societies in lands that have known little freedom."[58]

In retrospect, most commentators criticize the movement for its ethnocentricity and shortsightedness. Addressing the broader Alliance for Progress, William D. Rogers, who played an important role in implementing the Alliance, described the venture as a "crude and primitive" attempt to "coordinate the forces for change."[59] James A. Gardner noted that the forces were U.S. citizens working to change Latin American legal systems to more closely resemble U.S. systems. He characterized the lawyers as "legal missionaries" intent on bestowing U.S. expertise to the underdeveloped and ignorant lawyers of developing countries, and concluded that the movement was ethnocentric not only in

---

from Tasba Pri and returned from Honduras, many migrated to Puerto Cabezas, the capital of the department. During the 1980s, the population of Puerto Cabezas grew exponentially, far exceeding the capacity of the rustic infrastructure. *See* HURST HANNUM, AUTONOMY, SOVEREIGNTY, AND SELF-DETERMINATION: THE ACCOMMODATION OF CONFLICTING RIGHTS 209 (1990); Macdonald, *supra* note 2, at 135–37.

[57] In contrast to the current need for external assistance, most commentators argue that the Miskitos' historically strong commercial ties with the United Kingdom and the United States have not been based on dependency. *See generally* CRAIG L. DOZIER, NICARAGUA'S MOSQUITO SHORE: THE YEARS OF BRITISH AND AMERICAN PRESENCE (1985) (history of over four centuries of interaction between Miskitos and foreigners from perspective of foreigners).

[58] William O. Douglas, *Lawyers of the Peace Corps*, 48 A.B.A.J. 909, 913 (1962).

[59] WILLIAM D. ROGERS, THE TWILIGHT STRUGGLE: THE ALLIANCE FOR PROGRESS AND THE POLITICS OF DEVELOPMENT IN LATIN AMERICA 288 (1967).

origin, but also in character and implementation.[60] He did not criticize the motives of the participants, but described the legal assistance they provided as "a rather awkward mixture of goodwill, optimism, self-interest, arrogance, ethnocentricity, and simple lack of understanding."[61] This insensitivity to local cultures and issues is perhaps one of the reasons why the law and development movement lacked impact.

Thirty years later, the same patterns of ethnocentric zeal and cultural insensitivity are too often reflected in the educational assistance provided to the NAAR. While the USAID textbook project aimed to meet a need expressed by regional educators for pedagogical materials in the students' native languages, implementation of the project failed to incorporate guidance from regional educators and thus resulted in a product inappropriate for the students and in conflict with local values and realities.

However, lack of cultural sensitivity is not unique to foreign nations. The Atlantic Coast has had conflicts over assistance programs coordinated by the Nicaraguan government in Managua. When the Sandinistas gained power in 1979, one of their first projects was a widespread Spanish literacy campaign. The project aimed to reduce the illiteracy rate of the population from fifty percent to fifteen percent over the course of nine months.[62] The literacy campaign drew upon a pedagogical methodology developed in Cuba, Brazil, and Mexico that sought to develop both political awareness and literacy. In fact, one of the twenty-three themes used to organize the initial set of materials referred to the strengthening of transportation systems between the Atlantic Coast and western Nicaragua, reflecting the political goal of integrating the Atlantic Coast with the rest of the country.[63]

The Spanish language literacy campaign had roughly 50,000 participants on the Atlantic Coast.[64] Many, however, complained about the assimilative focus and the sole use of Spanish, which permitted coastal participants to become

---

[60] *See* JAMES A. GARDNER, LEGAL IMPERIALISM: AMERICAN LAWYERS AND FOREIGN AID IN LATIN AMERICA 283 (1980).

[61] *Id.* at 4.

[62] *See* ROBERT F. ARNOVE, EDUCATION AND REVOLUTION IN NICARAGUA 19 (1986) [hereinafter ARNOVE, EDUCATION AND REVOLUTION].

[63] In translation, the generative sentences are "The revolution opens up a road system to the Atlantic Coast. The Kurinwás is a navigable river." VALERIE MILLER, BETWEEN STRUGGLE AND HOPE: THE NICARAGUAN LITERACY CRUSADE 77 (1985).

[64] The October 1979 census estimated that roughly seventy-five percent of the population on the Atlantic Coast was illiterate. In 1980, approximately 50,000 participated in the literacy campaign in the region, allegedly reducing the illiteracy rate to roughly thirty percent. *See* ARNOVE, EDUCATION AND REVOLUTION, *supra* note 62, at 26.

literate only in their second language.[65] After the close of the campaign, the Sandinista government began a follow-up campaign in the major languages of the Atlantic Coast: English, Miskito, and Sumo. In 1980 and 1981, over 12,500 people participated in the follow-up campaign.[66]

The follow-up campaign had a very different impact from that of the Spanish language literacy campaign. As part of the follow-up campaign literacy curriculum, instructors encouraged their students to think about the possibility of autonomy for the region. However, when the Miskito leader of the political organization MISURASATA (Miskito, Sumo, Rama, Sandinistas All Together) was detained by the Sandinistas in February of 1981, many Miskitos withdrew from the campaign. The region thus entered a period of turmoil that was to last for a number of years. In the example of the follow-up literacy campaign, outside educational assistance provided in conjunction with local educators was central in galvanizing local political constituencies to form alliances seeking autonomy and formal structural change.

The problem of minority language rights is complex in the NAAR. Miskito speakers dominate numerically and politically, and educational programs in Sumo and Rama are few. The history of conflict between the indigenous groups only exacerbates these tensions. One anthropologist describes the Miskitos' "feeling of superiority over the shy and defensive Sumu," including their sense of greater intelligence, better hygiene, and stronger hospitality.[67] This intra-regional level conflict over educational programs is not addressed by the Autonomy Statute, which devolves administrative control over education to the regional level, where Miskitos dominate.

IV. SELF-DETERMINATION AND EDUCATIONAL CHANGE IN THE NAAR

Conceptually, the tension between self-determination as anti-imperialist and education as inherently imperialist is strong. In practice, however, education can play a critical role in the struggle for self-determination. When a nation alters its system of governance by reallocating power to newly autonomous regions, control over education is often one of the responsibilities that is most entirely devolved to the autonomous government.[68] The practical effect of these new

---

[65] The Center for Information and Documentation of the Atlantic Coast (CIDCA) estimated that sixty-three percent of the residents of the Atlantic coast are Spanish-speaking Latinos, twenty-four percent Miskito speakers, ten percent English speakers, 2.5 percent Sumo speakers, .47 percent Garifuno speakers, and .24 percent Rama speakers. *See* ARNOVE, EDUCATION AND REVOLUTION, *supra* note 62, at 42 n.23.

[66] *See id.* at 26. The government asserted an illiteracy rate of twenty-two percent in the region at the close of the follow-up literacy campaigns.

[67] MARY W. HELMS, ASANG: ADAPTATIONS TO CULTURE CONTACT IN A MISKITO COMMUNITY 222 (1971).

[68] *See generally* DOCUMENTS ON AUTONOMY AND MINORITY RIGHTS (H. Hannum, ed., 1993) (compiling autonomy statutes from various regions). Two countries with legal

legal provisions, however, may ultimately be frustrated by other more informal methods of control.

The decentralization of educational control was the focus of NAAR educational reforms in the years immediately following the adoption of the Autonomy Statute. In Latin America, most educational systems are coordinated and governed by central agencies. Given this strong centralist tradition, the decentralization of these State functions is a major change.[69] Education is a governmental function well suited to administrative and political decentralization. Most people have had at least some contact with formal educational institutions and have some degree of interest in their operation. Further, many people feel that their children's education should reflect the experiences of people in the local community. Local educators in particular usually favor some degree of local administrative control.

Dennis Rondinelli, a policy analyst specializing in development and decentralization issues, distinguished four varieties of decentralization in developing countries: deconcentration, delegation, devolution, and privatization.[70] Other authors divide decentralization into two types: political and administrative.[71] In the

---

provisions giving autonomous governments control over education are the Philippines and Spain. *See* Act No. 6734, Providing for an Organic Act for the Autonomous Region in Muslim Mindanao, art. XV §1 (1 Aug. 1989) ("The Autonomous Region shall establish, maintain and support a complete and integral system of quality education and adopt an educational framework that is meaningful, relevant and responsive to the needs, ideals and aspirations of the people in the Region."), Autonomy Statute of the Basque Country, Organic Law 3/1979, art. 15 (18 Dec. 1979) ("responsibility lies with the Autonomous Community of the Basque country for education in its entirety, regardless of what level, degree, kind or specialty it may be . . .").

[69] *See* CLAUDIO VÉLIZ, THE CENTRALIST TRADITION OF LATIN AMERICA (1980).

[70] *See* DENNIS RONDINELLI ET AL., DECENTRALIZATION IN DEVELOPING COUNTRIES: A REVIEW OF RECENT EXPERIENCE (Washington, DC: World Bank Staff Working Paper No. 581, Management and Development Series (No. 8), 1983). In DENNIS RONDINELLI ET AL., PLANNING EDUCATION REFORMS IN DEVELOPING COUNTRIES: THE CONTINGENCY APPROACH (1990), Rondinelli and his coauthors promote a contingency approach to implementing educational change in developing countries. While his analysis is flawed because of his assumption that changes will be developed by planners working in isolation, his method of implementing the changes resembles Michael Fullan's evolutionary planning or problem-coping techniques. *See* MICHAEL FULLAN, THE NEW MEANING OF EDUCATIONAL CHANGE (2d ed. 1991). He observed that educational systems are "people-centered," and thus rigid, bureaucratic techniques for managing change are inadequate. Furthermore, structural change, such as the change considered in the NAAR, is highly innovative in that it alters the foundation of the educational system. With people-centered environments and innovative changes, a flexible approach is key. Contingency analysis emphasizes extensive planning in conjunction with the ongoing amending of plans in response to actual, contextual events.

[71] *See* H.V. SAVITCH & MADELEINE ADLER, DECENTRALIZATION AT THE GRASS ROOTS: POLITICAL INNOVATION IN NEW YORK CITY AND LONDON (1974). Yet even administrative decentralization involves decisions on how new subunits should be managed and who should do the managing—arguably political decisions. *See* B.C. SMITH, DECENTRALIZA-

Atlantic Coast, for example, the Autonomy Statute assigns to the region the task of administering the educational system with the coordination of the corresponding central government ministry.[72] Placing principal responsibility in the hands of the autonomous government is an actual devolution of political and administrative control over the educational system—a very powerful form of decentralization. The transfer of responsibility for the administration of educational programs to the NAAR regional government may support educational initiatives, such as the bilingual/intercultural program, that are sensitive to regional needs. The Autonomy Statute gives a newly created Regional Council the right to promulgate resolutions concerning the administration of various municipal functions,[73] including education.[74]

The transfer of control over educational resources was an important element of the NAAR decentralization process. Nonetheless, the Ministry of Education in Managua still nominated people for positions in the regional educational system, and funding for the regional system still came from Managua. Indeed, central politicians and institutions appeared reluctant to relinquish control. While the region historically enjoyed a degree of *de facto* autonomy in the post-Autonomy Statute environment, the NAAR needed to develop formal structures to facilitate decentralized educational decision making.

Four governmental units administered education in Puerto Cabezas, the capital of the NAAR: the Instituto Nicaraguense de Desarrollo de las Regiones Autónomas (Nicaraguan Institute for the Development of the Autonomous Regions, known as INDERA), the Ministry of Education in Managua, the regional Ministry of Education in Puerto Cabezas, and the municipal Ministry of Education in Puerto Cabezas. Although the three levels of the Ministry of Education were part of the same structure, communication between the units was tense and fragmented. For example, INDERA, an institute with cabinet-level status in the central government, was outside the Ministry of Education structure, and it communicated primarily with the municipal Ministry of Education. All four units were involved in coastal education to one extent or another, yet the lack of coordination led to poor communication and duplication of efforts, limiting economic and managerial efficiency. Ultimately, this duplication of tasks diverted scarce funds from areas of urgent need. Poor communication fostered a top-heavy bureaucracy in which many educators dedicated time to supervising and coordinating the work of their unit while neglecting other units.

TION: THE TERRITORIAL DIMENSION OF THE STATE (1985) (arguing the distinction instead should be between decentralization and autonomy).

[72] *See* Autonomy Statute for the Regions of the Atlantic Coast of Nicaragua, Law No. 28, Sept. 7, 1987, *reprinted in* DOCUMENTS ON AUTONOMY AND MINORITY RIGHTS 386 (Hurst Hannum ed., 1993), at art. 8.1.

[73] *See id.* at arts. 17, 23.1.

[74] *See id.* at art. 8.2. However, the Regional Council has been extremely slow to approve any resolutions involving the region.

This complex administrative bureaucracy diminishes government responsiveness to societal needs and demands. One unit may become aware of a new community need, but this is unlikely to be communicated to other units in the structure. Thus, rather than focusing their efforts on determining community needs and allocating governmental resources accordingly, educators devote time to building up their unit to the detriment of the other units.

Communication among governmental units is understandably difficult within a rudimentary transportation and communication infrastructure. However, the situation could have improved if educators and administrators made inter-unit communication a higher priority. The regional and municipal Ministries of Education, which are both located in Puerto Cabezas, could have held regular joint sessions to update each other on recent projects. INDERA and the Ministry of Education in Managua similarly could have shared information on a regular basis. Officials in all units could have assumed formal responsibility for updating others within their unit on the progress of other units. Communication between the Coast and Managua is more difficult, but educators and administrators could have reported by radio, and the benefits of the periodic visits officials from Managua already made to other regions could have been maximized through a conscious effort to meet with educators in all units.

Instead, educational administrators motivated by the scarcity of local resources have looked to outside sources of funding and technical assistance. Because of a lack of local involvement in the process, the implementation of educational reform in the region has frequently fallen far short of the aspirations of regional educators. Incidents like the conflict over the *Siakni Bara Pihni* textbooks illustrate common problems in educational reform. In that case, a purported effort to strengthen the bilingual/intercultural education program—an outgrowth of local priorities in education—yielded materials that ignore or even attack the cultural realities and values of the region.

Fortunately, the Autonomy Statute supports a more locally responsive form of education. It establishes the right to promote the study of traditional cultures and to provide education in the native languages of the region, with a program respecting and supporting local values and traditions.[75] Yet, despite the Autonomy Statute, local educators have failed to realize meaningful control over the regional educational system. Scarcity of resources dictates cooperation with outsiders who provide material assistance, and the complex administrative structure effectively removes substantive control from the hands of local educators.

Although the Autonomy Statute was approved a decade ago, the NAAR has made little progress toward strengthening local control over education. Outsiders will likely play a role in the process, but outside assistance can have a lasting positive effect only to the extent that it supports local efforts to benefit students in the region through formal autonomy and control over education.

---

[75] *See id.* at arts. 8.5, 11.5.

In recent years, international law has clarified and strengthened provisions establishing the right of autonomy of indigenous peoples. As a result, in Nicaragua, as in many other places, indigenous peoples have gained increased control over their educational system. However, that educational system in many ways replicates the imperialistic aims of an earlier era. Minority indigenous groups, such as the Sumo, face threats to their intellectual autonomy from the enduring educational structures in Managua as well as from programs newly implemented by the Miskitos. In order to realize a lasting and meaningful autonomy, indigenous peoples in the region must work to develop an educational structure that minimizes the indoctrinating forces of education while using education as a tool of self-determination and autonomy.

CHAPTER 10

INDIGENOUS RIGHTS AND THE CASE OF THE YANOMAMI INDIANS IN BRAZIL

Gale Goodwin Gomez

I. INTRODUCTION

The United Nations' designation of 1993 as the International Year for the World's Indigenous Peoples was an extension of the recognition of the plight of indigenous populations that grew out of the quincentennial commemorations of Christopher Columbus' arrival in the New World. The year 1992 was instrumental in focusing the attention of dominant societies on their indigenous populations. Countries throughout North, Central, and South America, as well as the former European colonial powers, were given a view of their histories from a different perspective—that of the original inhabitants of the Americas.

The dominant societies were forced to examine the present state of these peoples and to listen to their voices. The initial desire of the so-called Western world to celebrate the 500-year anniversary was tempered by the responses of indigenous peoples, such as Suzan Shown Harjo, a Cheyenne-Creek, who stated, ''. . . we have no reason to celebrate an invasion that caused the demise of so many of our people and is still causing destruction today. The Europeans stole our land and killed our people.''[1]

For the Brazilian Yanomami, 1992 was also an important year; their traditional homeland was formally demarcated as an indigenous reserve. Ironically, this hard-fought victory has not guaranteed their right to life and land. This article describes their struggle for survival over the past two decades within the context of indigenous rights in Latin America. It concludes with an evaluation of their current situation, the role of the Pro-Yanomami Commission, and major concerns for the future.

II. HUMAN RIGHTS ABUSES IN LATIN AMERICA

The fact that, in the societies in which they live, indigenous people are the most marginalized and discriminated against reflects the political and economic

---

[1] *We Have No Reason to Celebrate an Invasion*, Interview with Suzan Shown Harjo, in RETHINKING COLUMBUS 4 (Bill Bigelow et al., eds., 1991).

effects of the last 500 years. In those cases where Indians have been assimilated into the general population, as in much of North and Central America—including Mexico, Costa Rica, Honduras, and El Salvador—their situation is similar to that of other economically disadvantaged groups. On the other hand, many indigenous communities in Latin America have been able to maintain their ethnic identities, their languages, and their traditional cultural and religious beliefs to a greater or lesser extent, depending on the specific local circumstances. For example, in Guatemala, the Mayan people make up fifty percent of the country's total population. In Bolivia, sixty-six percent of its inhabitants are identified as indigenous, while in Peru the percentage of indigenous inhabitants is thirty-nine, and in Ecuador it is twenty-nine.[2] Since the arrival of Columbus and the subsequent European invasion and occupation, indigenous peoples throughout the Americas have suffered every possible violation of their human rights. Countless historical, political, economic, and sociocultural factors have been given to account for this tragedy, but the underlying reality is that the indigenous communities of the Americas are the survivors of 500 years of premeditated genocide. In a special publication entitled *Human Rights Violations Against Indigenous Peoples in the Americas*, Amnesty International describes the current situation in North, Central, and South America with respect to the five types of human rights abuses that fall within its mandate. These include: extrajudicial execution, the judicial death penalty, "disappearance," torture and ill-treatment, arbitrary detention and unfair trial.[3]

The brutality and the magnitude of the abuses suffered by indigenous peasants in Guatemala, for example, is almost inconceivable. According to Amnesty International, during the 1980s thousands of people, particularly indigenous peasants, were reported "disappeared," entire villages were destroyed, and thousands extrajudicially executed as the Guatemalan military carried out its counterinsurgency program.[4] The suffering of these people and the efforts by some to help them was recognized by the awarding of the Nobel Peace Prize to Rigoberta Menchu. This award highlighted the culmination of international outrage over the Guatemalan government's blatantly genocidal acts.

Since 1983, Amnesty International has documented at least 4,200 cases in Peru of "disappearances" following detention by security forces.[5] At least 500 more killings have been documented in eighteen separate massacres by government forces.[6] A similar tale can be told of massive human rights violations in

---

[2] JULIAN BURGER, REPORT FROM THE FRONTIER: THE STATE OF THE WORLD'S INDIGENOUS PEOPLES 89 (1987)

[3] *See* AMNESTY INTERNATIONAL, HUMAN RIGHTS VIOLATIONS AGAINST INDIGENOUS PEOPLES IN THE AMERICAS 6 (1992).

[4] *See id.* at 12.

[5] *See id.* at 13.

[6] *Id.*

El Salvador during the civil war.[7] Additional instances of recent human rights violations against specific indigenous victims in other Latin American countries are described by Amnesty International throughout this special report.

The native populations of Central and South America were, from the earliest contact, treated with a total lack of respect by the European explorers and colonizers. Because of their deep-seated racism and cultural and religious intolerance, many of these Europeans believed not only that the indigenous populations were less than human and had no right to exist, but that it was, in fact, their noble duty to ''assimilate or annihilate'' them. Furthermore, the invaders believed that they were empowered by God to Christianize the native populations and to exploit the natural resources of the New World for their own benefit.

In hindsight, we might be tempted to say that these attitudes were the product of ignorance and, in this way, rationalize our forefathers' barbaric actions. How do we account, however, for the fact that such attitudes remain prevalent throughout the Americas and the world today? One modern-day version, for example, frames intolerance in terms of development: ''An area as rich as this, with gold, diamonds and uranium, cannot afford the luxury of preserving half a dozen Indian tribes which are holding up development.''[8] This statement, made in 1975 by the governor of the state of Roraima in northern Brazil, was in reaction to the international campaign on behalf of the Yanomami Indians, whose very survival continues to be threatened by the presence of gold prospectors on their land. Similar sentiments continue to be expressed regularly in the local presses throughout the Amazonian region. The principle of *terra nullius,* which provided the rationale for early exploration, continues to be invoked to support the exploitation, development, and colonization of what is considered to be ''empty land.'' These regions, such as the Amazon Basin today, are viewed as uninhabited and ''free for the taking'' despite the fact that indigenous communities have been living there for thousands of years.

The most basic of all human rights is the right to life as set forth in article 3 of the United Nations Universal Declaration of Human Rights.[9] For the Yanomami and for many indigenous peoples, the right to life, however, is directly linked to their rights to the lands they inhabit and the resources found on these lands. The indigenous societies that today still maintain their traditional ways of life and means of subsistence are those least affected by contact with the dominant societies in which they live. These are generally groups that are found in remote areas—such as the Amazon rain forest—which, until the last century, were either physically inaccessible or of little interest to the outside world. It is ironic that these are precisely the people who are now caught in the struggle to exploit the world's remaining natural resources.

---

[7] *Id.*

[8] *See* Burger, *supra* note 2, at 3.

[9] *See* Universal Declaration of Human Rights, G.A. Res. 217 (III 1948), art. 3.

In tropical forests there is an especially close relationship between the environment, its indigenous inhabitants, and their human rights. Consequently, the main source of conflict between the Yanomami and the outside world continues to be land and natural resources. The dramatic contrast between the relationship of indigenous people to land and nature and the attitude of Western, technological peoples toward the natural environment underlies much of the conflict between the two groups. Davi Kopenawa, the Yanomami leader, once made the astute observation that when the white man speaks of protecting the "environment," he is referring to *that part of nature which is left over* after he has stripped it for his needs.[10] The exploitation of the natural world by the white man is in sharp contrast to the indigenous view that the earth, the environment, and all of the natural world are inseparable from life itself.

III. THE YANOMAMI: ETHNOGRAPHIC BACKGROUND

There are over 20,000 Yanomami Indians living in the Amazon rain forest on both sides of the border between northern Brazil and southern Venezuela; the latest census conducted by the Brazilian National Health Foundation (March 1995) shows a population of 9,386 Yanomami in 188 communities in Brazil.[11] The Venezuelan Yanomami are more numerous, possibly exceeding 15,000 people.[12] They are seminomadic, hunter-horticulturalists, who also fish and gather forest products. They maintain gardens of bananas, plantains, manioc, sweet potatoes, and other crops. They live in communal dwellings of 30 to 150 or more people, and move their villages every three to five years as the soil and game in the area become depleted. Some relatively permanent settlements, located near religious missions or government outposts, are, to a large extent, a result of contact with the outside world and the Yanomami's acquired need for medical treatment and manufactured goods, especially metal tools.

Social groups are based on kinship, and extended families form the basis of a community. The interrelationships among villages are a continuation of this kinship network. Interaction between villages most often occurs during feasts, which are celebrated as part of the funerary ritual of a deceased relative. They frequently involve establishing alliances and resolving disputes, contracting marriages and renewing friendships, as well as bartering manufactured (e.g., knives, machetes, fish hooks) and traditional goods (e.g., resin, bows, arrows). The sociopolitical organization is egalitarian. Leaders of a community are usually respected, older men who influence by persuasion and example. There are no hierarchical or hereditary social or political positions. Many village leaders are also respected spiritual practitioners, or shamans, who play an important role in

---

[10] Author's personal communication.

[11] *See* DSY/FNS-RR, 03/95, *quoted in* CCPY UPDATE # 92, 1 (April 1997).

[12] MARCUS COLCHESTER, VENEZUELA: VIOLATIONS OF INDIGENOUS RIGHTS 8 (1996).

interceding with the spiritual world. Any man who chooses to do so may become a shaman after a lengthy and rigorous apprenticeship.

Their socioeconomic system requires extensive areas of land. Vast networks of trails link villages, which maintain trade and social alliances. Their system of shifting cultivation and their other subsistence activities are predicated on the availability of large tracts of land to promote soil regeneration and the replenishment of animal and plant stocks.[13] The Amazon rain forest, though ecologically fragile, is one of the most biologically diverse regions on earth. Every possible, useful forest product is gathered by the Yanomami for their daily needs. They eat much of what they gather, like wild fruits, especially from a variety of palm trees, grub larvae found in rotten palm trunks, and numerous types of wild honey. They use both crushed seeds of the annatto bush (*Bixa orellana*) and juice from the fruit of the genipap tree (*Genipa Americana* L.) for body painting. They also use hundreds of different species of trees, vines, and other plants for house construction materials, for medicinal and magical purposes, for hammocks, baskets, bows and arrows, and other necessities. The forest has, for countless generations, provided them with everything they need to survive physically, culturally, and spiritually.

IV. CONTACT AND EXPLOITATION

During the 1950s and 1960s, contact with the outside world was sporadic and limited to individuals or small groups, such as extractivists, government personnel, and missionaries. It was not until the 1960s that FUNAI, the Brazilian National Indian Foundation, made its initial contacts with the Yanomami. During the decade of the 1970s, however, two events brought the outside world into Yanomami territory in a major way and with devastating effects. One was the beginning of construction of the Northern Perimeter Highway (BR-210) from Manaus to Caracaraí; the other was the publication of the results of an aerial survey of the Amazon, carried out by the RADAM (Radar Amazonia) BRASIL project.

The RADAM BRASIL project produced satellite photographs of the Amazon Basin, indicating the location of potential mineral deposits. This, of course, brought immediate attention to the development potential of Amazonia and attracted mineral prospectors as well as large mining companies to the area. Since the discovery in 1975 of large deposits of cassiterite (tin ore) in the Serra de Surucucus region in the center of Yanomami territory, illegal invasions of the land by mineral prospectors have remained a continuous threat.[14] Subsequently, uranium, gold, diamonds, and titanium were also discovered on Yanomami

---

[13] ANTHROPOLOGY RESOURCE CENTER (ARC), THE YANOMAMI PARK: A CALL FOR ACTION 2 (1981) [hereinafter Anthropology Resource Center].

[14] Severo Gomes, *Legal Project n. 379/85 in* URIHI No. 2 (1986) at 17.

lands. Illegal invasions of the Yanomami territory by gold prospectors, or *garimpeiros*, began in earnest in 1976 and culminated in the gold rush of 1987.

These invasions brought disease and death in genocidal proportions to the Yanomami. Like other native peoples, the Yanomami have no natural immunities to the so-called white man's diseases such as malaria, measles, mumps, tuberculosis, venereal diseases, and common respiratory infections. Uncontrolled contact with the national society, especially gold prospectors, has resulted in 2,280 deaths since 1987; that represents over 20% of the Brazilian Yanomami population.[15]

The other event, which brought the Yanomami into forced contact with Brazilian society, was the construction of Brazil's Northern Perimeter Highway. Begun in 1973, it cut through the southeastern part of their territory in the Brazilian State of Roraima along 225 kms. Twenty-two percent of the Yanomami living near the construction areas died in the first year, principally from respiratory diseases contracted from construction workers.[16] The Yanomami living near the Ajarani River suffered a decrease in population from 400 in the 1960s to seventy-nine people in 1975.[17] The workers also introduced the indigenous population to prostitution and begging, which contributed to the social breakdown of these communities. Even after the highway construction was abandoned in 1976, the effects of contact continued to devastate the Yanomami in these peripheral areas. In fact, during 1977 and 1978, a measles epidemic killed half the population of four communities in the Upper Catrimani region.[18]

V. YANOMAMI CAMPAIGN

Between 1968 and 1978, anthropologists and missionaries petitioned the Brazilian government on eleven occasions for a protected land area for the Yanomami, but to no avail. Outraged by the ever-worsening situation of the Yanomami people, a group of concerned citizens in Brazil founded an independent, nonprofit, nongovernmental organization called the Commission for the Creation of the Yanomami Park (CCPY) that has recently been renamed The Pro-Yanomami Commission. In 1979, CCPY presented to the Brazilian government the first of several detailed proposals for the creation of the Yanomami Park, a protected indigenous reserve. The park proposal was the result of a comprehensive study of the historical, anthropological, judicial, ecological, and medical justifications for the demarcation of a single continuous protected area.

---

[15] CCPY, UPDATE # 83 2 (DECEMBER, 1995).

[16] ALCIDA R. RAMOS AND KENNETH I. TAYLOR, THE YANOMAMI IN BRAZIL 1979, 9 and 13 (1979).

[17] *See* Anthropology Resource Center, *supra* note 13, at 2.

[18] *See* RAMOS AND TAYLOR, *supra* note 16.

Since its founding, CCPY has coordinated an advocacy campaign to protect Yanomami rights and promote the creation of the park. The campaign has involved the collaboration of numerous human rights advocacy groups and environmental organizations in the U.S. and Europe, including (among others) the Anti-Slavery Society of London, the Indian Law Resource Center, Survival International, Cultural Survival, the Environmental Defense Fund, the National Wildlife Federation, the Natural Resources Defense Council, Friends of the Earth, and the Sierra Club.

The biggest threat to the Yanomami's human rights and, in fact, to their survival, are the recurrent invasions into their territory by illegal gold miners. Between 1987 and 1990, the Yanomami faced a gold rush of genocidal proportions with no medical care or outside help of any kind. Without warning, the Brazilian government expelled all medical (and other) personnel from the area, including medical teams from CCPY and two religious missions. An estimated 45,000 miners were illegally panning for gold in Yanomami territory during this period,[19] and hundreds of aircraft were flying into 110 clandestine airstrips daily to provide them with supplies and transportation.[20] The incidence of malaria among the Yanomami quadrupled; eighty to ninety percent of the populations of some villages were infected, and entire communities were wiped out.[21]

For two years the Brazilian government did nothing. This total lack of political will by the government of President José Sarney prompted accusations of "genocide by neglect" of the Yanomami people.[22] Because of the international outcry over this grave situation, an emergency health plan for the Yanomami was finally undertaken in January 1990. The intense domestic and international pressure led Fernando Collor de Mello, at that time Brazil's newly elected president, to order the expulsion of the *garimpeiros* by federal police in "Operation Free Jungle," at a cost to the government of nearly two million dollars.[23] Subsequently, anthropologists, missionaries, medical teams were allowed to return to work in the area after three years' interdiction.

Environmental and human rights groups, in an effort coordinated by CCPY, brought the ongoing tragedy of the Brazilian Yanomami to the attention of international press and to their respective governments. Through letters and personal contacts, pressure was brought to bear directly on the Brazilian government and on the World Bank because of its financial support for natural resource management projects in Brazil. Davi Kopenawa, the Yanomami leader, was

---

[19] *See* URIHI, No. 10, CCPY, 39 (1990).

[20] AÇÃO PELA CIDADANIA, YANOMAMI : A TODOS OS POVOS DA TERRA 40 (1990).

[21] *See* URIHI, *supra* note 19, at 5.

[22] *See* SURVIVAL INTERNATIONAL, YANOMAMI SURVIVAL CAMPAGN (1990), and AÇÃO PELA CIDADANIA, *supra* note 20 at 35.

[23] *See* URIHI, *supra* note 19, at 42.

honored with the Global 500 Award by the United Nations Environment Program in 1988 for his defense of the rain forest.

In the months preceding the U.N. Conference on Environment and Development (UNCED) held in Rio de Janeiro in June, 1992, the international campaign for the creation of the Yanomami Park intensified. In April 1991, Davi Kopenawa traveled to New York and met with United Nations' Secretary-General Perez de Cuellar, who took a personal interest in the Yanomami situation. Kopenawa also met with World Bank and U.S. officials in Washington, seeking support for the Yanomami Park. Protests were organized at Brazilian embassies and consulates worldwide and letter-writing campaigns inundated government offices in Brasília. "Between July and October 1991, FUNAI [the Brazilian National Indian Foundation] received 11,801 letters and petitions from individuals and organizations in 35 countries asking that Yanomami territory be demarcated."[24] The international pressure on Brazil's president to protect the Yanomami and their rain forest habitat was tremendous. Both conservationist and human rights groups in the United States lobbied senators and congressmen on behalf of the Yanomami. In anticipation of a visit by the Brazilian president, eight U.S. senators—including Al Gore and Edward Kennedy—urged President George Bush in a letter dated June 14, 1991, "to include the plight of the Yanomami people in your discussions next week with Brazilian President Fernando Collor de Mello."[25]

Finally, on November 15, 1991, President Fernando Collor surprised both supporters and opponents by announcing the administrative demarcation of the Yanomami territory.[26] Less than six months later, the physical demarcation of 68,000 sq. miles of Amazon rain forest (an area the size of Washington state) was completed. Despite strong objections from the military and from mining interests, President Collor signed the decree ratifying the demarcation and legally created the Yanomami Indigenous Reserve on May 25, 1992.[27] The political and financial scandal that forced Collor's resignation, however, left an unstable climate that further weakened prospects for the future of the reserve.

No sooner had the indigenous reserve been established than gold prospectors began re-invading Yanomami territory. By early 1993, an estimated 11,000 *garimpeiros* were once again working illegally within the reserve, seriously threatening the lives of the Yanomami and destroying the environment.[28] A

---

[24] *The Collor Administration and the Yanomami (Part 2) in* YANOMAMI URGENTE, No. 14, 7 (1991)

[25] *Id.*

[26] CCPY, "UPDATE 49" 1 (Nov. 18, 1991)

[27] CCPY, "UPDATE 57" 1 (June 1, 1992).

[28] THE N. Y. TIMES, Mar. 8, 1993, at A7 and CCPY, "UPDATE 63" 1 (Jan. 22, 1993).

second "Operation Free Jungle" was undertaken by the government to remove the gold prospectors.[29]

In July of that same year, sixteen Yanomami (including women and children) of the community of Haximu (just across the border in Venezuela) were killed and mutilated in two attacks by illegal Brazilian gold miners. [30] International pressure resulted in investigations into the incidents by the governments of both Brazil and Venezuela. Twenty-three suspects were named but only two clandestine gold miners were arrested by the Brazilian police. These two were released from police custody by a federal court judge.[31] Brazil's External Commission, established to investigate the massacres, concluded in its report that the incidents did indeed represent genocide and urged the government to increase its efforts to expel the *garimpeiros*.[32] To date, no one has ever been brought to trial for murdering a Yanomami.

Since that time, politicians, mining interests, and elements of the Brazilian military have remained determined to undermine the gains made on behalf of the Yanomami. Because a large part of the reserve coincides with the 150 km. international border with Venezuela, the issue of "national security" remains a serious threat to Yanomami land tenure. Kopenawa responded to the continued threats to the existence of the reserve:

> The whites don't want the land; they only want the gold, pieces of rock; they don't like the land; they only like gold, diamonds, money, that's all. That is why we Yanomami don't want them to keep harassing us, destroying the river, destroying the land, destroying the forest. They need to look at the law and respect it.[33]

VI. THE CURRENT SITUATION

Two recent government actions may have disastrous consequences for many of Brazil's Indians. The first is governmental Decree 1775, introduced on January 8, 1996.[34] This decree gives "interested parties," such as state and municipal authorities, ranchers, mining and logging companies, and settlers, the right to challenge demarcations of indigenous lands, past and future, that have not completed the final step of registration. Technically, 344 Indian areas are eligible for challenge under this new law. The Minister of Justice, Nelson Jobim, will make the final decisions on the documents presented. Brazilian Jurist Dalmo

---

[29] *Id.*

[30] CCPY, "UPDATE 71" 1 (Aug. 31, 1993).

[31] CCPY "UPDATE 73" 1 (Jan. 20, 1994).

[32] *Id.* at 2.

[33] Davi Kopenawa, Statement to CCPY (1995)(Gale Goodwin Gomez trans.).

[34] Decree No. 1775, Jan. 8, 1996, *described* in CCPY "UPDATE 85" 1 (Feb. 1996).

Dallari warns, "The decree is highly damaging to the Indians and favorable to land sharks and other adventurers who have invaded or want to invade Indian lands, and will be the cause of violent conflicts, with a foreseeably tragic outcome."[35] Brazilian NGOs and international organizations have called the new decree unconstitutional and have vigorously protested its enactment.

While the terms of the decree would theoretically exclude the Yanomami area because its demarcation has already been registered, many interested parties have interpreted the decree as permitting challenges to all demarcations. Those who want to abolish the Yanomami reserve have praised the decree. Among these are Almir Sa, president of the Legislative Assembly, and Congressman (and ex-gold miner) Elton Rohnelt from Roraima. Retired officers at the Military Club in Rio called for the immediate cancellation of the Yanomami reserve, declaring it a threat to national security.[36] Fortunately, however, the decree has had no direct impact on the Yanomami reserve.

The second, more recent, and most serious threat from the Brazilian government is a bill to allow mining in indigenous areas. This bill was introduced into the National Congress by Roraima representative and former FUNAI president Romero Juca, and it has already been approved in the Senate.[37] The justification given for the bill is that "the low exploration of Brazil's mineral potential causes enormous disadvantages to our economy."[38] This argument, however, takes no account of the fact that most indigenous lands were demarcated, at great cost and after much struggle, for the express purpose of protecting indigenous peoples from just such activities. Needless to say, the issue of indigenous human rights has been totally ignored by the proponents of the bill. Juca, who as president of FUNAI in the 1980s was supposed to defend the interests of Brazil's Indians, was recently described by CCPY as a man who "has been accused of using his office to favor loggers and has always championed the *garimpeiros*' cause."[39] Environmentalist and indigenous rights organizations will have their hands full once this bill passes in the House of Representatives and large-scale mining operations begin legally to exploit Indian lands. Such an outcome may be inevitable.

Keeping in mind the national climate promoted by such actions as Decree 1775 and the most recent bill to allow mining, it is not surprising that illegal invasions of the Yanomami Indigenous Reserve by *garimpeiros* continue despite the fact that it is fully demarcated and legally registered according to Brazilian law. In December 1995, the Organization of American States sent a mission to

---

[35] CCPY, "UPDATE 85" 2 (Feb. 1996).

[36] Id.

[37] CCPY, "UPDATE 93/94" 2 (May-July 1997).

[38] Id.

[39] Id.

Brazil to investigate alleged human rights violations against the Yanomami. A contemporaneous report by FUNAI states:

> the de-acceleration of the work of protecting the Yanomami area during the second half of 1995 has led to an increase in invasions. The removal of the garimpeiros is urgent, otherwise the Yanomami area will once again be totally invaded. If this happens all the work and the human and financial resources which have been invested will have been in vain.[40]

As of August 1997, there are at least twenty-four clandestine runways now in operation serving over 2,500 *garimpeiros.* Although President Fernando Henrique Cardoso personally gave his word nearly a year ago that the *garimpeiros* would be expelled and authorized the equivalent of six million dollars for the operation, the presidential promise remains unfulfilled, in spite of many appeals from national and international organizations and from the Yanomami themselves.''[41] The fact that the operation to expel the gold miners from the Yanomami territory continues to be delayed while the Brazilian congress considers a bill to permit mining on indigenous lands is suspect, to say the least. Such a situation is typical of the federal government's contradictory position with regard to protecting the rights of indigenous peoples, in general, and the Yanomami, in particular.

The continued presence of illegal gold miners not only pollutes the streams and rivers with deadly mercury, frightens away game animals, and results in violent conflicts between the miners and the Indians, but it dramatically increases the health risks to the Yanomami. There is a direct correlation between the presence of gold miners in the area and the mortality rate of the Yanomami, especially from malaria. Half of the total Yanomami population in Brazil (499.5 per 1,000 inhabitants) suffered from malaria in 1995.[42] This is over fifteen times the number of cases (30 per 1,000 inhabitants) considered by the World Health Organization to indicate a ''grave'' public health situation. Thirty-six of 172 total deaths registered during 1995 were due to malaria, the causes of seventy-four deaths were listed as unknown, while sixteen were caused by acute respiratory infections and six were homicides.[43] The spread of tuberculosis as well as respiratory and venereal infections is linked to the presence of gold miners. The incidence of tuberculosis among the Brazilian Yanomami in 1995 was 600 per 100,000 inhabitants, compared to fifty-six per 100,000 for Brazil as a whole in 1992 and an average of twenty per 100,000 for developed countries.[44]

---

[40] *See* ''UPDATE 85,'' *supra* note 35, at 2.

[41] *See* ''UPDATE 93/94,'' *supra* note 37 at 1.

[42] FNS/DSY Demographic Statistics for 1995, furnished to the author by Dr. Deise Alves Francisco, CCPY, Roraima, Brazil.

[43] *Id.*

[44] *Id.*

The Yanomami Health District (DSY) was created by the Brazilian government in 1991 as a means to reduce the high death rate. Although twenty-four health posts are presently operating in the Yanomami reserve under the auspices of seven different governmental, nongovernmental, and religious organizations, the health coverage is neither comprehensive nor consistent throughout the area. The Brazilian National Health Foundation (FNS), which coordinates these activities, has been plagued by frequent changes of personnel and inadequate funding. The World Bank, which funded a project for malaria control that provided substantial funding for the DSY until last year, is expected to finance a second health project in Amazonia. The World Bank is concerned, however, about "the federal government's intention to decentralise the activities of the FNS."[45] Such a move would place the responsibility for Yanomami health on local authorities, who "have neither the funds nor the trained staff to take over the work of the FNS."[46]

VII. THE WORK OF THE PRO-YANOMAMI COMMISSION

The advocacy work, which culminated in the creation of the Yanomami reserve, is only a part of the Pro-Yanomami Commission's (CCPY) effort to defend and protect the Yanomami people. Their physical survival remains as threatened as ever by the proverbial scourge of white man's diseases. CCPY began vaccination campaigns in Yanomami villages in 1980 and since 1983 has supported medical teams providing health care throughout Yanomami territory.

In 1990, following the devastating effects of the gold rush, Kopenawa requested that they open a health post in his village of Demini. Since then, CCPY has expanded its work to include health posts in two other regions, Toototobi and Balawaú, serving 1,207 Yanomami among thirty-five communities. Communication was found to be a major problem, however, in providing medical care throughout the Yanomami Health District because most Brazilian Yanomami do not speak Portuguese. Consequently, literacy education became the next priority.

The newest CCPY project, which is of great interest to the Indians, concerns education. One aspect of it is a bilingual literacy program at the village level that was initiated in July 1995 in Demini. Schools in other communities are already being planned. The literacy program is teaching the villagers to read and write their native Yanomami language, to speak, read, and write Portuguese, and to do basic arithmetic calculations.

The majority of Yanomami speak only their native languages, of which there are four: Yanomam, Yanomamï, Sanumá, and Ninam. Speakers of neighboring languages and dialects understand each other easily and intermarriage among these groups is not unusual. Those few Yanomami who also speak Portuguese are

---

[45] See "UPDATE 93/94," *supra* note 37.

[46] *Id.*

generally young men who have had prolonged contact with whites (particularly missionaries, cattle ranchers, construction workers, and mineral prospectors).

Another aspect of the education project is called "Video in the Villages." Its purpose is to equip isolated, indigenous communities with the capability to document and view their own important cultural events and ceremonies, as well as films of other indigenous communities. The video medium is also ideal for introducing preliterate peoples, such as the Yanomami, to important aspects of the national society.

One major goal of this two-part education project is to enable the Yanomami to deal directly with Brazilian officials and other outsiders who impact their survival and their future. Another goal is to train the Yanomami themselves to become literacy and health paraprofessionals in their own communities. Recently, three Yanomami men completed initial training to become microscope technicians who can diagnose malaria. Kopenawa describes the project as follows:

> We Yanomami need support for a school in Watorik [Demini]. We need to learn to write our own Yanomami language, to read, and to make accounts. And then we need to learn a little Portuguese, the Portuguese language, in order to defend our rights, our land. When a gold panner arrives in the reserve [we need] to be able to talk [to him]. When they want to pan gold near the village, we can talk [to them]—to not allow the gold panners to approach us here in the reserve. . . . And then when we have learned to read well and to make accounts, we are going to learn to work with the white health workers [as indigenous health agents].[47]

Until this decade the plight of the Yanomami had been told exclusively through nongovernmental organizations (specifically CCPY in Brazil), missionaries, and anthropologists. The Yanomami had no way to express directly their own beliefs, emotions, and concerns. Kopenawa has become well-known internationally as a spokesperson for his people. The ongoing CCPY health and education projects anticipate a new reality for the Yanomami, one in which they can play an active role in shaping their own future rather than having it determined by outside forces.

VIII. CONCLUSION

The basic right to life for the Yanomami, as is the case for many indigenous peoples, requires that they have control over their lands and resources. The traditional Yanomami ways of subsistence, their cultural and religious beliefs and practices, their languages, the organization of their social and political lives, the very essence of their existence depend upon the Amazon rain forest, which

---

[47] Davi Kopenawa, Statement to CCPY (1995)(Gale Goodwin Gomez trans.).

they have inhabited for, literally, thousands of years. Unfortunately, this same forest is coveted for its mineral resources by powerful interest groups that do not consider valid any indigenous claims to this land, whether legal or historical. The blatant disregard for the law by many local politicians, certain segments of the military, and both Brazilian and international business interests must be effectively dealt with if there is to be a positive resolution to the conflict between the Yanomami and the larger society that threatens to end their existence. The situation is analogous to that faced by Native North Americans a few hundred years ago, and this fact is not lost on most people when they hear about the plight of the Yanomami today.

Considering the impact of the last 500 years on the world's indigenous peoples, three questions come to mind in terms of potential outcomes for the Yanomami. First of all, can this conflict of interest between the traditional world and the modern world, between nature and industrialized man, be resolved? Second, does the Indian, the signer of broken treaties, always have to lose to the politically and economically more powerful adversary? Finally, has humankind learned nothing since the first explorers pillaged and destroyed the New World?

The fact that the Yanomami Indigenous Reserve was legally created, despite years of bureaucratic hassles and powerful opponents, has been a positive response to these questions. If the legal rights to this land cannot be guaranteed and protected, however, they are robbed of all meaning.

The ongoing health and education projects being conducted by CCPY, religious missions, Doctors of the World (MDM), the Brazilian National Health Foundation (FNS), and the Brazilian National Indian Foundation (FUNAI) are testimony to the belief that the Yanomami have the right to survive and thrive in the modern world. Thousands of people in Brazil and throughout the world continue to be involved in these efforts. Nevertheless, large segments of Brazilian society and the international business community must still be convinced of the validity of indigenous rights and the value of indigenous knowledge and culture as well as the global importance of protecting the Amazon Basin.

One very difficult issue to resolve, and one that is intertwined with all the others, is the conflict between the indigenous inhabitants' need to remain, unmolested, in the natural environment on which their lives depend and the desires of the industrial world to exploit the Amazon's natural resources. The future of the Amazon Basin and its peoples has such international importance that the Commission on Development and Environment of Amazonia was established to present a report prior to the United Nations Conference on Environment and Development, the so-called Earth Summit, held in Rio de Janeiro in June 1992. This document was prepared by the Inter-American Development Bank (IDB) and the United Nations Development Programme (UNDP) in collaboration with the Amazon Cooperation Treaty.[48] Its recommendations, which are

---

[48] COMMISSION ON DEVELOPMENT AND ENVIRONMENT FOR AMAZONIA, AMAZONIA WITHOUT MYTHS, iii. (1992).

based on the latest and most comprehensive scientific research conducted on the region, support ''the rights of the Indian and other peoples of the forest to the resources on which their economy is based,''[49] emphasize the importance of preserving biodiversity, and provide strategies for sustainable development.[50] The world would do well to read this report and heed its recommendations.

---

[49] *Id.* at 89.

[50] *Id.* at 65.

CHAPTER 11

ENVIRONMENTAL, ECONOMIC, SOCIAL, AND CULTURAL RIGHTS OF THE INDIGENOUS PEOPLES OF CHIAPAS, MEXICO

Richard J. Wilson

I. INTRODUCTION

This introduction will briefly summarize and bring up to date some of the major events following the armed insurgency of the Ejercito Zapatista de Liberación Nacional (EZLN, or Zapatistas) in Chiapas, Mexico, then describe the international legal actions taken on behalf of the indigenous peoples of that region in the Inter-American human rights system of the Organization of American States (OAS). This background is offered to give context to the more specific project of this essay: a discussion of the viable international legal claims by the peoples of Chiapas in response to violations of their environmental, indigenous, economic, social, and cultural rights by the government of Mexico.

A. Rebellion in Chiapas and Its Aftermath

The armed conflict in Chiapas was short-lived, but the consequences of the uprising, largely to indigenous peoples, have reverberated throughout Mexico and beyond, and will continue to do so for a long time. The uprising lasted for only the first few days in January 1994. It began on New Year's Day as a powerful protest against the inauguration of the North Atlantic Free Trade Agreement (NAFTA) and ended with a fragile peace that holds, though a massive army presence cordons the EZLN in the outer perimeter of the Lacandón rain forest in central Chiapas state.

Mexico has undergone a sea change since the rebellion, some of which is directly attributable to the armed uprising. Since the Zapatista conflict began, the most important events in the country include the assassination of Luis Donaldo Colosio in March 1994, the investigation of which has produced multiple conspiracy theories implicating actors, and perhaps family members, related to former president Carlos Salinas;[1] the November 1994 election of Ernesto Zedillo

---

[1] *See* Phil Davidson, *Ex-President of Mexico Attempts to Clear Name*, THE INDEPENDENT, Dec. 6, 1995, at 15.

as President, and the almost immediate collapse of the peso in international markets after his announcement that its price would no longer be controlled;[2] and local elections in October 1995, which eroded the power of the dominant Institutional Revolutionary Party (PRI), but left their power base intact in Chiapas state, where they won seventy of 111 municipalities.[3]

There is little doubt, however, that the EZLN has left a lasting political mark in Chiapas. In February 1995, newly elected President Zedillo, in an attempt to demonstrate his firmness in dealing with the rebellion, issued warrants for the arrest of Zapatista leaders and beefed up military presence in the state significantly. He lifted the warrants a month later and began negotiations with the Zapatistas again.[4] As an important statement of protest against the PRI, local indigenous people heavily boycotted the October 1995 local elections, and, alleging fraud by the PRI, briefly installed Amado Avedano, publisher of a local daily paper, *El Tiempo*, as "rebel governor."[5] Peace negotiations, guided by the thirty-four EZLN demands presented at the opening session of the negotiations, continue forward extremely slowly.[6] As early as March 1994, the Zapatistas reviewed a broad-ranging set of peace accords with the federal government and refused to put down their weapons until the negotiations were concluded.[7] Daily conflicts over land occupation and political power, however, continue to put the indigenous community in conflict with ranchers, local *caciques* (village leaders), and their political allies in the PRI; further bloodshed has occurred, with and without the army's participation. In February 1996, some progress was made with the signing of peace accords concluded in San Andres Larrainzar, Chiapas.[8]

---

[2] *See* Richard Lacayo, *The Plunger: The Peso Heads South*, Time, Jan. 9, 1995, at 44.

[3] *See Mexico: PRI Holds Chiapas Although Opposition Gains Ground*, INTERPRESS SERVICE, Oct. 16, 1995.

[4] *See* Medea Benjamin, *On the Road with the Zapatistas; Mexican Crackdown in Chiapas*, THE PROGRESSIVE, May 1995, at 28. Mexico is the only Latin American country engaged in a military build-up, largely in response to the Chiapas conflict. New expenditures for 1996 will be about fifteen billion pesos (two billion U.S. dollars). *See* William Perry, *Mexican Military Build-Up Continues*, JANE'S INTELLIGENCE REV., Apr. 1, 1996, at 3.

[5] *See* Bill Weinberg, *Rumbles of War, Rumors of Peace: Chiapas One Year Later*, THE NATION, Feb. 6, 1995, at 164.

[6] The thirty-four demands are included as an annex to a report by a human rights delegation of which I was a member, sponsored by the Ecumenical Program on Central America and the Caribbean (EPICA). *See* EPICA, Chiapas: THE REBELLION OF THE EXCLUDED 27, and Annex 1, at 32 (1994) [hereinafter EPICA Report]. The delegation conducted a fact-finding mission in Chiapas in February 1994. Many of the report's conclusions form the factual basis for the legal claims articulated here.

[7] *See* Tim Golden, *Rebel Leader Says Zapatistas Won't Disarm Yet*, N.Y. TIMES, Mar. 18, 1994, at A3.

[8] The text of the agreement is set out in Spanish in MEXPAZ: BOLETIN #60, Feb. 22, 1996, and is summarized in II MEXICO UPDATE −56, Jan. 23, 1996; and *Agreement*

The accords, endorsed by a ninety-eight-percent vote of the EZLN communities, commit the federal government to amending articles 4 and 115 of the Constitution to fully legitimize indigenous rights and guarantee indigenous participation in local government in Chiapas. The accords also call for creation of a new law for agrarian development; a new, local office of the National Human Rights Commission (CNDH) in Chiapas; the creation of a new commission for municipal reform, with guaranteed EZLN participation; and the outlawing of racial, ethnic, cultural, and religious discrimination. The agreements allow indigenous peoples of the region to apply their own customary laws within their communities.[9] There is little optimism for a prompt settling of the remaining issues on the table between the government and the rebels. A new round of negotiations was marred by violence against the Indian population, and issues that remain unsettled include important questions on political democracy, social justice, grassroots participation, human rights, the judicial system, national sovereignty, and democracy and the media.[10] There is little doubt, however, that the principles that motivate the EZLN, as well as its supporters inside and outside of Chiapas, will continue to affect the post-NAFTA character of Mexico.

Another positive effect of the rebellion is the solidarity shown by other indigenous communities of Mexico with the action taken in Chiapas and new pride and boldness in the assertion of rights in their own communities. Other indigenous communities have experienced rising consciousness of rights, and new progressive grassroots coalitions have emerged. Indigenous populations of Mexico are concentrated in what in colonial times was called the Republic of Indians: the states of Chiapas, Oaxaca, Tabasco, Michoacan, Guerrero, Puebla, Chihuahua, and Sonora, collectively known today as "Mexico *profundo*," or "deep Mexico."[11] The conflict in Chiapas has spread to Guerrero, where the state's governor recently resigned amid the scandal over the 1995 massacre of seventeen farm workers on their way to a peaceful community demonstration. Police were killed in ambush in the wake of the tragedy, and ultimately, several police and officials have been arrested and charged with the killings.[12] Major protests occurred in Oaxaca state in the wake of allegations of fraud in local

---

on Self-Rule and Separate Judicial Systems, Latin Am. Weekly Rep., Feb. 8, 1996, at 56. The constitutional articles to be amended will be discussed below, in text.

[9] *Id.*

[10] *See* Jesus Ramirez, *Violence Threatens Chiapas Peace Talks in Mexico*, Reuters World Service, Mar. 23, 1996; *Mexican Government, Rebels Reach Agreement on Democratic Reform Talks*, Agence France Presse, Mar. 11, 1996.

[11] *See* Jorge G. Castaneda, *Ferocious Differences: Differences Between Mexico and the U.S.*, Atlantic Monthly, July 1995, at 68.

[12] *See* Anthony De Palma, *7 Police Agents Are Slain in Ambush in Mexico*, N.Y. Times, Sept. 24, 1995, at A11; Anthony De Palma, *17 Police and 4 Officials Arrested in Mexican Peasants' Killings*, N.Y. Times, Jan. 11, 1996, at A5; Anthony De Palma, *Report on Massacre Provokes a Political Storm in Mexico*, N.Y. Times, Feb. 29, 1996; *Mexican Governor Quits Over Massacre*, U.P.I., Mar. 12, 1996.

elections,[13] and more than 1,000 protesters shut down oil production in the state of Tabasco to protest the failure of the state-owned oil companies to return revenues to the indigenous communities in the region.[14]

In the wake of the uprising, nearly 300 local organizations formed the Chiapas State Council of Campesinos and Indigenous Organizations (CEIOC).[15] Very recently, this coalition was expanded to the national level through the organization of the Broad Front for the Construction of a National Liberation Movement, created in January 1996 with more than 10,500 delegates from 269 grassroots organizations. The purpose of the organization, which includes activists from some of the most conflicted states, including Guerrero and Tabasco, is to "fight against the imperial capitalist regime in Mexico and the State party which sustains it."[16] The creation of this national coalition seems consistent with objectives of the EZLN to extend the influence of their actions beyond the local level to nationwide reforms. It remains to be seen, however, whether they will be able to accomplish their two most fundamental objectives: "truly free and democratic elections" at both the state and national levels, and a life of "peace and tranquility" for the native peoples of Chiapas.[17]

B. International Legal Action After the Fighting

In late January 1994, a petition was filed by several human rights groups with the Inter-American Commission on Human Rights (the Commission), part of the regional human rights enforcement mechanism within the OAS.[18] (The

---

[13] See Latin America Regional Reports: Mexico and Central America, Major Protests in Oaxaca; But Michoacan in Calm, Jan. 18, 1996, at 5.

[14] See Mexico: Miscellaneous; Mexican Oil Wells, Blocked by Protesters, REUTER TEXTLINE, Feb. 6, 1996.

[15] See EPICA Report, supra note 6, at 12.

[16] Maribel Gutierez, Integraron 269 Organizaciones el Frente Amplio para la Constitucion del Movimiento de Liberacion Nacional, LA JORNADA, Jan. 30, 1996. Translations of Spanish text, here and elsewhere in this chapter, are the author's.

[17] Tim Golden, Mexican Rebels Gather to Rule on Government's Peace Offer, N.Y. TIMES, June 1, 1994, at A15. Two popular accounts of the rebellion tell this story in much greater depth. See JOHN ROSS, BASTA!: LAND AND THE ZAPATISTA REBELLION IN CHIAPAS (1995); John Ross, Rebellion from the Roots: Indian Uprising in Chiapas (1995).

[18] The petition was filed by the Center for Human Rights Legal Action and the Center for Constitutional Rights, with other organizations co-signing, under the caption, In the Matter of Civilian Populations of Chiapas and Members of the Ejercito Zapatista de Liberación Nacional who have laid down their weapons or been placed hors de combat by sickness, wounds, detention, or other cause: Petition Against the Government of Mexico and Request for Precautionary Measures and On-Site Visit by the Inter-American Commission on Human Rights, Jan. 27, 1994. This petition was consolidated with the petition of various Native American and medical groups, coordinated by the Center for Human Rights & Constitutional Law in Los Angeles, under the caption, Petition for Interim and Permanent Measures Regarding the Systematic Violation of the American Convention on Human Rights and Other International Covenants in Chiapas, Mexico, Feb. 10, 1994.

work of the Commission and its companion organ, the Inter-American Court of Human Rights, which sits in San Jose, Costa Rica, will be described more fully below.) That petition, as originally filed, alleged violations of international human rights treaties to which the Mexican government had agreed to be bound. First, the petition alleged violations of the American Convention on Human Rights and the American Declaration of the Rights and Duties of Man. It sought protection of civil and political rights such as the right to life, physical security, personal liberty, fair and impartial trials, and equal protection of the laws without discrimination based on race or social origin.[19] Second, the petition alleges violations of the laws of war embodied in the Geneva Conventions, which protect civilian populations in times of armed conflict, protect prisoners taken in combat, and give access to areas of conflict for humanitarian services such as the Red Cross.[20] In each of these areas protected by law, there is strong evidence to show that army troops and local authorities abused both combatants and civilians by summary executions, torture, arbitrary detention without trial, and mass arrests, particularly of indigenous males. Moreover, the petitions themselves documented the impunity of government officials, police and military, and their civilian collaborators in the Mexican judicial system, thereby establishing the futility of exhausting domestic remedies before pursuing international adjudication of their claims.[21] The best reports on these abuses, and on the inefficacy of the Mexican judicial system, were published by international[22] and local[23] human rights organizations that closely examined these violations in the immediate wake of the hostilities and continue to monitor the situation.

It is clear, however, that violations of human rights of the indigenous peoples of Chiapas were not limited to the armed conflict that spanned such a short time in January 1994. The history of conflict between the government, cattle ranchers and *caciques*, and the indigenous peoples of the region, was much deeper and

---

[19] *See id.* at 5–7.

[20] *See id.* at 7–12.

[21] *See id.* at 12 13.

[22] *See* AMERICAS WATCH, THE NEW YEAR'S REBELLION: VIOLATIONS OF HUMAN RIGHTS AND HUMANITARIAN LAW DURING THE ARMED REVOLT IN CHIAPAS, MEXICO (1994); AMNESTY INTERNATIONAL, PREPARED STATEMENT OF CARLOS M. SALINAS, GOVERNMENT PROGRAM OFFICER, BEFORE THE SUBCOMMITTEE ON WESTERN HEMISPHERE AFFAIRS, COMMITTEE ON FOREIGN AFFAIRS, U.S. HOUSE OF REPRESENTATIVES (Feb. 2, 1994); PHYSICIANS FOR HUMAN RIGHTS & HUMAN RIGHTS WATCH/AMERICAS, WAITING FOR JUSTICE IN CHIAPAS (1994).

[23] *See, e.g.*, INFORME PRELIMINAR A LA COMISIÓN INTERAMERICANA DE DERECHOS HUMANOS, prepared for a hearing on Feb. 10, 1994, under the auspices of the Red Nacional de Organismos Civiles de Derechos Humanos "Todos Los Derechos para Todos," and the periodic reports of the Academia Mexicana de Derechos Humanos, the Coordinación de los Organismos no Gobernamentales de San Cristóbal de las Casas por la Paz, and the official governmental human rights agency, the Comisión Nacional de Derechos Humanos.

long-standing. These struggles date back to antiquity; some argue that the Mexican Revolution, fought mostly over land rights, never reached Chiapas. There is, for those who wished to see it before the uprising, a clear and well-documented pattern of abuses of civil and political rights of the indigenous populations over many years.[24]

Most human rights organizations reporting on the region, however, focus in large measure on the effects, rather than the causes, of the conflict in the region. The underlying struggle in Chiapas was and is for land and other natural resources, for autonomy and the right to self-determination among the indigenous peoples there. Those who control the land and government are overwhelmingly white or *mestizo* (mined white and Indian). They harbor deep hostility toward indigenous peoples who seek to retain their tribal territories, to claim land, or simply to claim anything better in life: stable work, education, health, and protection of the family and tribal traditions. These deeply ingrained patterns are based almost wholly in racial and ethnic discrimination; ranchers made repeated assertions in local newspapers that the only reason Indians don't have anything is because they are "lazy," or that they enjoy living in poverty because that is how they choose to live.[25]

Prior human rights reports by international delegations uniformly document efforts of the indigenous people to organize—whether through legal unionization as workers or in peaceful protest against government policies that deprived them of legal entitlements—followed by brutal repression by state authorities themselves or by paramilitary groups, *guardias blancas* (mercenary "white guards"), and *pistoleros* (hired gunmen), who act with complete impunity. The courts, to which the indigenous people turn for legal redress, largely respond by silence, lengthy delays, or overt hostility.

The most important undocumented violations of human rights in Chiapas, then, are those involving indigenous peoples and the environment, as well as the economic, social, and cultural rights to which Mexico has agreed to be bound under international law. Unfortunately, Mexico has been as lax in its international human rights obligations as it often is accused of being in the domestic

---

[24] *See* AMERICAS WATCH, HUMAN RIGHTS IN MEXICO: A POLICY OF IMPUNITY (1990); AMNESTY INTERNATIONAL, MEXICO: TORTURE WITH IMPUNITY (1991); AMNESTY INTERNATIONAL, MEXICO: CONTINUING HUMAN RIGHTS VIOLATIONS AGAINST MEMBERS OF THE TZELTAL INDIGENOUS COMMUNITY IN CHIAPAS (1993); AMNESTY INTERNATIONAL, MEXICO: HUMAN RIGHTS VIOLATIONS AGAINST CH'OL AND TZELTAL INDIAN ACTIVISTS (1992); AMNESTY INTERNATIONAL, MEXICO: THE PERSISTENCE OF TORTURE AND IMPUNITY (1993); MINNESOTA ADVOCATES FOR HUMAN RIGHTS, CONQUEST CONTINUED: DISREGARD FOR HUMAN AND INDIGENOUS RIGHTS IN THE MEXICAN STATE OF CHIAPAS (1992); WORLD POLICY INSTITUTE, CIVILIANS AT RISK: MILITARY AND POLICE ABUSES IN THE MEXICAN COUNTRYSIDE (1993). The U.S. State Department's Country Reports on Human Rights: 1993, Mexico (1994), as in past reports, document a pattern of human rights abuses in Chiapas.

[25] Ana Carrigan, *Chiapas: The First Post-Modern Revolution*, 19 FLETCHER F. WORLD AFF. 71, 90–91 (1995)

protection of human rights; the laws may exist in theory, but there is no effective domestic venue for their vindication. It is no coincidence, for example, that Chiapas state has "the highest number of pending petitions for land reform in the country."[26] Moreover, the rights in question here are themselves new and still underdeveloped in the international arena. Human rights discourse has focused on the protection of individual rights, and the protection of collective rights, such as those of tribal peoples or to a clean and healthy environment, are only recently the subject of scholarly writing and litigation. Even the economic, social, and cultural rights of indigenous individuals are seen as underdeveloped when compared to the protections afforded for violation of civil and political rights. Many of the international norms in all of these areas are only recently adopted or still in the drafting stages at the international level.

The purpose of this essay is to identify some of the areas in which economic, social, cultural, and environmental rights of the indigenous peoples have been violated, before and after the conflict of January 1994, and to suggest some ways in which quickly evolving international human rights law may provide a framework for analysis of those violations and a remedy for the wrongs. The chapter first provides historical background as a basis for the contemporary human rights violations. Then it sets up a framework for discussion of the various legal obligations which come into play in Chiapas and suggests that international human rights law has matured enough to permit adjudication of collective rights claims such as those here posed by indigenous peoples and their relationship to the environment. Finally, it examines the way in which the claims might be articulated against the government of Mexico at the Inter-American Human Rights Commission, and a brief conclusion suggests important areas of international human rights law which cannot yet be enforced, despite their violation in Chiapas.

II. BRIEF HISTORICAL OVERVIEW

A. Environmental Degradation

The history of Chiapas in this century is one that combines two closely related trends. The first trend is the massive exploitation and despoliation of the heart of the state, the Lacandón rain forest, either by the government and its agents, or by governmental policies that do not control or monitor rapid economic changes and growth in the region. The Lacandón rain forest, still the largest in North America, contains representation from forty per cent of the nation's plant varieties, thirty-six percent of its mammals, thirty-four percent of its reptiles and amphibians, sixty-six per cent of its birds, and twenty percent of its freshwater fish.[27] It nonetheless suffers more rapid and serious destruction

---

[26] MINNESOTA ADVOCATES FOR HUMAN RIGHTS, *supra* note 24, at 60.

[27] See Ejercito Zapatista de Liberación Nacional [EZLN], Letter to the Editor, LA JORNADA, Jan. 28, 1994.

than the Amazon basin, and has lost more than seventy percent of its forest cover in the last thirty years. In 1990, only thirty percent of the original forest area remained.[28]

The loss of forest cover was caused in part by intentional government policies, such as the 1960 "March to the Tropics" campaign of the government of Adolfo López Mateos, which encouraged massive migration to Chiapas of new settlers. The Ocosingo municipality, for example, has grown from 2,500 people to over 100,000 in the past twenty years.[29] As these massive arrivals of new settlers occurred, farming by the slash-and-burn technique not only decimated the rain forest but quickly leached the soil of available nutrients and required that the new settlers continue to carve away the forest to acquire fertile land for planting. Moreover, the massive influx of people throughout the state was done without any careful planning or forethought by either the agrarian reform authorities or social services agencies, whose resources were quickly outstripped by the new migrant populations.[30]

A decree of President Luis Echeverría gave forty percent of the forest, 614,321 hectares (1,517,373 acres), to sixty-six heads of families in the Lacandón.[31] The forest was exploited for its valuable wood and stripped to make grazing and farm land available. In 1988, wood exports brought in revenue of 23.9 billion pesos, 6,000 percent more than they had in 1980.[32] Even the slash-and-burn farmer contributes to the forest's diminution but, as an EZLN letter to the press notes, "the peasant cuts [the trees] to survive, the beast to plunder."

Another source of environmental destruction is state-sponsored exploitation of mineral and energy resources, the benefits of which are seldom enjoyed within Chiapas state. Pemex has eighty-six stations in Chiapas state, mostly in the northern part. They extract a total of 92,000 barrels of oil and 516.7 billion cubic feet of natural gas per day from the state. Eight new petroleum deposits are under exploration. These incursions strip away natural resources to make way for roads and new towns with the full cooperation of the government. However, only two-thirds of the municipal capitals of Chiapas have paved roads. Twelve thousand communities in the state have no means of transport and communication other than mountain trails. Chiapas state provides fifty-five percent of the national hydroelectric energy and twenty percent of Mexico's total

---

[28] *See* Jorge Ramon Gonzalez-Ponciano, *Frontera, Ecología y Soberanía Nacional: La Colonización de la Franja Fronteriza Sur de Marqués de Comillas*, ANUARIO 1990: INSTITUTO CHIAPANECO DE CULTURA 50, 54 (1991).

[29] One article put population growth in Ocosingo at a rate of 6.5 percent annually for the past two decades. *Mexico: Promised Land*, THE ECONOMIST, May 14, 1994.

[30] *See* Interviews by researchers at Na-Bolom Cultural Institute, San Cristobal de las Casas, Chiapas, Mexico (Feb. 9, 1994).

[31] *See* Gonzalez-Ponciano, *supra* note 28, at 56.

[32] *See* EZLN, *supra* note 27.

energy needs, but only one-third of the homes in Chiapas have electricity. The consequences of these government-sponsored actions are, according to the EZLN, "ecological destruction, agricultural scraps, hyperinflation, alcoholism, prostitution, and poverty."[33]

B. Displacement of Indigenous Peoples in Chiapas

A second historical trend in Chiapas has been the displacement of whole communities of indigenous peoples by large landowners, principally cattle ranchers, aided by governmental policies which either actively abetted their efforts or turned a blind eye to their abuses. The native people of Chiapas officially make up 27.5 percent of the population of the state, but many informed estimates suggest that they make up a majority.[34] They are principally from the Ch'ol, Tzeltal, Tzotzil, Zoque, and Lacandón groups. Over time, the ranchers have forced the native peoples, who have occupied the lands from the time of their Mayan ancestors, off of the most arable land and deeper and deeper into both the less productive mountainsides and the shrinking forests.

The *ejido*, or collective farm, provided many peasants with farmland through constitutional reforms enacted in the wake of the Mexican Revolution but, in Chiapas. the *ejido* became a convenient tool by which to control and limit the land claims of the indigenous peoples, who continued to earn their livelihoods from traditional agricultural patterns of corn, coffee, and fruit production. In all of Mexico today, more than one million people work some 28,000 small *ejidos*, though most of them are worked individually and are smaller than thirteen acres.[35] However, in 1976, the official policy of the government of President José López Portillo held that the country had run out of land for distribution, and each presidency since has followed that line.[36]

The rural population of the entire country is thirty percent; in Chiapas, it is sixty percent.[37] Chiapas produces thirty-five per cent of Mexico's coffee, more than half of which is exported to Europe and the United States.[38] In 1991, however, the country's agricultural sector produced only one-tenth of the gross

---

[33] *Id.*

[34] *Id.*

[35] *See* Jack Epstein, *In Rural Mexico, A Land War*, L.A. TIMES, May 8, 1988, at E2; Edward Cody, *Mexico to Revise Concept of Agrarian Ownership; Smallholders Could Sell or Rent Plots*, WASH. POST, Nov. 8, 1991, at A27.

[36] Epstein, *supra* note 35.

[37] *See* Academia Mexicana de Derechos Humanos, CHIAPAS IN FIGURES, Jan. 1 15, 1994.

[38] *See* EZLN, *supra*, note 27.

national product; the countryside attracted less than one percent of the $9.9 billion in foreign investment that flowed into Mexico.[39]

C. Constitutional Reforms in Anticipation of NAFTA Ratification

In an effort to open the extensive *ejidos* to foreign investment and promote the ratification of NAFTA, President Salinas sponsored amendments to the Mexican Constitution. Article 27 of the Constitution was amended in 1991, and later implemented through an Agrarian Law reform in 1992, to permit individual members of the *ejido*, with the permission of the other owners, to buy, sell, or rent their holdings or those of their neighbors.[40] The effect of this reform in Chiapas was to exacerbate the already difficult situation of its native peoples. Told by the government that there is no more land to which they may claim title, the large indigenous populations in the *ejidos* are left with an irresolvable dilemma: they can sell off their meager plots, with no place to go and no viable skills outside of farming, or they can remain on the land and face withering competition from either their richer local neighbors who consolidate their holdings or foreign investors who take advantage of the liberalized rules of NAFTA. This frustration undoubtedly contributed to the taking up of arms. One of the immediate after-effects of the armed conflict was massive relocation of internally displaced people who filed to the areas surrounding the larger villages and cities from their own villages and *ejidos*. They were often designated by the government as "refugees," when, in fact, there was strong evidence to show that the military and government relocated the people almost forcibly after fomenting anti-Zapatista propaganda. These people had little when they left and even less in the temporary shelters either provided to them by local government officials or scrambled together on their own.[41] Displaced from their lands originally by large farmers, the local indigenous peoples were forced to relocate yet again (this time with the active support of the local government), thus continuing a centuries-old pattern of making them refugees in their own homeland.

---

[39] *See* Diane Lindquist, *Mexican Official Touts Agricultural Reforms*, SAN DIEGO UNION-TRIBUNE, Jan. 31, 1992, at D1.

[40] *See* CONSTITUCIÓN POLÍTICA DE LOS ESTADOS UNIDOS DE MÉXICO, art. 27, para 10, No. VII (1990), and the Ley Agraria (Agrarian Reform Law), arts. 76–86, Diario Oficial, 26 de febrero de 1992. Two very different perspectives on the impact of these reforms on the indigenous peoples are found in James J. Kelly, Jr., *Article 27 and Mexican Land Reform: The Legacy of Zapata's Dream*, 25 COLUM. HUM. RTS. L. REV. 541 (1994) (arguing that 1992 amendments to article 27 are a threat to ancient indigenous tradition); and Adriana De Aguinaga, *The New Agrarian Law—Mexico's Way Out*, 24 ST. MARY'S L.J. 883 (1993) (arguing that amendments to the Agrarian Law in 1992 will lead to higher productivity in the agricultural sector, rural development, and greater competitive ability for Mexico in international markets). For a persuasive argument about the benefits to all involved in maintaining the traditional agricultural patterns of the region, *see* June Nash, *The Challenge of Trade Liberalization to Cultural Survival on the Southern Frontier of Mexico*, 1 IND. J. GLOBAL LEG. STUD. 367 (1994).

[41] *See* EPICA Report, *supra* note 6, at 18.

III. A FRAMEWORK FOR ANALYSIS OF INTERNATIONAL LEGAL OBLIGATIONS

Along with an understanding of the historical roots of the conflict in Chiapas, there must also be an understanding of the legal principles that apply to that conflict at the domestic and international levels. The theory developed in this section is not grounded in the same principles that underlie the first international legal claims filed immediately after the armed conflict. It does not look to the traditional sources of international law, found in the assertion of individual claims of civil and political rights, but rather to developing concepts of collective claims of the indigenous peoples to environmental protection, as well as to economic, social, and cultural rights.

A. What Law Applies?: The Interplay of Traditional Customary Law, Domestic State Law, and International Law Concepts

In setting up a framework for analysis of legal claims by indigenous peoples, there are many levels at which the law might be applied: there is tribal law and custom; state law; national law; and the international law of treaty or custom. In Mexico, as in the United States, codifications of law exist at both the federal level and at the state level in Chiapas. For some of the indigenous peoples of Chiapas, as in virtually any case involving natives with deep ancestral roots in a region, their principles for the resolution of conflict lie in tribal custom, a form of law that often consists of oral tradition and loosely knit practices, as well as rituals and rites that flow seamlessly between traditional and Western concepts of religion and law. The very ways in which the English language and law give meaning to legal concepts may be different in tribal culture. One example is the Australian Aboriginal peoples' understanding of the word "home," a concept which, in their language, may mean " 'camp,' 'hearth,' 'country,' 'everlasting home,' 'totem place,' 'life source,' [or] 'spirit centre.' "[42]

In Mexico, it can be ascertained whether the law applied inside the country is national law, state law, or the traditional tribal law that precedes the existence of the modern state. Article 4 of the Mexican Constitution provides that the practices and customs of the native peoples will be taken into account in all trials and agrarian proceedings. Mexico also ratified the International Labor Organization Convention (No. 169) Concerning Indigenous and Tribal Peoples in Independent Countries (ILO Convention 169),[43] one of the most progressive

---

[42] WILLIAM EDWARD HANLEY STANNER, WHITE MEN GOT NO DREAMING 230 (1979), *quoted in* Gary D. Meyers and John Mugambwa, *The Mabo Decision: Australian Aboriginal Land Rights in Transition*, 23 ENVTL. L. 1203, 1204 (1993).

[43] *See* Convention (No. 169) Concerning Indigenous and Tribal Peoples in Independent Countries, International Labor Conference, Draft Report of the Committee on Convention No. 107, App. I, C.C. 107/D.303 (*entered into force* Sept. 5, 1991), *reprinted in* 28 I.L.M. 1382 (1989) [hereinafter Convention No. 169]. *See* Chapter 2, Lee Swepston, *The ILO Indigenous and Tribal Peoples Convention (No. 169): Eighty Years After Adoption.*

treaties dealing with the rights of indigenous peoples. In article 8.1, ILO Convention 169 provides that due regard must be given the customary law of the indigenous peoples in interpreting national law. While neither of these provisions states that customary law is dispositive when conflicts between it and other law occur, they argue for strong deference to custom in the absence of a direct conflict.

The Inter-American Court of Human Rights recently recognized the applicability of customary tribal law on family structure of the Saramaca peoples in Suriname in the *Aloeboetoe Case*. The Court used customary practices of the Saramacans to determine monetary damages for victims of human rights violations, despite the lack of proof of a formal autonomy agreement with the government.[44] Because Mexico has ratified the American Convention on Human Rights, as discussed below, a strong argument can be made that the traditional practices of the native peoples of Chiapas are a source of law which must be ascertained, respected, and applied before other domestic law is applied indiscriminately.

Conflicts between domestic and international law also must be resolved. One rule is that the specific will always reign over the general; if there is domestic law that makes rights explicit, that source is a powerful measure of the obligations that the state has assumed. The same is true at the international level, where the specific language of treaties is more indicative of the obligations assumed by and between countries than is custom, the practice of states, or general principles of law.[45] The language of either domestic law or international treaties may make explicit reference as to which law, domestic or international, is to prevail or be applied in preference over the other. In an international tribunal, of course, international law applies first, unless it explicitly defers to domestic law.

In Mexico, international and domestic laws regarding the rights of indigenous peoples are consistent; they are remarkably similar in content and intent. Mexico's constitution provides the answer as to the relationship of domestic and international law. Article 133 gives equal status to international treaties, the federal constitution, and federal law, all of which are the supreme law of the land, thereby giving them precedence over state law.[46]

What treaties, then, are relevant to ascertaining Mexico's international legal obligations?[47] Mexico has signed and ratified a number of multilateral international treaties that define its obligations to respect the human rights of indigenous

---

[44] *See* Aloeboetoe case, Int. Am. Ct. H.R., Reparations, Judgment of Sept. 10, 1993, at 15–16.

[45] *See, e.g.*, Statute of the International Court of Justice, art. 38(a)(1), 59 Stat. 1055 (1945).

[46] *See* Frente Independiente de Pueblos Indios (FIPI), Pueblos Indígenas: Nuestros Derechos Constitucionales 8–9, 15 (1993).

[47] An interesting related question is whether a treaty signed between indigenous peoples of a country and the national government is enforceable in international law. Guidance on that question is found in a 1975 advisory opinion of the International Court

peoples and the environment. In the regional system of the OAS, where a complaint is now in process, the primary controlling instruments are the American Convention on Human Rights (American Convention),[48] to which Mexico acceded in 1982, and the American Declaration on the Rights and Duties of Man (American Declaration),[49] which is the original instrument that created the OAS human rights system in 1948.

In addition to the American Convention, the Mexican government has also ratified ILO Convention No. 169, as well as the International Convention on the Elimination of All Forms of Racial Discrimination.[50] Moreover, in 1992, it ratified the Rio Declaration on Environment and Development (Rio Declaration),[51] the Convention on Biological Diversity (Biodiversity Convention),[52] and the Framework Convention on Climate Change (Climate Convention),[53] all of which emerged from the proceedings of the U.N. Conference on the Environment and Development in Rio de Janeiro that year.[54] Finally, Mexico has long been a party to both of the major international treaties on human rights: the International Covenant on Civil and Political Rights (ICCPR Covenant),[55] and the

---

of Justice regarding the Western Sahara. In that case, the Court held that indigenous peoples had a right to act as a separate legal unit from the state in which they have exclusively inhabited territory. Such tribal peoples, in short, have the legal right to self-determination. ICJ Reports 1975, 38, 79 *et seq.* If it could be proven that the indigenous peoples of Chiapas have "exclusively inhabited" certain portions of the state, as is undoubtedly true in certain areas of the Lacandón rain forest, those peoples should have true legal autonomy as a matter of international law.

[48] American Convention on Human Rights, OAS Treaties Series No. 36, 1144 U.N.T.S. 123 (July 18, 1978); OEA/Ser L./V/II.82, doc. 6, rev. 1 at 25 (1992).

[49] American Declaration on the Rights and Duties of Man, OAS Res. XXX OEA/ Ser.L/V/II.82, doc. 6, rev. 1 at 17 (1992).

[50] *See* International Covenant on the Elimination of All Forms of Racial Discrimination, 660 U.N.T.S. 195 (Jan. 4, 1969). This convention, which clearly applies to the indigenous peoples of Chiapas, contains many provisions that support the arguments made in this section. In the interest of brevity, however, this general reference suffices.

[51] *See* Rio Declaration on Environment and Development, A/Conf.151/5/Rev.1, 13 June 1992, 31 I.L.M. 874 (1992).

[52] *See* United Nations Convention on Biological Diversity, Na.92 7807, June 5, 1992, 31 I.L.M. 818 (1992) [hereinafter Biodiversity Convention].

[53] *See* Framework Convention on Climate Change, U.N. Doc. A/AC 237/18 (Pt. II) Add.1, 31 I.L.M. 848 (1992) [hereinafter Climate Convention].

[54] U.N. Conference on the Environment and Development, A/CONF/151/5/Rev.1, June 13, 1992.

[55] International Covenant on Civil and Political Rights GA Res. 2200A (XXI), 21 U.N. GAOR Supp. (No. 16) at 52, U.N. Doc. A/6361 (1966), 999 U.N.T.S. 171 (March 23,1966).

International Covenant on Economic, Social and Cultural Rights (ESCR Covenant).[56] In the Inter-American system for the protection of human rights, each of these treaties must be read in conjunction with the American Convention to determine Mexico's obligations under international human rights law. Taken together, they create a rich tapestry of legal protections for the indigenous peoples of Chiapas that are enforceable at the international level.

There are also some draft declarations regarding indigenous peoples now under consideration at the international level. Mexico has played important roles in the drafting of each. The most important is the U.N. draft Declaration on the Rights of Indigenous Peoples,[57] a product of many years of study by the Working Group on Indigenous Populations. That document, having benefited from the participation of indigenous groups themselves throughout its evolution, is one of the most progressive instruments regarding indigenous rights. In the Americas, the Inter-American Commission on Human Rights has also prepared a draft instrument on indigenous rights.[58] In 1992, the Commission sent a questionnaire to the governments of all member States regarding their opinion as to issues and approaches to be included in the instrument. The responses of the Mexican government are important, and are mentioned below where relevant.[59]

Finally, there are several situations in which a country may be exempted from its obligations in international law, regardless of the existence of a treaty. While these exceptions are too numerous to develop fully here, some, such as specific reservations to treaty provisions, will be mentioned in the text below. Derogability from a treaty, the notion that a government may permissibly suspend its international legal obligations, is also discussed where relevant.

Another broad area that must be addressed is the question of the applicability of domestically adopted amnesty or pardon provisions which purport to exempt certain groups or persons from responsibility for legal wrongdoing. Specifically, there is some question as to the scope of an amnesty law that took effect on

---

[56] See International Covenant on Economic, Social and Cultural Rights, GA Res. 2200A (XXI) 21 U.N. GAOR Supp. (No. 16) at 49; U.N. Doc. A/6316 (1996) Jan. 3, 1976.

[57] See Commission on Human Rights, Sub-Commission on Prevention of Discrimination and Protection of Minorities, Ea/CN.4/Sub.2/1993/29, Aug. 23, 1993, Annex I, draft Declaration as Agreed Upon by the Members of the Working Group at its Eleventh Session. See Chapter 1, Julian Burger, *Indigenous Peoples and the United Nations.*

[58] See Inter-American Commission on Human Rights, Draft of the Inter-American Declaration on the Rights of Indigenous Peoples, OEA/Ser./L/V/II.90, doc. 9, rev. 1 (Sept. 21, 1995) [hereinafter draft Declaration]. See Chapter 4, Osvaldo Kreimer, *The Future Inter-American Declaration on the Rights of Indigenous Peoples: A Challenge for the Americas.*

[59] See generally ANNUAL REPORT OF THE INTER-AMERICAN COMMISSION ON HUMAN RIGHTS, 1992 1993, OEA/Ser.L/V/II.83, doc. 14, corr. 1, Mar. 12, 1993, at 263–312.

January 22, 1994, regarding the events in Chiapas.[60] While purportedly offered by the federal government as an incentive for the EZLN to begin peace negotiations, it has been suggested that military personnel or governmental officials may use the amnesty provisions to avoid responsibility for their wrongs. There is little doubt that these arguments are unavailing. First, many of the violations of the rights analyzed here took place long before the outbreak of open hostilities in the region—they are both long-standing and continuous—and the amnesty was adopted in response to events which occurred after January 1, 1994. Second, recent decisions from the Inter-American Commission make the defense of amnesty unavailable to the government as a matter of international human rights law. These two 1992 decisions of the Inter-American Commission on Human Rights suggest that Mexico cannot avoid its obligations to the victims of any human rights violations which have taken place in Chiapas, before or after January 1994. Those decisions involving the validity of amnesty laws in Argentina[61] and Uruguay[62] found that the amnesty laws, which precluded any punishment for persons responsible for such crimes as disappearance, torture, and political killings, were incompatible with the American Convention. Taken together with the Commission's 1987 Nicaragua decision denying immunity to government officials for violations of private property rights,[63] discussed below, these decisions convincingly rebut any potential claim which might be interposed by the government of Mexico to avoid the legal obligations of its army or its elected or judicial officials.

B. Toward a Jurisprudence of Collective Rights: Indigenous Peoples' Rights and Environmental Rights as Human Rights

In addition to complicated questions of what law applies, there is the added problem of developing, through litigation and analysis, a theory for the protection of collective rights such as those of indigenous peoples or the environment. Such theories are achieving currency in human rights theory,[64] but some argue that collective rights are inconsistent with an enforceable notion of human rights, and that individual claims should be the sole basis for the resolution of actual

---

[60] *See President Issues Amnesty Law and Sets Up Amnesty Commission for Chiapas Rebels*, BBC SUMMARY OF WORLD BROADCASTS, Jan. 26, 1994.

[61] *See* Cases 10.147 et al. Inter-Am. C.H.R., OEA/Ser.L/V/ II.83, doc. 14, corr.1, Mar. 12, 1993 at 41 (Argentina), Report No. 28/92.

[62] *See* Cases 10.029 et al., Inter-Am. C.H.R. (Uruguay), Report No. 29/92, Oct. 1992.

[63] *Id.* at 154 (discussed *infra*) notes 101–114 and accompanying test.

[64] *See generally* THE RIGHTS OF PEOPLES (James Crawford, ed., 1988); IAN BROWNLIE, TREATIES AND INDIGENOUS PEOPLES (1991); PEOPLES AND MINORITIES IN INTERNATIONAL LAW (Catherine Brolmann et al., eds., 1993); Douglas Sanders, *Collective Rights*, 13 HUM. RTS. Q. 368 (1991); Richard Hertz, *Legal Protection for Indigenous Cultures: Sacred Sites and Communal Rights*, 79 VA. L. REV. 691 (1993); Allen Buchanan, *The Role of Collective Rights in the Theory of Indigenous Peoples' Rights*, 3 TRANSNAT'L L. & CONTEMP. PROBS. 89 (1993).

disputes.[65] Moreover, definitions of terms, such as "indigenous peoples," can be key to the willingness of a tribunal to award relief. No judge is willing to award a verdict in favor of a hypothetical, undefined group. In one recent case in the United States, for example, the Mashpee tribe sued to recover tribal lands in Massachusetts. The threshold issue of whether the Mashpee could prove they constituted a "tribe" took forty days to resolve.[66]

Much help in a definition of "indigenous peoples" is provided by ILO Convention 169. Article 1 states that the instrument applies to the following groups:

(a)   tribal peoples in independent countries whose social, cultural and economic conditions distinguish them from other sections of the national community, and whose status is regulated wholly or partially by their own customs or traditions or by special laws or regulations;

(b)   peoples in independent countries who are regarded as indigenous on account of their descent from the populations which inhabited the country, or a geographical region to which the country belongs, at the time of conquest or colonisation or the establishment of present state boundaries and who, regardless of their legal status, retain some or all of their own social, economic, cultural and political institutions.[67]

There is little doubt that the tribal and indigenous peoples of Chiapas qualify for protection under either of these definitions.

Environmental rights are even more problematic, theoretically, than are the rights of indigenous peoples. Such rights, like those of indigenous peoples, are not limited by national borders and nation-states. But environmental degradation may have international consequences even when it is "local" in origin, as when, for example, poisons buried in one country seep into groundwater and cross

---

[65] See Jack Donnelly, *Third Generation Rights*, in PEOPLES AND MINORITIES IN INTERNATIONAL LAW, *supra* note 64, at 119.

[66] See Gerald Torres, *Translating Yonnondio by Precedent and Evidence: The Mashpee Indian Case*, 1990 DUKE L.J. 625, 633 (1990).

[67] Another definition, also applicable to the peoples of Chiapas, is that found in article I of the Draft of the Inter-American Declaration on the Rights of Indigenous Peoples. Indigenous peoples are "those who embody historical continuity with societies that existed prior to the conquest and settlement of their territories by Europeans," as well as those who were either (alternative I) "brought involuntarily to the New World," or (alternative II) "tribal peoples whose social, cultural and economic conditions distinguish them from other sections of the national community, and whose status is regulated wholly or partially by their own customs or traditions or by special laws or regulations." *See also* Russell Lawrence Barsh, *Indigenous Peoples: An Emerging Object of International Law*, 80 AM. J. INT'L L. 369, 373–376 (1986).

borders or enter the oceans, or when one country's factories release gases that deplete the entire Earth's ozone layer. Environmental rights, moreover, can be conceived of as relating to the rights of human beings who occupy ecosystems, or the environment can be seen as deserving of protection for its own sake.[68] In short, it is most difficult to give sharp definition to environmental rights for enforcement purposes.

The concept of indigenous peoples may provide the key link in the law to a shape and form for enforceable environmental rights. Indigenous peoples, by their very nature, are in communion with their environment by virtue of hunting, fishing, and planting of crops. Therefore, protection of the right to a clean and healthy environment is an element in the definition of the rights of indigenous peoples. As will be seen in many of the cases discussed below, the rights of indigenous peoples can only be understood in the context of a well-protected environment.

IV. MEXICO'S VIOLATIONS OF INTERNATIONAL LAW AND THE PROSPECTS FOR ENFORCEMENT OF THOSE RIGHTS IN THE INTER-AMERICAN HUMAN RIGHTS SYSTEM

This section looks more closely at the ways in which the Mexican government has failed the native peoples of Chiapas. It examines the explicit obligations that Mexico has voluntarily assumed by its adoption of international human rights treaties as its national law, and develops a theory by which these rights can be enforced in the Inter-American system for the protection of human rights. While this is not the only international venue for protection of human rights, it may be the most viable.

The organs charged with enforcement of the regional human rights treaties—the American Convention and the American Declaration—are the Inter-American Commission on Human Rights, in Washington, D.C., and the Inter-American Court of Human Rights, in San José, Costa Rica. The jurisdiction of the Court can only be invoked if agreed to by a party to the American Convention, and neither the United States nor Mexico has agreed to that jurisdiction. Thus, the ultimate adjudicative body on these issues is the Commission, which now has two consolidated petitions pending before it on the events that took place in Chiapas in January 1994.[69] The claims articulated below can be added to the claims to be adjudicated by the Commission, under conditions which will be discussed in the conclusion to this article.

---

[68] *See* Michael Bothe, *The Impact of International Law on the Protection of the Environment in Amazonia and Siberia, in* AMAZONIA AND SIBERIA: LEGAL ASPECTS OF THE PRESERVATION OF THE ENVIRONMENT AND DEVELOPMENT IN THE LAST OPEN SPACES 237, 245–249 (Michael Bothe et al., eds., 1993).

[69] *See supra* note 18.

The Commission is one of the few international bodies that has jurisdiction to hear complaints alleging collective rights.[70] While the earliest decision on a case brought by indigenous peoples was resolved by the Commission as violations of individual rights,[71] the author is aware of two prior matters dealing with collective rights—the *Yanomami Case* from Brazil[72] and the friendly settlement report on Miskito Indians in Nicaragua,[73] both discussed below—as well as at least three other pending claims before the Commission on these issues and related questions.[74]

Potential violations of the international human rights of the indigenous peoples of Chiapas are divided here, for convenience, into five broad areas: violations of the right to a healthy environment; violations of the right to life

---

[70] *See, e.g.,* the discussion of limitations on the rights of collectives under the Optional Protocol to the ICCPR, *in* Mary Ellen Turpel, *Indigenous Peoples' Rights to Political Participation and Self-Determination: Recent International Legal Developments and the Continuing Struggle for Recognition,* 25 CORNELL INT'L L.J.. 579 (1992)(discussing admissibility and merits decisions of the Human Rights Committee in *Mikmaq Tribal Society v. Canada*); and the general discussion at DOMINIC MCGOLDRICK, THE HUMAN RIGHTS COMMITTEE: ITS ROLE IN THE DEVELOPMENT OF THE INTERNATIONAL COVENANT ON CIVIL AND POLITICAL RIGHTS 254–256 (1994).

[71] *See* Ache Tribe Case, Case 1802, Inter-Am. C.H.R. (Paraguay 1977), *in* INTER-AMERICAN COMMISSION ON HUMAN RIGHTS, TEN YEARS OF ACTIVITIES, 1971–81, at 151.

[72] *See* Yanomami Case, Case No. 7615, Inter-Am. C.H.R. OEA/Ser.L/V/II.66, doc. 10, rev. 1 at 33 (1985).

[73] *See infra* notes 96–98 and accompanying text.

[74] One such petition is that of the International Human Rights Law Clinic at American University, of which I am the director, which was filed on behalf of indigenous peoples in the Araracuara region at the headwaters of the Amazon River in southeast Colombia, alleging violation of territorial and other rights in the placement of a radar installation co-sponsored by the U.S. Armed Forces. The petition is styled as *Petition of the Comunidades Indigenas del Medio Amazonas (CRIMA) on behalf of the Huitoto and Muiname peoples of Colombia,* filed Mar. 23, 1994. As of the date of publication of this article, the petition has not been opened. A second is a petition filed on behalf of the Huarorani peoples of Ecuador by the Sierra Club Legal Defense Fund, and discussed in Thomas S. O'Connor, *"We Are Part of Nature": Indigenous Peoples' Rights as a Basis for Environmental Protection in the Amazon Basin,* 5 COLO. J. INT'L ENVTL. L & POL'Y 193 (1994). A third was brought on behalf of Yurok, Karok, and Tolowa Indians in California, and is discussed in Christopher P. Cline, *Pursuing Native American Rights in International Law Venues: A Jus Cogens Strategy After Lyng v. Northwest Indian Cemetary Protective Association,* 42 HASTINGS L.J. 591 (1991). Two related issues in Mexico have to do with rights to protection of a healthy environment on the U.S.-Mexican border and free passage by tribal peoples of the U.S.-Mexican border. These issues are discussed, respectively, in Scott D. Cahalan, *NIMBY: Not in Mexico's Back Yard? A Case for Recognition of a Human Right to Healthy Environment in the American States,* 23 GA. J. INT'L & COMP. L. 409, 415 (1993)(discussing action brought in the Commission); and Megan S. Austin, *A Culture Divided by the United States-Mexico Border: The Tohono O'odham Claim for Border Crossing Rights,* 8 ARIZ. J. INT'L & COMP. L. 97 (1991) (proposing legislation to permit free border crossing by native peoples).

and cultural survival; violations of the right to full political participation and eventual full self-determination; violations of rights to property; and full protection of other economic and social rights. Each will now be discussed in turn.

A. Rights to Protection of a Healthy Environment

The need for effective protection of the ecosystem of Chiapas, and particularly of the Lacandón rain forest and other ecological reserves, should be obvious from the history of deforestation alone, as set out above. However, environmental damage has at least two immediate and important legal consequences. First, damage of one type leads inexorably to other significant adverse effects on the ecosystem. Deforestation, for example, is proven to have effects, at the very least, on animal diseases and extinctions, soil erosion and damage, groundwater conditions, and surface water flow and pollution.[75] Second, environmental damage cannot be separated from its impact on people. Thus, principle 1 of the Rio Declaration states that ''human beings are at the centre of concerns for sustainable development. They are entitled to a healthy and productive life in harmony with nature.'' Mexico signed the Rio Declaration. Thus, for example, the forced displacement of the indigenous peoples of Chiapas because of a degraded and uninhabitable environment is a viable allegation of violation of international law.[76]

The American Convention and Declaration have no specific provisions that guarantee environmental rights. However, the right to environmental protection is strongly implied by the cumulative effect of the Convention's rights to life (article 4), personal liberty and security (article 7), privacy (article 11), family (article 17), property (article 21), and freedom of movement and residence (article 22). In the landmark *Yanomami Case*, the Commission recognized the right of the Yanomami tribal peoples of Brazil to protection within a designated national park area, a protected environment, because of the cumulative effects of violations of their rights under the American Declaration to ''life, liberty and personal security (article I); the right to residence and movement (article VIII), and the right to preservation of health and well-being (article XI).''[77] Thus, specific claims dealt with in the following sections, particularly with regard to property, add strength to the more generalized claim of violation of the right to a clean and healthy environment.

The most explicit provision in the treaties of the Inter-American human rights system is found in article 11 of the Additional Protocol to the American

---

[75] *See generally* THE HUMAN IMPACT ON THE NATURAL ENVIRONMENT (A. Goudie, ed., 4th ed. 1994).

[76] *See* Maria Stavropoulou, *Indigenous Peoples Displaced from Their Environment: Is There Adequate Protection?*, 5 COLO. J. INT'L ENVTL. L. & POL'Y 105 (1994).

[77] Yanomami Case, *supra* note 72.

Convention on Human Rights in the Area of Economic, Social and Cultural Rights (Protocol of San Salvador), which explicitly provides that "[e]veryone shall have the right to live in a healthy environment. . . ."[78] Mexico has not ratified the Protocol of San Salvador, but, as indicated in the discussion here, it does provide for almost identical protections in domestic legislation and in other documents at the international level that it has signed.

In the General Law on Ecological Equilibrium and Environmental Protection, the Mexican government makes it a distinct "ecological policy" that "everyone has the right to enjoyment of a healthy environment."[79] While no effective enforcement mechanisms are set out in either these provisions or the Forestry Law,[80] Mexico has undertaken to protect such rights at the international level.

First, ILO Convention 169 explicitly protects the relationship of indigenous peoples to their environment in articles 4 and 7. Article 4 provides that special measures must be taken by governments to safeguard the environment of such peoples, and article 7 requires governments, in cooperation with the peoples concerned, to "protect and preserve the environment of the territories they inhabit." The U.N. draft Declaration on the Rights of Indigenous Peoples goes further, providing for ownership, development, and control by native peoples of their lands and territories, "including the total environment of the lands, air, waters, coastal seas, sea-ice, flora and fauna and other resources which they have traditionally owned or otherwise occupied or used."[81] This definition of territories gives meaning to the terms "resources" and "lands," as they are now used in articles 4 and 27 of the Mexican Constitution, respectively.

In this area, cases decided by the European Commission and Court of Human Rights have taken a leading role in determining that environmental deterioration can lead to violations of human rights such as the rights to privacy and family life, as well as the right to property, all of which are also contained in the American Convention. In *Arondelle v. United Kingdom*, for example, the European Commission held that noise pollution at Gatwick Airport near London resulted in intolerable stress for nearby residents and therefore violated the right to privacy.[82] If noise is enough to create an environmental human rights violation, how much worse is massive despoliation of traditional tribal lands in

---

[78] ORGANIZATION OF AMERICAN STATES, BASIC DOCUMENTS PERTAINING TO HUMAN RIGHTS IN THE INTER-AMERICAN SYSTEM 67, 72 (1992).

[79] Ley General del Equilibrio Ecológico y la Protección al Ambiente, art. 15, para. XI (1991).

[80] Ley Forestal, Diario Oficial, 22 de diciembre de 1992, at 16.

[81] Draft Declaration, *supra* note 58, at art. 26.

[82] *See* Arondelle v. United Kingdom, 26 Eur. Comm'n H.R. Dec. & Rep. 5 (1982). Cases are discussed in Dinah L. Shelton, *Environmental Rights in the European Community*, 16 HASTINGS INT'L & COMP. L. REV. 557, 566–69 (1993); and Richard Desgangne,

Chiapas by logging, mining and drilling, road building, and other activities whose effects on the environment are catastrophic?

Second, Mexico signed the Rio Declaration, which protects the sovereign right to exploit resources (principle 2), the obligation to cooperate in restoring the health and integrity of the Earth's ecosystem (principle 7), and the requirement that it enact effective environmental legislation (principle 11), which would presumably provide for liability and compensation for "the victims of pollution and other environmental damage," as guaranteed in principle 13. Neither the current Environmental Protection code, the Forestry Law, nor the NAFTA side agreements on the environment provide effectively for the protection and compensation of victims. The principles of the Rio Declaration, finally, make particular mention of indigenous peoples, by recognizing in principle 22 the "vital role" which the peoples play in environmental management, and by declaring that states "should recognize and duly support [indigenous peoples'] identity, culture and interests and enable their effective participation in the achievement of sustainable development." These concepts are forcefully reiterated in common article 1(2) of both the International Covenant on Civil and Political Rights and the International Covenant on Economic, Social and Cultural Rights, to both of which Mexico is a party. There, "peoples," not States, are guaranteed the right to "freely dispose of their natural wealth and resources." If this is so, the indigenous peoples of Chiapas, not the federal government of Mexico, should have control, use, and benefit of the ecosystem of Chiapas.

Finally, Mexico has the obligation to learn from its native peoples about preservation of environmental integrity. The Biodiversity Convention explicitly recognizes the obligation of governments to "respect, preserve and maintain knowledge of innovations and practices of indigenous and local communities embodying traditional lifestyles relevant for the conservation and sustainable use of biological diversity and promote their wider application with the approval and involvement of the holders of such knowledge."[83]

The Climate Convention has an even broader objective. It seeks for its parties to "protect the climate system for the benefit of present and future generations of humankind."[84] The parties are urged to "protect the climate system against human-induced change."[85] Such change occurs when human activity directly or indirectly "alters the composition of the global atmosphere."[86] There is no doubt that the vast environmental destruction, particularly deforestation such as that which continues each day in the Lacandón rain forest,

---

Integrating Environmental Values into the European Convention on Human Rights, 89 AM. J. INT'L L. 263 (1995).

[83] Biodiversity Convention, *supra* note 52, at art. 8(j).

[84] Climate Convention, *supra* note 53, at art. 3.1.

[85] *Id.* at art 3.4.

[86] *Id.* at art. 1.2.

contributes to climate change not only in Mexico but throughout the world. Mexico thus assumes the obligation to preserve life on the planet by learning from traditional practices of indigenous peoples how to protect life, and how to protect its precious forest resources in order to protect all of us and our children.

B. Violations of the Right to Life: The Potential for Cultural Genocide

The most basic of human rights, recognized explicitly or implicitly in each of the above treaties, is the right to life. The American Convention states, in article 4.1, that "[e]very person has the right to have his life respected. . . . No one shall be arbitrarily deprived of his life."[87] The right is made nonderogable in American Convention article 27.2, which means that it cannot be suspended under any circumstances, including states of emergency (although none was ever declared in Chiapas state). The right to life is also recognized in the American Declaration's article I; the Statute of the Inter-American Commission on Human Rights, at article 20(a), includes the right to life among those to which the Commission is to give "particular attention."

In one of its most important decisions to date, the Inter-American Court of Human Rights decided, in the *Velasquez Rodriguez Case*, that parties to the American Convention have an obligation to ensure free exercise of the rights recognized in that convention, including the right to life. The States parties to the American Convention agree, implicitly, to

> organize the government apparatus and, in general, all the structures through which public power is exercised, so that they are capable of juridically ensuring the free and full enjoyment of human rights. . . . States must prevent, investigate and punish any violation of the rights recognized by the Convention and, moreover, if possible attempt to restore the right violated and provide compensation as warranted for the damages resulting from the violation.[88]

Thus, Mexico has undertaken, by its signing of the American Convention, something that its domestic legal machinery has proven incapable of accomplishing for its indigenous peoples. The inability of the courts in Chiapas to resolve claims involving the murder or disappearance of indigenous peoples is, quite simply and clearly, a violation of international law.

Moreover, in the *Yanomami Case*, discussed above, the Inter-American Commission on Human Rights found that the Brazilian government had violated the right to life and other human rights by not taking timely and effective

---

[87] American Convention, *supra* note 48.

[88] Velasquez Rodriguez Case, Inter-Am. Ct. H.R., 1988, App. VI, at 70–71 (Aug. 31, 1988).

measures to prevent harm that led to the loss of life, cultural identity, and property among the Yanomami.[89]

Finally, the inexorable diminution in the size of tribal groups in Chiapas, albeit gradual, raises the important question of whether exploitation of the natural resources there forces the displacement, and ultimately the death, of the indigenous peoples of the region. Protection against such cultural genocide, or "ethnocide," is provided for in the draft U.N. Declaration on Indigenous Rights, which defines it as "any action which has the aim or effect of depriving [indigenous peoples] of their integrity as distinct peoples. . . of dispossessing them of their lands, territories or resources," or any form of population transfer or assimilation which undermines their rights.[90] The Genocide Convention, which Mexico has ratified, defines "genocide" as any of five types of acts, including those committed with the intent to destroy an ethnic group by "deliberately inflicting on the group conditions of life calculated to bring about its physical destruction."[91] Genocide is a crime against humanity, for which there is no exception or statute of limitations.

There is a compelling argument that the indigenous peoples of Chiapas, particularly the Lacandón group, have been gradually annihilated by the onslaught of civilization. That group now numbers only about 475, and is fast disappearing through death or assimilation.[92]

C. Rights to Political Participation, Cultural Preservation, Self-Determination, and Autonomy

The American Convention protects the right to participate in government, which includes the rights to "take part in the conduct of public affairs . . . to vote and to be elected in genuine periodic elections . . . by secret ballot that guarantees the free expression of the will of the voters."[93] Like the right to life, the Convention makes the right to participation nonderogable.[94] Article XX of the American Declaration also protects the right to political participation. A central complaint of the EZLN forces is that there is no real democracy in

---

[89] *See* Yanomami Case, *supra* note 72, at 24, 28, 33.

[90] *See* draft Declaration, *supra* note 58, at art. 3.

[91] Convention on the Prevention and Punishment of the Crime of Genocide, 78 U.N.T.S. 277, 280 (1948), at art. 2.

[92] *See* Gregory Katz, *Struggling for Survival; Lacandon Indians Fear Zapatista Unrest Could Wipe Out Tribe*, DALLAS MORNING NEWS, Feb. 20, 1994, at 1A. A related theory, suggesting that certain acts of government can result in "patrimonicide," can be found in Ndiva Kofele-Kale, *Patrimonicide: The International Economic Crime of Indigenous Spoliation*, 28 VAND. J. TRANSNAT'L L. 45 (1995).

[93] American Convention, *supra* note 48, at art. 23.

[94] *See id.* at art. 27.2.

Chiapas or, indeed, anywhere in Mexico.[95] Their call for the resignation of the president and for general elections is some measure of their lack of confidence in the vitality of democratic principles.

Common article 1(1) of the International Covenants on Civil and Political Rights, and on Economic, Social and Cultural Rights, to which Mexico is a party, states, as its opening provision, that "[a]ll peoples have the right of self-determination. By virtue of that right they freely determine their political status and freely pursue their economic, social and cultural development." Note again that the operative entity is "peoples," not States or governments. These provisions are powerful statements of law protecting the rights of the indigenous peoples of Chiapas, whether or not national legislation exists to give them autonomy or other limited forms of self-determination.

ILO Convention 169, which deals exclusively with the rights of indigenous peoples, further refines the obligations undertaken pursuant to the American Convention. In addition to the general franchise, it extends to tribal peoples several affirmative rights: 1) the right to decide their own priorities for the process of development as it affects their lives (article 7.1); 2) the right to be consulted whenever new laws are considered that might affect them directly (article 6.1(a)); and 3) the right to recognition and protection of their social, cultural, religious, and spiritual values (article 5(a)). The right to conservation of culture is also recognized in article 14(c) of the International Covenant on Economic, Social and Cultural Rights, to which Mexico is a party. These rights are to be provided, to the greatest extent possible, by institutions and methods that are part of the native dispute resolution system, not necessarily through the national legal system (articles 8 and 9). The demands of the EZLN, in fact, include these rights and institutions.

Mexico, in responding to a recent initiative from the Inter-American Commission on Human Rights to draft a regional treaty on the rights of indigenous peoples, has recognized its interest in offering these benefits to its own indigenous peoples. In response to a survey on rights to be included in the instrument, the Mexican government replied:

> Mexico believes that the instrument should establish the indigenous populations' right to govern their own affairs and to have their own authorities and institutions to represent them. It argues that the instrument must recognize the right of indigenous populations to govern their social affairs by their own rules, insofar as possible.[96]

---

[95] *See, e.g.,* the fourth objective of the EZLN's "Declaration from the Forest," which calls for "all those Mexicans who wish to join our just struggle" to join ranks. EZLN Declaración de la Selva Lacandona, on the internet at <http://www.ezln.org/primera-lacandona.htp>.

[96] INTER-AMERICAN COMMISSION ON HUMAN RIGHTS, REPORT ON THE FIRST ROUND OF CONSULTATIONS CONCERNING THE FUTURE INTER-AMERICAN LEGAL INSTRUMENT ON THE RIGHTS OF INDIGENOUS POPULATIONS, at 29.

In an extensive report on the Miskito native population of Nicaragua, prepared by the Inter-American Commission on Human Rights in 1984, the Commission discussed the evolution of the rights of ethnic groups and the right of the Miskitos to protection under international law. The Commission found that the American Convention itself protected cultural identity through: the explicit rights to protection of honor and dignity; freedom of thought and expression; the right to assembly and of association; the right to residence and movement; and the right to elect their authorities.[97] Although, at that time, the status of international law could not be invoked to afford the Miskitos full political autonomy and self-determination, the Commission also recognized the rights to protection of their language; their religion; and protection of cultural identity and productive organization, which includes the protection of ancestral and communal lands.[98] Many of the rights which were in formation in 1984 are now fully recognized in the enacted treaties to which Mexico is a party.

Finally, in the *Yanomami Case* discussed above, the Inter-American Commission found that an international treaty to which Mexico is also bound "recognizes the right of ethnic groups to special protection on their use of their own language, for the practice of their own religion, and, in general, for all those characteristics necessary for the preservation of their cultural identity."[99] The Mexican government does not recognize formal autonomy for its native populations, as do the governments of Nicaragua, for the Miskitos; Panamá, for the Kuna; or Suriname, for the Saramaca. Steps toward a true voice and control of their own affairs would be a strong prelude to an autonomy agreement.

The International Convention on the Suppression and Punishment of the Crime of "Apartheid," which Mexico also has ratified, defines the crime of apartheid as:

> measures calculated to prevent a racial group or groups from participation in the political, social, economic and cultural life of the country and the deliberate creation of conditions preventing the full development of such a group or groups, in particular by denying to members of a racial group or groups basic human rights and freedoms. . .[100]

Again, the crime of apartheid is an offense against humanity and can be prosecuted wherever and whenever it may have occurred in the past. The indigenous

---

[97] INTER-AMERICAN COMMISSION ON HUMAN RIGHTS, REPORT ON THE SITUATION OF HUMAN RIGHTS OF A SEGMENT OF THE NICARAGUAN POPULATION OF MISKITO ORIGIN 81, 414 (May 16, 1984).

[98] *See id.* at 81, 415.

[99] Yanomami Case, *supra* note 72.

[100] International Convention on the Suppression and Punishment of the Crime of "Apartheid," art. II(c), *reprinted in* 13 I.L.M. 50, 53 (1973).

people of Chiapas have a long and compelling history of deliberate and calculated governmental denial of their right to exercise most basic human rights.

D. Property Rights: Individual Title and Territorial or Ancestral Lands

Article 21 of the American Convention states that everyone has the right "to the use and enjoyment of his property." That right is subordinate to the "interest of society," but if a person is deprived of property for that reason or for "public utility," the owner is entitled to "payment of just compensation." This provision must be read in conjunction with the right to residence in article 22, and the right to privacy in article 11.2, which states that a person may not be the object of "arbitrary or abusive interference with his private life . . . [or] his home." Similar rights are contained in articles XXIII and IX (property and inviolability of the home), VIII (residence), and V (privacy) of the American Declaration. Taken together, these rights create a powerful set of protections for the indigenous people in Chiapas, whether they live in villages, private farms, *ejidos*, or in their traditional lands, the rain forest.

Article 21 of the Convention articulates three important concepts: 1) the principle of peaceful enjoyment of property; 2) a standard by which the State may deprive the private owner of it; and 3) the obligation of adequate compensation by the State when the owner is deprived of it. In an important decision in 1987, the Inter-American Commission held in *Carlos Martínez Riguero v. Nicaragua*[101] that the right to property under article 21 of the American Convention had been violated by Nicaragua in several respects, each of which relates to the above principles. First, it held that the government had illegally confiscated stock dividends earned by the complainant for his share of ownership in a private company alleged to have connections with the Somoza family, because the complainant had left the country after December 1977.[102] Second, it held that the government had failed to pay adequate compensation for a quarry the complainant owned that had been nationalized after the Sandinistas assumed power. The complainant estimated that the value of the seized assets exceeded $63,000,000 (US).[103]

---

[101] *See* Carlos Martínez Riguero v. Nicaragua, Res. No. 2/87, Case 7788, Annual Report of the Inter-American Commission on Human Rights 1986–1987, OEA/Ser.L/V/ 11.71, doc. 9, Rev. 1, Sept. 22, 1987 at 89.

[102] *See id.* at 110.

[103] *See id.* at 109. For another view on the viability of property rights in the Inter-American system, see Victor Marroquin-Merino, *The Protection of Property Rights in the Inter-American System: Banco de Lima Shareholder v. Peru*, 1 U. MIAMI Y.B. INT'L L. 218 (1991). The author notes that *Banco de Lima* was declared inadmissible by the Commission on grounds that it did not have jurisdiction to adjudicate "collective rights of the company" rather than "individual property rights of the individual shareholders." *Id.* at 249. The Commission's conclusion sounds similar to that reached with regard to the initial petitions filed here. *See infra* nn. 131 and 132 and accompanying text.

Thus, the Commission found violations of the right to property and to adequate compensation for its seizure by the government. Most important, however, the Commission implicitly rejected an immunity defense interposed by the government under a law adopted in June 1980. The immunity provision was cited by the complainant as a response to the government's assertion that there were domestic remedies that the complainant could have interposed to obtain domestic judicial relief.[104] While the Commission did not explicitly analyze the immunity claim, it ordered relief for the petitioner, finding that the petitioner had "convincingly rebutted the arguments of the Government of Nicaragua."[105] It thus recognized that the operation of domestic law does not vitiate the government's international legal obligations.

There is no question that "property" includes real estate. The Nicaraguan case cited above included claims of compensation for confiscation of real property, and many decisions under a similar provision in Protocol I to the European Convention on Human Rights extend the right to realty. Thus, under the Convention itself, indigenous peoples in Chiapas have the right to keep property to which they have legal title, whether collectively or individually owned, and when the State deprives them of that property, literally or constructively, it must pay for that expropriation. The Chiapas state government itself estimates that around 4,000 full and partial land takeovers have occurred in the region, peaking in June 1995.[106] An in-depth study of the issue of land seizures, published by the Frey Bartolome de las Casas Center for Human Rights in San Cristobal de las Casas, Chiapas, concludes that peasant farmers, driven from their land by large ranchers acting in collusion with police and other local government authorities, were rightful owners of the lands they repossessed in the wake of the Zapatista uprising.[107] That ownership entitles the small farmers to either rightful repossession of their land or to adequate compensation by the government for its loss.

There is a question as to whether traditional tribal lands, such as hunting and fishing areas within the Lacandón forest, are controlled by the indigenous peoples to such an extent that the government violates their rights to its use and enjoyment when it uses the lands adversely itself, or when it encourages or permits exploitation of the forest by commercial or private owners. In other

---

[104] *See* Carlos Martínez Riguero v. Nicaragua, *supra* note 101, at 100–103.

[105] *Id.* at 109.

[106] *See* Todd Robberson, *Mexican Indians Act on Long-Standing Land Claims*, Wash. Post, Feb. 27, 1994, at A31; Tim Golden, *Mexican Conflict Heats Up, with Peasants Seizing Land*, N.Y. Times, Mar. 14, 1994, at A2; Chris Aspen, *Mexico: Feature—Zapatista Rebels Hit Chiapas Coffee Output*, Reuter Textline, Feb. 21, 1996.

[107] *See* Patricia Jovita Gomez Cruz and Christina Maria Kovic, Con un Pueblo Vivo, En tierra Negada (1994). That study, as well as the EPICA report contain information about specific land takeovers, including case studies. *See* Cruz and Kovic, *supra*, at 139–85; EPICA Report, *supra* note 6, at 32.

words, is the Lacandón rain forest, whether a designated preserve or biosphere, "property" of its tribal peoples under the Convention?

In domestic law, the new constitutional amendments of 1991 provide some guidance. Article 4, for which there is not any regulatory law to date, states that the law "shall protect and promote the development of [the indigenous peoples'] languages, cultures, usages, customs, *resources and specific forms of social organization. . .*"[108] In addition, both the 1991 amendments to article 27 of the Constitution and the new Agrarian Law state that the law "shall protect the integrity of the lands (*tierras*) of indigenous groups."[109] "Lands," as used in that context, must have a different meaning than the *ejido* or the *comunidad*, each of which is fully defined in article 27 of the Constitution and the accompanying Agrarian Reform Law of 1992. As noted above, moreover, article 4 further guarantees that native customs and practices are to be given particular weight in agrarian proceedings.

The *Yanomami Case* in the Inter-American Commission, discussed above, also suggests that traditional tribal lands are under the control, if not the ownership, of indigenous peoples.[110] The complaint was filed on behalf of the peoples, collectively, and the recommendations included creation of a preserve of land for the Yanomami tribal peoples.[111]

An important recent decision by the Australian High Court uses international law to conclude that Aboriginal peoples have native title to their traditional tribal lands, so long as they were occupied by those peoples before the time of original colonial occupation, referred to as "annexation." The government, as defendant, thus could not invoke any traditional common law concept of property ownership in the State—*terra nullius* doctrine, radical title, or the doctrine of tenure—to defeat the claim of the tribal peoples.[112] This case takes an important step in protecting an ancient right to property ownership of indigenous peoples,

---

[108] MEX. CONST., art. 4, para. 1 (emphasis added).

[109] *Id.* The Agrarian Law consistently uses the term "tierras,' or land. *See, e. g.*, Ley Agraria (Agrarian Reform Law), art. 23, XI, y Capítulo II, "De las Tierras Ejidales," Diario Oficial, 26 de febrero de 1992.

[110] *See* Yanomami Case, *supra* note 72, at 33.

[111] *See id.* at 33.

[112] *See* Mabo and Others v. State of Queensland (1992) 107 A.L.R. 1. The *Mabo* decision has been the subject of intense study by academics and commercial interests. Its full impact at the international level is yet to be ascertained. *See, e.g.*, Gary D. Mayers and John Mugumbwa, *The Mabo Decision: Australian Aboriginal Land Rights in Transition*, 23 ENVTL. L. 1203, 1204–1218 (1993); Melissa Manwaring, *A Small Step or a Giant Leap? The Implications of Australia's First Judicial Recognition of Indigenous Land Rights: Mabo and Others v. State of Queensland, 107 A.L.R. 1 (1992)(Aust.)*, 34 HARV. INT'L L.J. 177 (1993); Dianne Otto, *A Question of Law or Politics? Indigenous Claims to Sovereignty in Australia*, 21 SYRACUSE J. INT'L L. & COM. 65 (1995).

despite their lack of formal title or even an understanding that "ownership" of the land is something which anyone can possess.

A separate legal question is whether deforestation and other despoliation of the environment in these territories deprives the indigenous peoples of its use and benefit to such an extent that compensation for their loss must be made by the government. An examination of domestic and international law, taken together, leads inexorably to the conclusion that the answer to these questions must be in the affirmative.

ILO Convention 169 further articulates the right to control of traditional territory as a property right. Article 14 of the Convention states that "rights of ownership and possession of the peoples concerned over the lands which they traditionally occupy shall be recognized." Even if the land is not "exclusively occupied" by native peoples, the article continues, if they have "traditionally had access [to the lands] for their subsistence and traditional activities," their rights to its use must be protected. Article 15 of the Convention extends special safeguards to the rights of native peoples to the natural resources of their traditional lands. Mexico seems to recognize these rights in its proposals for a draft instrument on indigenous peoples in the Americas. There, in response to questions about the right to private property and to its use and enjoyment, the government stated that "the territorial rights and the right to individual and collective property must be respected."[113]

Indigenous peoples who are removed from traditional lands or whose lands are plundered for their natural resources are entitled to governmental notice of these actions, and the native peoples must surrender these rights by free and informed consent, under the detailed provisions of articles 15 and 16 of ILO Convention 169. When such losses occur, as with the American Convention's property provisions, full compensation is required or, at their choice, the peoples must be provided with lands "of quality and legal status at least equal to that of the lands previously occupied by them."[114] Protection against forced removal of native peoples from their lands or territories is also provided for in article 10 of the U.N. draft Declaration on the Rights of Indigenous Peoples.

E. The Right to Adequate Living Standards: Livelihood, Education, Health, Food, Clothing, and Shelter

There is little doubt that the law of the Inter-American human rights system makes one of the most powerful cases for enforceable economic and social rights in Chiapas. These rights—to food, clothing, shelter, work, health, and education—are fully articulated in several instruments of the region, including

---

[113] INTER-AMERICAN COMMISSION ON HUMAN RIGHTS, *supra* note 96, at 17.

[114] International Labor Organsation Convention (No. 169) Concerning Indigenous and Tribal Peoples in Independent Countries, *supra* note 43, at arts. 15–16.

the OAS Charter itself,[115] the American Convention and Declaration, and the Protocol of San Salvador,[116] a supplemental instrument in the system which protects economic, social, and cultural rights. While Mexico signed the Protocol of San Salvador in 1988, it has not yet ratified it; still, it is legally bound to recognize the rights articulated in the other treaties mentioned above.

The American Convention contains only one article that explicitly deals with economic and social rights. Article 26 commits the States parties to "the full realization of the rights implicit in the economic, social, educational, scientific, and cultural standards set forth in the [OAS Charter]." The provision, however, contains qualifying language similar to that found in the International Covenant on Economic, Social and Cultural Rights which commits the ratifying countries to "undertake to adopt measures" to adopt these rights with the goal of "progressively" implementing them.[117] This "progressive implementation" language gives the Mexican government a powerful argument in response to demands of economic and social rights by the indigenous peoples of the region. The argument is that all efforts are being made to provide such rights, and that any effort at all is demonstrative of progressive implementation, which may take years or decades to fully achieve. Prominent international legal scholars have suggested that a minimum "floor" of State legal obligations for the protection of economic and social rights can be articulated, even under the progressive implementation standard.[118] The government's argument might well prevail, however, were it not for important decisions in the jurisprudence of the Inter-American human rights system.

Advisory Opinion No. 10 of the Inter-American Court of Human Rights, rendered in 1989, finds that the American Declaration, while not a formal treaty, is a "source of international obligations" by virtue of its relationship to the Charter of the OAS.[119] Thus, all of the provisions of the Declaration must be given full international legal effect. As such, economic and social rights are amply protected by the explicit language of those instruments.

---

[115] Charter of the Organization of American States, 2 U.S.T. 2394, T.I.A.S. No. 2361, 119 U.N.T.S. 3 (dec. 13, 1951).

[116] Additonal Protocol the American Convention on Human Rights in the Area of Economic, Social and Cultural Rights, Protocol of San Salvador (Nov. 17, 1988) in Basic Documents Pertaining to Human Rights in the Inter-American Systam, OAS, 1996.

[117] See International Covenant on Economic, Social and Cultural Rights, supra note 56, at art. 2(1).

[118] See, e.g., Asbjorn Eide, *Realization of Social and Economic Rights and the Minimum Threshold Approach*, in HUMAN RIGHTS IN THE WORLD COMMUNITY 158 (R. Claude and B. Weston, eds., 2d ed. 1992); Philip Alston, *The International Covenant on Economic, Social and Cultural Rights*, in MANUAL ON HUMAN RIGHTS REPORTING 39, 46–47 (1991).

[119] Inter-American Court of Human Rights, Advisory Opinion OC–10/89, July 14, 1989, at 43–51.

1. Rights to Livelihood

First, the Declaration, in articles XIV, XV, and XVI, protects the right to work, to fair wages, to rest and leisure, and to social security for unemployment and old age. The OAS Charter commits every Member State, in article 31(g), to dedicate every effort to the achievement of basic goals including "fair wages, employment opportunities, and acceptable working conditions for all." Article 43 of the Charter recognizes the right to work as "a right and a social duty," and promotes the right to collective bargaining and the workers' right to strike. ILO Convention 169 and the International Covenant on Economic, Social and Cultural Rights also specify these rights and others, including the protection of lawful trade union activities, and protections against bonded service and other forms of debt servitude.[120]

Agricultural workers are given special attention in the OAS Charter, article 31(d), which seeks "reforms leading to equitable and efficient land-tenure systems, increased agricultural productivity, expanded use of undeveloped land, diversification of production; improved processing and marketing systems for agricultural products; and the strengthening and expansion of facilities to attain these ends." ILO Convention 169, in article 20.3(b), explicitly protects against "working conditions hazardous to [indigenous workers'] health, in particular through exposure to pesticides or other toxic substances." Articles 21 through 23 of the ILO Convention commit States parties to full vocational training, and to protection of handicrafts and "traditional activities of the peoples concerned, such as hunting, fishing, trapping and gathering." All of these protections seem particularly important, given the express concerns of the EZLN and the indigenous peoples of Chiapas regarding the implementation of NAFTA and its impact on the region.

2. Rights to Education

Second, the Declaration, in article XII, protects the right to education, including equality of opportunity for all education and free education at the primary level. The OAS Charter, in article 31(h), seeks "eradication of illiteracy and expansion of educational opportunities for all," and articles 45 through 48 commit member states to a wide range of educational rights, including the obligation to "give primary importance within their development plans to the encouragement of education . . . as a foundation for democracy, social justice, and progress."

ILO Convention 169, in articles 26 through 31, guarantees full equality of educational opportunity to indigenous peoples, including protection of indigenous languages by education of native children in its usage. The International

---

[120] *See* Convention No. 169, *supra* note 43, at art. 20.3; International Covenant on Economic, Social and Cultural Rights, *supra* note 56, at arts. 6–9.

Covenant on Economic, Social and Cultural Rights creates similar obligations in its articles 13 and 14.

3. Rights to Health and Subsistence: Food, Clothing, and Shelter

The Declaration, in article XI, protects the right to health "through sanitary and social measures relating to food, clothing, housing and medical care, to the extent permitted by public and community resources." This right thus also contains an important qualifier to which the government may appeal as an excuse for noncompliance. However, other sources of the right are less qualified. The OAS Charter protects the right to proper nutrition and housing in articles 31(j) and (k), and ILO Convention 169 requires that governments ensure adequate health services and health care to indigenous peoples in article 25. The International Covenant on Economic, Social and Cultural Rights, in article 11, clearly protects the right to "adequate food, clothing and housing, and to the continuous improvement of living conditions," and article 12 protects the right to "the highest attainable standard of physical and mental health."

4. Special Protections of Economic and Social Rights of Indigenous Children

Article VII of the Declaration creates a higher standard of care for indigenous children when it states that "all children have the right to special protection, care and aid." This protection is reiterated in the American Convention's article 19; in ILO Convention 169, article 29; and in article 10.3 of the International Covenant on Economic, Social and Cultural Rights. The rights of children are fully enumerated in the 1989 U.N. Convention of the Rights of the Child,[121] which entered into force in 1990 and has been ratified by Mexico. Thus, while the Mexican government owes obligations of economic and social rights to all indigenous peoples, their children are entitled to special and extraordinary protections.

F. The Inter-American Commission's Initial Response to the Petitions

Thus far, the response of the Commission to the filing of the initial petitions alleging violations of civil, political and humanitarian rights has been disappointing. The Commission staff informed the petitioners, a group of concerned NGOs, that the petitions would not be opened as contentious complaints, but could only be accepted by the Commission under its powers to consider general conditions in a country unless individual victims were named in the petitions.[122] The power

---

[121] See Convention on the Rights of the Child, U.N. G.A. Res. 25 (XLIV), 44 U.N. GAOR, Supp. (No. 49), U.N. Doc. A./RES/44/25 (1989), 28 I.L.M. 1448 (1989).

[122] This was the customary practice of the Commission. American Convention on Human Rights, arts. 44–47; Regulations of the Inter-American Commission on Human Rights, arts. 44–50, 55–59 (1980) *in* Basic Documents Pertaining to Human Rights in the Inter-American System, OAS (May 1996).

to examine human rights situations on a countrywide basis is clearly contemplated in the American Convention and in the Commission's regulations,[123] but acceptance of the petitions only as general reports is a political judgment that effectively means that the petitions disappear into the Commission's archives. The Commission would rather not have to adjudicate the difficult legal questions involved in these cases by offering recommendations to the government of Mexico as to specific human rights violations. Moreover, a close reading of the Commission's regulations leads to an opposite conclusion about the nature of collective claims without naming the specific victims.

Most decisively, the American Convention (article 44) and the Commission's Regulations (article 26.1) both refer to the rights of "groups of persons" to file as victims. While this provision has never been interpreted by the Commission, its clear facial meaning refers to collectives. Moreover, the Commission has decided cases involving collective rights of groups, including the Yanomami and Miskito cases referred to so often in this chapter, without the requirement that each member of the group be specifically identified. If it has done so in some cases, there is no discernible reason for its denial in this one, other than politics. Finally, the Commission's regulations require only that the victim's name be given "if possible" (article 32(b)). This provision acknowledges the difficulty in obtaining names of victims of some human rights violations, and keeps informality as a legitimate goal of the Commission's adjudicative powers. Taken together, these provisions, and their interpretations by the Commission itself, argue that the Chiapas cases are viable human rights claims susceptible to resolution by the petition system.

V. CONCLUSION

This chapter provides an analysis that focuses on violations of human rights in Chiapas by the Mexican government. It concentrates intentionally on the rights of indigenous peoples, protection of the environment, the honoring of economic and social obligations of the Mexican government, and the special duties that it undertakes with regard to children. This is not to suggest that there are no violations of other rights; there were widespread violations of the humanitarian law and of civil and political rights during the January 1994 armed conflict. Nor does it deny that human rights violations have been committed by the forces of the EZLN. Such violations are, in fact, documented in the detailed reports to which this chapter makes reference. Finally, it elaborates on what are potentially enforceable human rights. Unfortunately, for example, the internally displaced people whose plight is documented here have no explicitly enforceable rights under traditional refugee law, although they certainly may be entitled to

---

[123] The American Convention, at article 41(c), permits the Commission to "prepare such studies or reports as it considers advisable." The Commission's Regulations, at articles 62 and 63, allow it to report on human rights in a State, or to include such observations in its annual report.

protection under humanitarian principles.[124] Another area that could be discussed is the evolving human right to democracy, which connotes the kind of government that is legitimated by the consent of the governed. In determining if democracy exists, one must examine whether there is evidence of consent to the process by which a populace is consulted by its government.[125] In Chiapas and the rest of Mexico, that definition has been honored in its breach for too long.

The purpose of this chapter has been, instead, to educate readers about the historical roots of the conflict in Chiapas and to relate human rights violations to this wider time frame, in which the native peoples of Chiapas have vastly more often been the victims rather than the violators of human rights. It also seeks to widen the perspective of human rights monitors to the range of human rights protections that Mexico has voluntarily assumed in the international arena. While all have watched, with great attention and hope for the future, the successful negotiation of the NAFTA agreements, we cannot ignore the existing obligations that the Mexican government assumed for protection of all of its citizens. The appeal of the EZLN is not one that any civilized government can ignore for its native peoples; it is a cry for true equality, for true democracy.

---

[124] See Roberta Cohen, *International Protection for Internally Displaced Persons, in* HUMAN RIGHTS: AN AGENDA FOR THE NEXT CENTURY 17, 24 (Louis Henkin and John Lawrence Hargrove, eds., 1994).

[125] *See* Thomas M. Franck, *Democracy as a Human Right, in* HUMAN RIGHTS: AN AGENDA FOR THE NEXT CENTURY at 73, 75.

CHAPTER 12

THE ROLE OF INDIGENOUS GROUPS IN CONSTITUTIONAL DEMOCRACIES: A LESSON FROM CHILE AND THE UNITED STATES

Kevin J. Worthen

Since the day Columbus' ships landed on American soil 500 years ago, few legal questions have produced as much deliberation, consternation, and emotion as the "Indian question."[1] Public officials, religious leaders, legal scholars, and

---

[1] Within two years of Columbus' maiden voyage, the "question of the aborigines of the new World had [already] been submitted by the [Spanish] government to a commission composed of theologians and canonists. . ." Ernest Nys, *Introduction, in* FRANCISCI DE VICTORIA, DE INDIS ET DE IVRE BELLI RELECTIONES 84 (1917). The natives' control of prime lands in both the United States and Chile, as well as periodic "uprisings" in these countries, kept the "Indian question" high on the policymakers' lists throughout the nineteenth century, as evidenced by massive military action against the native population in 1880–1881 in Chile and as late as 1890 in the United States. *See* JOSÉ BENGOA C., HISTORIA DEL PUEBLO MAPUCHE: SIGLO XIX Y XX 285–325 (1985); [hereinafter BENGOA] ANGIE DEBO, A HISTORY OF THE INDIANS OF THE UNITED STATES 290–94 (1970). Recent comprehensive legislation in Chile and ongoing Supreme Court litigation in the United States (there have been twenty-two Supreme Court cases involving Indian law issues in the past ten years), indicate that the issue continues to be of great interest to contemporary policymakers: Idaho v. Coeur D"Alene Tribe of Idaho — U.S. —, 117 S. Ct. 2028 (1997); Strate v. A-1 Contractors, — U.S. —, 117 S. Ct. 1404 (1997); Babbitt v. Youpee, — U.S. —, 117 S. Ct. 727 (1997); Seminole Tribe of Florida v. Florida, 519 U.S. 234, 116 S. Ct. 1114 (1996); Oklahoma Tax Comm'n v. Chickasaw Nation, 515 U.S. 450 (1995); Department of Taxation and Finance of New York v. Milhelm Attea & Bros., Inc., 512 U.S. 61 (1994); Hagen v. Utah 510 U.S. 399 (1994); South Dakota v. Bourland, 508 U.S. 679 (1993); Lincoln v. Vigil, 508 U.S. 182 (1993); Oklahoma Tax Comm'n v. Sac and Fox Nation, 508 U.S. 114 (1993); Negonsott v. Samuels, 507 U.S. 99 (1993); County of Yakima v. Confederated Tribes and Bands of the Yakima Indian Nation 502 U.S. 251 (1992); Blatchford v. Native Village of Noatak, 501 U.S. 775 (1991); Oklahoma Tax Comm'n v. Citizen Band Potawatomi Indian Tribe of Oklahoma, 498 U.S. 505 (1991); Employment Div. Dept. of Human Resources v. Smith, 494 U. S. 872 (1990); Mississippi Band of Choctaw Indians v. Holyfield, 490 U.S. 30 (1989); Duro v. Reina, 495 U.S. 676 (1990); Cotton Petroleum Co. v. New Mexico, 490 U. S. 163 (1989); Brendale v. Confederated Tribes and Bands of the Yakima Indian Nation, 492 U.S. 408 (1989); Oklahoma Tax Comm'n v. Graham, 489 U.S. 838 (1998); Employment Div. Dept. of Human Resources v. Smith, 485 U.S. 660 (1988); Lyng v. Northwest Indian Cemetary

private citizens have debated seemingly *ad nauseam* what the various govern-ments[2] should do with respect to the indigenous populations that inhabited the continents when the Europeans first arrived. Different answers to that question have been given at different times and places.[3] Widely different approaches have

---

Protective Assoc. 485 U.S. 493 (1988).

See Ley No. 19.253 del octubre de 1993.

[2] By the time English colonists arrived on the shores of the modern-day United States, kings, queens, popes, and legal scholars had all wrestled extensively with the proper relationship between the Spanish and Portuguese colonizers and the native popula-tion of the Americas. *See* S. LYMAN TYLER, THE INDIAN CAUSE IN THE SPANISH LAWS OF THE INDIES (1980); EUGENE H. KORTH, SPANISH POLICY IN COLONIAL CHILE 1–21 (1968); ROBERT A. WILLIAMS, JR., THE AMERICAN INDIAN IN WESTERN LEGAL THOUGHT 78–108 (1990). These discussions continued in Europe until the independence of the American nations. *See, e.g.,* FRANCIS PAUL PRUCHA, AMERICAN INDIAN POLICY IN THE FORMATIVE YEARS 5–25 (1962); KORTH, *supra, passim*; WILLIAMS, *supra,* at 151–249.

The early Spanish discussions influenced most of the Indian policy of both the English colonists and the United States. *See* TYLER, *supra,* at xxviii; Felix S. Cohen, *The Spanish Origin of Indian Rights in the Law of the United States,* 31 GEO. L.J. 1 (1942); Felix S. Cohen, *Original Indian Title,* 32 MINN. L. REV. 28 (1947).

[3] For example, the British followed a policy of entering into treaties with most indigenous groups with which they wished to deal. *See* Siegfried Wiessner, *American Indian Treaties and Modern International Law,* 7 ST. THOMAS L. REV. 567, 570 & n.16 (1995). This policy was continued by the United States until 1871. *See* FRANCIS PAUL PRUCHA, AMERICAN INDIAN TREATIES: THE HISTORY OF A POLITICAL ANOMALY 289 (1994). On the other hand, "[i]n Mexico, Central and South America, neither the Spanish nor the Portuguese appear to have pursued a treaty policy with respect to indigenous peoples" (with the notable exception of the Peace of Quillín entered into with the Mapuche in Chile. *See infra* note 18). Wiessner, *supra,* at 570 n.15.

Which policy was more harmful to the indigenous populations is far from certain. As Alexis de Tocqueville noted in the nineteenth century, with more than a little hyperbole:

> The Spaniards pursued the Indians with blood-hounds, like wild beasts; they sacked the New World with no more temper or compassion than a city taken by storm; but destruction must cease, and frenzy be stayed; the remnant of the Indian population, which had escaped the massacre, mixed with its conquerors, and adopted in the end their religion and their manners. The conduct of the Americans of the United States towards the aborigines is characterized, on the other hand, by a singular attachment to the formalities of the law. Provided that the Indians retain their barbarous condition, the Americans take no part in their affairs; they treat them as independent nations, and do not possess themselves of their hunting-grounds without a treaty of purchase: and if an Indian nation happens to be so encroached upon as to be unable to subsist upon its territory, they afford it brotherly assistance in transporting it to a grave sufficiently remote from the land of its fathers.

> The Spaniards were unable to exterminate the Indian race by those unparalleled atrocities which brand them with indelible shame, nor did they even succeed in wholly depriving it of its rights; but the Americans of the United States have accomplished this twofold purpose with singular felicity; tranquilly, legally, philanthropically, without shedding blood, and without violating a single great

been tried even within the same country at different times.[4] Yet more than 500 years after the discussion commenced, the answers still elude us. In many countries, the indigenous population faces social and economic challenges on a scale not encountered by the remainder of the country.[5] We in the Americas are still in search of the ideal answer to the legal status of the descendants of the original Americans.

This chapter does not purport to provide that ideal answer. It does, however, attempt to set forth a lesson to be learned from the Indian law experience of two countries—the United States and Chile—a lesson that can be a valuable starting point for addressing the role of indigenous peoples in the kinds of constitutional democracies that exist in our American nations.

---

principle of morality in the eyes of the world. It is impossible to destroy men with more respect for the laws of humanity.

ALEXIS DE TOCQUEVILLE, 1 DEMOCRACY IN AMERICA 422 23 (Henry Reeve trans., 1961).

[4] This has been especially true in the United States. "[O]ne of the most striking characteristics of formal federal policy toward Native Americans [in the United States] since the Revolutionary War has been its inconsistency. Massive swings between separationist and assimilationist attitudes, goals, and means have been the norm." Kevin J. Worthen, *One Small Step for Courts, One Giant Leap for Group Rights: Accommodating the Associational Role of "Intimate" Government Associations*, 71 N.C. L. REV. 595, 629 (1993). As one scholar has observed, "If there is one eternal verity which emerges from Indian law, history, and policy [in the United States], it is that, like little Alice [in Wonderland], we are never certain of the 'Rules of Battle. . . .' Consistently, the rules have changed, often for reasons that have little to do with Indian concerns or needs." Rennard Strickland, *The Absurd Ballet of American Indian Policy or American Indian Struggling With Ape on a Tropical Landscape: An Afterword*, 31 Me. L. REV. 213, 218 (1979).

[5] For example, the unemployment rate on Indian reservations in the United States was 48% in 1989, with the figure reaching 80% for reservations in South Dakota. *See* BUREAU OF INDIAN AFFAIRS, INDIAN SERVICE POPULATION AND LABOR FORCE ESTIMATES, Table 1, at 1 (1989). By comparison, the unemployment rate for the entire United States that year was only 5.3%. *See* U.S. DEPARTMENT OF COMMERCE, BUREAU OF THE CENSUS, 1994 STATISTICAL ABSTRACT OF THE UNITED STATES, Table 616, at 396 (1994). The suicide rate among Native American youth between the ages of 15 and 19 is more than twice that of the rest of American youth. *See* OFFICE OF TECHNOLOGY ASSESSMENT, INDIAN ADOLESCENT MENTAL HEALTH 16 (1990). The alcoholism mortality rate for Native American males ages 25 to 34 is nearly seven times that of other Americans. *See* U.S. Indian Health Service., U.S. DEPARTMENT OF HEALTH AND HUMAN SERVICES, TRENDS IN INDIAN HEALTH 1991, Table 4.24, at 50 (1991).

In Chile, a study of an area inhabited predominantly by the Mapuche Indians indicated that the child death rate was double that of the rest of the country (amounting to 45 deaths per 1,000 live births). It also indicated that the illiteracy rate (16%) more than doubled that of the rest of the country. *See* JOSÉ AYLWIN O., THE INDIGENOUS PEOPLES OF CHILE: HISTORICAL BACKGROUND AND CURRENT SITUATION 5 (1993), *citing* CENTRO LATINAMERICANO DE DEMOGRAFIA, ET AL., CENSO DE REDUCCIONES INDÍGENAS SELECCIONADAS: ANÁLISIS SOCIODEMOGRAPHICO (1991).

The lesson is this: membership in groups plays an important role for many indigenous peoples.[6] Any legal policy that fails to take this fact into account—that fails to provide a role for the indigenous group as a positive entity in the national society—is destined to fail. The Indian policies of Chile and the United States have not been successful because policymakers have failed to consider how the law might be shaped to provide indigenous groups—not just individual members of those groups, but the groups themselves—with the legal space they need to act as a positive mediating structure between the nation and the individual.

The experiences of indigenous populations in the legal systems of Chile and the United States illustrate two different ways in which the failure to understand the role of groups in a constitutional democracy can lead to frustrating failures in the implementation of constitutional policy. The Chilean experience shows how such a failure of understanding can cause a policy based on individual equality to flounder; the United States' experience demonstrates how a failure of understanding can lead to an ineffective policy based on separation. As much as those two policies seem to conflict with each other, both share the fatal flaw of failure to provide legal space for the proper workings of intermediate groups in democratic society.

I. THE CHILEAN EXPERIENCE: THE LIMITS OF INDIVIDUAL EQUALITY

On March 4, 1819, less than a year after Chilean forces had repulsed the last Spanish threat to the new nation's capital of Santiago,[7] Bernardo O'Higgins issued a decree laying the foundation for Chilean policy toward its indigenous population. Reflecting the new nation's dramatic break with its Spanish progenitors in other areas, O'Higgins rejected the Spanish tradition of ''guardianship''

---

[6] The same point is true for many nonindigenous peoples as well, a fact policymakers in other areas of the law would do well to heed. As two scholars have noted, ''[it] is no longer, and indeed never was, just a few small and relatively self-contained communities like the . . . Native Americans who are threatened by modern society's 'hydraulic' pressures toward conformity.'' Mary Ann Glendon & Raul F. Yanes, *Structural Free Exercise*, 90 MICH. L. REV. 477, 547 (1991).

[7] Chileans celebrate September 18, 1810—the date on which the Spanish governor resigned in favor of a newly created national junta—as their independence day. However, the junta that took over power on that day did not declare independence from Spain. It was merely rejecting Napoleon Bonaparte's efforts to place his brother Joseph on the Spanish throne. Like other juntas formed at the time in both Spain and Spanish America, the Chilean junta swore allegiance to the deposed heir to the Spanish throne, King Ferdinand. *See* LUIS GALDAMES, A HISTORY OF CHILE 157 (Isaac Cox trans., 1964). The idea of full separation gained ascendancy in the junta over the next few years, and the battle for full independence continued for the next decade. O'Higgins signed an act declaring Chile's independence in February of 1818. *See id.* at 197. The critical battle repulsing the last Spanish assault on Santiago occurred on April 5, 1818. *See id.* at 198–201.

for native populations, calling it "inhumane" and incompatible with "[t]he liberal system which Chile has adopted."[8] Instead, O'Higgins declared,

> this precious portion of our species [shall] henceforth . . . be Chilean citizens . . . free as the other inhabitants of the State with whom they will have equal voice and representation, possessing for themselves the power to enter all classes of contracts, defend their causes, contract marriages, [engage in] trade, practice the arts toward which they are inclined, and pursue a career in letters and arms to obtain political and military employment according to their abilities.[9]

This policy of individual equality before the law was full of promise for the indigenous peoples of Chile, as the Chilean revolutionaries looked forward to the day when all persons within the new nation's borders would join in a common brotherhood of peace and tranquility.[10] However, a brief review of the actual implementation of the policy shows how this concept of individual equality—an indispensable constitutional tool in the legal battle of many ethnic and racial minorities in the United States,[11] and throughout the world—is limited in its ability to resolve many problems facing indigenous peoples in the Americas because it fails to take into account the importance to many indigenous peoples of membership in the indigenous group.

---

[8] Decreto del Director Supremo Bernardo O'Higgins del 4 de Marzo de 1819. All translations of Spanish materials into English in this paper are the author's.

[9] *Id.*

[10] The feelings of the revolutionaries toward the largest indigenous group—the Mapuche—were captured in a short sketch written by the Chilean patriot Bernardo Vera y Pintado during O'Higgins' reign as supreme dictator. The sketch opens at the mouth of the river Bío-Bío, the dividing line between the Spanish and the Mapuche. A Chilean ship bearing the name of the great Mapuche warrior Lautaro arrives from the ocean, with several Mapuches watching from the beach. The captain of the ship delivers an oration praising "the indomitable Araucano" [the Spanish name for the Mapuche], and then informs a male Mapuche of the liberation of Chile. The Mapuche goes in search of his wife, inviting her to join the festivities. When she expresses reservations, the captain assures her, "We are not enemies; We are compatriots, children of Chile." The two Mapuche then board the boat, where all sing a hymn in praise of O'Higgins. *See* BENGOA, *supra* note 1, at 140–41, *quoting* Bernardo Vera y Pintado, *El Triunfo de la Naturaleza, Introduction* (presented August 20, 1819).

[11] As one scholar has noted, "[s]ince the [fourteenth] amendment was ratified in 1868, this [equal protection] clause has become a powerful guarantee of racial equality and a bulwark for ethnic and religious minorities." JUDITH A. BAER, EQUALITY UNDER THE CONSTITUTION: RECLAIMING THE FOURTEENTH AMENDMENT 17–18 (1983).

While there are several different indigenous groups living within the borders of Chile,[12] this chapter focuses mainly on the largest[13] group,[14] the Mapuches. Prior to the arrival of the Spanish, the Mapuches consisted of several subgroups, whose principal governing social group was the family.[15] These subgroups, which shared a common language, combined politically only in times of war, and even then did so in a very decentralized manner.[16] Despite, or some have argued, because of this loose political organization,[17] the Mapuches repulsed conquest

---

[12] In the 1993 Indian law, the Chilean government expressly recognized "as the principal [indigenous] ethnic groups of Chile: the Mapuche, Aymara, Rapa Nui or 'Easter Islanders,' the communities of the Atacamenans, Quechua, and Coya communities in the north of the country, [and] the communities of the Kaweskar or Alacalufes and Yaman or Yanganes of the southern channels." Ley No. 19.253 del Octubre de 1993, art. 1.

[13] Exact statistics concerning the indigenous groups of Chile are unreliable, among other reasons, because of the high percentage of mixed European and native persons, or *mestizos*, in the Chilean population. Most estimates are that *mestizos* account for more than 80% of the contemporary Chilean population. *See* THE STATESMAN'S YEAR-BOOK 348 (Brian Hunter, ed., 1991–92). Thus, status as a member of an indigenous group is largely a question of culture and self-identification.

The 1992 official census—which asked respondents if they identified themselves as Mapuche, Aymara, or Rapa Nui—indicates that there are 928,060 Mapuche, 48,477 Aymara, and 21,848 Rapa Nui over the age of 14 in the country. Extrapolating those figures to the total population of all ages (including those under 14), the figures would be 1,271,442 Mapuche (9.6% of the population), 66,413 Aymara (0.5% of the population), and 29,932 Rapa Nui (0.2% of the population). Most agree that the numbers with respect to the Rapa Nui are grossly exaggerated. *See* AYLWIN, *supra* note 5, at 17 & n.17.

[14] The term "group," rather than "tribe," is used advisedly because, unlike U.S. tribal entities, none of the Chilean indigenous groups currently has any attributes of political sovereignty. Moreover, the Mapuche does not have now, and historically has lacked, a comprehensive group-wide organization or system of self government. The absence of any kind of tradition of recognized sovereignty is one of the key distinctions between U.S. and Chilean Indian policy, and a proper subject for its own examination in another time and place. For present purposes, it suffices to note the absence of this fundamental component and to point out that it is a logical outgrowth of a policy of full individual equality, in which membership in the group is irrelevant to any governmental policy.

[15] *See* BENGOA, *supra* note 1, at 26–28. The Mapuche at one time consisted of several autonomous or semi-autonomous subgroups, such as the Abajinos or Nagpuleche, the Arribano or Huenteche, the Pehuneces, Puelches, and others. *See id.* at 69–124. The Spanish referred to them as the Araucanians because they inhabited the area of Arauco.

[16] *See id.* at 26–28, 62 64.

[17] Explaining this theory, Chilean anthropologist José Bengoa states, "According to this hypothesis, unlike the Incas and Mexicans, who had centralized governments and internal political divisions, the Mapuches had a social structure without hierarchy. In the Mexican and Andean situations, the conquistador struck the central political power and, upon conquering it, assured himself dominion of the Empire. In the case of the Mapuche, this was not possible because their subjection passed through every one of the thousands of independent families." *Id.* at 37.

attempts by the Incas, the Spanish, and the Chileans for over 300 years.[18] Their fierce and successful resistance to Spanish rule served as a rallying cry for the early Chilean revolutionaries,[19] especially O'Higgins.[20]

The history of this people contains a multitude of lessons for constitutional law. However, this chapter focuses on the history of Mapuche property rights under Chilean law, for it is with respect to property that the Chilean policy of individual equality has had the greatest impact on the Mapuches. This is not surprising because the relationship of the Mapuches to the land is so central to their culture. Indeed, the term "Mapuche" comes from two words in Mapudugun (the Mapuches' native tongue)—"Mapu" (earth) and "che" (people)—so that the term "Mapuche" literally means "People of the Earth."[21]

As is the case with many indigenous cultures, the relationship of the Mapuches to the land is much different from that envisioned by the Western Europeans who came to rule Chile.[22] For the Mapuches, as for many indigenous peoples, the land is a living thing. Moreover, the Mapuche concept of land is not limited to the physical elements. When the Mapuches talk of land or "Mapu," they are referring not just to the physical soil and the plants that grow there, but to a multidimensional metaphysical and spiritual sphere that extends upward to the sky, downward to the center of the earth, and outward beyond the physical space

---

[18] In a rare departure from their normal policy (*see supra* note 3), the Spanish in 1641 entered into a treaty with the Mapuches at Quillín in which they recognized the Mapuches as an independent nation and established the River Bío-Bío as a permanent frontier between the two peoples. *See* KORTH, *supra* note 2, at 175–77. The Bío-Bío continued to be the informal border between the Mapuches and the Chileans from the time that Chile gained its independence until the 1880s. *See* BENGOA, *supra* note 1, at 139.

[19] The history of the Mapuches' successful resistance against the Spanish invasion is well known in Chile. It is memorialized in the epic poem of the Spaniard Alonso de Ercilla y Zuñiga, LA ASRAUCANA. At the time of the Chilean revolution, the principal rebel leaders invoked this imagery, referring to themselves as the "descendants of Arauco." *See* GONZALO BULNES A., LOS MAPUCHES Y LA TIERRA 15 (1985), *quoting* Letter from Bernardo O'Higgins to Juan Florencio Terrada (February 20, 1812).

[20] O'Higgins' concern for the native population of Chile is evidenced by the fact that a frequent visitor to his governmental palace in Santiago recorded that he raised several Mapuche orphans, whom he occasionally addressed in their native tongue of Mapudugun. *See* BENGOA, *supra* note 1, at 138 n.10, *citing* MARIA GRAHAM, DIARIO DE MI RESIDENCIA EN CHILE 117 (1972).

[21] RENÉ RODRIGUEZ G., LOS MAPUCHES EN EL LARGO SENDERO DE LA HISTORIA DE CHILE 25 (1983).

[22] While there are a number of sources which set forth the Mapuche view of property, *see, e.g.,* José Aylwin O., *Tierra Mapuche: Derecho Consuetudinario y Legislación Chilena, in* ENTRE LA LEY Y LA COSTUMBRE: EL DERECHO CONSUETUDINARIO INDÍGENA EN AMÉRICA LATINA 333, 336–39 (Rodolfo Stavenhagen & Diego Iturralde eds., 1990), the description presented in this paper is based largely on presentations made by Juan Manculef H., a Mapuche, to a class of law students at the University of Chile in September and October 1994. A copy of Manculef's outline is on file with the author.

to the spiritual. The term "earth" or "land" refers not only to geographic physical space, but to a philosophical space as well, one that represents the essence of the Mapuche cosmology of good and evil.

Given the Mapuches' unique concept of land, it is not surprising that Chilean real property laws have had the greatest impact on the Mapuches, or that the application of those laws most clearly demonstrates the limits of a policy based on individual equality. The manner in which the policy of full individual equality was to play itself out with respect to the Mapuches and their land became evident soon after O'Higgins' 1819 decree. In 1823, Chile enacted a law requiring the *intendentes* of each region to appoint a person who, aided by a surveyor, would inform him as to the existence of native peoples in the region. The law provided that "the lands currently possessed by . . . the natives" were to be "declared as their perpetual and secure property."[23] The intent was to identify who "owned" what property, and record the information, thereby making the land available for purchase or development, according to the desires of the owners. Surplus land was then to be made available for colonization by natives or nonnatives.[24]

It is important to emphasize that there is no evidence that this requirement was introduced for the purpose of depriving the Mapuches of their land.[25] It was merely the first step in an effort to bring order to the property system nationwide, so that developed lands could be marketed effectively and undeveloped lands could be colonized. The law did not require that the Mapuches move off their land. Nor did it prevent them from claiming as much of the land as they were using. They were, after all, to have equal voice with the rest of Chilean society, an equal ability to participate in the process.

However, the effort to systematize land ownership initiated by the 1823 law, and carried out by other laws, did not fare well in areas dominated by the Mapuches. Many of the Mapuches had little contact with Chilean laws and little knowledge of the Spanish language in which those laws were administered. Their day-to-day existence was governed by Mapuche customs, not by decrees from Santiago. Thus, most did not understand what was expected of them in order to protect their legal rights. More fundamentally, the European concept of land ownership underlying the system—a concept that viewed real property as a commodity of production to be bought and sold—was so foreign to the Mapuche understanding of what land was, that many did not truly comprehend the significance of the legal acts in which they engaged. Yet, because of the Chilean

---

[23] Ley del 10 de junio de 1823, art. 3.

[24] Articles 4 and 5 of the 1823 law provided that surplus lands were to be sold at public auctions in portions no greater than ten sections so as to give as many Chileans as possible the chance to be landowners. *See id.* at arts. 4–5.

[25] As one scholar has noted, "There can be no doubt that the intentions of the first governors of the country were well intended." José Bengoa C., Breve Historia de la Legislación Indígena en Chile 15 (1990).

commitment to individual equality, the law gave them full authority to act, and to be acted upon, as if there were no difference between their understanding of the transaction and that of the more acculturated Chileans.

The result was a fiasco for both the Mapuches and the Chilean effort to systematize property ownership. An unscrupulous businessman would "purchase" property from a Mapuche who happened to be physically present on the land on the day the businessman arrived. The Mapuche—who in many cases did not speak Spanish,[26] and who in any event could not really comprehend "selling" the earth any more than we can conceive of selling existentialism or other philosophical or religious concepts—did not fully comprehend what the transaction was all about,[27] and often was not the one with primary claim to use of the land under Mapuche custom.[28] Sometime later, a different nonnative of similar scruples would purchase the same land from another Mapuche who happened to be there on a different day. Both purchasers would register their title, only to find, upon efforts to claim possession of the land, that there was a third Mapuche residing there on a somewhat permanent basis.[29] This effort to systematize land ownership in order to avoid property disputes—which worked fairly well in areas immediately adjacent to Santiago—was a complete disaster in the Araucania, where most Mapuches resided, precisely because the law gave them full individual equality in theory, while their different fundamental

---

[26] Congressional records of the time noted that the Mapuches involved in land transactions often did not understand Spanish, and that even when they did, the purchasers often brought interpreters with them who misrepresented the nature of the proposed transaction, indicating, for example, that the contract provided for the sale of 1,000 sections of land, when in reality it was 2,000. The natives were easily taken in by this fraud, the record notes, because they did not know how to read or write, even if they spoke Spanish. *See* Cámara de Diputados, sesión ordinaria No. 43 de septiembre de 1864, *cited in* MYLENE VALENZUELA R., LA LEGISLACIÓN MAPUCHE Y LA POLÍTICA INDÍGENA DEL ESTADO DE CHILE 21 (1992/1993) (unpublished Memoria para La Facultad de Derecho de la Universidad de Chile).

[27] As noted by Gonzalo Bulnes, "there arose from this fraudulent fiction of the pretended citizenship and equality . . . of the aborigines, a european style property right—personal, exclusive, private . . . alienable and encumberable by acts of the living and transmissible by testament as a result of death—all of which was an institution that never existed among the natives. *The native sold, therefore, a european right, that he had never had.* All was a fraud." BULNES, *supra* note 19, at 28.

[28] Mapuche chiefs also often sold the same land to two different individuals at two different times. *See* BENGOA, *supra,* note 1, at 158.

[29] In 1866, the Intendente of Arauco, Cornelio Saavedra, reported that loan agreements secured by real property in the area often involved lands that either did not belong to the supposed debtor or were uncultivated lands belonging to the government. One agreement involved property in "the possession of a peaceful owner who, because of his ignorance and little contact with civilized people, did not understand the significance of the notifications given him, with the result that his silence later involved him in a property lawsuit, because he had lost possession by means of a judgment [against the property]." Bulnes, *supra* note 19, at 26.

viewpoint concerning property made the application of the law radically unequal.[30]

This illustrates one reason why an indigenous policy based on individual equality can fall short of its goal. Because it focuses solely on the individual, the concept of individual equality usually fails to take into account the primary importance of groups in the lives of individuals.[31] Under the extreme theory of individual equality, there are, in the end, only two entities: the State and the individual.[32] While groups may exist, they are merely collections of individuals that are cognizable under the law only if the State decides to recognize them. Under this view, membership in a group is an irrelevant fact that the government cannot consider because individuals are all fundamentally similar. The groups to which they belong are not legally pertinent to any classification[33] because

---

[30] As former U.S. Supreme Court Justice Felix Frankfurter observed: "It was a wise man who said that there is no greater inequality than equal treatment of unequals." Dennis v. United States, 339 U.S. 162, 184 (1950) (Frankfurter, J., dissenting).

[31] As Professor David Williams has explained, "The equal protection clause imposes an ethos of individualism on the state; the 'ultimate goal' is to 'eliminat[e] entirely from governmental decisionmaking such irrelevant factors as a human being's race.'" David C. Williams, *The Borders of the Equal Protection Clause: Indians as Peoples*, 38 U.C.L.A. L. REV. 759, 765 (1991), *quoting* City of Richmond v. J.A. Croson Co., 488 U.S. 469, 495 (1989).

Professor Owen Fiss has explained that the concept of individual equality followed by the U.S. Supreme Court—a concept he calls antidiscrimination—is attractive to some precisely because "it avoids the need of making any statement about the basic societal units." Owen Fiss, *Groups and the Equal Protection Clause*, 5 PHIL. & PUB. AFF. 107, 123 (1975). The concept treats all groups as irrelevant to any meaningful distinctions, avoiding any need to determine "whether, in defining a class, the legislature has carved the universe at a natural joint." *Id.*, *quoting* Joseph Tussman & Jacobus tenBroek, *The Equal Protection of the Laws*, 37 CAL. L. REV. 341, 346 (1949)).

[32] Commenting on the state of the law in England at the turn of this century, John Figgis noted that "[s]ince the corporate society is only a *persona ficta*, with the name given it by the law, but no real inward life, we have on this view but two social entities, the State on the one hand and the individual on the other." JOHN N. FIGGIS, CHURCHES IN THE MODERN STATE 67 (1913). Figgis attacked this view as inadequate because it failed to account for the reality of the importance of groups in the lives of individuals: "What we actually see in the world is not on the one hand the State, and on the other a mass of unrelated individuals; but a vast complex of gathered unions, in which alone we find individuals, families, clubs, trade unions, colleges, professions, and so forth; and further, that there are exercised functions within these groups which are of the nature of government. . . . *Id.* at 70.

[33] This view of the limited relevancy of groups between the nation-state and the individual persists among many in Chilean society today, and it explains why many Chilean lawyers claim that until recently there has been no Chilean Indian policy. There has been no Chilean Indian policy, they contend, because there were no Chilean Indians once O'Higgins issued his decree. These lawyers are not so naive as to believe that the Mapuches and all other indigenous peoples magically disappeared the moment O'Higgins' pen touched the paper on that fall day in 1819. Rather, under their view, O'Higgins'

group membership does not constitute enough of a relevant portion of an individual's life to make any meaningful difference according to this theory.[34]

The reality is, however, that on some issues membership in a group does make a profound difference in some individuals' lives. And it not only tells a relevant portion of their story, it sometimes tells the entire story. The fact that one was Mapuche in the fullest cultural sense was not only a relevant factor with respect to property ownership in nineteenth-century Chile, membership in that group was the determinative factor with respect to one's ability to benefit from the Chilean property system.

In one sense the nineteenth-century Chilean lawmakers came to understand this reality, but only very superficially and then only very grudgingly. Faced with the specter of an increasingly chaotic land system in developing areas on the frontier of Mapuche territory, the government in 1853 issued special property rules for the newly formed province of Arauco, where many Mapuche lived.[35] As stated in the introduction to the law, the purpose was to protect both buyer and seller and, more important, to avoid the problems that ''produce uncertainty

---

decree rendered Indianness an irrelevant factor as far as the law was concerned. At that moment, the Mapuches, and all other indigenous peoples, became Chileans; any other type of group identification was irrelevant.

Consistent with this view, the Chilean government in 1988 opposed amendments to the International Labor Organization's Covenant on Indigenous Peoples, asserting that ''in Chile no difference exists between indigenous and non-indigenous peoples.'' COMISIÓN ESPECIAL DE PUEBLOS INDÍGENAS, CONVENINO NO. 169 SOBRE PUEBLOS INDÍGENAS Y TRIBALES EN PAISES INDEPENDIENTES 1989 21 (1990). One cannot discuss the issue of equality with Chileans long without hearing the oft-repeated phrase ''Todos somos Chilenos'' (We are all Chileans). Current members of the U.S. Supreme Court have expressed the same sentiment. *See, e.g.*, Adarand Constructors, Inc. v. Pena, 515 U.S. 200, 239 (1995)(Scalia, J., concurring)(''In the eyes of the government, we are just one race here. It is American.'').

[34] R. M. MacIver captured this position well when he wrote: ''The central conception of democracy, that which gives it its vitality underneath, is the conception that it is the person as person that counts; the person not as property owner, *not as the member of any class, not as the child of wealth or prestige, not as belonging to this or that race or group or religion,* but the person as person; the conception that as a person he should be given equal rights and equal opportunities with others, and that these various distinctions are from this point of view irrelevant.'' R. M. MacIver, *The Need for a Change of Attitude, in* CIVILIZATION AND GROUP RELATIONSHIPS 4 (R.M. MacIver, ed., 1945). This view has also been espoused by members of the current United States Supreme Court. *See* Miller v. Johnson, 515 U.S. 900 (1995)(''At the heart of the Constitution's guarantee of equal protection lies the simple command that the Government must treat citizens as individuals, not as simply components of a racial, religious, sexual, or national class''); Missouri v. Jenkins, 515 U.S. 70, 120–21 (1995) (Thomas, J., concurring)(''At the heart of this interpretation of the Equal Protection Clause lies the principle that the Government must treat citizens as individuals, and not as members of racial, ethnic or religious groups'').

[35] Decreto del 14 de marzo de 1853.

and lack of permanency in the properties located in those territories."[36] The decree required that all lands in the area be registered within one year. Furthermore, it required the government to approve all land transactions "within native territory in the province."[37] Consistent with the policy of individual equality, the decree did not differentiate between natives and nonnatives, but only between lands in different geographic locations.[38] Moreover, the decree did not give the government the authority to veto a deal because it was unfair. Once the officer was convinced that 1) the land actually belonged to the person selling it, 2) the seller freely consented to the transaction; and 3) the agreed-upon price had been paid, the sale was to be approved and recorded.[39] As development pushed southward, the area subject to the special property decrees expanded.[40]

While this initial State intervention was minimal, it established a familiar pattern for a system based exclusively on individual equality. When the policy of individual equality fails, the policymakers resort to governmental paternalism as the remedy. This is only natural because, if one believes that the only relevant actors in the legal scheme are the State and the individual, there is only one solution to a problem created by the perceived failure of a group of individuals to reap the benefits of conforming to the norms set by the State: have the State intervene on their behalf, both to educate them as to how to conform to the norm and to ensure that, in the meantime, they are not taken advantage of and that they do not interfere with the system. There is no thought given to allowing the group itself to mediate the differences. The nineteenth-century Chilean policymakers followed this predictable course toward State paternalism beginning in the 1850s. However, because they sincerely believed that the Mapuches should be equal to other citizens as far as practically possible, as noted above, the initial State intervention was minimal.

This minimal intervention proved unavailing, and the fraudulent transactions continued almost unabated.[41] Realizing that the policy of individual equality was

---

[36] *Id.*, introducción, para. 1.

[37] *Id.* art. 1.

[38] Though the text of the decree is quite clear in this respect, there was apparently some confusion at the time because the President issued a decree the following year clarifying that the March 14, 1853 law applied "'to all alienation of lands in native territory, whether or not Natives are parties to the contract." Decreto del 10 de marzo de 1854.

[39] *See* Decreto del 14 de marzo de 1853, arts. 1, 6.

[40] For example, in 1855, the restrictions imposed by the 1853 law were extended to the Province of Valdivia. *See* Decreto del 4 de diciembre de 1855. In 1856, they were extended to the colonization territory of Llanquihue. *See* Decreto del 9 de julio de 1856.

[41] There were several reasons why the problems continued. First, some of the officials charged with supervising the transactions, especially the public scribes, were themselves corrupt. As one member of the Chamber of Deputies asked rhetorically, "Is it possible that title can be forged and false testimonies given . . . without the intervention

not working as planned with respect to real estate, the government resorted to even more state paternalism. In 1866, the government enacted a law providing that the restrictions of the 1853 law were to continue to apply if a "native is one of the contracting parties" unless the purchase was being made by the government itself (who, presumably, could be trusted to treat the Mapuche properly).[42] Boundaries were to be set for all lands belonging to natives, and *títulos de merced* (literally translated "mercy titles" or "favor titles") were to be issued to the natives, and registered in the official records.[43] A Protector of Natives (an office existing under the Spanish, and ridiculed and rejected by O'Higgins in his 1819 decree[44]) was appointed to aid the Mapuches in boundary and contract proceedings.[45]

In the one grudging recognition that Mapuches viewed property differently than did other Chileans of the time, the 1866 law provided that natives who occupied a parcel of land as dependents of a *cacique* or chief would be considered common owners, and the land common property of them all, with the mercy title being issued to this *reducción* in the name of the cacique.[46] The issuance of these "common mercy titles" was the one clear departure from the policy of individual equality during the entire Chilean history with respect to the Mapuche, but it still fell far short of the mark—for Mapuches did not consider themselves as common owners of property; no one owned it in their view. Moreover, they did not consider themselves dependent on the *cacique* for their right to use the property. In the rush to bring order and equality to the law, the Chileans did not make an effort to understand this fully. Moreover, the Chilean government clearly contemplated that this form of common ownership would be a temporary

---

of the public officials of the Republic?" Don Angel Custodio Gallo, Cámara de Diputados, sesión ordinaria No. 34, agosto de 1870, *quoted in* VALENZUELA, *supra* note 26, at 25 n.28.

Second, many witnesses were willing to perjure themselves as to the relevant facts. A contemporary complained of the existence of groups of "oathtakers" ("jureros") who gave no account to the "obligation imposed by [testimonial] oaths." BULNES, *supra* note 19, at 33, *quoting* Perez Rosales.

Finally, those who were unwilling to engage in out-and-out fraud were nonetheless ingenious enough to get around the minimal restrictions imposed by the 1853 law. Some persuaded Mapuche "landowners" to sign loan agreements granting them a mortgage, which was then foreclosed upon without any government involvement. See VALENZUELA, *supra* note 26, at 27. Others entered into long-term leases. The government amended the law to apply to these forms of transfers in 1857. *See* Decreto del 23 de marzo de 1857.

[42] Ley de 4 de diciembre de 1866, art. 4.

[43] *Id.* art. 5.

[44] O'Higgins' 1819 decree expressly criticized the Spanish for forcing the Natives to live as a "class of minors under the guardianship of an official entitled General Protector of Naturals," and "abolished" the office "as unnecessary." Decreto del Director Supremo Bernardo O'Higgins del 4 de marzo de 1819.

[45] *See* Ley del 4 de diciembre de 1866, art. 8.

[46] *See id.* art 7, para. 5.

stopgap measure on the road to individual ownership of all lands. Thus, the law provided that if one eighth part of the native heads of family of the *reducción* requested it, the land was to be divided among the individual landowners.[47]

The 1866 law became the basis for the creation of today's *reducciones* in Chile, something that many in the United States easily confuse with our Indian reservations. However, it is important to keep in mind that the intent was not to require that the Mapuches move to areas designated arbitrarily by the government. The titles were, in theory, to be issued to lands claimed and inhabited by the Mapuches themselves.[48] Furthermore, unlike in the United States, there was no attempt to keep the Mapuches separated physically from the rest of the Chilean population. All the government wanted to do was to establish who owned what, and to colonize the area in as orderly a fashion as possible.[49] If, as seemed to be the case, the boundaries among the Mapuches themselves were not clear, the policymakers concluded, the government should establish the boundaries of the general area used by a particular group and issue a title to the whole group, so that colonization could proceed on the surplus lands.[50] In the meantime, the thinking seemed to be, the Mapuches would soon see the advantages of individual ownership, and the land would, at their request, be divided into individual parcels soon enough.

There are some indications that the new system worked in a few limited areas, at least from the government's standpoint. In 1869, the government declared that several geographic departments in the affected provinces were no

---

[47] *See id.* art. 7, para. 6.

[48] Bengoa explains the "location" or "reduction" process as follows: "The Location Commission would arrive at a place inhabited by natives and would proceed to take a census. It would establish the area these families permanently occupied, which [generally involved] a smaller area than was occupied by the itinerant cattle-raising Mapuche families. Generally, [the survey] included the area where the Mapuche families carried out their relatively stable agricultural activities, where they pastured and kept their cattle. In this manner, the territory actually occupied by each family was 'reduced.' . . . It is for that reason that [these] areas are called native reductions ['reducciones indígenas']." José Bengoa C., Quinquen: Cien Años de Historia Pehuenche 39–40 (1992).

[49] That the government's intent was to bring order to the colonization process is evidenced by the fact that "[t]he prohibition against [Mapuche] alienation [to private citizens] was limited to those lands suitable for colonization, and it was not established as a general prohibition, permitting unlimited appropriation of native lands in the rest of the areas." Valenzuela, *supra* note 26, at 49.

[50] In some areas the Location Commission proceeded with great haste and little care. On several occasions, Mapuche families displaced by earlier violence were arbitrarily grouped with families with which they shared no blood relationship. Bengoa, *supra* note 48, at 40. Moreover, once the families' lands were located, the surveyors "made an approximate map, without clearly establishing the contours of the land, estuaries, or rivers." *Id.* Finally, because the Location Commission did not arrive at many isolated locations, as many as one-third of the Mapuche families were never "located" and never received official title to any lands. *See id.*

longer "to be considered Native territory, so that [their] inhabitants can [now] enter into contracts without being subject to the [1866] law."[51]

However, success was extremely limited, even from the government's viewpoint, mainly because the Mapuches still effectively controlled most of the area from a military standpoint, and they refused to participate in the surveying or registration effort. Thus, the first mercy title was not granted until 1881, fifteen years after the law authorized their use, and shortly after the government had successfully ended the last Mapuche uprising.[52] Moreover, the location commission created to establish the boundaries never arrived in many remote areas.[53] Finally, because fraud continued despite the new restrictions, the law eventually forbade any private citizen from acquiring native lands in the affected area by any means.[54]

Again, however, it is important to emphasize that the restrictions applied only in certain geographic areas. It was not a restriction imposed on Mapuches as a group, but only on those individuals who lived in a certain area.[55] The group itself, and membership in the group, were largely irrelevant from the standpoint of the law. Furthermore, the restrictions were thought to be temporary. The Protector of Natives, joint titles, and prohibition on private sales and other forms of governmental paternalism would be tolerated in these areas, but only until the Mapuches were sufficiently "educated," so that their "naivete" did not interfere with the proper working of the property law system.[56] Then the policy

---

[51] Ley del 15 de julio de 1869.

[52] BENGOA, *supra* note 25, at 19.

[53] *See id.*

[54] This prohibition was originally imposed in 1874. *See* Ley del 4 de Agosto de 1874, art. 6. It was originally applied only to lands for which there was no recorded title. *See id.* However, as abuses continued, the prohibition was extended to the acquisition of native lands by "mortgage, lease, or any other contract by which they [the natives] are deprived, directly or indirectly, of the possession or ownership of land" in the restricted area "even when the native or *reducción* to which [the land] belongs has a registered title." Ley del 20 de enero de 1883, art. 1.

[55] *See* note 48, *supra.*

[56] This was made clear by a 1927 law which set up three sets of restrictions—based on the educational level of the head of the household—for alienating land to which individual title had been issued as a result of the division of a common mercy title. Those who had a high school diploma or a professional title from a university or the state (category 1) could alienate or encumber their lands immediately upon issuance of the title. *See* Ley No. 4169 del 29 de agosto de 1927, art. 10. Those who were married to a woman who could read and write or who had children over the age of 21 who could do so (category 2) could immediately encumber and alienate their lands, but only with judicial approval once the judge assured himself that the seller had freely consented to the sale, and the transaction was clearly useful and advisable. *Id.* Those who did not fall into the previous two categories (and were therefore the least "educated") could alienate and encumber their lands only after 10 years had passed, and then only after obtaining

of individual equality could apply with full force, as it already did with respect to all other aspects of the law.[57]

Once the native lands were formally surveyed and titles were issued, and the surplus lands began to be inhabited by colonists,[58] including, if they wished, Mapuche colonists,[59] what was to be the final step in this temporary process—the division of the common mercy titles into individual parcels—began. As noted earlier, the 1866 law provided that the common mercy titles were to be divided into individual parcels once one-eighth of the heads of household residing in the area requested it. For the next 125 years, the most important, if not the sole, Chilean Indian law issue was what percentage of the common owners could trigger the division process. Ebbs and flows in Indian policy, legislative victories and defeats for the Mapuches, were largely measured on the basis of that number.

---

the judicial approval required for those in category 2. *Id.* art. 12.

The law was subsequently amended so that those in the second and third categories could immediately alienate their land with judicial approval (as those in the second category could do under the 1927 law), and could do so without judicial approval after ten years. *See* Decreto No. 4111 del 12 de junio de 1931 arts. 54, 57.

[57] That full individual equality continued to be the driving force even while special property laws were being passed for some native areas is evidenced by the fact that as the mercy title lands were divided, each person was to obtain title to "a part of equal value" in the community, *see* Ley No. 4169 del 29 de agosto de 1927, art. 2, even though under Mapuche custom, some were entitled to more use of the land than others. *See* BENGOA, *supra* note 25, at 25.

[58] As noted above, many of the property laws affecting the Mapuche resulted from the chaos caused by private purchase and development of Mapuche lands. In order to bring order to the development, the Chilean government eventually forbade any purchase of lands by private individuals and sought to introduce a program under which the lands would be colonized in an orderly fashion. Native lands were to be surveyed and registered, and surplus lands were to be granted to colonists. *See* VALENZUELA, *supra* note 26, at 21 34. The most ambitious colonization program was established in 1874. It authorized the President to grant to each immigrant family from the United States or Europe, at no cost, up to 405 acres of land (150 hectares), with an additional 200 acres of land for each child over 10, and 100 acres for each child over four. *See* Ley del 4 de agosto de 1874, art. 11. Between 1850 and 1915, approximately 65,000 immigrant colonists took advantage of this and other colony laws, receiving approximately 378,000 acres (140,000 hectares) of land. *See* VALENZUELA, *supra* note 26, at 34.

[59] Several laws permitted the Mapuches to acquire property as colonists. An 1873 law established a native colony in the department of Angol, granting each native family 81 acres of land (with some allowance for an increase or decrease in that amount), a habitation, and some seed. *See* Decreto del 29 de octubre de 1873, art. 2. Native colonies were also created by other laws. *See, e.g.*, Decreto del 14 de octubre de 1880.

The 1874 law establishing the colonization program for foreigners, *see supra* note 58, provided that natives who had not established their right to possess lands under the 1866 law would be considered colonists for purposes of acquiring land. *See* Ley del 4 de agosto de 1874, art. 8. The 1927 law aimed at increasing the speed with which common mercy title lands were divided also provided that any individual dissatisfied with the property assigned him in the division could elect to obtain land as a colonist. *See* Ley No. 4169 del 29 de agosto de 1927, art. 4.

The low points for the Mapuches came in 1927, with the passage of legislation requiring division of *all* common mercy titles, including those for which no request had been made by the previously required 12.5 percent of the heads of household,[60] and again in 1979 when the government of General Pinochet issued a law requiring division upon the request of any single occupant of the land covered by a communal title.[61] The ''high'' point (such as it was) arrived with the election of Salvador Allende in 1970, heralded today as a great president by many Mapuches because he obtained the passage of legislation that permitted division only if a majority of the joint owners requested it.[62]

Throughout this entire time, however, the goal remained the same, as explained in the text of a 1931 decree: ''the submission of the natives to the legal regimen that applies in the rest of the country, which is the only way to fully incorporate them into civilization and to ensure that the lands that they occupy enjoy the benefit of credit and are properly worked and cultivated.''[63] Regardless of the percentage required, the firm belief throughout the entire time was that sooner or later all the Mapuches would come into full legal equality with the

---

[60] *See* Ley No. 4169 del 29 de agosto de 1927.

[61] *See* Decreto Ley No. 2568 del 28 de marzo de 1979, art. 10. The 1979 law clearly had more impact on the Mapuche in this respect than had any other division law. From 1931 until 1978 (a period of 47 years), 816 common titles (some of which were not mercy titles, but common titles issued under other laws affecting native lands in the south) were divided. *See* Cristian Vives, *Proyecto de Ley Sobre Indígenas: Integración o Asimilación?*, 274 Mensaje 711, 714 (1978), *citing* Ricardo Hepp, vicepresidente de INDAP, *in* El Mercurio, 6 de agosto de 1978. In the 11-year period from 1979 until 1990, 2,062 communities were divided. *See* Bengoa, *supra* note 25.

Although figures vary, there were approximately 3,000 common mercy titles issued between 1881 and 1929. Most of the divisions before 1979 were apparently of communal lands held under other laws. There were, therefore, approximately 900 common mercy titles still in existence when civilian government returned in 1990. *See* Bengoa, *supra* note 25, at 47. The 1993 law still permits division at the request of a majority of the resident holders of hereditary rights to the lands. *See* Ley No. 19.253 de Octubre de 1993, art. 16.

[62] *See* Ley No. 17.729 del 15 de septiembre de 1972, art. 14.

[63] Decreto con fuerza de ley No. 166 del 20 de mayo de 1931, introducción, para. 2. Mapuche resistance to the 1927 law requiring the division of all common titles apparently caught the government officials by surprise, they having apparently expected that the Mapuche would welcome the opportunity to be individual landowners like the majority of Chilean society. In an introduction to the decree, the president indicated that ''the forced and obligatory division of the native communities . . . is frequently contrary to the desires of the majority, and at times, the totality, of the interested communities, who refuse to obey the judicial sentences in view of the fact that the individual parcels of land assigned to them are of a very reduced extent.'' *Id.*, introducción, para. 1. The law was therefore amended to provide that division would occur only when one-third of the joint owners requested it. *See* Decreto No. 4111 de 12 de junio de 1931, art.2. However, as the statement in the text indicates, the goal remained the same: individualization of all property.

rest of Chilean society with respect to property rights,[64] not through the efforts of some Mapuche organization, but solely through the efforts of the state and the various individuals.

Nearly 130 years after the division process was first enacted into law, the day awaited by its architects has still not arrived, however. Even the 1993 law, properly heralded as the dawning of a new day for indigenous peoples in Chile, contains a special mechanism for dividing and resolving property disputes in these areas.[65]

The persistence of this "temporary" property problem highlights another reason why the policy of individual equality has failed in Chile. Because it denies the importance of group norms, such a policy too easily turns into a policy of uniformity. One of the appeals of the approach of individual equality is that the policymaker is required to establish only one standard, not several.[66] Once the standard is established, the goal is for everyone to adhere to that standard. Some temporary deviation from that standard may be tolerated to achieve some other goal (such as the orderly colonization of the remote areas of Chile), but ultimately everyone must conform with *the* established standard. Not surprisingly, the content of that single standard is likely to reflect the norms of the dominant culture;[67] since diverse group norms are not important, alternate approaches are neither accepted nor seriously considered.

In Chile this tendency toward uniformity occurred. Members of the dominant Chilean culture set the standard for the use and ownership of property. This standard reflected their views of property. The unvarying goal since the time that the standard was set has been for all Mapuches to view property as a "Chilean" does. The problem has been that this has proven to be almost impossible for many Mapuches, because it requires that they cease to view themselves as Mapuches. It forces them to choose between being a full citizen of the artificial

---

[64] For example, the 1927 legislation provided that once division was complete, the Mapuche could begin to encumber and alienate their individual parcels to private citizens, with different restrictions based on the amount of education obtained by the owner, all of which were temporary restrictions to be lifted after 10 years. *See supra* note 55.

[65] *See* Ley No. 19.253 del 5 de Octubre 1993, arts. 55–59.

[66] As Professor Fiss has observed, under an individualized theory of anti-discrimination, "equal protection rights are not only individualized, but also universalized and this is another source of its appeal. . . . In contrast, a mediating principle that is, for example, built on the concept of social groups might not be so universal in scope, since it is conceivable that some individual adversely affected by the state might not be a member of one of the protected groups." Fiss, *supra* note 31, at 128.

[67] As Professor Adeno Addis has observed, "The dominant cultural understanding and experience of a society tends to universalize itself as the inevitable norm for social life, marking the culture of the marginal as the 'Other,' either to be excluded or 'normalized.'" Adeno Addis, *Individualism, Communitarianism, and the Rights of Ethnic Minorities*, 67 NOTRE DAME L. REV. 615, 619 (1992).

Nation-State or a member of the organic social group that forms part of their consciousness. When a policy forces people to make such a choice, it will likely fail—because many people will, as many Mapuches did, choose to belong to the organic group rather than to the artificial State, and they will remain on the fringes of mainstream society.

This phenomenon was demonstrated in 1881, the time of the last great Mapuche uprising. As noted earlier, the Mapuches had successfully resisted conquest attempts by the Incas, the Spanish, and the Chileans for nearly 400 years, but by 1881, the discrepancy in military technology had caught up with them. The Chilean military, fresh from victory in the War of the Pacific against Peru and Bolivia, arrived with full fury to bring Arauco under control. By November 1881, the task had largely been accomplished. The military effectively controlled the entire area, and forts and towns had been established in all key sectors.[68]

Yet, on November 5, 1881, the Mapuches arose one last time in a general insurrection. According to José Bengoa, a prominent Chilean anthropologist, it was the first time in their entire history that all the groups of the very decentralized Mapuche had joined in a single insurrection.[69] They did not engage in this act to secure their political and military independence—that was now lost beyond recovery. As Bengoa notes, "the Mapuches knew perfectly well that they were going to lose and that the majority of them would die in this general insurrection."[70] So why did they make the effort? Again, to quote Bengoa, the last insurrection was "a cultural imperative that obligated [the Mapuches] to appear with their lances, in front of the *huinca* [the Mapuche word for non-Indians] forts and cities and say: We are still an independent people and we will cease to be such only in a ritual act of combat and death."[71]

At the front of the Mapuche troops attacking the city of Lumaco was Luis Marileo Colipí, a descendant of one of the founders of the Colipí dynasty among one powerful segment of the Mapuche—los Abajinos. Prior to the insurrection, Marileo Colipí owned more than 16,000 acres of land on which he ran a large cattle and farming business. The specific Mapuche group of which he was the leader had for some time successfully pursued a policy of peaceful negotiations with the Chileans. As a result, he was one of the richest landowners in the region, with a home in one of the Chilean cities—a model, the Chileans thought, of the chileanization of the Mapuche.

Thus, when news of the last general insurrection arrived via messengers carrying cords with knots in them to indicate the day of the uprising, Marileo

---

[68] *See* BENGOA, *supra* note 1, at 297–98.

[69] *See* BENGOA, *supra* note 1, at 298.

[70] *Id.* at 297.

[71] *Id.*

Colipí had a difficult choice to make: he had to decide whether he was a Chilean citizen, who possessed great material wealth and power, or a Mapuche, who would stand with his people in a seemingly futile effort, likely to result in the loss of that wealth and power, and perhaps his own life. Choosing the route often chosen by the Mapuches since that time when Chilean legal policy has forced them to make similar choices, Marileo Colipí chose to adhere to his indigenous culture. Thus, early in the morning of the day indicated by the knots in the cords, Marileo Colipí, largely unpracticed in the art of warfare, stood at the front of his warriors facing the walls surrounding the city of Lumaco. He lost the ensuing military battle. He also lost his lands, which were taken from him. Eventually, he traveled to Argentina, where he died in poverty.[72]

Most Chileans soon forgot Marileo Colipí. Those who remembered did not understand what they thought was his foolishness. They, like most Chilean policymakers since that time, did not understand that membership in organic groups does matter for some people in a very fundamental way—in a way that the policy of individual equality often does not, and perhaps cannot, recognize.

Critics may contend that the lessons about a policy based on individual equality are not entirely clear from the experience of the Mapuches and their land. After all, they may assert, the law did eventually grant special status to some Mapuches with respect to property laws, as evidenced by the continued existence of *títulos de merced*. Perhaps the problem is that the concept of individual equality was simply not carried out completely, not that it failed in some way.

There are several rebuttals to such assertions. However, the most telling is the history and current status of other indigenous peoples in Chile, such as the Aymara[73] in the North. Despite the fact that there have never been any special laws for the Aymaras,[74] they continue to exist as a people, facing many of the

---

[72] *See id.* at 301.

[73] The Aymara population of Chile became part of the Republic following the War of the Pacific in which Chile wrested control of this portion of their homelands from Peru and Bolivia. *See* JUAN VAN KESSEL, HOLOCAUSTO AL PROGRESO: LOS AYMARAS DE TARAPACÁ 176 (1992).

[74] As Juan van Kessel has explained: "In the case of the Aymaras, who were numerically weaker than the Mapuches, assimilation was pursued via a different strategy: ignore their existence in the legislation. Thus, their communities were never mentioned; *títulos de merced* were not granted; . . . collective property rights in communal lands were not established in the legislation. . . . Upon incorporation into the Chilean legal system, communal property ceased to exist, de jure, and the Aymara community itself ceased to exist for the legislator." *Id.* at 178. *See also* AYLWIN O., *supra* note 5, at 6 ("After incorporation of their ancestral territories to Chile, the Aymaras have been practically ignored by the authorities, who have never legislated in their favor and with respect to whom they have only implemented policies destined to attain their assimilation to the national society").

same types of difficulties as do the Mapuches,[75] and just as determined to revive and maintain their culture.[76] The policy of individual equality has impacted as dramatically on the Aymaras as it has on the Mapuches.

Perhaps most devastating for the Aymaras has been the impact of the equal application of Chilean water laws. Because water is so scarce in the Aymaras' traditional homeland, it forms a central part of their existence and their culture. As Juan van Kessel has observed, "what land is for the Mapuche, water is for the Aymara."[77] Aymara villages that are geographically separated often are part of the same political community, tied together by a common water source.[78] Traditionally, water and land resources in these geographically diverse and exceedingly arid communities are considered as a single resource (the water being

---

[75] Because many Aymara have not registered their real property as required by Chilean law, they "are subject to losing their property rights in their ancestral communal lands through the inscription of the same by third parties." José Aylwin O. & Eduardo Castillo V., Legislación Sobre Indígenas en Chile a Traves de la Historia 43 (1990). The individualization of the communal lands resulting from this equal application of the laws to the Aymara has caused not only the loss of Aymara lands, but also unity in the community itself, as members of a once unified community are forced to compete with one another for individual ownership of what were previously communal lands. *See* van Kessel, *supra* note 73, at 178–79.

[76] Juan van Kessel has chronicled the renewed interest and efforts of the Chilean Aymara, both urban and rural, to resist "the homogenizing pressure of the political and religious authorities" by retaining their ancient rituals and ceremonies. Juan van Kessel, Cuando Arde El Tiempo Sagrado 177 (1992). He notes that these efforts manifest themselves in other ways as well. "We mention only their growing presence in public and in mass communication, their new intercommunal organizations, their decided judicial defense of their land and water interests against the mining companies, their awakening in the political and educational fields, their participation in [the free trade zone in the first region of Chile], their growing self awareness and self pride, their participation in seminars, expositions, and events nationally and internationally and their manner of presenting themselves before authorities and the public: not as 'poor *campesinos*,' but as 'Aymaras, owners of the land, possessors of a grand culture and an ancient technology.'" *Id.* at 178.

[77] Taller de Estudios Aymara, Centro de Investigación de la Realidad del Norte, Desarrollo Andino y Cultura Aymara en el Norte de Chile 132 (Hector Gonzalez C. & Bernardo Guerrero J., eds., 1990).

[78] As Juan van Kessel has observed, when the Spanish arrived in Chile, they discovered that the typical Aymara community was divided into two parts or *sayas*. Each *saya* included a series of *ayllus*, or groups of extended families. The various *ayllus* were found in all ecological levels from the tops of the Andes to the valleys below. Each *allyu* in a *saya* had a special relationship with another *allyu* in the other *saya*. The related *allyu* exchanged products and labor with one another, with one typically being in the agricultural zone and the other higher up in pasture lands. Thus, a single community included persons living in geographically dispersed areas. *See* van Kessel, *supra* note 73, at 111.

A version of this same social organization exists in some Aymara communities today. *See id.* at 113.

part of the land on which it is used),[79] and the use of the land, as well as work assignments in the different areas, are assigned by community leaders on an annual basis according to the differing needs and capacities of the different families.[80]

In 1981, Chile enacted a new water code that dramatically departed from prior law by providing that water could be appropriated by someone other than the owner of the land to which it is appurtenant, and that the right could be bought, sold, acquired, and lost by prescription.[81] This change—which was designed not to destroy Aymara communities, but to free up water for new uses—has had unforeseen deleterious consequences for many traditional Aymara communities.

Because the water rights created by the code cannot be acquired by the community itself,[82] the community has lost control of the use of the water. Fearing the loss of the water, many individual members of the community have begun to file for individual water rights, leading to disputes among community members[83]—disputes that are resolved, not by traditional community leaders, but by Chilean judges applying the rules of the Chilean water code. The resulting disintegration of the traditional communities has been noted by more than one scholar.[84] Yet, when the aid of the General Director of Waters was sought by leaders of some affected Aymara communities, he indicated that there was little

---

[79] As the leader of one Aymara community explained, "anciently we had no problems because the waters were bound, earth and water in a single thing." Gumercindo Mamani, Interview between six Aymara leaders and the General Director of Waters, in Santiago (Mar. 13, 1987), *quoted in* JAAP LEMEREIS, LA LUCHA POR EL AGUA DE LOS AYMARAS DEL NORTE DE CHILE 99 (1987).

[80] *See* VAN KESSEL, *supra* note 73, at 113.

[81] Código de Aguas.

[82] The 1981 code provides that a "water community" can be created by "one or more persons having rights . . . to the water from the same canal." Código de Aguas, art. 186. However, all of the persons to be included in the community have to be named individually, *see id.* at art. 198, and the right belongs to the various individuals and not to the community itself, *see id.* at art. 193, thus enabling the transfer of individual shares of the right to persons outside the community. *See* AYLWIN & CASTILLO, *supra* note 75, at 41; LEMEREIS, *supra* note 79, at 20–21. Moreover, others who acquire rights in the same canal are entitled to become members of the community. *See* Código de Aguas, art. 199. Thus, the law does not allow a traditional community to hold water rights as a community. This was made clear by the General Director of Waters in a 1987 meeting with leaders of some Aymara communities when he informed them that under the new code, "the [traditional] community can have no property rights." Eugenio Lobo Parga, Interview with six Aymara leaders, in Santiago (Mar. 13, 1987), *quoted in* LEMEREIS, *supra* note 79, at 113.

[83] *See* AYLWIN & CASTILLO, *supra* note 75, at 42; LEMEREIS, *supra* note 79, at 100–01.

[84] *See* LEMEREIS, *supra* note 79, *passim*; AYLWIN & CASTILLO, *supra* note 75, at 41.

he could do because "the laws of the country have to apply equally to all citizens."[85] That such problems can arise after more than a century of the equal application of the laws to the Aymara and that many Aymara continue to resist full incorporation into the Chilean economic system despite the lack of land and water needed to maintain their traditional way of life, is powerful evidence that the pursuit of a single-minded policy of individual equality—the only policy ever followed by Chile with respect to the Aymaras prior to 1993—is a principal cause of the Chilean failure to resolve its "Indian question."

The Chilean experience thus demonstrates that a policy based solely on the concept of individual equality cannot adequately address the needs of both the nation and its indigenous peoples.[86] An individual equality based policy will fail in this respect because it fails to take proper account of the role of groups in the lives of many people, a role that is central to their worldview. With that lesson in mind, let us turn to the experience of the indigenous peoples of the United States.

II. THE UNITED STATES EXPERIENCE: THE LIMITS OF SEPARATION

At first glance, it seems safe to conclude that the United States avoided the pitfalls into which Chilean policymakers fell. The United States has never fully

---

[85] Eugenio Lobo Parga, Interview with six Aymara leaders, in Santiago (Mar. 13, 1987), *quoted in* LEMEREIS, *supra* note 79, at 101.

[86] There are, however, signs that things are changing in Chile. In 1993, the Chilean Congress enacted a comprehensive Indian law. *See* Ley No. 19.253 del 5 de octubre 1993. This law contains several provisions that indicate a movement away from the single-minded individual equality approach to Chilean Indian policy.

First and foremost, the law expressly recognizes on behalf of the state that there are indigenous peoples in Chile, who are different from the mainstream society, and from one another. The first article of the law provides that "the State recognizes that the natives of Chile are descendants of the human groupings that have existed in the national territory since precolombian times and which conserve ethnic and cultural expressions of their own." The article continues: "It is the duty of society in general and of the State in particular, through its institutions, to respect, protect and promote the development of these natives, their cultures, families and communities, adopting appropriate measures to that end, and to protect their indigenous lands." *Id.* art. 1. The same article recognizes that there are different indigenous groups in the country, identifying eight specifically. *See supra* note 12.

The law also permits the creation of indigenous communities with the status of legal persons entitled to own property. *See* Ley No. 19.253 del 5 de octubre 1993, arts. 9–11. Perhaps most importantly, it provides that at the request of one of the parties to a lawsuit involving members of the same indigenous groups, the custom of the group, rather than the precepts of civil law, will be the law of the case, as long as the custom is not incompatible with the constitution. *See id.* art. 54.

Just how dramatic this policy shift will be depends on how the law is actually implemented. The shift will not be wholesale, however, because the primary role in determining tribal customs and implementing other aspects of the law is given to a governmental agency (the National Corporation for Indigenous Development (CONADI)), and not to any indigenous group. *See id.* arts. 38–54.

pursued a formal policy of complete individual equality for its indigenous population.[87] As the U.S. Supreme Court indicated in 1974, the concept of equal protection[88]—the primary constitutional and legal embodiment of the concept of individual equality in the United States—has never applied in the same manner to Native Americans as it has to other ethnic and racial groups.[89] Instead, as the Court noted, "[o]n numerous occasions this Court specifically has upheld legislation that singles out Indians for particular and special treatment."[90] Thus, overreliance on the concept of individual equality can hardly be blamed for the continued struggle of Native Americans to fit into the United States' legal system, or for the continued social problems on American Indian reservations.

Notwithstanding this difference between the American experience and the Chilean experience, the inability of the United States to resolve its "Indian question" to the satisfaction of either the Native Americans or the general population is, at root, due to the same failure that existed in the Chilean system—the failure of the policy to fully take into account the importance of the tribal group to the existence and self-concept of many individual Native Americans.

In the United States, this failure manifested itself in a much different way than it did in Chile, but it was still the heart of the problem. While the Chilean

---

[87] As noted below, *see* text accompanying *infra* notes 99–102 and 104–107, the United States has adopted policies such as the General Allotment Act in the 1880s and the Termination policy of the 1950s which, if fully implemented, would have had the effect of dismantling tribal governments and treating all Native Americans solely as individual citizens, undifferentiated in all respects from other U.S. citizens. However, as also noted below, none of these programs was ever fully implemented. *See infra* notes 101, 112.

[88] *See* U.S. Const., amend. XIV ("No state shall . . . deny to any person within its jurisdiction the equal protection of the laws."). Although this provision by its terms applies only to state governments, and not to the national or federal government, the concept it embodies has been applied to the federal government with full force. *See* Adarand Constructors, Inc. v. Pena, 515 U.S. 200, 213–18; Bolling v. Sharpe, 347 U.S. 497, 500 (1954).

[89] *See* Morton v. Mancari, 417 U.S. 535 (1974). The Court in *Morton* indicated that "[a]s long as the special treatment [accorded Native Americans] *can be tied rationally to the fulfillment of Congress' unique obligation toward the Indians*, such legislative judgments will not be disturbed." *Id.* at 555 (emphasis added). As the Court recently made clear, congressional legislation granting special treatment to other racial groups will pass equal protection muster only "if they are narrowly tailored measures that further compelling governmental interests," *Adarand Constructors*, 515 U. S. at 227, a standard that is clearly more stringent than that applied in *Morton*.

[90] Morton, 417 U.S. at 554–55. The Court observed that "[l]iterally every piece of legislation dealing with Indian tribes and reservations, and certainly all legislation dealing with the BIA [the Bureau of Indian Affairs], single out for special treatment a constituency of tribal Indians living on or near reservations. If these laws, derived from historical relationships and explicitly designed to help only Indians, were deemed invidious racial discrimination, an entire Title of the U.S. Code (25 U.S.C.) would be effectively erased. . . ." *Id.* at 552.

experience demonstrates how that failure can result in an ineffective policy based on individual equality, the American experience shows how it can also result in a failed policy of separation.

The policy of the United States toward its native population, from the time of its independence from Great Britain until 1887, was to separate them—both philosophically and geographically—from the rest of American society. "Indian country"—a legal concept connoting a geographic location reserved for Native Americans into which non-Native Americans could not legally venture without permission of the central government—was established by the British even before the American Revolution.[91] After independence, the leaders of the new U.S. republic continued to rely on this concept of a separate geographic "Indian country" into which non-Native American entry was limited and non-Native settlement was prohibited, first via treaties with separate tribes,[92] and then eventually by congressional enactment.[93]

This policy of physical separation reached its zenith during the "removal period" of the early to mid-1800s,[94] when numerous tribes were moved out West—often to the "Indian Territory" of present-day Oklahoma and Kansas—to areas where the tribes were often promised freedom from incorporation into any future state or territory.[95]

---

[91] Some British colonies entered into agreements with various tribes under which "an absolute line was drawn between the whites and the Indians, and neither was to violate the territory of the other." FRANCIS PAUL PRUCHA, AMERICAN INDIAN POLICY IN THE FORMATIVE YEARS 15 (1962), *citing* the 1758 Treaty of Easton between Pennsylvania and the Six Nations of the Iroquois. A 1763 Proclamation, issued by King George III, contained the "first official delineation and definition of the Indian Country." *Id.* at 13. The Proclamation reserved "all the Lands and Territories lying to the Westward of the Sources of the Rivers which fall into the Sea from the West and North West" to the Native Americans, prohibited the king's subjects from settling in the territory, and ordered the removal of any non-Native American who had already settled in the area. *Id.* at 14.

[92] *See, e.g.*, Treaty with the Six Nations, Oct. 22, 1784, 7 Stat. 15 (Treaty at Fort Stanwix); Treaty with the Wyandots, Delawares, Chippawas, and Ottawas, Jan. 21, 1785, 7 Stat. 16 (Treaty of Fort McIntosh).

[93] The Trade and Intercourse Act of 1796, Act of May 19, 1796, Ch. 30, 1 Stat. 469, contained "the first designation of the Indian Country in a statute law." PRUCHA, *supra* note 91, at 49. The law set forth in detail "the boundary between the whites and the Indians." *Id.* For some time, a special passport was needed to enter legally the "Indian Country" south of the Ohio River. *Id.* at 145. The passport could be obtained from "the governor of one of the states or . . . a commander at a frontier military post." *Id.*

[94] One source states that the "removal schemes" lasted from 1816 until 1846. *See* FELIX S. COHEN, HANDBOOK OF FEDERAL INDIAN LAW 28 (1982 ed.). Others have indicated that the removal period encompassed the years from 1835 until 1861. *See* ROBERT N. CLINTON ET AL., AMERICAN INDIAN LAW: CASES AND MATERIALS 144 (1991). The different starting dates may reflect the fact that while the initial removal efforts were voluntary, *see* treaties listed in CLINTON ET AL., *supra*, at 145, the moves "became forced under the Jackson Administration in the 1830s." COHEN, *supra*, at 28.

[95] An 1856 treaty with the Creek and Seminole Tribes was typical. It provided that "no state or territory shall ever pass laws for the government of the Creek and Seminole

The effort to remove the Native Americans beyond the boundary of any white settlement proved unavailing with the discovery of gold in California and other events leading to the settlement of the western United States. However, while these changes ultimately rendered unrealistic the idea of an "Indian country" *outside* the boundaries of any state or territory, the policy of physical separation continued with the creation of "reservations" within newly established states and territories.[96]

More important than the physical separation mandated by the formal legal policy—which, properly limited, is not necessarily inconsistent with a legal policy in which a tribe's role as a positive group is recognized—was the philosophical separation imposed on Native Americans by law during most of our history. From the outset, the documents articulating formal national policy toward the indigenous peoples made it clear that they could not be full participants in United States society without giving up their ties to their tribes.

The original constitution of the United States, for example, excluded "Indians not taxed" from those to be counted for purposes of state representation in Congress,[97] "thereby suggesting that they were not part of the polity"[98] unless, of course, they choose to adopt the ways of the white man (in this instance, by being taxed). Until the 1920s, most Native Americans who chose to reside in "Indian country" and retain their ties to their tribes were legally considered

---

tribes of Indians, and [none of the tracts] of [Indian] country defined [in] the agreement shall ever be embraced or included within, or annexed to, any Territory or State, nor shall either, or any part of either, ever be erected into a Territory without the full and free consent of the legislative authority of the tribe owning the same." Treaty of Aug. 7, 1856, 11 Stat. 699. A nearly identical provision in an agreement with the Chickasaw Tribe was recently held not to foreclose the state of Oklahoma from imposing an income tax on tribal members who worked for the Tribe but resided outside "Indian Country." *See* Oklahoma Tax Commission v. Chickasaw Nation, 515 U.S. 450 (1995).

[96] COHEN, *supra* note 94, at 29. As one leading text notes, "Once westward settlement leap-frogged the Indian Territory to California, the effort to remove Indian tribes from the states was doomed. Thus, in California during the early 1850s, federal agents experimented with the creation of smaller reservations within the states." CLINTON ET AL., *supra* note 94, at 146. The typical pattern was that lands that had been reserved for the tribes would be exempted from the authority of newly created states whose exterior boundaries included those lands. *See e.g.*, Act of Jan. 29, 1861, ch. 20, § 1, 12 Stat. 127 (Kansas); Act of June 20, 1910, ch. 310, §§ 2, 20, 36 Stat. 558–59, 569–70 (Arizona and New Mexico); Act of Feb. 22, 1889, ch. 180, § 4, 25 Stat. 677 (North Dakota, South Dakota, Montana, and Washington).

[97] *See* U.S. CONST, arts. 1, § 2. As part of a compromise between the slave and non-slave states, the same provision provided that slaves (designated as "other persons") counted as "three-fifths" of a person for representation purposes. *Id.* Although the Fourteenth Amendment to the U.S. Constitution eliminated the 60% valuation for slaves following the Civil War, it retained the exclusion for "Indians not taxed." *Id.*, amend. XIV, § 2.

[98] CLINTON ET AL., *supra* note 94, at 142.

citizens of their tribes and not of the United States.[99] Under the terms of some laws and treaties, members of some tribes could become U.S. citizens prior to the 1920s, but only if they ceased to be members of their tribes, abandoning their native customs and, in some instances, physically leaving the tribal community.[100]

These laws directly imposed on Native Americans the same choice the Chilean system of individual equality indirectly imposed on persons such as Luis Marileo Colipí—the choice between being a member of the organic tribe or a citizen of the nation. Not surprisingly, many Native Americans made the same choice Marileo Colipí did, preferring to remain with their tribe—even in poverty—rather than assimilate into the mainstream society that refused to value, or even recognize, their customs and points of view. The thought that the tribe could act as a mediating institution to facilitate the individual tribal members' full entry into the society was never considered.

With the passage of the General Allotment Act of 1887,[101] an ultimately unsuccessful effort was made to completely end the physical separation of the Native Americans in order to hasten the assimilation process. Under the Act,

---

[99] In 1884, the U.S. Supreme Court indicated that the provision of the Fourteenth Amendment that granted U.S. citizenship to "all persons born or naturalized in the United States, and subject to the jurisdiction thereof" did not apply to Native Americans born within the territorial boundaries of the nation. Elk v. Wilkins, 112 U.S. 94 (1884). The Court observed that under the original constitution, Native Americans "owed immediate allegiance to their several tribes, and were not part of the people of the United States." *Id.* at 99. According to the Court, the Fourteenth Amendment had not changed the basic nature of this relationship, as evidenced by the fact that the Amendment provided that representatives of Congress "shall be apportioned among the several States according to their respective numbers, counting the whole number of persons in each State, *excluding Indians not taxed.*" *Id.* at 102, *quoting* U.S. Const., amend. XIV, § 2 (emphasis added). According to the Court, "Indians not taxed are still excluded from the count, for the reason that they are not citizens. Their absolute exclusion from the basis of representation, in which all other persons are now included, is wholly inconsistent with their being considered citizens." *Id.*

[100] As the leading Indian Law treatise explains:

Early treaties sometimes granted citizenship options to Indians. The Indians were required to make a choice: accept United States citizenship and receive an allotment, or retain tribal membership and remove with their tribe to a new location. [*See e.g.,* Treaty with the Cherokees, July 8, 1817, art. 8, 7 Stat. 156, 159]. Some treaties provided that those who remained behind and became citizens forfeited their tribal membership. [*See, e.g., id.*]. Under other treaties tribal rights or property, but not tribal membership, were forfeited [*See, e.g.,* Treaty with the Choctaws, Sept. 27, 1830, art. 14, 7 Stat. 333, 335].

COHEN, *supra* note 94, at 142.

[101] *See* Act of Feb. 8, 1887, ch. 119, 24 Stat. 388 (codified as amended in scattered sections of 25 U.S.C.). Individual allotment of some tribal lands was a part of some Indian treaties and statutes prior to 1887, *see* COHEN, *supra* note 94, at 129–30. The 1887 Act adopted it as a general policy for all reservations. *Id.* at 130–31.

the president was authorized to divide tribal lands into individual allotments for the individual members of the tribe.[102] However, even though the land-ownership policy had changed dramatically,[103] the concept that a Native American could not simultaneously be a member of his tribe and a citizen of the United States remained constant. There was no intent to allow Native Americans to become part of the mainstream society while retaining their tribal ties. The goal was to eliminate the tribe, thereby turning the previous choice of citizenship in the United States or the tribe into a truly Hobson's choice. Thus, in order to become a U.S. citizen under the terms of the Allotment Act of 1887, a Native American had to either obtain title to an individual allotment of land, which was no longer part of the tribe's lands, or move outside the boundaries of the reservation and ''adopt the habits of civilized life.''[104]

In 1924, almost seventy years after citizenship had been granted to the former black slaves, Congress approved a law granting citizenship to ''all non-citizen Indians born within the territorial limits of the United States.''[105] But even this law was part of an assimilationist policy whose goal was to remove from the Native Americans the desire to be members of their tribe. Even though it was now theoretically possible from a legal standpoint to be both a member of a tribe and a citizen of the United States, it was not acceptable from a social

---

[102] The original plan was to allot parcels of land to individual tribal members—160 acres to each head of household and 40 acres to each minor. Surplus lands were then to be made available to non-Native Americans. *See* CHARLES WILKINSON, AMERICAN INDIANS, TIME, AND THE LAW 19–20 (1987).

[103] Total tribal landholdings fell from over 138 million acres in 1887 to approximately 52 million acres in 1934, when the allotment process was halted. *See* WILKINSON, *supra* note 101, at 20. The effects varied from reservation to reservation, as the process was never fully effectuated. For example, none of the land in the Jicarilla Apache reservation is owned by individual allottees. *See* Merrion v. Jicarilla Apache Tribe, 455 U.S. 130, 133 (1982). By contrast, the Lake Traverse Reservation of the Wahpeton and Sisseton Bands of the Sioux Tribe was held to be terminated when 85% of the reservation had been purchased by non-Indians, and the remaining 15% (scattered among the non-Indian parcels) was held by individual tribal allottees. *See* DeCoteau v. District County Court, 420 U.S. 425, 427–28 (1975).

[104] Ch. 119, § 6, 24 Stat. 388, 390 (*codified as amended* at 25 U.S.C. § 349).

[105] Act of June 2, 1924, ch. 233, 43 Stat. 253 (codified as carried forward at 8 U.S.C. § 1401(b) (1988)).

The decision to grant citizenship to all Native Americans without requiring them to formally sever their ties with the tribe was reached and implemented gradually. In the words of the leading Indian law treatise: ''For a long period Indian naturalization was conditioned on the severing of tribal ties . . . , but this policy was gradually relaxed. . . . An 1890 statute permitted tribal Indians residing in Indian Territory to become naturalized citizens without any change in tribal or federal ties [*See* Act of May 2, 1890, ch. 182, § 43, 26 Stat. 81, 99]. But the view that citizenship should require at least partial or future . . . severing of tribal ties predominated until World War I.'' COHEN, *supra* note 94, at 644.

standpoint, and extremely difficult from a realistic legal viewpoint. As President Theodore Roosevelt explained, the ultimate hope was that the laws of this era would act "as a mighty pulverizing engine to break up the tribal mass."[106] Accordingly, during this time laws prohibited Native Americans from engaging in certain native dances and ceremonies,[107] and federal authorities in charge of reservations regulated many aspects of the daily lives of the Native Americans, such as hair length[108] and funeral procedures,[109] all in an effort to help them "become civilized," i.e., to break their ties with the tribe.

After a short period of less assimilationist pressure in the 1930s,[110] the "termination" era began.[111] Pursuant to a House Concurrent Resolution adopted in 1953, Congress expressed its desire to end any relationships between the

---

[106] A COMPILATION OF THE MESSAGES AND PAPERS OF THE PRESIDENTS 1789–1914 6674 (James D. Richardson, ed., 1896–1917).

[107] "Engaging in specified dances and ceremonials was made punishable in 1921, subjecting the offender to fines and imprisonment." COHEN, *supra* note 94, at 141, *citing* K. PHILP, JOHN COLLIER'S CRUSADE FOR INDIAN REFORM 1920–1954, 56–57 (1977).

[108] *See* COHEN, *supra* note 94, at 141, *citing* Comm'r Ind. Aff. Ann. Rep., H.R. Doc. No. 5, 57th Cong., 2d Sess. 13–16 (1902).

[109] One Indian agent reported that he forbade the burning of a deceased Native American's property when the deceased was cremated because it "destroys ambition for the accumulation of property, which is the chief fundamental foundation of the structure of our civilization." Comm'r Ind. Aff. Ann. Rep., H.R. Exec. Doc., No. 1, 51st Cong., 1st Sess. 117 (1899) *quoted in* COHEN, *supra* note 94, at 141.

[110] In 1934, Congress enacted the Indian Reorganization Act, Ch. 576, 48 Stat. 984 (*codified as amended* at 25 U.S.C. §§ 461, 462, 463, 464, 465, 466–70, 471 73, 474, 475, 476–78, 479 (1988)). The act prohibited further allotment of reservation lands, *see* 25 U.S.C. § 461, authorized the acquisition of lands for the tribe, *see* 25 U.S.C. §§ 464–65, and the addition of these lands to the tribal reservation, *see* 25 U.S.C. § 467. It also authorized the Secretary to approve constitutions and corporate charters for tribes who opted to organize under its terms. *See* 25 U.S.C. §§ 476–478. More than 150 tribes adopted constitutions under these provisions, *see* CLINTON ET AL., *supra* note 94, at 155, but several including the largest tribe—the Navajo—rejected the provisions, *see id.* at 154, and continue to govern themselves without any written constitution. *See* Kerr-McGee Corp. v. Navajo Tribe, 471 U.S. 195, 198–99 (1985).

[111] Although the formal resolution approving the termination policy was not adopted until 1953, *see infra* note 112, congressional hearings leading to the resolution began in 1940, *see, e.g., Hearings on S. 2103 Before the Comm. on Indian Affairs*, H.R. 76th Cong., 3d Sess. (1940), and statutes granting states jurisdiction over the reservations of selected tribes—legislation which seriously undermined, if not eliminated, tribal autonomy—was enacted throughout the 1940s. *See, e.g.,* Act of June 8, 1940, ch. 276., 54 State. 249, *codified* at 18 U.S.C. § 3243 (all reservations in Kansas); Act of May 31, 1946, ch. 279, 60 Stat. 229 (Devils Lake Reservation in California); Act of June 30, 1948, ch. 759, 62 Stat. 1161 (Sac and Fox reservation in Iowa). Thus, one leading text indicates that the "Termination Era" commenced in 1940, *see* CLINTON ET AL., *supra* note 94, at 155; another that it began in 1943. *See* COHEN, *supra* note 94 at 152.

federal government and the tribes.[112] Specific legislation officially "terminating"[113] more than 100 tribes and bands soon followed.[114] Even for the tribes who were not directly affected, the message was clear: Native Americans' relationship with their tribe was incompatible with full membership in American society—a message that completely precluded any consideration of using the tribe as a positive force in the lives of Native Americans.

Over the last thirty years, official federal policy has for the first time begun to recognize the central place of the tribe in the resolution of the "Indian question," as the federal government has pursed a policy of greater tribal self-determination.[115] However, the Supreme Court has limited the extent of tribal

---

[112] *See* H.R. Con. Res. 108, 83rd Cong., 1st Sess. 67 Stat. 132 (1953). The seminal provisions of the resolution provided:

> Whereas it is the policy of Congress, as rapidly as possible, to make the Indians within the territorial limits of the United States subject to the same laws and entitled to the same privileges and responsibilities as are applicable to other citizens of the United States, to end their status as wards of the United States, and to grant them all of the rights and prerogatives pertaining to American citizenship; and

> Whereas the Indians within the territorial limits should assume their full responsibilities as American citizens: Now, therefore, be it *Resolved by the House of Representatives (the Senate concurring)*, That it is declared to be the sense of Congress that, at the earliest possible time, all of the Indian tribes and the individual members thereof located within the States of California, Florida, New York and Texas, and all of the following named Indian tribes and individual members thereof, should be freed from Federal supervision and control and from all disabilities and limitations specially applicable to Indians. . . .

[113] The various termination bills varied somewhat from one another. Typically, the statute required termination of federal trusteeship over the tribe, mandatory distribution of tribal assets to individual tribal members, and in some cases, disbandment of the tribe. *See* Robert Clinton, *Isolated in Their Own Country: A Defense of Federal Protection of Indian Autonomy and Self-Government*, 33 STAN. L. REV. 979, 1025 (1981); *see also*, Charles Wilkinson & Eric Biggs, *The Evolution of the Termination Policy*, 5 AM. IND. L. REV. 139, 152 53 (1977).

[114] During the "Termination Era," 109 tribes and bands were terminated. *See* Wilkinson & Biggs, *supra* note 113, at 151. The large number of tribes terminated may be misleading unless placed in context. One statute, for example, terminated 61 bands in western Oregon. The total membership of all the terminated Oregon bands, however, was only 2,081, and only 2,158 acres of land were involved. *See id.* at 151. In all "no more than [three] per cent of all federally recognized Indians were involved" in the termination process before it was halted. *Id.* Moreover, tribal status was eventually restored to some of the terminated tribes. *See, e.g.*, Menominee Restoration Act, 25 U.S.C. §§ 903–903f (1988).

[115] During this time, legislation has been enacted to strengthen tribal control over federally funded programs for Native Americans, *see* The Indian Self-Determination and Education Assistance Act of 1975, Pub. L. No. 93–638 (*codified at* 25 U.S.C. 450a and elsewhere in titles 25, 42, and 50 U.S.C.), and to give tribes greater authority over adoption and child custody proceedings involving tribal children, *see* the Indian Child Welfare Act of 1978, Pub. L. No. 95–608 (*codified at* 25 U.S.C. §§ 1901 1963). For a

sovereignty,[116] and there continues to be strongly expressed public opposition to the existence and autonomy of native tribes.[117] Thus, many Native Americans continue to believe that tribal membership and national citizenship fit together roughly at best, and uneasiness about their ability to be both citizens and tribal members persists.[118]

Until that uneasiness is alleviated, the United States will continue to struggle with its "Indian question." For many Native Americans, the tribe continues to be the "heart and spirit" of their existence,[119] an affiliation that they will not,

---

general description of the legislation and policies of the past 30 years, *see* CLINTON ET AL., *supra* note 94, at 158–64.

[116] *See, e.g.*, Strate v. A-1 Contractors, — U.S. —, 117 S. Ct. 1404 (1997)(tribe has no jurisdiction over lawsuit arising out of traffic accident between non-tribal members on federally granted right-of-way through the reservation); South Dakota v. Bourland, 508 U.S. 679 (1993)(tribe has no jurisdiction to regulate hunting and fishing by non-Native Americans on federal lands within the reservation); Duro v. Reina, 495 U.S. 676 (1990) (tribe has no jurisdiction to prosecute crime committed on the reservation by a Native American who is not a member of the tribe); Brendale v. Confederated Tribes and Bands of Yakima Indian Nation, 492 U.S. 408 (1989)(limiting tribal authority to regulate land use on portion of reservation previously opened to non-Native American settlement). The effect of the *Duro* decision has been reversed by legislation. *See* Act of Oct. 28, 1991, Pub. L. No. 102 137, 105 Stat. 646 (1991).

[117] Anti-tribal and anti-Native American feelings unfortunately continue to surface. In some areas, resentment concerning treaty rights that enable tribal members to hunt and fish without being subject to the same rules and regulations applicable to non-tribal citizens of the state has led to the proliferation of bumper stickers proclaiming "Save a Salmon; can an Indian," "Spare a fish, spear an Indian," and "Save a deer, shoot an Indian." *See* Williams, *supra* note 31, at 759 & n.1. Protesting a Navajo employment preference policy enacted by the Navajo Tribal Council, the president of a Denver-based drilling-supply firm informed the council of his feelings in the following terms in 1986:

> Given the historical facts, we consider ourselves to be members of the conquering race and you to be members of the vanquished and inferior race. We hold your land and property to be spoils of war, ours by right of conquest. Through the generosity of our people, you have been given a reservation where you may prance and dance as you please obeying your kings and worshipping your false gods.

Letter from Ronald Vertrees to the Navajo Tribal Council, *quoted in* Hugh Nibley, *Promised Lands*, CLARK MEMORANDUM, Spring 1993, at 7.

[118] As one prominent Native American scholar explained: "Termination is out of fashion and dead as an announced policy, but termination with a small 't' is not. For tactical purposes other names might be used, but the long range goal will not change." Philip S. Deloria, *The Era of Indian Self-Determination: An Overview*, in INDIAN SELF-RULE: FIRST-HAND ACCOUNTS OF INDIAN-WHITE RELATIONS FROM ROOSEVELT TO REAGAN 191, 192 (Kenneth R. Philp, ed., 1985).

[119] RUSSEL L. BARSH & JAMES Y. HENDERSON, THE ROAD: INDIAN TRIBES AND POLITICAL LIBERTY viii (1980). Henderson and Barsh sum up the point quite well:

> The entire history of the federal relationship with tribes is a history of attempts to subvert [tribal] consciousness and replace it with the naked, alienated individualism and formal equality of contemporary American society. Indian people

and perhaps cannot, easily set aside.[120] Unless the law can provide a meaningful and permanent place for the tribal group in American society, many Native Americans will remain on the fringe. Policymakers in the United States, like those in Chile, have too often failed to understand the importance of groups in both the lives of many of their citizens and the life of the nation itself.[121] Understanding the importance of such groups could lead to the beginning of a new indigenous policy, one that views the groups in a positive light.

III. TOWARD AN ANSWER: THE ROLE OF INTERMEDIATE GROUPS IN A CONSTITUTIONAL DEMOCRACY

The Chilean and American experiences with their indigenous populations demonstrates the futility of following a policy that fails to provide an adequate and positive role for groups in the legal structure. The Chilean system has ignored indigenous groups. The United States has recognized their existence, but has then generally forced individual Native Americans to choose between full membership in the American society or full membership in the tribe. Neither has sought to focus on the way in which the group itself might be empowered to solve the problems that individual members of the group face and to contribute to the overall well-being of the nation.

That such failures should occur in the types of liberal democracies that exist in the Americas is, in one respect, not surprising, because these systems are largely based on liberal individualist philosophies.[122] Therefore, it should be expected that there would be little in the way of group rights in the constitutions of American democracies. Yet some intermediate groups—groups between the individual and the nation—have played an important role in such democracies.

Some intermediate groups have acted as "mediating structures" in different societies, especially in the United States.[123] A "mediating structure" is a group,

---

have resisted and endured, but the poverty and hate which follow upon failure to assimilate obligingly into the American "melting pot" are the high price they have paid for it.

Id.

[120] As Barsh and Henderson note, for many native Americans, "[t]ribalism is not an association of interest but a form of consciousness which faithfully reflects the experience of Indians." *Id.*

[121] *See* text accompanying *infra* notes 127–132.

[122] As Professor Glendon has noted: "The legal systems of continental Western Europe [from which many Latin American legal systems evolved], like the American system, assign a high priority to the free development of the autonomous individual." Mary Ann Glendon, *Individualism and Communitarianism in Contemporary Legal Systems: Tensions and Accommodations*, 1993 B.Y.U. L. Rev. 385, 407.

[123] *See* Peter L. Berger & Richard J. Neuhaus, To Empower People: The Role of Mediating Structures in the Public Policy 2 (1977).

usually an organic or quasi-organic group,[124] that acts as a buffer between the individual and the megastructures of society, such as the Nation-State.[125] It is a group that has connections with both the individual and the State. It has both a public face (which it presents to the State) and a private face (which it presents to its members). These groups help their members make the transition from isolated individuals to productive members of the larger society[126] by helping them, on the one hand, learn the responsibilities and duties of membership in the democratic State, and on the other hand, providing them with protection against the extreme assimilationist pressures that frequently emanate from the same State. In order to operate properly, these groups must have both a sufficient connection with the State itself—a stake in the system, if you will—and, at the same time, sufficient freedom from State interference that they can exercise some measure of autonomy over their own members.

Intermediate groups whose relationship with their members are not unlike those between indigenous tribes and their members have performed important mediating functions in the United States. Among other things, they "buttress individual freedom by serving to buffer the power and relativize the ideology of the State," and "prevent citizens from becoming too dependent on government for solutions to their problems."[127] Such groups also teach their members "civic virtue," i.e., "the republican virtues of moderation, self-restraint, sturdy independence of mind and respect for the rights of others," that are important to any fully functioning democracy.[128] The importance of these functions to the proper operation of a democracy is illustrated by a brief examination of the way in which the development of civic virtue is critical to democracies and the manner in which intermediate groups can facilitate the development of this essential quality.

Resting as it does on the concepts of popular sovereignty and maximum individual freedom, the form of democracy adopted by the United States requires that the ultimate caretakers of the democratic flame—the people—possess certain attributes and attitudes. They must obey the law not solely because they are afraid that they will be caught and punished, but because they recognize that obedience to the overall system of law is good for the whole society of which they are a part.[129] As historian Gordon S. Wood explained:

---

[124] Examples include families, churches, and voluntary associations. *See id.* at 3.

[125] "Megastructures" are the "large institutions of public life," those institutions which order the public aspects of our lives *Id.* at 2. According to Berger and Neuhaus, "the most important large institution in the ordering of modern society is the modern state itself." *Id.*

[126] Id. at 2–3.

[127] Glendon, *supra* note 122, at 390–91.

[128] *Id.*

[129] As one political theorist has noted, "The conviction that . . . action controlled by inner authority leads to an harmonious social and political world forms an important condition of modern democracy." John W. Chapman, *Voluntary Association and the*

In a monarchy each man's desire to do what was right in his own eyes could be restrained by fear or force. In a republic, however, each man must somehow be persuaded to submerge his personal wants into the greater good of the whole. This willingness of the individual to sacrifice his private interests for the good of the community—such patriotism or love of country—the eighteenth century termed "public virtue."[130]

This essential attitude of public or civic virtue can often best be taught through membership in intermediate groups. It is difficult, if not impossible, for a Nation-State to generate this critical attitude because it is an attitude of the heart that one can learn only from those with whom one has a close relationship. As the French philosopher Alexis de Tocqueville explained, "[f]eelings and opinions are recruited, the heart is enlarged, and the human mind is developed by no other means than by the reciprocal influence of men upon each other."[131] The relationship between a person and the Nation-State is generally too diffuse and removed for this kind of reciprocal influence to exist. Thus, society in the United States has come to rely on more intimate groups, such as families, churches, and other intermediate groups that exist between the individual and the state, to generate this kind of attitude.[132]

Political Theory of Pluralism, in VOLUNTARY ASSOCIATIONS 87, 93 (J. Roland Pennock & John W. Chapman, eds., 1969), *quoting* ZEVEDIE BARBU, DEMOCRACY AND DICTATORSHIP: THEIR PSYCHOLOGY AND PATTERNS OF LIFE 73 (1965)). George Washington framed the same sentiment this way: "it is substantially true that virtue or morality is a necessary spring of popular government." 2 GEORGE DE HUZR ET AL., BASIC AMERICAN DOCUMENTS 108–09 (1953), *quoted in* RICHARD VETTERLI & GARY BRYNER, IN SEARCH OF THE REPUBLIC: PUBLIC VIRTUE AND THE ROOTS OF AMERICAN GOVERNMENT 70 (1987).

[130] GORDON S. WOOD, THE CREATION OF THE AMERICAN REPUBLIC 1776–1787 68 (1969).

[131] 2 ALEXIS DE TOCQUEVILLE, DEMOCRACY IN AMERICA 131 (Henry Reeve, trans., 1961).

[132] The way in which intermediate groups carry out this function is perhaps best illustrated by the manner in which it occurs in the most organic intermediate group—the family. In the family, children are compelled to learn to deal with authority, responsibility, and duty in an atmosphere of love that permits these lessons to be learned effectively. As one scholar has noted, "[s]omething about the combined permanence, authority, and love that characterize the formal family uniquely makes possible the . . . teaching of [moral and civic duty]." Bruce C. Hafen, *The Constitutional Status of Marriage, Kinship, and Sexual Privacy—Balancing the Individual and Social Interests*, 81 MICH. L. REV. 463, 477 (1983). Thus, "American society has relied to a considerable extent on the family not only to nurture the young, but also to instill the habits required by citizenship in a self-governing community. We have relied on the family to teach us to care for others, [and] to moderate . . . self-interest. . . ." WALTER BERNS, THE FIRST AMENDMENT AND THE FUTURE OF AMERICAN DEMOCRACY 222 (1976).

Other forms of intermediate groups such as churches, schools, and even local government have also performed this same educational role in the United States. *See* Worthen, *supra* note 4, at 603–04.

Given this, and other[133] important roles that intermediate groups can perform in a democracy, the preservation of such groups and the provision of legal and philosophical space for them to perform their proper role is important not only to indigenous peoples, but to all persons in democratic nations. Recognition of this fact could provide the basis for the resolution of the "Indian question." By accepting the indigenous group as a positive entity—not something to be ignored or attacked, but something to be encouraged—the nations of the Americas may begin a process of reconciliation with their native populations that both the nation and the members of the indigenous groups will find satisfactory.

If policymakers began to view indigenous groups as potential allies in the democratic process of nation building by encouraging membership in such groups and granting a measure of autonomy to them, the individual members of the group would feel less alienated from the larger society, and more willing to search for common goals and norms. Somewhat paradoxically, national governments could obtain more integration on critical matters by permitting more freedom to the group to define for itself how its members should interact with the larger society.[134]

This is not to say, however, that the solution to the "Indian question" or any other group rights problems is obvious or simple. Difficult questions have, and will, continue to arise when we begin to consider how intermediate group rights can and should be recognized in a constitutional democracy that values individual liberty. Groups, even groups like Native American tribes, can limit individual freedom in ways that are damaging to the lives of their individual members.[135] Legal limits on group autonomy have to be set to avoid abuses.

---

[133] Professor Mary Ann Glendon has observed that intermediate groups can also "nurture the sorts of political skills that a republic requires in its citizens as well as its statesmen" and promote the "delivery of services such as health, education, and child care more economically, efficiently, and humanely" than can large governments. Glendon, *supra* note 122, at 390–91.

[134] As José Bengoa explained concerning the Mapuche:

> Mapuche society of the first half of the nineteenth century was very flexible toward outside influences, precisely because it possessed complete territorial and political freedom. . . . When total political independence exists, a society can openly expose itself to cultural change. It is not afraid it will disappear. By contrast, when a society is subjugated—whether politically, territorially, or economically—by another that oppresses it; it transforms itself into a conservative society, it closes ranks around its traditional culture and clings to it with all its might.

BENGOA, *supra* note 1, at 155. While Bengoa's remarks seem to indicate that complete independence is necessary in order for the indigenous society to completely come to terms with the larger nation, I remain optimistic that such dramatic measures are not necessary.

[135] Concerns that the rights of individual tribal members were "seriously jeopardized by the tribal government's administration of justice," 113 Cong. Rec. 13, 473 (1967)(Statement of Sen. Ervin), led to the passage of the Indian Civil Rights Act of 1968, Pub. L. No. 90–284, 82 Stat. 77 (1968) (*codified at* 25 U.S.C. §§ 1301–1303). The ICRA statutorily imposes on Indian tribes many, but not all, of the prohibitions imposed

Moreover, not all groups are the same; some have more ties with the larger society than do others. Legal incentives to produce the necessary State loyalty may, therefore, be required.

Furthermore, determining what constitutes an intermediate group and how much legal and philosophical space should be allotted to it are not easy tasks. Serious thought and debate must be undertaken in order to come up with even tentative answers to these most basic questions. Such a theory will also require some new and deep thinking about the concepts of sovereignty and autonomy, concepts that carry different connotations in different contexts.

None of this will be easy. However, as difficult as it may be, the experience of indigenous peoples in Chile and the United States indicates that we must begin to seriously address these difficult questions rather than futilely pursue constitutional policies that ignore the important role of groups to both individual and societal well-being.

---

on the federal and state governments by the Bill of Rights and the Fourteenth Amendment to the U.S. Constitution. *See* Kevin J Worthen, *Two Sides of the Same Coin: The Potential Normative Power of American Cities and Indian Tribes*, 44 VAND. L. REV. 1273, 1302 n.146 (1991). Allegations of abuse of tribal authority after passage of the Act triggered a study by the U.S. Civil Rights Commission involving more than 170 witnesses in hearings held at five different locations. *See* REPORT OF THE U.S. COMMISSION ON CIVIL RIGHTS, THE INDIAN CIVIL RIGHTS ACT 85 n.3 (1991)(Statement of Commissioner Allen).

CHAPTER 13

DOES SECTION 35 OF THE CONSTITUTION ACT, 1982, HAVE ANY REAL MEANING? AN ANALYSIS OF THE "REASONABLE LIMITS" TEST IN *SPARROW V. THE QUEEN*

Bob Freedman

I. INTRODUCTION

In a thought-provoking journal article,[1] Tom Berger, a former Justice of the Supreme Court of British Columbia, asks the reader to study a rather interesting question that arises in *Sparrow v. The Queen*.[2] He notes that although the British Columbia Court of Appeal upheld the aboriginal[3] fishing rights at issue in that case, at the same time, the court placed a limitation on the aboriginal rights contained in section 35 of the Constitution Act, 1982.[4] Berger points out that:

> Since aboriginal rights under s. 35 do not come within the *Charter*, they are not subject to ss. 1 or 33. The B. C. Court of Appeal held that

---

[1] *See* Tom Berger, *The Charter: A Historical Perspective*, 23 U.B.C. L.Rᴇᴠ. 603 (1989).

[2] Sparrow v. The Queen 36 D.L.R. (4th) 246 (B. B. C. A. 1986).

[3] The term ''aboriginal'' is used in this chapter to embrace all First Nations people in Canada.

[4] Part II of the Constitution Act, 1982 (Can.), being Schedule B of the Canada Act, 1982 (U.K.) ch. 11. Section 35 is in these terms:

35. (1) The existing aboriginal and treaty rights of the aboriginal peoples of Canada are hereby recognized and affirmed.

(2) In this Act, ''aboriginal peoples of Canada'' includes the Indian, Inuit and Metis peoples of Canada.

(3) For greater certainty, in subsection (1) ''treaty rights'' includes rights that now exist by way of land claims agreements or may be so acquired.

(4) Notwithstanding any other provisions of this Act, the aboriginal and treaty rights referred to in subsection (1) are guaranteed equally to male and female persons.

there was an aboriginal right to fish at the mouth of the Fraser River,
and the Musqueam Band enjoys that right, but they said there must be
a limitation on that right (at 277). Where did that limitation come from?
Section 1 does not apply because it is not a ''Charter'' case. The truth
is that the Court invented it out of thin air. They said there is a compelling state interest in the conservation of the fishery. In reaching this
decision, the Court tracked American jurisprudence.[5]

In essence, Berger is pointing to the idea that, because the aboriginal rights
provision contained in section 35 of the Constitution Act, 1982 is outside the
confines of the Canadian Charter of Rights and Freedoms,[6] it is not subject to
the ''reasonable limits'' test contained in section I of the Charter,[7] nor to the
legislative override provision in section 33 of the Charter.[8]

When the *Sparrow* case was heard by the Supreme Court of Canada,[9] a
similar limitation was placed on section 35 rights. The Supreme Court also did
not provide a very detailed explanation for why it was limiting such rights. It
should be noted that *Sparrow* is probably the most important decision thus far
rendered by the Supreme Court on the topic of aboriginal rights. In its decision,
the Court used the following language to describe its rationale for limiting section
35 rights:

> There is no explicit language in [s. 35] that authorizes this Court
> or any other court to assess the legitimacy of any government legislation
> that restricts aboriginal rights. Yet, we find that the words ''recognition
> and affirmation'' incorporate the fiduciary relationship referred to ear-
> lier and so import some restraint on the exercise of sovereign power.
> *Rights that are affirmed are not absolute.* Federal legislative powers
> continue, including, of course, the right to legislate with respect to
> Indians pursuant to s. 91(24) of the *Constitution Act, 1867.* These pow-
> ers must, however, now be read together with s. 35(1). In other words,
> federal power must be reconciled with federal duty and the best way

---

[5] Berger, *supra* note 1, at 606.

[6] *See* Part I of the Constitution Act, 1982, being schedule B of the Canada Act,
1982, ch. 11 (U.K.) [hereinafter the Charter].

[7] Section I of the Charter sets out a ''reasonable limits'' test on the rights contained
in the document: ''The Canadian Charter of Rights and Freedoms guarantees the rights
and freedoms set out in it subject only to such reasonable limits prescribed by law as
can be demonstrably justified in a free and democratic society.''

[8] Section 33 allows the federal and provincial governments to derogate from certain
rights set out in the Charter: ''(1) Parliament or the legislature of a province may expressly
declare in an Act of Parliament or of the legislature, as the case may be that the Act or
a provision thereof shall operate notwithstanding a provision included in section 2 or
sections 7 to 15 of this Charter.''

[9] *See* Sparrow v. The Queen 70 D.L.R. (4th) 385 (S.C.C. 1990).

to achieve that recognition is to demand the justification of any government regulation that infringes upon or denies aboriginal rights.[10]

Under the section 35 "test," it must be determined whether the legislation in question has the effect of interfering with an existing aboriginal right. If so, there is a *prima facie* infringement of section 35(1). The onus of proving infringement lies with the individual or group challenging the legislation.

Of relevance to the issue of infringement will be such questions as:

(1) Is the limitation reasonable?

(2) Does the regulation impose undue hardship?

(3) Does the regulation deny to the holders of the right their preferred means of exercising that right?

(4) Does the regulation unnecessarily infringe on the interest protected by the fishing right?

In essence, the Supreme Court of Canada has incorporated into section 35 the analysis that it uses to determine the constitutionality of legislation under section 1 of the Charter.[11]

If a *prima facie* infringement is found, the next step in the analysis addresses the issue of "justification." This branch of the test concerns what would or would not constitute the legitimate regulation of a constitutional aboriginal right. At this stage of the analysis the duty is on the Crown to demonstrate that the regulation is justifiable. The Court describes the justification in this way:

> First, is there a valid legislative objective? Here the court would inquire into whether the objective of Parliament in authorizing the department to enact regulations regarding fisheries is valid. The objective of the department in setting out the particular regulations would also be scrutinized. An objective aimed at preserving s. 35(1) rights by conserving and managing a natural resource, for example, would be valid. Also valid would be objectives purporting to prevent the exercise of s. 35(1) rights that would cause harm to the general populace or to aboriginal peoples themselves, or other objectives found to be compelling and substantial.[12]

---

[10] *Id.* at 409.

[11] The Supreme Court of Canada has set out a test to determine whether the infringement of a Charter right is justified under section 1. The test was originally developed in *R. v. Oakes* [1986] 1 S.C.R. 103, and refined in *R. v. Edwards Books and Arts Ltd.* [1986] 2 S.C.R. 713.

[12] Sparrow v. The Queen 70 D.L.R. (4th) 385 (S.C.C. 1990).

If a valid legislative objective is found, the analysis then moves to a second stage within the justification analysis; that is, the special trust relationship and responsibility of the government toward aboriginal peoples must be given first consideration in determining whether the legislation can be justified.

The practical effect of such a trust relationship in the context of fisheries regulation is the allocation of the fisheries resources in a manner that gives top priority to aboriginal food fishing over other user groups such as commercial and sports fishermen. The Court said the following:

> We acknowledge that the justification standard to be met may place a heavy burden on the Crown. However, government policy with respect to the British Columbia fishery, regardless of s. 35(1), already dictates that, in allocating the right to fish, Indian food fishing is to be given priority over the interest of other user groups. . . . The objective is to guarantee that those plans treat aboriginal peoples in a way ensuring that their rights will be taken seriously.[13]

The justification analysis also comprises these considerations:

(1) Whether there has been as little infringement as possible, in order to effect the desired result;

(2) Whether, in a situation of expropriation, fair compensation is available; and

(3) Whether the aboriginal group in question has been consulted with respect to the conservation measures being implemented?

---

[13] The fishing rights of First Nations have been further limited by the Supreme Court of Canada in what has become known as the "fishing trilogy": *R. v. Van der Peet* 137 D.L.R. (4th) 289 (S.C.C. 1996); *R. v. Gladstone* 137 D.L.R. (4th) 648 (S.C.C. 1996.); *R. v. N.T.C. Smokehouse Ltd.* 137 D.L.R. (4th) 528 (S.C.C. 1996). At issue in these cases was the question of whether First Nations have the right to sell fish as an aboriginal right, pursuant to section 35 of the Constitution Act, 1982. In *Van der Peet* the Court set out an onerous test to determine whether there is an "existing aboriginal right," saying that in order for there to be an "existing aboriginal right" under section 35, an activity must be an element of a practice, custom or tradition—integral to the distinctive culture of the particular aboriginal group claiming the right—prior to the European contract. In *Van der Peet* and *Smokehouse,* the Court held that there was an aboriginal right to sell fish.

In *Gladstone* the Court held that there was such a right. However, the Court expanded on the rights limitation theme in *Sparrow.* The Court said that it is necessary to look at economic issues respecting non-aboriginal fisheries, and to "compelling and subtantial objectives" pursuant to which government could act in order to justify the infringement of an aboriginal right. In addition to applying the conservation concerns that were used in *Sparrow* as a basis upon which to infringe an aboriginal right, the Court said that reasons concerning the pursuit of economic and regional fairness, and the recognition of the historical reliance upon, and participation in, the fishery by non-aboriginal groups could be taken into account. This is essentially a rejection of the view taken in *Sparrow* that the "public interest" could not be used to justify the infringement of aboriginal rights.

The Court's reliance on the fiduciary relationship between the government and Canada's aboriginal peoples within the context of its justification analysis is significant in that the Court indicates that the government's fiduciary obligation is embodied within section 35. The Court clearly states that the contemporary recognition and affirmation of aboriginal rights must be defined in light of the trust-like historic relationship between government and aboriginal peoples.[14] This establishes a broad federal obligation to act in the best interest of aboriginal peoples across Canada where a "high standard of honourable dealing with respect to aboriginal peoples" is expected.[15]

Despite the heavy burden placed on the Crown to justify any infringement of aboriginal rights, the Supreme Court is performing, in effect, a rather significant and potentially ominous task. The Court is choosing to place a limit on the exercise of aboriginal rights without defining the nature and content of those rights in a meaningful fashion. What is particularly disturbing about this aspect of the *Sparrow* decision is that any future aboriginal right, such as the right of self-government, is effectively being curtailed before such a matter can be worked out in legislation or in the courts.

Several commentators have begun to argue that section 35, by affirming existing aboriginal and treaty rights, may contain the seeds of an aboriginal right to self-government.[16] The issue of concern, particularly in this context, is that by holding that section 35 rights can be limited, there is the potential for the right of self-government, or indeed for any aboriginal right, to be curtailed, perhaps to the point of nonexistence, as in the case of the right of aboriginal peoples to commercial sale of fish. Although we do not know at this point what the content and meaning of the aboriginal rights guaranteed in section 35 are, the Supreme Court of Canada has now placed some sort of limitation on rights that now exist or may be acquired in the future.

The question that Tom Berger is asking us to examine is this: why is the Supreme Court of Canada placing some sort of limitation on section 35 rights before their scope and meaning is clarified? The problem with limiting rights in this way is quite simple: judges and lawyers, trained according to the case

---

[14] *Sparrow supra* note 12 at 408.

[15] *Id.* at 409.

[16] *See, e.g.,* Michael Asch and Patrick Macklem, *Aboriginal Rights And Canadian Sovereignty: An Essay on R. v. Sparrow*, 29 ALTA. L. REV. 492 (1991); John Borrows, *A Genealogy of Law: Inherent Sovereignty and First Nations Self-Government*, 30 OSGOODE HALL L.J. 1 (1992); Bob Freedman, *The Space for Aboriginal Rights of Self-Government in British Columbia: The Effect of the Decision of the British Columbia Court of Appeal in Delgamuukw v. British Columbia*, 28 U.B.C. L. REV. 49 (1994); Patrick Macklem, *First Nations Self-Government and the Borders of the Canadian Legal Imagination*, 36 McGILL L.J. 382 (1991); Bruce Ryder, *The Demise and Rise of the Classical Paradigm in Canadian Federalism: Promoting Autonomy for the Provinces and First Nations*, 36 McGILL L.J. 308 (1991).

method, will seek to place boxes around those rights and debate will be focused on the application of the *Sparrow* "test," rather than on determining how the laws and customs of aboriginal peoples can be given effect today.[17]

The Supreme Court of Canada has provided us with very little guidance about why it has limited aboriginal rights. It seems, at first glance, as though the Court is acting in a positive manner to protect aboriginal rights. The Court makes this point: ". . . Our history has shown, unfortunately all too well, that Canada's aboriginal peoples are justified in worrying about government objectives that may be superficially neutral but which constitute de facto threats to the existence of aboriginal rights and interests."[18] In other words, the reasoning seems to be that historically, various levels of government have acted in ways that threaten aboriginal peoples. However, recent case law has held that governments owe some sort of ill-defined fiduciary or trust-like duty toward aboriginal peoples.[19] The argument then runs that if section 35 rights are left "unprotected," governments may continue to restrict aboriginal rights. As a result, the Court sees the limitation on section 35 rights as a mechanism by which governments may be held to an extremely high standard of justification before they will be permitted to legislate in violation of the aboriginal rights protected by section 35 of the Constitution Act, 1982.

Viewed from another perspective, however, the Supreme Court is acting in a manner that limits the potential scope of section 35 rights. Rather than simply protecting aboriginal peoples from the "nasty government," the limitation section in *Sparrow* may also serve to limit the very exercise of aboriginal rights before anyone has the chance to figure out exactly what rights are contained in section 35 of the Constitution Act, 1982.

II. PURPOSE AND BOUNDARIES OF THE INQUIRY

Because of the lack of explanation given by both the British Columbia Court of Appeal and by the Supreme Court of Canada as to why section 35 rights have been limited in *Sparrow*, it is necessary to develop certain hypotheses that might explain both the reasoning behind such a limitation of rights, and the

---

[17] We would do well to heed the words of Professor Lyon, who says the following about section 35(1):

> the context of 1982 is surely enough to tell us that this is not just a codification of the case law on aboriginal rights that had accumulated by 1982. Section 35 calls for a just settlement for aboriginal peoples. It renounces the old rules of the game under which the Crown established courts of law and denied those courts the authority to question sovereign claims made by the Crown.

Noel Lyon, *An Essay on Constitutional Interpretation,* 26 Osgoode Hall L.J. 95, 100 (1988).

[18] Sparrow v. The Queen 70 D.L.R. (4th) 385, (S.C.C. 1990), 409–10.

[19] *See* Guerin v. The Queen [1984] 2 S.C.R. 335.

implications of those explanations. Three hypotheses are advanced in this chapter for the limitation of section 35 rights. The *first* hypothesis is, quite simply, that there has been and continues to be a cultural bias inherent in Canadian law and politics toward aboriginal peoples. It is suggested that it is this bias that has informed, and continues to inform, the way in which legal and political decisions are made about aboriginal persons.

The *second* hypothesis is that the Supreme Court of Canada is wedded to the idea of rights limitation as it exists in section 1 of the Charter. The analysis of section 1 has played a major role in the way in which the Court approaches all questions related to competing rights.[20] The *third* hypothesis, which is in some ways related to the first, is that Canadian courts continue to be wedded to the notion that the *rule of law* can be given effect only within the division of powers in the Constitution Act, 1867 between the Provinces and Canada. This was the view taken by a majority of the British Columbia Court of Appeal in *Delgamuukw v. British Columbia.*[21] Under both hypotheses, the idea is that Canadian courts have difficulty with the notion that section 35 could contain unfettered or absolute rights, or even rights that can be exercised by aboriginal peoples using their own institutions and decision-making procedures. In both cases, the idea is that courts and politicians are concerned with maintaining *order.* Absent from this perspective is any consideration of the culture and perspective of aboriginal peoples, despite the comments of the Supreme Court in *Sparrow* that we must be sensitive to the aboriginal perspective.[22]

There continues to be an assumption that aboriginal peoples are incapable of making their own decisions or, if they are, then these decisions are not to be trusted, because they may infringe on the rights enjoyed by nonaboriginal Canadians. While it is obvious that all rights must be limited in a democratic

---

[20] In *Sparrow*, the Supreme Court refers to this idea:

The constitutional recognition afforded by [section 35(1)], therefore, gives a measure of control over government conduct and a strong check on legislative power. *While it does not promise immunity from government regulation in a society that, in the twentieth century, is increasingly more complex, interdependent and sophisticated, and where exhaustible resources need protection and management, it does hold the Crown to a substantive promise. The government is required to bear the burden of justifying any legislation that has some negative effect on any aboriginal right protected under section 35(1).*

Sparrow v. The Queen 70 D.L.R. (4th) 385 (S.C.C. 1990), 410 (emphasis added).

[21] *See* Delgamuukw v. British Columbia, [1993] 5 W.W.R. 97.

[22] In this context, the Supreme Court said the following:

it is possible, and, indeed, crucial, to be sensitive to the aboriginal perspective itself on the meaning of the rights at stake. For example, it would be artificial to try to create a hard distinction between the right to fish and the particular manner in which that right is exercised.

Sparrow v. The Queen 70 D.L.R. (4th) 385 (S.C.C. 1990), 411.

society in which there are different demands on scarce resources, the limitation of aboriginal rights is done largely by nonaboriginal Canadians *to* and *for* aboriginal peoples, often in a rather paternalistic fashion, rather than through consensus and consent. Perhaps we may begin to understand the motivation for such limitation of rights more clearly by examining some of the seeds from which contemporary law and policy about aboriginal peoples emanates.

III. CULTURAL BIAS AND THE CANADIAN LEGAL IMAGINATION

The formation of social policies and laws are largely a product of the norms, values, and ideologies that prevail in a given country or society at a particular time. It has been observed that:

> Social policies are affected by the demographic composition, the level of productivity of a society (be it an industrialized, a preindustrial, or a developing country), the way the social structure operates, assumptions made about human nature, the assumptions extant in a society. Policies that social institutions produce reflect the dominance of some values over others, and social problems are defined according to normative conceptions and the degree of tenacity with which they are held.[23]

This raises the crucial question of exactly *who* it is that makes policy and law and upon what kinds of assumptions are those laws and policies made.

Berger and Luckmann argue that reality is socially constructed.[24] Whatever passes for "knowledge" in a society, whether valid or invalid, helps to constitute the "reality" of that society. This socially constructed reality is not solely determined by objective facts. Rather, the conception of the rights of aboriginal peoples is determined by:

(1) The interpretations and ordering of perceptions of certain facts into paradigms; and

(2) The power and influence of the perceivers and interpreters of the data.[25]

Using this framework, the British perceived the title to land in North America as residing in the Crown. The only "rights" held by the aboriginal peoples were "personal and usufructuary, dependent on the goodwill of the

---

[23] Louis Lowy, *Introduction, in* PUBLIC POLICIES FOR AN AGING POPULATION 1 (Markson and Batra, eds., 1980).

[24] P. BERGER AND T. LUCKMANN, THE SOCIAL CONSTRUCTION OF REALITY (1966).

[25] *See* CAROLL L. ESTES AND MEREDITH MINKLER, READINGS IN THE POLITICAL ECONOMY OF AGING 25 (1984).

sovereign."[26] Through the actions of the judiciary and various legislatures, both of which were controlled by the British and/or influenced by the British notion of parliamentary supremacy, this "perception" became the imposed "reality" of the situation faced by aboriginal peoples. The "logical" extension of this principle allowed for the unilateral extinguishment and impairment of these rights at the will of the sovereign. Absent from this perspective is any recognition of the aboriginal peoples' notions of the same.

It is in the context of this unequal power relationship that many laws and policies continue to be made *for* and *about* aboriginal peoples in Canada. It is largely because judges, lawyers, and policymakers have little or no knowledge or appreciation of the culture and mores of aboriginal peoples that they can continue to ignore their rights. It will be argued throughout this chapter that it is this lack of appreciation of aboriginal differences that allows the Supreme Court of Canada to limit aboriginal rights in section 35 of the Constitution Act, 1982.

Professors Asch and Macklem have suggested a useful term to explain the way in which aboriginal rights have been conceptualized in the Canadian legal discourse. This idea is called the "contingent rights approach" and is described in this way:

> A contingent rights approach views the existence or non-existence of aboriginal rights to be contingent on the exercise of state authority. It therefore assumes the legitimacy of executive and legislative authority over First Nations and imagines rights as emanating from state recognition of a valid aboriginal claim to freedom from state interference. An aboriginal right to fish, for example, is dependent upon the state conferring such a right on the relevant aboriginal population by legislative or executive action.[27]

This concept encompasses the idea that from the outset the Canadian legal imagination accepts without question the "fact" that title to lands in Canada ultimately vests in the Crown and that aboriginal rights may only be exercised with the acquiesence of the State. There is no room in this scheme for the idea that, as the original inhabitants of Canada, the aboriginal peoples have a valid claim to this land. Nor is there any questioning of how, exactly, the Crown acquired title to the land.[28]

---

[26] St. Catherine's Milling and Lumber Co. v. The Queen, 14 App. Cas. 46 (J.C.P.C. 1888).

[27] Asch and Mecklem, *supra* note 16, at 495.

[28] While it is beyond the scope of this chapter to answer any of these questions, it should be noted that European notions of "discovery" and "conquest" and a host of other legal fictions were used to wrest sovereignty and title to land from aboriginal peoples. For a discussion of the rather curious misinterpretation of legal terms which allowed the Crown to gain sovereignty over the land and aboriginal peoples *see, e.g.,*

It may be argued that the contingent rights approach, and the subsequent law and policy that emanate from it, are largely a product of the cultural bias exhibited toward aboriginal peoples. The term "cultural bias" is meant to connote a wide range of negative attitudes held about aboriginal peoples. Such an idea encompasses the notion of bias based on difference in color, attitudes, and beliefs. As Professor Turpel notes, "the expression 'cultural difference' conjures up more than differences of appearance (colour). It allows us to consider profound differences in understanding of social and political life."[29]

The idea that European attitudes based on colonialism influence contemporary attitudes about aboriginal peoples has been canvassed by American Professor Robert A. Williams, Jr. He maintains that it is necessary to examine such attitudes in order to analyze in a detailed fashion the underlying assumptions that are held about native peoples. In a recent article, Williams examines the writings of Albert Memmi, a Tunisian Jew, who was subject to European racism and imperialism, particularly when he was a prisoner in a Nazi work camp

---

KENT MCNEIL, COMMON LAW ABORIGINAL TITLE (1989); BRIAN SLATTERY, THE LAND RIGHTS OF INDIGENOUS CANADIAN PEOPLES, AS AFFECTED BY THE CROWN'S ACQUISITION OF THEIR TERRITORIES (1979); and BRUCE CLARK, NATIVE LIBERTY, CROWN SOVEREIGNTY (1990).

It should be noted that recent judicial decisions have begun to question and reject the idea of "discovery" and other fictions, such as the land in Australia and Canada being *terra nullius*. See, for example, the decision of Mr. Justice Brennan in *Mabo v. Queensland* [1992] 107 A.L.R. 1, and the dissenting judgment of Mr. Justice Lambert in *Delgamuukw v. British Columbia* [1993] 5 W.W.R. 97.

It should also be noted that in both *Mabo* and *Delgamuukw,* the notion that all land rights vest in the Crown, free and clear of aboriginal interests and potential title to the land, has been rejected by the majority in both *Mabo v. Queensland* [1992] 107 A.L.R. 1, 35–36, as but one example, and in *Delgamuukw v. British Columbia* [1993] 5 W.W.R. 97, 125, and throughout the dissenting judgment of Mr. Justice Lambert. In both cases, it is recognized that the rights of the Crown and of subsequent grantees may be burdened by aboriginal title. This idea was recognized almost seventy-five years ago by the Judicial Committee of the Privy Council in *Amodu Tijani v. Southern Nigeria (Secretary)*, [1921] 2 A.C. 399. Viscount Haldane, on behalf of the Judicial Committee of the Privy Council, said:

> Their Lordships think that the learned Chief Justice in the judgment thus summarised, which virtually excludes the legal reality of the community usufruct, has failed to recognize the real character of the title to land occupied by a native community. That title, as they have pointed out, is prima facie based, not on such individual ownership as English law has made familiar, but on a communal usufructuary occupation, which may be so complete as to reduce any radical right in the Sovereign to one which only extends to comparatively limited rights of administrative interference.

Amodu Tijani v. Southern Nigeria (Secretary) [1921] 2 A.C. 399, 409–10

[29] Mary Ellen Turpel, *Aboriginal Peoples and the Canadian Charter: Interpretive Monopolies, Cultural Differences,* 6 C.H.R.Y.B. 3, 4–5 (1989–1990).

during World War Two.[30] Memmi wrote about his experiences as a colonized Jew in order to construct a "genealogy of European racist imperial discourse." Williams notes that this discourse is instructive in analyzing Euro-based attitudes toward native peoples in North America.

Memmi defines racism in this way: "Racism is the generalized and final assigning of values to real or imaginary differences, to the accuser's benefit and at his victim's expense, in order to justify the former's own privileges or aggression."[31] He then identifies four strategies employed by European-based cultures to maintain their power and superiority over non-European races:

(1) Stressing the *real* or *imaginary differences* between the racist and his victim.

(2) *Assigning values* to these differences, to the advantage of the racist and the detriment of his victim.

(3) Trying to make them *absolutes* by *generalizing* from them and claiming that they are final.

(4) *Justifying* any present or possible *aggression or privilege*.[32]

One can look to Canadian policy and judicial decisions to find examples of these strategies.

The predominant view of the Canadian government's attitude toward aboriginal peoples was stated by then-Prime Minister Pierre Trudeau: "We can't recognize aboriginal rights because no society can be built on historical 'might have beens.' "[33] This sort of political thinking was contained in the federal government's White Paper on Indian Policy, which was released in 1969:

---

[30] See Robert A. Williams, Jr., *The Contemporary Language of European Racism in the Narrative Traditions of Federal Indian Law*, 31 Ariz. L. Rev. 237, 261 262 (1989).

[31] Albert Memmi, *Attempt at a Definition, in* Dominated Man: Notes Toward a Portrait 185 (1968).

[32] *Id.* at 186 (emphasis added).

[33] Pierre Trudeau, *quoted in* William T. Badcock, Who Owns Canada? Aboriginal Title and Canadian Courts 5 (1976).

Professor Richard Falk has pointed out that this type of attitude, principally generated in the West from the Enlightenment mindset, is based

> [on] a belief in the sufficiency of human reason, especially as manifest in science and technology, and a vestigial distaste for any intrusion on the terrain of human rights by recourse to religion, tradition and emotion. The ideological foundations of this secularist approach are often implicit, generating a cult of modernization that has for several centuries occupied center-stage in the West. One result has been a dualism between progress and backwardness that has been damaging to non-modernizing peoples.

The policies proposed recognize the simple reality that the separate legal status of Indians and the policies which have flowed from it have kept the Indian people apart and behind other Canadians. . .

In the pages which follow, the Government has outlined a number of measures and a policy which it is convinced will offer another road for Indians, a road that would lead gradually away from the different status to full social, economic and political participation in Canadian life. . .

Indian people must be persuaded, must persuade themselves, that this path will lead them to a fuller and richer life.[34]

The thrust of the White Paper echoes the American policy of the late nineteenth century. Both sought to assimilate the Indians by eliminating the tribal unit. It should be noted, however, that the White Paper was never effectuated, due in large part to the protests that were made by aboriginal peoples against the plan.

This policy sums up in a neat package the nonsensical reasoning that has been applied to aboriginal peoples. The aboriginal peoples are conceived of as a "problem" in need of a solution. This view completely ignores the question of *why* the aboriginal peoples find themselves in such disarray. In other words, without taking into account the laws and policies that have largely caused these problems, any attempt to solve these problems is largely nonsense. For example, the placement of aboriginal peoples in residential schools, where attempts were made, often by using physical abuse, to remove the language and culture of those aboriginal peoples, must be taken into account when one examines the social problems in many aboriginal communities today. What is perhaps most telling about government policy toward aboriginal peoples, whether in the White Paper or in the Indian Act,[35] is the reflection of the paternalistic attitude adopted by the government. These policies reflect the government's belief that they know what is best for their aboriginal "children." The problem with the White Paper was that it sought, with the stroke of a pen, to eliminate the dependent status of aboriginal peoples as though hundreds of years of domination could suddenly be removed both politically and financially. This was to be done, of course,

---

RICHARD FALK, CULTURAL FOUNDATIONS FOR THE INTERNATIONAL PROTECTION OF HUMAN RIGHTS 1–2 (1989).

[34] *See* STATEMENT OF THE GOVERNMENT OF CANADA ON INDIAN POLICY (1969). It is interesting to note that Prime Minister Jean Chretien was the Minister of Indian and Northern Affairs at the time that the White Paper was released.

[35] *See* Indian Act, R.S.C., ch. 149 (1985) (Can.). It should be noted that Ron Irwin, the minister of Indian Affairs and Northern Development, proposed that the Indian Act be gradually eliminated.

without any discussion with aboriginal peoples on how best to organize their own communities.

The attitude that prevents aboriginal peoples from realizing their constitutional rights is explained by Tom Berger:

> We have pursued policies designed to suppress Native languages, Native culture and the Native economy. Our attitude has been founded on the belief that Native society is moribund, that their "culture" consists of crafts and carvings, dances and drinking—that it is at best a colourful reminder of the past, and that what we observe today is no more than a pathetic and diminishing remnant of what existed long ago.
>
> The Native people are seen as people locked into their past. Such an assumption becomes self-fulfilling. By not allowing them the means to deal with their present problems on their own terms, their culture may, in fact, tend to become degraded and static.[36]

While Berger paints in graphic detail a negative picture of how aboriginal peoples are often viewed by the Euro-based society, it should be noted that we do have a choice in how we, as a society—whether in policy making or in the courts—deal with aboriginal peoples.

Unfortunately, it is all too apparent that Canadian courts have largely chosen to concentrate on the differences between aboriginal peoples and the dominant, Euro-based culture. As but one example of this judicial attitude, one can cite the following passage from the decision of Chief Justice Davey of the British Columbia Court of Appeal in *Calder v. A.G.B.C.*:

> [The Nishga] were at the time of settlement a very primitive people with few of the institutions of civilized society. . . . I have no evidence to justify a conclusion that the aboriginal rights claimed by the successors of these primitive peoples are of a kind that it should be assumed the Crown recognized them when it acquired the mainland of British Columbia by occupation.[37]

---

[36] Tom Berger, *Native History, Native Claims and Self-Determination, in* INDIANS AND THE LAW 12 (Boldt and Long eds., 1982).

[37] Calder v. A.G.B.C. 13 D.L.R. 64 (B.C.C.A. 1970), 66. One could also cite the comments of Chief Justice McEachern throughout the trial decision in *Delgamuukw v. B.C.* 3 W.W.R. 97 (B.C.S.C 1991) . In particular, I note that the Chief Justice said that "[t]he plaintiff's ancestors had no written language, no horses or wheeled vehicles, slavery and starvation was not uncommon, wars with neighbouring peoples were common, and there is no doubt, to quote Hobbes, that *aboriginal life in the territory was, at best, 'nasty, brutish and short.' "* Delgamuukw v. B.C. 3 W.W.R. 97 (B.C.S.C. 1991), 126 (emphasis added). These comments raise the more general question of whether courts are particularly useful arenas for solving what are, in large measure, political disputes.

Beside the assertion of the inferiority of these "primitive" people, Chief Justice Davey's comments also reflect a more troubling aspect of Canadian judicial discourse in the field of aboriginal rights.

There is the assumption that aboriginal rights are dependent upon the exercise of Canadian sovereign authority. This type of thinking is carried forward in the *Sparrow* decision. The Supreme Court of Canada, demonstrating the contingent rights approach described earlier, "unquestioningly accepted that the British Crown, and thereafter Canada, obtained territorial sovereignty over the land mass that is now Canada by the mere fact of European settlement."[38] In its decision, the Supreme Court essentially precluded the possibility of unfettered aboriginal rights in the following passage:

Gary Yabsley raises this question in a recent essay:

> in times of constitutional transformation, courts are an inappropriate instrument for redefining the constitutional order. Indeed, the court is not created for such a purpose. Courts, by their nature, tend to be retrospective and conservative. Their function is to preserve, to the greatest degree possible, the foundation of the old order. When that order ceases to adequately respond to the stresses of modern society, this is a political problem involving society as a whole, and must be dealt with as such.

Gary R. Yabsley, *First Nations, Self-Government, and the Canadian Constitution, in* Constitutional Entrenchment of Aboriginal Self-Government 3–4 (1992).

[38] Asch and Macklem, *supra* note 16, at 500. The idea that sovereignty brought with it unencumbered title to land is simply incorrect. Allodial title is title not held of a superior lord. Land owned by the Crown is always held allodially because, in the common law, there is no lord superior to the Sovereign. Mr. Justice Lambert describes the operation of common law principles of property holding in these terms:

> "Fee simple" is a description of an estate. It means that the land is held, unconditionally and without restraint on alienation, either directly or indirectly from the holder of the radical, allodial or root title. The concept that the Crown in right of British Columbia could hold an estate in fee simple from the Crown Imperial is both incorrect constitutionally and incorrect in terms of estates in land. The Crown's title is paramount and not held of any superior lord who could impose restraints on it. The title remains an allodial title and its nature was not changed by the imposition of a statutory scheme, though for the purposes of administration of the statutory scheme the Crown may be said to hold land in fee simple. The concept in English common law that Sovereignty may carry with it the root title may not have been well understood, and the concept of fee simple title may have been much better understood in British Columbia at the relevant times. So it was provided by the Proclamation, and the Ordinance, that the Crown held the land "in fee simple" meaning without restraint on alienation, and with a power to make grants in accordance with the legislation, and the meaning that no one in British Columbia could in future acquire any rights in land in British Columbia without complying with the statute. The person to whom the Crown granted any interests in the land would be able to take the land in fee simple or in accordance with the terms of a subordinate interest.

Delgamuukw v. British Columbia 15 W.W.R. 97 (B.C.C.A. 1993), 307.

It is worth recalling that while British policy toward the native population was based on respect for their right to occupy their traditional lands, a proposition to which the Royal Proclamation of 1763 bears witness, *there was from the outset never any doubt that sovereignty and legislative power, and indeed the underlying title to such lands vested in the Crown.*[39]

This statement indicates the Court's belief that any assertion of aboriginal rights must be subsumed under the sovereign authority of the Canadian State.

So the idea that aboriginal rights must be limited is based in large part on the colonialism and paternalism that has operated from the time of first contact between aboriginal peoples and the Europeans. All along, there has been the idea that the aboriginal peoples must be controlled in order to achieve overall order in the territories. It is the idea of *order* that provides the basis for the *second* theory advanced in this chapter, that aboriginal peoples cannot be conceptualized as being capable of exercising unrestricted power over their own lives. It is to the topic of rights limitation in the Canadian legal discourse, and its connection in the aboriginal context to the rule of law, that this chapter now turns.

IV. RIGHTS LIMITATION IN THE CONTEXT OF ABORIGINAL RIGHTS

The following discussion will focus on the role of section 1 of the Charter as a limit on absolute rights and freedoms. One may hypothesize that the judicial analysis present in such cases as *Oakes*[40] and *Edward's Books*[41] has deeply influenced the Supreme Court of Canada in terms of rights analysis since the

---

The assertion of sovereignty does not give the Crown a free, clear and unencumbered title. In *Mabo v. Queensland*, Mr. Justice Brennan accepts that sovereignty and radical title are related, but he goes on to limit the impact of his finding with respect to radical title in the next paragraph:

The radical title is a postulate of the doctrine of tenure and a concomitant of sovereignty. As a sovereign enjoys supreme legal authority in and over a territory, the sovereign has power to prescribe what parcels of land what interests in those parcels should be enjoyed by others and what parcels of land should be kept as the sovereign's beneficial demesne.

But it is not a corollary of the Crown's acquisition of a radical title to land in an occupied territory that the Crown acquired absolute beneficial ownership of that land to the exclusion of the indigenous inhabitants.

Mabo v. Queensland 107 A.L.R. 1 (H.C.A. 1992), 33–34 (emphasis added).

[39] Sparrow v. The Queen 70 D.L.R.(4th) 385 (S.C.C. 1990), 404 (emphasis added).

[40] *See* R. v. Oakes [1986] 1 S.C.R. 103.

[41] *See* R. v. Edwards Books and Arts Ltd. [1986] S.C.R. 713.

coming into force of the Charter in 1982.[42] While section 52 of the Constitution Act, 1982 grants the constitution its legislative supremacy, the Charter is the constitution's lifeline. Without the inclusion of the Charter, the constitution would simply not have the same impact. And what the Charter is to the constitution, section 1 is to the Charter.

Section 1 is the essence of the Charter. It serves the dual purpose of existing as both the guarantee and potential source of limitation of Charter rights and freedoms. As Chief Justice Dickson explained in the *Oakes* decision:

> It is important to observe at the outset that s. 1 has two functions: first, it constitutionally guarantees the rights and freedoms set out in the provisions which follow; and, secondly, it states explicitly the exclusive justificatory criteria (outside of s. 33 of the Charter) against which limitations on those rights and freedoms must be measured.[43]

Section 1, however, does not reach beyond the confines of the Charter. Any other rights and freedoms guaranteed by the constitution are supposedly then not subject to limitation by section 1 or by any other provision. The absence of constitutionally entrenched limitations to aboriginal rights makes the question of whether aboriginal rights can ''supersede'' the Charter a legitimate one under these circumstances.

The *sui generis* nature of aboriginal rights, as they were so described in the *Guerin* decision,[44] makes their reconciliation with the values of a European-based democracy much more difficult than is the case with Charter rights. The coexistence of aboriginal and Charter rights within the framework of Canadian society necessitates the posing of fundamental questions about the interaction of the two divergent strands of rights.

Civil rights, by their very nature, can never be absolute in a democratic society. There are many competing rights and freedoms within a society. Inevitably, these often come into conflict with each other. Indeed, they can also conflict with the values of the society itself. When there is an attempt to protect civil rights by the State, this necessarily involves the making of compromises:

> When we speak of the protection of civil liberties in a society, we are really speaking about the nature of the compromises which that

---

[42] In this section, an attempt will be made to sketch out what is presumed to be the thinking of the Supreme Court of Canada with regard to the limitation of rights in general. It should be obvious by this point that I do not necessarily agree with the ''analysis'' in this section. The information is presented to allow the reader to understand how the Supreme Court of Canada generally approaches issues in relation to section 1 of the Charter.

[43] R. v. Oakes [1986] 1 S.C.R. 103, 224–25.

[44] *See* Guerin v. The Queen [1984] 2 S.C.R. 335.

society has made between civil libertarian values . . . and the competing values recognized by social and economic regulation, which limits individual freedom in pursuit of collective goals, such as public order and morality, safety, fair dealing, and a more equitable distribution of wealth.[45]

When there is a clash between competing rights or freedoms or between them and a greater social value, it is clear that some degree of abridgement of these rights must be enacted in order to preserve the harmony of the society as a whole. In a situation such as this, "it may become necessary to limit rights and freedoms in circumstances where their exercise would be inimical to the realization of collective goals of fundamental importance."[46] What is required in such a scenario is a compromise whereby the rights and freedoms of individuals are modified to the least possible extent to achieve a harmony between them and the greater goals of society.

The absence of an explicit constitutional provision that authorizes the limitation of aboriginal rights does not entail that aboriginal rights are not subject to limitation. The American Bill of Rights is a prime example of this. It is a guarantee of rights that does not provide any explicit authority to limit the rights guaranteed in it, but nevertheless has had, and continues to have, its enshrined rights limited by American courts when "necessary":

> American courts have had to struggle with [the problem of limiting rights] without the aid of a limitation clause like s. 1 in their Bill of Rights. They have, however, never accepted that the guaranteed rights were absolutes and have developed a variety of constitutional justifications, which have enabled them to uphold limitations on speech, and equality [for example], despite the unqualified language of the First and Fourteenth amendments.[47]

It is relatively easy to understand the functional place of Charter rights in Canadian society. Charter rights are based upon the values and mores of Canadian society. Subsequently, it is not difficult to impose limitations upon those rights when a higher social value necessitates such an imposition since the higher value originates from the same cultural and political biases that the Charter rights are derived from.

Under this argument, while aboriginal rights must also take a back seat to "higher" social values, such as conservation in an era of competition for ever more scarce resources, they cannot do so in the same manner as Charter rights.

---

[45] Peter Hogg, Canadian Constitutional Law 627–628 (1985).

[46] R. v. Oakes [1986] 1 S.C.R. 103, 225.

[47] Hogg, *supra* note 45, at 686.

The worldview of aboriginal peoples is vastly divergent from that held by European-based peoples. This fact makes it much more difficult to reconcile the existence of aboriginal rights within a European-based constitutional system such as that of Canada. The very nature of aboriginal rights, as collective rights, is at odds with the Charter, the latter being based, for the most part, on individual rights.

Presumably, the Supreme Court's decision in *Sparrow* is an attempt to reconcile the rights limitation idea above with the *sui generis* nature of aboriginal rights in the constitution. Thus, although the court essentially limits the potential scope of section 35, it has chosen to subject government to a higher standard than that found in the section 1 test in order to justify the infringement of aboriginal rights.

The section 35 test differs from the section 1 test in that if a valid legislative objective is found, the courts will take into account the "special trust relationship and the responsibility of the government vis-a-vis aboriginals."[48] This means that, as a result of this fiduciary relationship between the government and aboriginal peoples, there is an increased obligation on the part of government not to infringe upon or deny aboriginal peoples their aboriginal and treaty rights. Any legislation that adversely affects aboriginal and treaty rights must be fully justified. As the Court said in the *Sparrow* decision: "The government is required to bear the burden of justifying any legislation that has some negative effect on any aboriginal right protected under s. 35 (1)."[49]

Despite the influence of section 1 of the Charter, which may provide an explanation for *why* the Supreme Court has constructed a "reasonable limits" test on the exercise of the rights contained in section 35 of the Constitution Act, 1982, a troubling question remains: what is the basis behind the limitation of aboriginal rights in a particular case? In my opinion, it is precisely because the term *"sui generis"* is applied uncritically by courts that aboriginal rights can be limited to the point of extinction. In *Delgamuukw*, Mr. Justice Lambert defined the term *"sui generis"* in this way:

> The meaning of sui generis is that the thing so described is in a class or category of its own. *It does not mean that the class or category is in any respect inferior to or lesser than any other class or category.* The solution to further problems in relation to aboriginal title should be sought in a deeper understanding of the nature of the aboriginal title itself, in aboriginal terms, and not in attributing consequences under the common law on the basis that those consequences flow from a common law classification for tenure purposes of the aboriginal title or right as either proprietary or personal.[50]

---

[48] Sparrow v. The Queen 70 D.L.R. (4th) 385 (S.C.C. 1990), 413.

[49] *Id.* at 410.

[50] Delgamuukw v. British Columbia [1993] 5 W.W.R. 97, 282 (emphasis added).

Yet, despite the discussion in *Sparrow* concerning the seriousness of aboriginal rights, these rights have been defined in an extremely narrow way in judicial decisions thus far. In the next section of this chapter, discussion turns to why rights are often defined narrowly.

V. COMPELLING GOVERNMENT INTEREST AND ATTENUATION

Professor Stephen Gottlieb has argued that much of the commentary on constitutional rights and liberties has centered on the sources of or justification for such rights. He maintains that scholars have focused particularly upon the judicial recognition of fundamental rights which have been developed from open-ended clauses of the American constitution. He points out that "surprisingly little" writing has looked at the "flip-side" of these rights; that is, the "interests asserted by the government in support of restricting an individual's constitutional rights."[51] He calls this idea "compelling government interests."

Professor Gottlieb notes that many rights have been "found" in the American constitution. A right to privacy, for example, was found in the due process clause of the Fourteenth Amendment by the U.S. Supreme Court in *Griswold v. Connecticut*.[52] While many commentators have criticized this supposedly "non-constitutionally based" creation of rights, there has been relatively less criticism of the "creation" of tests by courts to allow government to infringe rights. In this regard, Professor Gottlieb says:

> . . . compelling interests lack a strong textual foundation in the Constitution: at no point does the Constitution mandate or define compelling interests, or establish their weight or supremacy. Like fundamental rights, some governmental interests can be justified on the basis of penumbras surrounding constitutional rights. Others may be justified as among the purposes for which particular government powers were authorized.[53]

Thus, the "compelling government interest" test is, in reality, a fiction created by the courts to rationalize restrictions placed on the exercise of rights by

---

[51] Stephen E. Gottlieb, *Compelling Government Interests: An Essential But Unanalyzed Term in Constitutional Adjudication*, 68 B.U. L. Rev. 917 (1988). Professor Gottlieb correctly points out that "governmental" interests are misnamed, because governmental interests are either the interests of the public collectively or are invalid. *See id.* at 919 n.11. Thus, when the term " government[al]" is used in the literature surrounding rights analysis, or in any type of writing, it is important to keep in mind that this term assumes that some notion of the "public interest" is chosen over another. In the context of aboriginal rights, one must always consider the issue of racism, both past and present, when something is done by or in the name of government or in the supposed "public interest."

[52] *See* Griswold v. Connecticut, 381 U.S. 479, 483 (1965).

[53] *See* Gottlieb, *supra* note 51, at 919.

government, while preventing government from overstepping its bounds. However, because the test is really a statement rather than a precise set of guidelines, the line at which government can no longer act is one that is constantly evolving.

The "compelling government interest" test was developed in 1938 by the U.S. Supreme Court in a famous footnote within the *United States v. Carolene Prods. Co.* decision.[54] Professor Gottlieb describes the creation and evolution of the test in this way:

> The [U.S. Supreme] Court recognized in 1938 that it would have to be less deferential [to legislatures] in cases raising claims based on clear textual rights, abuse of the democratic system, and certain minority rights. To practice judicial activism in those areas, the Court could not allow protected rights to give way to any assertion of legislative powers. The Court's solution was to subject the means and purposes of legislative or administrative action to careful scrutiny: a legislative or administrative enactment impinging on the critical rights defined in *Carolene Products* could be sustained only where a compelling government purpose was furthered by the least restrictive available means. [*Shelton v. Tucker*, 364 U. S. 479, 488 (1960)]. As utilized by the Warren Court, the compelling interest test was an almost automatic tool for overturning legislation.[55]

If the idea of compelling interest applies in *Sparrow*, is it included because the limitation of rights is assumed to be necessary by the Supreme Court of Canada in *all* cases, or is the potentially unrestricted nature of aboriginal rights in section 35 what is so troubling to the Court?[56] What is disturbing about the creation of a reasonable limits test in *Sparrow*, if it is in some way connected to the idea of the balancing of rights and compelling government interest, is that, as noted earlier, the test is read in by the Court before any action has been taken by aboriginal peoples under section 35.

---

[54] *See* United States v. Carolene Prods. Co., 304 U.S. 144, 152 n.4 (1938).

[55] Gottlieb, *supra* note 51, at 923.

[56] It should be noted that, in its decision in Sparrow, the Supreme Court of Canada rejected the "public interest" rationale for limiting aboriginal rights:

> The Court of Appeal below held, at page 96, that regulations could be valid if reasonably justified as "necessary for the proper management and conservation of the resource *or in the public interest.*" We find the "public interest" justification to be so vague as to provide no meaningful guidance and so broad as to be unworkable as a test for the justification of a limitation on constitutional rights.

Sparrow v. The Queen 70 D.L.R. (4th) 385 (S.C.C. 1990), 412 (emphasis added).

Despite this passage, one is left to wonder why, exactly, the Court still chose to limit aboriginal rights in *Sparrow*.

In other words, no First Nation has yet attempted to exercise a broad right of self-government based on section 35 and run into conflict with some other element of Canadian society. Most exercises of self-government are done either under the Indian Act, or in small increments under section 35. In British Columbia, following the decision of the Court of Appeal in *Delgamuukw v. British Columbia*, the idea of inherent rights of self-government as *contingent* rights dependent on State authority has been approved by the majority.[57]

However, the Court has essentially foreclosed the possibility of attempting to work out the meaning of section 35 without state or legal interference. Rather than assuming that section 35 contains rights which, when exercised by aboriginal peoples, may serve to improve their lives without infringing on the rights of others, the Court has assumed the opposite, *ab initio*: namely, that section 35 is a source of potentially conflicting rights with Euro-Canadian society which must be limited before any trouble develops.[58] All of this is done under the laudable umbrella of ''conservation concerns.'' It should be noted that in the context of *Sparrow*, it was *assumed* that conservation concerns were at stake. There was an absence of any evidence of such a concern at trial, or in the appellate decisions in the case. In some instances, there will be a conflict over scarce resources, while in other cases, there will not be any conflict.

Unfortunately, the *Sparrow* ''test'' subjects every First Nation to prove its rights, at great time and expense, should the matter go to court. Each potential right under section 35 must go through a trial and appeals all the way to the Supreme Court of Canada each and every time a right is asserted. Each of these cases draws a number of intervenors in support and in opposition, where the focus of the case often shifts away from the particular factual circumstances of a First Nation to a free-ranging discussion on the place of First Nations in Canadian society, their histories, etc. While the huge documentary record and

---

[57] *See* Delgamuukw v. British Columbia [1993] 5 W.W.R. 97. *See also* decision of the Supreme Court of Canada in R. v. Gardner; R. v. Jones, 138 D.L.R. (4th) 204 (S.C.C. 1996) , where the Court rejected the idea that there are broad rights of self-government in section 35 of the Constitution Act, 1982. Instead the Court said that. like aboriginal rights, rights of self-government must be proved according to the test in *Van der Peet, supra* note 13.

[58] The Supreme Court makes this point:

The presence of numerous intervenors representing commercial fishing interests, and the suggestion on the facts that the net length restriction is at least in part related to the probable commercial use of fish caught under the Musqueam food fishing licence, indicate the possibility of conflict between aboriginal fishing and the competitive commercial fishery with respect to economically valuable fish such as salmon. We recognize the existence of this conflict and the probability of its intensification as fish availability drops, demand rises and tensions increase.

Sparrow v. The Queen 70 D.L.R. (4th) 385 (S. C. C. 1990), 403.

legal arguments may be warranted in some of these cases, surely it is not a requirement of virtually every case that this scenario be followed.

In his paper, Professor Gottlieb also describes the dangers inherent in what may be termed "attenuation."[59] This refers to the idea that when the government acts to protect certain constitutionally entrenched rights, such as the protection of national security, other rights may be infringed or ignored entirely in the name of the greater public good. In an extreme example, the protection of national security was used as one of the justifications for U.S. internment of Japanese-Americans.[60]

In Canada, the War Measures Act was invoked during the October Crisis in 1970.[61] The civil liberties of Canadian citizens in Quebec were suspended in the name of "national security." The term "national security" is quite vague and amorphous. It allows the government, if the courts acquiesce, to limit or suspend other civil rights for the "greater public good." Thus, even though it is presumed that the *rule of law* may protect citizens from unjustified government action, the idea of attenuation presents a far more covert danger. Certain broad and vaguely worded government powers found in the constitution, or even in legislation, may serve as a basis upon which government may infringe other rights which are supposed to be constitutionally protected.

VI. THE RULE OF LAW IN CANADIAN CONSTITUTIONAL THOUGHT

A third hypothesis that may explain why the Supreme Court of Canada has chosen to limit section 35 rights concerns the Court's possible adherence to the *rule of law*. In this section, the history of the rule of law will be examined briefly, and some of the problems inherent in the principle will be set out. The decision of the Supreme Court of Canada in *Re Manitoba Language Rights*[62] will then be used to focus discussion on how Canadian courts have attempted to apply the rule of law. The idea is that this principle might have some influence on the way in which the Court decided the *Sparrow* case.

The rule of law has been described by Professors Hutchinson and Monahan in this way: "The Rule of Law's central core comprises the enduring values of regularity and restraint, embodied in the slogan of 'a government of laws, not men.' Its very generality is the reason for its durability and contestability."[63] It is the amorphous character of the term which may allow the Supreme Court of

---

[59] *See* Gottlieb, *supra* note 51.

[60] *See, e.g.,* Hirbayashi v. United States, 320 U.S. 81 (1943).

[61] *See* War Measures Act, R.S.C. 1970, c. w—2 (Can.).

[62] *See* Re Manitoba Language Rights [1985] 1 S.C.R. 721.

[63] Allan C. Hutchinson and Patrick Monahan, *Introduction,* in THE RULE OF LAW: IDEAL OR IDEOLOGY ix (Allan C. Hutchinson and Patrick Monahan, eds.).

Canada in *Sparrow* to set limits on section 35 rights without necessarily considering the consequences of such actions.

The case of *Entick v. Carrington*[64] is often relied on as one of the earliest judicial expressions of the rule of law. In this case, the English government attempted to act under the doctrine of ''State necessity,'' rather than under any statute or rule of common law. The House of Lords denied the existence of this doctrine and held that the government had to act under some rule of law, found either in statute or in the common law. One may also cite *Dr. Bonham's Case*[65] for early judicial recognition of the existence of the rule of law. In this case, Chief Justice Coke wrote:

> . . . it appears in our books, that in many cases, the common law will control Acts of Parliament, and sometimes adjudge them to be utterly void: for when an Act of Parliament is against common right and reason, or repugnant, or impossible to be performed, the common law will controul it, and adjudge such acts to be void.[66]

The rule of law was developed out of the chaos that existed in seventeenth-century England. Both parliamentary supremacy and the rule of law were seen as safeguards or limits on the exercise of arbitrary power by the Crown.

Although it is possible to understand why the rule of law may have emerged as a limitation on the exercise of power by the Crown and Parliament, it is more difficult to see why the principle has been relied on as though it exists in a statute or in the common law as some sort of positive guide to behavior. Professor Hayek has provided a useful explanation for this phenomenon: ''It is a deeply ingrained tendency of the human mind that whenever it discovers an orderly pattern, it believes that this must have been designed by a mind like itself and assumes that there can be no order without such conscious design.''[67] Professor Hayek describes the rule of law as a ''meta-legal'' principle. He continues his discussion with the following comments about the principle:

> Since the Rule of Law means that the government must never coerce an individual except in enforcement of a rule which has been announced beforehand and from which the particular act of coercion necessarily follows, it is of course a limitation upon the powers of all government and especially a limitation upon legislation.

> But the ultimate legislator can never by law limit his own powers, because he can also abrogate any law he has made. *The Rule of Law,*

---

[64] *See* Entick v. Carrington, 19 St. Tr. 1030 (K.B. 1765)

[65] *See* Dr. Bonham's Case, 77 Eng. Rep. 652 (H.L. 1607)

[66] *Id.* at 652.

[67] F.A. HAYEK, THE POLITICAL IDEAL OF THE RULE OF LAW 30 (1955).

is therefore, not a rule of the law but a rule about the law, a meta-legal doctrine, or a political ideal. It will be effective only in so far as a legislator feels himself bound to abide by it. In a democracy this means in effect that whether the Rule of Law will be obeyed or not will depend on whether it is accepted by public opinion, that is, in effect, on whether it is part of the sense of justice prevailing in the community.[68]

Inherent in this discussion is the idea that the rule of law really refers to the sense that some sort of order exists (or should exist) in a particular sociolegal system. Many writers describe this aspect of the doctrine, rather than attempt to define what, exactly, the rule of law means.

Professor Hayek argues that a primary goal of the rule of law is that *"the individual should be able to plan his own affairs successfully; he should be in a position to predict from the circumstances which he can be presumed to know or foresee what he will be allowed to do and what not."*[69] In this sense, one may presume that Professor Hayek refers to the rule of law as a mechanism by which order and certainty are established. The rule of law means that the legal rules of a system should be written down or made known in some other way so that the individual may plan his or her affairs.

The possible order and certainty that may exist in the name of the rule of law by having a constitution with clearly delineated rights and freedoms is disturbed in *Sparrow*. While the task of determining what rights are to be found in section 35 is certainly a difficult one, the decision in *Sparrow* has made such a task much more difficult because we now have to question the whole notion of whether section 35 contains any meaningful rights at all that are beyond the reach of government. The order and certainty aspects of the rule of law are largely thrown out by the Supreme Court of Canada.

It is the refusal by the Court to state the premise under which it chooses to limit rights in *Sparrow* that makes the task of interpreting the limitation in section 35 so difficult. If the rule of law is to serve as a plausible explanation for why rights are limited in *Sparrow*, we have to confront yet another problem inherent in the doctrine. This is the recognition that the rule of law has many different meanings.

At least two distinct meanings of the concept can be set out, although many other meanings can be discerned from the two broad statements in the following passage:

The Rule of Law originally had two quite distinct meanings. It referred either to an entire way of life, or merely to several specific public

---

[68] *Id.* at 33 (emphasis added).

[69] *Id.* at 44 (emphasis added).

institutions. The first of the models can be attributed to Aristotle, who presented the Rule of Law as nothing less than the rule of reason. The second version sees the Rule of Law as those institutional restraints that prevent governmental agents from oppressing the rest of society.[70]

In the first case, the rule of law refers to an overall notion of "justice and fairness." In the second, it refers to the Diceyan notion of controls on government, such as those contained in administrative law.[71] When speaking about the rule of law in the first sense, one must keep in mind the potential for an ethnocentric application of such terms as "justice and fairness." While the two conceptions of the rule of law certainly overlap, in the first formulation, we are concerned with how to achieve an overall social order. The roots of this idea are in the writings of Hobbes and others who were concerned with achieving order out of the chaos that existed around them. The second principle is a more narrow one: it essentially dictates that there must be specific laws and rules to govern behavior. Thus, the idea of no search without a warrant in *Entick v. Carrington* would come under this heading.

One writer has commented on some of the more troubling aspects of Dicey's writings about the rule of law:

> The most influential restatement of the Rule of Law since the 18th century has been Dicey's unfortunate outburst of Anglo-Saxon parochialism. In his version the Rule of Law was both traditionalized and formalized. . . . He began by finding the Rule of Law inherent in the remote English past, in the depth of the early middle ages. Its validity

---

[70] Judith N. Shklar, *Political Theory and The Rule of Law, in* THE RULE OF LAW: IDEAL OR IDEOLOGY, *supra* note 63, at 1.

[71] Dicey set out the following definition of the rule of law, one which is thought to be *the* classic definition of the term:

> We mean, in the first place, that no man is punishable or can be lawfully made to suffer in body or goods except for a distinct breach of law established in the ordinary legal manner before the ordinary Courts of the land.

> We mean in the second place, when we speak of the "rule of law" as a characteristic of our country, not only that with us no man is above the law, but (what is a different thing) that here every man, whatever be his rank or condition, is subject to the ordinary law of the realm, and amenable to the jurisdiction of the ordinary tribunals.

> There remains yet a third and a different sense in which the "rule of law" or the predominance of the legal spirit may be described as a special attribute of English institutions. We may say that the constitution is pervaded by the rule of law on the ground that the general principles of the constitution . . . are with us the result of judicial decisions determining the rights of private persons in particular cases brought before the Courts.

A.V. DICEY, THE LAW OF THE CONSTITUTION 172, 177–178, 208 (1885).

> rested on its antiquity, on its having grown . . . but the political arrangements of the English constitution did concern him. They were part of the Rule of Law. The Rule of Law was both trivialized as the peculiar patrimony of one and only one national order, and formalized by the insistence that only one set of inherited procedures and court practices could sustain it. Not the structure or purposes of judicial rigour, but its forms became significant for freedom.[72]

The rule of law, while universal in its appeal, does not have a universal meaning. The aboriginal people's notion of justice and fairness, for example, may be different from the prevailing Euro-Canadian view.

There are several criticisms that must be made about Dicey's formulation of the rule of law. As noted earlier, the rule of law is essentially a liberal principle that maintains that individuals should be free to conduct their lives with as few constraints as possible and that they should know the rules under which they may conduct their lives. Thus, the rule of law dictates that the laws in a given system should be "predictable, nonretroactive, and equally applicable to all citizens."[73] If this is an accurate description of the workings of the rule of law, then certain problems arise from it. Particularly from the point of view of aboriginal peoples, it can be argued that "the fixed quality of law that creates the possibility of a Rule of Law also creates the possibility that the law will be fixed in an unjust manner."[74]

Another problem that one encounters in trying to attach meaning to the rule of law concerns the very malleability of the term:

> At times, the Rule of Law has been used to legitimize and galvanize a challenge to entrenched power; at others, the ruling elite has relied upon it to sanction its power and resistance to would-be usurpers. Like any ideal, it only exists in the political consciousness and conscience. Indeed, its ideological attraction and political durability are largely attributable to its historical plasticity, the facility to accommodate itself to changing governmental situations and political forces. In short, it is the will-o'-the-wisp of constitutional history.[75]

---

[72] Shklar, *supra* note 70, at 5–6.

[73] J.M. Balkin, *The Rule of Law as a Source of Constitutional Change*, 6 CONSTITUTIONAL COMMENTARY 21 (1989).

[74] *Id.* at 21. The author goes on to argue, that the Rule of Law requires not only that *some* law be applied, but the additional requirement that "a statement of reasons for decisions [be given] to demonstrate the connection between the decision and the existing body of law." *Id.* at 22. In *Sparrow*, the Supreme Court of Canada does not give a very detailed reason of why it has placed a reasonable limits test on section 35 rights.

[75] Allan C. Hutchinson and Patrick Monahan, *Democracy and the Rule of Law*, in THE RULE OF LAW: IDEAL OR IDEOLOGY, *supra* note 63, at 99.

According to this description, the rule of law is really an *ideal* rather than a specific set of positive legal principles.[76] As a result, it can be used to effect a variety of very different outcomes, depending on the motive(s) of the person using it.[77]

If the Supreme Court has the rule of law in mind in *Sparrow*, it seems that the term is being used as a synonym for maintaining the status quo. This idea operates in two ways. In the *first* sense, the Court may feel bound by such traditional doctrinal aspects of constitutional law as parliamentary supremacy and the rule of law as representing specific mechanisms by which the fabric of Canadian constitutional law operates (and should operate). These ideals may be held by the Court even though both terms can convey a number of different meanings.

The term *status quo* may also be used in a *second* way to indicate that the Court may approve of the existing constitutional order as being composed of two different levels of government—federal and provincial—as repositories for power in Canada. The notion that section 35 may introduce a new actor into the scene is viewed as a conflict with the "law and order" notion of the rule of law. This was the view taken by a majority of the British Columbia Court of Appeal in *Delgamuukw*.[78]

The following passage sets out some of the dangers that exist in relying so heavily on Dicey's formulation of the Rule of Law. The passage should be read with the particular question in mind of how the criticism set out by the writer would apply to aboriginal peoples:

> The danger with Dicey's conflation of nineteenth-century constitutional arrangements and *the* rule of law is that, if we freeze the latter notion into the institutional background of a particular period, we abandon its larger flavour. If it then becomes as *description* the ruling paradigm for discussing constitutionality and the rule of law, it can only

---

[76] Professor Heuston points out that Dicey described his principle as "the Rule of Law," which gave the impression that it was a legal principle. Heuston argues that "it is in truth only a constitutional principle based upon the practice of liberal democracies of the Western world." R.V. HEUSTON, ESSAYS IN CONSTITUTIONAL LAW 40–41 (1964). The problem alluded to by Heuston is that many theorists and, indeed, the Supreme Court of Canada, treat Dicey's three formulations of the "Rule of Law" as a set of immutable legal principles.

[77] Sir Ivor Jennings has commented at length about the imprecise nature of the rule of law. He points out that the term can stand for public order, the notion of equality, and even the notion of liberty. In his estimation, the rule of law is essentially an imprecise attitude built on the idea of liberal and democratic principles, which are also imprecise terms. *See* SIR IVOR JENNINGS, THE LAW AND THE CONSTITUTION 42–59 (1952).

[78] *See* Delgamuukw v. British Columbia [1993] 5 W.W.R. 97.

work in opposition to an effective analysis of contemporary constitutional conditions by suppressing the fact that there are underlying propositions and beliefs that inform the idea itself. The Diceyan concept is the archetype of what modern American writers have styled 'legal formalism,' the main danger of which is to disguise if not suppress 'the inevitably political and redistributive functions of law.'[79]

This passage points out the danger that the rule of law may be accepted as though it expresses a clear set of principles, rather than the more realistic idea that the concept expresses some sort of ideal which is held by certain segments of the population.

One can discern much in the thought process of the Supreme Court of Canada from its definition and description of the rule of law in *Re Manitoba Langauge Rights*. In this case, the Supreme Court of Canada relied on the rule of law to give temporary effect to a number of unilingual acts passed by the Manitoba Legislature between 1890 and 1985, although such acts were declared unconstitutional.[80] In this section, the *Manitoba* case will be used to focus discussion on the operation and limitations inherent in the rule of law.

It is important to delve into the mindset of the Supreme Court in the *Manitoba* case in order to understand the way in which it applied the rule of law and how this thinking permeates other decisions of the Court. The essential problem is that the Court seems to treat the rule of law as a set of positive legal principles that are comprehensible, clear, and provide a particular meaning that can be followed in all legal reasoning. In my opinion, the meaning of the rule of law is far from clear and plain and it is often dependent on the result that a particular court wishes to achieve.

---

[79] IAN HARDEN AND NORMAN LEWIS, THE NOBLE LIE: THE BRITISH CONSTITUTION AND THE RULE OF LAW 4 (1986).

Professor Weinrib has commented along the same lines:

The paradox of the Rule of Law is that it simultaneously states both an ideal and an apparent falsehood. As an ideal, the Rule of Law implies a contrast to the rule of men and evokes an image of stability, impersonality, and lack of arbitrariness. But as long as men have experienced the demands of law, they have also experienced in law the demands of other men. Law as we know it is neither spontaneous nor self-executing nor immune to change: its creation, administration, and interpretation are invariably acts of human agency and are exposed to all the mischief which human action can produce. If law inescapably implies the rule of some men over others, can a notion of the Rule of Law with its implicit contrast to the rule of men be in any sense intelligible or coherent?

Ernest J. Weinrib, *The Intelligibility of The Rule of Law, in* THE RULE OF LAW: IDEAL OR IDEOLOGY, *supra* note 63, at 59.

[80] *See* Re Manitoba Language Rights [1985] 1 S.C.R. 721.

This case gives us a unique opportunity to examine the definitions relied on by the Court in explaining the rule of law, as well as the particular manner in which the principle was used in this case. By examining the way in which the concept was used in the *Manitoba* case, it is possible to formulate an opinion as to the extent to which the Court was influenced to carry the idea of *order* forward in the *Sparrow* decision.

As noted earlier, the problem facing the Supreme Court of Canada in *Manitoba* concerned the consequences that would follow from declaring that almost all of the legislation passed by the Manitoba Legislature was unconstitutional and of no force and effect. The Manitoba Legislature was under a legal obligation to pass legislation in Canada's two official languages—English and French. Between 1890 and 1985, however, legislation was passed and disseminated in English only.

This practice was declared unconstitutional by the Supreme Court of Canada,[81] which was now faced with the dilemma of how to remedy the problem. The most direct outcome, if the decision were taken literally, was that all legislation passed in English only after 1890 was null and void. Thus, Manitoba would have no statutory law at all. The Court feared that this would lead to legal chaos and it also reasoned that this would undermine ''the principle of the rule of law.''[82]

The Supreme Court fashioned a compromise by giving temporary effect to the otherwise unconstitutional laws until Manitoba had a reasonable amount of time to draft and pass equivalent laws in French. The Court began its discussion or justification of this compromise by describing the rule of law in the following terms:

> In the present case, declaring the Acts of the Legislature of Manitoba invalid and of no force or effect would, without more, undermine the principle of the rule of law. The rule of law, a fundamental principle of our Constitution, must mean at least two things. First, that the law is supreme over officials of the government as well as private individuals, and thereby preclusive of their influence of arbitrary power.

> Second, the rule of law requires the creation and maintenance of an actual order of positive laws which preserves and embodies the more general principle of normative order.[83]

The definitions used by the Court are instructive.

---

[81] *Id.*

[82] *Id.*

[83] *See* Re Manitoba Language Rights [1985] 1 S.C.R. 721, 748–749.

We can see the Diceyan influence in the first definition set out by the Court, while in the second there is a combination of Diceyan thinking mixed in with the Hobbesian notion of preserving social order. The Court quoted from Wade and Phillips' work on constitutional law as follows:

> ... the rule of law expresses a preference for law and order within a community rather than anarchy, warfare and constant strife. In this sense, the rule of law is a philosophical view of society which in the Western tradition is linked with basic democratic notions.[84]

These statements may help us to discern some of the Court's thinking in *Sparrow*.

Based on the Wade and Phillips definition, the rule of law is a Western political/philosophical notion which is required to maintain order out of potential chaos. The assumption implicit in this view, if it is extended to explain the Court's reasoning in *Sparrow*, is that somehow an undiluted section 35 would give too much power to aboriginal peoples which, in turn, might lead to some sort of chaos.

It is interesting that Wade and Phillips' term, "democratic notions," is understood in a narrow fashion. Apparently, aboriginal notions of self-government as being potentially contained within section 35 might be seen as too chaotic for Euro-Canadian sensibilities. Or, as noted earlier, Canadian courts may feel that there is no room in the Canadian legal imagination for another layer of government.

In *Manitoba*, the Supreme Court quoted from the work of Dr. Raz: "... the 'rule of law' means literally what it says: the rule of law ... [has]two aspects: (1) that people should be ruled by the law and obey it, and (2) that the law should be such that people will be able to be guided by it."[85] The Supreme Court concluded that "the rule of law simply cannot be fulfilled in a province that has no positive law."[86] What is troubling about the Court's reasoning is that it is difficult to reconcile the call for clarity leading to observance of the law as called for in *Manitoba* with the introduction of a "reasonable limits" test in *Sparrow*.

In other words, if the goal of the rule of law is to give certainty to the law, then the placement of section 35 beyond the reach of sections 1 and 33 of the Charter, coupled with the notion of parliamentary supremacy—that the federal and provincial governments have *chosen* to place section 35 outside the Charter—should intuitively protect section 35 rights from being emasculated. However, as we have seen, the rule of law is not the concrete term that the Supreme

---

[84] *Id.* at 748–49, (*quoting* E.S.C. WADE AND G.G. PHILLIPS, CONSTITUTIONAL AND ADMINISTRATIVE LAW 89 (1977)).

[85] *Id.* at 750 (*quoting* J. RAZ, THE AUTHORITY OF LAW 212–213 (1979)).

[86] *Id.*

Court would like to make it. It is inherently flexible and malleable and it is often used to unquestioningly protect the status quo.

VII. CONCLUSION

The same Court that can use the rule of law to achieve "order" in *Manitoba* can also act to create disorder in *Sparrow* through its analysis of section 35. The Supreme Court makes the statement in *Manitoba* that the preamble to the Constitution Act, 1982 refers to the rule of law, and the Court goes on to say that the rule of law has "always been understood as the very basis of the English Constitution characterizing the political institutions of England from the time of the Norman Conquest."[87] This rather limited discussion of the rule of law is troubling.

We are concerned with the constitution of *Canada,* not simply with influential, but confusing, English terms. As Professor Lyon has pointed out, there is more to Canadian constitutional decision making than the mere borrowing and implementation of English legal terms.[88] What is objectionable, then, is not that the Court invokes the rule of law in *Manitoba*, but rather that it assumes that the term has a particular, neutral meaning which can be objectively determined and which can be categorically applied in a particular case. Given the different criticisms of this term in the literature, it is difficult to accept the Court's rather limited discussion of the meaning of the rule of law.

In *Sparrow*, the Supreme Court of Canada operates with many sleights of hand to limit section 35 rights. Under the guise of paternalism, the rule of law is turned on its head. The clear intention of Parliament and the provincial legislatures to place section 35 beyond the limits and confines of section 1 of the Charter is completely ignored.

The Supreme Court says that it is using a generous, liberal, and purposive interpretation in *Sparrow* to analyze section 35. The problem is that the decision contains seeds of the very paternalism that has been faced by aboriginal peoples since the "discovery" of North America by the Europeans. The historical analysis that the Court describes is actually used to reaffirm the controlled, *"done to,"* status of aboriginal peoples through the limitation of their rights in section 35.

When we try to forecast the Supreme Court's behavior in future cases, such as we are attempting to do in the context of *Sparrow*, we are faced with two uncertainties. The *first* has to do with the way in which the Court will choose to invoke an idea, such as the rule of law, and the sort of assumptions upon which it will act. The *second* problem has to do with the more covert problem at issue in *Manitoba*: the issue of maintaining social order. What aspect of

---

[87] *Id.*

[88] *See* Noel Lyon, *The Central Fallacy of Canadian Constitutional Law,* 22 McGILL L.J. 40 (1976).

"social order" is being maintained in *Sparrow*, given the Court's discussion of the term in *Manitoba*?

Returning to the *Sparrow* case, what we must keep in mind is that the limitation of section 35 rights was done without any real explanation by the Supreme Court of Canada. While one should not jump to the conclusion that some sort of parallel can be drawn between the reasoning in *Sparrow* and that of other, more odious rights limitation cases, one should also not treat the Supreme Court of Canada's actions lightly.

The federal and provincial legislatures, by enacting the Constitution Act, 1982, have chosen to place section 35 outside the section 1 test in the Charter, and beyond the section 33 override. While such rights may be limited, it is at least incumbent on the highest court in the land to provide some explanation and guidance, beyond crass paternalistic language, as to why such rights might be limited.

As this chapter demonstrates, there are a number of plausible hypotheses, based on other rights limitation cases, for why the Court has felt compelled to act as it has in *Sparrow*. Whether the court is acting because it feels compelled to "balance" interests which would undoubtedly arise from a conflict between section 35 rights and other Constitutional rights, or because of a notion that aboriginal peoples cannot be trusted with absolute rights in section 35 and the possible rights that might arise thereunder, remains open to speculation.

CHAPTER 14

TWO STEPS FORWARD AND ONE STEP BACK: THE FRUSTRATING PACE OF BUILDING A NEW ABORIGINAL–CROWN RELATIONSHIP IN CANADA

Bradford W. Morse

I. INTRODUCTION

Indigenous peoples occupied what is now called Canada for thousands of years. They consisted of dozens of separate, discrete nations with their own governments, legal systems, religions, cultures, languages, ways of life, and territories. The Inuit (still often called by the pejorative label of "Eskimos" in the United States) lived in many small villages from northeastern Quebec and Labrador across the Arctic and sub-Arctic region to Alaska, as well as in Greenland and Siberia. To their immediate south were many other nations sharing a single race who acquired from Europeans the mistaken common description of "Indians," but otherwise were as distinct from each other as were individual nations in other regions of the world. The descendants of these two main groups—the Indian and Inuit peoples—comprise the original population of Canada. A third distinct group, known as the Métis, developed after contact with Europeans and reflect a unique merger of Indian, French, and British cultures, languages, and lifestyles, through intermarriage and intercultural adaptation, so as to become ultimately a distinct people. The Indian, Inuit, and Métis peoples, now collectively described as the Aboriginal peoples of Canada,[1] welcomed the visitors from across the Atlantic, taught them how to survive and flourish in what was to them a foreign land, and then were steadily dispossessed of their homelands, subjugated under colonial law, and nearly exterminated.[2]

---

[1] The term "Aboriginal peoples" will generally be used herein, except where the context requires a reference to a specific group.

[2] Estimates of the Aboriginal population in Canada at the time of contact range from 500,000 to three million people. The 1871 census estimated the Aboriginal population as having plummeted to 102,000 because of introduced diseases, armed conflict, starvation, and relocation. CANADA, REPORT OF THE ROYAL COMMISSION ON ABORIGINAL PEOPLES, LOOKING FORWARD, LOOKING BACK, VOL. 1 (1996) at 13.

The Aboriginal population in Canada is now undergoing a renascence. It is growing rapidly in numbers, economic influence, and political importance. At the same time, Aboriginal peoples face monumental crises, as all but three of their languages are on the brink of disappearance, traditional cultural practices are endangered, family violence and disintegration is widespread, unemployment rates are astronomically high, and many of their territories are threatened by large-scale natural resource industries. Nothing is static, but it is clear that the status quo cannot and should not be sustained.

The situation in Canada is typified by diversity; some of the communities achieve major successes while others seek to resist the temptation to despair. Presenting an overview, as I will attempt to do through this essay, is fraught with dangers, because to each generalization there are always exceptions. Furthermore, optimistic or pessimistic assessments naturally reflect the baseline reference points selected and the perspective of the commentator. Both glowing testimonials and condemnations are often possible regarding the same topic, depending upon where one sits in the country, as the divergences are so great. Nevertheless, the commonalities among Aboriginal peoples, especially among the Indian nations—or First Nations as they choose to call themselves—transcend the differences.

This chapter is intended to provide a general overview of the political and legal position of the Indian, Inuit and Métis peoples in contemporary Canada. One of the many major challenges that confront Aboriginal people, namely, the struggle to reestablish their own governments, will serve as a primary focal point for consideration. To set the stage for such analysis, however, this contribution will briefly describe the historical background, then provide information on the current situation of Aboriginal peoples in Canada. To facilitate greater understanding, comparisons will also be drawn between the position of Indian Nations in the United States and that of Canadian First Nations.

II. HISTORICAL BACKGROUND OF THE RELATIONSHIP BETWEEN THE CROWN AND ABORIGINAL PEOPLES

Aboriginal peoples were obviously the first inhabitants of Canada. In the thousands of years before the arrival of Europeans, they developed a wide variety of systems of government that reflected their many different cultures and spiritual beliefs, as well as their particular economic, social, and geographic circumstances. With the arrival of the European settlers, and the establishment of colonial governments, treaties began to be negotiated and signed by the Crown and, starting in the mid-1600s, with many Indian Nations.[3] Treaty-making was initially the primary vehicle for determining the relationship between the Crown

---

[3] For a recent detailed discussion of this relationship in Canadian history and the pre-contact era, *see* CANADA, REPORT OF THE ROYAL COMMISSION ON ABORIGINAL PEOPLES, LOOKING FORWARD, LOOKING BACK, VOL. 1 (1996).

and First Nations. The treaty process was not, however, extended throughout all of Canada and it was rare for treaties to be fully honored by the Crown.

France and Great Britain vied for Aboriginal alliances, while at the same time recognizing Aboriginal independence and territorial rights. This approach was continued by Great Britain after France ceased to be a colonial rival, as a result of the outcome of the Seven Years' War. On October 7, 1763, the British Crown issued a Royal Proclamation which, in many ways, is the Magna Carta of Aboriginal rights in Canada, although it originally also had application to the American colonies.[4] In a striking preamble, the Proclamation states:

> And whereas it is just and reasonable, and essential to Our Interest and the Security of Our Colonies, that the several Nations or Tribes of Indians, with whom We are connected, and who live under Our Protection, should not be molested or disturbed in the Possession of such Parts of Our Dominions and Territories as, not having been ceded to, or purchased by Us, are reserved to them, or any of them, as their Hunting Grounds. . . .[5]

The Proclamation clearly recognized Indian nations as nations. Further, it provided that Aboriginal nations should not be molested in their possession of any unceded land. It prohibited colonial governments from granting away Aboriginal lands, and ordered settlers not to invade Indian territory unless made available for settlement by colonists as a result of cessions or surrenders to the Crown through public meetings called for that purpose.[6] These provisions angered many American colonists and were a contributing factor to the American Revolution. The Supreme Court of Canada decision in *R. v. Sioui*[7] supports the view that Indian sovereignty was originally recognized:

> The mother countries [Great Britain and France] did everything in their power to secure the alliance of each Indian nation and to encourage nations allied with the enemy to change sides. When these efforts met with success, they were incorporated in treaties of alliance or neutrality. This clearly indicates that the Indian nations were regarded in their relations with the European nations which occupied North America as

---

[4] The Royal Proclamation, R.S.C., App. II, No. 1 (1985). *See* BRIAN SLATTERY, THE LAND RIGHTS OF INDIGENOUS CANADIAN PEOPLES (1979); and JOHN D. HURLEY, CHILDREN OR BRETHREN: ABORIGINAL RIGHTS IN COLONIAL IROQUOIA (1985).

[5] The Royal Proclamation, R.S.C., App. II, No. 1 at 4–5 (1985). *See* 12 BRITISH ROYAL PROCLAMATIONS RELATING TO AMERICA 212 218 (Clarence S. Brigham, ed., 1911). The Royal Proclamation has legal force and has been expressly recognized by section 25 of the Constitution Act, 1982.

[6] For the purposes of this section, the use of the terms "Indian" and "Aboriginal" are intended to mean the same thing.

[7] *See* R. v. Sioui [1990] 1 S.C.R. 1025.

independent nations. The papers of Sir William Johnson . . . , who was in charge of Indian affairs in British North America, demonstrate the recognition by Great Britain that nation-to-nation relations had to be conducted with the North American Indians.[8]

In rendering its decision in that case, the Supreme Court of Canada quoted with approval the observations of the U.S. Supreme Court in *Worcester v. State of Georgia*[9] regarding British policy in the mid-1700s:

> Such was the policy of Great Britain towards the Indian nations inhabiting the territory from which she excluded all other Europeans; such her claims, and such her practical exposition of the charters she had granted; *she considered them as nations capable of maintaining the relations of peace and war; of governing themselves, under her protection; and she made treaties with them, the obligation of which she acknowledged.*[10]

In the view of the Supreme Court of Canada, a similar policy was continued by Great Britain after the fall of New France:

> The British Crown recognized that the Indians had certain ownership rights over their land, it sought to establish trade with them which would rise above the level of exploitation and give them a fair return. It also allowed them autonomy in their internal affairs, intervening in this area as little as possible.[11]

Land rights accompanied by the right of Aboriginal self-government, exercised by Aboriginal peoples with diverse historical experiences and acknowledged by the Crown in the Royal Proclamation of 1763 and elsewhere, have never been relinquished in any general way by Aboriginal peoples. The Supreme Court of Canada in *R. v. Sioui* did, however, unanimously state, as the U.S. Supreme Court had already declared over 150 years earlier in *Worcester*, that the former status as fully "independent nations" had changed with the arrival of European nations—but without articulating the implications of that change or how the extent of autonomy had been circumscribed. Where the two final courts of appeal have differed to date has been that the U.S. Supreme Court recognized internal or residual sovereignty as surviving colonization such that Indian nations were

---

[8] *Id.* at 1053.

[9] *See* Worcester v. Georgia, 31 U.S. (6 Pet.) 515 (1832).

[10] R. v. Sioui [1990] 1 S.C.R. 1025, 1054 (emphasis in original).

[11] *Id.* at 1055.

transformed into "domestic dependent nations,"[12] while the Supreme Court of Canada has yet to confirm the common law's recognition of this status.[13]

The negotiations leading to the drafting of the British North America Act, 1867[14] (now known as the Constitution Act, 1867),[15] which was the original source for Canada's independence, did not include Aboriginal peoples nor were they consulted in any way on the development of Canada's constitution. Subsection 91(24) of this Act allocated to the federal government exclusive legislative authority for "Indians, and Lands reserved for Indians." It was pursuant to this responsibility that the federal government passed the first comprehensive Indian Act in 1876,[16] consolidating the pre-Confederation legislation previously passed with respect to Indians by the two colonies of Upper and Lower Canada coupled with initial federal legislation in this field. While the Indian Act was being administered, the Crown in right of Canada continued to enter into treaties with First Nations. The intense period of treaty negotiations from 1867–1899, with a few subsequent treaties being concluded up until 1923, would suggest that the recognition of nationhood, including the capacity to make treaties, was alive and well. However, after the enactment of the Indian Act and various laws of general application, the effective exercise of traditional governments was severely curtailed or eliminated without Aboriginal consent, giving rise to many of the difficulties still experienced in relations between First Nations and the rest of Canada. The Indian Act was used as a blunt instrument to foster assimilation through imposing a municipal-style elected government, outlawing traditional religious practices, and extending primary power to federal officials.

The federal government used its Constitution Act section 91(24) power to create a statutory definition of "Indian" for the purposes of the Indian Act that was far more limited in scope than the word "Indians" in section 91(24) itself. It excluded, as Indians, many people who, prior to its passage, would have been considered by their communities and by themselves as Indians. Its orientation was patrilineal; Indian women would lose their status as Indians through marriage to a non-Indian or an Aboriginal person who was not registered. This applied even in relation to matrilineal societies. The definition system was also patronizing, as any Indian who obtained a university degree or membership in

---

[12] Cherokee Nation v. Georgia, 30 U.S. (5 Pet.) 1 (1831).

[13] *See* R. v. Gardner [1996] 138 D.L.R.(4th) 204 (S.C.C.) (popularly called *Pamajewon* after one of the defendants).

[14] British North America Act, 1867, c. 3 (U.K.), 30–31 Vic.

[15] *See* Constitution Act, 1867 (being Schedule B to the Canada Act 1982 (U.K.), 1982, ch. 11 (formerly called the British North America Act, 1867)).

[16] *See* An Act to amend and consolidate the laws respecting Indians, S.C. 1876, ch. 18. For a review of the current Act, regulations, and summaries of relevant case law, *see* THE 1997 ANNOTATED INDIAN ACT (Shin Imai & Donna Hawley, eds., 1996).

a profession was enfranchised.[17] The Métis and Inuit were specifically excluded from the scope of the Act. By a Supreme Court of Canada decision,[18] the Inuit were deemed to fall within the meaning of "Indians" contained in section 91(24), even though they remained outside the Indian Act. The Métis have never been afforded such recognition by government or by the courts; however, there is clearly a reasonable argument to be made that they, too, fall within the meaning of "Indians" contained in section 91(24).[19] The significance of being so included is that it empowers, and arguably obligates, the federal government to forge a political and legal relationship with the Aboriginal group so affected.

Early commentary by the Supreme Court of Canada on the special relationship tended to characterize Aboriginal peoples as wards of the State, and the State's role merely as a political trust rather than a legally enforceable one.[20] More recent decisions have given some legal meaning and force to the concept of a fiduciary relationship between the Crown and Aboriginal peoples. Judgements in the *Guerin* case[21] characterized the fiduciary relationship dramatically differently from earlier descriptions of wardship. It borrowed heavily from the law of trusts to craft a legally enforceable duty on the Crown that also indicated that a high standard was imposed upon the Crown as its honor is at stake in its dealings with Aboriginal peoples. Similarly, the common law doctrine of Aboriginal title regained new vitality as a result of the Supreme Court of Canada's decision in *Calder,*[22] while treaty rights were recognized as retaining legal meaning in a number of decisions starting in the 1960s.[23] These trends were advanced with the passage of the Constitution Act, 1982 as it recognized and affirmed "existing aboriginal and treaty rights" in subsection 35(1).

Although the situation has improved dramatically for Indian, Inuit, and Métis peoples in Canada over the last twenty-five years, this comes on the

---

[17] These provisions were finally repealed by amendments to the Act in the form of the infamous Bill C–31 in 1985, Indian Act, R.S.C. 1985 (1st Supp.), c. 32.

[18] See Reference re Eskimos [1939] 2 D.L.R. 417 (S.C.C.).

[19] See Clem Chartier, *Indian: An Analysis of the Term as Used in Section 91(24) of the British North America Act, 1867,* 43 SASK. L. REV. 27 (1978–1979); and Bradford W. Morse & John Giokas, *Do the Métis Fall Within Section 91(24) of the Constitution Act, 1867?, in* ABORIGINAL SELF-GOVERNMENT: LEGAL AND CONSTITUTIONAL ISSUES 140–276 (1995). This argument has been adopted by the Royal Commission on Aboriginal People in its final report. For the opposite position, *see* BRYAN SCHWARTZ, FIRST PEOPLES, SECOND THOUGHTS: ABORIGINAL PEOPLES, CONSTITUTIONAL THOUGHTS REFORM AND CANADIAN STATECRAFT (1986).

[20] *See, e.g.,* St. Ann's Island Shooting & Fishing Club Ltd. v. The King [1950] 2 D.L.R. 225 (S.C.C.).

[21] *See* Guerin v. The Queen [1984] 2 S.C.R. 335.

[22] *See* Calder v. Attorney-General of British Columbia [1973] S.C.R. 328.

[23] *See, e.g.,* R. v. White (1964) 50 D.L.R. (2d) 613 (B.C.C.A.); R. v. Taylor (1981) 34 O.R. (2d) 360 (Ont. C.A.); R. v. Simon [1985] 2 S.C.R. 387 (S.C.C.); and R. v. Sioui [1990] 1 S.C.R. 1025.

heels of many generations of oppression and efforts at complete assimilation or elimination. Traditional religious practices were suppressed, cultural beliefs denigrated, children removed and transported to residential schools, traditional knowledge demeaned, and longstanding economies and ways of life overturned or rendered obsolete. As a result of these developments, the authority and functions of traditional Aboriginal governments were significantly eroded or totally overwhelmed. Despite well over 300 years of active efforts at colonization and disposition, Aboriginal peoples never accepted assimilation and continued to struggle to survive. Indeed, it is a testimony to their determination and fortitude that their unique cultures, traditions and languages have survived and remain an integral part of the Canadian mosaic today.

III. CURRENT SITUATION

A. Overview

The Aboriginal peoples of Canada consist of three major groups, namely, the Indians, Inuit, and the Métis. The total population comprises approximately 1.2 million people or 4.4 percent of the country.[24] This compares to a larger indigenous population of 2.2 million in the United States, which reflects only 0.90 percent of the total American population.[25] According to the Canadian Department of Indian Affairs and Northern Development (DIAND), there are approximately 55,700 Inuit residing primarily in northern Canada, who are affiliated with the Inuit of Greenland, Russia, and Alaska (all of whom belong to the Inuit Circumpolar Conference).[26] Because of the Indian Act, the overall Indian population has been segregated into those who are registered, or have status, under that Act, and those who are not recognized as legally being Indians for the purposes of that statute or the services made available by DIAND and Health Canada. The 1996 statistics of DIAND recorded 602,700 registered Indians, of whom approximately 86,000 gained status through the 1985 amendments to the Act (Bill C–31).[27] If one subtracts the registered Indian and Inuit populations from the federal overall total for Aboriginal peoples, it leaves an estimated Métis and non-status Indian population of 624,300 people.[28] The Congress of Aboriginal Peoples (which is a national organization that represents many off-reserve Indians and some Métis) estimates the latter two groups as comprising

---

[24] *See* Indian and Northern Affairs Canada, 1995–1996 Performance Report 2 (1996).

[25] The World Almanac and Book of Facts 379 (1997).

[26] Indian and Northern Affairs Canada, *Inuit in Canada* 1 (1996) <http://www.i-nac.gc.ca/pubs/information/info16.html>.

[27] Indian and Northern Affairs Canada, *Indians in Canada and the United States* 1 (1996) <http://www.inac.gc.ca/pubs/information/info37.html>.

[28] This figure is derived from a calculation based on the information Indian and Northern Affairs Canada, *supra* notes 24, 26, and 27.

750,000 people.[29] There are 256,400 registered Indians who reside outside of reserves, or 42 percent of the total status Indian population.[30]

Today, the Aboriginal population receives $5.6 billion annually from the Government of Canada alone,[31] which is directed primarily toward 608 First Nations recognized under the Indian Act. Approximately 80 percent of that money is administered directly by those First Nations, while a portion of the balance is distributed through the provinces. Provincial governments also provide approximately $5 billion in direct and indirect funding and services. Despite this significant annual allocation, Aboriginal people are on the bottom of every list where that is a negative place to be—such as data regarding life span, income, education levels, and so forth—and on the top of the list, where that is the worst place to be—such as statistics concerning unemployment, suicide, diabetes, incarceration, and child welfare rates, etc.

The experience of racism has plagued Canadian society, and the threat to traditional lands been a hallmark of Canadian-Aboriginal relations for well over one hundred years. As is the case for American Indians, the negative effects from the residential school system (which existed from the mid-1800s to the 1970s) and the numbers of Indian children taken from their parents through the 1960s and 1970s by the child welfare system, have magnified both social problems and a deep sense of victimization from racism. These twin experiences have robbed generations of their parenting skills, eroded cultural knowledge and linguistic comprehension, fostered family disintegration, and sapped self-respect. The rapid growth of the indigenous population and its increasing urbanization since the end of World War II—to the extent that there are now more Aboriginal people living outside of what remains of their lands than are living on them—is dramatically altering the situation of Aboriginal peoples. Despite this fact, the approach of the federal government has been to focus almost exclusively upon people who are living on reservations, or in Canadian terms "reserves," through programs and services in direct bilateral relations, and to leave people in urban areas largely to the provinces. Often this has meant that the latter receive extremely little special attention, although this is an area in which positive changes have been slowly occurring in Canada in recent years. This federal focus on land-based peoples has stemmed largely from federal interpretation of its constitutional authority for "Indians, and Lands reserved for Indians"—buttressed by treaties, federal legislation since the early days of nationhood, and fiscal factors. It is paralleled by the approach adopted by the federal government in the United States toward Indian nations and Alaskan Natives.

---

[29] Bradford W. Morse & Robert K. Groves, *Canada's Forgotten Peoples: The Aboriginal Rights of Métis and Non-Status Indians*, 2 LAW & ANTHRO. 139 (1987).

[30] INDIAN AND NORTHERN AFFAIRS CANADA, *supra* note 27.

[31] *See* INDIAN AND NORTHERN AFFAIRS CANADA, 1995–1996 PERFORMANCE REPORT 3 (1996).

The revival of treaty-making in 1973, as a result of the Supreme Court of Canada decision in *Calder*,[32] was established as a matter of federal policy leading to the negotiation of the James Bay and Northern Quebec Agreement in August of 1977,[33] the Northeastern Quebec Agreement in 1978,[34] and the Western Arctic (or Inuvialuit) Agreement of 1984.[35] More recently, it has resulted in seven major treaties being signed within the last five years: the Gwich'in Agreement, [36] the Nunavut Land Claims Agreement,[37] the Sahtu Dene and Métis Agreement, [38] the Vuntut Gwich'in First Nation Final Agreement,[39] the First Nation of Nacho Nyak Dun Final Agreement,[40] the Teslin Tlingit Council Final Agreement, and the Champagne and Aishihik First Nations Final Agreement.[41]

The sacredness of treaties and the necessity to honor them, along with the recognition that they have been far more often broken than honored in their implementation, is a major issue that is in the forefront of Crown–First Nations relations in many regions of Canada today. Historic treaties contained no dispute resolution mechanism, as do those reached over the past twenty years, and Canadian courts have resisted providing a forum for civil actions for breach of treaty.[42] Indian views of the terms of the treaties, based upon oral histories passed down from generation to generation, differ radically from the written versions that influence judicial and non-Aboriginal governmental views.

Although great progress has been made over the past two decades, the Aboriginal population remains the poorest of the poor, with lower life expectancies, educational levels, and employment rates, as well as extraordinary over-representation in the prisons and child welfare agencies across the country.

---

[32] *See* Calder v. Attorney-General of British Columbia [1973] S.C.R. 328.

[33] EDITEUR OFFICIEL DU QUEBEC, THE JAMES BAY AND NORTHERN QUEBEC AGREEMENT (1976); *reprinted* with all subsequent amendments in 1997.

[34] INDIAN AND NORTHERN AFFAIRS CANADA, THE NORTHEASTERN QUEBEC AGREEMENT (1978).

[35] INDIAN AND NORTHERN AFFAIRS CANADA, THE WESTERN ARCTIC CLAIM: THE INUVIALUIT FINAL AGREEMENT (1984).

[36] INDIAN AND NORTHERN AFFAIRS CANADA, GWICH'IN FINAL AGREEMENT (1992).

[37] INDIAN AND NORTHERN AFFAIRS CANADA, AGREEMENT BETWEEN THE INUIT OF THE NUNAVUT SETTLEMENT AREA AND HER MAJESTY IN RIGHT OF CANADA (1993).

[38] INDIAN AND NORTHERN AFFAIRS CANADA, SAHTU DENE AND MÉTIS COMPREHENSIVE LAND CLAIM AGREEMENT (1993).

[39] INDIAN AND NORTHERN AFFAIRS CANADA, VUNTUT GWICH'IN FIRST NATION FINAL AGREEMENT (1993).

[40] INDIAN AND NORTHERN AFFAIRS CANADA, FIRST NATION OF NACHO NYAK DUN FINAL AGREEMENT (1993).

[41] INDIAN AND NORTHERN AFFAIRS CANADA, TESLIN TLINGIT COUNCIL FINAL AGREEMENT (1993); and INDIAN AND NORTHERN AFFAIRS CANADA, CHAMPAGNE AND AISHIHIK FIRST NATIONS FINAL AGREEMENT (1993).

[42] *See, e.g.,* Pawis v. The Queen (1979) 102 D.L.R. (3d) 602 (F.C.T.D.).

There are now, however, 372 First Nation-managed schools serving 31 percent of the status Indian students who live on reserves, as opposed to only 53 percent in the 1975–1976 school year.[43] The number of students remaining in school to grade 12 has grown dramatically from less than 15 percent in 1970–1971 to over 77 percent in 1993–94.[44] Postsecondary enrollment has also mushroomed from 432 registered Indian students in 1970–1971 to 26,800 in 1994, with estimates that upwards of 150,000 Aboriginal people have attended tertiary educational institutions.[45] Community infrastructure has also improved significantly with over 85 percent of dwellings on reserve now possessing adequate water and sewage systems in comparison to only 50 percent less than twenty years ago.[46]

B. Financial Expenditures

The Department of Indian Affairs and Northern Development's budget for the 1995–1996 fiscal year included expenditures of $5.2 billion CDN, of which $3.9 billion was directed exclusively toward Aboriginal peoples.[47] This included $1.1 billion for social assistance and welfare services,[48] $1.1 billion for education[49] and $362 million for payment of land claims settlements[50] In addition, the Department of Justice announced the renewal of the Aboriginal Justice Initiative in March of 1996 with $6.7 million per year[51] while the Solicitor General's budget for Indian policing on reserves was $23.36 million.[52] Heritage Canada maintains responsibility to fund the core operations budgets of Aboriginal friendship centers in urban areas and political organizations as well as Aboriginal language initiatives, while Health Canada funds all health initiatives, including uninsured health care for status Indians and the Inuit at a cost in 1995–1996 of $997 million.[53] A range of other departments and federal agencies (for example,

---

[43] INDIAN AND NORTHERN AFFAIRS CANADA, THE OUTLOOK ON PRIORITIES AND EXPENDITURES 1995–1996 to 1997–1998 (1995) at 11[hereinafter OUTLOOK ON PRIORITIES].

[44] *Id.*

[45] *Id. See also* INDIAN AND NORTHERN AFFAIRS CANADA, CREATING OPPORTUNITY: PROGRESS ON COMMITMENTS TO ABORIGINAL PEOPLES 18 (1995) [hereinafter PROGRESS ON COMMITMENTS].

[46] OUTLOOK ON PRIORITIES, *supra* note 43 at 10.

[47] INDIAN AND NORTHERN AFFAIRS CANADA, *supra* note 24 at 3–4.

[48] OUTLOOK ON PRIORITIES, *supra* note 43 at 13.

[49] *Id.*

[50] INDIAN AND NORTHERN AFFAIRS CANADA, *supra* note 24 at 3.

[51] LIBERAL PARTY OF CANADA, A RECORD OF ACHIEVEMENT: A REPORT ON THE LIBERAL GOVERNMENT'S 36 MONTHS IN OFFICE 108 (1996).

[52] INDIAN AND NORTHERN AFFAIRS CANADA, *supra* note 24 at 3.

[53] *Id.*

the Canada Mortgage and Housing Corporation allocated $263 million on Aboriginal housing[54] and Human Resources Development Canada provided $211 million to Aboriginal organizations for job and skills training during the 1995–1996 fiscal year[55]) also fund specific programs that are of importance to all Aboriginal people.[56]

It is important to note that the lion's share of federal expenditures are to the Inuit and on-reserve Indians, while the off-reserve population is largely left to their own devices or to be assisted by the provinces. Federal data suggest that off-reserve Aboriginal people pay approximately $3 billion per year in taxes,[57] while on-reserve Indians, who are exempt from income and a number of taxes on goods consumed on reserve by virtue of provisions in the Indian Act,[58] pay an unknown amount of taxes for goods consumed off reserve or concerning those taxes buried within the purchase price of goods and services.

C. Land Base

There are 2,370 reserves across the country, totalling 7.4 million acres held by the Crown in trust for 608 bands or First Nations.[59] This reflects less than one-half of one percent of the land mass of the country south of the sixtieth parallel for the original owners,[60] despite legal recognition of land rights and even though they represent four percent of the total population.[61] A further 25.25 million acres were dedicated for exclusive Aboriginal use through the three land claims settlements reached under modern claims negotiations in the 1970s and 1980s, two of which are in northern Quebec.[62] Seven other aboriginal title claims have been negotiated and implemented so far this decade, thereby creating a

---

[54] *Id.*

[55] *Id.*

[56] *See* INDIAN AND NORTHERN AFFAIRS CANADA, *supra* note 24.

[57] CANADA, REPORT OF THE ROYAL COMMISSION ON ABORIGINAL PEOPLES, LOOKING FORWARD, LOOKING BACK, VOL. 5, RENEWAL: A TWENTY–YEAR COMMITMENT 29 and 47 (1996).

[58] *See* Indian Act, R.S.C., ch. I–5, § 87 and § 90 (1985). Treaty No. 8 contains an express tax exemption provision; however, First Nations assert that they are exempt from all federal and provincial taxation because of their aboriginal and treaty rights. This argument has yet to find favor with the courts.

[59] INDIAN AND NORTHERN AFFAIRS CANADA, *supra* note 27 at 2.

[60] CANADA, REPORT OF THE ROYAL COMMISSION ON ABORIGINAL PEOPLES, VOL. 2, RESTRUCTURING THE RELATIONSHIP 422 (1996) [hereinafter RESTRUCTURING THE RELATIONSHIP].

[61] INDIAN AND NORTHERN AFFAIRS CANADA, *supra* note 24.

[62] *See supra* notes 33, 34, and 35.

total of 143 million acres of additional land dedicated for exclusive Aboriginal use in Quebec, the Northwest Territories and Yukon Territory.[63]

There are forty-seven sets of negotiations underway in British Columbia, where an Agreement-in-Principle for a modern treaty was reached in March of 1996 among the Nisga'a Nation (who launched the *Calder* case that led to a renewal of the treaty process in Canada in 1973), the Government of Canada and the provincial government.[64] Once a final treaty is reached, the Nisga'a will have exclusive use and governmental authority over 1,900 square kilometres of land (about ten percent of their traditional territory), $190 million, guarantees of commercial fishing rights, comanagement of natural resources and a broad range of jurisdictional powers for their government.[65] Similar negotiations are also occurring in Labrador as well as parts of Quebec, Ontario and the Northwest Territories.[66]

By comparison, the 554 federally recognized Indian tribes in the United States possess 56 million acres or 3 percent of the total land mass as reservations.[67] The Alaskan Natives achieved a legislatively imposed claim settlement—rather than a freely negotiated one—in 1971 that set aside 40 million acres and almost $1 billion as a full and final resolution of their aboriginal title to the entire state.[68] American Indian tribes, like First Nations in Canada, have been dispossessed of almost all of their original territories through forced relocations and broken treaties. This has been compounded by coerced and improper sales of reservation lands, resulting in a decline in landholdings of 90 million acres by 1934.[69]

D. Legal Status and Constitutional Structure

The Constitution Act, 1867[70] assigned exclusive responsibility to Parliament under section 91(24) for "Indians, and Lands reserved for the Indians." This gave Parliament two heads of legislative jurisdiction as it could enact laws for both the people referred to in the Constitution as "Indians" and also in relation to all of the lands that remained unceded territory (which is not the same as Indian reserves set aside under the Indian Act). Parliament has exercised this

---

[63] INDIAN AND NORTHERN AFFAIRS CANADA, *supra* note 27 at 2.

[64] INDIAN AND NORTHERN AFFAIRS CANADA, *supra* note 24 at 21.

[65] *Id.* at 20.

[66] *Id.* at 21.

[67] RESTRUCTURING THE RELATIONSHIP, *supra* note 61 at 423 (1996).

[68] Russel Barsh, *Indian Land Claims Policy in the United States*, 58 N. DAK. L. REV. 7 at 48–49 (1982).

[69] *See* RENNARD STRICKLAND ET AL., FELIX S. COHEN'S HANDBOOK OF FEDERAL INDIAN LAW 138 (2d ed. 1982).

[70] *See* Constitution Act, 1867, *supra* note 15.

authority since 1868 by passing legislation in relation to some of the Indian people and some of their lands.

The jurisdiction of Parliament regarding "Indians" was determined by the Supreme Court of Canada (in *Reference re Eskimos* in 1939)[71] to include the Inuit, although this jurisdiction has never been utilized to enact Inuit-specific legislation. Parliament has, however, frequently altered the Indian Act to vary the definition of Indians narrowly or broadly over the years. While the federal 91(24) jurisdiction was traditionally viewed as permissive, rather than mandatory, this may have changed as a result of the development of the fiduciary obligation doctrine by the courts upon the Crown in right of Canada[72] and the terms of section 35 of the Constitution Act, 1982. It is interesting to note that the federal government did quickly assume both its jurisdiction in theory and in practice in Quebec by taking over all expenditures for health and social services for the Inuit after the Supreme Court's decision.

The position of the Métis in regard to section 91(24) has remained a subject of legal and political debate for many years; the federal and Alberta governments take the view that the Métis do not fall within section 91(24), while all other provinces and most commentators, as well as the Métis, assert the contrary perspective. Although, in this author's opinion, the Métis as a distinct people are encompassed within section 91(24) as "constitutional Indians," the continuing uncertainty in this regard has left the Métis as a political football passed back and forth between the two levels of government. As a result, there has been no special legislation outside Alberta and few governmental initiatives designed to meet their needs.[73]

In addition to the Indian Act, the federal government has absorbed the role formerly reserved to the Imperial government of negotiating treaties in the name of the Crown. Literally hundreds of treaties were negotiated with the Indian nations in the preconfederation era in what are now the Atlantic provinces, southern Quebec, southern Ontario, and Vancouver Island.[74] Since 1867, the Crown in right of Canada has entered into eleven numbered treaties in northern Ontario, the prairie provinces, northeastern British Columbia, and parts of the

---

[71] *See* Reference re Eskimos [1939] 2 D.L.R. 417 (S.C.C.).

[72] *See* Guerin v. The Queen [1984] 2 S.C.R. 335. The courts have tentatively begun to extend the fiduciary obligation doctrine to the provinces. For further information, *see* Leonard I. Rotman, *Provincial Fiduciary Obligations to First Nations: The Nexus Between Governmental Power and Responsibility*, 32 Osgoode Hall L.J. 735 (1994); and Parallel Paths: Fiduciary Doctrine and the Crown–Native Relationship in Canada (1996).

[73] *See* Paul L.A.H. Chartrand, Manitoba's Métis Settlement Scheme of 1870 (1991); and Morse & Giokas, *supra* note 19, at 140–276.

[74] *See* Alexander Morris, The Treaties of Canada with the Indians of Manitoba and the Northwest Territories (1880, reprinted 1971); Canada, Indian Treaties and Surrenders 1680 to 1890 (1992).

Yukon and Northwest Territories,[75] as well as the Williams Treaty of 1923 in eastern Ontario.[76] Adhesions to these treaties, which often cover large tracts of land, have also been negotiated.[77] These postconfederation treaties, along with those from the earlier era in Upper Canada, on their face share in common the surrender of exclusive land rights to the Crown by the Indian parties in return for annuities, confirmation of wildlife and fishing harvesting rights, the preservation of certain lands for exclusive Indian use as reserves, and other commitments. The Indian understanding of many of these treaties derived from their oral histories, however, differs dramatically from the written version in English.

The Inuit, with a few minor exceptions, did not sign treaties. This is probably a result of geography, as their territory in the far north held little appeal to the waves of immigrants seeking agricultural land or to the natural resources industry until after World War II and the discovery of subsurface potential. The Indian nations to the south of the Inuit also were not involved in treaty negotiations until the last twenty-five years. The land rights of the Métis were recognized in some locales (e.g., through signing the adhesion to Treaty No. 3[78] in Ontario) as a distinct indigenous people. The more common approach was for the Métis frequently to join in the treaties with their Indian relatives or to take scrip under the Manitoba Act[79] and subsequent Dominion land legislation. The implementation of these federal laws is currently being contested before the Manitoba courts by the Manitoba Métis Federation and the Native Council of Canada.[80] Scrip entitled the holder to exchange this certificate for a specified number of acres of land to be held in fee simple by the individual (rather than collectively as in the case of reserve lands) or for cash.

As is the case in Canada, the federal government plays the dominant role in Indian affairs in the United States for constitutional reasons. The American Constitution allocates power to Congress regarding commercial relations with Indian nations,[81] while the president possesses the ability to enter into treaties

---

[75] Patrick Macklem, *The Impact of Treaty 9 on Natural Resource Development in Northern Ontario*, in Aboriginal and Treaty Rights in Canada 97 (Michael Asch ed., 1997).

[76] Canada, *supra* note 2 at 162.

[77] Olive P. Dickason, Canada's First Nations: A History of Founding Peoples from Earliest Times 273 (1992).

[78] Canada, Report of the Royal Commission on Aboriginal Peoples, vol. 4, Perspectives and Realities 261 (1996) [hereinafter Perspectives and Realities].

[79] *See* Manitoba Act, 1870 (formerly An Act to amend and continue the Act 32 33 Victoria chapter 3; and to establish and provide for the Government of the Province of Manitoba, 1870, 33 Vict., ch. 3 (Can.)), *reprinted* in R.S.C. 1985, App. II, No. 8.

[80] *See* Dumont v. Canada (Attorney-General) [1990] 1 S.C.R. 279.

[81] *See* U.S. Const. art. I, § 8, cl. 3.

with other sovereign nations, including Indian tribes.[82] The U.S. Supreme Court has created a new basis for Congressional power—the plenary power doctrine—to justify more federal jurisdiction than the commerce clause would naturally support.

The Supreme Court of the United States has performed a much more fundamental role than has its equivalent in Canada or in virtually any other country around the world with an indigenous population. Not only has it articulated foundational principles of the common law, such as the aboriginal title doctrine and its recognition,[83] but it has also developed a political compromise cast as a legal doctrine to protect the fragile independence and territorial ambitions of the United States on the one hand, while also acknowledging the strength of the moral, historical, and legal arguments of the Indian nations on the other.[84] As a result, a doctrine of discovery was fashioned, drawing upon embryonic international law principles to justify ultimate ownership of the soil resting with the colonists and exclusive international status belonging to the United States. The Indian nations were held to have simply lost their stature as foreign nations through the force of history.[85] The Court softened the compromise by recognizing that Indian nations continued to possess inherent powers of sovereignty rather than delegated ones.[86] Nevertheless, their status as "domestic dependent nations"[87] meant that this residual sovereignty was always subject to diminution

---

[82] Congress passed legislation in 1871 that prohibited the negotiation of any further treaties with Indian nations. For a review of the development of this legislation, which did not invalidate any of the previously negotiated treaties, *see* Siegfried Wiessner, *American Indian Treaties and Modern International Law,* 7 ST. THOMAS L. REV. 567, at 575–583 (1995).

[83] *See* Cherokee Nation v. Georgia, *supra* note 13; Worcester v. Georgia, *supra* note 10; and, generally, STRICKLAND, *supra* note 69. The theory of aboriginal title articulated in the early decisions of the Marshall Court have been adopted by the judiciary in Australia (Mabo v. Queensland, (1992) 107 A.L.R. 1), New Zealand (*see* David Williams, *Aboriginal Rights in Aoteroa (New Zealand)* 2 LAW & ANTHRO. 423 (1987)), and Canada (Calder v. Attorney-General of British Columbia, *supra* note 22) over the intervening 160 years.

[84] *See* Nell Jessup Newton, *Federal Power Over Indians: Its Sources, Scope and Limitations* 132 U. PA L. REV. 195 (1984); and Steven Paul McSloy, *"Because the Bible Told Me So": Manifest Destiny and American Indians* 9 ST. THOMAS L. REV. 37 (1996).

[85] *See* Robert A. Williams, Jr., *The Algebra of Federal Indian Law: The Hard Trail of Decolonizing and Americanizing the White Man's Indian Jurisprudence,* — WIS. L. REV. — [1986].

[86] *See* McSloy, *supra* note 84 at 38, who articulates this so well when he states:

How were American Indian lands taken? The answer is not, as it turns out, by military force. The wars, massacres, Geronimo and Sitting Bull—all that was just cleanup. The real conquest was on paper, on maps and in laws. What those maps showed and those laws said was that Indians had been "conquered" merely by being "discovered."

[87] Cherokee Nation v. Georgia, 30 U.S. (5 Pet.) 1, 12 (1831).

or elimination by Congress[88] for which Congress took upon itself the role of trustee. The Court subsequently developed new rationales for Congressional authority beyond the express language of the Constitution, such as the plenary power doctrine.[89] More recently, the Court has begun to chip away at tribal sovereignty where it felt that the land in question had lost its Indian character through demographic shifts, [90] or where it was inappropriate, in the judges' views, for Indian sovereignty to encompass non-Indians[91] or nontribal member Indians in criminal matters.[92] Therefore, residual sovereignty continues to survive, subject to explicit Congressional legislative overrides and judicial redefinitions.

The Canadian Constitution Act, 1982 dramatically changed the political and legal relationship among governments and Canadians generally, as well as between all Aboriginal groups and the rest of Canada. It entrenched the Canadian Charter of Rights and Freedoms,[93] which was inspired by the American Bill of Rights and international covenants on human rights. The Charter establishes the supremacy of the enumerated individual and collective rights, as interpreted by the judiciary rather than the supremacy of Parliament, which had been the case since the Reformation.[94] Not only does section 25 of the Charter protect "aboriginal, treaty or other rights or freedoms" of the Aboriginal peoples from being abrogated or derogated by the remaining provisions of the Charter, but section 35 confirms the "existing aboriginal and treaty rights" as part of the "supreme law of Canada" (§ 52(1)). The term "aboriginal peoples" is also defined in subsection 35(2) so as to clearly include "the Indian, Inuit and Métis peoples," while their unique rights have been guaranteed equally among female and male Aboriginal persons through the 1983 package of constitutional amendments adding subsection 35(4). These latter amendments also made certain that prior and future land claims settlements will receive the same constitutional status as

---

[88] State governments do not possess similar powers to intrude upon or erode tribal jurisdiction, unless Congress delegates such authority to the states by legislation, as was done in 1953 through Public Law No. 280, 67 Stat. 588 (1953).

[89] *See* Robert N. Clinton, *Redressing the Legacy of Conquest* 46 ARK. L REV. 77 (1993).

[90] *See* Brendale v. Confederated Tribes and Bands of the Yakima Indian Nation, 492 U.S. 408 (1989).

[91] *See* Oliphant v. Suquamish Indian Tribe, 435 U.S. 191 (1978).

[92] *See* Duro v. Reina, 495 U.S. 696 (1990). The effect of this decision was swiftly overturned by Congress. *See* 25 U.S.C. § 1301(4). The Court's theory, however, still stands as a continuing threat to tribal sovereignty in other circumstances or if the legislative reversal is ever repealed.

[93] *See* Canadian Charter of Rights and Freedoms, Part I of the Constitution Act, 1982, Schedule B of the Canada Act, 1982, ch. 11 (Eng.) [hereinafter Canadian Charter].

[94] *See* PETER W. HOGG, CONSTITUTIONAL LAW OF CANADA (4th ed., 1997).

treaties[95] (§§ 25(b) and 35(3)), so as to encompass the two comprehensive claims settlements reached in the 1970s in Quebec, and that no future amendments to the constitutional provisions that explicitly apply to Aboriginal peoples can occur without having a First Ministers' Conference to which their representatives would be invited (§ 35.1) to discuss any proposed constitutional amendments.[96] This latter provision guarantees consultation on amendments under active consideration, but does not provide a veto or even a vote.

The effect of these provisions has had a significant impact upon the jurisprudence, as well as upon the political structure and public profile, of the Aboriginal peoples in Canada. The precise nature of the changes in the case law outstrips the scope of this paper; however, suffice it to say that the Canadian perceptions of what constitutes the legally recognized rights of Aboriginal peoples has expanded exponentially. For example, the definition of what is a treaty has been broadened considerably by the decisions of the Quebec Court of Appeal and Supreme Court of Canada in the *Sioui*[97] case, and it is now clear as a result of the latter court's decision in *R. v. Sparrow*[98] that aboriginal and treaty rights can render federal and provincial laws inapplicable to Aboriginal people in appropriate situations. The Court also recognized in *Sioui* that Aboriginal peoples at least once constituted independent, sovereign nations (without commenting upon their current status) who could enter into treaties as such with the Crown and its representatives. The Supreme Court has also developed a new doctrine called ''fiduciary obligations'' in the *Guerin*[99] and *Sparrow* cases and stated that it applies to restrain the behavior of both federal and provincial governments in the way they deal with Indian, Inuit, and Métis peoples. One other recent and important decision of the Supreme Court that has a bearing on these issues is the *Simon*[100] case, in which the Court made clear that eighteenth-century peace and friendship treaties continue to confirm legally significant treaty rights that are not limited to status Indians, but can apply to any descendant of the treaty beneficiaries.

---

[95] The addition of subsection 35(3) provides a definition of ''treaty rights'' expressly to encompass prior and subsequent land claims agreements within its scope while paragraph 25(b) was repealed and replaced with wording that ensures that this section is also intended to include past and future land claims agreements.

[96] Constitutional Amendment Proclamation, 1983, SI 84–102, Schedule. For a description of this stage in the constitutional negotiations, *see* Norman K. Zlotkin, *The 1983 and 1984 Constitutional Conferences: Only the Beginning*, (1994) 3 C.N.L.R. 3.

[97] *See* R. v. Sioui [1990] 1 S.C.R. 1025.

[98] *See* R. v. Sparrow [1990] 1 S.C.R. 1075.

[99] *See* Guerin v. The Queen [1984] 2 S.C.R. 335.

[100] *See* R. v. Simon [1985] 2 S.C.R. 387.

1. Section 35, Constitution Act, 1982—What does it mean?

Part II of the Constitution Act, 1982, as amended in 1984, now reads:

35. (1) The existing aboriginal and treaty rights of the aboriginal peoples of Canada are hereby recognized and affirmed.

(2) In this Act, "aboriginal peoples of Canada" includes the Indian, Inuit, and Métis peoples of Canada.

(3) For greater certainty, in subsection (1) "treaty rights" includes rights that now exist by way of land claims agreements or may be so acquired.

(4) Notwithstanding any other provision of this Act, the aboriginal and treaty rights referred to in subsection (1) are guaranteed equally to male and female persons.

35.1 The government of Canada and the provincial governments are committed to the principle that, before any amendment is made to Class 24 of Section 91 of the "Constitution Act, 1867," to Section 25 of this Act or to this Part,

(a) a constitutional conference that includes in its agenda an item relating to the proposed amendment, composed of the Prime Minister of Canada and the first ministers of the provinces, will be convened by the Prime Minister of Canada; and

(b) the Prime Minister of Canada will invite representatives of the aboriginal peoples of Canada to participate in the discussions on that item.

The meaning of what constitutes "aboriginal and treaty rights" remains uncertain, as is the meaning of the expressions "existing" and "recognized and affirmed." The inclusion of Métis in the definition of Aboriginal peoples has not resulted in an acceptance of federal governmental authority to include them within the meaning of "Indians" contained in Constitution Act, 1867 section 91(24). It has, however, aided individual Métis in several lower court cases to establish their wildlife harvesting rights on a basis equivalent to registered Indians.[101]

---

[101] *See, e.g.,* R. v. McPherson [1992] 4 C.N.L.R. 144 (Man. Prov. Ct.); R. v. Muswagon [1992] 4 C.N.L.R. 159 (Man. Q.B.); R. v. Ferguson [1994] 1 C.N.L.R. 117 (Alta. Q.B.).

2. What Is an "Aboriginal Right?"

Generally speaking, "aboriginal rights" in their broadest sense can be defined as those rights that the Aboriginal peoples possess because of their occupation of North America before the coming of Europeans. These rights presumably encompass all aspects of distinctive Aboriginal societies, self-government, and include rights to land and to practice their cultures and traditions, although the courts have yet to consider fully the scope of "aboriginal rights" outside the context of the use of lands and waters and their renewable natural resources.[102]

Canadian law is constantly evolving with respect to the meaning and scope of what constitutes an "aboriginal right."[103] Generally, however, they are considered to be *sui generis* and are decided on a case-by-case basis.

3. What Is an "Existing Aboriginal Right?"

An "aboriginal right" is an "existing right" if:

1) the Aboriginal people concerned possessed the "aboriginal right" as an aspect of their occupation of the land prior to colonialism;

2) the right encompasses an activity that is "an element of a practice, custom or tradition, integral to the distinctive culture of the aboriginal group claiming the right;"[104]

3) although there may be an interruption in its exercise and the way in which the activity is practiced may have been modernized or adapted to the presence of newcomers, to qualify as an "aboriginal right" today there must be continuity between the current practice and those practices that existed prior to contact with European society; and

4) the right was not extinguished before 1982, although its exercise may have been regulated extensively.

---

[102] *See* SHIN IMAI ET AL., ABORIGINAL LAW HANDBOOK 7 (1993). *See also* R. v. Gardner (1996) 138 D.L.R. (4th) 204 (S.C.C.), in which the Supreme Court of Canada rejected the assertion that the activity of gaming and its regulation were within the Aboriginal rights protected under the Constitution.

[103] *See, e.g.,* R. v. Nikal [1996] 1 S.C.R. 1013; R. v. Lewis (1996) 133 D.L.R. (4th) 700 (S.C.C.); R. v. Gladstone (1996) 137 D.L.R. (4th) 47 (S.C.C.); R. v. Van der Peet (1996) 137 D.L.R. (4th) 289 (S.C.C.); and R. v. N.T.C. Smokehouse Ltd. (1996) 137 D.L.R. (4th) 528 (S.C.C.).

[104] R. v. Van der Peet [1996] 2 S.C.R. 507, 549 (S.C.C.).

Prior to constitutional entrenchment in 1982, "aboriginal rights" could be extinguished in the following ways:

— by treaty between the Aboriginal people concerned and the Crown;

— by Crown activity which is inconsistent with the continued exercise of the aboriginal right in question; or

— by the Crown taking some action which demonstrates an intention to extinguish specific "aboriginal rights."

The Supreme Court of Canada held in the landmark *Sparrow*[105] decision that section 35 gives constitutional affirmation to those aboriginal and treaty rights that had not been extinguished prior to 1982 and protects them against such future invasion and restriction that is regarded by the judiciary as unwarranted. In the Court's opinion, the reality that an "aboriginal right" was not explicitly recognized as a right, or may have been highly regulated prior to 1982, does not mean that it was extinguished. The Supreme Court also clarified the extinguishment doctrine by raising the standard, so that the legislation at issue must exhibit a clear and plain intention to extinguish before the courts can conclude that the "aboriginal right" under consideration has in fact been extinguished.[106] More recently, the Supreme Court of Canada has indicated that extinguishment is no longer possible after 1982 for rights protected by subsection 35(1), although they can be regulated or infringed by federal or provincial legislation that meets the justificatory test outlined in the *Sparrow* decision.[107]

The *Sparrow* ruling held that, unless there is a compelling reason of an overriding nature for enacting a law which intrudes upon an "aboriginal right" that can be fully justified, and unless that law only interferes with the right in the least intrusive way possible in the circumstances, the law will be regarded to have infringed section 35 of the Constitution Act, 1982 and will be declared unconstitutional.[108] Pursuant to the test developed in *Sparrow*, if there is interference with an activity that is within the scope of an "aboriginal right," the party seeking to uphold the legislation must show that:

1) there was an otherwise constitutionally valid reason for making the law, such as it was essential for conserving and managing the resource (which in the *Sparrow* case involved the fishery), or preventing the exercise of a right in a way which would cause harm to the general populace or Aboriginal peoples, or other objectives

---

[105] *See* R. v. Sparrow (1990) 70 D.L.R. (4th) 385 (S.C.C.).

[106] *See id.* at 403.

[107] *See* R. v. Gladstone (1996) 137 D.L.R. (4th) 47 (S.C.C.).

[108] *See* R. v. Sparrow, *supra* note 105, at 418.

which are "compelling and substantial" rather than merely being in the "public interest" or "reasonable";

2) the law upholds the honour of the Crown so as to be in keeping with the unique contemporary relationship, grounded in history and policy, between the Crown and Canada's Aboriginal peoples that include fiduciary obligations on the Crown; and

3) the government has addressed remaining critical factors, such as infringing the "aboriginal right" as little as possible, providing fair compensation to the Aboriginal peoples affected if the right was extinguished, and consulting with the Aboriginal group concerned.[109]

The *Sparrow* standard has been watered down by several decisions of the Supreme Court of Canada delivered in 1996. In *Van der Peet* the majority of the Court declared that the purpose of subsection 35(1) was "directed towards the reconciliation of the pre-existence of Aboriginal societies with the sovereignty of the Crown."[110] This purpose was then elaborated upon in *Gladstone* in dicta that suggested that the federal government could unilaterally reallocate constitutionally protected "aboriginal rights" to non-Aboriginal users to meet objectives of "economic and regional fairness, and the recognition of the historical reliance upon . . . the fishery by non-Aboriginal groups."[111] The majority went on to say that "[i]n the right circumstances, such objectives are in the interests of all Canadians and, more importantly, the reconciliation of Aboriginal societies with the rest of Canadian society may well depend on their successful attainment."[112] This creates the specter that majority electoral strength may influence legislators to trade off resources or other constitutionally protected rights to placate non-Aboriginal demands with judicial approval. What is particularly amazing about these comments from the Supreme Court is that they are not even within the context of negotiated settlements, but rather are in reference to unilaterally imposed legislative regimes. This approach contains the seeds that could render constitutional protection a hollow shell in the future.

4. What Are "Treaty Rights"?

The phrase "treaty rights" in subsection 35(1) relates to the commitments that were made when the treaties were negotiated and signed by the Crown and

---

[109] *See id.* at 416.

[110] R. v. Van der Peet [1996] 2 S.C.R. 507, 539 (S.C.C.).

[111] R. v. Gladstone [1996] 2 S.C.R. 723, 775 (S.C.C.).

[112] *Id.* at 775 (emphasis in original).

First Nations. The source of "treaty rights" is, therefore, fundamentally different from that of "aboriginal rights," as it is based upon the specific obligations and responsibilities contained within the government-to-government negotiated agreements, rather than from any historic occupation of territory. The breadth of treaty promises, whether or not they should be read literally or given a contemporary meaning—as is done with constitutional provisions—and even what constitutes a treaty, are all matters subject to considerable debate in Canada. This is in part a reflection of the fact that so many treaties have never been fully implemented. Most of the land-surrender treaties in Canada were signed between 1800 and the early 1920s; however, treaty-making between Indian nations and the Crown began in the mid-1600s.[113] The written texts in English of almost all of the land-surrender treaties in Ontario and the three prairie provinces use real property conveyancing language of "yield, cede and surrender" to provide that the Indian nation signatories gave up their title to massive territories in exchange for retaining small blocks as reserves, modest individual annuity payments, and the right to pursue their traditional avocation of wildlife harvesting in certain circumstances. Other treaties may not refer to land surrenders or may provide for other understandings.[114]

The Canadian judiciary has had considerable difficulty selecting the appropriate characterization of the legal nature of treaties and has considered defining them as contracts at one end of the spectrum or as treaties in the international sense at the other. Thus far, both of these characterizations have been rejected; the prevailing interpretation is to regard Crown-Indian treaties as falling somewhere in between with aspects of each legal concept—applying in part but not in full—thereby rendering Indian treaties truly *sui generis*.

The early treaties are often referred to as the "historic" treaties to distinguish them from the treaty-making process that was revived by the federal government in 1973 after the *Calder* decision. As a result of the 1984 amendment to the Constitution Act, 1982, which added subsection 35(3), constitutional recognition is provided to modern day treaties and land claims agreements in the same manner provided for historic treaties in subsection 35(1). This provision captures the James Bay and Northern Quebec Agreement of 1975, the Northeastern Quebec Agreement of 1978, the Inuvialuit Agreement of the western Arctic of 1984, the Nunavut Agreement of the eastern Arctic of 1993, and the four recent agreements in the Yukon as well as the Gwich'in and Sahtu settlements in the Mackenzie Valley region of the Northwest Territories.

---

[113] For a discussion of a vital eighteenth-century treaty that has yet to be recognized by Canada, John Burrows, *Wampum at Niagara: The Royal Proclamation, Canadian Legal History and Self-Government*, in ABORIGINAL AND TREATY RIGHTS IN CANADA 155 (Michael Asch, ed., 1997).

[114] For more information, *see* CANADA, REPORT OF THE ROYAL COMMISSION ON ABORIGINAL PEOPLES 5 VOLS. (1996); and several of the essays in ABORIGINAL AND TREATY RIGHTS IN CANADA (Michael Asch, ed., 1997).

5.   What Does "Recognized and Affirmed" Mean?

It is essential to realize that section 35 of the Constitution Act, 1982 is in Part II, and, therefore is not part of the Canadian Charter of Rights and Freedoms.[115] As a consequence, aboriginal and treaty rights affirmed by subsection 35(1) are not expressly "guaranteed" as rights contained within the Charter are by virtue of section 1. Although they are not guaranteed, aboriginal and treaty rights are nevertheless "recognized and affirmed" by the Constitution, which is itself declared by section 52 to be the supreme law of the land. As part of this country's highest law, these rights warrant the greatest legal and political respect.

In the unanimous *Sparrow* decision, the Court described the purpose of constitutionalizing aboriginal and treaty rights in these terms:

> the context of 1982 is surely enough to tell us that this is not just a codification of the case law on "aboriginal rights" that had accumulated by 1982. Section 35 calls for a just settlement for aboriginal peoples. It renounces the old rules of the game under which the Crown established courts of law and denied those courts the authority to question sovereign claims made by them.[116]

Aboriginal and treaty rights are definitely enforceable in the ordinary provincial and federal courts, amd their violation can render a federal or provincial law inoperative or invalid. The courts have on numerous instances since 1982 relied upon subsection 35(1) to acquit individuals accused of hunting and fishing violations.[117] The provision has also been used to create a preferential scheme for allocating these resources so as to give priority to Aboriginal users.[118] Constitutional entrenchment has not led, however, to frequent judicial determination of legislation as unconstitutional, as has been the case with the Charter. Litigants have primarily called upon subsection 35(1) as a shield to quasi-criminal charges, rather than as a sword to strike down statutory provisions.[119] The pattern of test case litigation developed in the 1960s and 1970s regarding aboriginal and treaty rights has, therefore, been maintained after constitutional recognition and affirmation. This reflects in large part the absence of financial resources among Aboriginal groups to initiate major civil litigation, the general reluctance to

---

[115] *See* Canadian Charter, *supra* note 93.

[116] Noel Lyon, *An Essay on Constitutional Interpretation* 26 OSGOODE HALL L.J. 95, 100 (1988), quoted by the Supreme Court of Canada in R. v. Sparrow [1990] 1 S.C.R. 1075, 1105–1106.

[117] *See, e.g.*, R. v. Sparrow, *id.*; R. v. Gladstone, *supra* note 104; R. v. Adams [1996] 3 S.C.R. 101; R. v. Cote [1996] 3 S.C.R. 139; R. v. Jack, John and John [1996] 2 C.N.L.R. 113 (B.C.C.A.)

[118] Author's personal observations based upon a review of the reported litigation.

[119] Author's personal observations based upon a review of the reported litigation.

place the interpretation of major Aboriginal issues before the courts rather than pursuing them through negotiations in which Aboriginal people are a direct party with control over the outcome, the complexity of the legal matters involved, and the usual presence of a viable alternative in the form of negotiations. As a result, section 35 is primarily invoked by the defense when the Crown initiates the court action through laying a charge.[120]

6. What Is the Purpose of Subsection 35(4)?

Subsection 35(4) was intended to provide a "Charter-like" guarantee to Aboriginal women that aboriginal and treaty rights will be equally available to both men and women; this would naturally include the right to self-government if it were recognized as being within subsection (1). In October of 1994, the majority opinion of the Supreme Court of Canada stated:

> The right of the Aboriginal people of Canada to participate in constitutional discussions does not derive from any existing Aboriginal or treaty right protected under s. 35. Therefore, s. 35(4) of the Constitution Act, 1982, which guarantees Aboriginal and Treaty rights referred to in s. 35(1) equally to male and female persons, is of no assistance to the respondents.[121]

In this particular case, the Native Women's Association of Canada was unsuccessful in persuading the Court that the right they were alleging was an aboriginal or treaty right. The Court did, however, confirm the effect of subsection 35(4) as a full guarantee of gender equality in reference to any specific rights found as existing within subsection 35(1).[122]

7. Does the Charter Apply to Aboriginal Governments?

The Canadian Charter of Rights and Freedoms was introduced as part of the Constitution Act, 1982. The rights and fundamental freedoms contained in the Charter are guaranteed both to individuals and groups; the Charter contains both individual and collective rights. The Charter is designed to provide protection from inappropriate actions of governments but has no application in private matters.

---

[120] This has been the pattern since long before the advent of the Constitution Act, 1982. *See* JACK WOODWARD, NATIVE LAW (1989).

[121] Native Women's Ass'n of Canada v. Canada [1994] 3 S.C.R. 627, 665. The Inuit Tapirisat of Canada and the Assembly of First Nations intervened in opposition to NWAC and in support of the federal position.

[122] *See id.* at 665.

Some Aboriginal women have been advocating the application of the Canadian Charter of Rights and Freedoms to Aboriginal self-government regimes.[123] This has been viewed by other Aboriginal peoples, both men and women, as undermining the collective fight for the recognition of the "inherent right" of self-government. The then National Chief of the Assembly of First Nations, in responding to this issue before the Royal Commission on Aboriginal Peoples, stated that the

> Assembly of First Nations did not resist equality rights or individual rights. Its resistance concerning the Canadian Charter of Rights and Freedoms was in order to keep options open for traditional forms of government such as those based on clans, confederacy, or hereditary chiefs. The Assembly of First Nations advocated an Aboriginal Charter of Rights, but it did not want to see the Canadian Charter of Rights and Freedoms become another instrument of oppression.[124]

On the other hand, the Native Women's Association of Canada (NWAC) has actively sought the application of the Charter as the best means readily available to protect the interests of Aboriginal women from potential discrimination by Aboriginal governments. While not opposing the development of an Aboriginal Charter, NWAC argues that the Canadian Charter guarantees gender equality now, and that excluding the existing Charter would reflect a shift from a certain, safe position to one in which their protection would be in doubt.[125] Furthermore, the Canadian Charter applies uniformly across the country, whereas leaving the matter to First Nations would require Aboriginal women to struggle, on a community-by-community basis, to obtain equivalent safeguards.[126] This divergence of views has yet to be resolved; however, the current federal government has insisted that the Charter, including the protection provided by section 25 to aboriginal and treaty rights, should apply to Aboriginal governments as it does to all other governments in Canada.

Section 32 (1) of the Charter states that the Charter applies:

(a) to the Parliament and government of Canada in respect of all matters within the authority of Parliament including all matters relating to the Yukon Territory and Northwest Territories; and

---

[123] Author's personal observations. For a very interesting assessment of this overall issue, *see* Peter W. Hogg and Mary Ellen Turpel, *Implementing Aboriginal Self-Government: Constitutional and Jurisdictional Issues*, 74 CDN. BAR REV. 187 (1995).

[124] MICHAEL CASSIDY, OVERVIEW OF THE FIRST ROUND (1992), *quoting* National Chief Ovide Mercredi.

[125] For a summary of some of the concerns from Aboriginal women about discrimination they have suffered from Indian Act governments and the necessity to ensure fairness and accountability from newly constituted Aboriginal governments, *see* PERSPECTIVES AND REALITIES, *supra* note 78 at 71 83.

[126] Author's personal observations.

(b) to the legislature and government of each province in respect of all matters within the authority of the legislature of each province.

It appears that the concept of an "Aboriginal" government is not envisioned by this section.[127] As a result, there is considerable uncertainty as to whether or not the Charter applies. This lack of clarity is further emphasized by the fact that the Charlottetown Accord Draft Legal Text of 1992,[128] in article 27, proposed an amendment to section 32 in order to include an express statement that the Charter applied to "all legislative bodies and governments of the Aboriginal peoples of Canada." Aboriginal governments operating under a delegated authority, for example, the Sechelt First Nation of British Columbia, or under a negotiated agreement recognized by operation of federal legislation, as in the James Bay and Northern Quebec Agreement, would presumably fall under the provisions of the existing section 32 to the extent that the Charter currently applies to these governments. The Indian Act itself, as regular federal legislation, is subject to the Charter, so that First Nations that exercise power as bands under that Act may be covered by the Charter, unless section 25 applies.

Certainly, there are no clear answers on this subject because the Canadian courts have yet to rule definitively on this point. Because of the legal uncertainty, it would seem that the only way to resolve the Charter's application definitively, short of a constitutional amendment, would be to explicitly address the matter in any self-government agreement or for the Supreme Court of Canada to rule on the matter.

8. Section 25 of the Canadian Charter of Rights and Freedoms

Section 25 of the Canadian Charter of Rights and Freedoms provides that:

---

[127] If the Charter does not apply, Aboriginal governments would not be afforded the opportunity to invoke section 33 of the Charter, which states:

33.(1) Parliament or the legislature of a province may expressly declare in an Act of Parliament or the legislature, as the case may be, that the Act or a provision thereof shall operate notwithstanding a provision included in section 2 or sections 7 to 15 of this Charter.

If the Charter is found to apply to Aboriginal governments, some concern has been expressed that section 33 could be used to deny individual rights. On the other hand, some Aboriginal leaders fear that the Charter will apply but that they will not have access to section 33 as they are not included within the phrase "Parliament or the legislatures" in the section. This gives rise to concerns that section 25 may be inadequate to protect laws that advance Aboriginal languages, cultures, religions, and economic opportunities from charges of discrimination and that Aboriginal governments will not possess the safeguard of section 33 in such an eventuality.

[128] CANADA, CHARLOTTETOWN ACCORD–DRAFT LEGAL TEXT (October 9, 1992).

25. The guarantee in this Charter of certain rights and freedoms shall not be construed so as to abrogate or derogate from any aboriginal, treaty or other rights or freedoms that pertain to the aboriginal peoples of Canada including:

(a) any rights or freedoms that have been recognized by the Royal Proclamation of October 7, 1763; and

(b) any rights or freedoms that now exist by way of land claims agreements or may be so acquired.

There is considerable legal uncertainty around this section as well. It has been argued that the main purpose of section 25 is to make clear that the prohibition of racial discrimination in section 15 of the Charter is not to be interpreted as abrogating aboriginal or treaty rights that are possessed by a class of people defined by culture or race.[129] In other words, it is designed as a shield to guard against diminishing aboriginal and treaty rights in situations where non-Aboriginal peoples might challenge the special status or rights of Aboriginal peoples as contrary to equality guarantees. The shield protection of section 25, if it exists, would apply to Charter guarantees generally, not just to section 15. Likewise, it would not be limited to temporary initiatives designed to ameliorate adversity, as is the case with affirmative action efforts protected under subsection 15(2).

This conflict between the application of the Charter to Aboriginal governments exercising self-government and the rights of Aboriginal individuals to Charter protection was dealt with by the Royal Commission on Aboriginal Peoples as follows:

This approach distinguishes between the right of self-government proper and the exercise of government powers flowing from that right. In so far as the right of self-government is an Aboriginal right, section 25 protects it from suppression or amputations at the hands of the Charter. However, individual members of Aboriginal groups like other Canadians enjoy Charter rights in their relations with governments, and this protection extends to Aboriginal governments. In this view, then, the Charter regulates the manner in which Aboriginal governments exercise their powers, but it does not have the effect of abrogating the right of self-government proper.[130]

---

[129] William Pentney, *The Rights of the Aboriginal Peoples of Canada and the Constitution Act, 1982: Part I, The Interpretive Prism of Section 25*, 22 U.B.C. L. REV. 21 (1985).

[130] ROYAL COMMISSION ON ABORIGINAL PEOPLES, PARTNERS IN CONFEDERATION 39 (1993). For a detailed discussion of this topic, *see* Kent McNeil, *Aboriginal Governments and the Canadian Charter of Rights and Freedoms*, 34 OSGOODE HALL L.J. 61 (1996), who concludes that the Charter does not apply to Aboriginal governments at all.

Section 28 of the Charter provides that, "Notwithstanding anything in this Charter, the rights and freedoms referred to in it are guaranteed equally to male and female persons." The argument has been made that section 28 may be the only section that has the potential to limit the shield created by section 25.[131] In making this point it has been suggested that the opening words contained in section 28 are intended to be more comprehensive and inclusive than the general "guarantee" in section 25, so that the relationship of the two can be interpreted as extending the application of section 28 to section 25 rights and freedoms.[132] This would seem to provide a guarantee that Aboriginal governments could not make laws and administrative decisions that discriminate solely on the basis of gender.

9. Post-1982 Attempts to Refine the Constitution Act, 1982[133]

Aboriginal and treaty rights were embodied in the written Constitution in 1982, following sporadic yet intense negotiations that had begun five years earlier. Three sections of the Constitution Act, 1982 related directly to Aboriginal peoples, i.e., sections 25, 35, and 37. Section 25 was designed by the drafters, parliamentarians, and Aboriginal leaders to protect Aboriginal legal rights generally and any legislation outlining the special rights of Aboriginal peoples from potential adverse effects that might flow from the Canadian Charter of Rights and Freedoms. There was particular concern felt that the guarantee of non-discrimination based upon race could undermine if not eliminate any statutory- or policy-based initiatives that benefitted Aboriginal peoples *qua* Aboriginal.[134] Section 25 provides an interpretive prism so that the Charter will not be read in such a way as to abrogate or derogate from "any aboriginal, treaty or other rights or freedoms," including those recognized by the Royal Proclamation of October 7, 1763. It was amended in 1984, so that these protections would apply equally to rights acquired in present or future land claims settlements.[135]

Section 35, by contrast, embodied a positive constitutional recognition. In its original form upon enactment, it stated that:

(1) The existing aboriginal and treaty rights of the aboriginal peoples of Canada are hereby recognized and affirmed.

(2) In this Act, "aboriginal peoples of Canada" includes the Indian, Inuit and Métis peoples of Canada.

---

[131] Kent McNeil, *Aboriginal Governments and the Canadian Charter of Rights and Freedoms*, 34 OsGOODE HALL L.J. 61 (1996) at 79.

[132] *Id.* at 76.

[133] *See* Canadian Charter, *supra* note 95.

[134] BRUCE H. WILDSMITH, ABORIGINAL PEOPLES AND SECTION 25 OF THE CANADIAN CHARTER OF RIGHTS AND FREEDOMS (1988).

[135] Constitutional Amendment Proclamation, 1984, SI 84–102, Schedule.

Section 37 provided for the convening of a First Ministers' Conference (FMC) on Aboriginal Constitutional Matters by no later than April 17, 1983 (one year after proclamation), involving representatives of the Aboriginal peoples, along with the Prime Minister, the Premiers, and delegates from the two Territorial governments. Among other things, section 37 mandated the "identification and definition of the rights of those peoples to be included in the Constitution of Canada."

An accord reached at the first FMC held in March 1983 led to the first, and so far the only, amendments to the Constitution Act, 1982. Section 25 was clarified so as to protect future as well as existing land claims settlements.[136] Section 35 was also changed to indicate that "treaty rights" included rights under existing and future land claims agreements, and to guarantee aboriginal and treaty rights equally to male and female persons.[137] Subsection 35.1 was added, calling for the convening of a First Ministers' Conference, to include representatives of the Aboriginal peoples of Canada, before any constitutional amendments directly affecting Aboriginal peoples could be enacted.[138] Because section 37 had expired without completing its objectives, subsection 37.1 was added to require two further FMCs be called before April 17, 1987.[139] (A third was added for 1984 by way of the terms of the political accord reached at the March 1983 FMC; it was not included within the constitutional amendment as it would be spent before the amendment could take effect.)[140]

The three First Ministers' Conferences that followed focused almost exclusively upon the right of Aboriginal self-government. The debate centered upon the question of whether the right of Aboriginal self-government already existed as flowing from inherent and unextinguished Aboriginal sovereignty and/or from existing treaty rights so as to be included in subsection 35(1)—the commonly called "full box" theory—or whether it did not exist so that the approval of the federal and provincial governments by way of a constitutional amendment was necessary.[141] The government of Canada took the "contingent right" approach, which required the content of self-government to be defined later to some degree by agreement among federal and provincial governments prior to any entrenchment of a new right of self-government in the Constitution.[142] This approach

---

[136] *Id.* For a description of the negotiations, *see* Zlotkin, *supra* note 96.

[137] *Id.*

[138] *Id.*

[139] *Id.*

[140] *See* Zlotkin, *supra* note 96.

[141] For a detailed discussion of these negotiations, *see* Michael Asch, Home and Native Land: Aboriginal Rights and the Canadian Constitution (1984); and Georges Erasmus, *Twenty Years of Disappointed Hopes* in Drumbeat: Anger and Renewal in Indian Country (Boyce Richardson, ed., 1990).

[142] *See* David C. Hawkes, Aboriginal Peoples and Constitutional Reform: What Have We Learned? (1989).

was unacceptable to Aboriginal peoples, because it presupposed that the right was to be created by the Constitution and somehow "given" to them, rather than being recognized as preexisting so that it flowed from the Creator and their historic status as nations. The reaction of provincial and territorial governments was mixed, and negotiations ended without agreement. Just prior to the adjournment of the 1987 Conference, the four national Aboriginal peoples' organizations tabled a common draft constitutional amendment that would have, if adopted, recognized and affirmed the "inherent right" of self-government for all Indian, Inuit, and Métis peoples of Canada.[143] In this proposal, negotiations would be initiated at the request of Aboriginal peoples, and would include: self-government, lands, resources, enhancement of language and culture, and equity of access to federal initiatives for Indian, Métis, and Inuit persons. It was proposed that the rights defined in the agreements would be protected in the Constitution in the same manner as were existing treaty rights. This position never received an official reaction from the governments; the Prime Minister terminated the conference and this process without discussion on the proposal.

A constitutional amendment package known as the Meech Lake Accord,[144] negotiated by the First Ministers in 1987 and focused primarily on meeting the constitutional concerns of Quebec, was rejected by Aboriginal peoples as they were excluded both from its provisions and its development. Public opposition to the accord grew for a wide variety of reasons, including the fact that it offered both too little and too much for Quebec from different perspectives. The proposed constitutional amendments, which, given some of the accord's contents, necessitated passage by all ten provinces as well as the Parliament of Canada under the required version of the amending formula, were not approved by the Legislature of Manitoba prior to the expiration of the three-year deadline required by the Constitution Act, 1982. Speedy passage in the dying days of this time frame was repeatedly blocked by the only First Nations member of the Manitoba Legislature, Elijah Harper, on the basis that the accord not only provided no benefits to Aboriginal peoples but that it also might be to their legal detriment.

The Federal government's constitutional proposals of September 1991[145] moved somewhat away from the "contingent right" approach insisted upon in 1987. The new proposal suggested:

---

[143] See Assembly of First Nations et al., Joint Aboriginal Proposal for Self-Government, First Ministers' Conference on Aboriginal Constitutional Matters, CICS Doc. 800–23/030, Mar. 27, 1987.

[144] CANADA, MEECH LAKE ACCORD (1987). For further information on its contents, see PETER HOGG, MEECH LAKE CONSTITUTIONAL ACCORD ANNOTATED (1988).

[145] See CANADA, SHAPING CANADA'S FUTURE TOGETHER 7 (1991).

an amendment to the Constitution to entrench a general justiciable right to Aboriginal self-government in order to recognize Aboriginal peoples' autonomy over their own affairs within the Canadian federation.[146]

The intent behind this proposal was that the right of self-government would become enforceable in the courts in ten years, or before that time, if negotiated agreements on content and scope could be successfully concluded.

Because of the ambiguous language of the document, it was difficult for others to determine precisely what the government of Canada was proposing: was it recognizing an already-existing ''inherent right'' of self-government in the Constitution, while postponing its justiciability, or was it proposing to entrench a newly created right, one conferred on Aboriginal peoples by the federal and provincial governments? Some of the language in the proposal suggested that the right was inherent, while other language appeared to imply a new right. For example, the word ''recognize'' in the phrase ''. . . in order to recognize Aboriginal peoples' autonomy . . .'' suggested that the right already existed, whereas the use of the past tense in a proposed overreaching ''Canada clause'' to be added to the beginning of the Constitution to the effect ''. . . that the Aboriginal peoples were historically self-governing . . .'' implied that they were no longer self-governing peoples. Likewise, the proposal to ''. . . entrench a general justiciable right to Aboriginal self-government . . .'' suggested that the right was not currently included in section 35 of the Constitution Act, 1982 so as to be immediately enforceable without an amendment, a position unacceptable to Aboriginal peoples.

In response to the federal proposal, the Assembly of First Nations reformulated the view, shared by most other Aboriginal peoples, that their right to self-government was an ''inherent right,'' flowing from their original occupation of the land:

> Our Creator, Mother Earth, put First Nations on this land to care for and live in harmony with all her creation. We cared for our earth, our brothers and sisters in the animal world, and each other. These responsibilities give us our inherent, continuing right to self-government. This right flows from our original occupation of this land from time immemorial.[147]

Similarly, the Native Council of Canada stated that:

> Part of the problem is the failure to see that Aboriginal rights do not come from European documents or agreements or pieces of paper,

---

[146] *Id.*

[147] Assembly of First Nations First Circle on the Constitution, FIRST NATIONS AND THE CONSTITUTION: DISCUSSION PAPER, at 8, Nov. 21, 1991.

although they may be acknowledged or recognized or defined on paper. Aboriginal rights are "inherent" in Aboriginal peoples. They are inherited from our ancestors.[148]

The Right Honorable Joe Clark, the federal minister responsible for Constitutional Affairs at that time and a former Prime Minister, explained why the government of Canada was reluctant to recognize the "inherent right to self-government" of Aboriginal peoples in the Constitution in these terms:

> Our concern with that term is straightforward. We believe that the word—undefined or unmodified—could be used as the basis for a claim to international sovereignty or as the justification of a unilateral approach to deciding what laws did or did not apply to Aboriginal peoples. Our concern with inherency is not with the word but with the meaning. If it can be shown that an amendment can be drafted to ensure that an inherent right does not mean a right to sovereignty or separation, or the unilateral determination of powers, we will look at that. If Aboriginal Canadians can help define what inherency would mean in practical terms—in terms of authorities and jurisdiction and powers—in such a way that the integrity of this federation is not put in question, we would welcome that. We are not opposed to inherency.[149]

Aboriginal leaders did not share Mr. Clark's concerns. Rosemarie Kuptana, then President of the Inuit Tapirisat of Canada, addressed the issue directly in remarks to the Special Joint Parliamentary Committee on a Renewed Canada by stating:

> "Inherent" does not connote a desire to separate from the Canadian state. To the extent it is international, it is simply the international language of human rights. It is used in the preamble of the United Nations' Covenant on Human Rights. The word "inherent" connotes the notion of right that can be recognized but not granted, rights that may be unlawfully violated but that can never be extinguished.[150]

In answering questions before the Special Joint Parliamentary Committee on a Renewed Canada in January 1992, Yvon Dumont of the Métis National Council asserted:

---

[148] Native Council of Canada, *Towards a New Covenant*, Jan. 27, 1992.

[149] The Right Honorable Joe Clark, Transcript of Speech Presented to the Native Council of Canada, at 6 (Nov. 7, 1991).

[150] Minutes of Proceedings and Evidence of the Special Joint Committee of the Senate and the House of Commons on a Renewed Canada, Issues No. 37, at 32:12, Jan. 9, 1992, *quoting* Rosemarie Kuptana.

We want to make it very clear . . . that the Métis saw themselves as nation-builders within Canada . . . we wish to continue to be part of Canada. We are not seeking sovereignty from Canada, we are not seeking separation; we are seeking recognition within the Canadian federation.[151]

Subsequent intense efforts at negotiations in response to the federal proposals of 1991 resulted in agreement of all First Ministers with the national Aboriginal leaders in a form called the Charlottetown Accord[152] in August of 1992, which offered more compromise and more promise from an Aboriginal perspective. This constitutional package addressed most of Quebec's demands as well as extensive provisions on Aboriginal issues, instituting an elected Senate and increasing provincial powers generally at the expense of federal jurisdiction. It was ultimately rejected, however, by Canadians and by the majority of on-reserve Indians at a national referendum in October of 1992. The Charlottetown Accord concluded what was termed the "Canada Round" of constitutional negotiations among federal, provincial, territorial and Aboriginal political leaders. It attempted to reconcile the different and often competing constitutional aspirations of Quebec, Aboriginal peoples, western provinces, women, linguistic communities, racial and ethnic minorities, as well as other interests seeking constitutional change. The provisions of the Accord, which affected Aboriginal peoples most relevant to this discussion, included explicit recognition of the "inherent right" of self-government for all Aboriginal peoples, the development of a treaty clarification process, and agreement that the Canadian Charter of Rights and Freedoms would apply to Aboriginal self-governments.

10. Federal Agenda with Respect to Aboriginal Peoples—"Red Book" Commitments

The Liberal Party, under the leadership of Jean Chrétien, undertook extensive consultations and meetings and listened to thousands of Canadians to devise an agenda and plan for a new government. The result of this process was the creation of an election manifesto in 1993 entitled, *Creating Opportunity: The Liberal Plan for Canada*,[153] better known as the *Red Book.*

The *Red Book* provided the platform for the Liberal Party, and the agenda by which now Prime Minister Chrétien and the federal government sought to

---

[151] Minutes of Proceedings and Evidence of the Special Joint Committee of the Senate and the House of Commons on a Renewed Canada, Issue No. 36, at 36:41, Jan. 9, 1992, *quoting* Yvon Dumont.

[152] Canada, *Consensus Report on the Constitution*, August 28, 1992 (popularly called the Charlottetown Accord after the city in which the last of the negotiations took place).

[153] *See* LIBERAL PARTY OF CANADA, CREATING OPPORTUNITY: THE LIBERAL PLAN FOR CANADA (1993).

meet the objectives of the country and of Canadians. The *Red Book* included a full chapter on Aboriginal peoples and stated that "the priority of a Liberal government will be to assist Aboriginal communities in their efforts to address the obstacles to their development and to help them marshal the human and physical resources necessary to build and sustain vibrant communities."[154] Specifically,

> Our goal for Canada must be a future where: Aboriginal people enjoy a standard of living and quality of life and opportunity equal to those of other Canadians; First Nations, Inuit and Métis peoples live self-reliantly, secure in the knowledge of who they are as unique peoples; all Canadians are enriched by Aboriginal cultures and are committed to the fair sharing of the potential of our nation; Aboriginal people have the positive option to live and work wherever they choose; and perhaps most importantly, Aboriginal children grow up in secure families and healthy communities, with the opportunity to take their full place in Canada.[155]

These goals are premised on the fact that "many Aboriginal people face enormous problems, both in their communities and in the cities across Canada where they live: absence of meaningful employment and economic opportunities, unequal educational opportunity and results, poor housing, unsafe drinking water, and lack of health services. They suffer also from the destruction and lack of respect for Aboriginal languages, values, and culture."[156]

For the first time in Canadian history, a party was elected to form the national government with a detailed campaign platform on Aboriginal issues that reflected the recognition that past and "current ways of dealing with these conditions are not working" and that "it is a time for change."[157] In pursuit of these objectives, the Liberal government "will be committed to building a new partnership with Aboriginal peoples that is based on trust, mutual respect, and participation in the decision-making process."[158] Specifically, the Liberal government undertook to:

— develop a more comprehensive process for consultation between federal ministers and Aboriginal representatives with respect to decision-making that directly affects First Nations, Inuit, and Métis people

---

[154] *Id.* at 96.

[155] *Id.* at 98.

[156] *Id.* at 97.

[157] *Id.*

[158] *Id.* at 98.

— explore new fiscal arrangements with Aboriginal peoples;

— seek the advice of treaty First Nations on how to achieve a mutually acceptable process to interpret the treaties in contemporary terms, while giving full recognition to their original spirit and intent;

— support the Inuit in a process for the negotiation of regional self-government agreements for Inuit living outside the future territory of Nunavut;

— take the lead in trilateral negotiations involving the provinces to define the nature and scope of federal and provincial responsibility for Métis and off-reserve Indians; and

— provide assistance to enumerate the Métis.[159]

Most of these objectives were to be achieved primarily through the process of negotiating and implementing self-government. As the Royal Commission on Aboriginal Peoples has stated:

Self-government is the way forward and the main source of hope for Aboriginal people. It is the key to renewing the vigour of communities and societies, a prerequisite for ending the cycle of poverty and despair, and a means of enhancing both the self-respect of Aboriginal people and mutual respect between Aboriginal and non-Aboriginal people. In short, it is the potential turning point of modern Aboriginal history.[160]

As such, the pursuit of self-government by Aboriginal peoples and the federal government alike, is about restoring human rights and human dignity to Aboriginal peoples as a whole. It is also an effort designed to ensure the protection of the rights of individuals under Aboriginal self-government and as residents of Canada.

In May 1994, the Honorable Ronald Irwin (then Minister of Indian Affairs and Northern Development) and the Honorable Anne McLellan (then Federal Interlocutor for the Métis and non-status Indians) set out the main elements of a proposed approach to implementing the "inherent right," which included the following:

1) recognition of the inherent right as an existing "aboriginal right" under section 35 of the Constitution Act, 1982;

---

[159] *Id.*

[160] ROYAL COMMISSION ON ABORIGINAL PEOPLES, DISCUSSION PAPER 2: FOCUSING THE DIALOGUE (1993).

2) that the exercise of the right should be within the existing constitutional framework, including application of the Canadian Charter of Rights and Freedoms;

3) that the negotiations among governments and Aboriginal groups are the only practical and effective way to implement the right and ensure harmonious jurisdictional relationships;

4) a preference to negotiate through processes at the provincial, treaty or regional level;

5) a willingness to consider protecting certain aspects of negotiated agreements as section 35 treaties, where all parties so agree; and

6) an indication that financing of self-government should be a shared responsibility of all governments, including Aboriginal governments.[161]

In December 1994, the Cabinet agreed that the Minister of Indian Affairs and the Federal Interlocutor could further test, with provinces, territories, and Aboriginal leaders, a more detailed version of the main elements of this proposed policy approach, and were to return to the Cabinet with final recommendations on how best to proceed with the implementation of the "inherent right" once this last round of consultations was completed.[162] These further consultations were undertaken and, although they did not lead to dramatic change in the positions of key players, some important alterations in the proposed federal position were made.

The approach of the current federal government differs from that of previous governments in several very significant respects:

1) it is based on a recognition of an "inherent right" as already existing in section 35 of the Constitution Act, 1982 rather than offering to create a delegated authority;

2) where parties agree, it allows for the constitutional protection of certain aspects of negotiated agreements as section 35 treaty rights, which was not possible previously;

3) it allows for more matters to be negotiated and for a broader potential range of Aboriginal jurisdiction than was the case under previous federal policy; and

---

[161] The Honorable Ronald Irwin, Speech Presented to the Federal, Provincial/Territorial Meeting with Ministers and Aboriginal Leaders (May 1994).

[162] Personal observation of the author who was Executive Assistant at the time to the Hon. Ronald A. Irwin, Minister of Indian and Northern Affairs.

4) it allows for negotiation processes to be initiated by Métis and Indian people off a land base and provides for the enumeration of their members who may be covered by self-government arrangements, neither of which was formerly permitted.[163]

E. Federal "Inherent Right" Policy

On August 10, 1995, following eighteen months of consultations with provinces, territories, and national, regional, and local Aboriginal organizations, Ministers Irwin and McLellan announced the federal government's policy approach to implementing the "inherent right" of Aboriginal self-government.[164] The policy is grounded on the premise that the "inherent right" of self-government is an existing right within section 35 of the Constitution Act, 1982. Furthermore, the negotiation of self-government agreements is described as one of the top priorities of the Department of Indian Affairs and Northern Development, as identified in its business plan.[165]

Firstly, the government of Canada asserts that the Aboriginal peoples currently have the right to govern themselves. The government believes that Aboriginal peoples not only deserve, but that they already possess, the constitutionally recognized right to decide fundamental issues that affect their communities and exercise the responsibility that is required to achieve true self-government.[166] This policy shift has created the opportunity for a historic turning point in the relationship between Aboriginal and non-Aboriginal peoples in Canada. The federal policy to recognize the "inherent right" of Aboriginal peoples to self-government, which is not without controversy, will result, if implemented, in new arrangements that revive hope and establish a true partnership in the context of an evolving federation.

Restoring Aboriginal governments can empower Aboriginal communities to assert far more significant control over their lives so as to meet their needs, cultures, philosophies, and goals for the future in such vital fields as education, health, child care, housing, and economic opportunities. The federal approach is to declare itself willing to negotiate the details of implementation of the "inherent right" of self-government with First Nations or Aboriginal groups and the relevant provincial or territorial government.

Second, the federal government recognizes the inherent right to self-government as an "existing" "aboriginal right" so as to be enforceable through the

---

[163] *Id.*

[164] GOVERNMENT OF CANADA, ABORIGINAL SELF-GOVERNMENT: FEDERAL POLICY GUIDE (1995) [hereinafter FEDERAL POLICY GUIDE].

[165] INDIAN AND NORTHERN AFFAIRS CANADA, 1996–1997 BUSINESS PLAN i–ii (1996) [hereinafter BUSINESS PLAN].

[166] FEDERAL POLICY GUIDE, *supra* note 164 at 3.

courts by virtue of being "recognized and affirmed" by subsection 35(1) of the Constitution Act, 1982.[167] The Canadian government also accepts that the "inherent right" may find expression in treaties, and within the general context of the Crown's unique relationship with treaty First Nations.[168] Although government accepts judicial authority to define the scope of the "inherent right," it would clearly rather see the right and practical arrangements be elaborated through negotiations.[169] The Government of Canada favors negotiation over litigation for various reasons including the fact that: the judicial process is very expensive and time-consuming; the result is always uncertain until a decision is rendered and tends to result in all-or-nothing judgements; the length of the process will mean that jurisdiction will be up in the air for many years pending the outcome of the final appeal; the courts are poorly equipped to address extremely complex intergovernmental matters, especially when all the issues are not even apparent; and the judiciary has previously indicated that these matters are more appropriately dealt with by negotiations in any event. In *MacMillan Bloedel v. Mullin,* Mr. Justice Macfarlane stated:

> I think it fair to say that, in the end, the public anticipates that the claims will be resolved by negotiation and by settlement. This judicial proceeding is but a small part of the whole of a process which will ultimately find its solution in a reasonable exchange between governments and the Indian nations.[170]

Delimiting self-government jurisdiction through lawsuits would entail an immense amount of litigation on a subject-by-subject, First Nation-by-First Nation, and conflict-by-conflict basis in every province or territory.[171] At the end of the day, any judgments upholding the right of self-government would almost inevitably still require negotiations among the parties to analyze the impact of the decisions and to identify the next steps necessary to respect and fulfill the decisions.

The federal government's opinion is that both the "inherent right" and the specific jurisdictions of Aboriginal governments must be exercised within the

---

[167] *Id.*

[168] *Id.*

[169] *Id.*

[170] MacMillan Bloedel v. Mullin [1985] 2 C.N.L.R. 58, 77 (B.C.C.A).

[171] For a recent series of Supreme Court of Canada decisions that both reflect the use of this case-by-case approach and also establish principles of law that require its utilization, *see* R. v. Gladstone (1996) 137 D.L.R. (4th) 47 (S.C.C.) R. v. Van der Peet (1996) 137 D.L.R. (4th) 289 (S.C.C.); R. v. N.T.C. Smokehouse Ltd. (1996) 137 D.L.R. (4th) 528 (S.C.C.); R. v. Adams (1996) 138 D.L.R. (4th) 657 (S.C.C.); R. v. Cote (1996) 138 D.L.R. 385 (S.C.C.); and R. v. Gardner (1996) 138 D.L.R. (4th) 204 (S.C.C.)

framework of the Constitution as it stands. Aboriginal governments and agencies would have to function harmoniously with the institutions operated by other governments. Similarly, federal, provincial, territorial, regional, and municipal non-Aboriginal governments will need to conduct their sovereign or delegated jurisdiction, as the case may be, in harmony with sovereign Aboriginal governments. The government of Canada argues that it is in the interest of both Aboriginal and non-Aboriginal governments to create a cooperative approach to promote a positive relationship with a minimum of conflicts of laws, which is so vital to the effective and efficient operations of any federation. One can readily inspect the American experience to see the flood of jurisdictional conflict litigation, primarily between state and tribal governments, that occurs in the absence of intergovernmental arrangements.

The government of Canada asserts that the Canadian Charter of Rights and Freedoms binds all existing governments, and must likewise affect any future Aboriginal governments in order to ensure that it continues to apply to all governments in Canada.[172] As a result, all Canadians—Aboriginal and non-Aboriginal alike—will continue to enjoy the Charter's guarantee of rights and freedoms. It must be realized, however, that the Charter does contain section 25, which likely shields the right of self-government as an "aboriginal right" from any negative interpretations or applications of individual rights principles while still subjecting the exercise of governmental powers by Aboriginal governments to Charter scrutiny. The federal position is that the Canadian Criminal Code[173] should also continue to apply to all Aboriginal peoples after self-government is fully implemented regardless of the situs of the crime.[174] While criminal procedure, pretrial diversion, and sentencing rules may differ between Aboriginal justice systems and mainstream systems, the substantive criminal law would continue to remain uniform throughout Canada under the federal view. This negotiating position, if it prevails, would obviously lead to a situation in which First Nations and other Aboriginal communities in Canada would possess significantly less criminal law jurisdiction than tribal governments in the United States.

Third, the federal "inherent right" policy is predicated on the belief that Aboriginal governments would negotiate different degrees of authority in areas otherwise falling into federal and provincial jurisdiction, reflecting the result of separate negotiations and the divergent conditions that exist across the country. The federal position is that some heads of jurisdiction have effects beyond the boundaries of Aboriginal communities and that a limited range of subject matters are of clearly overriding national and provincial interest to the extent that federal or provincial laws in these spheres should prevail in instances of conflicts of

---

[172] FEDERAL POLICY GUIDE, *supra* note 164, at 4.

[173] Criminal Code, R.S.C., ch. C–34 (1985).

[174] FEDERAL POLICY GUIDE, *supra* note 164, at 7.

laws that cannot otherwise be resolved.[175] The federal view is that the core of self-government agreements should recognize that Aboriginal peoples have the right to decide matters "internal to their communities, integral to their unique cultures, identities, traditions, languages and institutions, and with respect to their special relationship to their land and their resources."[176] Self-government arrangements should respect the special, spiritual relationship that Aboriginal peoples have with their lands and their resources.[177] Self-government negotiations to date, as well as the Federal Policy Guide, indicate that agreements will likely set out areas of jurisdiction and conflicts of law rules in some detail, so as to provide as much precision as possible to reduce future disputes.

The fourth key principle underlying the federal position is that the fiscal resources required by Aboriginal governments should be shared among federal, provincial, territorial, and Aboriginal governments and institutions.[178] Specific financial transfer arrangements would need to be negotiated by the other relevant governments and the Aboriginal groups concerned, as are the financial transfers that exist now from the federal government to all provinces and territories. The federal position declares that "[a]ll participants in self-government negotiations must recognize that self-government arrangements will have to be affordable and consistent with the overall social and economic policies and priorities of governments,"[179] while at the same time taking into account the particular requirements and revenue raising capacities of the Aboriginal governments involved.

Last, the federal preference is for the process to commence by an Aboriginal community or group declaring its readiness to start negotiations, followed by preliminary meetings among representatives of the federal government, the Aboriginal group, and the relevant province or territory to clarify how the substantive discussions should proceed.[180] So far, over fifty framework agreements or memoranda of understanding have been negotiated to identify the agendas for substantive negotiations to follow, the procedures to govern the negotiation process, the anticipated time frames in which different steps will occur, and the mechanism for terminating negotiations if they are unsuccessful. The comprehensive land claims negotiations that are underway in certain nontreaty areas

---

[175] *Id.* at 6–7.

[176] *Id.* at 3. The federal position paper language is remarkably similar to the test enunciated by the Supreme Court of Canada one year later without any reference to the federal policy in *R. v. Van der Peet* (1996) 137 D.L.R. (4th) 289 (S.C.C.).

[177] *Id.*

[178] *Id.* at 14.

[179] *Id.*

[180] *Id.* at 23.

of Canada (British Columbia, Quebec, Yukon, Northwest Territories, and Labrador) are now being used to address self-government matters, as all parties have consented to expand their scope.

The federal government strenuously argues that provincial governments are essential parties to these negotiations and must be a signatory to the agreements reached, because many of the subjects are generally within provincial jurisdiction under the Canadian Constitution, or because the exercise of governmental powers under the agreements may have effects beyond the Aboriginal lands or group involved.[181] The federal thinking is applied to territorial governments north of the sixtieth parallel, although they do not possess any sovereign jurisdiction, as they exercise most of the powers of a province under delegated authority from Parliament. Given the obvious desire of First Nations to obtain constitutional protection under section 35 for any agreements that confirm or elaborate upon their powers of governance, it is preferable to have the relevant province or territorial government be a signatory to the agreement that specifies constitutional entrenchment, so as to drastically reduce the possibility that these governments might challenge the constitutionality of such entrenchment in the future. There is a question as to whether or not a province's consent is required for agreements that trench upon provincial jurisdiction to obtain constitutional protection under section 35. It could be argued that recognition of rights from a collateral agreement is an indirect constitutional amendment not in accordance with the formal requirements of the amending formula set out in Part V of the Constitution Act, 1982. Clearly, having the province as a party to the negotiations and the final agreement decreases significantly the likelihood of a challenge from this quarter.

The reality is that Aboriginal and provincial or territorial governments will be compelled to interact extensively in the future. It is, therefore, in their mutual best interest to harmonize the exercise of their respective jurisdictions on a pragmatic, effective basis so as to meet the common goals of their respective citizens. First Nations, for example, will want the graduates from schools governed by their laws to be recognized by provincially controlled tertiary institutions, while those universities will want to attract First Nations students and their tuition revenue. Having all three governments in the same negotiating forum from the outset should be conducive to building a cooperative relationship for the future. On the other hand, Aboriginal parties naturally assert that provincial refusal to participate should not constitute a *de facto* veto. The very foundation of the "inherent right" theory is that it is an immediately exercisable and enforceable right, such that an appropriate Aboriginal group should be able to exercise its authority or negotiate an agreement on a bilateral basis with the federal government alone.

---

[181] *Id.* at 4.

F. Self-Government Jurisdiction

The essential object of self-government negotiations should be to reach practical arrangements that will work on the ground, rather than to seeking a common national legal definition of the "inherent right" in the abstract.[182] Naturally, self-government arrangements will differ dramatically across the nation in order to reflect the different cultures, values, traditions, ways of life, and economic conditions that exist.[183]

Aboriginal governments and institutions will obviously require the jurisdiction and authority to act in a number of areas in order to give practical effect to the "inherent right" to self-government. The debate that is underway presently in Canada among Aboriginal, federal, and provincial government representatives is over what should be the limits of Aboriginal jurisdiction, if any, and who can set them. "Broadly stated, the Government views the scope of Aboriginal jurisdiction or authority as likely extending to matters that are internal to the group, integral to its distinct Aboriginal culture, and essential to its operation as a government or institution."[184] Under this perspective, the areas that the federal government would recognize as appropriate negotiation topics could include all, some, or parts of the following heads of authority:

— establishment of governing structures, internal constitutions, elections, and leadership selection processes;

— membership;

— marriage;

— adoption and child welfare;

— Aboriginal language, culture, and religion;

— education;

— health care;

— social services;

— administration/enforcement of Aboriginal laws, including the establishment of Aboriginal courts or tribunals and the creation of

---

[182] *Id.* at 24. See Clem Chartier, *Aboriginal Self-Government and the Métis Nation* in ABORIGINAL SELF-GOVERNMENT IN CANADA: CURRENT TRENDS AND ISSUES 199, 209–211 (John H. Hylton, ed., 1994).

[183] *Id.* at 17–21.

[184] *Id.* at 5.

offences of the type normally created by local or regional governments for contravention of their laws,

— policing;

— property rights, including succession and estates;

— land management, including: zoning; service fees; land tenure and
access; and expropriation of Aboriginal land by Aboriginal governments for their own public purposes;

— natural resources management;

— agriculture;

— hunting, fishing, and trapping on Aboriginal lands;

— taxation in respect of direct taxes and property taxes of members;

— transfer and management of monies and group assets;

— management of public works and infrastructure;

— housing;

— local transportation; and

— licensing, regulation, and operation of businesses located on Aboriginal lands.[185]

In some of the foregoing areas, developing very precise rules will likely be
required to ensure harmonization of laws, in order to resolve conflicts with
existing federal and provincial legislation and minimize future discord. A more
general recognition of Aboriginal jurisdiction or authority may be sufficient in
certain spheres through a simple paramountcy rule, whereby those Aboriginal
laws that conflict with existing federal or provincial legislation covering the
exact same subject matter would be regarded as paramount to the extent of any
conflict. This would not render the federal or provincial law *ultra vires*, but
merely inapplicable in the face of the more precise Aboriginal law in force in
that specific Aboriginal community.

There are a number of other legal fields that may go beyond matters that
are integral to Aboriginal cultures or traditions or that are strictly internal to an
Aboriginal group. To the extent that the federal government has jurisdiction in

---

[185] *See id.* at 5–6.

these areas, it has declared that it is prepared to negotiate measures that would confirm a level of Aboriginal jurisdiction.[186] In these subject areas, laws and regulations tend to have impacts that go beyond any individual communities and territorial borders by virtue of the nature of the subject matter. Therefore, the federal government argues that primary lawmaking authority should likely remain at the federal or provincial level, as the case may be, and their legislation would override any conflicting Aboriginal laws,[187] however complementary, and "meet or beat" legislation would readily be possible. The subjects identified as falling into this category by the federal government are:

— divorce;

— labour/training;

— administration of justice issues, including matters related to the administration and enforcement of laws of other jurisdictions which might include certain criminal laws;

— penitentiaries and parole;

— environmental protection, assessment, and pollution prevention;

— fisheries co-management;

— migratory birds co-management;

— gaming; and

— emergency preparedness.[188]

Many Aboriginal groups dispute this federal characterization and believe that primary legislative jurisdiction over these heads of power should also rest with Aboriginal governments.[189] They have further criticized the federal government for the process it used to develop its position, namely consultations in general followed by the release of a federal position, rather than negotiating what the precise terms of the federal policy should be.[190]

---

[186] *Id.* at 6.

[187] *Id.*

[188] *Id.* at 7.

[189] For some comments in this regard given to the media *see* Jack Aubry, *Natives Offered 'Historic' Self-Government Powers,* Ottawa Citizen, Aug. 11, 1995, at A1.

[190] *See* Jack Aubry, *Ottawa Lays Out Indian Proposal,* Toronto Star May 4, 1995, at A16.

There are also a number of areas where the federal government has stated that it sees no compelling reasons for Aboriginal governments or institutions to exercise any lawmaking authority, while compelling reasons do exist in its view for federal jurisdiction to remain intact. These subject matters are not characterized by the government as either integral to Aboriginal societies, or internal to Aboriginal territories. They can be grouped under two main headings: powers related to Canadian sovereignty, defense, and external relations; and other national interest powers. The federal policy argues that it is essential to the proper functioning of a Nation-State for the Government of Canada to retain its exclusive legislative jurisdiction over the following subject matters:

Powers Related to Canadian Sovereignty, Defence and External Relations:

— international/diplomatic relations and foreign policy;

— national defence and security;

— security of national borders;

— international treaty-making;

— immigration, naturalization, and aliens; and

— international trade, including tariffs and import/export controls.

Other National Interest Powers:

— Management and regulation of the national economy, including:

  • regulation of the national business framework, fiscal and monetary policy;

  • a central bank and the banking system;

  • bankruptcy and insolvency;

  • trade and competition policy;

  • intellectual property;

  • incorporation of federal corporations; and

  • currency.

— Maintenance of national law and order and substantive criminal law, including:

- offenses and penalties under the *Criminal Code* and other criminal laws;

- emergencies and the "peace, order and good government" power of section 91 of the *Constitution Act, 1867*.

— Protection of the health and safety of all Canadians.

— Federal undertakings and other powers, including:

- broadcasting and telecommunications

- aeronautics

- navigation and shipping

- maintenance of national transportation systems

- postal service; and

- census and statistics.[191]

While the Canadian government has rejected recognizing legislative power in these areas, it has indicated it is prepared to consider negotiating "administrative arrangements where it might be feasible and appropriate."[192] One possibility of such an arrangement might be the licensing of a local closed circuit cable television system by an Aboriginal government while the federal government would retain general legislative jurisdiction over telecommunication, television, and radio.

Needless to say, the federal position is a highly controversial one and has been criticized from various directions. From what might be characterized as the political right, the policy has been challenged as being without a legal foundation, despite official endorsement from the federal Department of Justice.[193] Some of those who reject the theory that the "inherent right" has already been recognized by subsection 35(1) still support the concept of Aboriginal governance, but believe that no such right of self-government yet exists. They assert that either a constitutional amendment is required to create the right (the "contingent right" theory) or legislation delegating local government powers is necessary.[194] Other critics argue that the government of Canada has gone too far in its policy and

---

[191] *See* FEDERAL POLICY GUIDE, *supra* note 164, at 7.

[192] *Id.* at 8.

[193] Confidential information made available to the author.

[194] Author's personal observations.

conceded too much jurisdictional scope for Aboriginal governments.[195] Several provinces fall into each of these two camps. There are, of course, also those who oppose the very concept of Aboriginal governments as contrary to their notion of equality. They assert that Aboriginal governments are race-based and should be prohibited as constituting racial discrimination, rather than appreciating that their existence stems from the reality that they were political nations prior to European arrival.[196]

On the other side of the spectrum, some Aboriginal leaders have denounced the federal policy as paternalistic and mislabeled.[197] This attack argues that placing parameters on what is negotiable, or even pushing the concept of negotiation over immediate recognition, is antithetical to the perspective that the "inherent right" is equivalent to international sovereignty. According to almost all Aboriginal peoples, "the inherent right" comes from the Creator and, therefore, it predates the arrival of the Europeans. Mr. Justice Judson of the Supreme Court of Canada supported this basic notion in *Calder* v. *Attorney-General of British Columbia* when he stated:

> Although I think that it is clear that Indian title in British Columbia cannot owe its origin to the *Proclamation of 1763*, the fact is that when the settlers came, the Indians were there, organized in societies and occupying the land as their forefathers had done for centuries.[198]

The "inherent right" to self-government reflects the continuation of jurisdiction from the pre-contact era of full sovereignty. This claim is based primarily upon the following principles:

(1) before the coming of the Europeans, the Aboriginal peoples were organized as self-governing societies;

(2) Aboriginal societies were recognized by the Crown as nations capable of entering into treaties;

(3) Aboriginal peoples did not generally give up their right to self-government expressly in the treaties; and

(4) although the right to self-government may have been restricted, it was never specifically extinguished by treaties or valid legislation.

---

[195] *Id.*

[196] For an interesting discussion of this issue from an Aboriginal perspective, *see* Paul L.A.H. Chartrand, *Aboriginal Self-Government: The Two Sides of Legitimacy in* How Ottawa Spends: A More Democratic Canada. . . ? 1993–94 (Susan D. Phillips, ed., 1993) 234, 236.

[197] Author's personal observations.

[198] Calder v. Attorney-General of British Columbia, *supra* note 22, at 328.

Within the Constitution Acts, from 1867 up to and including 1982, express mention is made of only two sovereign levels of government capable of making laws, i.e., the federal and provincial governments. Although the "inherent right" to Aboriginal self-government has not been judicially confirmed as an "aboriginal" or "treaty right," there is no Supreme Court of Canada decision that would preclude such a finding.[199] Furthermore, modern land claims agreements pursuant to subsection 35(3), which often include self-government types of issues, are constitutionally entrenched.

The important distinction between, on the one hand, the constitutional entrenchment after an agreement has been negotiated, and the immediate constitutional recognition that there is an existing right which can result in negotiations of an agreement or unilateral exercise of the right on the other, is significant. This difference goes to the core of the debate as illustrated in the foregoing discussion on the meaning of "inherent right" versus a "contingent right," which can solely be realized if an agreement is ever actually reached. This distinction influences the amount of leverage that Aboriginal groups have in any negotiations, determines the perceptions of the parties, affects the ability to litigate the issue in the absence of any agreement, and effectively decides whether the negotiations can be described as government-to-government in nature.

The Royal Commission on Aboriginal Peoples, in a preliminary document entitled *Partners in Confederation,*[200] expressed its endorsement of an "inherent right" to self-government as does one of its primary research advisors, legal scholar Brian Slattery. He stated that:

> Over the years, the right was whittled away by the provisions of the Indian Act. However, it seems the right of self-government as such was never extinguished. The important consequence is that, when section 35 of the Constitution Act, 1982 took effect, the right of self-government was still extant and featured among the "existing aboriginal and treaty rights" recognized in the section.[201]

It is highly informative to contrast the Canadian position with that prevailing in the United States. An "inherent right" of Indian nations to governance has been recognized by the U.S. Supreme Court virtually since its creation.[202] Tribal

---

[199] The Supreme Court of Canada's decision in *R. v. Gardner, supra* note 14, does not, however, give great comfort in this regard.

[200] *See* ROYAL COMMISSION ON ABORIGINAL PEOPLES, *supra* note 130.

[201] Brian Slattery, *First Nations and the Constitution: A Question of Trust,* 71 CAN. BAR REV. 261, 279 (1992).

[202] *See, e.g.,* Johnson v. M'Intosh, 21 U.S. (8 Wheat.) 543 (1823); Worcester v. Georgia, 31 U.S. (6 Pet.) 515 (1832); and Cherokee Nation v. Georgia, 30 U.S. (5 Pet.) 16, 20 (1831).

governments in the United States have limits placed on their right of self-government by treaty, by federal law, and by their status as protected domestic nations
as interpreted by the dominant society's judicial system. This latter status pre-
cludes them from entering into treaties with other nations, while American courts
have also denied to tribes the right to assert criminal jurisdiction over non-
Indians.[203] Apart from this, however, the tribal governments have almost unlimited civil jurisdiction, including marriage, divorce, child welfare, estates, trusts,
taxation, licensing, real and personal property, torts, wildlife, natural resources,
administration of justice, social services, education, health care, culture, language, religion, policing, corrections, utilities, membership, highway traffic, and
commercial transactions. They maintain law and order and administer civil and
criminal justice within their territories, subject to specific federal statutory limitations. There is, however, no constitutional recognition of Aboriginal peoples
and their rights in the United States. Thus, while Indian governments in the
United States hold inherent powers of self-government or residual sovereignty,
these powers are limited and are subordinated to the overriding or plenary power
of Congress, without any brake on the exercise of Congressional authority.[204]

G. Status of Self-Government Agreements

Canadian federal policy anticipates that agreements on self-government will
be given legal effect through a variety of mechanisms, including using new or
existing treaties, legislation, contracts, and nonbinding memoranda of understanding as the parties decide. It has described its position on the critical issue
of the constitutional status of agreements negotiated in these terms: ''The Government of Canada is prepared, where the other parties agree, to constitutionally
protect rights set out in negotiated self-government agreements as treaty rights
within the meaning of section 35 of the Constitution Act, 1982. Implementation
of the inherent right in this fashion would be a continuation of the historic
relationship between Aboriginal peoples and the Crown,''[205] which is reflected
in subsection 35(3) with land claims agreements. Self-government rights could
be protected under section 35 as new treaties, additions to existing treaties, or
as part of major land claims agreements dealing with Aboriginal title. The federal
government summarized its view of what should receive constitutional protection as follows:

> Treaties create mutually binding obligations and commitments which
> are constitutionally protected. Recognizing the solemn and enduring

---

[203] *See* Oliphant v. Suquamish Indian Tribe, 435 U.S. 191 (1978).

[204] For further information on the American situation *see,* STRICKLAND, *supra* note
69; CHARLES F. WILKINSON, AMERICAN INDIANS, TIME AND THE LAW (1987); FRANK POM-
MERSHEIM, BRAID OF FEATHERS: PLURALISM, LEGITIMACY, SOVEREIGNTY AND THE IMPOR-
TANCE OF TRIBAL COURT JURISPRUDENCE (1995); and VINE DELORIA, JR. & CLIFFORD M.
LYTLE, AMERICAN INDIANS, AMERICAN JUSTICE (1983).

[205] Federal Policy Guide, *supra* note 164 at 8.

nature of treaty rights, the Government believes that the primary criterion for determining whether or not a matter should receive constitutional protection is whether it is a fundamental element of self-government that should bind future generations. Under this approach, suitable matters for constitutional protection would naturally include:

(1) a listing of jurisdictions or authorities by subject matter and related arrangements;

(2) the relationship of Aboriginal laws to federal and provincial laws;

(3) the geographic area within which the Aboriginal government or institution would exercise its jurisdiction or authority, and the people to be affected thereby; and

(4) matters relating to the accountability of the Aboriginal government to its members, in order to confirm its legitimacy and the legitimacy of its laws within the Constitution of Canada.[206]

This approach suggests that matters of a technical or temporary nature would not generally be appropriate to obtain constitutional protection as treaty rights. Similarly, those commitments that must be flexible to accommodate changing conditions or be periodically renegotiated, such as the detailed aspects of program delivery and funding agreements, would not seem to reflect the type of enduring arrangements that fit within the realm of constitutional entrenchment.

Collateral agreements could be reached on these kinds of matters and be binding on the parties, so as to be legally enforceable in a forum identified within the agreements themselves. Therefore, some components of the overall self-government arrangements negotiated will be implemented through treaties, while others will be within intergovernmental agreements. Additional mechanisms that will play a role in this process include legislation and nonbinding memoranda of understanding. Federal and provincial or territorial legislation can be used:

— to ratify and give effect to agreements, including treaties, as has been done with modern comprehensive claims agreements for over 20 years;

— to implement particular provisions of agreements; or

— as a stand-alone mechanism when the parties do not want to use a treaty as the vehicle to implement the self-government agreement.[207]

---

[206] Id.

[207] Id. at 9.

Similarly, Aboriginal governments or communities would wish to confirm their agreements through legislation or referenda.

The historic treaties are central to the unique relationship that exists between Treaty First Nations and the Crown in right of Canada. Implementing the ''inherent right'' through negotiating self-government agreements does not necessitate the reopening, changing or displacing existing treaties. The federal thinking is that agreements on self-government would be negotiated by those Treaty First Nations that desire to do so in a manner that can expand upon the relationship already established by their treaties and complement their terms in this regard.[208] Exploratory discussions of this nature are underway with Treaty First Nations in Saskatchewan and Alberta concerning postconfederation treaties.

The true test of the durability of any complex agreement is how it will be respected and implemented once ratified. The modern experience in land claims negotiations has demonstrated that it is essential to negotiate a separate implementation plan for all agreements simultaneously with the negotiations of the substantive final agreements. In the self-government context, this would mean that implementation plans would specifically address the activities that need to be undertaken, the human and fiscal resources required, the time lines for action and transitional measures that have been agreed upon to give effect to the substantive agreements or treaties. ''Issues related to affordability, efficiency, capital requirements, duplication of services, feasibility and capacity will have to be addressed.''[209] An enforcement mechanism, such as mediation followed by arbitration, is also vital. Starting with the Inuvialuit settlement in the Western Arctic in 1984, arbitration provisions have become common in comprehensive land claims agreements, as a method of overcoming judicial reluctance to enforce modern treaties, in addition to providing a lower cost alternative to the courts. Furthermore, negotiating arbitral clauses offers an opportunity to seek an expedited process for achieving decisions and guarantees an equal role to the Aboriginal signatory in the selection of the arbitrator(s). Experience to date has also shown that arbitration provides an opportunity to draw upon nonlegal expertise of arbitrators and to use a far higher percentage of Aboriginal people than is the case with the Canadian judiciary.

It is obvious that establishing new Aboriginal governments, or completely revamping existing Indian Act governments, into real Aboriginal ones with sovereign authority will involve significant new financial expenditures. The federal government takes the position, however, that there will not be a new source of funding for implementation and transition costs.[210] As a result, it has declared that all federal costs associated with the implementation of self-government agreements will have to be accommodated within existing federal expenditures

---

[208] *Id.*

[209] *Id.* at 16.

[210] *Id.*

given the fiscal crisis and debt burden that confronts the government of Canada. The federal view is that all three parties to the negotiations should share the future costs of Aboriginal governments.[211] Once fully implemented, First Nations would be free to redesign their budgets and redistribute funds into those activities they view as most important, subject to adhering to any national program standards or statutory requirements agreed to through the negotiations.

The pace, timing, and progress of self-government negotiations will also naturally vary across the country. Self-government negotiations in conjunction with land claim negotiations, for instance, tend to be on a somewhat slower pace as the general preference of Aboriginal groups is to focus on land and natural resources aspects to negotiations first, which may themselves take many years to complete. Self-government negotiations associated with the former community-based delegated powers approach are on a faster track, as many of these have been underway since the mid 1980s and are now at the point where decisions need to be taken to finalize negotiations or to terminate them. The Manitoba Dismantling initiative, which commenced officially through the signing of a Framework Agreement on December 7, 1994[212] to confirm First Nations' jurisdictions through negotiations, while also transferring to them the functions of DIAND, has its own internal timetable to reach a Final Agreement. The comprehensive claims and self-government negotiations under the British Columbia Treaty Commission process proceed at a pace no faster than the capacity of the parties can permit, which is somewhat restricted for the federal and provincial governments by their participation in 48 separate negotiations, with well over 125 First Nations, simultaneously. Sectoral arrangements, because they deal with a single or several areas of jurisdiction at one time, can and are proceeding more expeditiously than the more comprehensive negotiations.

Since the announcement of the ''inherent right'' approach in August of 1995, several self-government negotiations that were initiated before the policy have undergone the transition to the ''inherent right'' approach and have resulted in many signed or initialed agreements. These include the Fort Frances (Ontario) Education Framework Agreement,[213] the Nisga'a Tribal Council Agreement-in-Principle (British Columbia),[214] the Innu Nation (Newfoundland), the Inuvialuit/ Gwich'in (Northwest Territories) and Dogrib (Northwest Territories) Framework Agreements[215] as well as over twenty signed or initialled framework agreements through the British Columbia Treaty Commission process.[216] The

---

[211] *Id.* at 14–15.

[212] BUSINESS PLAN, *supra* note 165 at 31–33.

[213] INDIAN AND NORTHERN AFFAIRS CANADA, *Pride in Partnership: Ontario* 1–2 (November 1996).

[214] INDIAN AND NORTHERN AFFAIRS CANADA, *supra* note 24 at 20.

[215] BUSINESS PLAN, *supra* note 165 at 26–28.

[216] INDIAN AND NORTHERN AFFAIRS CANADA, *supra* note 24 at 20.

Mi'kmaq education negotiations have progressed from a framework agreement in 1994, through an agreement-in-principle in 1996, to a final agreement signed in early 1997,[217] so that all that now remains is legislation to confirm full Mi'k-maq jurisdiction over education within their communities.

In addition, the federal government is engaged in preliminary discussions with a number of other Aboriginal communities or organizations that have expressed an initial interest in setting up a process of negotiations. New self-government initiatives entered into by the Government of Canada will likely focus its priority efforts on establishing tables at which affordable agreements can be concluded within a few years to deliver tangible gains for Aboriginal communities as soon as possible.

The speed and time frames of these various negotiating tables are very important. It is estimated that approximately seventeen self-government agreements could be concluded over the next five years.[218] It is further anticipated that, over a ten-year period, approximately thirty-five self-government agreements may be achieved and implemented.[219] Since the formal announcement of the federal Inherent Right Policy on August 10, 1995, over ninety negotiations have commenced, or been renewed under this policy,[220] involving 347 of the 608 First Nations from British Columbia, Yukon, the western Northwest Territories, Alberta, Saskatchewan, Manitoba, Nova Scotia, and parts of Ontario, Quebec, and Newfoundland. In addition, the Inuit are engaged in self-government negotiations in Labrador, northern Quebec and the western Arctic.[221] The next likely series of initiatives consists of eleven proposals which will involve up to 149 First Nations.

The creation of the new huge territory of Nunavut (which represents the eastern half of the Northwest Territories (NWT) with a territory larger than that of almost all governments in the world) is one example of self-government on a large and unique scale. It will require the establishment on April 1, 1999, of a new public government for all residents of this territory that is being carved out of the existing NWT and its government. Although it will be a public government with territorial powers delegated by Parliament, there will be effective Inuit control as over 80 percent of the population are Inuit.[222] The Nunavut

---

[217] INDIAN AND NORTHERN AFFAIRS CANADA, *Education Jurisdiction Transferred to Mi'kmaq of Nova Scotia,* communique (February 14, 1997).

[218] Confidential information made available to the author.

[219] *Id.*

[220] INDIAN AND NORTHERN AFFAIRS CANADA, *supra* note 24 at 24.

[221] PROGRESS ON COMMITMENTS, *supra* note 45 at 11.

[222] INDIAN AND NORTHERN AFFAIRS CANADA, *supra* note 24 at 43–44. *See also* the websites on Nunavut maintained by the Nunavut Implementation Commission and by Indian and Northern Affairs Canada at <ttp://www.inac.gc.ca>.

Territorial Government will have legislative and administrative jurisdiction in almost all provincial spheres of power that impact upon the daily lives of people, but will be subject to parliamentary override as it is not a sovereign government under the Canadian Constitition. Groups in the western part of the NWT also have an opportunity to develop unique self-government arrangements in conjunction with establishing regional public governments that are not readily available south of the sixtieth parallel.

Negotiations are actively underway at present in the Beaufort-Delta region to create such an arrangement incorporating aspects of both public and Aboriginal governments in the same area. Furthermore, there are four First Nations self-government agreements in Yukon Territory which were brought into force by legislation proclaimed in 1995 with processes in place to complete negotiations with the remaining 10 First Nations in the Yukon. The federal government's participation in these negotiations is naturally being guided by its Inherent Right Policy and existing commitments. The next step will be to confirm constitutional protection of these self-government agreements, reflecting ''inherent right'' language under subsection 35(1), which is currently being negotiated in the Yukon.

IV. CONCLUSION

The opportunities for real progress are now present in Canada. Negotiations will definitely not be easy nor will results be evident overnight. Progress is also always vulnerable to political windows closing, key leaders moving on, public opinion changing, and judicial redefining of the Aboriginal–Crown relationship in ways that are either positive or very negative. There is nothing static in this situation, nor is there any inevitability to forward advancement, as many people seem to presume, based upon the generally positive developments of the last three decades. Nevertheless, with the federal acceptance of the ''inherent right'' of self-government, constitutional protection of aboriginal and treaty rights, a renewed emphasis on creating economic opportunities for Aboriginal people, increased success in education and an improved rate of achieving land claims settlements, there is good reason to hope that the first steps to completing this great unfinished business of Canada's history are underway.

CHAPTER 15

AMERICAN INDIANS IN THE INTERNATIONAL ARENA: A BRIEF HISTORY FROM A UNITED STATES PERSPECTIVE

Kirke Kickingbird

The status of American Indians in the United States is generally regarded by most people as an issue of national domestic concern. This was not always the case. As early as 1789, and well into the next century, European affairs and Indian affairs received equal emphasis.[1] At the present time, however, the average American citizen is not likely to give much attention to the legal status of Native people.

There seems to be a belief among the general public that the "Vanishing American"[2] vanished into domestic dominions when the Department of the Interior, the "home" department of American government,[3], was created in 1849 and Indian affairs were handed off to Interior by the Department of War.[4] There is also some sentiment that Indians vanished politically when, in a power struggle between the chambers of the U.S. Congress,[5] Congress passed the 1871 act to stop making treaties with the tribes.[6] What is often overlooked is the fact that Congress continued to pursue future intergovernmental contracts, but did so under the title of "Agreements."[7] Still other American citizens assume that

---

[1] "Washington and Congress were as deeply concerned over Indian as over European relations." SAMUEL ELIOT MORRISON, 2 OXFORD HISTORY OF THE AMERICAN PEOPLE 52 (NEW AMERICAN LIBRARY 1972) [hereinafter *Morrison*].

[2] The term derives from the fact that the American Indian population fell to 250,000 around the turn of the century. *See* S. LYMAN TYLER, A HISTORY OF INDIAN POLICY 234 (1973).

[3] "It was created by act of Congress approved March 5, 1849, and in the original law was called the Home Department." JAMES D. RICHARDSON, X MESSAGES AND PAPERS OF THE PRESIDENTS, INDEX, 204 (1903).

[4] *See* LAURENCE F. SCHMECKEBIER, THE OFFICE OF INDIAN AFFAIRS 43 (1927).

[5] *See* F. COHEN, HANDBOOK OF FEDERAL INDIAN LAW 106–107 (Michie, ed. 1982).

[6] *See* Indian Contract Act, 25 U.S.C. § 71 (1871).

[7] For the period after 1871, *see* CHARLES J. KAPPLER, II INDIAN LAWS AND TREATIES (1904).

Indians must have been virtually annihilated in some massive military response to Custer's defeat at the hands of the Sioux.[8] Finally, there are those who assume that the dismantling of the reservations into homestead allotments[9] must have expunged Indians from existence, following the failure before the U.S. Supreme Court of the tribal court challenge to this division in the 1903 case of *Lone Wolf v. Hitchcock*.[10]

These pieces of American Indian law are only part of a larger picture. The legal status of American Indian governments is not nearly so diminished as is presumed.[11] And, the five-hundred-year-old history of relations between Indians and whites in North America—of which nearly four hundred of those years focused on international relations—appears to be returning to its original foundations.

I. INTERNATIONAL FOUNDATIONS OF INDIAN–WHITE RELATIONS: 1492–1787

Columbus' arrival in the New World began a tale of domestic history as taught in American classrooms. Yet it was really the beginning of a tale of international relations between non-Indian governments and tribal governments in the Western Hemisphere that has persisted until this very moment. Initially, the international impact was direct, and remained so under the U.S. Constitution, well after the establishment of the American government as we know it today. And, when international law and relations ceased to be a direct force in the United States' dealings with American Indian governments, U.S. law about American Indians became so suffused with international law concepts that the indirect impact continues to shape legal relationships.[12]

In sorting out the implications of the contact between the New World and the Old, the legal scholars of Spain set out a framework for relations between nations that would form the foundation of modern international law. The ideas

---

[8] United States military force as a direct cause of the deaths of Indians appears to have limited significance. One estimate for the period 1789 to 1898 indicates that 4,000 Indians were killed, versus 7,000 U.S. soldiers killed. *See* Wilcomb E. Washburn, The Indian in American 207 (1975).

[9] *See* D.S. Otis, The Dawes Act and the Allotment of Indian Lands (1973).

[10] *See* Lone Wolf v. Hitchcock, 187 U.S. 553 (1903).

[11] Some writers are not aware of the impact of the American Indian on American law and offer comments such as the following: "Of Indian law and Swedish law, it is fair to say, not a trace remains." Lawrence M. Friedman, A History of American Law 15 (1973). American Indian influence extends to a variety of institutions, including the United States Constitution. *See generally* Kirke Kickingbird & Lynn Shelby Kickingbird, Indians and the U.S. Constitution: A Forgotten Legacy (1987).

[12] *See* Felix S. Cohen, *The Spanish Origin of Indian Rights in the Law of the United States, in* The Legal Conscience 230 (1960).

emerging from Spain would ultimately be adopted in the work of Grotius and Vattel.[13]

Contact with American Indians impacted the spirit of the Age of Discovery. The writings of Amerigo Vespucci [14] and interviews with Dutch explorers who had visited America and the Indians gave Sir Thomas More his vision for the book *Utopia*[15] and its government that operated on the consent of the governed.[16]

Spanish explorer Peter Martyr's *Decades of the New World,* [17] captivated European intellectuals.[18] Montaigne read the works of many of the European explorers, including Martyr, and made it a point to interview three Indians touring Europe who visited the French court of King Charles IX in 1562. This became the inspiration for his essay, *Of the Cannibals* (1578–80),[19] in which he discussed the ideal country and its government.[20]

Indians also came to Europe under less than "voluntary" conditions. The Patuxent warrior, Squanto, is presented in American history as befriending the Pilgrims. Often omitted from this tale is Squanto's kidnapping in 1614 by English fishermen, who sold him as a slave in Spain. Squanto escaped and made his way to England. He learned English and returned to New England as a guide for a party of English explorers. Equipped with English as a result of his international adventures, Squanto was able to greet the Pilgrims and guide them through their first winter.[21]

As Europeans came to North America in search of wealth, they found an opportunity for trade. These economic alliances were bolstered by military and political alliances. The international rivalries required treaty relations between the Europeans and the Native governments.[22]

Travel by American Indians eastward across the Atlantic continued. Two sons of a Delaware chief in the Hudson Valley were in Amsterdam in 1612.[23]

---

[13] *See id.* at 248.

[14] *See* AMERIGO VESPUCCI, MUNDUS NOVUS (NEW WORLD) (1505).

[15] *See* SIR THOMAS MOORE, Utopia (1516).

[16] *See* Cohen, *supra* note 12, at 324.

[17] *See* PETER MARTYR, DECADES OF THE NEW WORLD (1516)(English trans. 1555).

[18] *See* SAMUEL ELIOT MORRISON, THE EUROPEAN DISCOVERY OF AMERICA, THE NORTHERN VOYAGES, 487 (1971).

[19] *See* MONTAIGNE, OF THE CANNIBALS (1578).

[20] *See* DONALD H. FRAME, THE COMPLETE ESSAYS OF MONTAIGNE (1948).

[21] *See* 15 HANDBOOK OF NORTH AMERICAN INDIANS 82 (1978).

[22] *See* KIRKE KICKINGBIRD ET AL., INDIAN TREATIES 2, 10 (1980).

[23] *See* HANDBOOK OF NORTH AMERICAN INDIANS, *supra* note 21, at 82.

Pocahontas accompanied her husband, John Rolfe, to England in 1616, where she was received as an ''American princess.'' Sadly, while planning for her family's return to America in 1617, Pocahontas contracted smallpox and died.[24]

Unwittingly, Champlain's decision in 1609 to support the Hurons in their rivalry against the Iroquois sealed the fate of French interests around the Great Lakes.[25] The British and the Iroquois looked for alliances to overwhelm their enemies and found one another. The subsequent fall of Montreal brought an end to the French and Indian Wars and to French interests in Canada.

As the French and Indian Wars drew to a close in 1763, the Cherokee sent a diplomatic mission to London that was composed of three chiefs. One of them was Outicite,' or Mankiller, who was often a guest of Thomas Jefferson's father.[26]

In 1775, Guy Johnson (Superintendent of the Six Nations), Captain Daniel Clause, and the young Mohawk chief Joseph Brant, set out for England to ask the Crown to protect the lands of the Six Nations from colonial encroachment.[27]

The American colonies had grown restive under the taxes required to support British troops that were defending the colonists from their own folly and the resentments of the Indian governments. The decision to declare independence plunged them into war. The new American government needed alliances with militarily powerful nations. Unfortunately, the Iroquois Confederacy was shattered because of its divided loyalties during the American Revolution.

The American government turned to France, but not before it turned to the Delaware Nation and its allied tribes. The American government signed its first treaty with Indian governments in 1778. The Delaware were offered a seat in Congress as a token of their good faith.[28]

Even as the bloody war ended, the United States sought to fashion a future policy for dealing with the Indians. It chose as its primary methodology the treaty, a contract between nations, a long-established means for sovereign governments to relate to one another.

---

[24] *See* VIRGINIUS DABNEY, VIRGINIA, THE NEW DOMINION 26–28 (1971).

[25] *See* SAMUEL ELIOT MORRISON, 1 OXFORD HISTORY OF THE AMERICAN PEOPLE 97 (New American Library 1972).

[26] *See* J. RALPH RANDOLPH, BRITISH TRAVELERS AMONG THE SOUTHERN INDIANS, 1660–1763 143 (1973).

[27] *See* WALTER H. MOHR, FEDERAL INDIAN RELATIONS, 1774–1788, 45 (1933).

[28] *See* Article VI, Treaty with the Delawares, 1778, *cited in* II KAPPLER'S LAWS AND TREATIES 3.

In 1786, the Mohawk chief Joseph Brant returned to England to secure British aid in the matter of Iroquois land rights. Brant received monetary compensation for the Iroquois for tribal lands that had been lost during the Revolution.[29]

II. CONTINUATION OF INTERNATIONAL RELATIONS WITH INDIANS: LATTER 1787–1830

The end of the Revolutionary War did not bring an end to international rivalries. The British, French, and Spanish continued their intrigues at the edges of U.S. territory. The United States remained in constant fear that the Indian governments would ally with European powers.

When Napoleon found his European endeavors underfunded, he recapitalized his efforts by selling the Louisiana Territory. The treaty of purchase required the United States to honor established Spanish and Indian treaties, and to make new treaties with the Indian nations west of the Mississippi in establishing relations with one another.[30]

Alliances among foreign nations in Europe were not the only concerns of the American government. An alliance of Indian nations loomed on the political horizon as Tecumseh sought to forge the tribes from the Great Lakes to the Gulf of Mexico into one implacable force. At the same time, the British sought to reopen the American Revolution in what American history knows as the War of 1812.[31]

The interests of the Native American governments were no more monolithic than those of their European counterparts. Thus, fighting as part of the American forces defending Jackson's flank at the Battle of New Orleans (January 8, 1815), a combined international force of Cherokee, Choctaw, Creeks, and Tennesseeans helped defeat the British forces of Lord Pakenham.[32]

The nations of North America now turned their attentions to one another. The use of international instruments known as treaties continued. But some of the battlegrounds for these conflicts shifted from forest and prairie to the U.S. Supreme Court, where the international foundations for Indian-white relations were invoked to resolve these disputes.

Under the Louisiana Purchase, the United States was obligated to respect Spanish-Indian treaties in the area and make new treaties with the tribal governments for the future disposition of lands the tribes claimed. At the same time,

---

[29] *See* MOHR, *supra* note 27, at 121.

[30] *See* Article VI, Treaty of April 30, 1803, for cession of Louisiana.

[31] *See* MORRISON, *supra* note 1, at 109–111.

[32] *See* ANGIE DEBO, THE RISE AND FALL OF THE CHOCTAW REPUBLIC 41 (1934).

President Jefferson began discussions about either assimilating Indians as farmers east of the Mississippi as the game diminished, or removing eastern tribes into the Louisiana Territory, if they wished to maintain a traditional hunting culture. White farmers and land speculators clamored for Indian removal in order to secure ownership of the tribal lands east of the Mississippi.[33]

Concepts of Indian sovereignty and government were discussed by the U.S. Supreme Court as early as the 1830s. From that time to the present, the Supreme Court has followed a consistent course of upholding Indian sovereignty and the ability of tribes to exercise their powers of self-government. The United States acknowledged the political equality and sovereignty of Indian governments by asking tribes to negotiate treaties.

The principle that an Indian tribe is a political body with the powers of self-government was clearly enunciated by Chief Justice Marshall in the 1830s in the second of the two Cherokee cases, *Worcester v. Georgia.*[34] Indian tribes or nations, he declared," . . . had always been considered as distinct, independent, political communities, retaining their original natural rights. . . ."[35] To this situation was applied the accepted rule of international law: ". . . the settled doctrine of the law of nations is, that a weaker power does not surrender its independence—its right to self-government—by associating with a stronger, and taking its protection."[36]

From these premises the federal courts concluded that Indian tribes have all the powers of self-government of any sovereign, except insofar as those powers have been modified by treaty or repealed by an act of Congress. Hence, over large fields of criminal and civil law—and particularly over questions of tribal membership, inheritance, tribal taxation, tribal property, domestic relations, and the form of tribal government—the laws, customs, and decisions of the proper tribal governing authorities have, to this day, the force of law.[37]

All of the colonial powers, and later, the United States, recognized the sovereignty of Indian nations by entering into over 800 treaties with Indians. Under international law, treaties are a means for sovereign nations to relate to each other. The fact that Europeans and the United States made treaties with Indian nations demonstrates that they recognized the sovereignty of Indian nations.

---

[33] *See* AMERICAN INDIAN POLICY REVIEW COMMISSION, I FINAL REPORT OF THE AMERICAN INDIAN POLICY REVIEW COMMISSION 51 58 (1977).

[34] *See* Worcester v. Georgia, 31 U.S. 515 (1832) [hereinafter *Worcester*]. *Worcester* and the earlier *Cherokee Nation v. Georgia*, 30 U.S. 1 (1831), are two of the foundation cases in American Indian law. Both involve the Cherokee Nation.

[35] *Worcester, supra* note 34, at 559.

[36] *Id.* at 560–561.

[37] *See* FELIX COHEN, HANDBOOK OF FEDERAL INDIAN LAW XXIV (1942)

In the *Worcester v. Georgia* decision mentioned above, the U.S. Supreme Court said that:

> the very fact of repeated treaties with them recognized (the Indians' right to self-government) and the settled doctrine of the law of nations is that a weaker power does not surrender its independence—its right to self government—by associating with a stronger, and taking its protection. . . .[38]

And when critics complained that Indian tribes were not "nations" in the European sense, the Court responded that:

> The words "treaty" and "nation" are words of our language, selected in our diplomatic and legislative proceedings, by ourselves, having each a definite and well understood meaning. We have applied them to Indians as we have applied them to other nations of the earth. They are applied to all in the same sense.[39]

While the exercise of sovereign powers by Indian governments has been restricted to some extent by the terms of treaties and statutes passed by Congress to carry out those treaties, there can be no doubt that the United States and other nations have recognized the inherent sovereignty of Indian nations and their right to self-government.[40]

The first half of the nineteenth century found traffic continuing to move across the Atlantic in both directions. The twenty-year-old Count Albert-Alexandre de Pourtales of Switzerland, who accompanied Washington Irving on his Tour on the Prairies, had "seen, in Geneva, the six Osage Indians who had created such a sensation in Europe in the summer of 1827."[41] The young count hoped to see the Osage warriors in their homeland.

The painter George Catlin had completed 500 works on American Indian subjects by the 1840s and took his "Indian gallery" on a tour of Europe, leaving New York on November 25, 1839.[42] In 1843, nine Ojibway arrived in England and joined forces with Catlin by performing tribal dances at his painting exhibition. Although the Ojibway made fun of a nation ruled by a young woman, they gave a command performance at Buckingham Palace for Queen Victoria and Prince Albert.[43]

---

[38] *Worcester, supra* note 34, at 559–61.

[39] *Id.* at 559.

[40] *See* COHEN, *supra* note 37, at 122; U.S. Department of Interior, *Solicitor's Opinion, Powers of Indian Tribes*, INTERIOR DEP'T, 55 I.D. 14, Oct. 25, 1934.

[41] *See* ALBERT DE POURTALES, ON THE WESTERN TOUR WITH WASHINGTON IRVING, THE JOURNAL AND LETTERS OF COUNT DE POURTALES 6 (George F. Spaulding ed., 1968).

[42] MARK SUFRIN, GEORGE CATLIN, PAINTER OF THE INDIAN WEST 111 (1991).

[43] *See id.* at 118.

A party of Iowa led by White Cloud arrived in London in 1844, and Catlin took them to Paris in 1845 to meet King Louis Philippe, Victor Hugo, Eugene Delacroix, Charles Baudelaire, and Baron Alexander von Humboldt.[44]

Yet, while Indians were being actively recognized on the Continent, their situation at home was beginning to become unsettled. The continuing arrival of settlers, whose expansion began to encroach on Indian lands, created new tensions that threatened the stability of Indian-white relations.

III. "REMOVAL" AND THE DIMINUTION OF INTERNATIONAL RELATIONS: 1830–1934

The U.S. government settled on the Indian Removal Act[45] in 1830 as the policy mechanism to force the Indian governments to move west of the Mississippi. The means of executing this policy was the treaty instrument.

But removal as a means of resolving the "Indian problem" was not without its own set of difficulties. The population moving west threatened to push the Indians into the arms of potential British, Spanish/Mexican, or even Texican alliances. However, access to these potential alliances with foreign nations was finally cut off by the end of the Mexican War (1846–1848) and by the settlement of the Oregon Country border between the United States and Britain (1846).[46]

This was also the period of time in which the Department of the Interior was created and responsibility for Indian affairs was transferred to the new department, although the Department of War would continue to participate in Indian matters. One purpose of creating the "home" department, as Interior was called in the legislation, was to make room for increased international responsibilities at the Department of State. To achieve this, various domestic and housekeeping chores were transferred to the Department of the Interior. The Bureau of Indian Affairs was handed to Interior as part of these domestic duties.[47]

---

[44] See id. at 123–124.

[45] See Indian Removal Act, 4 U.S. Stat. 411–413 (1830).

[46] Morrison sets the end date for potential foreign alliances with the Indian tribes earlier. "The problem of United States–Indian relations, which for many years had involved international rivalries, became localized after the Florida treaty was ratified in 1821." MORRISON, supra note 1, at 187.

[47] "In passing from this survey of our foreign relations, I invite the attention of Congress to the condition of the Department of the Government to which this branch of the public business is entrusted. Our intercourse with foreign powers has of late years greatly increased, both in consequence of our own growth and the introduction of many new states into the family of nations. In this way the Department of State has become overburdened. It has been by the recent establishment of the Department of the Interior that the Department of State has been relieved of some portion of the domestic business. If the residue of the business of that kind such as the distribution of Congressional documents, the keeping, publishing, and distribution of the laws of the United States, the execution of the copyright law, the subject of reprieves and pardons, and some other subjects relating to interior administration should be transferred from the Department of State, it would unquestionably be for the benefit of the public service. Indian affairs."

While international interests now had limited access to the Indian govern-ments and vice versa, the international instruments known as treaties continued to be the primary means of Indian-U.S. relations for the next twenty-five years. Even after adopting the euphemism of "agreements" to replace "treaties" after 1871, the contracting process between Indian governments and the U.S. govern-ment continued for almost a half century after "treaty-making" allegedly ended.[48]

Unfortunately, the white men who directed Indian policy at this juncture wanted the Indians to consent to their own destruction in some of these agree-ments. American Indians proved to be just as intractable as any people confront-ing a dictatorship of governmental officials. The Plains Indian treaties contained a "fail-safe" device, which required a supermajority of seventy-five percent tribal agreement before their reservations could be broken apart.

America's policymakers were undaunted by the impossible task of achieving a supermajority. They visited the tribes, got a fifty-one percent agreement from the tribes for dismantling the reservations, and returned to Washington to get Congress to pass legislation approving their manipulations. Urged on by rail-roads, farmers, ranchers, and mineral companies who wanted the Indian lands, Congressmen sought to assure reelection by complying with their constituents' demands and approving the agreements.

Tribal leaders were stunned by Congress' failure to follow the treaties' requirement for a supermajority. The Kiowa, Comanche, and Apache leaders in Indian Territory (now Oklahoma) filed a challenge to Secretary of the Interior Hitchcock's efforts to allot their reservations. This case, known as *Lone Wolf v. Hitchcock*,[49] proved to be one of the events that helped frame Indian affairs as a "domestic" issue.

Lone Wolf, the Kiowa leader, invoked the rationale that the treaty instru-ment could not be unilaterally changed by the United States and that the super-majority requirement was an essential element that had to be met before allotment could take place. Lone Wolf argued that Indian treaties should be treated in the same fashion as international treaties. The ultimate irony was that was exactly how the Indian governments were treated.

Prior to the *Cherokee Cases*,[50] Chief Justice Marshall had asserted that a treaty could supersede an earlier statute.[51] The reverse proposition, that a statute

---

Millard Filmore, Third Annual Message (Dec. 6, 1852), *quoted in* V. RICHARDSON, *supra* note 3, at 168.

[48] *See* KICKINGBIRD ET AL., *supra* note 22, at 17.

[49] *See* Lone Wolf v. Hitchcock, 187 U.S. 553 (1903).

[50] *Worcester* and *Cherokee, supra* note 34.

[51] *See* Foster v. Neilson, 27 U.S. 253, 314–315 (1829).

could supersede an earlier treaty, was adopted judicially at mid-century.[52] The doctrine was applied to a Cherokee treaty two decades later.[53] The doctrine was most prominently remembered when the Supreme Court decided that Congress could unilaterally change a treaty with China in the *Chinese Exclusion Case.*[54]

The Supreme Court applied this same doctrine in *Lone Wolf* and rationalized its decision by saying that the approval, disapproval, or change of treaties by legislation was a ''political question'' and therefore a matter for Congress or the Executive to decide, not a question for the judiciary.

The result was similar to the Titanic's smashing into an iceberg. Just as swiftly as the Titanic and 1,500 passengers slid beneath the chilly waters of the North Atlantic, American Indians seemed to slide beneath the icy calm of domestic tranquility. The impact becomes more tangible in terms of reservation lands. Between 1887 and 1934, Indian holdings fell from 138,000,000 to 48,000,000 acres of land.[55]

IV. RESURGENCE OF INDIAN INTERNATIONAL RELATIONS: 1934–1944

President Franklin D. Roosevelt's New Deal included Indians.[56] Indian policy focused on revitalizing Indian government, reconsolidating the reservation land base, supporting economic development, and assisting tribes with cultural survival. These policies received support in the legislative framework of the Indian Reorganization Act[57] and related legislation.[58]

The administration's concerns were not confined to the United States' borders. These issues moved into an international arena and became a Western hemisphere issue. One result was an inter-American agreement embodied in the Treaty of Patzcuaro in 1940, which created an Interamerican Indian Institute. It became a milestone on the American Indian's road back to the international scene.[59]

---

[52] *See* Taylor v. Morton, 23 F. Cas. 784 (C.C.D. Mass. 1855)(No. 13,799).

[53] *See* The Cherokee Tobacco, 78 U.S. 616 (1871). ''A treaty may supersede a prior act of Congress, and an act of Congress may supersede a prior treaty. In the cases referred to [citations omitted] these principles were applied to treaties with foreign nations. Treaties with Indian nations . . . cannot be more obligatory.'' 78 U.S. at 621.

[54] *See* The Chinese Exclusion Case, 130 U.S. 581 (1889).

[55] *See* COHEN, *supra* note 37, at 216.

[56] *See* HARRY A. KERSEY, JR., THE FLORIDA SEMINOLES AND THE NEW DEAL, 1933–1942 48 (1989).

[57] *See* Indian Reorganization Act, 25 U.S.C. § 461 (1934).

[58] *See* Oklahoma Indian Welfare Act, 25 U.S.C. § 501 (1936).

[59] *See* 4 HANDBOOK OF NORTH AMERICAN INDIANS 108 (1988).

World War II brought these policies to an abrupt stop. Attention shifted to the global conflict. After the war, measures to prevent a future global conflict changed the world.

Between the World Wars, Deskaheh—a Cayuga chief—was appointed Speaker of the Six Nations Council, and sent to oppose Canadian governmental policies designed to constrict the governmental authority of the Six Nations, to encroach on their lands, and to force assimilation of the tribal members. The Canadian government in Ottawa refused the Six Nations entreaties.

Seeking alternative redress, Deskaheh went first to England in 1921 to ask King George V to uphold the treaty rights guaranteed by George III of England. English authorities decided that Canadian Indians, like those in the United States, were a domestic issue. In 1923 Deskaheh set out for Geneva to bring his case before the League of Nations.[60] Even though Deskaheh persuaded delegates from Ireland, Panama, Persia, and Estonia to support an address before the League of Nations and suggest a referral of the Canada–Six Nations dispute to the International Court of Justice, his mission ultimately failed. A particularly troublesome point was whether these North American Indians constituted an independent state.[61]

The world as Deskaheh knew it no longer existed after World War II. The change in political, economic, and military conditions after the war would force even further change.[62]

A. Indigenous Peoples and the International Labor Organization: 1940s–1960s

The League of Nations, established in 1919, was disbanded in 1946. The International Labor Organization (ILO), which was originally established as an independent agency of the League, became a specialized agency of the United Nations after 1946.[63]

In 1951, the ILO convened a Committee of Experts on Indigenous Labor to examine the treatment of native people as part of national workforces.[64] This

---

[60] *See id.* at 210.

[61] *See* RUSSEL BARSH, THE CHALLENGE OF INDIGENOUS SELF-DETERMINATION, 26 U MICH. J.L. REFORM 277, 280 at n. 15 (1993).

[62] Professor Siegfried Wiessner explores how vast these changes are in his article, *American Indian Treaties and Modern International Law*, 7 ST. THOMAS L. REV. 567 (1995).

[63] *See* INTERNATIONAL LABOUR OFFICE, CONSTITUTION OF THE INTERNATIONAL LABOUR ORGANISATION, 5, 72 (1988).

[64] *See* Committee of Experts on Indigenous Labour, *Partial Revision of the Indigenous and Tribal Populations Convention*, 1957 (No. 107), International Labour Conference, 75th Session, Report VI(1), at 3 (1988).

resulted in the 1953 publication of the book, *Indigenous Peoples*, which compiled data on economics and living conditions, as well as on national and international treatment.[65]

The Committee of Experts on Indigenous Labor was convened again in 1954,[66] and by 1956, the ILO had issued the law and practice report, *Living and Working Conditions of Indigenous Populations in Independent Countries*.[67] The report was submitted to the 39th Session of the General Assembly of the ILO. It was specifically concerned with the ILO's Andean Indian Program.

The report and related discussions generated substantial interest in the ILO Conference Session and resulted in proposals for the adoption of a policy statement. In 1957, the ILO Conference Session adopted the Indigenous and Tribal Populations Convention 1957 (No. 107), which broadened the focus from South America to all countries. On June 2, 1959, Convention No.107 went into force and effect after adoption by twenty-seven nations.[68]

In 1962, a panel of consultants on Indigenous and Tribal Populations met and made recommendations regarding national policies and training of personnel; international exchange of experience; training of national personnel in integration techniques; and the special problems of nomadic and seminomadic populations. This panel of consultants subsequently held a technical meeting in 1968 in Niger to address the problems of nomadism in the Sahelian region of Africa.[69]

B. Other International Action Recognizing the Rights of Indigenous Peoples: 1970s–1980s

The next decade provided a framework that clearly included the Western hemisphere. In 1971, the United Nations Sub-Commission on Prevention of Discrimination and Protection of Minorities appointed a special rapporteur to prepare a study on the treatment of indigenous populations.[70] Part of the information gathering process included the September 1977 International NGO Conference on Discrimination Against Indigenous Populations in the Americas, held at the Palais des Nations in Geneva. One of the products from the meeting was

---

[65] *See id.* at 4.

[66] *See id.* at 3.

[67] *See id.* at 4.

[68] *See id.* at 5.

[69] *See id.* at 6.

[70] *See* Sub-Commission on Prevention of Discrimination and Protection of Minorities, *Study of the Problem of Discrimination Against Indigenous Populations*, U.N. ESCOR, Comm. on Hum. Rts., 36th Sess., U.N. Doc. E/CN.4/Sub. 2/1983/21/Add. 18 (1983).

the Draft Declaration of Principles for the Defence of the Indigenous Nations and Populations of the Western Hemisphere.[71]

As the decade closed, in 1979, the Organization of American States (OAS) General Assembly authorized a Five Year Inter-American Indian Action Plan. The principles in the plan included: self-determination; equality; participation in benefits; human dignity; and cooperation in the protection of resources and economic development.[72]

The international focus on issues affecting Indians of the Americas continued to gain momentum as the 1980s opened. In November 1980 the Eighth Inter-American Indian Congress met. Across the Atlantic an International NGO Conference on Indigenous People and the Land was held in Geneva in 1981.[73]

Even more significant actions were taken the next year. In 1982, establishment of the United Nations Working Group on Indigenous Populations was authorized by an Economic and Social Council (ECOSOC).[74] This was followed in 1985 by an action of the U.N. General Assembly, which created the Voluntary Fund for Indigenous Populations to aid indigenous participation in the deliberations of the Working Group on Indigenous Populations.[75] In that same year, the Ninth Inter-American Indian Conference was held in Santa Fe, New Mexico.[76]

From March 18–26, 1986, the 12th Conference of American States that are members of the International Labor Organization was held in Montreal. At this conference, the attending government, employer, and labor members drew attention to the loss of cultural identity faced by millions of indigenous peoples.[77] By September of that year, the ILO had convened a meeting of experts to discuss revision of the Indigenous and Tribal Populations Convention 1957 (107).[78]

The discussion about revision of Convention No. 107 and development of draft language for such a revision moved more quickly than anyone imagined possible. Discussions on the proposed draft language were scheduled for the ILOs 1988 annual conference. The ILO treaty procedure calls for "double discussion"—meaning that proposals are discussed in two consecutive years during

---

[71] *See* Committee of Experts on Indigenous Labour, *supra* note 64, at 13–14.

[72] *See id.* at 11.

[73] *See id.* at 14.

[74] *See* E.S.C. Res. 34, U.N. ESCOR, 38th Sess., Supp. No. 1 at 26, U.N. Doc. E/1982/59 (1982). *See* Chapter 1, Julian Burger, *Indigenous Peoples and the United Nations*.

[75] *See* Committee of Experts on Indigenous Labour, *supra* note 64, at 9.

[76] *See* Lee Swepston, *A New Step in the International Law on Indigenous and Tribal Peoples: ILO Convention 169 of 1989*, 15 OKLA. CITY U.L. REV. 677, 691 (1990).

[77] *See* Committee of Experts on Indigenous Labour, *supra* note 64, at 7.

[78] *See id.* at 1.

the annual conference.[79] Discussions on the revision of Convention No. 107 moved so slowly during the 1988 session and the early part of the 1989 session that participants were skeptical that work on the proposed revisions could be completed. To everyone's surprise, by the end of the second session the ILO General Assembly had managed to adopt a revised convention: the Indigenous and Tribal Populations Convention 1989 (No. 169).[80]

V. A NEW ERA FOR INDIGENOUS PEOPLES: 1990s AND BEYOND

On December 18, 1990, the General Assembly of the United Nations adopted a resolution declaring 1993 as the International Year for the World's Indigenous People.[81]

The ILO was just one of the organizations to take action on creating an indigenous rights instrument. In 1992, the Inter-American Commission on Human Rights sent questionnaires to OAS Member States and organizations representing indigenous peoples to gather information that would aid in drafting a Legal Instrument on the Rights of Indigenous Peoples.[82] By 1993, the U.N. Working Group on Indigenous Populations completed an instrument entitled the draft Declaration on the Rights of Indigenous Peoples.[83] That same year, the United Nations also proclaimed the "International Decade of the World's Indigenous People" (1995–2004). With this act, it called on governments around the world to use the decade to address the problems of native peoples.[84]

In 1995, Dr. Erica-Irene Daes of Greece, chairperson rapporteur of the U.N. Working Group on Indigenous Populations, wrote of the U.N. draft Declaration on the Rights of Indigenous Peoples:

> I would like to emphasize my belief that the eventual adoption of the Draft Declaration should not be the end, but merely the beginning of the defense and empowerment of the world's indigenous peoples

---

[79] *See* Swepston, *supra* note 76, at 684.

[80] *See* Russel Lawrence Barsh, *An Advocate's Guide to the Convention on Indigenous and Tribal Peoples*, 15 OKLA. CITY U.L. REV. 209, 210–211 (1990).

[81] *See* G.A. Res. 164, U.N. GAOR, 45 Sess., Supp. No. 49, at 277, U.N. Doc. Aes/ 4.5/164 (1990). *See also* Kirke Kickingbird, *A Reflective Look at the Year for the World's Indigenous People*, 19 AM. INDIAN L. REV. 260 (1994).

[82] *See* INTER-AMERICAN COMMISSION ON HUMAN RIGHTS, REPORT OF THE FIRST ROUND OF CONSULTATIONS ON THE INTER-AMERICAN LEGAL INSTRUMENT ON THE RIGHTS OF INDIGENOUS PEOPLES (1993).

[83] *See* United Nations Draft Declaration on the Rights of Indigenous Peoples, U.N. ESCOR, Comm. on Hum. Rts., 11th Sess., Annex. I, U.N. Doc. E/CN.4/Sub. 2 (1993).

[84] *See* G.A Res. 48/163, U.N. GAOR, 48th Sess., Supp. No. 49, at 281, U.N. Doc. A/48/49 (1993).

through international law. The rights of indigenous peoples will continue to evolve through practice. Even more importantly, the Draft Declaration after its proclamation, will provide a basis for increasing the formal, representative role of the indigenous peoples themselves in the operations and decision making of the United Nations system, through which they will increasingly guide the future interpretation and implementation of their own rights. The work that lies ahead is more challenging and exciting, and more likely to bring about genuine changes in the lives of indigenous people, than the work we already have behind us.

Let us move ahead, then, with the courage, fairness and confidence that this significant cause deserves. Indigenous Peoples should remain, nonetheless, here as elsewhere in their lives, the interpreters of their own situation and the masters of their lives.[85]

The next steps in the process call for the U.N. Commission on Human Rights to ask Member States to review the draft Declaration on the Rights of Indigenous People before the Commission and the General Assembly take up the issue. Although Dr. Daes predicted ultimate adoption of the Declaration, the process is likely to be one that is difficult and controversial.

At the United Nations, and in the Western hemisphere, the issues that concern indigenous people are: maintaining cultural integrity; controlling use and development of their geographical territory; achieving recognition of their right to formulate and control programs that impact indigenous people; protecting existing treaty rights; and developing modern agreements with national governments regarding the allocation of power between indigenous peoples and national governments.

In the decades since World War II, the primary actors working in international fora on behalf of indigenous people have been from North America. However, during this period, the participation has begun to shift from non-Native people to Native people. In recent years, there has been a greater participation by representatives of Native people from Central and South America.[86]

Much of the international dialogue concerning indigenous rights has been shaped by the experiences of American Indians in the United States and the

---

[85] Erica-Irene A. Daes, *Equality of Indigenous Peoples Under the Auspices of the United Nations Draft Declaration on the Rights of Indigenous Peoples*, 7 St. Thomas L. Rev. 499 (1995).

[86] *See* Swepston, *supra* note 76, at 686. *See also* Russel Lawrence Barsh, *Indigenous Peoples in the 1990s: From Object to Subject of International Law*, 7 Harv. Hum. Rts. J. 33, 81 83 (1994).

policies they have confronted.[87] To a certain extent, the indigenous people of the United States have achieved the goals to which other native people in the hemisphere only aspire. Through U.S. statutes and court decisions treaty rights have been upheld;[88] tribal court authority has been recognized and supported;[89] land rights have been recognized;[90] and modern contractual arrangements have been established between the national and tribal governments.[91] There have even been agreements between state and tribal governments. Cultural rights and traditional religions have been acknowledged and accommodated by the United States in a variety of ways.[92]

Despite the progress tribal governments have made in the United States, there is much that remains to be done. The status of indigenous peoples does not go unchallenged, even in the United States. The existing programs and laws that benefit Native people must be defended and expanded. Obviously, this provides a direct benefit to Native Americans in the United States. But the U.S. policies, developed under tribal guidance during the last three decades, can also provide guidance for other indigenous people and nations in this hemisphere and elsewhere.

The struggle is not over in the United States, nor in the Western hemisphere, nor at the United Nations. It will continue as long as the dreams and ambitions of indigenous people continue. It will continue and be aided by all those who champion freedom and justice and the dignity of all people. It will continue, as Dr. Daes predicted, until indigenous peoples are masters of their own lives.

---

[87] *See* Barsh, *supra* note 86, at 77. *Washington v. Washington State Commercial Passenger Fishing Ass'n,* 443 U.S. 658 (1979), confirmed the validity of treaties signed in 1854 with Indians of the Pacific Northwest and led the Court to state: "a treaty, including one between the United States and an Indian tribe, is essentially a contract between two sovereign nations." 443 U.S. at 675.

[88] *See* Santa Clara v. Martinez, 436 U.S. 49 (1978); National Farmers Union Ins. Cos. v. Crow Tribe, 471 U.S. 845 (1985); Iowa Mutual Ins. Co. v. LaPlante, 480 U.S. 9 (1987).

[89] *See* Alaska Native Claims Settlement Act, 43 U.S.C § 1601; Alabama and Coushatta Indian Tribes of Texas, 25 U.S.C. § 732 (1988); Ysleta del Sur Pueblo, 25 U.S.C. § 1300g (1988); Maine Indian Claim Settlement, 25 U.S.C. § 1721; Mashantucket Pequot Indian Land Claims Settlement, 25 U.S.C. § 1751 (1988); the

[90] Massachusetts Indian Land Claims Settlement Act, 25 U.S.C. §1771 (1988); and the Catawba Indian Tribe of South Carolina Land Claims Settlement Act of 1993, 25 U.S.C. § 941 (1994).

[91] Since 1975, the Indian Self-determination Act has provided authority for tribes to contract to operate programs for Indians run by the federal government. See Indian Self-determination Act, 25 U.S.C. § 450 (1975). Tribes gained even more flexibility in program authority and design and use of federal funds under the 1987 amendments creating the Tribal Self-Governance Demonstration Project, Title III of P.L. 100–472; 25 U.S.C. §§ 458aa–458gg.

[92] *See* American Indian Religious Freedom Act, 42 U.S.C. § 1996 (as amended); Religious Freedom Restoration Act, 42 U.S.C. §§ 2000bb–2000bb-4; Native American Graves Protection Act, 25 U.S.C. § 3001; and Archeological Resource Protection Act of 1979, 16 U.S.C. §§ 470aa–470ll.

APPENDICES

UNITED NATIONS DRAFT DECLARATION ON THE RIGHTS OF INDIGENOUS PEOPLES SUB-COMMISSION RESOLUTION 1994/45*

The Sub-Commission on Prevention of Discrimination and Protection of Minorities,

Recalling its resolutions 1985/22 of 29 August 1985, 1991/30 of 29 August 1991, 1992/33 of 27 August 1992, 1993/46 of 26 August 1993,

Taking into account, in particular, paragraph 3 of its resolution 1993/46, in which it decided to postpone until its forty-sixth session consideration of the draft United Nations declaration on the rights of indigenous peoples agreed upon by the members of the Working Group on Indigenous Populations, to request the Secretary-General to submit the draft declaration to the appropriate services in the Centre for Human Rights for its technical revision, and to submit, if possible, the draft declaration to the Commission on Human Rights with the recommendation that the Commission adopt it at its fifty-first session,

Recalling Commission on Human Rights resolution 1994/29 of 4 March 1994, in which the Sub-Commission was urged to complete its consideration of the draft United Nations declaration at its forty-sixth session and to submit it to the Commission at its fifty-first session together with any recommendations thereon,

Bearing in mind General Assembly resolution 47/75 of 14 December 1992, paragraph 12 of Commission on Human Rights resolution 1993/30 of 5 March 1993, paragraph 6 (a) of Commission resolution 1993/31 of 5 March 1993 and paragraph II.28 of the Vienna Declaration and Programme of Action(A/Conf.157/23),

Having considered the report of the Working Group on Indigenous Populations on its twelfth session (E/CN.4/Sub.2/1994/30 and Corr.1), in particular the general comments on the draft declaration and the recommendations contained in chapters II and IX respectively of the report,

---

Taking into account the technical review of the draft declaration prepared by the Centre for Human Rights (E/CN.4/Sub.2/1994/2 and Add.1),

1. Expresses its satisfaction at the conclusion of the deliberations on the draft United Nations declaration on the rights of indigenous peoples by the Working Group on Indigenous Populations and the general views of the participants as reflected in the report of the Working Group on its twelfth session;

2. Expresses its appreciation to the Chairperson-Rapporteur of the Working Group, Ms. Erica-Irene Daes, and to the present and former members of the Working Group for their contributions to the process of elaboration of the draft declaration;

3. Expresses its appreciation to the Centre for Human Rights for its technical revision of the draft declaration;

4. Decides:

    (a) To adopt the draft United Nations declaration on the rights of indigenous peoples agreed upon by members of the Working Group as contained in the annex to the present resolution;

    (b) To submit the draft declaration to the Commission on Human Rights at its fifty-first session with the request that it consider the draft as expeditiously as possible;

    (c) To request the Secretary-General to transmit the text of the draft declaration to indigenous peoples and organizations, Governments and intergovernmental organizations and to include in the note of transmittal the information that the draft declaration is to be submitted to the Commission on Human Rights at its fifty-first session;

5. Recommends that the Commission on Human Rights and the Economic and Social Council take effective measures to ensure that representatives of indigenous peoples are able to participate in the consideration of the draft declaration by these two bodies, regardless of their consultative status with the Economic and Social Council.

ANNEX

DRAFT UNITED NATIONS DECLARATION ON THE RIGHTS OF INDIGENOUS PEOPLES

36th meeting, 26 August 1994 [adopted without a vote]

Affirming that indigenous peoples are equal in dignity and rights to all other peoples, while recognizing the right of all peoples to be different, to consider themselves different, and to be respected as such,

Affirming also that all peoples contribute to the diversity and richness of civilizations and cultures, which constitute the common heritage of humankind,

Affirming further that all doctrines, policies and practices based on or advocating superiority of peoples or individuals on the basis of national origin, racial, religious, ethnic or cultural differences are racist, scientifically false, legally invalid, morally condemnable and socially unjust,

Reaffirming also that indigenous peoples, in the exercise of their rights, should be free from discrimination of any kind,

Concerned that indigenous peoples have been deprived of their human rights and fundamental freedoms, resulting, inter alia, in their colonization and dispossession of their lands, territories and resources, thus preventing them from exercising, in particular, their right to development in accordance with their own needs and interests,

Recognizing the urgent need to respect and promote the inherent rights and characteristics of indigenous peoples, especially their rights to their lands, territories and resources, which derive from their political, economic and social structures and from their cultures, spiritual traditions, histories and philosophies,

Welcoming the fact that indigenous peoples are organizing themselves for political, economic, social and cultural enhancement and in order to bring an end to all forms of discrimination and oppression wherever they occur,

Convinced that control by indigenous peoples over developments affecting them and their lands, territories and resources will enable them to maintain and strengthen their institutions, cultures and traditions, and to promote their development in accordance with their aspirations and needs,

Recognizing also that respect for indigenous knowledge, cultures and traditional practices contributes to sustainable and equitable development and proper management of the environment,

Emphasizing the need for demilitarization of the lands and territories of indigenous peoples, which will contribute to peace, economic and social progress and development, understanding and friendly relations among nations and peoples of the world,

Recognizing in particular the right of indigenous families and communities to retain shared responsibility for the upbringing, training, education and well-being of their children,

Recognizing also that indigenous peoples have the right freely to determine their relationships with States in a spirit of coexistence, mutual benefit and full respect,

Considering that treaties, agreements and other arrangements between States and indigenous peoples are properly matters of international concern and responsibility,

Acknowledging that the Charter of the United Nations, the International Covenant on Economic, Social and Cultural Rights and the International Covenant on Civil and Political Rights affirm the fundamental importance of the right of self-determination of all peoples, by virtue of which they freely determine their political status and freely pursue their economic, social and cultural development,

Bearing in mind that nothing in this Declaration may be used to deny any peoples their right of self-determination,

Encouraging States to comply with and effectively implement all international instruments, in particular those related to human rights, as they apply to indigenous peoples, in consultation and cooperation with the peoples concerned,

Emphasizing that the United Nations has an important and continuing role to play in promoting and protecting the rights of indigenous peoples,

Believing that this Declaration is a further important step forward for the recognition, promotion and protection of the rights and freedoms of indigenous peoples and in the development of relevant activities of the United Nations system in this field,

Solemnly proclaims the following United Nations Declaration on the Rights of Indigenous Peoples:

PART I

Article 1

Indigenous peoples have the right to the full and effective enjoyment of all human rights and fundamental freedoms recognized in the Charter of the United Nations, the Universal Declaration of Human Rights and international human rights law.

Article 2

Indigenous individuals and peoples are free and equal to all other individuals and peoples in dignity and rights, and have the right to be free from any kind of adverse discrimination, in particular that based on their indigenous origin or identity.

Article 3

Indigenous peoples have the right of self-determination. By virtue of that right they freely determine their political status and freely pursue their economic, social and cultural development.

Article 4

Indigenous peoples have the right to maintain and strengthen their distinct political, economic, social and cultural characteristics, as well as their legal systems, while retaining their rights to participate fully, if they so choose, in the political, economic, social and cultural life of the State.

Article 5

Every indigenous individual has the right to a nationality.

PART II

Article 6

Indigenous peoples have the collective right to live in freedom, peace and security as distinct peoples and to full guarantees against genocide or any other act of violence, including the removal of indigenous children from their families and communities under any pretext.

In addition, they have the individual rights to life, physical and mental integrity, liberty and security of person.

Article 7

Indigenous peoples have the collective and individual right not to be subjected to ethnocide and cultural genocide, including prevention of and redress for:

(a) Any action which has the aim or effect of depriving them of their integrity as distinct peoples, or of their cultural values or ethnic identities;

(b) Any action which has the aim or effect of dispossessing them of their lands, territories or resources;

(c) Any form of population transfer which has the aim or effect of violating or undermining any of their rights;

(d) Any form of assimilation or integration by other cultures or ways of life imposed on them by legislative, administrative or other measures;

(e) Any form of propaganda directed against them.

Article 8

Indigenous peoples have the collective and individual right to maintain and develop their distinct identities and characteristics, including the right to identify themselves as indigenous and to be recognized as such.

Article 9

Indigenous peoples and individuals have the right to belong to an indigenous community or nation, in accordance with the traditions and customs of the community or nation concerned. No disadvantage of any kind may arise from the exercise of such a right.

Article 10

Indigenous peoples shall not be forcibly removed from their lands or territories. No relocation shall take place without the free and informed consent of the indigenous peoples concerned and after agreement on just and fair compensation and, where possible, with the option of return.

Article 11

Indigenous peoples have the right to special protection and security in periods of armed conflict.

States shall observe international standards, in particular the Fourth Geneva Convention of 1949, for the protection of civilian populations in circumstances of emergency and armed conflict, and shall not:

(a) Recruit indigenous individuals against their will into the armed forces and, in particular, for use against other indigenous peoples;

(b) Recruit indigenous children into the armed forces under any circumstances;

(c) Force indigenous individuals to abandon their lands, territories or means of subsistence, or relocate them in special centres for military purposes;

(d) Force indigenous individuals to work for military purposes under any discriminatory conditions.

PART III

Article 12

Indigenous peoples have the right to practise and revitalize their cultural traditions and customs. This includes the right to maintain, protect and develop the past, present and future manifestations of their cultures, such as archaeological and historical sites, artifacts, designs, ceremonies, technologies and visual and performing arts and literature, as well as the right to the restitution of cultural, intellectual, religious and spiritual property taken without their free and informed consent or in violation of their laws, traditions and customs.

Article 13

Indigenous peoples have the right to manifest, practise, develop and teach their spiritual and religious traditions, customs and ceremonies; the right to maintain, protect, and have access in privacy to their religious and cultural sites; the right to the use and control of ceremonial objects; and the right to the repatriation of human remains.

States shall take effective measures, in conjunction with the indigenous peoples concerned, to ensure that indigenous sacred places, including burial sites, be preserved, respected and protected.

Article 14

Indigenous peoples have the right to revitalize, use, develop and transmit to future generations their histories, languages, oral traditions, philosophies, writing systems and literatures, and to designate and retain their own names for communities, places and persons.

States shall take effective measures, whenever any right of indigenous peoples may be threatened, to ensure this right is protected and also to ensure that they can understand and be understood in political, legal and administrative proceedings, where necessary through the provision of interpretation or by other appropriate means.

PART IV

Article 15

Indigenous children have the right to all levels and forms of education of the State. All indigenous peoples also have this right and the right to establish and control their educational systems and institutions providing education in their own languages, in a manner appropriate to their cultural methods of teaching and learning.

Indigenous children living outside their communities have the right to be provided access to education in their own culture and language.

States shall take effective measures to provide appropriate resources for these purposes.

Article 16

Indigenous peoples have the right to have the dignity and diversity of their cultures, traditions, histories and aspirations appropriately reflected in all forms of education and public information.

States shall take effective measures, in consultation with the indigenous peoples concerned, to eliminate prejudice and discrimination and to promote tolerance, understanding and good relations among indigenous peoples and all segments of society.

Article 17

Indigenous peoples have the right to establish their own media in their own languages. They also have the right to equal access to all forms of non-indigenous media.

States shall take effective measures to ensure that State-owned media duly reflect indigenous cultural diversity.

Article 18

Indigenous peoples have the right to enjoy fully all rights established under international labour law and national labour legislation.

Indigenous individuals have the right not to be subjected to any discriminatory conditions of labour, employment or salary.

PART V

Article 19

Indigenous peoples have the right to participate fully, if they so choose, at all levels of decision-making in matters which may affect their rights, lives and destinies through representatives chosen by themselves in accordance with their own procedures, as well as to maintain and develop their own indigenous decision-making institutions.

Article 20

Indigenous peoples have the right to participate fully, if they so choose, through procedures determined by them, in devising legislative or administrative measures that may affect them.

States shall obtain the free and informed consent of the peoples concerned before adopting and implementing such measures.

Article 21

Indigenous peoples have the right to maintain and develop their political, economic and social systems, to be secure in the enjoyment of their own means of subsistence and development, and to engage freely in all their traditional and other economic activities. Indigenous peoples who have been deprived of their means of subsistence and development are entitled to just and fair compensation.

Article 22

Indigenous peoples have the right to special measures for the immediate, effective and continuing improvement of their economic and social conditions, including in the areas of employment, vocational training and retraining, housing, sanitation, health and social security.

Particular attention shall be paid to the rights and special needs of indigenous elders, women, youth, children and disabled persons.

Article 23

Indigenous peoples have the right to determine and develop priorities and strategies for exercising their right to development. In particular, indigenous peoples have the right to determine and develop all health, housing and other economic and social programmes affecting them and, as far as possible, to administer such programmes through their own institutions.

Article 24

Indigenous peoples have the right to their traditional medicines and health practices, including the right to the protection of vital medicinal plants, animals and minerals.

They also have the right to access, without any discrimination, to all medical institutions, health services and medical care.

PART VI

Article 25

Indigenous peoples have the right to maintain and strengthen their distinctive spiritual and material relationship with the lands, territories, waters and coastal seas and other resources which they have traditionally owned or otherwise occupied or used, and to uphold their responsibilities to future generations in this regard.

Article 26

Indigenous peoples have the right to own, develop, control and use the lands and territories, including the total environment of the lands, air, waters, coastal seas, sea-ice, flora and fauna and other resources which they have traditionally owned or otherwise occupied or used. This includes the right to the full recognition of their laws, traditions and customs, land-tenure systems and institutions for the development and management of resources, and the right to effective measures by States to prevent any interference with, alienation of or encroachment upon these rights.

Article 27

Indigenous peoples have the right to the restitution of the lands, territories and resources which they have traditionally owned or otherwise occupied or used, and which have been confiscated, occupied, used or damaged without their free and informed consent. Where this is not possible, they have the right to just and fair compensation. Unless otherwise freely agree upon by the peoples concerned, compensation shall take the form of lands, territories and resources equal in quality, size and legal status.

Article 28

Indigenous peoples have the right to the conservation, restoration and protection of the total environment and the productive capacity of their lands, territories and resources, as well as to assistance for this purpose from States and through international cooperation. Military activities shall not take place in the lands and territories of indigenous peoples, unless otherwise freely agreed upon by the peoples concerned.

States shall take effective measures to ensure that no storage or disposal of hazardous materials shall take place in the lands and territories of indigenous peoples.

States shall also take effective measures to ensure, as needed, that programmes for monitoring, maintaining and restoring the health of indigenous peoples, as developed and implemented by the peoples affected by such materials, are duly implemented.

Article 29

Indigenous peoples are entitled to the recognition of the full ownership, control and protection of their cultural and intellectual property.

They have the right to special measures to control, develop and protect their sciences, technologies and cultural manifestations, including human and other genetic resources, seeds, medicines, knowledge of the properties of fauna and flora, oral traditions, literatures, designs and visual and performing arts.

Article 30

Indigenous peoples have the right to determine and develop priorities and strategies for the development or use of their lands, territories and other resources, including the right to require that States obtain their free and informed consent prior to the approval of any project affecting their lands, territories and other resources, particularly in connection with the development, utilization or exploitation of mineral, water or other resources. Pursuant to agreement with the indigenous peoples concerned, just and fair compensation shall be provided for any such activities and measures taken to mitigate adverse environmental, economic, social, cultural or spiritual impact.

PART VII

Article 31

Indigenous peoples, as a specific form of exercising their right to self-determination, have the right to autonomy or self-government in matters relating to their internal and local affairs, including culture, religion, education, information, media, health, housing, employment, social welfare, economic activities, land and resources management, environment and entry by non-members, as well as ways and means for financing these autonomous functions.

Article 32

Indigenous peoples have the collective right to determine their own citizenship in accordance with their customs and traditions. Indigenous citizenship does not impair the right of indigenous individuals to obtain citizenship of the States in which they live.

Indigenous peoples have the right to determine the structures and to select the membership of their institutions in accordance with their own procedures.

Article 33

Indigenous peoples have the right to promote, develop and maintain their institutional structures and their distinctive juridical customs, traditions, procedures and practices, in accordance with internationally recognized human rights standards.

Article 34

Indigenous peoples have the collective right to determine the responsibilities of individuals to their communities.

Article 35

Indigenous peoples, in particular those divided by international borders, have the right to maintain and develop contacts, relations and cooperation, including activities for spiritual, cultural, political, economic and social purposes, with other peoples across borders.

States shall take effective measures to ensure the exercise and implementation of this right.

Article 36

Indigenous peoples have the right to the recognition, observance and enforcement of treaties, agreements and other constructive arrangements concluded with States or their successors, according to their original spirit and intent, and to have States honour and respect such treaties, agreements and other constructive arrangements. Conflicts and disputes which cannot otherwise be settled should be submitted to competent international bodies agreed to by all parties concerned.

PART VIII

Article 37

States shall take effective and appropriate measures, in consultation with the indigenous peoples concerned, to give full effect to the provisions of this Declaration. The rights recognized herein shall be adopted and included in national legislation in such a manner that indigenous peoples can avail themselves of such rights in practice.

Article 38

Indigenous peoples have the right to have access to adequate financial and technical assistance, from States and through international cooperation, to pursue freely their political, economic, social, cultural and spiritual development and for the enjoyment of the rights and freedoms recognized in this Declaration.

Article 39

Indigenous peoples have the right to have access to and prompt decision through mutually acceptable and fair procedures for the resolution of conflicts and disputes with States, as well as to effective remedies for all infringements of their individual and collective rights. Such a decision shall take into consideration the customs, traditions, rules and legal systems of the indigenous peoples concerned.

Article 40

The organs and specialized agencies of the United Nations system and other intergovernmental organizations shall contribute to the full realization of the provisions of this Declaration through the mobilization, inter alia, of financial cooperation and technical assistance. Ways and means of ensuring participation of indigenous peoples on issues affecting them shall be established.

Article 41

The United Nations shall take the necessary steps to ensure the implementation of this Declaration including the creation of a body at the highest level with special competence in this field and with the direct participation of indigenous peoples. All United Nations bodies shall promote respect for and full application of the provisions of this Declaration.

PART IX

Article 42

The rights recognized herein constitute the minimum standards for the survival, dignity and well-being of the indigenous peoples of the world.

Article 43

All the rights and freedoms recognized herein are equally guaranteed to male and female indigenous individuals.

Article 44

Nothing in this Declaration may be construed as diminishing or extinguishing existing or future rights indigenous peoples may have or acquire.

Article 45

Nothing in this Declaration may be interpreted as implying for any State, group or person any right to engage in any activity or to perform any act contrary to the Charter of the United Nations.

APPENDIX 2

UNITED NATIONS CONVENTION ON THE RIGHTS OF THE CHILD*

Adopted and opened for signature, ratification and accession by General Assembly resolution 44/25 of 20 November 1989

2 September 1990, in accordance with Article 49

PREAMBLE

The States Parties to the present Convention,

Considering that, in accordance with the principles proclaimed in the Charter of the United Nations, recognition of the inherent dignity and of the equal and inalienable rights of all members of the human family is the foundation of freedom, justice and peace in the world,

Bearing in mind that the peoples of the United Nations have, in the charter, reaffirmed their faith in fundamental human rights and in the dignity and worth of the human person, and have determined to promote social progress and better standards of life in larger freedom,

Recognizing that the United Nations has, in the Universal Declaration of Human Rights and in the International Covenants on Human Rights, proclaimed and agreed that everyone is entitled to all the rights and freedoms set forth therein, without distinction of any kind, such as race, colour, sex, language, religion, political or other opinion, national or social origin, property, birth or other status,

Recalling that, in the Universal Declaration of Human Rights, the United Nations has proclaimed that childhood is entitled to special care and assistance,

Convinced that the family, as the fundamental group of society and the natural environment for the growth and well-being of all its members and particularly children, should be afforded the necessary protection and assistance so that it can fully assume its responsibilities within the community,

Recognizing that the child, for the full and harmonious development of his or her personality, should grow up in a family environment, in an atmosphere of happiness, love and understanding,

Considering that the child should be fully prepared to live an individual life in society, and brought up in the spirit of the ideals proclaimed in the Charter of the United Nations, and in particular in the spirit of peace, dignity, tolerance, freedom, equality and solidarity,

Bearing in mind that the need to extend particular care to the child has been stated in the Geneva Declaration of the Rights of the Child of 1924 and in the Declaration of the Rights of the Child adopted by the General Assembly on 20 November 1959 and recognized in the Universal Declaration of Human Rights, in the International Covenant on Civil and Political Rights (in particular in articles 23 and 24), in the International Covenant on Economic, Social and Cultural Rights (in particular in article 10) and in the statutes and relevant instruments of specialized agencies and international organizations concerned with the welfare of children,

Bearing in mind that, as indicated in the Declaration of the Rights of the Child, the child, by reason of his physical and mental immaturity, needs special safeguards and care, including appropriate legal protection, before as well as after birth,

Recalling the provisions of the Declaration on Social and Legal Principles relating to the Protection and Welfare of Children, with Special Reference to Foster Placement and Adoption Nationally and Internationally; the United Nations Standard Minimum Rules for the Administration of Juvenile Justice (The Beijing Rules) ; and the Declaration on the Protection of Women and Children in Emergency and Armed Conflict,

Recognizing that, in all countries in the world, there are children living in exceptionally difficult conditions, and that such children need special consideration,

Taking due account of the importance of the traditions and cultural values of each people for the protection and harmonious development of the child,

Recognizing the importance of international co-operation for improving the living conditions of children in every country, in particular in the developing countries,

Have agreed as follows:

PART I

Article 1

For the purposes of the present Convention, a child means every human being below the age of eighteen years unless under the law applicable to the child, majority is attained earlier.

Article 2

1. States Parties shall respect and ensure the rights set forth in the present Convention to each child within their jurisdiction without discrimination of any kind, irrespective of the child's or his or her parent's or legal guardian's race, colour, sex, language, religion, political or other opinion, national, ethnic or social origin, property, disability, birth or other status.

2. States Parties shall take all appropriate measures to ensure that the child is protected against all forms of discrimination or punishment on the basis of the status, activities, expressed opinions, or beliefs of the child's parents, legal guardians, or family members.

Article 3

1. In all actions concerning children, whether undertaken by public or private social welfare institutions, courts of law, administrative authorities or legislative bodies, the best interests of the child shall be a primary consideration.

2. States Parties undertake to ensure the child such protection and care as is necessary for his or her well-being, taking into account the rights and duties of his or her parents, legal guardians, or other individuals legally responsible for him or her, and, to this end, shall take all appropriate legislative and administrative measures.

3. States Parties shall ensure that the institutions, services and facilities responsible for the care or protection of children shall conform with the standards established by competent authorities, particularly in the areas of safety, health, in the number and suitability of their staff, as well as competent supervision.

Article 4

States Parties shall undertake all appropriate legislative, administrative, and other measures for the implementation of the rights recognized in the present Convention. With regard to economic, social and cultural rights, States Parties shall undertake such measures to the maximum extent of their available resources and, where needed, within the framework of international co-operation.

Article 5

States Parties shall respect the responsibilities, rights and duties of parents or, where applicable, the members of the extended family or community as provided for by local custom, legal guardians or other persons legally responsible for the child, to provide, in a manner consistent with the evolving capacities of the child, appropriate direction and guidance in the exercise by the child of the rights recognized in the present Convention.

Article 6

1. States Parties recognize that every child has the inherent right to life.

2. States Parties shall ensure to the maximum extent possible the survival and development of the child.

Article 7

1. The child shall be registered immediately after birth and shall have the right from birth to a name, the right to acquire a nationality and as far as possible, the right to know and be cared for by his or her parents.

2. States Parties shall ensure the implementation of these rights in accordance with their national law and their obligations under the relevant international instruments in this field, in particular where the child would otherwise be stateless.

Article 8

1. States Parties undertake to respect the right of the child to preserve his or her identity, including nationality, name and family relations as recognized by law without unlawful interference.

2. Where a child is illegally deprived of some or all of the elements of his or her identity, States Parties shall provide appropriate assistance and protection, with a view to re-establishing speedily his or her identity.

Article 9

1. States Parties shall ensure that a child shall not be separated from his or her parents against their will, except when competent authorities subject to judicial review determine, in accordance with applicable law and procedures, that such separation is necessary for the

best interests of the child. Such determination may be necessary in a particular case such as one involving abuse or neglect of the child by the parents, or one where the parents are living separately and a decision must be made as to the child's place of residence.

2. In any proceedings pursuant to paragraph 1 of the present article, all interested parties shall be given an opportunity to participate in the proceedings and make their views known.

3. States Parties shall respect the right of the child who is separated from one or both parents to maintain personal relations and direct contact with both parents on a regular basis, except if it is contrary to the child's best interests.

4. Where such separation results from any action initiated by a State Party, such as the detention, imprisonment, exile, deportation or death (including death arising from any cause while the person is in the custody of the State) of one or both parents or of the child, that State Party shall, upon request, provide the parents, the child or, if appropriate, another member of the family with the essential information concerning the whereabouts of the absent member(s) of the family unless the provision of the information would be detrimental to the well-being of the child. States Parties shall further ensure that the submission of such a request shall of itself entail no adverse consequences for the person(s)concerned.

Article 10

1. In accordance with the obligation of States Parties under article 9, paragraph 1, applications by a child or his or her parents to enter or leave a State Party for the purpose of family reunification shall be dealt with by States Parties in a positive, humane and expeditious manner. States Parties shall further ensure that the submission of such a request shall entail no adverse consequences for the applicants and for the members of their family.

2. A child whose parents reside in different States shall have the right to maintain on a regular basis, save in exceptional circumstances personal relations and direct contacts with both parents. Towards that end and in accordance with the obligation of States Parties under article 9, paragraph 1, States Parties shall respect the right of the child and his or her parents to leave any country, including their own, and to enter their own country. The right to leave any country shall be subject only to such restrictions as are prescribed by law and which are necessary to protect the national security, public order (ordre public), public health or morals or the rights

and freedoms of others and are consistent with the other rights recognized in the present Convention.

Article 11

1. States Parties shall take measures to combat the illicit transfer and non-return of children abroad.

2. To this end, States Parties shall promote the conclusion of bilateral or multilateral agreements or accession to existing agreements.

Article 12

1. States Parties shall assure to the child who is capable of forming his or her own views the right to express those views freely in all matters affecting the child, the views of the child being given due weight in accordance with the age and maturity of the child.

2. For this purpose, the child shall in particular be provided the opportunity to be heard in any judicial and administrative proceedings affecting the child, either directly, or through a representative or an appropriate body, in a manner consistent with the procedural rules of national law.

Article 13

1. The child shall have the right to freedom of expression; this right shall include freedom to seek, receive and impart information and ideas of all kinds, regardless of frontiers, either orally, in writing or in print, in the form of art, or through any other media of the child's choice.

2. The exercise of this right may be subject to certain restrictions, but these shall only be such as are provided by law and are necessary:

(a) For respect of the rights or reputations of others; or

(b) For the protection of national security or of public order (ordre public), or of public health or morals.

Article 14

1. States Parties shall respect the right of the child to freedom of thought, conscience and religion.

2. States Parties shall respect the rights and duties of the parents and, when applicable, legal guardians, to provide direction to the child in the exercise of his or her right in a manner consistent with the evolving capacities of the child.

3. Freedom to manifest one's religion or beliefs may be subject only to such limitations as are prescribed by law and are necessary to protect public safety, order, health or morals, or the fundamental rights and freedoms of others.

Article 15

1. States Parties recognize the rights of the child to freedom of association and to freedom of peaceful assembly.

2. No restrictions may be placed on the exercise of these rights other than those imposed in conformity with the law and which are necessary in a democratic society in the interests of national security or public safety, public order (ordre public), the protection of public health or morals or the protection of the rights and freedoms of others.

Article 16

1. No child shall be subjected to arbitrary or unlawful interference with his or her privacy, family, home or correspondence, nor to unlawful attacks on his or her honour and reputation.

2. The child has the right to the protection of the law against such interference or attacks.

Article 17

States Parties recognize the important function performed by the mass media and shall ensure that the child has access to information and material from a diversity of national and international sources, especially those aimed at the promotion of his or her social, spiritual and moral well-being and physical and mental health. To this end, States Parties shall:

(a) Encourage the mass media to disseminate information and material of social and cultural benefit to the child and in accordance with the spirit of article 29;

(b) Encourage international co-operation in the production, exchange and dissemination of such information and material from a diversity of cultural, national and international sources;

(c) Encourage the production and dissemination of children's books;

(d) Encourage the mass media to have particular regard to the linguistic needs of the child who belongs to a minority group or who is indigenous;

(e) Encourage the development of appropriate guidelines for the protection of the child from information and material injurious to his or her well-being, bearing in mind the provisions of articles 13 and 18.

Article 18

1. States Parties shall use their best efforts to ensure recognition of the principle that both parents have common responsibilities for the upbringing and development of the child. Parents or, as the case may be, legal guardians, have the primary responsibility for the upbringing and development of the child. The best interests of the child will be their basic concern.

2. For the purpose of guaranteeing and promoting the rights set forth in the present Convention, States Parties shall render appropriate assistance to parents and legal guardians in the performance of their child-rearing responsibilities and shall ensure the development of institutions, facilities and services for the care of children.

3. States Parties shall take all appropriate measures to ensure that children of working parents have the right to benefit from child-care services and facilities for which they are eligible.

Article 19

1. States Parties shall take all appropriate legislative, administrative, social and educational measures to protect the child from all forms of physical or mental violence, injury or abuse, neglect or negligent treatment, maltreatment or exploitation, including sexual abuse, while in the care of parent(s), legal guardian(s) or any other person who has the care of the child.

2. Such protective measures should, as appropriate, include effective procedures for the establishment of social programmes to provide necessary support for the child and for those who have the care of the child, as well as for other forms of prevention and for identification, reporting, referral, investigation, treatment and follow-up of instances of child maltreatment described heretofore, and, as appropriate, for judicial involvement

Article 20

1. A child temporarily or permanently deprived of his or her family environment, or in whose own best interests cannot be allowed to remain in that environment, shall be entitled to special protection and assistance provided by the State.

2. States Parties shall in accordance with their national laws ensure alternative care for such a child.

3. Such care could include, inter alia, foster placement, kafalah of Islamic law, adoption or if necessary placement in suitable institutions for the care of children. When considering solutions, due regard shall be paid to the desirability of continuity in a child's upbringing and to the child's ethnic, religious, cultural and linguistic background.

Article 21

States Parties that recognize and/or permit the system of adoption shall ensure that the best interests of the child shall be the paramount consideration and they shall:

(a) Ensure that the adoption of a child is authorized only by competent authorities who determine, in accordance with applicable law and procedures and on the basis of all pertinent and reliable information, that the adoption is permissible in view of the child's status concerning parents, relatives and legal guardians and that, if required, the persons concerned have given their informed consent to the adoption on the basis of such counseling as may be necessary;

(b) Recognize that inter-country adoption may be considered as an alternative means of child's care, if the child cannot be placed in a foster or an adoptive family or cannot in any suitable manner be cared for in the child's country of origin;

(c) Ensure that the child concerned by inter-country adoption enjoys safeguards and standards equivalent to those existing in the case of national adoption;

(d) Take all appropriate measures to ensure that, in inter-country adoption, the placement does not result in improper financial gain for those involved in it;

(e) Promote, where appropriate, the objectives of the present article by concluding bilateral or multilateral arrangements or agreements, and endeavour, within this framework, to ensure that the placement of the child in another country is carried out by competent authorities or organs.

Article 22

1. States Parties shall take appropriate measures to ensure that a child who is seeking refugee status or who is considered a refugee in accordance with applicable international or domestic law and procedures shall, whether unaccompanied or accompanied by his or her parents or by any other person, receive appropriate protection and humanitarian assistance in the enjoyment of applicable rights set forth in the present Convention and in other international human rights or humanitarian instruments to which the said States are Parties.

2. For this purpose, States Parties shall provide, as they consider appropriate, co-operation in any efforts by the United Nations and other competent intergovernmental organizations or non-governmental organizations co-operating with the United Nations to protect and assist such a child and to trace the parents or other members of the family of any refugee child in order to obtain information necessary for reunification with his or her family. In cases where no parents or other members of the family can be found, the child shall be accorded the same protection as any other child permanently or temporarily deprived of his or her family environment for any reason, as set forth in the present Convention.

Article 23

1. States Parties recognize that a mentally or physically disabled child should enjoy a full and decent life, in conditions which ensure dignity, promote self-reliance and facilitate the child's active participation in the community.

2. States Parties recognize the right of the disabled child to special care and shall encourage and ensure the extension, subject to available resources, to the eligible child and those responsible for his or her care, of assistance for which application is made and which is appropriate to the child's condition and to the circumstances of the parents or others caring for the child.

3. Recognizing the special needs of a disabled child, assistance extended in accordance with paragraph 2 of the present article shall be provided free of charge, whenever possible, taking into account the financial resources of the parents or others caring for the child,

and shall be designed to ensure that the disabled child has effective access to and receives education, training, health care services, rehabilitation services, preparation for employment and recreation opportunities in a manner conducive to the child's achieving the fullest possible social integration and individual development, including his or her cultural and spiritual development.

4. States Parties shall promote, in the spirit of international cooperation, the exchange of appropriate information in the field of preventive health care and of medical, psychological and functional treatment of disabled children, including dissemination of and access to information concerning methods of rehabilitation, education and vocational services, with the aim of enabling States Parties to improve their capabilities and skills and to widen their experience in these areas. In this regard, particular account shall be taken of the needs of developing countries.

Article 24

1. States Parties recognize the right of the child to the enjoyment of the highest attainable standard of health and to facilities for the treatment of illness and rehabilitation of health. States Parties shall strive to ensure that no child is deprived of his or her right of access to such health care services.

2. States Parties shall pursue full implementation of this right and, in particular, shall take appropriate measures:

(a) To diminish infant and child mortality;

(b) To ensure the provision of necessary medical assistance and health care to all children with emphasis on the development of primary health care;

(c) To combat disease and malnutrition, including within the framework of primary health care, through, inter alia, the application of readily available technology and through the provision of adequate nutritious foods and clean drinking water, taking into consideration the dangers and risks of environmental pollution;

(d) To ensure appropriate pre-natal and post-natal health care for mothers;

(e) To ensure that all segments of society, in particular parents and children, are informed, have access to education and are supported in the use of basic knowledge of child health and nutrition, the advantages of breastfeeding, hygiene and environmental sanitation and the prevention of accidents;

(f) To develop preventive health care, guidance for parents and family planning education and services.

3. States Parties shall take all effective and appropriate measures with a view to abolishing traditional practices prejudicial to the health of children.

4. States Parties undertake to promote and encourage international co-operation with a view to achieving progressively the full realization of the right recognized in the present article. In this regard, particular account shall be taken of the needs of developing countries.

Article 25

States Parties recognize the right of a child who has been placed by the competent authorities for the purposes of care, protection or treatment of his or her physical or mental health, to a periodic review of the treatment provided to the child and all other circumstances relevant to his or her placement.

Article 26

1. States Parties shall recognize for every child the right to benefit from social security, including social insurance, and shall take the necessary measures to achieve the full realization of this right in accordance with their national law.

2. The benefits should, where appropriate, be granted, taking into account the resources and the circumstances of the child and persons having responsibility for the maintenance of the child, as well as any other consideration relevant to an application for benefits made by or on behalf of the child.

Article 27

1. States Parties recognize the right of every child to a standard of living adequate for the child's physical, mental, spiritual, moral and social development.

2. The parent(s) or others responsible for the child have the primary responsibility to secure, within their abilities and financial capacities, the conditions of living necessary for the child's development.

3. States Parties, in accordance with national conditions and within their means, shall take appropriate measures to assist parents and others responsible for the child to implement this right and shall in case of need provide material assistance and support programmes, particularly with regard to nutrition, clothing and housing.

4. States Parties shall take all appropriate measures to secure the recovery of maintenance for the child from the parents or other person sharing financial responsibility for the child, both within the State Party and from abroad. In particular, where the person having financial responsibility for the child lives in a State different from that of the child, States Parties shall promote the accession to international agreements or the conclusion of such agreements, as well as the making of other appropriate arrangements.

Article 28

1. States Parties recognize the right of the child to education, and with a view to achieving this right progressively and on the basis of equal opportunity, they shall, in particular:

(a) Make primary education compulsory and available free to all;

(b) Encourage the development of different forms of secondary education, including general and vocational education, make them available and accessible to every child, and take appropriate measures such as the introduction of free education and offering financial assistance in case of need;

(c) Make higher education accessible to all on the basis of capacity by every appropriate means;

(d) Make educational and vocational information and guidance available and accessible to all children;

(e) Take measures to encourage regular attendance at schools and the reduction of drop-out rates.

2. States Parties shall take all appropriate measures to ensure that school discipline is administered in a manner consistent with the child's human dignity and in conformity with the present Convention.

3. States Parties shall promote and encourage international cooperation in matters relating to education, in particular with a view to

contributing to the elimination of ignorance and illiteracy throughout the world and facilitating access to scientific and technical
knowledge and modern teaching methods. In this regard, particular
account shall be taken of the needs of developing countries.

Article 29

1. States Parties agree that the education of the child shall be di-
    rected to:

(a) The development of the child's personality, talents and mental and
    physical abilities to their fullest potential;

(b) The development of respect for human rights and fundamental
    freedoms, and for the principles enshrined in the Charter of the
    United Nations;

(c) The development of respect for the child's parents, his or her own
    cultural identity, language and values, for the national values of
    the country in which the child is living, the country from which he
    or she may originate, and for civilizations different from his or
    her own;

(d) The preparation of the child for responsible life in a free society,
    in the spirit of understanding, peace, tolerance, equality of sexes,
    and friendship among all peoples, ethnic, national and religious
    groups and persons of indigenous origin;

(e) The development of respect for the natural environment.

2. No part of the present article or article 28 shall be construed so as
    to interfere with the liberty of individuals and bodies to establish
    and direct educational institutions, subject always to the observance
    of the principle set forth in paragraph 1 of the present article and
    to the requirements that the education given in such institutions
    shall conform to such minimum standards as may be laid down by
    the State.

Article 30

In those States in which ethnic, religious or linguistic minorities or persons
of indigenous origin exist, a child belonging to such a minority or who is indigenous shall not be denied the right, in community with other members of his or
her group, to enjoy his or her own culture, to profess and practise his or her
own religion, or to use his or her own language.

Article 31

1. States Parties recognize the right of the child to rest and leisure, to engage in play and recreational activities appropriate to the age of the child and to participate freely in cultural life and the arts.

2. States Parties shall respect and promote the right of the child to participate fully in cultural and artistic life and shall encourage the provision of appropriate and equal opportunities for cultural, artistic, recreational and leisure activity.

Article 32

1. States Parties recognize the right of the child to be protected from economic exploitation and from performing any work that is likely to be hazardous or to interfere with the child's education, or to be harmful to the child's health or physical, mental, spiritual, moral or social development.

2. States Parties shall take legislative, administrative, social and educational measures to ensure the implementation of the present article. To this end, and having regard to the relevant provisions of other international instruments, States Parties shall in particular:

(a) Provide for a minimum age or minimum ages for admission to employment;

(b) Provide for appropriate regulation of the hours and conditions of employment;

(c) Provide for appropriate penalties or other sanctions to ensure the effective enforcement of the present article.

Article 33

States Parties shall take all appropriate measures, including legislative, administrative, social and educational measures, to protect children from the illicit use of narcotic drugs and psychotropic substances as defined in the relevant international treaties, and to prevent the use of children in the illicit production and trafficking of such substances.

Article 34

States Parties undertake to protect the child from all forms of sexual exploitation and sexual abuse. For these purposes, States Parties shall in particular take all appropriate national, bilateral and multilateral measures to prevent:

(a) The inducement or coercion of a child to engage in any unlawful sexual activity;

(b) The exploitative use of children in prostitution or other unlawful sexual practices;

(c) The exploitative use of children in pornographic performances and materials.

Article 35

States Parties shall take all appropriate national, bilateral and multilateral measures to prevent the abduction of, the sale of or traffic in children for any purpose or in any form.

Article 36

States Parties shall protect the child against all other forms of exploitation prejudicial to any aspects of the child's welfare.

Article 37

States Parties shall ensure that:

(a) No child shall be subjected to torture or other cruel, inhuman or degrading treatment or punishment. Neither capital punishment nor life imprisonment without possibility of release shall be imposed for offences committed by persons below eighteen years of age;

(b) No child shall be deprived of his or her liberty unlawfully or arbitrarily. The arrest, detention or imprisonment of a child shall be in conformity with the law and shall be used only as a measure of last resort and for the shortest appropriate period of time;

(c) Every child deprived of liberty shall be treated with humanity and respect for the inherent dignity of the human person, and in a manner which takes into account the needs of persons of his or her age. In particular, every child deprived of liberty shall be separated from adults unless it is considered in the child's best interest not to do so and shall have the right to maintain contact with his or her family through correspondence and visits, save in exceptional circumstances;

(d) Every child deprived of his or her liberty shall have the right to prompt access to legal and other appropriate assistance, as well as the right to challenge the legality of the deprivation of his or her liberty before a court or other competent, independent and impartial authority, and to a prompt decision on any such action.

Article 38

1. States Parties undertake to respect and to ensure respect for rules of international humanitarian law applicable to them in armed conflicts which are relevant to the child.

2. States Parties shall take all feasible measures to ensure that persons who have not attained the age of fifteen years do not take a direct part in hostilities.

3. States Parties shall refrain from recruiting any person who has not attained the age of fifteen years into their armed forces. In recruiting among those persons who have attained the age of fifteen years but who have not attained the age of eighteen years, States Parties shall endeavour to give priority to those who are oldest.

4. In accordance with their obligations under international humanitarian law to protect the civilian population in armed conflicts, States Parties shall take all feasible measures to ensure protection and care of children who are affected by an armed conflict.

Article 39

States Parties shall take all appropriate measures to promote physical and psychological recovery and social reintegration of a child victim of: any form of neglect, exploitation, or abuse; torture or any other form of cruel, inhuman or degrading treatment or punishment; or armed conflicts. Such recovery and reintegration shall take place in an environment which fosters the health, self-respect and dignity of the child.

Article 40

1. States Parties recognize the right of every child alleged as, accused of, or recognized as having infringed the penal law to be treated in a manner consistent with the promotion of the child's sense of dignity and worth, which reinforces the child's respect for the human rights and fundamental freedoms of others and which takes into account the child's age and the desirability of promoting the child's reintegration and the child's assuming a constructive role in society.

2. To this end, and having regard to the relevant provisions of international instruments, States Parties shall, in particular, ensure that:

(a) No child shall be alleged as, be accused of, or recognized as having infringed the penal law by reason of acts or omissions that were not prohibited by national or international law at the time they were committed;

(b) Every child alleged as or accused of having infringed the penal law has at least the following guarantees:

  (i)   To be presumed innocent until proven guilty according to law;

  (ii) To be informed promptly and directly of the charges against him or her, and, if appropriate, through his or her parents or legal guardians, and to have legal or other appropriate assistance in the preparation and presentation of his or her defence;

  (iii) To have the matter determined without delay by a competent, independent and impartial authority or judicial body in a fair hearing according to law, in the presence of legal or other appropriate assistance and, unless it is considered not to be in the best interest of the child, in particular, taking into account his or her age or situation, his or her parents or legal guardians;

  (iv) Not to be compelled to give testimony or to confess guilt; to examine or have examined adverse witnesses and to obtain the participation and examination of witnesses on his or her behalf under conditions of equality;

  (v)   If considered to have infringed the penal law, to have this decision and any measures imposed in consequence thereof reviewed by a higher competent, independent and impartial authority or judicial body according to law;

  (vi) To have the free assistance of an interpreter if the child cannot understand or speak the language used;

  (vii) To have his or her privacy fully respected at all stages of the proceedings.

3. States Parties shall seek to promote the establishment of laws, procedures, authorities and institutions specifically applicable to children alleged as, accused of, or recognized as having infringed the penal law, and, in particular:

(a) The establishment of a minimum age below which children shall be presumed not to have the capacity to infringe the penal law;

(b) Whenever appropriate and desirable, measures for dealing with such children without resorting to judicial proceedings, providing that human rights and legal safeguards are fully respected.

4. A variety of dispositions, such as care, guidance and supervision orders; counseling; probation; foster care; education and vocational training programmes and other alternatives to institutional care shall be available to ensure that children are dealt with in a manner appropriate to their well-being and proportionate both to their circumstances and the offence.

Article 41

Nothing in the present Convention shall affect any provisions which are more conducive to the realization of the rights of the child and which may be contained in:

(a) The law of a State party; or

(b) International law in force for that State.

PART II

Article 42

States Parties undertake to make the principles and provisions of the Convention widely known, by appropriate and active means, to adults and children alike.

Article 43

1. For the purpose of examining the progress made by States Parties in achieving the realization of the obligations undertaken in the present Convention, there shall be established a Committee on the Rights of the Child, which shall carry out the functions hereinafter provided.

2. The Committee shall consist of ten experts of high moral standing and recognized competence in the field covered by this Convention. The members of the Committee shall be elected by States Parties from among their nationals and shall serve in their personal capacity, consideration being given to equitable geographical distribution, as well as to the principal legal systems.

3. The members of the Committee shall be elected by secret ballot from a list of persons nominated by States Parties. Each State Party may nominate one person from among its own nationals.

4. The initial election to the Committee shall be held no later than six months after the date of the entry into force of the present Convention and thereafter every second year. At least four months before the date of each election, the Secretary-General of the United Nations shall address a letter to States Parties inviting them to submit their nominations within two months. The Secretary-General shall subsequently prepare a list in alphabetical order of all persons thus nominated, indicating States Parties which have nominated them, and shall submit it to the States Parties to the present Convention.

5. The elections shall be held at meetings of States Parties convened by the Secretary-General at United Nations Headquarters. At those meetings, for which two thirds of States Parties shall constitute a quorum, the person selected to the Committee shall be those who obtain the largest number of votes and an absolute majority of the votes of the representatives of States Parties present and voting.

6. The members of the Committee shall be elected for a term of four years. They shall be eligible for re-election if renominated. The term of five of the members elected at the first election shall expire at the end of two years; immediately after the first election, the names of these five members shall be chosen by lot by the Chairman of the meeting.

7. If a member of the Committee dies or resigns or declares that for any other cause he or she can no longer perform the duties of the Committee, the State Party which nominated the member shall appoint another expert from among its nationals to serve for the remainder of the term, subject to the approval of the Committee.

8. The Committee shall establish its own rules of procedure.

9. The Committee shall elect its officers for a period of two years.

10. The meetings of the Committee shall normally be held at United Nations Headquarters or at any other convenient place as determined by the Committee. The Committee shall normally meet annually. The duration of the meetings of the Committee shall be determined, and reviewed, if necessary, by a meeting of the States Parties to the present Convention, subject to the approval of the General Assembly.

11. The Secretary-General of the United Nations shall provide the necessary staff and facilities for the effective performance of the functions of the Committee under the present Convention.

12. With the approval of the General Assembly, the members of the Committee established under the present Convention shall receive emoluments from United Nations resources on such terms and conditions as the Assembly may decide.

Article 44

1. States Parties undertake to submit to the Committee, through the Secretary-General of the United Nations, reports on the measures they have adopted which give effect to the rights recognized herein and on the progress made on the enjoyment of those rights:

(a) Within two years of the entry into force of the Convention for the State Party concerned;

(b) Thereafter every five years.

2. Reports made under the present article shall indicate factors and difficulties, if any, affecting the degree of fulfillment of the obligations under the present Convention. Reports shall also contain sufficient information to provide the Committee with a comprehensive understanding of the implementation of the Convention in the country concerned.

3. A State Party which has submitted a comprehensive initial report to the Committee need not, in its subsequent reports submitted in accordance with paragraph 1 (b) of the present article, repeat basic information previously provided.

4. The Committee may request from States Parties further information relevant to the implementation of the Convention.

5. The Committee shall submit to the General Assembly, through the Economic and Social Council, every two years, reports on its activities.

6. States Parties shall make their reports widely available to the public in their own countries.

Article 45

In order to foster the effective implementation of the Convention and to encourage international co-operation in the field covered by the Convention:

(a) The specialized agencies, the United Nations Children's Fund, and other United Nations organs shall be entitled to be represented at the consideration of the implementation of such provisions of the present Convention as fall within the scope of their mandate. The Committee may invite the specialized agencies, the United Nations Children's Fund and other competent bodies as it may consider appropriate to provide expert advice on the implementation of the Convention in areas falling within the scope of their respective mandates. The Committee may invite the specialized agencies, the United Nations Children's Fund, and other United Nations organs to submit reports on the implementation of the Convention in areas falling within the scope of their activities;

(b) The Committee shall transmit, as it may consider appropriate, to the specialized agencies, the United Nations Children's Fund and other competent bodies, any reports from States Parties that contain a request, or indicate a need, for technical advice or assistance, along with the Committee's observations and suggestions, if any, on these requests or indications;

(c) The Committee may recommend to the General Assembly to request the Secretary-General to undertake on its behalf studies on specific issues relating to the rights of the child;

(d) The Committee may make suggestions and general recommendations based on information received pursuant to articles 44 and 45 of the present Convention. Such suggestions and general recommendations shall be transmitted to any State Party concerned and reported to the General Assembly, together with comments, if any, from States Parties.

PART III

Article 46

The present Convention shall be open for signature by all States.

Article 47

The present Convention is subject to ratification. Instruments of ratification shall be deposited with the Secretary-General of the United Nations.

Article 48

The present Convention shall remain open for accession by any State. The instruments of accession shall be deposited with the Secretary-General of the United Nations.

Article 49

1. The present Convention shall enter into force on the thirtieth day following the date of deposit with the Secretary-General of the United Nations of the twentieth instrument of ratification or accession.

2. For each State ratifying or acceding to the Convention after the deposit of the twentieth instrument of ratification or accession, the Convention shall enter into force on the thirtieth day after the deposit by such State of its instrument of ratification or accession.

Article 50

1. Any State Party may propose an amendment and file it with the Secretary-General of the United Nations. The Secretary-General shall thereupon communicate the proposed amendment to States Parties, with a request that they indicate whether they favour a conference of States Parties for the purpose of considering and voting upon the proposals. In the event that, within four months from the date of such communication, at least one third of the States Parties favour such a conference, the Secretary-General shall convene the conference under the auspices of the United Nations. Any amendment adopted by a majority of States Parties present and voting at the conference shall be submitted to the General Assembly for approval.

2. An amendment adopted in accordance with paragraph 1 of the present article shall enter into force when it has been approved by the General Assembly of the United Nations and accepted by a two-thirds majority of States Parties.

3. When an amendment enters into force, it shall be binding on those States Parties which have accepted it, other States Parties still being bound by the provisions of the present Convention and any earlier amendments which they have accepted.

Article 51

1. The Secretary-General of the United Nations shall receive and circulate to all States the text of reservations made by States at the time of ratification or accession.

2. A reservation incompatible with the object and purpose of the present Convention shall not be permitted.

3. Reservations may be withdrawn at any time by notification to that effect addressed to the Secretary-General of the United Nations, who shall then inform all States. Such notification shall take effect on the date on which it is received by the Secretary-General.

Article 52

A State Party may denounce the present Convention by written notification to the Secretary-General of the United Nations. Denunciation becomes effective one year after the date of receipt of the notification by the Secretary-General.

Article 53

The Secretary-General of the United Nations is designated as the depositary of the present Convention.

Article 54

The original of the present Convention, of which the Arabic, Chinese, English, French, Russian and Spanish texts are equally authentic, shall be deposited with the Secretary-General of the United Nations.

IN WITNESS THEREOF the undersigned plenipotentiaries, being duly authorized thereto by their respective governments, have signed the present Convention.

ILO CONVENTION CONCERNING INDIGENOUS AND TRIBAL PEOPLES IN INDEPENDENT COUNTRIES (NO. 169)*

72 ILO Official Bull. 59, entered into force September 5, 1991

The General Conference of the International Labour Organisation,

Having been convened at Geneva by the Governing Body of the International Labour Office, and

Having met in its seventy-sixth session on 7 June 1989, and

Noting the international standards contained in the Indigenous and Tribal Populations Convention and Recommendation, 1957, and

Recalling the terms of the Universal Declaration of Human Rights, the International Covenant on Economic, Social and Cultural Rights, the International Covenant on Civil and Political Rights, and the many international instruments on the prevention of discrimination, and

Considering that the developments which have taken place in international law since 1957, as well as developments in the situation of indigenous and tribal peoples in all regions of the world, have made it appropriate to adopt new international standards on the subject with a view to removing the assimilationist orientation of the earlier standards, and

Recognising the aspirations of these peoples to exercise control over their own institutions, ways of life and economic development and to maintain and develop their identities, languages and religions, within the framework of the States in which they live, and

Noting that in many parts of the world these peoples are unable to enjoy their fundamental human rights to the same degree as the rest of the population of the States within which they live, and that their laws, values, customs and perspectives have often been eroded, and

---

Calling attention to the distinctive contributions of indigenous and tribal peoples to the cultural diversity and social and ecological harmony of humankind and to international co-operation and understanding, and

Noting that the following provisions have been framed with the cooperation of the United Nations, the Food and Agriculture Organization of the United Nations, the United Nations Educational, Scientific and Cultural Organization and the World Health Organization, as well as of the Inter-American Indian Institute, at appropriate levels and in their respective fields and that it is proposed to continue this co-operation in promoting and securing the application of these provisions, and

Having decided upon the adoption of certain proposals with regard to the partial revision of the Indigenous and Tribal Populations Convention, 1957 (No. 107), which is the fourth item on the agenda of the session, and

Having determined that these proposals shall take the form of an international Convention revising the Indigenous and Tribal Populations Convention, 1957,

Adopts this twenty-seventh day of June of the year one thousand nine hundred and eighty-nine the following Convention. which may be cited as the Indigenous and Tribal Peoples Convention, 1989;

PART I. GENERAL POLICY

Article 1

1. This Convention applies to:

(a) Tribal peoples in independent countries whose social, cultural and economic conditions distinguish them from other sections of the national community, and whose status is regulated wholly or partially by their own customs or traditions or by special laws or regulations;

(b) Peoples in independent countries who are regarded as indigenous on account of their descent from the populations which inhabited the country, or a geographical region to which the country belongs, at the time of conquest or colonisation or the establishment of present State boundaries and who, irrespective of their legal status, retain some or all of their own social, economic, cultural and political institutions.

2. Self-identification as indigenous or tribal shall be regarded as a fundamental criterion for determining the groups to which the provisions of this Convention apply.

3. The use of the term "peoples" in this Convention shall not be construed as having any implications as regards the rights which may attach to the term under international law.

Article 2

1. Governments shall have the responsibility for developing, with the participation of the peoples concerned, co-ordinated and systematic action to protect the rights of these peoples and to guarantee respect for their integrity.

2. Such action shall include measures for:

(a) Ensuring that members of these peoples benefit on an equal footing from the rights and opportunities which national laws and regulations grant to other members of the population;

(b) Promoting the full realisation of the social, economic and cultural rights of these peoples with respect for their social and cultural identity, their customs and traditions and their institutions;

(c) Assisting the members of the peoples concerned to eliminate socio-economic gaps that may exist between indigenous and other members of the national community, in a manner compatible with their aspirations and ways of life.

Article 3

1. Indigenous and tribal peoples shall enjoy the full measure of human rights and fundamental freedoms without hindrance or discrimination. The provisions of the Convention shall be applied without discrimination to male and female members of these peoples.

2. No form of force or coercion shall be used in violation of the human rights and fundamental freedoms of the peoples concerned, including the rights contained in this Convention.

Article 4

1. Special measures shall be adopted as appropriate for safeguarding the persons, institutions, property, labour, cultures and environment of the peoples concerned.

2. Such special measures shall not be contrary to the freely-expressed wishes of the peoples concerned.

3. Enjoyment of the general rights of citizenship, without discrimination, shall not be prejudiced in any way by such special measures.

Article 5

In applying the provisions of this Convention:

(a) The social, cultural, religious and spiritual values and practices of these peoples shall be recognised and protected, and due account shall be taken of the nature of the problems which face them both as groups and as individuals;

(b) The integrity of the values, practices and institutions of these peoples shall be respected;

(c) Policies aimed at mitigating the difficulties experienced by these peoples in facing new conditions of life and work shall be adopted, with the participation and co-operation of the peoples affected.

Article 6

1. In applying the provisions of this Convention, Governments shall:

(a) Consult the peoples concerned, through appropriate procedures and in particular through their representative institutions, whenever consideration is being given to legislative or administrative measures which may affect them directly;

(b) Establish means by which these peoples can freely participate, to at least the same extent as other sectors of the population, at all levels of decision-making in elective institutions and administrative and other bodies responsible for policies and programmes which concern them;

(c) Establish means for the full development of these peoples' own institutions and initiatives, and in appropriate cases provide the resources necessary for this purpose.

2. The consultations carried out in application of this Convention shall be undertaken, in good faith and in a form appropriate to the circumstances, with the objective of achieving agreement or consent to the proposed measures.

Article 7

1. The peoples concerned shall have the right to decide their own priorities for the process of development as it affects their lives, beliefs, institutions and spiritual well-being and the lands they occupy or otherwise use, and to exercise control, to the extent possible, over their own economic, social and

cultural development. In addition, they shall participate in the formulation, implementation and evaluation of plans and programmes for national and regional development which may affect them directly.

2. The improvement of the conditions of life and work and levels of health and education of the peoples concerned, with their participation and co-operation, shall be a matter of priority in plans for the overall economic development of areas they inhabit. Special projects for development of the areas in question shall also be so designed as to promote such improvement.

3. Governments shall ensure that, whenever appropriate, studies are carried out, in co-operation with the peoples concerned, to assess the social, spiritual, cultural and environmental impact on them of planned development activities. The results of these studies shall be considered as fundamental criteria for the implementation of these activities.

4. Governments shall take measures, in co-operation with the peoples concerned, to protect and preserve the environment of the territories they inhabit.

Article 8

1. In applying national laws and regulations to the peoples concerned, due regard shall be had to their customs or customary laws.

2. These peoples shall have the right to retain their own customs and institutions, where these are not incompatible with fundamental rights defined by the national legal system and with internationally recognized human rights. Procedures shall be established, whenever necessary, to resolve conflicts which may arise in the application of this principle.

3. The application of paragraphs I and 2 of this Article shall not prevent members of these peoples from exercising the rights granted to all citizens and from assuming the corresponding duties.

Article 9

1. To the extent compatible with the national legal system and internationally recognised human rights. the methods customarily practised by the peoples concerned for dealing with offences committed by their members shall be respected.

2. The customs of these peoples in regard to penal matters shall be taken into consideration by the authorities and courts dealing with such cases.

Article 10

1. In imposing penalties laid down by general law on members of these peoples account shall be taken of their economic, social and cultural characteristics.

2. Preference shall be given to methods of punishment other than confinement in prison.

Article 11

The exaction from members of the peoples concerned of compulsory personal services in any form, whether paid or unpaid, shall be prohibited and punishable by law, except in cases prescribed by law for all citizens.

Article 12

The peoples concerned shall be safeguarded against the abuse of their rights and shall be able to take legal proceedings, either individually or through their representative bodies, for the effective protection of these rights. Measures shall be taken to ensure that members of these peoples can understand and be understood in legal proceedings, where necessary through the provision of interpretation or by other effective means.

PART II. LAND

Article 13

1. In applying the provisions of this Part of the Convention governments shall respect the special importance for the cultures and spiritual values of the peoples concerned of their relationship with the lands or territories, or both as applicable, which they occupy or otherwise use, and in particular the collective aspects of this relationship.

2. The use of the term ''lands'' in Articles 15 and 16 shall include the concept of territories, which covers the total environment of the areas which the peoples concerned occupy or otherwise use.

Article 14

1. The rights of ownership and possession of the peoples concerned over the lands which they traditionally occupy shall be recognised. In addition, measures shall be taken in appropriate cases to safeguard the right of the peoples concerned to use lands not exclusively occupied by them, but to which they have traditionally had access for their subsistence and traditional activities. Particular attention shall be paid to the situation of nomadic peoples and shifting cultivators in this respect.

2. Governments shall take steps as necessary to identify the lands which the peoples concerned traditionally occupy, and to guarantee effective protection of their rights of ownership and possession.

3. Adequate procedures shall be established within the national legal system to resolve land claims by the peoples concerned.

Article 15

1. The rights of the peoples concerned to the natural resources pertaining to their lands shall be specially safeguarded. These rights include the right of these peoples to participate in the use, management and conservation of these resources.

2. In cases in which the State retains the ownership of mineral or sub-surface resources or rights to other resources pertaining to lands, governments shall establish or maintain procedures through which they shall consult these peoples, with a view to ascertaining whether and to what degree their interests would be prejudiced, before undertaking or permitting any programmes for the exploration or exploitation of such resources pertaining to their lands. The peoples concerned shall wherever possible participate in the benefits of such activities, and shall receive fair compensation for any damages which they may sustain as a result of such activities.

Article 16

1. Subject to the following paragraphs of this Article, the peoples concerned shall not be removed from the lands which they occupy.

2. Where the relocation of these peoples is considered necessary as an exceptional measure, such relocation shall take place only with their free and informed consent. Where their consent cannot be obtained, such relocation shall take place only following appropriate procedures established by national laws and regulations, including public inquiries where appropriate, which provide the opportunity for effective representation of the peoples concerned.

3. Whenever possible, these peoples shall have the right to return to their traditional lands, as soon as the grounds for relocation cease to exist.

4. When such return is not possible, as determined by agreement or, in the absence of such agreement, through appropriate procedures, these peoples shall be provided in all possible cases with lands of quality and legal status at least equal to that of the lands previously occupied by them, suitable to provide for their present needs and future development. Where the peoples concerned express a preference for compensation in money or in kind, they shall be so compensated under appropriate guarantees.

5. Persons thus relocated shall be fully compensated for any resulting loss or injury.

Article 17

1. Procedures established by the peoples concerned for the transmission of land rights among members of these peoples shall be respected.

2. The peoples concerned shall be consulted whenever consideration is being given to their capacity to alienate their lands or otherwise transmit their rights outside their own community.

3. Persons not belonging to these peoples shall be prevented from taking advantage of their customs or of lack of understanding of the laws on the part of their members to secure the ownership, possession or use of land belonging to them.

Article 18

Adequate penalties shall be established by law for unauthorised intrusion upon, or use of, the lands of the peoples concerned, and governments shall take measures to prevent such offences.

Article 19

National agrarian programmes shall secure to the people concerned treatment equivalent to that accorded to other sectors of the population with regard to:

(a) The provision of more land for these peoples when they have not the area necessary for providing the essentials of a normal existence, or for any possible increase in their numbers;

(b) The provision of the means required to promote the development of the lands which these peoples already possess.

PART III. RECRUITMENT AND CONDITIONS OF EMPLOYMENT

Article 20

1. Governments shall, within the framework of national laws and regulations, and in co-operation with the peoples concerned, adopt special measures to ensure the effective protection with regard to recruitment and conditions of employment of workers belonging to these peoples, to the extent that they are not effectively protected by laws applicable to workers in general.

2. Governments shall do everything possible to prevent any discrimination between workers belonging to the peoples concerned and other workers, in particular as regards:

(a) Admission to employment, including skilled employment, as well as measures for promotion and advancement;

(b) Equal remuneration for work of equal value;

(c) Medical and social assistance, occupational safety and health, all social security benefits and any other occupationally related benefits, and housing;

(d) The right of association and freedom for all lawful trade union activities, and the right to conclude collective agreements with employers or employers' organisations.

3. The measures taken shall include measures to ensure:

(a) That workers belonging to the peoples concerned, including seasonal, casual and migrant workers in agricultural and other employment, as well as those employed by labour contractors, enjoy the protection afforded by national law and practice to other such workers in the same sectors, and that they are fully informed of their rights under labour legislation and of the means of redress available to them;

(b) That workers belonging to these peoples are not subjected to working conditions hazardous to their health, in particular through exposure to pesticides or other toxic substances;

(c) That workers belonging to these peoples are not subjected to coercive recruitment systems, including bonded labour and other forms of debt servitude;

(d) That workers belonging to these peoples enjoy equal opportunities and equal treatment in employment for men and women, and protection from sexual harassment.

4. Particular attention shall be paid to the establishment of adequate labour inspection services in areas where workers belonging to the peoples concerned undertake wage employment, in order to ensure compliance with the provisions of this Part of this Convention.

PART IV. VOCATIONAL TRAINING, HANDICRAFTS AND RURAL INDUSTRIES

Article 21

Members of the peoples concerned shall enjoy opportunities at least equal to those of other citizens in respect of vocational training measures.

Article 22

1. Measures shall be taken to promote the voluntary participation of members of the peoples concerned in vocational training programmes of general application.

2. Whenever existing programmes of vocational training of general application do not meet the special needs of the peoples concerned, governments shall, with the participation of these peoples, ensure the provision of special training programmes and facilities.

3. Any special training programmes shall be based on the economic environment, social and cultural conditions and practical needs of the peoples concerned. Any studies made in this connection shall be carried out in cooperation with these peoples, who shall be consulted on the organisation and operation of such programmes. Where feasible, these peoples shall progressively assume responsibility for the organisation and operation of such special training programmes, if they so decide.

Article 23

1. Handicrafts, rural and community-based industries, and subsistence economy and traditional activities of the peoples concerned, such as hunting, fishing, trapping and gathering, shall be recognised as important factors in the maintenance of their cultures and in their economic self-reliance and development. Governments shall, with the participation of these peoples and whenever appropriate, ensure that these activities are strengthened and promoted.

2. Upon the request of the peoples concerned, appropriate technical and financial assistance shall be provided wherever possible, taking into account the traditional technologies and cultural characteristics of these peoples, as well as the importance of sustainable and equitable development.

PART V. SOCIAL SECURITY AND HEALTH

Article 24

Social security schemes shall be extended progressively to cover the peoples concerned, and applied without discrimination against them.

Article 25

1. Governments shall ensure that adequate health services are made available to the peoples concerned, or shall provide them with resources to allow them to design and deliver such services under their own responsibility and control, so that they may enjoy the highest attainable standard of physical and mental health.

2. Health services shall, to the extent possible, be community-based. These services shall be planned and administered in co-operation with the peoples concerned and take into account their economic, geographic, social and cultural conditions as well as their traditional preventive care, healing practices and medicines.

3. The health care system shall give preference to the training and employment of local community health workers, and focus on primary health care while maintaining strong links with other levels of health care services.

4. The provision of such health services shall be co-ordinated with other social, economic and cultural measures in the country.

PART VI. EDUCATION AND MEANS OF COMMUNICATION

Article 26

Measures shall be taken to ensure that members of the peoples concerned have the opportunity to acquire education at all levels on at least an equal footing with the rest of the national community.

Article 27

1. Education programmes and services for the peoples concerned shall be developed and implemented in co-operation with them to address their special needs, and shall incorporate their histories, their knowledge and technologies, their value systems and their further social, economic and cultural aspirations.

2. The competent authority shall ensure the training of members of these peoples and their involvement in the formulation and implementation of education programmes, with a view to the progressive transfer of responsibility for the conduct of these programmes to these peoples as appropriate.

3. In addition, governments shall recognise the right of these peoples to establish their own educational institutions and facilities, provided that such institutions meet minimum standards established by the competent authority in consultation with these peoples. Appropriate resources shall be provided for this purpose.

Article 28

1. Children belonging to the peoples concerned shall, wherever practicable, be taught to read and write in their own indigenous language or in the language most commonly used by the group to which they belong. When this is not practicable, the competent authorities shall undertake consultations with these peoples with a view to the adoption of measures to achieve this objective.

2. Adequate measures shall be taken to ensure that these peoples have the opportunity to attain fluency in the national language or in one of the official languages of the country.

3. Measures shall be taken to preserve and promote the development and practice of the indigenous languages of the peoples concerned.

Article 29

The imparting of general knowledge and skills that will help children belonging to the peoples concerned to participate fully and on an equal footing in their own community and in the national community shall be an aim of education for these peoples.

Article 30

1. Governments shall adopt measures appropriate to the traditions and cultures of the peoples concerned, to make known to them their rights and duties, especially in regard to labour, economic opportunities, education and health matters, social welfare and their rights deriving from this Convention.

2. If necessary, this shall be done by means of written translations and through the use of mass communications in the languages of these peoples.

Article 31

Educational measures shall be taken among all sections of the national community, and particularly among those that are in most direct contact with the peoples concerned, with the object of eliminating prejudices that they may harbour in respect of these peoples. To this end, efforts shall be made to ensure that history textbooks and other educational materials provide a fair, accurate and informative portrayal of the societies and cultures of these peoples.

PART VII. CONTACTS AND CO-OPERATION ACROSS BORDERS

Article 32

Governments shall take appropriate measures, including by means of international agreements, to facilitate contacts and co-operation between indigenous and tribal peoples across borders, including activities in the economic, social, cultural, spiritual and environmental fields.

PART VIII. ADMINISTRATION

Article 33

1. The governmental authority responsible for the matters covered in this Convention shall ensure that agencies or other appropriate mechanisms exist to administer the programmes affecting the peoples concerned. and shall

ensure that they have the means necessary for the proper fulfilment of the functions assigned to them.

2. These programmes shall include:

(a) The planning, co-ordination, execution and evaluation, in cooperation with the peoples concerned, of the measures provided for in this Convention;

(b) The proposing of legislative and other measures to the competent authorities and supervision of the application of the measures taken, in cooperation with the peoples concerned.

PART IX. GENERAL PROVISIONS

Article 34

The nature and scope of the measures to be taken to give effect to this Convention shall be determined in a flexible manner, having regard to the conditions characteristic of each country.

Article 35

The application of the provisions of this Convention shall not adversely affect rights and benefits of the peoples concerned pursuant to other Conventions and Recommendations, international instruments, treaties, or national laws, awards, custom or agreements.

PART X. FINAL PROVISIONS

Article 36

This Convention revises the Indigenous and Tribal Populations Convention, 1957.

Article 37

The formal ratifications of this Convention shall be communicated to the Director-General of the International Labour Office for registration.

Article 38

1. This Convention shall be binding only upon those Members of the International Labour Organisation whose ratifications have been registered with the Director-General.

2. It shall come into force twelve months after the date on which the ratifications of two Members have been registered with the Director General.

3. Thereafter, this Convention shall come into force for any Member twelve months after the date on which its ratification has been registered.

Article 39

1. A Member which has ratified this Convention may denounce it after the expiration of ten years from the date on which the Convention first comes into force, by an act communicated to the Director-General of the International Labour Office for registration. Such denunciation shall not take effect until one year after the date on which it is registered.

2. Each Member which has ratified this Convention and which does not, within the year following the expiration of the period of ten years mentioned in the preceding paragraph, exercise the right of denunciation provided for in this Article, will be bound for another period of ten years and, thereafter, may denounce this Convention at the expiration of each period of ten years under the terms provided for in this Article.

Article 40

1. The Director-General of the International Labour Office shall notify all Members of the International Labour Organisation of the registration of all ratifications and denunciations communicated to him by the Members of the Organisation.

2. When notifying the Members of the Organisation of the registration of the second ratification communicated to him, the Director-General shall draw the attention of the Members of the Organisation to the date upon which the Convention will come into force.

Article 41

The Director-General of the International Labour Office shall communicate to the Secretary-General of the United Nations for registration in accordance with Article 102 of the Charter of the United Nations full particulars of all ratifications and acts of denunciation registered by him in accordance with the provisions of the preceding Articles.

Article 42

At such times as it may consider necessary the Governing Body of the International Labour Office shall present to the General Conference a report on the working of this Convention and shall examine the desirability of placing on the agenda of the Conference the question of its revision in whole or in part.

Article 43

1. Should the Conference adopt a new Convention revising this Convention in whole or in part, then, unless the new Convention otherwise provides:

(a) The ratification by a Member of the new revising Convention shall ipso jure involve the immediate denunciation of this Convention, notwithstanding the provisions of Article 39 above, if and when the new revising Convention shall have come into force:

(b) As from the date when the new revising Convention comes into force this Convention shall cease to be open to ratification by the Members.

2. This Convention shall in any case remain in force in its actual form and content for those Members which have ratified it but have not ratified the revising Convention.

Article 44

The English and French versions of the text of this Convention are equally authoritative.

DRAFT INTER-AMERICAN DECLARATION ON THE RIGHTS OF INDIGENOUS PEOPLES

(Approved by the Inter-American Commission on Human Rights on February 26, 1997, at its 1333rd session, 95th regular session)

PREAMBLE

1. *Indigenous institutions and the strengthening of nations*

The member states of the OAS (hereafter the states),

Recalling that the indigenous peoples of the Americas constitute an organized, distinctive and integral segment of their population and are entitled to be part of the national identities of the countries of the Americas, and have a special role to play in strengthening the institutions of the state and in establishing national unity based on democratic principles; and,

Further recalling that some of the democratic institutions and concepts embodied in the constitutions of American states originate from institutions of the indigenous peoples, and that in many instances their present participatory systems for decision-making and for authority contribute to improving democracies in the Americas.

Recalling the need to develop their national juridical systems to consolidate the pluricultural nature of our societies.

2. *Eradication of poverty and the right to development*

Concerned about the frequent deprivation afflicting indigenous peoples of their human rights and fundamental freedoms; within and outside their communities, as well as the dispossession of their lands, territories and resources, thus preventing them from exercising, in particular, their right to development in accordance with their own traditions, needs and interests.

Recognizing the severe impoverishment afflicting indigenous peoples in several regions of the Hemisphere and that their living conditions are generally deplorable.

And recalling that in the Declaration of Principles issued by the Summit of the Americas in December 1994, the heads of state and governments declared that in observance of the International Decade of the World's Indigenous People, they will focus their energies on improving the exercise of democratic rights and the access to social services by indigenous peoples and their communities.

3. *Indigenous culture and ecology*

Recognizing the respect for the environment accorded by the cultures of indigenous peoples of the Americas, and considering the special relationship between the indigenous peoples and the environment, lands, resources and territories on which they live and their natural resources.

4. *Harmonious Relations, Respect and the Absence of Discrimination*

Reaffirming the responsibility of all states and peoples of the Americas to end racism and racial discrimination, with a view to establishing harmonious relations and respect among all peoples.

5. *Territories and Indigenous Survival*

Recognizing that in many indigenous cultures, traditional collective systems for control and use of land, territory and resources, including bodies of water and coastal areas, are a necessary condition for their survival, social organization, development and their individual and collective well-being; and that the form of such control and ownership is varied and distinctive and does not necessarily coincide with the systems protected by the domestic laws of the states in which they live.

6. *Security and indigenous areas*

Reaffirming that the armed forces in indigenous areas shall restrict themselves to the performance of their functions and shall not be the cause of abuses or violations of the rights of indigenous peoples.

7. *Human Rights instruments and other advances in international law*

Recognizing the paramountcy and applicability to the states and peoples of the Americas of the American Declaration of the Rights and Duties of Man, the American Convention on Human Rights and other human rights instruments of inter-American and international law; and

Recognizing that indigenous peoples are a subject of international law, and mindful of the progress achieved by the states and indigenous organizations, especially in the sphere of the United Nations and the International Labor Organization, in several international instruments, particularly in the ILO Convention 169.

Affirming the principle of the universality and indivisibility of human rights, and the application of international human rights to all individuals.

8. *Enjoyment of Collective Rights*

Recalling the international recognition of rights that can only be enjoyed when exercised collectively.

9. *Advances in the provisions of national instruments*

Noting the constitutional, legislative and jurisprudential advances achieved in the Americas in guaranteeing the rights and institutions of indigenous peoples.

DECLARE:

SECTION ONE. INDIGENOUS PEOPLES

Article I. Scope and definitions

1. This Declaration applies to indigenous peoples as well as peoples whose social, cultural and economic conditions distinguish them from other sections of the national community, and whose status is regulated wholly or partially by their own customs or traditions or by special laws or regulations.

2. Self identification as indigenous shall be regarded as a fundamental criterion for determining the peoples to which the provisions of this Declaration apply.

3. The use of the term ''peoples'' in this Instrument shall not be construed as having any implication with respect to any other rights that might be attached to that term in international law.

SECTION TWO. HUMAN RIGHTS

Article II. Full observance of human rights

1. Indigenous peoples have the right to the full and effective enjoyment of the human rights and fundamental freedoms recognized in the Charter of the OAS, the American Declaration of the Rights and Duties of Man, the American Convention on Human Rights, and other international human rights law; and nothing in this Declaration shall be construed as in any way limiting or denying those rights or authorizing any action not in accordance with the instruments of international law including human rights law.

2. Indigenous peoples have the collective rights that are indispensable to the enjoyment of the individual human rights of their members. Accordingly the states recognize *inter alia* the right of the indigenous peoples to collective action, to their cultures, to profess and practice their spiritual beliefs, and to use their languages.

3. The states shall ensure for indigenous peoples the full exercise of all rights, and shall adopt in accordance with their constitutional processes such legislative or other measures as may be necessary to give effect to the rights recognized in this Declaration.

Article III. Right to belong to indigenous peoples

Indigenous peoples and communities have the right to belong to indigenous peoples, in accordance with the traditions and customs of the peoples or nation concerned.

Article IV. Legal status of communities

Indigenous peoples have the right to have their legal personality fully recognized by the states within their systems.

Article V. No forced assimilation

1. Indigenous peoples have the right to freely preserve, express and develop their cultural identity in all its aspects, free of any attempt at assimilation.

2. The states shall not undertake, support or favour any policy of artificial or enforced assimilation of indigenous peoples, destruction of a culture or the possibility of the extermination of any indigenous peoples.

Article VI. Special guarantees against discrimination

1. Indigenous peoples have the right to special guarantees against discrimination that may have to be instituted to fully enjoy internationally and nationally-recognized human rights; as well as measures necessary to enable indigenous women, men and children to exercise, without any discrimination, civil, political, economic, social, cultural and spiritual rights. The states recognize that violence exerted against persons because of their gender and age prevents and nullifies the exercise of those rights.

2. Indigenous peoples have the right to fully participate in the prescription of such guarantees.

SECTION THREE. CULTURAL DEVELOPMENT

Article VII. Right to cultural integrity

1. Indigenous peoples have the right to their cultural integrity, and their historical and archeological heritage, which are important both for their survival as well as for the identity of their members.

2. Indigenous peoples are entitled to restitution in respect of the property of which they have been dispossessed, and where that is not possible, compensation on a basis not less favorable than the standard of international law.

3. The states shall recognize and respect indigenous ways of life, customs, traditions, forms of social, economic and political organization, institutions, practices, beliefs and values, use of dress, and languages.

Article VIII. Philosophy, outlook and language

1. Indigenous peoples have the right to indigenous languages, philosophy and outlook as a component of national and universal culture, and as such, shall respect them and facilitate their dissemination.

2. The states shall take measures and ensure that broadcast radio and television programs are broadcast in the indigenous languages in the regions where there is a strong indigenous presence, and to support the creation of indigenous radio stations and other media.

3. The states shall take effective measures to enable indigenous peoples to understand administrative, legal and political rules and procedures, and to be understood in relation to these matters. In areas where indigenous languages are predominant, states shall endeavor to establish the pertinent languages as official languages and to give them the same status that is given to non-indigenous official languages.

4. Indigenous peoples have the right to use their indigenous names, and to have the states recognize them as such.

Article IX. Education

1. Indigenous peoples shall be entitled: a) to establish and set in motion their own educational programs, institutions and facilities; b) to prepare and implement their own educational plans, programs, curricula and materials; c) to train, educate and accredit their teachers and administrators. The states shall endeavor to ensure that such systems guarantee equal educational and teaching opportunities for the entire population and complementarity with national educational systems.

2. When indigenous peoples so decide, educational systems shall be conducted in the indigenous languages and incorporate indigenous content, and they shall also be provided with the necessary training

and means for complete mastery of the official language or languages.

3. The states shall ensure that those educational systems are equal in quality, efficiency, accessibility and in all other ways to that provided to the general population.

4. The states shall take measures to guarantee to the members of indigenous peoples the possibility to obtain education at all levels, at least of equal quality with the general population.

5. The states shall include in their general educational systems, content reflecting the pluricultural nature of their societies.

6. The states shall provide financial and any other type of assistance needed for the implementation of the provisions of this article.

Article X. Spiritual and religious freedom

1. Indigenous peoples have the right to freedom of conscience, freedom of religion and spiritual practice, and to exercise them both publicly and privately.

2. The states shall take necessary measures to prohibit attempts to forcibly convert indigenous peoples or to impose on them beliefs against their will.

3. In collaboration with the indigenous peoples concerned, the states shall adopt effective measures to ensure that their sacred sites, including burial sites, are preserved, respected and protected. When sacred graves and relics have been appropriated by state institutions, they shall be returned.

4. The states shall encourage respect by all people for the integrity of indigenous spiritual symbols, practices, sacred ceremonies, expressions and protocols.

Article XI. Family relations and family ties

1. The family is the natural and basic unit of societies and must be respected and protected by the state. Consequently the state shall recognize and respect the various forms of indigenous family, marriage, family name and filiation.

2. In determining the child's best interest in matters relating to the protection and adoption of children of members of indigenous peoples, and in matters of breaking of ties and other similar circumstances, consideration shall be given by courts and other relevant

institutions to the views of the peoples, including individual, family and community views.

Article XII. Health and well-being

1. Indigenous peoples have the right to legal recognition and practice of their traditional medicine, treatment, pharmacology, health practices and promotion, including preventive and rehabilitative practices.

2. Indigenous peoples have the right to the protection of vital medicinal plants, animal and mineral in their traditional territories.

3. Indigenous peoples shall be entitled to use, maintain, develop and manage their own health services, and they shall also have access, on an equal basis, to all health institutions and services and medical care accessible to the general population.

4. The states shall provide the necessary means to enable the indigenous peoples to eliminate such health conditions in their communities which fall below international accepted standards for the general population.

Article XIII. Right to environmental protection

1. Indigenous peoples have the right to a safe and healthy environment, which is an essential condition for the enjoyment of the right to life and collective well-being.

2. Indigenous peoples have the right to be informed of measures which will affect their environment, including information that ensures their effective participation in actions and policies that might affect it.

3. Indigenous peoples shall have the right to conserve, restore and protect their environment, and the productive capacity of their lands, territories and resources.

4. Indigenous peoples have the right to participate fully in formulating, planning, managing and applying governmental programmes of conservation of their lands, territories and resources.

5. Indigenous peoples have the right to assistance from their states for purposes of environmental protection, and may receive assistance from international organizations.

6. The states shall prohibit and punish, and shall impede jointly with the indigenous peoples, the introduction, abandonment, or deposit of radioactive materials or residues, toxic substances and garbage in contravention of legal provisions; as well as the production, introduction, transportation, possession or use of chemical, biological and nuclear weapons in indigenous areas.

7. When a State declares an indigenous territory as protected area, any lands, territories and resources under potential or actual claim by indigenous peoples, conservation areas shall not be subject to any natural resource development without the informed consent and participation of the peoples concerned.

SECTION FOUR. ORGANIZATIONAL AND POLITICAL RIGHTS

Article XIV. Rights of association, assembly, freedom of expression and freedom of thought

1. Indigenous peoples have the right of association, assembly and expression in accordance with their values, usages, customs, ancestral traditions, beliefs and religions.

2. Indigenous peoples have the right of assembly and to the use of their sacred and ceremonial areas, as well as the right to full contact and common activities with their members living in the territory of neighboring states.

Article XV. Right to self government

1. Indigenous peoples have the right to freely determine their political status and freely pursue their economic, social, spiritual and cultural development, and accordingly, they have the right to autonomy or self-government with regard to *inter alia* culture, religion, education, information, media, health, housing, employment, social welfare, economic activities, land and resource management, the environment and entry by nonmembers; and to determine ways and means for financing these autonomous functions.

2. Indigenous peoples have the right to participate without discrimination, if they so decide, in all decision-making, at all levels, with regard to matters that might affect their rights, lives and destiny. They may do so directly or through representatives chosen by them in accordance with their own procedures. They shall also have the right to maintain and develop their own indigenous decision-making institutions, as well as equal opportunities to access and participate in all state institutions and fora.

Article XVI. Indigenous Law

1. Indigenous law shall be recognized as a part of the states' legal system and of the framework in which the social and economic development of the states takes place.

2. Indigenous peoples have the right to maintain and reinforce their indigenous legal systems and also to apply them to matters within their communities, including systems related to such matters as conflict resolution, crime prevention and maintenance of peace and harmony.

3. In the jurisdiction of any state, procedures concerning indigenous peoples or their interests shall be conducted in such a way as to ensure the right of indigenous peoples to full representation with dignity and equality before the law. This shall include observance of indigenous law and custom and, where necessary, use of their language.

Article XVII. National incorporation of indigenous legal and organizational systems

1. The states shall facilitate the inclusion in their organizational structures, the institutions and traditional practices of indigenous peoples, and in consultation and with consent of the peoples concerned.

2. State institutions relevant to and serving indigenous peoples shall be designed in consultation and with the participation of the peoples concerned so as to reinforce and promote the identity, cultures, traditions, organization and values of those peoples.

SECTION FIVE. SOCIAL, ECONOMIC AND PROPERTY RIGHTS

Article XVIII. Traditional forms of ownership and cultural survival. Rights to land, territories and resources

1. Indigenous peoples have the right to the legal recognition of their varied and specific forms and modalities of their control, ownership, use and enjoyment of territories and property.

2. Indigenous peoples have the right to the recognition of their property and ownership rights with respect to lands, territories and resources they have historically occupied, as well as to the use of those to which they have historically had access for their traditional activities and livelihood.

3.i) Subject to 3.ii.), where property and user rights of indigenous peoples arise from rights existing prior to the creation of those states, the states shall recognize the titles of indigenous peoples relative thereto as permanent, exclusive, inalienable, imprescriptible and indefeasible.

ii) Such titles may only be changed by mutual consent between the state and respective indigenous peoples when they have full knowledge and appreciation of the nature or attributes of such property.

iii) Nothing in 3.i.) shall be construed as limiting the right of indigenous peoples to attribute ownership within the community in accordance with their customs, traditions, uses and traditional practices, nor shall it affect any collective community rights over them.

4. Indigenous peoples have the right to an effective legal framework for the protection of their rights with respect to the natural resources on their lands, including the ability to use, manage, and conserve such resources; and with respect to traditional uses of their lands, interests in lands, and resources, such as subsistence.

5. In the event that ownership of the minerals or resources of the subsoil pertains to the state or that the state has rights over other resources on the lands, the governments must establish or maintain procedures for the participation of the peoples concerned in determining whether the interests of these people would be adversely affected and to what extent, before undertaking or authorizing any program for planning, prospecting or exploiting existing resources on their lands. The peoples concerned shall participate in the benefits of such activities, and shall receive compensation, on a basis not less favorable than the standard of international law for any loss which they may sustain as a result of such activities.

6. Unless exceptional and justified circumstances so warrant in the public interest, the states shall not transfer or relocate indigenous peoples without the free, genuine, public and informed consent of those peoples, but in all cases with prior compensation and prompt replacement of lands taken, which must be of similar or better quality and which must have the same legal status; and with guarantee of the right to return if the causes that gave rise to the displacement cease to exist.

7. Indigenous peoples have the right to the restitution of the lands, territories and resources which they have traditionally owned or

otherwise occupied or used, and which have been confiscated, occupied, used or damaged, or when restitution is not possible, the right to compensation on a basis not less favorable than the standard of international law.

8. The states shall take all measures, including the use of law enforcement mechanisms, to avert, prevent and punish, if applicable, any intrusion or use of those lands by unauthorized persons to take possession or make use of them. The states shall give maximum priority to the demarcation and recognition of properties and areas of indigenous use.

Article XIX. Workers' rights

1. Indigenous peoples shall have the right to full enjoyment of the rights and guarantees recognized under international labor law and domestic labor law; they shall also have the right to special measures to correct, redress and prevent the discrimination to which they have historically been subject.

2. To the extent that they are not effectively protected by laws applicable to workers in general, the states shall take such special measures as may be necessary to:

a. effectively protect the workers and employees who are members of indigenous communities in respect of fair and equal hiring and terms of employment;

b. improve the labor inspection and enforcement service in regions, companies or paid activities involving indigenous workers or employees;

c. ensure that indigenous workers:

   i) enjoy equal opportunity and treatment as regards all conditions of employment, job promotion and advancement; and other conditions as stipulated under international law;

   ii) enjoy the right to association and freedom for all lawful trade union activities, and the right to conclude collective agreements with employers or employers' organizations;

   iii) are not subjected to racial, sexual or other forms of harassment;

   iv) are not subjected to coercive hiring practices, including servitude for debts or any other form of servitude, even if they have their origin in law, custom or a personal or collective arrangement, which shall be deemed absolutely null and void in each instance;

v) are not subjected to working conditions that endanger their health and safety;

vi) receive special protection when they serve as seasonal, casual or migrant workers and also when they are hired by labor contractors in order that they benefit from national legislation and practice which must itself be in accordance with established international human rights standards in respect of this type of workers, and,

vii) as well as their employers are made fully aware of the rights of indigenous workers, under such national legislation and international standards, and of the recourses available to them in order to protect those rights.

Article XX. Intellectual property rights

1. Indigenous peoples have the right to the recognition and the full ownership, control and protection of their cultural, artistic, spiritual, technological and scientific heritage, and legal protection for their intellectual property through trademarks, patents, copyright and other such procedures as established under domestic law; as well as to special measures to ensure them legal status and institutional capacity to develop, use, share, market and bequeath that heritage to future generations.

2. Indigenous peoples have the right to control, develop and protect their sciencies and technologies, including their human and genetic resources in general, seed, medicine, knowledge of plant and animal life, original designs and procedure.

3. The states shall take appropriate measures to ensure participation of the indigenous peoples in the determination of the conditions for the utilization, both public and private, of the rights listed in the previous paragraphs 1. and 2.

Article XXI. Right to development

1. The states recognize the right of indigenous peoples to decide democratically what values, objectives, priorities and strategies will govern and steer their development course, even where they are different from those adopted by the national government or by

other segments of society. Indigenous peoples shall be entitled to obtain on a non-discriminatory basis appropriate means for their own development according to their preferences and values, and to contribute by their own means, as distinct societies, to national development and international cooperation.

2. Unless exceptional circumstances so warrant in the public interest, the states shall take necessary measures to ensure that decisions regarding any plan, program or proposal affecting the rights or living conditions of indigenous peoples are not made without the free and informed consent and participation of those peoples, that their preferences are recognized and that no such plan, program or proposal that could have harmful effects on those peoples is adopted.

3. Indigenous peoples have the right to restitution or compensation no less favorable than the standards of international law, for any loss which, despite the foregoing precautions, the execution of those plans or proposals may have caused them; and measures taken to mitigate adverse environmental, economic, social, cultural or spiritual impact.

SECTION SIX. GENERAL PROVISIONS

Article XXII. Treaties, acts, agreements and constructive arrangements

Indigenous peoples have the right to the recognition, observance and enforcement of treaties, agreements and constructive arrangements, that may have been concluded with states or their successors, as well as historical Acts in that respect, according to their spirit and intent, and to have states honor and respect such treaties, agreements and constructive arrangements as well as the rights emanating from those historical instruments. Conflicts and disputes which cannot otherwise be settled should be submitted to competent bodies.

Article XXIII.

Nothing in this instrument shall be construed as diminishing or extinguishing existing or future rights indigenous peoples may have or acquire.

Article XXIV.

The rights recognized herein constitute the minimum standards for the survival, dignity and well-being of the indigenous peoples of the Americas.

Article XXV.

Nothing in this instrument shall be construed as granting any rights to ignore boundaries between states.

Article XXVI.

Nothing in this Declaration may be construed as permitting any activity contrary to the purposes and principles of the OAS, including sovereign equality, territorial integrity and political independence of states.

Article XXVII. Implementation

The Organization of American States and its organs, organisms and entities, in particular the Inter-American Indian Institute, the Inter-American Commission of Human Rights shall promote respect for and full application of the provisions in this Declaration.